'Tom McTague has produced a brilliant and unique piece of historical writing which will change how we think about Britain's schizophrenic relationship with Europe since the Second World War . . . Unfolding like a play with many acts and players, this extraordinary debut work of history is a reminder that everything is connected but nothing is inevitable'

John Bew, author of *Citizen Clem*

'From Macmillan's doomed application to Cameron's failed re-negotiation, Tom McTague clinically exposes the hesitations, contradictions and wilful self-delusion that have characterised Britain's relationship with the European project since its inception, and the slow-burning opposition from Powell to Farage which, in retrospect, makes the ultimate debacle of Brexit seem almost inevitable'

John Campbell, author of *Roy Jenkins: A Well-Rounded Life*

'A tour de force by an exceptional journalist, Tom McTague's account of Britain's relationship with Europe between the Second World War and Brexit is beautifully written, full of erudition and as broad as one could hope in its horizons. A remarkable achievement'

Matthew d'Ancona, Editor at Large, *The New World*

'McTague has an acute ear for the echoes and re-echoes of political history and a journalist's nose for narrative. It's that potent combination that makes this a sparkling re-telling of Britain's love-hate relationship with the post-War European project so unique. From inception in 1945 to rejection in 2016, McTague reveals with the precision of a political archaeologist how the arguments that tore the country apart after Brexit are as old as the federalist project itself. This is political history at its finest'

Peter Foster, author of *What Went Wrong With Brexit*

'A vivid and detailed account of British politicians and their small-island contortions on Europe, culminating in the abject self-harm of Brexit'

John Kampfner, author of *In Search of Berlin*

'This compelling, hugely well-informed narrative of how we came to leave Europe – a narrative involving the eternal interplay between character and fate as well as an exploration of the underestimated swirl of intellectual currents – will stand for many years as the authoritative political history'

David Kynaston, author of *Austerity Britain, 1945–1951*

'A riveting and revelatory new narrative of modern Britain that shows where we've come from, how we got here, and who we are'

Ian Leslie, author of *Conflicted*

'A sweeping, impressive and ambitious history of modern Europe – and Britain's turbulent relationship with it. With a deft touch and deep research, Tom McTague has captured a tale of big personalities – from Enoch Powell to Dominic Cummings – and even bigger events'

Helen Lewis, author of *The Genius Myth*

'Profound and intellectually scintillating, this book is one of the first true works of history analysing Britain's fraught relationship with Europe post-1945'

Sir Anthony Seldon, author of *The Impossible Office*

'*Between the Waves* is powerful, precise, morally engaged, wonderfully alert to character, context and the greater purpose of political life'

Rory Stewart, author of *Politics on the Edge*

'Lucid and witty, Tom McTague's magisterial rethinking of postwar British history exposes the fatal ambiguity of our attitudes to Europe. Conspirators and fantasists abound in his sweeping account. Like a physician or psychiatrist, he diagnoses the maladies of anti-Europeanism, but knows there was to be no remedy, as Brexit only worsened British economic and social diseases. Here is a compelling and illuminating tour through recent history, from a wise and authoritative pen'

Polly Toynbee, author of *An Uneasy Inheritance*

BETWEEN THE WAVES

TOM McTAGUE

BETWEEN THE WAVES

The Hidden History of a Very British Revolution
1945–2016

PICADOR

First published 2025 by Picador
an imprint of Pan Macmillan
The Smithson, 6 Briset Street, London ECIM 5NR
EU representative: Macmillan Publishers Ireland Limited, 1st Floor,
The Liffey Trust Centre, 117–126 Sheriff Street Upper,
Dublin 1 DOI YC43
Associated companies throughout the world

ISBN 978-1-5290-8309-5

The publishers gratefully acknowledge permission to reproduce quotations from 'Little Gidding' from *Four Quartets* by T. S. Eliot and from 'The Importance of Elsewhere' from *The Complete Poems* by Philip Larkin, both published by Faber and Faber Ltd.

1 3 5 7 9 8 6 4 2

A CIP catalogue record for this book is available from the British Library.

Typeset by Dante MT Std by Palimpsest Book Production Ltd.,
Falkirk, Stirlingshire.
Printed and bound in the UK using 100% Renewable Electricity by
CPI Group (UK) Ltd

For Mum and Dad, who let me question

Contents

List of Illustrations *xi*

Part One: 'The end of all our exploring'

Introduction *3*

Chapter 1 *11*

Chapter 2 *36*

Chapter 3 *61*

Chapter 4 *90*

Chapter 5 *110*

Part Two: 'Through the Unknown Gate'

Chapter 6 *127*

Chapter 7 *148*

Chapter 8 *175*

Chapter 9 *204*

Chapter 10 *233*

Chapter 11 *266*

Part Three: 'History is Now'

Chapter 12 *299*

Chapter 13 *331*

Chapter 14 *360*

Chapter 15 *392*

Chapter 16 *427*

Conclusion *459*

Acknowledgements *473*

Bibliography *477*

Notes *483*

Index *519*

'It is mad to believe in astrology—that is to say, in the sciences that judges future events. The science is either completely false, or else the things necessary for its practice are unknowable or unattainable by the human mind. But the result is the same: to think one can know the future by that means is a dream.'

Francesco Guicciardini, *Maxims and Reflections*

'In political activity, then, men sail a boundless and bottomless sea; there is neither harbour for shelter nor floor for anchorage, neither starting-place nor appointed destination. The enterprise is to keep afloat on an even keel; the sea is both friend and enemy, and the seamanship consists in using the resources of a traditional manner of behaviour in order to make a friend of every hostile occasion.'

Michael Oakeshott,
Rationalism in Politics and Other Essays

List of Illustrations

1. Admiral François Darlan. (Getty)
2. Fernand Bonnier de la Chapelle. (Alamy)
3. General Charles de Gaulle and Henri Giraud at the Casablanca Conference in January 1943, with Winston Churchill and Franklin D. Roosevelt seated in the background. (Getty)
4. Jean Monnet. (Getty)
5. Ernest Bevin with Robert Schuman and Dean Acheson. (Getty)
6. Clement Attlee with Harry Truman, Dean Acheson and George Marshall. (Getty)
7. Dwight D. Eisenhower with Winston Churchill, Richard Nixon, Sam Rayburn and Sir Harold Caccia. (Getty)
8. Hugh Gaitskell addresses the Labour Party Conference. (Getty)
9. Harold Wilson. (Getty)
10. Anthony Eden and Harold Macmillan with Edward Heath. (Getty)
11. Edward Heath and Enoch Powell at the Conservative Party Conference. (Getty)
12. Meat porters in Smithfield marching to Parliament. (Getty)
13. Michael Foot reads *The Sun* during the general election campaign. (Getty)
14. Barbara Castle, Enoch Powell, Arne Haugestad, Neil Marten, Peter Shore, Jack Jones, Ronald Bell and Michael Foot at a press conference of the referendum on British membership of the European Common Market. (Getty)

15. Margaret Thatcher campaigning for a Yes vote to stay in the EEC. (Getty)
16. Jeremy Thorpe, Edward Heath and Roy Jenkins during a press conference. (Getty)
17. Peregrine Worsthorne. (*The Telegraph*)
18. Professor Michael Oakeshott. (Getty)
19. T. E. Utley. (Images4Media)
20. Hugh Fraser with Antonia Fraser and Jonathan Aitken. (Getty)
21. Peter Young with a group of conservative European student leaders at a secret anti-Soviet conference in Poland. (Courtesy of the author)
22. George Miller-Kurakin and other conservative activists disrupt the 1986 Copenhagen Peace Congress. (*The Independent*)
23. Charles Douglas-Home with his fiancée, Jessica. (Getty)
24. Roger Scruton. (Shutterstock)
25. Norman Stone. (Getty)
26. Rodney Leach. (Alamy)
27. Margaret Thatcher giving the 'Bruges speech' in September 1988. (Alamy)
28. Jacques Delors. (Alamy)
29. Patrick Robertson. (Alamy)
30. Douglas Hurd and John Major at the Maastricht summit. (Getty)
31. Bill Cash. (Getty)
32. Jacob Rees-Mogg. (Getty)
33. Dr Alan Sked. (Alamy)
34. Dougie Smith. (*Daily Mail*)
35. James Goldsmith. (Getty)
36. Gordon Brown and Tony Blair during a press conference. (Getty)
37. Dominic Cummings. (Getty)
38. Robert Kilroy-Silk and Nigel Farage. (Getty)
39. David Cameron announces his resignation after the EU referendum. (Getty)
40. Gisela Stuart and Michael Gove listen to Boris Johnson at Vote Leave's headquarters. (Getty)

Part One

'THE END OF ALL OUR EXPLORING'

Introduction

Algiers in late 1942 was a city on the edge, a bustling hive of intrigue and ambiguity, espionage and violence. Formally, the city still remained part of Vichy France, locked in a collaborationist embrace with Adolf Hitler's Nazi Germany. Yet, in reality, like much of North Africa, it had long since fallen to the Allies. The result was an equivocal mess of competing loyalties and aspirations. Portraits of Marshal Philippe Pétain were still on public display across the city and Vichyite thugs roamed the streets looking for Jews even as General Dwight Eisenhower and his Allied forces took up residence and French Resistance units continued to plot and to rage.

The cause of this strange, uneasy state of affairs was the presence of one man: Admiral François Darlan, the Marshal's second in command, who happened to be in Algiers visiting his sick son when the Allied invasion began – or so he claimed. The British and Americans had hoped to install another French general, Henri Giraud, yet almost immediately after landing in North Africa it had become clear that he did not have the authority to command the 125,000 French forces still in the region whom the Allies wanted to avoid fighting.

The British and Americans needed to move quickly if they wanted to force a French ceasefire. The US general Mark Clark was given the go-ahead to negotiate with Darlan directly, wresting from the French commander a formal order to his troops not to resist the Allies, issued 'in the name of the Marshal' back in France. Though this order was swiftly disowned by Pétain himself, it worked. Suddenly, the Allies could advance on the Germans – and fast.

As a result, however, the Allies were now working with a regime that had not formally broken with the collaborationist government in France. For the British, this was calamitous. For the past two years, Winston Churchill had held up an entirely different man as leader of the real France, the *free* France: Charles de Gaulle.

De Gaulle was untarnished by collaboration, having fled France in 1940 refusing to accept the terms of Pétain's surrender. Despite being little more than a junior member of the last government of the Third Republic, de Gaulle had grown into something much more than this in London: an emblem of France unbowed and unbroken. With his broadcasts on the BBC, he had held up a different idea of France from the one that was shaming itself in Paris and Algiers.

If Britain now recognized Darlan as the legitimate leader of the French in North Africa, where did that leave de Gaulle and the idea for which he and Britain were supposed to be fighting? Where did it leave the future of Europe? In 1941, Churchill and Franklin Roosevelt had signed the Atlantic Charter, committing themselves to the principles of freedom and self-determination. How could they possibly deal with Darlan, this proconsul of Vichy, as anything other than a temporary expedient?

Today, it is hard to comprehend the stakes involved, the prospect of a France unmoored from its Gaullist future. Yet there was little in 1942 to suggest de Gaulle would emerge as the leader of a free, democratic France after the war. In Washington, Roosevelt saw in him the spectre of a future dictator, one he could not control. In London, meanwhile, Churchill's primary concern was to avoid any Anglo-American split. 'The question [. . .] we must ask ourselves is not whether we like or do not like what is going on,' he warned MPs in a closed session of Parliament. It was, he said, 'what are we going to do about it?' With the

Americans now in the war, the invasion of North Africa was a joint expedition. 'Neither militarily or politically are we directly controlling the course of events.'[1] A new American world order was emerging, which would have profound effects for Britain and the whole of Europe.

Behind the scenes, the British were furious. 'Darlan is Vichy, and Vichy is the rule of the wealthy and selfish interests which have ruined France,' read one note compiled by the British Political Warfare Executive team based in Algiers, a clandestine body set up to disseminate propaganda behind enemy lines.[2] By this time, British forces had spread through the surrounding hills and villages, including some from a unit called 'GHQ Liaison Regiment', code-named Phantom, several members of which would go on to play a curiously outsized role in the great drama of British post-war history.

Overseeing Britain's secret effort in the war was Churchill's foreign secretary, Anthony Eden, who was appalled at the alliance with Darlan. 'We are fighting for international decency, and Darlan is the antithesis to this,' Eden wrote on a Foreign Office note on 17 November 1942. The note itself had described Darlan as a 'temporary expedient' and posed, bluntly, the central challenge now facing the government: 'At what point and by what methods Darlan is to be eliminated must be governed by military considerations.'[3] The solution to these questions would soon come from the barrel of a gun.

At just after 2.30 p.m. on Christmas Eve 1942, a young royalist Frenchman – a pied noir, born and raised in North Africa – called Fernand Bonnier de la Chapelle arrived at the southern gates of the Palais d'été in Algiers filled with dreams of glory. Bonnier had been part of an underground resistance in the city that had been cultivated by the Allies before the war and had been appalled when it emerged Darlan would remain in place. Bonnier then joined a unit of seventy other Frenchmen armed and trained by the British Special Operations Executive, the celebrated branch of British intelligence created by Churchill to 'set Europe ablaze'. These fighters were drawn from various groups operating in Algiers at the time, all opposed to Darlan and the stain of Vichy. The group, given pay, rations and uniforms by the British, was controlled by the Special Operations Executive's Brandon mission, which was due to move on Tunisia in support of the British First Army to finally push the Germans out of North Africa.[4] On the evening of 18 November, however, a group of these patriotic young Frenchmen met in a barn on the outskirts of Algiers and drew straws for a more specific and deadly task.[5]

On 19 November, when Brandon moved east, it was Bonnier who stayed behind – the fateful figure who had drawn the shortest straw. Bonnier joined another clandestine British operation, code-named Massingham, where he attended a course in small arms and sabotage.[6] By mid-December, his two weeks of training completed, Bonnier neither 'returned to unit' with his former comrades on the Brandon mission nor was he tasked for other duties by Massingham. Instead, he loitered in Algiers, waiting.[7]

In the background, the Allied armies under Eisenhower remained stuck in Tunisia, not yet able to push the German forces out of Africa, but Churchill and Roosevelt had agreed that they needed to meet in person to discuss the war's next phase. Should Darlan have joined them, he would have been recognized and legitimated in the eyes of the world. If he was to be eliminated, it would need to happen quickly.

Exactly who ordered Bonnier to put an end to this shameful period remains clouded in the mists of war. Was it the British, who saw Darlan tightening his grip? Or perhaps the Gaullists in London? Maybe it was Giraud himself, still demanding supreme command of the Allied forces in their assault on Tunisia.

What we do know is that, after Bonnier arrived at the Palais d'été at just after 2.30 p.m. on Christmas Eve, he was admitted to a small waiting room, primed for his moment of destiny.[8] For half an hour he waited. Then his chance arrived: at just after

3 p.m., Admiral Darlan walked past. Thrusting forward, Bonnier opened fire before attempting a frantic escape out of an open window to a waiting car. But tragedy struck: hearing the commotion, a nearby spahi cavalryman had rushed in and grabbed Bonnier from behind, wrestling him to the ground. One of Darlan's aides remembered Bonnier in these final moments, 'excited eyes, very blue, with the pupils dilated as if by a drug.'[9] Darlan himself lay on the floor, still, eyes open, blood flowing from his mouth, dying.

For six weeks, the Allies had tolerated Darlan as a necessary evil. By Christmas, the collaboration risked sullying not just the Allied war effort but the ability of France to re-emerge into the European family of nations after the war. Darlan's violent removal presaged not only the end of Vichy, but the beginning of modern France and, with it, modern Europe.

To get there, however, the politics still needed to be fixed. With Darlan gone, Giraud and de Gaulle remained – one backed by the United States, the other by Britain. To ensure the issue did not become an open wound in the relationship, in 1943 Churchill and Roosevelt dispatched three of their most trusted political representatives to manage the situation. Representing the US president was Robert Murphy, the chargé d'affaires at the embassy in Vichy who had cultivated the secret network in Algiers that had tried to install Giraud in the first place and that almost certainly included Bonnier. Representing the British prime minister was the suave Conservative minister, Harold Macmillan, whose political career had, until the war, been one largely defined by backbench mediocrity. Completing the triumvirate of political fixers was a French businessman and bureaucrat who was working for the British in Washington at the time, and who, like de Gaulle, had left France for Britain in 1940 to avoid the shame of collaboration. That man was Jean Monnet, the future founding father of modern Europe.

For Macmillan, Monnet and de Gaulle, the following year in Algiers would be a pivotal moment in their careers, each bearing witness to a new dawn for Europe, and for Britain's place within it. They did not know it yet, but that future was theirs. Each would go on to play a decisive role in the great continental revolution to come; a transformation that would present Britain with the problem to which it has never quite found an answer: the question of Europe.

This book is the story of that struggle, chronicling the events, personalities and ideas that first took Britain into Jean Monnet's Europe, only to then take it back out a little over forty years later. It is a story of high drama and low intrigue, vaulting personal ambition and deep-grained romanticism – all dragged along by the great tide of history, whose direction is rarely visible at the time.

'What we call the beginning is often the end,' T. S. Eliot wrote in the last of his *Four Quartets*, 'Little Gidding', first published in 1942. The poem is a meditation on the deep continuities of time connecting the poet not just to the living who were then fighting for national survival over the skies of England and in the deserts of North Africa, but to the dead who came before them. 'A people without history is not redeemed from time,' Eliot observed, 'for history is a pattern of timeless moments.' The poem became a favourite to conservative iconoclasts of the twentieth and twenty-first centuries, including many of those who would lead the great Tory counter-revolution of the 1980s, enraptured by Eliot's evocation of England and its history.

Roger Scruton, perhaps the most influential of all post-war conservative thinkers, later wrote that the power of Eliot's poetry lay in its ability to convey both an atmosphere of England and an idea of life in which the present was forever moored to the past.

> We shall not cease from exploration
> And the end of all our exploring
> Will be to arrive where we started
> And know the place for the first time.

Through the unknown, remembered gate
When the last of earth left to discover
Is that which was the beginning;
At the source of the longest river
The voice of the hidden waterfall
And the children in the apple-tree
Not known, because not looked for
But heard, half-heard, in the stillness
Between two waves of the sea.[10]

These lines capture the story of Britain's post-war struggle over 'Europe'; a story of the waves of events and ideas, memories and dreams, personalities and politics which have rolled over the country since the grim years of 1941 and 1942, when bombs rained down on London and the country faced into the abyss.

Britain, of course, is itself set 'between the waves', lying in the stillness that separates 'us' from 'them', as Edward Heath would later lament. This, however, is not a story of geography, but of history; a process that is neither ordained nor ordered, but rather chaotic and contingent, shaped by character and chance and circumstance. There is no arc of history, no permanent settlement – only endless struggle.

The world that exists today is the product of men like Monnet and Macmillan, often through their failures as much as their successes. Yet it is also the product of those who struggled against them, filled with ideas of history shaped by the poetic imaginings of those such as T. S. Eliot.

As Monnet, Macmillan and de Gaulle plotted out the future of Europe in Algiers in 1943, one such figure of poetic opposition happened to arrive in the city: John Enoch Powell. Then just a young lieutenant colonel in Britain's directorate of intelligence, Powell had been sent to Algiers to head up a team of thirty officers tasked with disrupting the last German supply lines operating in Tunisia.[11] Though little more than a bit-part player in this high Algerian drama, Powell's time in North Africa forever shaped his own dreams and ambitions for an entirely different future from the one then being planned across the city. Indeed, Powell's ideas about the new European order would come to define British resistance to it. That resistance would ebb and flow through the years of Britain's subsequent decline, suffering defeat after defeat until, years after Powell's own death, the tide would turn.

It is a remarkable quirk of fate that these four men came together at the same time and in the same place. In them we find the source of many of the ideas that grew to dominate British, French and European politics for much of the next seventy-five years: ideas of nation and order, identity and belief. These were men of vision and intellect, but also – some more than others – messianic self-belief, wild passions and cataclysmic fantasies. Throughout their lives, each suffered great reversals, only to see their ideas adopted by new generations of politicians who would fight for them all over again. The story of Britain's relationship with Europe is, in many ways, a story of the battle between the ideas that these four men encapsulated. This is that story.

Bonnier, however, would not live to see this future. 'I am calm, London has been advised,' he is reported to have said in his cell on Christmas Day 1942.[12] During the night, Bonnier had asked his jailer if there was anything unusual happening outside, as if he were expecting something to save him, even speaking of a simulated firing squad with blank cartridges. When the moment came, at 7.30 a.m. on 26 December, the cartridges were not blank. 'Much to his surprise,' Churchill noted in his memoirs, '[he was] executed by firing squad.'[13]

Bonnier died a martyr for a future he could not have imagined, but one of which he is forever part. 'We are born with the dead,' Eliot observed in 'Little Gidding'. 'See, they return, and bring us with them.'

Chapter 1

When Enoch Powell was despatched to Algiers in February 1943, his mind had already turned east and to dreams of India. He would stay in Algiers barely four months before returning overland to Cairo, with a friend, on a fourteen-day, 3,000-mile journey across the desert, in a truck they nicknamed Pinafore. Powell later described this adventure as one of the few good things he had done with his life. It is also a window into the soul of this radical, bloody-minded man who would have such a profound effect on the country for which he was fighting.

In 1943, Powell was fighting for an imperial idea of Britain, an empire spanning the globe, with an ambiguous nation floating somewhere at its heart. This nation was not simply Great Britain, or even the United Kingdom, but a greater Britain that included Australia and New Zealand and Canada. Beyond that, of course, were the colonies, realms of the empire with their own histories, which were not white and never quite British enough to form part of the nation, though still bound in loyalty to the Crown. Indeed, it was the multinational element of the empire that seemed to tap Powell's most romantic imperial delusions. For him, the empire was unimaginable without India, and India unimaginable without the empire. Together, they represented a great Anglo-Indian civilization that stood apart from continental Europe and the upstart United States.

The idea of Britain that Powell was fighting for is laid out in vivid colour in an essay he wrote in North Africa over the

Christmas of 1942, containing his 'strategic and political convictions as they have built themselves up during the last three years'.[1] Powell titled the essay '1943'.

'The decisions of 1943 will determine our history and our greatness for centuries,' he declared. Europe, he wrote, must return to its pre-war borders and Britain return to its position as a global power. To do this, Powell saw the need for a new British base in what had been French Indo-China – an 'Eastern Malta', which would allow Britain to better defend its vast Asian territories.

With these visions of imperial expansion lighting his way, Powell turned to his own ambitions, which, at this time, had become fixated on the idea of becoming viceroy of India. To do so, though, he first needed to serve in the Raj. Powell's commitment to this idea was such that, before leaving Algiers for Cairo in the early summer of 1943, he turned down a promotion that would have kept him in North Africa. He wanted to serve the empire in India and was prepared to drop down to the rank of major to do so. Powell's friends warned him that he was foolish not to take the promotion, but he was driven by a primal fear that the United States – and not the forces of the Crown – would be first to retake Britain's colonies during the war. This, he said, would be the end of the empire 'not later than the lifetime of my children, should I have any.'[2] For Powell, the empire was the be-all and end-all, the source of his passion, and America was its chief threat – a conviction that never left him.

Powell's journey back to Cairo, then, was the first leg of a journey he hoped would conclude with his administration of India. He decided to return to Egypt by land because it was the safest way to transport sensitive intelligence files from Algiers. The only problem was he couldn't drive. So, Powell enlisted his friend, Michael Strachan, a driving instructor who could teach him along the way.

Strachan later wrote an account of his journey with Powell that summer, describing their first morning on the road together.

Having made it sixty miles out of Algiers, they found a disused railway cutting where they could stop for breakfast. Powell lit a fire, throwing petrol over it to get it going, causing the flames to flare up and singe his closely cropped moustache. He then cut his finger preparing the sausages, before allowing the water for the tea to boil over, which put the fire out. When Strachan offered to help, Powell shot back: 'You keep away. If they want to be bloody-minded, I'll show them, by God I will.'[3]

Strachan's vignette captures something of the essence of Powell, grumbling in full dress uniform, hair neatly trimmed, eyes green with a wild, startling intensity: 'Very penetrating and rather sinister,' in Strachan's words.[4] These were the eyes that would unnerve parliamentary colleagues years later as he stared intently, pouring out his intellectual contempt for the latest government policy that fell short of his idea of Britain.

Throughout the journey, Strachan and Powell kept to a rigid timetable. Each night, they stopped at 7.30 p.m. and made dinner, before bedding down in the back of the van at 10 p.m. They passed through Tunis, Tripoli, Benghazi, Tobruk and El Alamein, before finally arriving in Cairo, from where Powell hoped to be transferred to India. When the pyramids appeared in view, this pair of young officers broke into a chorus of 'Rule, Britannia!', 'Land of Hope and Glory' and 'God Save the King'.

Powell later wrote a poem capturing this moment, published in 1951. After the endless expanse of sand, he describes how the great monuments of pharaonic power 'rose sharp and blue against the desert's brown'. Yet it was not the pyramids themselves which captured Powell's imagination, but the fact that they were, for now, *British*. 'To our astonished sight,' he writes, 'Descried, above it all, the Imperial Crown'.[5]

Beyond this mirage of royal dominion, the experience seems to have lodged in Powell's very being. Years later, he would write a review of *Arabian Sands* – a chronicle of the British explorer Wilfred Thesiger's journeys across the desert. Travelling through such emptiness, Powell wrote, 'seems to remove the purpose from journeying and substitute in its place a kind of timeless contentment, almost as though the soul were soothed by this emblem of its own metaphorical journey across the desert of the world'.[6] In the lifeless emptiness of the Sahara, Powell had glimpsed his own mortality.

While there is no childhood trauma that explains this morbid streak, Powell's upbringing in the lost world of imperial Birmingham offers a clue. He was born in 1912, deep into the Indian summer of Edwardian Britain, an apparently golden age of comfort and civilization soon to be lost in the cataclysm of world war. Birmingham, the city of his birth, bathed particularly contentedly in the evening sunshine of this world; one of the great manufacturing hubs of empire, it was a thriving city of tradesmen and wealth, order and hierarchy, radicalism and reaction.

Yet this was no age of harmony and order. Edwardian Britain was a place of feverish division, trapped between a decaying Victoriana of the previous century and the horrors of the militarized modernity to come. This was a time of suffragette rebellion and armed insurrection in Ulster, Liberal radicalism and Conservative fury; a time divided between those who wanted to maintain the order that was slipping from their grasp and others eager to drag the country into a future of their imagining.

One of the great divides at the time was between enthusiastic imperialists like Joseph Chamberlain, that great titan of Liberal Birmingham, and the lowly 'Little Englanders' who saw the empire's shame and corruption. This division would last beyond the passing of Edwardian Britain and through the changing seasons of Britain's decline thereafter. No other Englishman has ever embodied this divide quite as profoundly as Enoch Powell, a lower-middle-class child of Edwardian Birmingham who grew not only to represent the global imperialism of his childhood, but also, in time, the provincial nationalism that replaced it; an icon of two very different Britains indelibly connected to each other.

For most of Powell's early life, it seemed he was destined for a brilliant career in academia rather than politics. From a young age, he displayed an almost monastic dedication and rigor that revealed itself in extraordinary achievement. In 1925, he won a scholarship to Birmingham's most prestigious school, King Edward's, where J. R. R. Tolkien had been a schoolboy a little over a decade earlier. By the age of fourteen, he had completed his first translation of Herodotus; by seventeen, he had won a scholarship to read classics at Cambridge; and, at twenty-two, he was made a fellow of Trinity College.

At Cambridge, Powell's intellectual hero was A. E. Housman, the austere classicist and poet whose collection, *A Shropshire Lad*, had proved wildly popular among homesick soldiers during the First World War, with its lamentations on mortality and evocative descriptions of the English homeland for which they were fighting – an idyll not dissimilar to Tolkien's Shire, first set out in *The Hobbit* in 1937.

After graduating from Cambridge in 1933, Powell became fixated with Friedrich Nietzsche, consuming everything he had written, 'not just the main works but the minor works as well, all of them, and every scrap of published correspondence,' as he later described it.[7] Powell's infatuation with Nietzsche was part of a deeper love affair he was developing with German culture at this time. This, in many ways, was Powell's first love, an infatuation quickly crushed by the reality of the Nazi regime. When news emerged of Hitler's 'night of the long knives', Powell wrote that he had lost a 'spiritual homeland,' one that he realized – like so many of his fantasies – was 'not of this world.' His dream had been an illusion, 'all fantasy, all a self-created myth', as he put it. 'I was left only with my geographical homeland.'[8] Britain and its empire became the new focus of Powell's imaginings, the unreality of which would take time to reveal itself.

At the age of twenty-five, Powell was appointed to the Chair of Greek at the University of Sydney in New South Wales, becoming the youngest professor in the British Empire. Elated, he began what was then a sixteen-day journey by flying boat from Poole Harbour to Singapore, before swapping for a 'land plane'. The route was intoxicating for a young imperialist like Powell, skimming his way around the world, touching down three or four times a day on lakes, rivers and seas, flying at such low altitude that it became 'an immense geography lesson in the extent and majesty of the British Empire.'[9] After stops in Rome and Crete, Powell passed through Alexandria, Lake Galilee, Basra, Abu Dhabi, Karachi, Jaipur, Allahabad, Calcutta, Rangoon, Singapore and many other places, almost all under British control. 'One was witnessing the ubiquity of a power on which the sun had not yet set,' he later recalled. 'I saw; I felt; I marvelled.'[10]

By this time, Powell was convinced war with Germany was imminent, an obsession that filled his letters to his parents. On 19 March 1938, he told them that 'one of these fine days the U.K. will declare war and you will get a cable to say I am returning.'[11] Powell gave vent to his fury at the British government for its failure to face up to this reality in his inaugural lecture as professor of Greek, in May that year. 'The world has recently been treated for nearly a decade to the unusual spectacle of a great empire deliberately taking every possible step to secure its own destruction,' he told his audience.[12] To Powell's mind, the root of the problem was the 'prejudice' of the empire's people, who, he said, were 'incapable of thinking for themselves, as never to perform the few logical steps necessary for proving that they would shortly be involved in a *guerre à outrance*, which could be neither averted nor escaped.'[13] As became customary in his life, Powell saw himself as both defender of British greatness and prophet of its self-inflicted decline.

That month, he told his parents he expected war in another week. By September, he told them the prospect was causing him 'continual and suffocating anxiety.'[14] A week later, he wrote home again following Chamberlain's first visit to Hitler at Berchtesgaden: 'I do here in the most solemn and bitter manner curse the Prime Minister of England for having cumulated all his other betrayals of the national interest and honour, by his last terrible exhibition of dishonour, weakness and gullibility.' He concluded the letter with a declaration that war was 'our only chance of salvation,' and that his highest ambition was to die fighting in it.[15]

Powell's attitude to the war was a foretaste of the absolutism that would define his life. As he later put it, he could not let go of a logical argument until he had taken it to what he believed was its rational conclusion, however controversial, or, at times, fantastical. It was this way of thinking that saw him become a militant atheist, unable to accept the 'extreme unrealism' of the New Testament that he had read in its early Ancient Greek.[16]

Powell was far from a simple rationalist, but a man gripped by the fiercest of passions that would, in time, overwhelm his career. An early outlet for Powell's emotion was poetry, much of it, like Housman, fixated on mortality and the passing of time. In his introduction to his *Collected Poems*, published decades later, he wrote of the 'sheer, almost physical agony' he felt at the onset of spring. 'The succession of the seasons is like a recurrent inescapable catastrophe,' he wrote, 'which sweeps away what is young and beautiful, and what is beautiful because it is young.'[17] This sense of loss, and the endless attempt to avert this catastrophe, lies at the heart of Powell's conservatism. Powell touches on these themes in one of his most famous verses, in which he writes:

> I only love the strong and bold,
> The flashing eye, the reddening cheek,
> But more than all I love the fire
> In youthful limbs, that wakes desire
> And never satisfies.[18]

Here, Powell reveals some of the preoccupations that would stay with him for the rest of his life: his own mortality and the heroism of youth, but also the inevitable disappointment at falling short, the inability to meet the desires of early passion. For Powell, the glory of a heroic death, martyrdom in the service of a cause bigger than himself, was his great and unfulfilled desire and something that he searched for throughout his life. When Hitler invaded Czechoslovakia in 1939, Powell wrote: 'Oh to be at war, to have a chance to kill and be killed!'[19] From as early as 1938, he was convinced he would die in battle, a martyr for the British Empire in its civilizational struggle with Nazism. Indeed, Powell's biographer Simon Heffer concludes that Powell never came to terms with *not* dying in the war.

When war was finally declared, Powell immediately returned to Britain and signed up to die. As the war progressed, it also began to sharpen his political views. In May 1942, Powell wrote to his parents that he believed war made people conservative. 'In the last analysis the people undertake to support them not for the present nor the future,' he wrote, 'but for the memory of a dream, the associations of infancy and childhood.'[20]

Powell, then, believed that nations fought for the *idea* they had of themselves, an idea forged in childhood. For Powell, this idea would always be the Birmingham of his youth, the city of empire, and the order and hierarchy and greatness that he imagined, defined by its institutions and cohesion, and its sense of belief. These themes would recur throughout his life, a memory of a dream of Britain that was forever lost. The power of these visions was such, however, that they would be picked up by new generations who would go on to shape and lead a very different Britain from the one Powell sought to preserve. Yet, if wars are waged for an idea of home, as Powell argued, their 'inescapable catastrophe' is that, in practice, they transform the old world into something irreversibly new.

In March 1943, as Powell sifted through the intelligence coming in from the front line and Jean Monnet and Harold Macmillan plotted the future of France, Britain's prophet-in-chief, Winston Churchill, sketched out his vision for the future, inspired by the extraordinary outpouring of support at home for the proposals contained in the Liberal economist William Beveridge's 'Social Insurance and Allied Services' report, which had been published in November 1942. The Beveridge Report, as it became known, remains a landmark document in modern British history, promising universal services, homes and benefits after the war, sent to every British serviceman at home and abroad. For many of the rank and file in the British army, here was a vision of home worth fighting for.

The core message of Churchill's address was that the mistakes of the interwar years must not be repeated – that 'squalid epoch of bickering and confusion', as he called it. The country needed to change for the better. The tenor, tone and content of Churchill's speech that day reflected the nation's mood. To a large degree, it was an acknowledgement of political reality. But it was also one of the best examples of Churchill's interventions during this time, which helped shape Britain's new idea of itself, a post-war national identity which has remained with us. Churchill gave voice to this idea better than anyone, both elevating the public discourse and, at times, overwhelming it.

In his speech, Churchill presented the country with a vision of itself as one of the world's three indispensable powers, a leader in Europe but not entirely of it. He told his audience that after the war there would be a new United Nations, headed by the three victorious powers: 'the British Commonwealth of Nations, the United States, and Soviet Russia.'[21] This triumvirate would lead this new world organization to safeguard against future wars. Its job would be to disarm the guilty states, bring to justice their criminal leaders and resurrect the old nations of Europe destroyed by the Nazis. Under this world organization would be a new Council of Europe, as well as a Council of Asia. The Council of Europe, in particular, Churchill declared, would be 'a stupendous business,' restoring the true greatness of the continent. As ever, however, Britain's place within this new continent was unclear.

When Churchill spoke of this new Europe, he was careful to play down its threat to Britain. It would have to fall into line with 'the high permanent interests of Britain, the United States, and Russia.' For most people in Britain, however, the future of Europe was far less pressing than the future of Britain. Each of the main parties in Churchill's national government was committed to the broad principles set out in the Beveridge Report, and Churchill himself was determined to be personally tied to its recommendations. He declared Beveridge a personal friend and that, once the war was over, the time would be ripe for 'another great advance' in conditions at home.

For Churchill, this meant taking all the different insurance schemes and making them 'unified, compulsory, and national.' This, Churchill declared, would bring 'the magic of averages to the rescue of the millions.'[22] It was the basis for the welfare state to come. The old Britain had melted away in the heat of war and a new one had already formed. These new national-insurance schemes Churchill promised would be joined by a new national education system, 'broader and more liberal' than what had been there before; towns and cities would be replanned and rebuilt, and the old class divisions flattened out. 'Tradition may play its part,' Churchill declared, 'but broader systems must now rule.'

Buried within the speech, however, was a warning. Britain, Churchill said, must not try to build a society 'in which nobody counts for anything except a politician or an official.' Here was a chink of light between the Conservatives and Labour that would, in the decades to come, grow into a chasm, shattering the consensus that Churchill then embodied.

Churchill had mapped many of the contours of the post-war order – Europe and the United Nations, democratic socialism at home and supranational democracy abroad. He also recognized the emerging power of the United States and Russia that would largely determine the post-war world. And yet the one part of the map he struggled to see clearly was the one closest to home: British decline and the emergence of Europe. It was nevertheless a speech that enraptured those who heard it.

In Macmillan's wartime diaries, he notes the moment he heard Churchill's speech over the radio while dining in Algiers. 'I remember hearing the broadcast after dinner,' the future prime minister writes. 'It was a Sunday; a great battle had been raging for the last two days on which was to turn the outcome of the African campaign and the possibility of an early landing of our armies on the continent of Europe.' Macmillan was with General Alexander, Eisenhower's deputy commander. 'Both of us were enthralled by Churchill's ideas,' Macmillan wrote.[23]

For the French triumvirate of Charles de Gaulle, Henri Giraud and Jean Monnet, also in Algiers at the time, the great question remained not the future of Britain, but that of France – and the man who seemed destined to lead the French out of the war was not de Gaulle, but Giraud. As late as 12 February, Macmillan wrote to Churchill that he saw a grave danger of the 'cabal' around the anointed general 'becoming too strongly entrenched to be removed.'[24] Indeed, it was not until 30 May 1943 that de Gaulle even arrived in Algiers to assert his leadership, his travel only made possible by the political compromise worked out by Monnet, Macmillan and their American counterpart, Robert Murphy, for the creation of what they called the Comité Francais de Libération Nationale (CFLN), in which both de Gaulle and Giraud would sit alongside four others, two chosen by each. One of those figures would be Monnet himself, 'the inspirer' of these events.

Without Monnet's guiding hand during this time, such a compromise might never have come. It seems extraordinary that a man who never once held elected office or fought for his country could have wielded such power, yet his undeniable influence is testament to his remarkable skill as a political operator. Monnet first rose to prominence in the First World War, where he had become the French government's principal representative on the Allied Supreme Economic Council, which ensured narrow nationalism did not interfere with the war effort. Such was his standing that, after the war, he was appointed deputy secretary general of the new League of Nations in Geneva and awarded an honorary knighthood by the British.

Over the next twenty years, Monnet slowly drifted from this position of political power back to the world of business, scarred by the failure of the League of Nations to establish itself as a credible body. If such an organization was to succeed in future, it needed more secure foundations, he concluded. By 1938, Monnet was approaching fifty and was little more than a 'petty financier', according to de Gaulle. His life changed again when the Second World War broke out.

After the capitulation to Hitler at Munich in 1938, the French prime minister, Édouard Daladier, sent for Monnet and dispatched him on a secret mission to Washington to negotiate the purchase of American warplanes. When Hitler invaded Poland the following year and the Allies recreated the old Supreme War Council, Daladier proposed 'a Frenchman who is a friend of Roosevelt' to take charge of joint Allied purchases abroad.[25] It was as if nothing had changed in twenty years.

Unlike the First World War, however, when Britain and France held the German advance at bay, the Allied armies collapsed in 1940. It was at this point that Monnet became involved in one of the great 'what ifs' of European history. On the afternoon of 16 June 1940, Churchill offered France an 'indissoluble union' with Britain to keep it in the war. The declaration was drafted by Monnet alongside British officials, with the support of de Gaulle, who was also in London, proposing the federal union of Britain and France and the creation of joint defence, foreign and economic policies, common citizenship and a single war cabinet. For Pétain, then deputy prime minister, any such union with Britain was pointless, a 'marriage to a corpse', as he put it. Germany had won the war. The French government duly collapsed and Pétain took charge. Within twenty-four hours, the First World War hero had announced the country's surrender.

For Monnet and de Gaulle, the surrender was cataclysmic, a defeat that left both facing the defining decision of their lives: should they continue to serve the France that now existed, or reject its legitimacy and fight for something else, for a different idea of France? Within a month, Monnet had submitted his resignation to Pétain's government and asked Churchill for a job in the United States 'in order to serve the true interest of my country.'[26] Churchill arranged for Monnet to join the British Supply Council in Washington on an annual tax-free salary of $10,000. Monnet became a British official with the same job Daladier had once proposed for him: to prise open the vast treasure chest of American weaponry. De Gaulle, meanwhile, stayed in London and began his slow transformation into the figure who would come to dominate post-war French politics.

Where Monnet's vision of the world was pragmatic, cooperative, international and transatlantic, de Gaulle's was defiant, proud and resolutely national. These two visions of France would clash for the rest of their lives and beyond, with dramatic consequences for Britain.

In Washington, Monnet's influence quickly grew. Soon, the Roosevelt administration began seeking his counsel on issues way beyond the formal scope of his job, including on French North Africa. It was therefore natural that, after Darlan's assassination, Roosevelt turned to Monnet as the man both he and the British could trust to manage the competition for power between Giraud and de Gaulle in a way that protected the Allied war effort.

This was the source of Monnet's power in Algiers in 1943: he was both a de facto emissary of the president of the United States and a trusted official of the British. When de Gaulle eventually arrived in Algiers, it was no surprise that Monnet was there to greet him. Over dinner that night, the future contours of French and European politics were forming, as the pair debated the future of the post-war order. In a note taken by Macmillan, who was in attendance, a fiery de Gaulle raged about the 'Anglo Saxon dominance of Europe' that could not be allowed to continue after the war.[27] If it did, de Gaulle declared, France would have no choice but to lean towards Germany and Russia. 'Monnet still finds it difficult to make up his mind as to whether the general is a dangerous demagogue or mad or both,' Macmillan noted in his diary.[28]

Over the course of the next few months, de Gaulle's authority, charisma, pride and relentlessness would see him slowly take control of the committee that Monnet and Macmillan had created to build a united French front ahead of the country's liberation. By the end of June, de Gaulle was its head, and by August the committee itself was recognized by the US and Britain as the de facto government in exile. In the space of a few months, de Gaulle had grown from one member in a committee to the leading figure in a government-in-waiting.

Though this is testament to the power of de Gaulle's personality, without Monnet's guiding hand during these months, ensuring

American and British support for the committee despite its slow Gaullist takeover, outcomes might have been very different. As late as August, the Americans were insisting that they would not allow Giraud to be sidelined, although that eventually came to pass.

The committee, meanwhile, continued to discuss the new Europe that was about to emerge. On 5 August, a note from Monnet warned that, unless democratic systems were installed immediately after the war, a rash of authoritarian nationalist governments bent on protectionism might emerge. Monnet warned his colleagues on the committee that the British, Americans and Russians had their own worlds to fall back on, but Europe did not. France needed to produce ideas for a 'European new order,' Monnet said, allowing it to stand alongside Britain and the United States in a new Atlantic Free World.[29]

One morning, a colleague found Monnet deep in thought, a map of Europe spread out on his desk with striped pencil lines across it. 'Showing me the regions of the Ruhr and Lorraine, he explained that all the trouble came from that part of the world,' his close colleague Étienne Hirsch recalled. 'It was from their coal and steel that Germany and France forged the instruments of war.' Monnet told Hirsch that, to stop another war, it would be necessary to 'extract' the region from France and Germany. In the depths of 1943, with Germany engaged in a civilizational battle to the death, such a proposal seemed madness. Hirsch recalled thinking it was 'sheer utopia to think of gouging areas that were such sources of wealth out of sovereign states.'[30]

This episode offers a revealing glimpse into the mind of Europe's founding father. Monnet's genius was his ability to combine high idealism with deep pragmatism, to transform his vision for peace into practical solutions. At a lunch given by de Gaulle on 17 October, Monnet went further, setting out his idea for Europe's future, in which the continent's great states would be united on an equal footing within a 'single economic entity with free trade.' Monnet did not specify the future of Germany, which many in France wanted to see divided, but the principle would be the same regardless: each member must be treated as an equal. Monnet's Europe would not be the plaything of one dominant power. His intention was to place the basic industries of coal and steel under an international authority. De Gaulle was sceptical. 'After a war such as this, it is hard to see French and Germans belonging together to an economic union,' he told Monnet.[31] Instead, the general favoured an economic union with the Low Countries and perhaps the Rhineland, detached from Germany. France, of course, would take the lead.

Monnet persisted. In August 1944, *Fortune* magazine published a profile of 'Mr Jean Monnet of Cognac'. In it, Monnet declared the need for a 'true yielding of sovereignty' after the war, 'some kind of central union' and 'a big European market without customs barriers.' This would prevent a return to nationalism, which Monnet described as 'the curse of the modern world.' The Ruhr should be internationalized under a European authority, he added. This was heady stuff, and Monnet knew it. 'But where to begin?' Monnet asked. 'And how far to go?' Then there was the biggest question of all: 'Could England be brought in? For without England . . . the concept of a unified Europe turns all too quickly into a Germanized Europe all over again.'[32]

The idea of Europe was alive, born into a world that was not quite ready for it, but soon would be. Its central problem was there for all to see – a problem to which Monnet, de Gaulle, Macmillan and Powell would offer profoundly different answers over the years to come.

The war in Europe ended on 8 May 1945. Although Japan was still to be subdued, in political terms Britain's life as a post-war nation had begun. In London, Winston Churchill confirmed a general election would be held in July, the first since 1935, after Clement Attlee refused his offer to maintain the wartime coalition until victory had been achieved in the East. In Paris, meanwhile, Jean Monnet was attempting to keep open a flow of credit from the United States in order to rebuild the country's shattered economy.

And, in Washington, the new president, Harry Truman – who had replaced Franklin Roosevelt after his death in April – was preparing for the Allied invasion of Japan.

For Enoch Powell, serving in India, Nazi Germany's fight to the death in Berlin had been 'a wonderful performance,' as he put it in a letter to his friend, Michael Strachan. 'I think only Germans are capable of such a feat,' Powell wrote.

With the war in Europe over, Powell's mind turned once again to thoughts of action. When the US dropped its atomic bomb on Hiroshima, Powell even wrote to his parents that he feared the enemy would 'let him down' by surrendering. When the end came, he expressed his 'shock' that the fighting was over. He had 'missed the war – every bit of it', he complained.

Powell was ordered home for demobilization early the following year, and he made plans to fly back to Britain to start what he called his 'third life'. For Powell, of course, the preservation of the British Empire remained axiomatic. India was everything he had dreamed of. The British, he later wrote, had found themselves 'married to India, as Venice was married to the sea.' When he left for home in early 1946, he did so with 'real reluctance and regret,' he wrote to Strachan, 'because of the unending fascination of this incredible Empire in which potentially we have in our hands power and wealth that would make America seem insignificant, and where nevertheless an evil spell seems to bind both the land itself and us.'[33]

To continue serving the empire, Powell understood he must leave academia. The route back to India and the viceroyalty lay through Westminster. And so, when he finally arrived home, in February 1946, weeping as he saw the green fields from the airport window, he immediately looked up the number of Conservative Central Office. Within twenty-four hours, he had spoken with the deputy chairman of the party; within two weeks, he had joined the party's parliamentary secretariat and was placed on the party's official candidates' list. The first day he arrived at the party's headquarters, he declared that he'd joined the Conservative Party 'to ensure the continuance of British rule in India.'[34] Powell, who had supported Labour in the 1945 election, had concluded – correctly, as it transpired – that the Conservative Party was most likely to do this. One official there that day, the future MP 'Cub' Alport, suggested he join the party's research department, phoning ahead to say 'a strange bird was on the way who might be of use.'[35]

Within a year, however, Powell's dream was shattered. In February 1947, the prime minister Clement Attlee – who had defeated Churchill in a landslide in July 1945 – announced that India would be independent within the year. For Powell, it was a shock so severe, he remembered 'spending the whole of one night walking the streets of London trying to come to terms with it,' just as he had been crushed by the reality of Germany in the 1930s.[36] And, just as he never came to terms with his failure to die for the empire, Powell never got over the loss of India, admitting in later life that he would always dream of the time British ships patrolled the earth's seas.

Powell quickly understood that not only were his dreams of viceroyalty over, but the British Empire itself had no future. 'The logically inevitable outcome will be the eventual and probably the rapid loss to the Empire of all its other non-European parts,' Powell wrote.[37] He was correct. With what would later be seen as his customary absolutism, Powell would soon become the fiercest *anti*-imperialist in British politics. Powell could support empire, he said, but not the 'sham' of Commonwealth, in which, as he saw it, countries could abandon their loyalty to the Crown only for Britain to pretend they had not.

The focus of Powell's life after 1947 became the resurrection of the British nation, the battered oak tree, still standing 'amid the fragment of demolished glory' of empire, as he would later put it.[38] He eventually entered Parliament in February 1950, as the Member for Wolverhampton South West. It was a watershed moment in British political history, although few imagined so at the time. And one of his first acts as an MP was to rebel against the Conservative Party leadership on the subject from which he would soon become personally inextricable: Europe.

The issue in question was the declaration by the then French foreign minister, Robert Schuman, inspired by the man of Algiers: Jean Monnet. At the war's conclusion, Monnet had returned to France to lead the country's efforts to rebuild its economy. Placed at the head of a new General Planning Commission by de Gaulle, Monnet implemented an emergency plan to grow the economy: a transformative national effort which laid the foundations of the *trente glorieuses* to come. This economic revolution was known as the Monnet Plan.

Yet France's domestic recovery relied on benign international conditions, principally the supply of German coal and American financing. A new plan was needed: a European plan. For Monnet and Schuman, this was the European Coal and Steel Community, a radical new idea that would put French and German production under a common High Authority, ensuring supply and managing competition, much as Monnet had tried to do during the First and Second World Wars.

Monnet and Schuman desperately wanted Britain to join the initiative, but were unable to persuade the Labour government, which did not believe any such scheme could possibly go ahead without them. Schuman, though, decided otherwise. 'World peace cannot be safeguarded without the making of creative efforts proportionate to the dangers which threaten it,' he declared, acknowledging the momentous nature of the announcement.

The problem for France was that the danger was becoming overwhelming. In 1947, the Americans had stepped in to save Greece after Britain declared it could no longer afford to support the country itself. Then came the Marshall Plan, a financial lifeline for Europe, designed to 'permit the emergence of political and social conditions in which free institutions can exist,' as the US secretary of state George C. Marshall declared. In return for its aid, the Americans demanded a plan, designed in Europe, for the whole of Europe. 'It should be a joint one, agreed to by a number of, if not all, European nations,' Marshall said. America was creating 'Europe' and, crucially, would not accept a German-shaped hole at its centre. The US needed Germany as a bulwark against the rising power of Soviet Russia. The Cold War was already beginning to remake the world.

For France, the imminent rehabilitation of Germany posed an immediate challenge: how could it stop history repeating itself? The obvious answer to France's strategic challenge lay in its entente with Britain. But Britain could not afford any new entanglements in Europe. Limits that had been imposed on German coal and steel production were not going to last much longer. Soon, France would, once again, find itself dwarfed by the might of its neighbour.

It was at this moment that Monnet persuaded the French foreign secretary to take the plunge on an alliance with Germany *without* Britain. If France could not strip Germany of its core industrial capacity, it could place it under a new supranational High Authority instead. To win German approval for this, however, would require France doing the same thing. Passing through Paris in May 1950, just days before the London conference, the new US secretary of state Dean Acheson gave his consent to the plan – without telling the British government. History was moving.

This, then, was the context of Schuman's great declaration. 'Europe will not be made all at once, or according to a single plan,' he said. 'It will be built through concrete achievements which first create a de facto solidarity.' At the heart of Europe lay France and Germany, the two great powers of the continent. Britain had been left behind. 'The French government proposes that action be taken immediately on one limited but decisive point,' Schuman went on. 'It proposes that Franco-German production of coal and steel as a whole be placed under a common High Authority.'

Schuman was clear that this new organization would be open to the other countries of Europe, including Britain. He was also clear what it meant: 'A first step in the federation of Europe.' The proposal was daring, controversial and revolutionary. It went against the conservative instincts of the French foreign ministry, which saw the alliance with Britain as the basis of its strategic defence. De Gaulle himself was hostile and many of the Gaullists in the National Assembly followed suit. In Britain, Labour's foreign secretary Ernest Bevin was furious. But what could he or Britain do? London had no overwhelming need to revolutionize its foreign policy to answer French concerns about German strength.

It was not simply a question of practicalities. Here was an elemental idea that would soon create its own momentum, changing the face of Europe to such an extent that it would become Britain's greatest foreign-policy challenge of the post-war era. The true significance of the proposal, though, was not France replacing Britain with Germany, but France transferring its insurance against German domination from Britain to America. With Britain's withdrawal from Greece, America had become a permanent European power. Britain's weakness had brought the United States into Europe, and in doing so had created the conditions for France to make its leap in the dark without Britain. The world had changed, but Britain was not quite ready to face up to what it meant yet.

A few days later, Churchill's wartime foreign secretary Anthony Eden stood up in the House of Commons to move an Opposition motion condemning the Labour government for refusing to take part in the discussions on the Schuman Plan. The Labour government's response was that the French government – at Monnet's insistence – had made entry into the talks conditional on accepting the principle of a supranational High Authority to manage each state's coal and steel production. Because Britain could never accept such a condition, Attlee's government argued, there was no point attending. It was an argument of principle, not pragmatism. Eden was equally driven by idealism, but believed there was a way through that could protect British sovereignty *and* its influence in Europe. This debate would rage for decades thereafter.

Looking back on that scene in 1950, the most striking thing, alongside the calibre of the combatants, is the clarity of the arguments expressed. Many of the Members of Parliament speaking over the two days of debate in June 1950 had either served in uniform or in government during the global cataclysms of the twentieth century. At the same time, we can observe notes of wishful thinking and myopia that would come to define Britain's debate over Europe – as much from the pro-European side as the anti.

The day before Eden rose to his feet, war had broken out in Korea after Kim Il Sung ordered his forces to storm the border with the south, supported by Communist China. For Eden, the invasion was proof that this was not a moment for Britain to break away from its European allies, to become a little England. 'Sometimes we stand too near to great events to see them in their true perspective,' Eden declared: 'That the Schuman Plan can be such an event I have no doubt.'[39] To his credit, Eden saw the proposal for what it was: not a small act of economic cooperation but something much bigger, a moment of seismic potential. Monnet's proposal removed the primary source of tension between France and Germany and therefore had to be supported. 'It must not, it cannot, be allowed to fail,' Eden stated.

He argued that, because it was in Britain's interest for the proposal to succeed, it followed that Britain needed to be at the table to ensure it did so. But this was not the only reason for attending the talks. Eden argued that there was an inherent danger in allowing Franco-German relations to develop separately from Britain. Any political separation could easily extend into a host of other areas, including defence. In effect, Churchill's wartime foreign secretary could see the power of Monnet's idea – that, once it had been accepted for coal and steel, it would make sense to extend it into other areas. What would Britain do then?

Eden's analysis was as brilliant as it was prescient, and yet it fell into the same trap of exceptionalism and avoidance that has bedevilled the British debate ever since. Eden told the House of Commons that, while the proposed project did envisage a 'common high authority' whose decisions would bind national governments, the British could negotiate safeguards that would make such an arrangement acceptable. Britain, it seemed, could join the European project while remaining an exception to its rules.

Replying for the Labour government, Stafford Cripps said other countries with much smaller steel and coal industries might be prepared to place them under a High Authority, but it was an entirely different question for Britain. In 1950, Britain remained the wealthiest and most powerful country in Western Europe, with a large industrial economy. It would have been almost impossible for *any* government, Conservative or Labour, to have put such a core part of its national economy under the control of a new supranational authority managed by its weaker competitors, let alone a Labour government which had just nationalized that very industry. 'I hope I have said enough on this point to show that no responsible British Government could enter into such a matter blindfold[ed] and without the fullest consideration,' Cripps concluded.[40]

Cripps also pointed to the French government's clear declaration that the pooling of sovereignty was the 'first concrete foundation of the European Federation.' Cripps said Britain's participation in a Western European political federation was not compatible with its obligations either to the Commonwealth, the wider Atlantic community, or as a world power. Britain's problem was that it was too weak to stop the project, but too powerful to need to join.

Notably, Cripps was not going out on a limb in his opposition to Monnet's supranational project. In 1950, the fiercest and most emotive resistance to the new European High Authority came from the Labour benches. At the time, Britain had a vast unionized workforce, earning far more than the average continental worker. For the Labour government, these were privileges it was anxious to protect; indeed, it was the party's very raison d'être to do so. On top of this, there was something less quantifiable about Britain's attitude to Europe that was, and remains, important: its imaginative understanding of itself. It wasn't just that the ministers of the Crown felt Britain was substantially different from its European counterparts; this was felt by many in the country as well.

In the debate over the Schuman Plan in 1950, this sense was articulated by the Labour Member of Parliament for Wandsworth Central, Harold Adams, who sarcastically rebuked Churchill and his party for being willing to sell out their country. Adams began by dismissively anticipating a Churchillian intervention, or, as he described it, 'another champagne speech by the Right Honourable Member for Woodford.' He continued, 'There are many of us who have learned to recognize the deception that lurks beneath the beaded brim. We shall much prefer the honest draught of British beer which will follow.' Churchill, Adams warned, was 'prepared to go outside this country to seek a muzzle for Socialism at home.' In 1950, it was left to Churchill to criticize what he called Labour's 'Palmerstonian jingo.'

The debate over the Schuman Plan is notable for two other moments whose importance would only become apparent years later. It provided Edward Heath with the opportunity to impress his colleagues with a maiden speech of profound eloquence and understanding that marked him out as a future star. It also provided Enoch Powell with an opportunity to lay down a very different kind of mark. In 1950, Heath and Powell placed themselves on opposite tracks that would, in time, destroy both their careers.

Heath used his speech to strike a number of important notes, accusing Labour of a fatalistic pessimism about Britain's ability to shape whatever new Europe was emerging. Heath then told Members of Parliament that, having recently come back from Germany, he could report that its new leaders really did want a harmonious relationship with France, as well as a unified Europe to stand against the threat from the east. 'I believe that in that desire the German Government are genuine, and I believe, too, that the German Government would be prepared to make economic sacrifices in order to achieve those political results'. Like Eden, Heath was also able to see the long-term implications of the project. Once it had bedded in, Heath said, Germany might very well become a 'major factor in Europe' again. Heath finished by urging the government to believe in British power and to lead Europe in the direction that was best for Britain.

Heath is a remarkable British politician in many ways, but chief among them is his uniquely open pro-Europeanism. No other prime minister in Britain's post-war history would be as unhesitatingly European as Heath. Not only did he understand better than most the power of the idea captured and made real by modern Europe's founding genius, Monnet, but he did not feel the need to hide it, nor to dilute it.

To Heath, the flaw in socialist scepticism was not that it was stuck in a lost past of British greatness – as 'little England' Euroscepticism would later be parodied – but that it had given up believing in British greatness at all. In 1950, and throughout much of the debate that followed, it was the pro-Europeans who were most concerned with protecting and projecting British power on the continent. As ever with Britain's European travails, the story is not a simple one. In 1950, was it really the Attlees and Powells in Parliament who held delusions about British power, or was it those who believed Britain could still lead Europe in whichever direction it wanted?

When Churchill himself rose to speak, he managed to capture much of Britain's confusion at this time. Trying to clarify the Conservative Party's position, he said he would not agree to any supranational authority which had 'the power to tell Great Britain not to cut any more coal or make any more steel'. But he argued the government should still attend the negotiations, at least to test what they might be able to negotiate. Churchill went on to say he was not in favour of British involvement in 'the tangles and intricacies of rigid constitution-making' that would be required to build a federal union of Europe. The real question, he said, was 'what association should Britain have with the Federal Union of Europe if such a thing should come to pass in the course of time?' He said he could not conceive of Britain ever being an ordinary member of such a union, but argued it should become 'intimately associated with it' while maintaining its empire, Commonwealth and 'fraternal association with the United States in the English-speaking world.' With all this in mind, he said, 'we could not accept full membership of a federal system of Europe.'[41] Essentially, Britain could have it all.

In response, Attlee was scathing. For the Labour leader, the problem with Schuman's plan was its fundamental idea, not some trifling negotiating point. Schuman and Monnet were proposing something entirely new, a supranational authority with the power to bind national governments. It was not possible to accept this principle with conditions, Attlee said. 'It is really making nonsense of an acceptance to think that one can accept a principle and then whittle it away until there is no principle left.' Churchill, grumbling in the background, is recorded in Hansard dismissing Attlee's argument as 'metaphysics, not politics.'[42] But here lay perhaps the most fundamental rupture point in Britain's troubled post-war relationship with Europe. Was it a question of principle, as Attlee suggested, which must be faced head on, or could a political compromise be found to maintain Britain's presence in the new Europe without having to sign up to all its articles of faith? Churchill believed Britain should have an intimate relationship with Europe, but without being bound by the decisions of the new High Authority, nor being a full member of the club, so that it could maintain its global responsibilities and relationships as before. Churchill's position would come to be that taken by almost all British governments thereafter, some with more success than others, but always skirting around the question identified by Attlee: to accept the principle or avoid its implications?

When the debate finished and the vote to censure the government was taken, Harold Macmillan and Edward Heath joined Winston Churchill and Anthony Eden in voting to condemn Clement Attlee's judgement. For Enoch Powell, however, the principle did matter, and he chose to abstain rather than back his own side. The Conservative chief whip, Patrick Buchan-Hepburn, told Powell: 'I don't think we shall be able to put you in the government, at any rate not at first, after what you've done.'[43] It would be Powell's first act of parliamentary rebellion, a step that cost him the chance of an early promotion on the parliamentary ladder. It would also be the first step in a long career of rebellion that would, in time, cost him the chance to become Conservative Party leader and prime minister, but would transform British politics and its relationship with Europe.

Chapter 2

In the early 1950s, the ascendency of the men of Algiers began. In Britain, Harold Macmillan joined Winston Churchill's cabinet following the Conservative Party's victory in 1951. In the United States, Dwight Eisenhower was being courted by both political parties to be their presidential nominee for the 1952 election. And, in France, Jean Monnet had established himself as one of the most influential figures of the Fourth Republic, the man charged with revolutionizing the country's economy at home and its place in Europe abroad. But, for General de Gaulle, the martial hero of France, the future offered little but pain and resentment.

On 6 February 1948, de Gaulle's daughter Anne had died in his arms, aged just twenty. Anne had Down's syndrome and was therefore vulnerable to the bronchitis she had contracted earlier that winter. 'I am a man annihilated,' de Gaulle told the priest of his home village of Colombey-les-Deux-Églises, where he had decamped after resigning as chairman of the provisional government of the French Republic in 1946.[1] In public, de Gaulle might have been an austere and haughty figure, but there was another side to him: loving and gentle, and even vulnerable. Anne was de Gaulle's third child, born on New Year's Day in 1928, a time when disabled children were often seen as something to be hidden from society, placed in ill-equipped hospitals far away from their families. De Gaulle and his wife refused to bend to these expectations. 'Believe me, Anne is my joy and strength,' de Gaulle said. 'She is the grace of God in my life.'[2]

It is difficult to be sure of how much de Gaulle knew about the eugenic horror unfolding in Nazi Germany in the years running up to the Second World War, but, given the appalling scale of the 'cleansing' taking place, it seems impossible that he was entirely unaware. When de Gaulle faced the great decision of his life in 1940 – to resist or collaborate – the choice, then, was not just political, but personal. He fled with his wife and daughter to England, escaping not only a regime that wanted to extinguish France as a great power, but one that wanted to extinguish his most vulnerable child. To lose Anne four years after France's liberation left de Gaulle in a state of stricken grief. A dark gloom seems to have descended over him and his household from that moment – a gloom that never entirely lifted. Every Sunday after Anne's death, de Gaulle and his wife would visit their daughter's grave in the small parish church in the village, where all three rest beside each other today.

This period of de Gaulle's life was particularly difficult. In 1948, he was not only mourning the loss of his daughter, but also the France that he believed still needed saving. In 1944, after France's liberation, de Gaulle had become the country's interim leader, tasked with overseeing the transition to a new republic, the culmination of his great struggle for supremacy over Giraud that began in Algiers in 1943. Though he had dominated the French government in exile, imposing his will on the committee through force of personality, he was unable to do the same with the new National Assembly whose primary job was to draw up a new constitution for the country. De Gaulle watched in horror as the Assembly agreed a constitution which, as he saw it, re-established the same fractious parliamentary politics he so loathed about the Third Republic. In a customary fit of pique, he resigned and returned to Colombey to wait for the country to come crawling back to him. It would be more than a decade before it did.

For de Gaulle, these were the wilderness years, a time of powerlessness and frustration, made worse by the continuing rise of those he was with in Algiers and the arrival of the new world they soon set about creating. First, the Americans had been brought into what had, until then, been known as the Western Union, to form a new North Atlantic Treaty Organization in 1949, with Dwight Eisenhower becoming its first Supreme Allied Commander in Europe in 1951, before going on to win the presidency as a Republican in November 1952. During this time, Jean Monnet had also become the first president of the High Authority of the European Coal and Steel Community in Luxembourg, promptly declaring himself head of a new European government in the process. None of these developments sat well with de Gaulle, who had raged against the coming Anglo-Saxon domination of Europe in Algiers during the war and now seemed to be seeing it come to pass. But when René Pleven, the prime minister of France, called for the creation of a European army to sit alongside the Coal and Steel Community, including German forces, it proved too much.

Once again, the scheme was the brainchild of Jean Monnet. The Pleven Plan, as it came to be known, envisaged a European army of 100,000 men, controlled by a new European minister of defence and placed under the supreme command of NATO, which was in effect controlled from Washington. Here was Monnet's Atlantic Free World in action: Europe, America and the British Commonwealth, all working together, the three constituent parts of the Western world, with France a second-order power in a new Europe.

The motivation for this new pillar of Europe was the same as that which had inspired the European Coal and Steel Community: the Cold War. In order to balance against the rising threat from Moscow, the United States, as the leader of the West, needed Germany not only to be resurrected economically, but militarily as well. But this raised the very spectre which had always haunted France: German power. The French needed a plan. On 23 August, Monnet drafted a handwritten letter to René Pleven urging him to grab the opportunity. What was needed, Monnet declared, was 'a political concept.'[3] For Monnet, of course, this was Europe.

Monnet told Pleven that Western Europe needed to be 'federated around an expanded Schuman Plan' if it was to remain relevant in the world. The Coal and Steel Community, in other words, was just the nucleus of a new Europe which would, over time, expand to take on other responsibilities, managing German power by Europeanizing it.

The Pleven Plan for a European army was formally presented to the world in February 1951. A draft agreement was ready by May the following year and signed by the six members of the Coal and Steel Community in Paris. The revolution that Monnet had helped bring about in 1950 was rapidly developing into something much more profound. Here were the foundations of a proto-European state, firmly placed within the American-dominated Atlantic Free World. The future seemed set. Indeed, once the new European army plan was agreed, a third European community was proposed – a *political* community. The idea was to place a democratic roof over these first two European pillars. A draft treaty was drawn up to create a directly elected 'people's chamber', as well as a senate appointed by each of the six members and a supranational executive. While de Gaulle was out of power, demanding a revolution at home, one was happening in Europe without him.

In fact, things were happening at such a pace, Britain was starting to feel uneasy. While very few saw Britain's future as a full federal member of a political Europe, there were some who saw the dangers of *not* being involved – most prominent among them, Harold Macmillan. In March 1953, Macmillan wrote a memorandum to the cabinet asking whether they were 'really sure we want to see a six-power federal Europe, with a common army, a common iron and steel industry . . . ending in a common currency and monetary policy?' If such a state ever came into being, Macmillan warned, it would not be in Britain's interests. 'Will not Germany ultimately control this state,' he asked, 'and may we not have created the very situation in Europe to prevent which, in every century since the Elizabethan age, we have fought long and bitter wars?'[4]

But what could Britain do? Macmillan wanted 'the Six' to become something more like the Commonwealth that Britain was building from the rubble of its empire. Anthony Eden, the foreign secretary, meanwhile, came up with a plan to place Monnet's various communities under a different roof, which Britain could help to control: the Council of Europe. The Council was a grand gathering of European states that had been set up after the war, just as Churchill called for in the speech that Macmillan had listened to in such rapture in Algiers. It was just as idealistic and forward-looking as Monnet's supranational communities, but far less revolutionary in principle. The Council of Europe was an intergovernmental organization – a body, in other words, which did not create a new 'high' interest above those of its national members, but which instead brought the old nation states together in an attempt to find common ground. To fold Monnet's federal project into this old intergovernmental system was a threat to the very idea of supranationalism which lay at the centre of the new Europe being built. As such, Monnet moved quickly to see off the idea.

The suggestions being put forward by Macmillan and Eden were not outlandish, and certainly not isolationist. They were imaginative and ambitious attempts to avoid the choice Britain faced but could not make: to join Monnet's new Europe and accept the loss of sovereignty, or to stay out and accept the loss of influence that entailed. At every turn during the decades that followed, Britain would seek a way to avoid the essential dilemma it faced, divided between those who came down clearly on one side or the other and the pragmatists for whom it was always a finely balanced judgement. Again and again, British governments would play for time, searching for a way out of the puzzle but never quite succeeding, settling for an uneasy compromise they could live with until the dilemma resurfaced in a different form. Like some kind of Promethean tragedy, Britain would go on suffering the same fate, bound on the cliffs of the new reality they could neither accept nor do anything to change.

This was the context for the inaugural ceremony of the European Coal and Steel Community in Luxembourg on 10 August 1952, when its president, Jean Monnet, stood up to declare 'Europe's First Government.'[5] Up until 1952, Monnet's entire experience of government had been his brief spell in the French Committee of National Liberation in Algiers in 1943. And yet, here he was, declaring himself president of the first government of Europe, determined to show it was not just another League of Nations, but something real and lasting, with its own authority separate from the nation states which made up its membership. In his inaugural address, Monnet declared that something new had been born, something that went beyond mere international cooperation: a new European community, taking national sovereignty and 'subordinating it to the common interest,' as he put it. As president of the new High Authority, Monnet said he was responsible not to nation states, but to the new European Assembly and European Court of Justice. 'All these institutions can be modified and improved in the light of experience,' he said. 'But there is one point on which there will be no turning back: these institutions are supranational and, let us not shrink from the word, federal.'[6]

At the founding moment of today's Europe, then, we see the idea that lies behind it. The project was for a supranational Europe, where the individual interests of each nation would be slowly subordinated to a new common interest to avoid war and increase prosperity. But what of Britain, the most powerful European country at the time, whose alliance with France was the foundation of French security policy? In his inaugural address, Monnet announced that one of his first steps as president would be to establish an association with the UK.

Soon after, on 21 August, Monnet travelled to London, where he was greeted by the British official Roger Makins, who declared with the kind of pomposity that became a cliché of Britain's attitude to Europe: 'Now that you are a fact, we shall deal with you.'[7] And deal with it he did, sending a delegation to Monnet's

High Authority in Luxembourg to 'lay the foundations for an intimate and enduring association between the Community and the United Kingdom,' as Eden put it.[8] The relationship between Britain and Monnet's new Europe might have got off to a slightly uncomfortable start, but it seemed to have found its footing. The relationship would be as close as possible, outside formal membership. It would be more than a decade before any British government considered an alternative.

Yet, even if Monnet's Coal and Steel Community was a fact, the other pillars of this prospective proto-state were not. At certain times, 'progress' can look inevitable, history proceeding gracefully. Yet, underneath, there is always churn, the true propeller of events. And so it proved in France. For the French public, the Pleven plan was not some uncontroversial step on the way to a united Europe, but a momentous and painful dilemma which had to be ratified by the National Assembly. Just a few years after being occupied and humiliated by Germany, France was being asked to share an army under the ultimate control of an outside power, the United States, and its junior partner, Britain. To many, it was simply too much – not a sign of progress, but an expression of national decline. After all, Britain had no intention of subordinating *its* army.

For de Gaulle, Britain's refusal to join proved that the new European army was not something France should accept either. Emerging from Colombey, he attacked Monnet, Britain and the United States for trying to create this new Europe at France's expense. 'Nothing is more curious than the public and private interventions of the United States to compel our country to ratify a treaty that would condemn her to decay,' de Gaulle fumed. 'Great Britain is also demanding that we join the so-called "European" army though nothing in the world would induce her to join herself.' With furious sarcasm, he concluded that Britain's position could be summed up like this: 'Sacrificing one's sovereignty, abandoning one's soldiers to the discretion of others, losing one's dominions, that is good for Paris, not for London!'[9]

The Europe of Jean Monnet, as it became known, had become a red rag to the Gaullist bull.

For the next two years, the European Defence Community lived on in a kind of coma – not quite dead, but losing its fight for life. It was eventually put out of its misery by an even greater blow to French pride. In May 1954, halfway across the world in Dien Bien Phu in Vietnam, the French army fell to an apparently ragtag bunch of separatist guerrillas. The result was a crisis of morale so deep that it toppled another French government, catapulting the charismatic strongman Pierre Mendès-France into power on a platform of national rejuvenation. Mendès-France quickly grasped a series of nettles, pulling French forces out of Indochina before finally putting the European Defence Community to the National Assembly for ratification, without endorsing it himself.

On 30 August 1954, with Jean Monnet in the public gallery, the National Assembly voted against ratification of the Treaty of Paris by 319 votes to 264, thanks to Gaullist opposition. When the result was confirmed, the triumphant majority in the Assembly burst into a chorus of 'La Marseillaise'. Monnet's Europe had suffered its first defeat and would never be the same again. From now on, a certain caution was injected into the project, and it lost some of its original forthrightness and dignity. Away went Monnet's talk of European governments and the subjugation of national interests, the defence of the idea of Europe and its federal potential. Instead, the focus shifted to that apparently more scientific but dismal world of economics, which would soon become the new driver of integration. Monnet, meanwhile, was so dismayed, he announced that he would resign from the European Coal and Steel Community when his term expired in early 1955, 'in order to be free to work across the board for European unity,' as his biographer François Duchêne put it.[10] He went on to create 'The Action Committee of the United States of Europe', which would consume the rest of his life – a new pressure group bringing together the political leaders and trades unions of Europe to promote the ideal of European union.

While Monnet sat in the National Assembly in Paris watching his dreams burn in a fire of French nationalism, Anthony Eden was watching his own political ambitions slowly wilt in the heat of Winston Churchill's ego. By that summer, Churchill was seventy-nine and in desperately poor health, but not yet willing to let go of power – in part because of Eden's own health problems. In April the previous year, Eden had almost died from a series of botched operations on his bile duct. Had he not suffered this misfortune, he might well have taken over in June 1953 when Churchill himself suffered a serious stroke leaving him unable to function as prime minister. In 1954, Britain was a country governed by men collapsing under the strain of their responsibilities.

Eden was Churchill's foreign secretary and heir apparent, one of the greatest figures of his generation, who had distinguished himself in both world wars. He was perhaps the most qualified, experienced and internationally respected candidate to be prime minister in Britain's post-war history – apart from Churchill himself. And yet, within two years of finally realizing his dream in 1955, he resigned, broken and unwell, his time in office marked by an historic failure that perhaps did more than anything to push Britain into a future neither he, nor Churchill, nor Attlee, nor anyone else in the upper echelons of power thought possible or desirable beforehand: the Europe of Jean Monnet.

In a speech to Colombia University in the United States in January 1952, Eden had addressed the thorny issue of Monnet's new Europe. For Eden, the simple reality was that Britain, whatever the pros or cons of such a project, would never fold itself into such a federal union. 'We know in our bones we cannot,' he told the audience that day.[11] To do so would violate the 'unalterable marrow' of the British nation. Part of the problem was that the British people looked beyond Europe to a greater, global Britain. 'What you've got to remember,' Eden told his private secretary, Evelyn Shuckburgh, 'is that if you looked at the postbag of an English village and examined the letters coming from abroad, ninety percent would come from way beyond Europe.'[12] And he was right.

In 1954, as Eden prepared for the premiership, it really was the case that Britain had a hinterland beyond Europe, displayed in all its pomp and majesty at Queen Elizabeth II's coronation the year before, following the death of George VI in February 1952. Indeed, on that occasion there seemed little reason to doubt the strength of this great global nation or its place at the centre of the Western world. The day before the ceremony, the New Zealander Edmund Hillary had conquered Mount Everest with Sherpa Tenzing Norgay. When he reached the summit, Hillary did the only thing anyone in his position would have done: he planted the Union flag. Back in New Zealand, the country's prime minister declared his pride that an 'Englishman' had been the first to climb the world's highest mountain.[13] The Australian prime minister, R. G. Menzies, felt similarly, declaring that the Queen inherited 'a crown that will always be the sign and proof that, wherever we may be in the world, we are one people.'[14]

While the Queen's coronation offered the world an image of continuity, it also served to veil the profound changes taking place. Today, we can see that the coronation happened at a moment of quiet revolution, in which the country was set on its path from global power to post-imperial nation. A sense of the change can be glimpsed in the extraordinarily convoluted debates over the Queen's title. Back in 1936, her father had been crowned George VI 'of Great Britain, Ireland and the British Dominions beyond the Seas', as well as 'Emperor of India'. By the time of his death in 1952, however, much of this was out of date. The Canadians and Australians did not want to be lumped in with Britain's African and Asian colonies, Ireland had been partitioned and India was a republic.

Anticipating such a problem, the government machine had come up with an elegant answer to present to cabinet upon the King's death. Elizabeth, it was agreed, would be proclaimed 'Queen of this Realm and of all Her other Realms and Territories', as well as 'Head of the Commonwealth'. Thereafter, each of her realms and territories would decide their own title. In Australia, she would be Queen of Australia; in Canada, Queen of Canada, and so on. At home, meanwhile, she would be queen 'of the United Kingdom of Great Britain and Northern Ireland, and of Her other Realms and Territories'.

In many respects, all of this looks utterly arcane and irrelevant. Yet these subtle changes to the Queen's position capture a substantive change in Britain's relationship with the old British world that Clement Attlee, Anthony Eden and almost all front-rank British politicians at that time felt a duty to protect at the expense of Britain's relations with Europe. In almost comically British fashion, a transformation had taken place with hardly anyone noticing. Apart, that is, from Enoch Powell.

On 3 March 1953, Powell made a speech in the House of Commons that he regarded for the rest of his life as the finest of his career. He identified three changes to the Queen's title, 'all of which seem to me to be evil.' The first was that the Crown had been divided. Where the sovereign had once been monarch of a single realm, Powell argued, she now reigned over multiple realms. If this was the case, it opened the door for different sovereigns to reign too. Second, Powell noted the suppression of the word 'British', which, he said, made the new title 'literally meaningless.' A monarch had to be designated a territory over which they reigned, he said. 'To say that he is Monarch of a certain territory and his other realms and territories is as good as to say that he is King of his Kingdom. We have perpetrated a solecism in the title we are proposing to attach to our Sovereign.'[15] In this, Powell was obviously correct.

Powell's third evil was the most consequential, encapsulating the problem of Britain's new role in the world, or at least the role it was attempting to create for itself. What did it mean for the Queen to be head of a Commonwealth which was no longer British and which included republics like India? 'The status of India resulting from these changes and declarations is an ungraspable one in law or in fact,' Powell said. He argued that the title had been designed to be as vague as possible to cover up the fact that the empire had gone. 'I therefore say that this formula "Head of the Commonwealth" and the declaration in which it is inscribed are essentially a sham,' he declared. 'They are essentially something which we have invented to blind ourselves to the reality of the position.'[16]

Powell's speech marks an important moment in his own political journey, and the country's. Once an imperial absolutist who believed in the myth of a great global civilization united in its loyalty to the Crown, Powell now believed that Britain needed to come to terms with its post-imperial state to protect the nation at its centre: Britain. Powell was calling for nationalism to replace imperialism. It was an argument he would return to again and again, gaining such traction – if not understanding – that both the Conservative and Labour parties would struggle to break free from its hold on public life in later years.

The refusal of almost the entire British political class to face the reality of what Powell had identified hampered its ability to address the choice presented by the new Europe emerging on the continent. For Attlee, Churchill, Eden and others, Britain's responsibilities to the Commonwealth were a central reason they could not enter such a distinctly European club. Opposing full British membership of Europe was, for most front-rank British politicians, a display of internationalism, proof of Britain's continued commitments to the world beyond the continent, the opposite of Powellite British nationalism. In the early 1950s, most British politicians still saw Britain as far more than just another European nation.

It was only once Britain's power began to wane more obviously that Britain's governing class turned to Europe, not because they accepted Powell's argument, but in an effort to protect British influence. Powell, of course, drew the opposite conclusion. For Powell, Britain should not attempt to replace its lost role in the world with either a sham Commonwealth or a new Europe. Instead, he argued, Britain needed to rebuild from the rubble of its empire.

Powell's arguments would be repeatedly rejected and defeated over the coming decades, as British governments pursued a European future. Yet the idea was never fully extinguished, and it would grow in intensity as the decades went on, eventually being taken up by a new generation of politicians. Britain's future would be more Powellite than he or anyone else in 1953 could have imagined. Far from a reflection of imperial nostalgia, it was a reflection of Britain's post-imperial reality.

By the time Anthony Eden finally became prime minister in April 1955, it looked for all the world as if Monnet's great European project was running out of steam. Eden's decision to keep Britain out of the European Defence Community had helped throttle its early momentum. If Britain could wield such influence from outside, what did it really have to lose by staying out?

This was the context for one of the most important moments in Europe's post-war history, when the foreign ministers of the six Coal and Steel Community nations met in the Sicilian town of Messina in June 1955, hoping to reinvigorate Monnet's grand project after the failure of the Defence Community. The summit did not seem like a particularly big deal for Britain at the time. Given the setback dealt by the French the year before, there was little indication that this meeting of foreign ministers would lay another foundation stone for the new Europe. Indeed, the first item on the agenda for the foreign ministers to discuss at the summit was how to replace Jean Monnet as president, following his resignation in the wake of the rejection of his project.

Even if Monnet himself was gone, his beliefs endured, carried in the hearts of his disciples. Of these, none was more vital for the project than the Belgian foreign minister Paul-Henri Spaak, who, like Monnet, was a committed Anglophile and follower of Churchill, desperately keen for Britain to join. Spaak would take Monnet's idea and drive it further than ever, putting London back in the same bind in which it found itself in 1950 and from which it has never truly been able to escape.

After dealing with Monnet's replacement, the foreign ministers at the summit turned to a proposal put forward by Belgium, the Netherlands and Luxembourg, calling for the establishment of 'a united Europe by the development of common institutions, the gradual fusion of national economies, the creation of a common market and the gradual harmonisation of . . . social policies.'[17] This visionary – and radical – proposal spooked some of the larger members, like France, still recovering from the fiasco over the European Defence Community. Some around the table in Messina saw a future in which there would be many different bodies, each set up along the lines of the Coal and Steel Community, each dealing with different policy areas, and perhaps with different memberships. Europe, in a sense, would be built piece by piece, unmoored to some grand plan or idea. Indeed, this was the kind of Europe, perhaps, that Britain could be a part of, staying out of some areas which did not suit, but joining others that might. For the Benelux countries, however, European unity needed a Monnet-style idea at its core, common institutions and, most radically of all, a common market, which ensured Europe came ever more closely together, injecting an internal logic into the project. This was the nightmare for Britain.

The foreign ministers in attendance at Messina did not choose between these paths, but rather kicked the decision into a series of study groups, brought together under Spaak's chairmanship. It was a tactic which would cause Britain problems for decades to come. Profound changes were being considered, but they had been smuggled out in dull diplomatic packaging. The Dutch ambassador told his British colleague in Rome that the meeting was never intended to achieve anything, while the Luxembourg representative, Joseph Bech, declared the most significant thing about Messina was it had *not* committed the Six to a Schuman-style High Authority. Even Monnet declared the summit a 'timid step towards the making of Europe.'[18] For most observers in London, there was little to worry about. Even if France agreed to some radical new step forward, how would it pass the National Assembly?

The next few months, however, would prove anything but timid. Chairing the committee to look at the various options, Spaak injected a dynamism and drive into the process that few thought possible. Like Monnet before him, Spaak endeavoured to do all he could to keep Britain involved, inviting London to the talks in the hope that the British might join whatever emerged.

A myth has grown over the years that Eden was some sort of little Englander, too narrow-minded to see the potential of the European project developing before him. The reality is quite the opposite. Eden was a high-minded Tory internationalist, committed to peace and supportive of European unity. Even discounting his efforts before and during the war, Eden had been remarkably successful as foreign secretary after Churchill's return as prime minister, working tirelessly to keep European cooperation alive after the crisis sparked by the French veto of the European Defence Community. Britain was not an absent partner in these early years of European integration, even if it chose to remain outside its new supranational project. Indeed, it was not British nationalism which was proving the main obstacle to European cooperation at this time, but French nationalism. Eden just did not think Britain should or could be part of a federal project of such radicalism as that being proposed, a view entirely of the mainstream at the time, not only uncontroversial but realistic. A majority did not exist in Parliament or the country to fold Britain into such a union.

Nor was Eden's government blind to the risks of *not* joining the new Europe. A note circulated to the cabinet in 1955 by the then chancellor, R. A. 'Rab' Butler, offers a textbook example of good governance, accurately assessing the nature of the European project and both the risks of taking part in Spaak's deliberations and the risks of not taking part. Butler makes a series of reasonable, perceptive and responsible recommendations, which were largely adopted, though later bitterly regretted.

Rab Butler's note to the cabinet states with clear-eyed simplicity that the Six wanted to establish a united Europe with shared institutions and a common European market with harmonized standards. None of these things were acceptable to the British government, which still had an international sterling zone, global trading commitments and nationalized industries paying workers more than those on the continent. What's more, based on discussions with the Dutch and others, the Treasury concluded – again, correctly – that the Benelux proposals were chiefly political in nature, rather than economic, intended to further bind West Germany into the West. The fundamental point, just as it had been when Attlee rejected the invitation to join the Schuman negotiations, was that the project was almost certainly going to be supranational, 'a manifestation of the "community" idea,' as Butler put it. It was to be a new Europe, organized around the same principle as the Coal and Steel Community. The question, once everything else was stripped away, was really quite simple: could Britain accept this principle or not? At the time, the answer seemed a straightforward no.

In 1955, Butler concluded that Britain had 'repeatedly made it clear that we cannot accept as an objective for ourselves the creation of or participation in a common market.' Britain did not mind the Europeans pushing ahead themselves, though Butler admitted this might soon cause problems. 'Developments of this kind may lead to some form of discriminatory bloc in Europe.'[19]

Butler had identified Britain's essential dilemma, unchanged from 1950: to join a project whose very purpose you reject, or to stay out and face a powerful bloc whose interests will soon clash with your own? This would be the same challenge faced by every subsequent British prime minister. At each stage, Britain fought the logic of the European project, rejected its ambitions, dodged, weaved and obfuscated, played for time, demanded special opt-outs, only then to panic about its lost influence when it was granted them. All this was evident in 1955, as Eden's government wrestled with how to respond to Spaak's invitation to join the discussions about the new Europe.

Butler's note contained another recurring theme in the great British struggle over Europe: the belief that London might be able to lead the continent down a different path. 'It may be possible to guide their thought towards suggestions for forms of co-operation in which we would be willing to join,' as Butler put it. This belief would never completely die, no matter how many times it jutted up against the reality of Europe's commitment to the ideal at the centre of its project.

After finally deciding to join the negotiations, Britain sent a man called Russell Bretherton to be its representative. In his first report back to London, he warned his political masters that the committee had shown a 'firm determination to implement the Messina proposals.' The project, he confirmed, was predominantly political – a project for a united Europe. More than that, he also quickly realized that British 'influence' was a double-edged sword. 'If we take an active part in trying to guide the final propositions,' he wrote to a colleague, 'it will be difficult to avoid later on the presumption that we are, in some sense, committed to the result. On the other hand, if we sit back and say nothing it's pretty certain that many more things will get into the report which would be unpleasant from the U.K. point of view whether we in the end took part in the Common Market or not.'[20]

Bretherton would later make clear that he believed Britain could have got almost anything it wanted from the new Common Market – if only it had agreed in principle to join. By October 1955, Eden's government, like Attlee's five years earlier, had concluded it could not accept the principle. In a note drawn up by the internal cabinet committee dealing with the Europe question, four main points were set out determining against membership. First, the report argued, membership would weaken

Britain's relationship with the Commonwealth. Second, Britain was more than just a European power – it was a world power. Third, membership would inevitably lead to further integration and perhaps federation, which the public would not accept. And fourth, British industry would no longer be protected against European competition.[21] Here, in four succinct points, was the case against British membership, a potent combination of short-sightedness and clear-eyed reality.

The clash between Britain's principled objections and Spaak's direction of travel finally came to a head in November 1955. According to the French diplomat Jean-François Deniau,* Bretherton, under orders to return home, said:

> Mr Chairman, Gentlemen. I would like to thank you sincerely for your hospitality and to let you know that it is going to cease from today . . . I must tell you that the future treaty you are talking about and are tasked with drafting (a) has no chances of being concluded; (b) if it is concluded, it has no chance of being ratified; (c) if it is ratified, it has no chance of being applied. Moreover, please note, that if it were, it would be totally unacceptable to Great Britain. You are talking of agriculture which we don't like, of customs dues on which we have nothing to say, and of institutions which horrify us. *Monsieur le Président, Messieurs, au revoir et bonne chance.*[22]

The scene seems to capture Britain's sense of superiority at the time, but it is unlikely Bretherton, a committed and serious British civil servant, would ever have uttered such a bon mot, even if he had been able to think of it. What he actually said, according to official documents, is a rather banal, technocratic restatement of Britain's position opposing the creation of a common market. Bretherton told Spaak that his proposed new European market trampled over 'the competence of existing

* The man credited with drafting the preamble of the Treaty of Rome.

and broader institutions,' by which he meant Britain's favoured intergovernmental bodies like the Organisation for European Economic Co-operation.[23]

In fact, the Whitehall machine had concluded – in official guidance given to ministers – that it was in 'the real and ultimate interest of the U.K. that the Common Market should collapse, with the result that there would be no need for the U.K. to face the embarrassing choice of joining it or abstaining from joining it.'[24] Faced with a choice it could not make, it chose to wish the choice away. Spaak was furious, replying, somewhat emotionally, revealing his real hurt, 'England has not moved at all, and I am not going to move either.'[25]

In truth, Britain was simply not in a position to join in 1955. According to the official record: 'A decision to join the common market would call for such major adjustments in United Kingdom policy as to rule it out as a short-term possibility.'[26] In other words, no prime minister at that point could have accepted such a loss of sovereignty for such economic disruption. Whatever the pros and cons of the venture, there was no way the House of Commons would abandon its Commonwealth in such a way either.

In 1955, it wasn't the deliberations in Brussels that were concerning people in London, but the delicate issue of Britain's relationship with Egypt. For years, British troops had been stationed there to defend the Suez Canal under the terms of a 1936 treaty between London and Cairo. Since 1945, however, these troops had come under sustained attack by Arab nationalists who, understandably, saw Britain's presence as a humiliating colonial hangover. The crisis first boiled over in 1951 when the Egyptian government announced it was no longer bound by the treaty. Within days, some 60,000 British troops were mobilized and sent to the region, which started a chain of events that would culminate in the country's greatest foreign-policy calamity since the war.

The problem for Britain was that it simply could not afford

to keep tens of thousands of troops stationed in Egypt indefinitely. Britain was no longer rich enough to sustain its global position, as demonstrated in Greece in 1947. London needed a political settlement with Cairo. In the last Queen's Speech of Churchill's time as prime minister, in November 1953, this was spelled out: 'My Government have been discussing with the Egyptian Government means of settling the differences between the two countries,' the young Queen Elizabeth declared.[27] This statement of government policy might have sounded somewhat banal and inoffensive, but it caught the attention of Enoch Powell, who only twelve years earlier had been stationed in Cairo, writing his long essay on the future glory of the British Empire.

Rising to speak in the debate, Powell told MPs that any move abrogating the existing treaty of 1936 'would not only be a fateful, but a fatal step' for Britain.[28] Britain could not hope to continue projecting the same degree of global power while withdrawing its forces from such a crucial location. Once again, Powell saw the fatal combination of reality and delusion that marks Britain's governing class. The government could see the numbers on the balance sheet did not add up, but did not want to face up to the wider consequences of what that meant. Nevertheless, Eden's government needed a deal with Egypt.

Under the terms of the deal, the last British troops stationed in the Canal Zone left Port Said at 12.15 a.m. on 13 June 1956. Six weeks later, on 26 July, the Egyptian president, Gamal Abdel Nasser, exploited Britain's weakness and moved his forces in to take control of the canal. Egypt now had its hand on Britain's windpipe, as Harold Macmillan – now chancellor – put it. Two thirds of Western Europe's oil supplies came through the canal and London was down to its last six weeks of reserves. But, with no troops in the area, what could Britain do?

In July 1956, Eden was faced with a diplomatic and economic catastrophe, partly of his own making, with few good options. The problem was that an immediate military response was seen as too risky; any route through the UN effectively meant a Soviet veto; and doing nothing was tantamount to appeasement, barely a decade after the end of the Second World War. To many at the time, Nasser was just another dictator seeking to extend his power. 'No more Adolf Hitlers,' declared the *Daily Herald*.[29] The *Daily Mirror* attacked the Egyptian leader as 'Grabber Nasser'.[30]

Soon, world figures began arriving in London in an attempt to find a solution. The American diplomat Robert Murphy – another veteran of Algiers – met Eden and concluded, rather gloomily, that the prime minister 'had not adjusted his thoughts to the altered world status of Great Britain.'[31] The fatal moment came when a French delegation arrived at Chequers to present Eden with just the kind of plan he had been looking for: Israel would invade the Suez Canal Zone and then the British and French would intervene as peacemakers to 'separate the combatants.'[32] In the most fateful moment of his career, Eden accepted.

On 30 October 1956, just a week before Americans went to the polls to elect their next president, Israeli forces crossed into Egypt, as planned, and Britain's Seaborne Assault Force set sail from Malta, en route to Port Said at the mouth of the canal. The Americans were furious and began preparing a security resolution imposing economic sanctions on Britain and France unless they agreed an immediate ceasefire. The crisis had begun because Britain had not been able to afford to garrison Egypt, and the country certainly could not afford an economic war with the US. Eden backed down and called off the operation twenty-four hours after its launch. It was a calamity. In retirement, Eden recalled a conversation with a young Enoch Powell in the 1940s, in which Powell had warned him to watch the Americans in the Middle East. 'Ah, Enoch, dear Enoch!' Eden began. 'He once said something to me I never understood. He said . . . "In the Middle East our great enemies are the Americans." You know, I had no idea what he meant . . . I do now.'[33]

By 5 January 1957, Eden had received medical advice that gave him no choice but to resign. A career of profound dignity and achievement had ended in failure and illness, revealing the delusion at the heart of Britain's post-war grand strategy. Britain and its Commonwealth was not one of the concentric circles that made up the Western world, neatly placed at the centre, but a declining power in an American world. In purely practical terms, little changed. But it was a psychological break, a moment that presaged a loss of confidence among Britain's elite and a spur for a change of policy. Suez not only transformed Britain's feelings towards itself, but its feelings towards the new Europe emerging on its doorstep. After 1956, Britain would stick ever more closely to the United States. The French, meanwhile, turned increasingly to Germany as a future partner. As German Chancellor Adenauer said to the socialist French prime minister Guy Mollet at the time, 'Europe will be your revenge.'[34]

In April 1956, the Spaak Report had published its conclusions, setting out the proposal for a new European Common Market and Atomic Energy Community to be agreed at a summit in Rome the following year. In comparison to the pained debates over the European Defence Community, the Treaties of Rome caused little more than a rumbling of political opposition, even though they were objectively far more radical. The opening words in the preamble committed the six founding members to 'an ever-closer union among the peoples of Europe,' in which they would take 'common action to eliminate the barriers which divide Europe.'

Even if such heady words are dismissed as mere aspiration – a kind of European version of life, liberty and the pursuit of happiness – the subsequent clauses cannot be. Article one of the Treaty of Rome established a new European Economic Community, committing the founding members to the progressive approximation of economic policy, the elimination of customs duties and all restrictions on movement of people, goods, services and capital. It also created a common European tariff, agricultural policy and a new set of institutions to represent the Community, including an assembly, council, commission and court. It was an extraordinarily ambitious programme which would change

Europe for ever. And yet it was ratified within the year, not only in Germany and the Benelux countries, but in France as well, that great bastion of Gaullist nationalism, which had been roused to song at the defeat of another federal project only two years earlier.

A number of factors combined to reduce the tension. Suez had revealed the limitations of France's alliance with Britain. A wild offer by Mollet at the height of the Suez crisis, for Britain and France to form a union, had been rejected by Eden, just as Churchill's offer to France during the war had been rejected by Pétain. Unlike the idea of a common European army, the Common Market deal was far less emotive. Crucially, in the background, the looming presence of Charles de Gaulle stayed silent. When, on 9 July, the treaties were presented to the National Assembly, the EEC Treaty was ratified by 342 votes to 234, and the Euratom Treaty (establishing the European Atomic Energy Community) by 332 votes to 240, despite most of the Gaullists voting against. France had taken its great leap forward into its European future without Britain.

Just as Europe was not the major issue for Britain in 1956, it was not France's principal concern either. By 1957, the Arab nationalism that had driven Britain out of Egypt in 1956 was threatening to drive France out of its slice of North Africa. But, unlike Egypt, which had never been a British colony, Algeria was formally a part of France, as much as Corsica or Normandy. When a series of armed nationalist attacks took place in November 1954, France's interior minister, François Mitterrand, summed up the French attitude: 'Algeria is France and the only negotiation is war.'[35] And so, war it was.

When Mollet visited Algiers in 1957, the month after winning power on a platform of peace, he was pelted with tomatoes by the angry pied noirs, who believed he was willing to sell them out. The trip was a turning point for France and for Europe, and Algeria became the catalyst for a revolution that would change Britain's relationship with Europe too. Mollet had gone to Algiers intending to appoint a liberal general by the name of Georges

Catroux, but instead appointed the hard-line Robert Lacoste, with a mission to restore order at any price.

This was the situation as Paul-Henri Spaak sat in Brussels, chairing the intergovernmental committee that would change Europe. Mollet was dealing not only with a revolution in European affairs, but also with a growing insurrection in Algeria that threatened the Fourth Republic. By 1957, the French army – desperate to restore the country's honour, as well as their own, after the humiliation of Dien Bien Phu – had begun to act outside the law, using torture in an effort to destroy the Algerian revolutionaries. Mollet's government soon fell – but not until June 1957, a few months after his government had signed the Treaty of Rome. The new government only managed to hobble on for five months, as the crisis began to infect the very core of the French body politic.

By early 1958, the situation had become critical. On 13 May, a demonstration in Algiers saw rioting pied noirs break into the city's government house, ransacking the building in the process. To address the situation, the new French prime minister, Pierre Pflimlin, appointed General Raoul Salan as the army's new commander-in-chief in Algiers, granting him emergency powers to deal with the crisis. Two days later, on 15 May, Salan addressed a crowd of pied noirs, assuring them Algeria would remain French, before ending with a cry of: '*Vive la France! Vive l'Algérie!*' And then, after a short pause: '*Vive le General de Gaulle!*'

It was the moment de Gaulle had been waiting for – and, indeed, preparing for. 'In the past, our country from the bottom of its heart showed its confidence in me to lead it to salvation,' he said. 'Today, in the face of the ordeals that are once again confronting us, I let it be known that I am ready to assume the powers of the Republic.'[36] For months, de Gaulle had been in communication with the leading army figures in Algiers, who were now seemingly intent on insurrection against their own government. The British embassy in Paris was so worried about the situation, it wrote to London that the country 'might well be on the way to becoming a sort of South American Republic or at best a kind of Franco-Spain.'[37]

The Fourth Republic was faced with a choice of military insurrection or the man committed to its destruction: Charles de Gaulle. In other words, it faced a choice between a fight to the death and an honourable suicide – and it chose suicide. In June 1958, Charles de Gaulle returned as prime minister of France, the last of the Fourth Republic, before becoming the first president of the Fifth less than a year later. For those back in London, his re-emergence offered hope as well as trepidation. While it was well understood that the old general could be impossible, as stubborn and impetuous as he was proud and unbiddable, he shared many of Britain's instincts, particularly when it came to the increasingly troublesome issue of Europe. It is hard to conceive of a world in which the Treaty of Rome could have emerged in the form it did, had the crisis in Algeria spiralled out of control a couple of years earlier, catapulting de Gaulle into power before Paul-Henri Spaak worked his magic. History rests on such moments. Charles de Gaulle returned to the Élysée just too late to save Britain from the choice it did not want to make. In power, he would make it pay for its indecision.

Chapter 3

As Charles de Gaulle was preparing to put the Fourth Republic out of its misery in Paris, Harold Macmillan was preparing for his first general election as prime minister in London. The result would cap a remarkable turnaround in a career that, until Algiers, had amounted to little.

Like many of his generation, Macmillan's life was principally defined by his service in the First World War. Wounded at the Battle of the Somme in 1916, he had lain for ten hours in a shell hole in no man's land, treating himself with morphine and alternating between feigning death as German soldiers skirted past and reading Aeschylus in the original Greek. Such apparently unflappable insouciance would become a hallmark of his political career, a trait which one French journalist would later dub 'Macmillisma'. But, rather like the man himself, such a reputation concealed far more than it revealed. Macmillan was a political operator and showman; he was also so racked with nerves before set-piece events, he would often be physically sick.

'How was Harold Macmillan when you met him?' Rab Butler asked in an interview with the biographer D. R. Thorpe in 1975. 'Was he the Duke's son-in-law or the crofter's great-grandson?'[1] This cutting little aside, though coloured by Butler's animosity towards the man who had denied him the premiership, captures something of the character of one of Britain's most consequential post-war figures. Macmillan was both a wealthy, Eton-educated Conservative grandee and a man who came from of a long line of weather-beaten crofters from the Western Isles of Scotland. Macmillan's ability, like that of many successful politicians, was to be able to play both roles, and to believe them when he did so.

Macmillan's shapeshifting reflects something of the ambiguity of his wider legacy. A study of his career reveals him as both a consensual, noblesse-oblige Tory *and* a ruthless Machiavel who flirted with Oswald Mosley's New Party in the 1930s, intrigued against Anthony Eden, and then, once in Number Ten, proved as slow as almost everyone else in British public life to spot the country's predicament.

Macmillan believed that the protection of British prosperity and influence meant not joining a federal Europe, and sought instead a new European 'Free Trade Area' that would give Britain the benefit of easy access to Monnet's Common Market without the need to sign up to the supranationalism at its core. De Gaulle quickly put paid to this idea, having grasped the obvious advantages to French industry, agriculture and diplomatic influence of keeping the new European bloc small.

Despite this setback, Macmillan and his 'middle way' reigned supreme at home. 'Butskellism' was the order of the day: the corporatist consensus presided over by successive chancellors Hugh Gaitskell and Rab Butler in the 1950s. And the public liked it, too. In the October 1959 election, Macmillan's Conservative Party was returned with a landslide one-hundred-seat majority, which saw Margaret Thatcher enter Parliament for the first time.

Few voices were actively standing outside this apparently all-powerful economic consensus. Enoch Powell, as ever, was one. In 1958, a seemingly innocuous clash between the Treasury and Macmillan's Number Ten over spending restraints had prompted Powell to lead a suicidal protest from his position as chief secretary to the Treasury. Infuriated by the prime minister's refusal to accept the Treasury's more austere spending plans, Powell and the entire Treasury team resigned. As the Conservative grandee

Quintin Hogg – Lord Hailsham – wrote in his diary at the time, the resignations appeared 'unreasonable to the point of being perverse'.[2] While Powell's critics would see this as a fitting epitaph for Powellism, Hogg's assessment was not shared by a young academic called Ralph Harris, the director general of a new free-market think tank, the Institute for Economic Affairs, which had been set up the year before, inspired by the writings of the Austrian-British economist Friedrich Hayek.

Harris would go on to become one of the most influential public intellectuals in post-war Britain – though, at the time, he and his institute were widely dismissed as eccentric. Brought up on a 'bleak council estate' in north London, as he put it, Harris found his way to Cambridge via a scholarship to a local grammar school in Tottenham, quickly becoming enthralled by Hayek's *The Road to Serfdom*, published in 1944, a cry for individual liberty that Harris would hold to for the rest of his life. After graduating from Cambridge with a first in 1947, Harris joined the Conservative Political Centre, then under the control of Rab Butler, before standing for Parliament in both the 1951 and 1955 elections, the latter of which saw him 'narrowly [escape] being elected', as he later put it.[3] 'Never again, thereafter, was Ralph tempted to act as a politician,' wrote Geoffrey Howe, years later, in posthumous memory of his friend and intellectual sparring partner.[4] Despite never being elected, Harris would have a far more profound effect on British politics than most MPs, through his work at the IEA alone.

Having decided against a career in politics, Harris entered academia and then journalism, before finally arriving at the berth that would make his name, joining the IEA as its first general director – and sole employee – in January 1957. The IEA was the brainchild of Antony Fisher, a Sussex farming entrepreneur who decided to use the profits of his Buxted Chickens company to create an 'educational charity' to promote free markets, having also been inspired by Hayek's work, which he'd read in condensed form in the *Reader's Digest*.

Though intellectually formidable, Harris was a man of easy charm and humour, with the familiar air of an English eccentric: toothbrush moustache, pipe clenched between his teeth, always armed with a portable pepper grinder, just in case.

Harris was joined at the IEA by Arthur Seldon, another man of formidable intellect who grew up in the most working class of environments in interwar London before finding his way into academia. Seldon was born to Jewish émigré parents who had escaped the pogroms that gripped Kiev shortly after the turn of the new century, and he was drawn first to the Liberals, having witnessed Oswald Mosley's blackshirts in the 1930s and 'associated the Tories with appeasement'.

Together, Harris and Seldon made a formidable team, and both saw the clash between Powell and Macmillan as a victory for the prime minister's 'middle way' over the Conservative Party's 'liberal wing'. Harris and Seldon agreed to seek out Powell and invite him to write a paper for the IEA, published in 1960, with the title, 'Saving in a Free Society'.

For the IEA, Powell was a particularly attractive disseminator, his growing gravitas allowing the institute's ideas to reach a wider audience. For Powell, the IEA offered an outlet for his interest in the economic questions of the day, from the role of the state to the causes of inflation. Writing in *The Spectator* in March 1959, Powell praised the IEA's work and observed that 'a lot of people in a lot of places have been rediscovering uses and even beauties in the laws of supply and demand.'[5] Long before Thatcherism was even a thought, let alone a word, Powellism largely revolved around challenging the economic orthodoxy of the day.

Powell was not alone in worrying about the country's direction of travel. Writing in *The Daily Telegraph* in February 1960, a journalist called T. E. Utley, known outside of print as Peter Utley, wondered what the Conservative Party under Macmillan was trying to achieve. 'The Tories have shown that they can win General Elections. Have they still got a philosophy of government?' he wondered.[6] Utley would go on to be one of the most influential conservative journalists in Britain. An extraordinary figure, who was adopted at birth and blind from the age of nine, he had developed a remarkable capacity to memorize information and dictate in clear, logical prose. After being educated at home and then at Cambridge, he entered Fleet Street and quickly established himself as one of the most recognizable Tory evangelists in the country, the black eyepatch adding a formidable aura to his fierce intellect. Utley's challenge to Macmillan in 1960 was a straw in the wind for a later, more concerted challenge to the post-war consensus. 'The Conservative Party, for all Mr. Macmillan's glittering triumphs in different parts of the world, is as much the captive of its confused and sentimental Left wing as ever in its history,' he declared.[7]

At the time, however, few were paying much attention to such musings. Certainly not Macmillan, who had bigger concerns. Despite his political supremacy at home, the nature of Britain's diplomatic predicament remained the same. In 1960, having failed to fold the Common Market into his proposed European Free Trade Area, Macmillan did the next best thing and created an alternative economic bloc of his own: the European Free Trade Association, or EFTA. The problem was, the original continental bloc was stronger, a reality that quickly began to cause real consternation in Whitehall. In April 1960, a memorandum was drawn up by the Treasury's Sir Frank Lee, which, more than any other official document, marks a turning point in Britain's post-war European policy. Today, the document is jarring only in how painfully conventional its conclusions appear. Yet, at the time, they were revolutionary.

In Lee's assessment, the Common Market posed a long-term challenge not only to Britain's economic interests, but also to its influence. The Six, he wrote, would soon emerge as a power 'comparable in size and influence to the United States and the USSR.' Such a scenario would leave Britain out in the cold, undermining both its influence with the US *and* within the

Commonwealth: 'We should find ourselves replaced as the second member of the North Atlantic Alliance and our relative influence with the United States in all fields would diminish.' Sooner or later, this reality would start to undermine EFTA as well: 'The independence which we have sought to preserve by remaining aloof from European integration would be of doubtful value, since our diminished status would suggest only a minor role for us in international affairs.'[8]

This, in a nutshell, was the case for joining Monnet's project. Within two months, Lee's advice became official government policy. Britain would seek to join the Common Market, with a young Edward Heath placed in charge of the negotiations. It was a remarkable U-turn from the consensus that had prevailed since 1950. Two decades on from its finest hour, Britain was prepared to join a federal European community whose central idea was the subordination of national sovereignty to something entirely new: a common European authority.

But, even if Macmillan had changed British government policy, he had yet to arrive at the logical conclusion of what this meant: joining the Common Market meant accepting the Treaty of Rome in its entirety. Nor had his overall strategy changed. In a paper called 'The Grand Design' which he shared with the cabinet that December, the prime minister set out the whole point of his new European policy: 'The need to organise the great forces of the Free World – U.S.A., Britain and Europe – economically, politically and militarily in a coherent effort to withstand the Communist tide all over the world.'[9] Macmillan's conception of the free world had not changed from that which Churchill had sketched out in 1942, or, for that matter, that which Monnet had believed still existed in 1950. The decision to pursue British entry into 'Europe', in other words, was not part of some great awakening. On the contrary, Macmillan's strategy was part of a plan to protect Britain's global power and influence.

The belief that Europe could protect British power and

prosperity was adopted by almost every subsequent government of the twentieth century, the conclusion of a political class committed, a priori, to the pursuit of influence. A curious detail of this calculation is that Enoch Powell – who, despite his resignation in 1958, returned to government in July 1960 as health minister – did not demur, accepting Macmillan's application to join, rather than resigning. The Labour Party, however, was a different matter.

While Labour was, by instinct, internationalist, it was never comfortable with supranationalism. The central ideology of the Labour Party was democratic socialism – improving the economic condition of the working class by seizing control of the political levers. When Monnet's European project was born, the British parliamentary system remained an extraordinarily powerful tool in the socialist arsenal. British parliamentary democracy had produced a national health service, national electricity network, national railways and, of course, national mines. It is hardly surprising that, in 1950, Labour did not want to hand over any of Parliament's power to a High Authority based in Luxembourg.

This was the standard socialist view, shared not only by Attlee, but by the heroes of working-class Labour, from Ernest Bevin on the right of the party to Aneurin Bevan on the left. In August 1957, just a few months after the signing of the Treaty of Rome, Bevan dismissed the new Common Market as a return to 'free markets – and the jungle.'[10]

When Attlee was replaced as Labour leader in 1955 – by another public-school moderate, Hugh Gaitskell – most of the party's senior figures shared a deep scepticism toward the European project. At the party's 1961 conference, a pro-Common Market resolution from the right was heavily voted down. Indeed, in the wake of this conference, the darling of the left, Harold Wilson, noticeably sharpened his anti-European rhetoric.

When Macmillan sought Parliament's approval to begin negotiating the potential terms of British entry into Europe, Wilson warned that there was no more 'dangerous illusion than that *laissez-faire* and the cold east wind' would improve Britain's economic prospects. What was needed was 'positive, purposive, economic planning', he said. This would be the guiding purpose of his premiership when he eventually took charge in 1964. For Wilson, though, such economic planning did not seem possible in the Common Market. 'I say frankly to the House that as I read the Treaty of Rome, and the intentions of those who at present operate it, the measures necessary . . . cannot be implemented without substantial amendments to the relevant articles to the Treaty.'[11]

It was not just the economics that were difficult for Labour at the time. In an illustration of how important the Commonwealth remained to members of both major parties, Wilson declared that, if Britain must choose between its old colonial ties and its immediate economic interests in Europe, the decision was simple: 'We are not entitled to sell our friends and kinsmen down the river for a problematical and marginal advantage in selling washing machines in Dusseldorf.'[12] For Wilson, a cultured and highly educated man, the Commonwealth remained the place where Britain's 'friends and kinsmen' could be found. Europe, in contrast, was where you sold washing machines.

From the moment Robert Schuman took his great leap into the dark in 1950, Britain's response to its Europe problem has been shaped by a series of hopes and fears, delusions and pragmatic calculations, each rooted in history and circumstance. In 1960, most British politicians remained emotionally committed to the world beyond Europe, whereas they felt no such commitment to the continent.

For Wilson, in 1960, the most vital issue was not the economic case for joining Europe, which he argued was in the balance, but whether joining the Common Market 'explicitly or implicitly means a move towards a federal Europe.' If it did, Wilson said, British membership should be out of the question. He concluded by summarizing the problem faced by almost all British governments since the country found its way into the bloc. 'There should be no doubt on this federal issue,' he said. 'There should be no double talk with Europe about it. Our position should be stated so that there is no accusation of bad faith, of dragging our feet, of perfidious Albion, if, subsequently, Europe seeks to move towards federation and then, and only then, we make clear our opposition to it.'[13]

From the moment Macmillan changed his mind about Europe in 1960, Britain's policy has been beset by this very problem, including under Wilson himself. Britain was attempting to join a club for explicitly political reasons, while refusing to face up to the political reality of the club it was joining. Presented with a dilemma it did not want, it first sought to find a way to avoid it, before reluctantly deciding it had no choice but to seek entry. But it did so not because it shared the convictions of the project's founding fathers, but because it came to believe membership was the only way to maintain Britain as a first-rank global power. But, as the Suez Crisis had so aptly demonstrated, Britain had already ceased to be a first-rank power. The banal truth was that, in or out of Europe, the old world Macmillan and Wilson were trying to protect had gone, as Powell had already seen.

There was, of course, a significant minority in the Labour movement which opposed the conventional scepticism towards Europe of the left, most notably the modernizing Gaitskellite Roy Jenkins. Yet, in the early 1960s, Labour scepticism remained firmly in the ascendency. At the Labour Party Conference in October 1962, just as Harold Macmillan's negotiations with Europe were reaching their climax, Labour leader Hugh Gaitskell set out his position. Joining a European Common Market, Gaitskell declared, meant 'the end of Britain as an independent nation state.'

'It may be a good thing or a bad thing but we must recognise that this is so. We must be clear about this: it does mean, if this is the idea, the end of Britain as an independent European state. I make no apology for repeating it. It means the end of a thousand years of history.'[14]

Joining the European Economic Community, of course, did

not mean that. Yet there is an honesty to Gaitskell's analysis, a willingness to grasp the radicalism at the heart of the European project. Signing the Treaty of Rome demanded a real surrender of national sovereignty. But, more importantly, it meant a *political* commitment to a project whose future direction Britain would not be able to set. It meant, as Jean Monnet had set out so clearly in 1950, the creation of a new collective European interest above the old national interest.

Gaitskell was enough of a realist to admit it was not an easy dilemma. If Britain could somehow join the Common Market without undermining its links to the Commonwealth, its foreign policy or its economic sovereignty, then he would support it. But it was far from 'an open-and-shut issue,' he said, adding that, if the Labour Party ended up opposing membership, 'the only right and proper and democratic thing is to let the people decide the issue.' And so, as early as 1962, the idea of a referendum emerged into the national debate. Gaitskell's speech would resonate through the Labour Party for a quarter of a century thereafter.

As 1962 faded into 1963, the Labour Party remained a largely Eurosceptic party, even though the term had not yet been invented. In the Commons, Michael Foot dismissed Monnet's project as a 'rich nations' club'. Influential left-wing voices in the media also agreed. The historian A. J. P. Taylor used his column in Lord Beaverbook's *Sunday Express* to regularly rail against the new Europe emerging on Britain's doorstep. Within a month of the new year, however, Hugh Gaitskell would be dead, replaced by Harold Wilson. Dead, too, were Harold Macmillan's European dreams, shot down by the man he had helped to seize power in Algiers two decades earlier.

The defining moment came on 14 January 1963, when Charles de Gaulle approached the lectern at the Élysée Palace in Paris to deliver his verdict on Macmillan's application. For eighteen months, the prime minister and his lead negotiator, Edward Heath, had been trying to agree terms for Britain's entry. But then came de Gaulle's judgement: *Non*. 'The entry of Britain would completely alter the entire set of arrangements, understandings, compensations, rules that have been agreed between the Six,' he declared. Once Britain joined, the cohesion of its original members would fall apart, he claimed. Worse: 'It would take on the appearance of a colossal Atlantic community under American dependence and direction.' Europe might have been born with American money, under American diplomatic pressure, but that mattered little to de Gaulle. Why should it?

De Gaulle shared Britain's distrust of European supranationalism, but understood that it offered France an opportunity. 'What is the point of Europe?' he asked his confidante Alain Peyrefitte in October 1962. 'The point is that one is not dominated by either the Russians or the Americans.' As a bloc of six, Europe was both big enough to matter on the world stage and small enough for France to remain a dominant player. 'Europe is the means by which France can become again what she has ceased to be since Waterloo,' de Gaulle declared. 'First in the world.'[15]

In many ways, de Gaulle's Europe policy was a mirror image of Macmillan's – both in its ambition and delusion. The goal for each man was the restoration of his country's global grandeur. While Macmillan saw that Britain's role in the world was to be the lynchpin in the Atlantic alliance, de Gaulle saw this as subservience to an American empire – an assessment, ironically, shared by Enoch Powell.

The paradox of de Gaulle's presence in the Élysée from 1958 was that it offered reassurance to Britain about the new Europe being built, while also acting as the main barrier to entry. 'The tragedy is that we agree with de Gaulle on almost everything,' Macmillan noted in his diary. 'We are anti-federalists; so is he. We fear a German revival and have no desire to see a revived Germany. These are de Gaulle's thoughts too.'[16]

De Gaulle's veto robbed Macmillan of his purpose. 'All our policies at home and abroad are in ruins,' the prime minister confided in his diary. The observation is revealing in more ways than one. Sir Michael Fraser, director of the Conservative research department, later recalled that Europe had become the party's *deus ex machina*. 'It was to create a new contemporary political argument with insular Socialism; dish the Liberals by stealing their clothes; give us something *new* after 12–13 years; act as a catalyst of modernisation; give us a new place in the international sun.'[17]

Europe had become a magic shield that could protect Britain from reality. It could rejuvenate the economy and offer a new arena in which Britain could be great again. Writing in *The Spectator* in May 1963, T. E. Utley captured the mood of many disappointed Tories: 'The prevailing impression of Conservative policy over the last 11 years is one of extreme incoherence,' he wrote. 'Essentially, we remain in much the same position as we were in 1951.' Beyond all the noise and fury, in other words, the general trend held: Britain was a country at peace, with rising home ownership and full employment; still a world power, but slowly falling behind its peers, without any real idea of how to change course. Utley was scathing of the prime minister in particular: 'Mr Macmillan, like General de Gaulle, had seized power with the aid of the Right only in order to betray the Right.' Macmillan had pursued a policy of 'indiscriminate surrender' in Africa, he claimed, and had meekly accepted the role of America's 'European agent' while prioritizing full employment and the welfare state over 'the revival of enterprise and the defence of the pound.'[18] This, too, was the view of Enoch Powell.

In an interview with Utley in *The Sunday Telegraph* later that year, Powell said he was 'deeply worried' by the trends towards 'national self-abasement' internationally and 'the habit of looking automatically to government for the solution whenever confronted by any kind of problem' domestically. Powell argued such habits played directly into Labour's hands. 'They oblige even Tory Governments to operate within the framework of an implicitly Socialist public opinion', he declared .[19] It is difficult to read such sentiments, expressed by Powell in 1963, and not hear the voice of Margaret Thatcher almost two decades later.

For Macmillan, it was not the friendly fire from Tory critics like Utley or Powell which sapped his political strength, but the collapse of his strategy in Paris and the hounding from Labour's new leader Harold Wilson over the Profumo sex scandal then gripping his government. During 1963, Macmillan visibly aged and tired, unable to summon the energy to keep pace with the world and those seeking to replace him. When his doctor told him a prostate issue would require surgery, the news jolted him from the indecision over his future that had gripped him since de Gaulle's veto. Even though Macmillan had been told his condition was treatable, it seemed he'd lost his desire for power and resigned.

Harold Wilson, in contrast, was everything Macmillan was not: a new man for a new age, with a mission to restore Britain that did not require the permission of Charles de Gaulle. In this, Wilson was inestimably helped by the Conservative Party's rather unexpected choice to replace Macmillan, late in 1963, with the achingly patrician Alec Douglas-Home. To become prime minister, Douglas-Home had first to renounce his earldom.

Within a year, Douglas-Home would narrowly lose the election to Labour, presaging a new era in British politics. After thirteen years and three election defeats, Labour was back in power. The new prime minister was a sharp-witted grammar-school Yorkshireman and precocious Oxford don, who stood not for consensus, but modernity – science, technology, progress, liberation. Britain was falling behind and needed to be brought up to speed with the rest of the world, dragged into the future with a new planned economy that would unleash the 'white heat of technology' and set the country free. Under the Tories, Britain had lost its mission. Under Labour, it had found a new one.

The sense of one era giving way to the next was captured by the death of Winston Churchill in January 1965, just a few months after Wilson had become prime minister. Churchill's death marked the passing not just of Britain's greatest warlord, but also, it seemed, the imperial nation he once embodied.

By 1965, the winds of change had blown through the empire and waves of Commonwealth immigration had brought new communities to Britain, as well as new tensions born of old prejudices. The 1960s was the era of Beatlemania and the miniskirt, cheap holidays abroad and the motorway – though, of course, also the era of mods and rockers rioting in seaside resorts and TV characters like Alf Garnett, the reactionary old man of *Till Death Us Do Part*.

To face this new world, the Conservative Party understood it needed its own modern man. A few months after his defeat in 1964, Douglas-Home resigned – but not until he had overhauled the rules for choosing a new party leader. For the first time, there would be a simple election of Conservative MPs. Three candidates emerged to replace Douglas-Home, the strong favourite being Edward Heath, the bright new representative of Macmillisma, though of more humble origins and with a greater commitment to modernization. Heath believed that Britain needed to be freed from its post-war shackles, not by socialist planning, but by pragmatic technocratic reform – and Europe. Heath's main opponent was the former chancellor Reginald Maudling, who, despite being a year younger than Heath, was less of a modernizing choice. The third leadership candidate was Enoch Powell, who stood not because he thought he had a chance of victory, but, in his wife's words, to show himself papabile, or capable of being Pope.

When the result was announced, Heath won 150 votes to Maudling's 133 and Powell's 15. So began a decade in British politics during which power would swap between Wilson and Heath, two representatives of modernism and reform, who would each nevertheless come to be known for their failure to modernize Britain. Yet it would also be the era of Enoch Powell, the great loser of the 1965 leadership election, who would never again hold a government position, but whose influence on British politics would grow to an extraordinary degree.

For the first two years of his premiership, Wilson looked unstoppable, the defining figure of a new Britain, with the gravitas and vision to haul it into the new world. While he may have only sneaked into power, the narrowness of his victory masks the scale of his achievement. In 1964, Wilson overturned a one-hundred-seat Conservative majority with the biggest swing to the party since 1945.

In 1964, Wilson had led on a platform promising a New Britain, 'mobilising the resources of technology under a national plan.' The Labour manifesto promised to reverse the decline of the previous thirteen years, 'affording a new opportunity to equal, and if possible surpass, the roaring progress of other western powers.' As ever, the plan almost immediately bumped up against the reality of Britain's predicament. On the night Wilson became prime minister, he was informed the deficit for 1964 was forecast to be £800 million – double the amount he had publicly predicted during the campaign. The Treasury presented Wilson with three choices: devalue the pound; impose new import quotas; or introduce temporary tariffs on imported goods.

Maintaining the value of sterling was considered a key plank of British power and prestige in the world, without which not only would its presence east of Suez be in jeopardy, but with it its special relationship with the US, privileged position within the Atlantic alliance, and even its leadership of the Commonwealth itself, where many countries still held reserves in sterling. As shadow chancellor, Wilson had warned that any future devaluation 'would be regarded all over the world as a defeat.'

Within twenty-four hours of kissing the Queen's hand, Wilson had stepped onto a political high wire from which he would never be able to dismount. By refusing to devalue, Wilson saved himself from an immediate crisis but was left permanently exposed to the economic winds that would buffet him for the rest of his premiership.

Of course, none of this was visible at the time. 'Wilson's first two years as Prime Minister were brilliant,' said Denis Healey.[20] Election promises to increase pensions and abolish prescription charges were kept, the value of the pound was maintained and, in 1965, his National Plan was finally published, the expression of all that he stood for. This was how Britain would pull itself out of decline. This was Wilsonism. This was modernity. In 1966, Wilson went back to the country seeking a mandate for his vision. And he got it, winning a ninety-eight-seat majority. In the space of three years, since becoming Labour leader, Wilson had turned a one-hundred-seat Conservative majority on its head. Heath's modern Toryism had been crushed by Wilson's modern socialism. A new Britain really was being built.

The year 1966 was both the crowning achievement of Harold Wilson's premiership and the moment from which he never quite recovered. Within months of what had seemed like an era-defining victory, the pound once again came under pressure, unable to sustain its value without ever-increasing costs at home. Wilson had staked his reputation on maintaining the value of the pound, but the hope that the government could grow its way out of trouble had all but vanished, leaving Wilson facing the unpalatable choice of austerity or devaluation. He chose austerity.

Wilson's refusal to devalue in 1966 prioritized British influence over his own economic planning, robbing him of his purpose and leaving a void at the heart of his government. Into that void came Europe. Where Wilson had once been sceptical of Europe as a barrier to economic planning, it now became the answer. Like Macmillan before him, Wilson needed a mission, a 'bounce to get back,' in the words of his soon-to-be chancellor Roy Jenkins. By October, he had secured the support of his cabinet for a new attempt to join the Common Market. But, even though Europe had become the alternative to the scuppered National Plan, the very act of pursuing entry into the Common Market only made devaluation more likely. To the markets, it sent a signal that old ideas of Commonwealth trade and British commitment to an extra-European role in the world were changing.

If 1966 was the year Wilson began to lose his reputation as the prophet of modernity, it had disappeared entirely by the end of 1968. Over the course of these two painful years, Wilson formally reapplied for membership of the Common Market, gave up the fight against devaluation and, finally, announced the withdrawal of British forces 'east of Aden'. Whatever the rights and wrongs of each individual decision, collectively they amounted to a repudiation of his government's raison d'être. Wilson had rejected Europe, painting it as a threat to national economic control and to Britain's influence beyond the continent. Yet, as prime minister, faced with the reality of Britain's domestic situation, he turned to Europe and withdrew from the world.

For those in Wilson's cabinet still opposed to entry, there remained one solace: Charles de Gaulle. Richard Crossman, a Bevanite Eurosceptic, spoke for many when he told a colleague not to panic because 'The General will save us from our own folly.'[21] And he did, rejecting Wilson's application in 1968. But even a figure as resolute as General de Gaulle would not be around for ever.

In May 1968, a young academic called Roger Scruton found himself in Paris, watching on as gangs of student revolutionaries smashed shop windows, hurled cobblestones at the police and demanded the removal of 'the Old Fascist and his regime', as some of his friends put it.[22]

The Old Fascist, of course, was de Gaulle, father of the Fifth Republic and saviour of French honour, who was by then approaching a decade in the Élysée after returning to power in 1958. Earlier in the day, Scruton had been reading de Gaulle's *Mémoires de Guerre*. 'All my life, I have had a certain idea of France,' de Gaulle began. This idea was of a country rooted in its past, in the notion of itself as a great country filled with mystique and power, ambition and grandeur. For Scruton, these ideas had allowed de Gaulle to save France, not just in 1940, but again in 1958 when the country seemed on the brink of anarchy.

Facing his friends that evening in May 1968, Scruton demanded to know what idea of France compelled them; what vision of France were they fighting for? His friends produced the works of Michel Foucault, which – in Scruton's account – declared that wherever there is power there is oppression, and wherever there is oppression there is the right to destroy. The violence on display in Paris was not just an expression of frustration with the government, but the living manifestation of Foucault's ideology, Scruton believed. True or not – there were many ideological currents driving the events of 1968 – to Scruton, such ideas were appalling. People did not need 'liberating' from their culture or the order and institutions that had been built by their forebears. These were the treasures of their inheritance.

Suddenly, Scruton found himself filled with 'the consciousness of death,' the sense that all he loved was being sacrificed on the altar of progress.[23] Such thoughts would stay with him for the rest of his life, driving him to become one of the most influential and controversial academics in Britain, a key figure in the conservative counter-revolution to come. In 1968, though, it wasn't only Scruton who felt the cold breath of mortality, but de Gaulle himself.

With the government unable to restore order, de Gaulle became increasingly panicked. At one point, the ageing general lost his nerve to such an extent he secretly fled the country to a French military base in Germany. And, although de Gaulle eventually regained control, he would never again recover the authority he once had. Within a year of May 1968, he would be gone, resigning the day after losing a quixotic referendum that was neither necessary nor relevant to the crisis at hand, but which he had insisted on elevating into a question of personal authority.

Suddenly, a new world had opened up – not only for France, but for Britain as well. With de Gaulle out of power, Britain might finally find its way into Europe. Yet, 1968 was a year of upheaval for Britain, too. This was the year that Enoch Powell finally burst onto the national stage with a speech of such violent foreboding it would forever change the face of British politics.

Powell's speech, in his home city of Birmingham, on 20 April 1968, remains the most incendiary in modern British history. To this day, the phrase 'Rivers of Blood' elicits a sense of unease. The speech cost Powell his job in the shadow cabinet and – eventually – the chance of high office, and it turned immigration into a toxic subject. The speech also lit a flame that has yet to go out, a flame that would burn Powellism into British politics in ways that would far outlast its propagator's own political career.

Powell had always been a figure of wary bipartisan respect in the House of Commons, admired for the intensity of his intellect and the independence of his spirit, even if he was seen as something of a crank pursuing marginal causes like monetarism, free-floating currencies and an end to price controls. However, what set Powellism alight was not the boggy terrain of economics, but the emotional kindling of race and immigration.

Until the early 1950s, immigration into Britain from the Commonwealth was relatively limited, amounting to around 3,000 per year. From then on, however, it began to rapidly increase, reaching more than 136,000 in 1961, the year before Powell began attending cabinet.[24]

Britain was not unique in this regard. For centuries, the story of migration had been one of mass European emigration, populating the lands of the 'New World' and the colonies of the old. From 1945, this trend went into reverse, as labour shortages and the experiences of wartime service brought new communities to Britain, Europe and the United States, which then settled and grew.

With rising public unease in Britain, the Macmillan government passed a new 'Commonwealth Immigrants Act' in 1962, which sought to deal with 'the problems caused by the uncontrolled entry into the United Kingdom of British subjects from overseas,' but which, effectively, targeted those coming from non-white countries.

Formally, the 1962 Act divided British subjects into different classes according to how their passports were issued. Anyone who had a British (or Irish) passport issued in the UK was exempt from controls. But those who had received their British passport from a colonial government overseas lost their right of entry.

The number of Commonwealth citizens arriving in Britain soon fell from 136,000 in 1961 to just 57,000 in 1963. And yet, in

Britain itself, the 'Commonwealth' population continued to grow, rising from just over 500,000 West Indian and Asian-born residents in 1961 to around 1.15 million in 1971.[25]

Part of the reason for this rise – beyond natural demographic change and wider family settlement – was a steady flow of East African Asians moving to Britain throughout the 1960s, culminating in a mass exodus from this corner of the Commonwealth in 1967–8. Among those moving to Britain at this time was a young Hindu doctor called Rashvir Sunak, from Kenya, and his wife Usha, who had been born and raised in Tanganyika, in present-day Tanzania. Together, they would go on to have a son called Rishi.

The Sunaks of East Africa were able to move to Britain at this time because of a strange quirk of decolonization. After Kenya became independent in 1962, many Asians in the country chose to renew their British passport rather than take up Kenyan citizenship. This meant that, rather than receiving their passport from the pre-independence colonial office, which would have disqualified them from the automatic right to move to Britain, they instead received their British passport from the postcolonial high commissions. Their passports were therefore issued by the British government, so many escaped the restrictions of the 1962 Act.

For the Labour government, however, the legal technicalities were soon deemed irrelevant. As public hostility grew, the home secretary James Callaghan moved to further restrict the rights of Commonwealth citizens from being able to move to Britain, passing a new Immigration Act in 1968 which would later become infamous as a form of state-sanctioned racism, putting into legislation the right of entry for the almost exclusively white residents of the Commonwealth who had at least one parent or grandparent born in Britain, while further tightening restrictions on everybody else. Another Immigration Act would follow in 1971, further entrenching this divide – and even coming up with a new word to describe those with an ancestral connection to Mother Britain: 'patrial'.

For Enoch Powell, the new controls of 1968 did not go far enough. From 1964, with the Conservative Party in Opposition, Powell had begun to speak out on the subject in ever more strident terms, upsetting even his friends at the IEA, who wrote to him criticizing his language.* But, for Powell, the issue was becoming another obsession, and in 1968 he concluded that he needed to shock the Conservative Party into action.

The great explosion in British political life took place in the drab, anonymous setting of a small upstairs room in the Midland Hotel in Birmingham. Powell knew the language he deployed would cause immediate controversy. Earlier in the week, he had told Clement Jones, a journalist for the Wolverhampton *Express & Star*, that he was 'going to make a speech at the weekend and it's going to "fizz" like a rocket; but whereas all rockets fall to earth, this one is going to stay up.'[26]

The essence of Powell's speech was that the rate of immigration from Britain's former colonies had risen to such a level it would destroy the nation itself. Powell warned that, unless it was immediately halted and even reversed, civil disorder was inevitable. 'Like the Roman, I seem to see "the River Tiber foaming with much blood",' he declared. This was the line for which the speech would forever be known. But it was far from the only section suffused with violent prophecy. Powell repeated the words of one angry white constituent who had told him that soon 'the black man will have the whip hand over the white man.'

Powell was alive to the outrage he would cause. 'I can already hear the chorus of execration,' he said in his address. 'How dare

* Ralph Harris wrote to Powell on 1 March 1968, 'arguing that his views on immigration were inconsistent with the general libertarian philosophy he had applied in other areas,' Simon Heffer records in *Like the Roman* (Chapter 10, 'The Silent Member'). Powell replied on 8 March: 'It does seem to me right and necessary that any country should have the legal discretion whether or not to admit within its boundaries those who wish to settle there, and, for this purpose, to distinguish between "its own people" and the rest of the inhabitants of the world.'

I say such a horrible thing?' Powell's answer was that he did not have the right *not* to do so. It was a question of national survival. He described the man worrying about black domination as 'a decent, ordinary fellow Englishman' who was only expressing what hundreds of thousands of others were saying and thinking in the areas of the country which Powell said were 'undergoing the total transformation to which there is no parallel in a thousand years of English history.'

Powell believed that it had become a matter of 'extreme urgency' and called for the further inflow of immigrants to be stopped, alongside the promotion of 'the maximum outflow.' He claimed that these demands were the official policy of the Conservative Party, which was not quite true—the official Tory position was that the government should 'help immigrants already here to rejoin their families in their countries of origin, or to return with their families to these countries, if they so wish'.* Powell's rhetoric then began to grow in intensity. 'We must be mad, *literally mad*, as a nation to be permitting the annual inflow of some 50,000 dependents.' It was, he said, 'like watching a nation busily engaged in heaping up its own funeral pyre.'

Powell then recounted another anonymous anecdote about an old lady whose once respectable street had been transformed into 'a place of noise and confusion' after all the white families left. The woman herself remained but would not rent the rooms in her boarding house to the new immigrants. 'She is becoming afraid to go out. Windows are broken. She finds excreta pushed

---

* The Conservative Party's 1966 manifesto set out this pledge as part of a series of policies to 'deal with the problem of immigration' (Conservative Party manifesto 1966, *Action Not Words*, Political Speech Archives), although by the time of Powell's speech in 1968 there had been discussions in the shadow cabinet about encouraging people to return to former colonies. The party's 1970 manifesto, 'A Better Tomorrow', declared there would be 'no further large scale permanent immigration' into the UK and promised to 'give assistance to Commonwealth immigrants who wish to return to their countries of origin.' (Political Speech Archives) There was no policy to encourage the 'maximum outflow' of immigrants. (FactCheck: Enoch Powell's 1968 speech, Channel 4 News)

through her letter box. When she goes to the shops, she is followed by children, charming, wide-grinning piccaninnies. They cannot speak English, but one word they know. "Racialist," they chant.'

The black-and-white footage of the event retains its shock value to this day, and as such continues to be shared online by those who see in Powell a kind of prophet, including many with straightforwardly racist views.* The specific use of the slur 'piccaninnies' would in later decades colour the career of a very different populist conservative who would change the life of the country. Powell maintained that neither the speech nor he himself was 'racialist' in any sense and that he was merely quoting his constituent, who would not rent her rooms to immigrants. Yet, in introducing her story, he specifically allowed her to 'speak for me'. It is also not the case that Powell's language was only subsequently considered beyond the pale. The speech caused an immediate and unprecedented furore, and some of Powell's shadow cabinet colleagues threatened to resign if he was not sacked. The Tory leader, Ted Heath, was so outraged he rang round the shadow cabinet seeking support for his plan to sack Powell immediately. Margaret Thatcher told Heath that Powell's language was 'strong meat,' but that she sympathized with the overall point he was making. She advised Heath to 'let things cool down' rather than heighten the crisis by sacking him. Heath nevertheless telephoned Powell on Sunday evening to dismiss him. They never spoke again.

The public reaction was of equal intensity, though altogether different from Heath's. In east London, workers took to the streets in support of their unlikely new tribune. Within weeks of the speech, Gallup found that, of those questioned, 74 per cent agreed

* The British National Party's youth wing, for example, promoted Powell with a poem sung by its mascot 'Billy Brit': 'In 1912 a lion was born./Enoch was his name./A gentleman. A British hero./Through truth, the man found fame./He gave a speech called "Rivers of Blood"./And never gave up the fight./Enoch Powell spoke for me and Enoch Powell was white.' (Milmo and Rawlinson, '10 things you should know about the BNP when you watch Question Time tonight', *The Independent*, 22 October 2009)

with what Powell had said and 69 per cent felt Heath was wrong to sack him.[27] Powell's political fortunes had been transformed overnight. Before the speech, just 1 per cent of those polled by Gallup felt Powell was the right man to replace Heath if there were a vacancy. After the speech, he became the favourite. In his diary, the Labour cabinet minister Richard Crossman wrote that Powell had 'stirred up the nearest thing to a mass movement since the 1930s.'[28]

At the Conservative Party Conference that autumn, Powell was the star draw, his every move met with near hysteria. In September 1968, T. E. Utley asked, in *The Sunday Telegraph*, 'How strong is the Powell challenge?' He described Powell's mission as 'The conversion of the Conservative Party from an outmoded imperialism to a realistic patriotism, and from a largely dirigiste and paternalistic view of economic policy to a radical policy of economic liberalism.' For Utley, Powell was a latter-day Joseph Chamberlain, seeking to 'alter the nature of the Conservative Party – to transform it from a "safe" party, to be turned to for sound administration in a crisis – into a . . . dynamic party with a defined political belief and social faith.' Utley speculated that, much like Chamberlain, Powell was unlikely ever to lead the party, but that his platform offered the Tory party 'a rare chance to achieve a permanent and solid foothold in areas of society which are assumed to belong by right to its opponents – in other words, among the working class.' Utley then concluded with a warning: 'Containing Powellism, if not Powell, will, I believe, be the main preoccupation of Tory internal politics for the next decade at least.'[29]

By 1969, Enoch Powell was a figure of extraordinary fame and influence, who could not deliver a speech without finding himself accosted by left-wing activists who accused him of being a racist and a Nazi, but also by actual racists who thought they had found in Powell an unlikely leader. Powell was once again racked by his inner contradictions: a man of high intellect, driven by passions he could barely contain; an ascetic loner from a world of European high culture, who had become a tribune not only for the provincial England he loved but many of the extremists that he did not. Powell believed Parliament was the stage on which national life should play out, where its great philosophical debates found their voice and meaning. Yet, here he was leading a populist uprising against Parliament and what he saw as its failures to fulfil its role by letting the 'evil' of immigration go unchecked.

It was not only immigration that was beginning to estrange Powell from his party. With his sacking, he was free to sharpen his critique of everything he thought was wrong in the country and in the Conservative Party. Over the following months, Powell would tour the country, giving more than a hundred speeches, setting out not simply a critique of the prevailing orthodoxy of the day, as he saw it, but an alternative platform for government. The country was stuck in the past. It was spending too much. The state was too big. Free markets, monetarism and free-floating currencies were the answer. And then, Powell opened up a new front in his long battle: Europe.

At 3 p.m. on Friday, 21 March 1969, Powell addressed the Harwich Conservative Association's women's rally in Clacton Town Hall, Essex.[30] Here, in the heart of what would later become Brexit country, Powell began his campaign against British entry into Europe – a campaign he would lose not just once, but again and again. Yet, the very fact that he entered the debate at all helped create the conditions for the eventual triumph of Powellite Euroscepticism.

Powell was fifty-seven, at the height of his influence and ambition. Should the Conservative Party lose the coming election, he was well placed to become leader. Labour had a one-hundred-seat majority and so it would be an uphill battle for Heath to replace Wilson as prime minister in the election, expected in 1970. Wilson had promised to bring the 'white heat of technology' to Britain's tired economy, but, by the time Powell got to his feet in Clacton, most of this heat had fizzled out into the usual post-war malaise. In an attempt to turn things around, Wilson had finally agreed to seek British entry into Europe. After de Gaulle's '*non*', Wilson had declared he would not take no for an answer. Britain was begging to be allowed in.

'To watch the British mopping up their daily ration of bad news, you might think that they not only liked it but throve on it,' Powell raged in Clacton. Britain, he said, had been through the indignity of Suez, the loss of influence in Africa and Asia, the shame of economic decline and, finally, in Powell's view, the shock of mass immigration. 'All these experiences and more have added up to a mood somewhere between dejection and desperation,' he declared to his receptive audience.[31]

Powell argued that it was time Britain stopped complaining. It was no good blaming the United States for Suez, or de Gaulle for his veto. Like Scruton, Enoch Powell had already fallen under de Gaulle's spell. 'The face which we see in de Gaulle's mirror is our own', Powell had written in 1967. But, unlike de Gaulle's France, Britain no longer seemed to know itself. 'What sort of people do we think we are? We have been hovering over the answer for years . . . a nation of ditherers who refuse to make up our minds.' It was time for Britain to make its own way in the world.

The conclusion was a logical culmination of Powell's journey ever since the loss of India. He dismissed the Commonwealth as a sham and the United States as a rapacious empire which did not have Britain's interests at heart. It was time, in Powell's view, for Britain to end its attempts to join the Common Market.

Powell's charge sheet against the European Economic Community would echo through British politics for decades to come. Europe might be a free-trading club internally, but it hid from the rest of the world behind a protectionist wall. It relied on 'complex, bureaucratic institutions' that would progressively become more powerful, undermining British democracy. To prosper, Powell argued, Britain needed to face up to its own problems, which were of its own making. For Powell, this meant abandoning price controls and instead embracing free markets, monetarism and free-floating currencies. This was wildly out of step not only with the political consensus at the time, but with the narrower political consensus within the Conservative Party itself. For the next fifty years, Powell's arguments would be rejected, defeated, marginalized and ridiculed. Yet they would not go away, always hovering in the distance, pulling the country off the course its leaders had set, but with which the country itself never quite seemed at ease. Always lurking in the conversation was the great issue of immigration, which would transform over the decades from a Commonwealth question into a European one.

Over the following months, Powell would return to the question of Europe again and again. With the 1970 general election fast approaching, his interventions offered Labour a golden opportunity to paint the Conservative opposition as divided and reactionary. Any move by Heath in Powell's direction opened him up to the charge that he was captured by the extreme right. 'I know Enoch is *persona non grata,*' Wilson joked, 'but despite these highly publicised governessy slaps on the wrist he gets from time to time for speaking out of turn, the last two years show that what Enoch says today Edward will be proclaiming as Tory policy anything from three to six months later.'[32]

Writing in the *New Left Review* in May 1970, the Scottish political theorist and essayist Tom Nairn had arrived at a similar conclusion. Powell, Nairn argued, was a far more profound figure than the 'immigrationmania' of his speech in 1968. As Nairn had spotted, Powell's ambition was more than simply to halt immigration into Britain, but to refashion the very idea of British nationalism.

To do so, Nairn argued, Powell had resorted to a form of mystical historiography. In 1961, speaking to the Royal Society of St George, Powell had certainly spoken in such terms, dismissing the empire as a 'strange fantastic structure' constructed around England without having any effect on the imperial nation itself. In this dreamlike retelling of Britain's imperial past, 'England underwent no organic change as the mistress of a world empire'. Britain had returned from its years of 'distant wandering' with a fresh love for the Shire.

The binding symbols of England's historic unity had nothing to do with empire, but rather focused on 'the kingship of England' and its Parliament: that palace 'near the great city which the Romans built at a ford of the River Thames', as Powell put it. This was the place to which 'men resorted out of all England to speak on behalf of their fellows'. And so the source of Powell's reverie is revealed, the wellspring of his parliamentary absolutism. To dilute the sovereignty of Parliament is to dilute England itself.

To Nairn, the real significance of Powellism was not its coherence as a myth, but its political potential. Powellism, Nairn argued, was merely a 'preliminary ground-clearing exercise' for the revolution to come, creating a 'ready-made formula' for a future leader to adopt when the next crisis demanded it. In 1970, however, that vision of the future appeared a long way off.

Despite the devaluation crisis, when Harold Wilson went to the Queen in May 1970 to ask for a dissolution of Parliament, he had every reason to be confident. Since November 1967, the economy had begun to rebound and the Labour Party had suddenly found itself ahead in the polls again. Wilson was on course to be the first Labour leader to be elected to two consecutive full terms in office, and in so doing become the defining figure of Britain's post-war era.

For Powell, it was a unique election. For the first time in his political career, his fortunes were not tied to those of the Conservative Party. He knew that, if Heath won, his own hopes of the Tory leadership were as good as over. And yet, the more popular Powell became, the more likely it was that the Conservative Party would win. Even if voters decided to vote Conservative only because they agreed with Powell about Europe or immigration, it pushed Heath closer to power. Douglas Hurd – Heath's political secretary at the time – later described Powell as acting like 'a solitary prophet, filled with scorn for his former friends and colleagues, waiting for the nation to turn to its real leader.'[33] It would be the last election where he urged the public to 'vote, and vote Tory.'

The day before the election, the final opinion polls seemed to show a clear lead for Labour – 8.7 per cent, according to *The Times*. Yet, as the results began to trickle in, it became clear the polls were wrong – and badly so. Heath had won, Wilson was out, and Powell's hopes were crushed. The swing to the Conservatives was higher in the West Midlands than anywhere else, and Powell would claim credit for helping his party over the line. But, as Wilson accepted defeat and Heath travelled to the palace to take the Conservative Party back into power for the first time in six years, Powell was powerless and disconsolate. It wasn't just Wilson that had lost the election, but Powell, too – and, more importantly, *Powellism*. 'It was the end,' his wife, Pam, recalled; 'we just had to put a brave face on it.'[34]

Heath's victory, and Powell's defeat, coincided with another moment of profound significance. On 9 November 1970, Charles de Gaulle died at home in Colombey-les-Deux-Églises, whereupon he was buried next to his daughter Anne. 'General de Gaulle is dead,' declared President Pompidou, voice trembling with emotion. 'France is a widow.' De Gaulle, two weeks before his eightieth birthday, had been playing solitaire in his living room when he had a heart attack. 'In 1940, de Gaulle saved our honour,' Pompidou told the nation. 'In 1944, he conducted us to liberation and victory. In 1958, he saved us from civil war. He gave France its governing institutions, its independence.'[35] He had blocked Britain from joining Europe for not being European enough. Coinciding with de Gaulle's passing, Britain finally seemed to have a genuine European as prime minister. It would never do so again. More than that: Britain had elected a Gaullist.

Chapter 4

It is often forgotten how transformative Edward Heath *almost* became. Though, domestically, he would come to be seen as a middle-of-the-road *Macmillanista*, he had come to power as an apparent radical. To begin with, he was 'Selsdon man', the nickname given to him by Harold Wilson following a meeting of the shadow cabinet in the run-up to the general election, at a country hotel in Selsdon Park, near Croydon.[1] It was here that Heath agreed to what appeared to be a complete break from the post-war consensus, with an agenda of tax cuts and free markets. While Heath would abandon much of this programme – setting the stage for Thatcher's trial of strength a decade later – in foreign affairs, he remained anything but conventional throughout his premiership. In the four years he was prime minister, Heath pursued a revolution in British foreign policy that was every bit as radical as the one Powell was demanding – but, unlike Powell, he got halfway to achieving it.

Heath not only saw Britain's future in Europe, but he was so committed to membership that he actively did not want any kind of 'special relationship' with the United States which might dilute the country's commitment to its new club. Not a single British prime minister before or since has shared such an exclusively European vision of Britain's future. From 1945 to 2016, only Heath came to the conclusion that the special relationship was actively undermining Britain's attempts to be a European power and therefore should be abandoned.

Heath's European vision also had an emotional depth unlike that of any other prime minister. Though shaped by his experiences in the Second World War, there was something else which drew Heath to Europe: music. Heath was born in the Kentish resort of Broadstairs, the eldest child of bright, ambitious working-class parents, who devoted their lives to young Teddy and his musical gifts. Heath's father might have been a carpenter and his mother a maid, but they were determined their son would rise to a higher status, scrimping and saving to buy him a piano. After winning a place at a local fee-paying grammar school, he went to Oxford, where he won a prestigious organ scholarship and became president of both the university Conservative Association (OUCA) and the Union – a path trodden by many an aspiring prime minister over the years, but rarely one from such humble beginnings.

One of the key moments in the young Heath's life was a trip he made to Germany in 1937, aged twenty-one, where he received an invitation to attend a Nazi rally in Nuremberg, witnessing the full sinister effect of Hitlerian theatre. 'Here was the mob orator,' Heath later described, 'the demagogue playing on every evil emotion in his audience.'[2] Afterwards, he was invited to a party given by Himmler. Heath returned to Germany in 1939, travelling as far as Danzig and then on to Warsaw, days before Hitler's invasion of Poland, escaping to England just forty-eight hours before the outbreak of the war.

These experiences of Europe in the 1930s burned into Heath's soul: the sense of a continent and a culture – *his* culture – collapsing into barbarism. Back home, Heath immediately signed up for service, but had one last piece of unfinished business from Oxford. He had been invited, along with his Oxford contemporary Hugh Fraser, to represent British universities on a debating tour of the United States. Fraser was everything Heath was not: gregarious and aristocratic, glamorous and sociable, with friends in the right places, including Joseph Kennedy, the US ambassador to Britain, and his children, notably Jack, who was just a year older than Hugh.

Having signed up to fight, Heath first consulted both the War Office and the Foreign Office, who were happy for him to travel. The trip to the United States might have brought these two unlikely Tory bedfellows together, had Fraser not already been called up for active service, commissioned while still at Oxford into the Lovat Scouts, set up by his own father, Simon Fraser, the 14th Lord Lovat, scion of an old Jacobite clan from the Highlands of Scotland. Fraser soon transferred to the new intelligence unit known as Phantom, which, in 1942, was dispatched to Algiers to aid in the battle then being waged against Erwin Rommel's Afrika Korps. And so, Fraser's place on the tour was taken by another Oxford man, Peter Street.

Heath's trip to the United States lasted three months, but did not make as much of an impression on him as his forays through Europe. While he was struck by the classless egalitarianism of American society, it did not leave him with any sense of 'close cousinship and common destiny', as his biographer, John Campbell, put it.[3] Heath was European and America was a foreign land. They were not kin.

After returning home in early 1940, Heath spent a frustrating few years of tedious military service at home. While Enoch Powell and Hugh Fraser were in Algiers in late 1942 and early 1943, Ted Heath was in England, plodding over the open moors on training exercises. It was not until 3 July 1944, three weeks after D-Day, that Heath arrived on the continent, landing under enemy fire at Arromanches. From this point, he saw heavy action, making his way across France, Belgium, Holland and eventually into Germany, where he was posted to Hanover as part of the army of occupation. For Heath, the experience of occupation rather than war itself seemed to have the most profound effect. 'Having known the ruined German cities as they were before the war, he felt an obligation to European culture to try to restore them,' Campbell noted.[4]

Writing in his 1977 book *Travels: People and Places in My Life*, Heath reflected on his experiences: 'I knew that those evil things had been beaten back and their perpetrators brought to justice. But at what cost? Europe had once more destroyed itself. This must never be allowed to happen again.'[5]

After returning from Europe, Heath was adopted as the Conservative Party candidate in Bexley, a commuter town conveniently located between Broadstairs and London – an area of neat, recently built semi-detached homes, densely populated with white-collar workers and the new middle classes. These were Heath's people. Yet, when the election came in 1950, he only narrowly made it, squeezing past his Labour opponent with a majority of just 133, thanks in no small part to the local Communist candidate, Charles Job, who took 481 votes. Colonel Heath was now an MP.

From the moment he entered Parliament, Europe defined him. In his maiden speech, he urged Attlee's Labour government to take part in negotiations to join the European Coal and Steel Community. Under Macmillan, he became Britain's chief negotiator. Finally, as prime minister, he committed himself to entry.

Heath's elevation to the premiership in 1970, the year after de Gaulle's resignation, created a unique opportunity for Britain's pro-Europeans. The last major obstacle in the way of British entry had been removed just as Britain had elected its first – and only – truly European prime minister. While Heath's manifesto commitment in 1970 was only to explore the terms of British membership, 'no more, no less,' he was not going to pass up such an opportunity. Taking Britain into Europe was the mission of his life and the central purpose of his premiership. To do so, he first had to persuade Europe that Britain had changed, and then to persuade Britain that, in joining Europe, everything would stay the same. It was in his pursuit of the latter where Heath began to stretch the boundaries of legitimacy.

After agreeing terms with Europe – accepting the Treaty of Rome in full – Heath returned to Parliament and declared that joining the community did not 'entail a loss of national identity or an erosion of essential national sovereignty.' Heath's declaration can be defended in technical terms, if by 'essential' we take Heath to mean that Britain was not becoming a province of a new superstate and could always leave in the future if it so wished. But of course joining Europe involved an erosion of 'essential national sovereignty': this was the whole point, the animating spirit of Monnet's project.

In a television address to the nation, Heath declared that Europe was the answer the country had been searching for. 'For twenty-five years we've been looking for something to get us going again,' he said. 'Now here it is. We must recognise it for what it is. We have the chance of new greatness. Now we must take it.'[6] This was hyperbole, of course, but also true to Heath's own instincts. Europe was the only way to end the years of drift and decline, he believed. Lining up against him, however, was the might of the Labour Party and the Tory malcontents, including Enoch Powell.

After 'Rivers of Blood', Powell had toured the country whipping up support for an almost entirely different type of Toryism from that of the prime minister: anti-immigration, Eurosceptic, free market, opposed not only to European federalism, but to the Commonwealth, the special relationship and, indeed, any global role based on what he saw as the chimerical notion that Britain could remain a great power.

Yet, if the two were in a battle for the soul of the party, by the autumn of 1971, it looked very much as though Ted Heath was winning. At the party conference that October, members overwhelmingly backed Heath over Powell on the twin issues of Europe and immigration. After an impassioned speech by Powell urging the party not to surrender the sovereignty of Parliament, a pro-Common Market motion was carried by 2,474 votes to 324.[7]

Even if Heath seemed to have won his party's support, it was far from a foregone conclusion that he would win the support of the House of Commons. A rump of Conservative opponents could combine with the Labour Party to form a blocking majority.

The crucial moment was 28 October 1971 – the first time the House of Commons would vote on a motion supporting entry into Monnet's Europe 'on the basis of the arrangements which have been negotiated.' In other words, this was not a theoretical decision, depending on what could or could not be negotiated, but a vote on a set of terms already agreed. For six days, the House debated the motion, marching back and forth over the same ground that had been trodden for the past decade.

In his final call to arms before the vote, Heath returned to his core beliefs in a way that remains striking today. For Heath, this was the last chance to create a real united Europe, to finally end the distinction between 'we' and 'they' that, he said, had dominated much of the debate over Europe for the previous decade. 'Some, I think, have been overwhelmed by a fear that this country in an organization such as the Community must always be dominated by "they",' he said. 'But we are approaching the point where, if this House so decides tonight, it will become just as much our Community as their Community. We shall be partners, we shall be cooperating, and we shall be trying to find common solutions to common problems of all the members of an enlarged Community.'[8]

Heath was brave enough to make the case for Europe in a way that no other prime minister has, before or since. He saw membership as neither a least worst option nor a necessary evil: Heath believed in Europe.

When the House of Commons finally divided on the issue that had confounded British politics for two decades, the men from Algiers waited expectedly. Jean Monnet took his seat in the gallery to watch the occasion, just as he had in the National Assembly in 1954. 'This is what I have been waiting for during the last twenty-five years,' he told French television.[9] In Dover, his old boss Harold Macmillan waited on the white cliffs to light a ceremonial bonfire that would be answered by expectant supporters in France. Enoch Powell, meanwhile, skulked through the 'no' lobby with the bulk of the Labour Party and thirty-eight Conservative colleagues, most of whom came from the old romantic right of the party, led by figures such as Richard Body, Neil Marten and Edward 'Teddy' Taylor, a combative, working-class Glaswegian who resigned as a minister in Heath's Scottish Office to oppose British entry and would never again hold ministerial office.

When the results were announced on 29 October 1971, sixty-nine Labour MPs had voted with the government to give Heath a majority for British accession to the European Communities. Labour loyalists and Eurosceptics reacted with immediate and unconstrained fury. 'Fascist bastard!' one screamed at the leader of the Labour rebels, Roy Jenkins. Another went further: 'Rat-fucker! Rat-fucker!'[10] Heath had won. Monnet had won. Macmillan had won. And Powell had lost.

On 22 January 1972, basking in the glory of his victory, the British prime minister hosted a lunch at the British embassy in Brussels for the grand old men of Europe, including the *père de l'europe* himself, Jean Monnet. Heath was in town to sign the Treaty of Accession, a moment of extraordinary pride and accomplishment, which he wanted to mark in style. Alongside Heath and Monnet, Harold Macmillan was invited, too. The men of Algiers had been brought together again, victorious, but only after the death of their great rival and compatriot. 'Perhaps it is a good thing de Gaulle is dead,' Macmillan remarked to the British diplomat Nicholas Barrington as they travelled in the official car to the embassy. 'But I am alive and I am very happy.'[11]

Monnet was eighty-three by this time, his influence long since faded. Yet his vision was still burning. Never before had Britain been led by a man as committed to Monnet's European dream as Heath, a believer not only in the Churchillian sense that it was good for the continent, but someone who believed it was good for Britain as well. For Monnet, the occasion was a delight. As he toasted the glorious future that now lay in store for Europe, he heaped praise on Heath for finally bringing it about. After a long, difficult labour, a new world had been born. Britain had accepted the Treaty of Rome in full, without exception. It had signed up to the goal of Europe's ever closer union and the reality of its High Authority. It was not the end of a thousand years of British history, but it was something new and profound and radical. For the first time, Parliament had given away its sole right to make the laws of the land. It had done so voluntarily, without a major national catastrophe or defeat in war. Britain had become a European country, led by a European prime minister, with a European future.

Yet, in just over two years, Heath would be cast out of power, his premiership ripped from its roots by the most ferocious storm faced by any government since 1945. Heath's premiership would end in a failure of such dizzying proportions, it led not only to his own demise, but to an altogether different kind of revolution from the one he intended. Indeed, the force of the coming conservative counter-revolution would, in time, animate a whole new generation of radicals who were later to challenge his one solid achievement: Europe.

Even before the signing ceremony in Brussels, clouds cast a shadow over the occasion. Two days before, news had dropped that unemployment had passed the million mark for the first time since 1947.[12] Heath had come to power promising to manage the economy better than Labour; eighteen months into his premiership, he seemed to be faring no better.

In March 1972, Heath gambled on an economic boom that he hoped would fix his problems. There was less than a year to go until Britain entered the Common Market and he was desperate to make sure the economy was in good shape. Heath believed Britain could accelerate away from its problems once inside, allowing it to modernize its industry and hold back inflation through sensible deals with the unions – all without the need for any major confrontation. While the Treasury wanted a neutral Budget, Heath had no time for such caution. He wanted a European budget to take Britain into the Community running at full speed.

By the time Britain entered the European Economic

Community, of course, it was not the Treasury's forecasts that proved ill-founded, but Heath's. The prime minister's attempt to create a virtuous cycle of growth and industrial modernization never materialized. Membership of the Common Market was not to blame for this, but nor had it saved Britain from its difficult choices. Instead, Heath found himself back in the same old hamster wheel of inflation and industrial strife that had crippled the previous government. The budget of 1972 was founded on a misguided faith in the transformative power of Europe.

In the end, Heath, no less than Powell, believed in an idealized vision of Britain and Europe: a Britain that was gentle and reasonable, and a Europe where the great powers would put aside old rivalries to run the continent's affairs. Both of these visions would soon jut up against the reality of economics, identity, class and national interest.

By the time it joined the European Economic Community on 1 January 1973, Britain had entered a new era of heightened industrial strife, and Northern Ireland had collapsed into dangerous levels of sectarian violence. It was not just these explosions of domestic disorder that cost Heath power, but the international disorder that blew in from the Middle East following the Yom Kippur War of 1973, leading to the first oil-price shock of the postcolonial world after the Arab powers imposed an oil embargo on the countries which had supported Israel. Among them was Britain. The result was a 70 per cent increase in the price of oil.[13] Any of these crises would have been daunting enough for a single government to deal with; taken together, they proved too much.

The oil crisis undermined the economy and left the government more dependent on domestic coal supplies just as the miners began their second campaign of industrial action. In a television address, Heath said Britain needed to prepare for the most difficult Christmas since the war. In the end, unable to reach a deal with the miners over pay, Heath reluctantly went to the country in January 1974, asking a simple question: Who Governs? The usual snide observation is that the country replied, 'Not you.'

Yet the country was not enamoured by the alternative, either. Facing Heath was Harold Wilson, still just about holding the Labour Party together with a policy on Europe promising to renegotiate the terms of Britain's membership before putting it to a referendum.

If Heath's record left a lot to be desired, so too did the prospect of Harold Wilson's return. Neither had tamed inflation, modernized the economy, reset industrial relations or put Britain on the path to a glorious new future. They were the modernizers who had not modernized.

Another factor then reasserted itself: Enoch Powell. On the day after Heath called the election, Powell announced he could not stand for the party because of its policy on Europe. And then, with just days to go before polling day, Powell went further and declared to an audience of supporters back in Birmingham that, if they wanted to remain a democracy and not 'become one province in a new European super-state', a new prime minister was needed. Powell had not said 'Vote Labour', but that was his message. Two days later, at Shipley, he was even more explicit, declaring his support for 'the party which is committed to fundamental renegotiation of the Treaty of Brussels and to submitting to the British people thereafter.'[14] When a heckler yelled out 'Judas!' Powell responded with electric anger: 'Judas was paid! Judas was paid! I am making a sacrifice!' And indeed he was – sacrificing himself for a cause he believed in, just as he had always yearned.

When the result was announced, Powell was jubilant, retiring to his bathroom to sing the Te Deum. 'I had had my revenge on the man who had destroyed the self-government of the United Kingdom,' he later reflected.[15] While neither party had secured a majority, Labour had narrowly emerged as the largest party, albeit with 200,000 fewer votes. Powell had not given up his ambition to become prime minister either. Eight days after the election, he appeared on *Any Questions*, declaring that he had 'the unfulfilled ambition, but not an ignoble one, of leading the Tory party.'[16]

Throughout the spring and summer of 1974, he was approached by Conservative associations to be their candidate at the next election, but said he could not stand on a platform that did not move on the question of Europe.

With his political future in doubt, Northern Ireland offered the prospect of an honourable return to Parliament. After he had announced his resignation at the beginning of the February election, he had been approached by the Ulster Unionists to see if he would stand under their banner. With Wilson now hinting at an election later in the year, Powell risked finding himself exiled for years if he did not make a swift decision. Once again, he confounded Westminster by agreeing to stand as an Ulster Unionist at the next election. The decision was not entirely out of the blue. Throughout Heath's premiership, Powell had been a thorn in his side not only on the questions of Europe and immigration, but also on Northern Ireland.

British troops had first been sent into the province in Harold Wilson's first stint as prime minister, in what he hoped would be a 'limited mission' to help the authorities in Northern Ireland restore order amid spiralling sectarian violence. Such a mission turned out to be neither limited nor successful. Thirteen people were killed in Northern Ireland in the first full year of 'the Troubles', a euphemistic name for Ulster's descent into violent disorder. The following year, 1970, the number killed jumped to twenty-five, before reaching 174 in 1971 and 467 in 1972. This was the context for Heath's decision in 1972 to abolish the Stormont parliament and take on the direct responsibility for restoring security and order in the province.

This act is not some minor footnote in Britain's post-war history, but a seismic moment that effectively erased Northern Ireland as a self-governing, semi-independent state within the United Kingdom, as had existed for the previous fifty years. Until 1972, Northern Ireland had its own prime minister and House of Commons, as well as its own Senate and dominion-style governor. Stormont was not some glorified county council that could be placed into special measures, but the centre of political life in Ulster.

When Heath abolished Stormont, it was far from clear what would go in its place. Neither the Tories nor Labour were at all interested in the British state permanently taking over Stormont's responsibilities, but nor could the UK simply up and leave, as it had in Cyprus or India. The result was confusion.

At first, the plan was to rebuild the old state, but with the province's nationalists brought into government in a power-sharing agreement with unionism. Between 1972 and 1974, however, the bulk of Ulster unionism could not accept such a bargain and began flirting with much more radical options. It was at this time that two transformative ideas briefly came to prominence. The first was the seemingly paradoxical idea that loyalist Northern Ireland should declare unilateral independence from the United Kingdom. This was briefly adopted as the policy of the breakaway Ulster Vanguard Party, whose members included the future Nobel prize winner David Trimble. Vanguard declared that, by abolishing Stormont, the British government had 'unwittingly forged a nation that cannot entrust to them its security or national destiny', and so it must take care of itself.

The alternative idea was the complete opposite: total integration with Britain. The key to this proposal was not to rebuild the Northern Irish state, but to turn the province into another Scotland or Wales. The most prominent supporter of this idea was Enoch Powell, who believed the solution to the violence was to end the ambiguity about Northern Ireland's constitutional position by governing it in the same way as the rest of the UK. In 1971, shortly before a speaking tour of Northern Ireland, Powell declared that 'Stormont itself is a threat to the British link because it is an assertion of separateness.'[17] Despite Powell's opposition to Stormont, he also opposed Heath's imposition of direct rule on the grounds that it would mean Ulster being governed by ministerial decree, unlike the rest of the country.

Whatever his motivations at this time, Powell was once again building a solid argument on weak foundations. The problem was not just that there was a lack of enthusiasm for total integration among the political elite in Westminster, but this was also the case in Northern Ireland itself. The DUP's Ian Paisley flatly rejected Powell's call for Northern Ireland to show its total loyalty to Parliament. 'If the Crown-in-Parliament decided to put Ulster into a united Ireland, according to Mr Powell, we would have to obey if we were loyal,' Paisley replied, with cutting logic of his own.[18] Powell was holding out an idea of the United Kingdom that did not exist.

For Powell, Ulster was the logical extension of the arguments he had been making since the independence of India and loss of face at Suez: just as the colonies had asserted their nationhood, so too must the mother country. This was the mission of Powell's career, swapping his old imperial fantasy of a united empire for the national vision of a united British nation, organic and whole, stretching from the Kentish cliffs to the steeples of Fermanagh.

Two months before Heath's defeat in 1974, he had overseen the establishment of a new Northern Ireland Executive made up of six Protestants and five Catholics, signing the Sunningdale Agreement in December 1973. This should have been a moment of great significance. It was not. In that election, a slate of anti-power-sharing unionists won eleven of the twelve parliamentary seats available in Northern Ireland. 'Dublin is just a Sunningdale away,' their election posters warned.

The immediate cost was borne by Ted Heath, who had finished only four seats short of Labour. Between 1970 and 1974, he had been able to count on eight Ulster Unionists who had taken the Conservative whip in Parliament. Their replacements would do no such thing. Heath's attempts to resurrect Stormont, therefore, played a significant role in his own downfall.

In May 1974, the Ulster Workers' Council called a general strike across the province over the power-sharing agreement reached under Heath. The two-week strike was extraordinary in its scope – acting, in effect, as a total rejection of the British government's authority to govern Northern Ireland without unionist consent. Ports were blocked, roads closed, petrol stations bombed, paramilitaries deployed. This was not simply a display of civil disobedience. On day three of the strike, the Ulster Volunteer Force exploded four bombs in the Republic, killing thirty-three people. The strike provoked Harold Wilson into a speech of ferocious ill-temper, which only further entrenched support for the loyalist cause. 'What we are seeing in Northern Ireland is not just an industrial strike,' Wilson thundered in a national televised address on 25 May, eleven days into the strike. 'It is a deliberate and calculated attempt to use every undemocratic and unparliamentary means for the purpose of bringing down the whole constitution of Northern Ireland so as to set up there a sectarian and undemocratic state, from which one third of the people of Northern Ireland will be excluded.'[19]

When Wilson then called a second election for 3 October, Powell doubled down on his support for Labour on the mainland, telling an anti-Common Market rally in Bristol that there was only one course of action for voters who wanted the question of Britain's membership reopened. Asked whether he was urging a Labour vote, he replied, 'I should have thought that was the clear implication of what I have said in the last three-quarters of an hour.'[20] His break from the Tory party was now total.

By the time the results were in on 11 October, Wilson had sneaked over the line with the smallest of majorities – three. Interviewed the next day, Powell declared, 'I am popularly supposed to have won two, not to say three elections.'[21] The truth, however, was that Powell's influence had already crested. It would now be up to the public to decide the country's fate once and for all. Powell had helped to keep alive the question of Britain's membership of Europe, at the cost of his chance of becoming Conservative Party leader himself. Another era was beginning, under new Conservative leadership, with new ideas about Britain and Europe.

*

After Ted Heath's defeat in October, his third election loss, his grip on the Conservative Party was fatally weakened. Over the next few weeks, Tory MPs began a somewhat slapdash 'Ted must go' campaign. Their problem was not so much the residual support in the parliamentary party for Heath, but the fact that there was no obvious replacement. All the potential candidates were flawed. The shadow chancellor and former home secretary Robert Carr was the obvious Heathite candidate, but he was too closely tied to the old regime. Keith Joseph was the leading candidate of the free-market right, but he had blown his chances with an inflammatory speech warning that too many children were being born to 'mothers least fitted to bring children into the world.' Few thought the former education secretary – now shadow environment secretary – Margaret Thatcher was a serious candidate.

For much of 1974, Thatcher's working assumption had been that Joseph would challenge Heath for the leadership and she would back him. It was only after his self-immolation that she began to seriously consider a tilt at the leadership herself. In her memoirs, Thatcher wrote that she 'heard herself saying: "Look, Keith, if you're not going to stand, I will, because someone who represents our viewpoint *has* to stand."'[22] Joseph told her she would have his full support.

When Thatcher went home that night and told her husband, Denis, of her decision, he said, 'You must be out of your mind. You haven't got a hope.' He wasn't alone. At the time, many considered Thatcher to be little more than a stalking horse, a challenger whose role was simply to test whether Heath could be wounded enough for him to be replaced. *The Economist* described her as 'precisely the sort of candidate who ought to be able to stand, and lose harmlessly.'[23] Soon after, Thatcher went to see Heath to tell him of her decision. 'If you must,' came his reply. 'You'll lose.'[24] Even Airey Neave, the man who would soon become her campaign manager, remained uncommitted until as late as January 1975, waiting on the decision of the chairman of the influential backbench 1922 Committee, Edward du Cann, whom he would have backed had he decided to stand. Eventually, du Cann announced he would not stand because he could not 'let down' his wife, who did not want to lose the family's country house in Somerset, which, without his side earnings from the City, would have been unaffordable. Upon such considerations Thatcher's rise depended.

When she announced that she would stand for the leadership, only one national publication backed her, *The Spectator*, then edited by the Powellite George Gale. 'What seems to me to be distinctive about Mrs Thatcher's candidature . . . is that implicit in it is the conviction that Mr Heath's leadership of the Conservative Party has been a very bad one,' wrote Patrick Cosgrave, the magazine's political editor.[25] Thatcher was the only option left.

While Thatcher was certainly to the right of Heath, she had no reputation as a radical. To Powell, she did not represent much of a change at all. 'If the Conservative Party is seeking a successor to Mr Heath who will re-establish the principles which were trampled on in office,' Powell declared, dismissively, 'it is no use looking among the members of the cabinet which, without a single resignation or public dissent, not merely swallowed but advocated every single reversal of election pledge or party principle.'

He then aimed his fire even more squarely at Thatcher: '"Oh," they say, "but she – sorry, he – used to grumble a lot in private." Maybe, but it is not among private murmurers and grumblers, disloyal colleagues, willing to wound but afraid to strike, holding one opinion outside the cabinet room but inside acquiescing in the opposite, that the leadership needed is to be found.'[26]

Until 1974, Thatcher's career had certainly been marked by ideological conformity and party loyalty. Aged forty-nine, married, with two children, she had enjoyed a steady though not spectacular career in Parliament, rising slowly through the ranks to become shadow education secretary in 1967 and then education secretary in 1970. While she was known to be to the right of her leader, even sympathetic to Powell and Powellism, she had not wavered in her support for Heath while he was prime minister. She had backed Britain's accession to the Common Market, accepted the wage and price controls Heath had implemented to bring down inflation, and campaigned sincerely and effectively for his re-election both in February and October. It was only in the last few months of Heath's leadership that she felt liberated enough to tacitly criticize him for drifting away from what she saw as conservative principles in government. It was the Conservative Party's twin defeats in 1974 that changed her life and that of the country.

After the first defeat in February, Thatcher had joined her cabinet colleague Keith Joseph in setting up a new think tank called the Centre for Policy Studies (CPS), ostensibly to study the success of Europe's social market economies. Heath's defeat in February had liberated Joseph from the timidity he had shown in office. Joseph was restless for change and, following Enoch Powell's departure, he was now the leading figure on the free-market right of the party. Over the course of the next few months, with the help of the CPS, he set about dismantling the record of the last Tory government and therefore that of its leader, Ted Heath. As the centre's deputy chairman, Thatcher could not escape her complicity in these attacks.

In some ways, Thatcher was a strange fit for a senior role in a think tank like this. The CPS's director, and Thatcher's adviser, Alfred Sherman, later described her as a person of 'beliefs, not ideas'.[27] Thatcher was a practical conservative who believed in values like self-reliance, thrift, patriotism and individual responsibility, which dovetailed with the free-market ideas that had been pushed by Powell and the IEA since the 1960s.

Yet, it wasn't only Powell who was dismayed at the choice being presented to Conservative MPs in 1975. Frustrated with the paucity of the offer, another candidate from the Tory right decided to throw his hat in the ring: Hugh Fraser. 'This is not just about personalities,' Fraser declared; 'it is about the feeling inside the

Tory Party.'[28] The feeling Fraser wanted to express was essentially Powellite, despite Powell no longer being in the party; the sense that, under Heath's leadership, the party had abandoned old Tory principles, creating the space for Labour to return to power.

Fraser saw Thatcher as just another shade of the technocratic, middle-class grey that was sapping the party's very soul. In 1975, as one colleague put it years later, he had raised the Jolly Roger for a very different kind of Toryism. Though he was never likely to win, Fraser was not a nobody either. He had distinguished himself at Oxford and in the war, winning both the Belgian Croix de Guerre and the Dutch Order of Orange, as well as the military MBE, like Powell himself. After the war, Fraser immediately entered Parliament in 1945, aged only twenty-seven, beating both Heath and Powell into the Commons. In that election, he had been joined on the campaign trail by his friend John F. Kennedy, who was then a journalist and already something of a household name because of his family connections.

Over the next two decades, Fraser steadily climbed the political ladder in Westminster, serving in the governments of Churchill, Eden, Macmillan and Douglas-Home. In 1962, as colonial secretary, he had stayed with Kennedy, by then president of the United States, on his way back from government business in British Guiana. The two spent the afternoon with their wives, swimming in the White House pool. Until the arrival of Ted Heath in 1965, Fraser was a figure of real political potential, a man of bravery and honour, celebrity and glamour, representative of a still-powerful strain of old Toryism that could trace its roots back through Churchill and Disraeli to the rebellious Jacobite romanticism of his ancestors.

In Fraser's leadership pitch, he offered a vision of Toryism which he saw as being markedly different from that of Heath – or, indeed, Thatcher. He spoke of the Tory party as 'a pragmatic party, a constitutional party, a nationalist party and a populous party' – all the things that he felt it had stopped being under Heath. For Fraser, the very idea of European supranationalism ran counter to all of the old Disraelian threads which made the Tory party successful. Instead, it was 'international, undemocratic, élitist and not in the interests of our people.'[29]

To help with his leadership bid, Fraser called on some of his friends and ideological soulmates. The recently elected Jonathan Aitken was brought on board alongside the philosopher Roger Scruton and Cambridge academic John Casey, who had only recently taken over the editorship of the prestigious *Cambridge Review*, setting in motion what *The Guardian* would later call 'a kind of intellectual revolution, a long march through the periodicals to "challenge the left-liberal orthodoxy with conservative values".'[30] Together, they began to organize and campaign for their friend in the hope of reminding the Conservative hierarchy that their vision of Toryism still existed.

When the day of the ballot came, Fraser and his supporters believed they would make a good show of themselves. Heath, meanwhile, never took Thatcher seriously. When the results were announced, it was Thatcher who had won – and far more impressively than anticipated, securing 130 votes to Heath's 119. Fraser managed just fifteen votes, far less than he was expecting. 'We thought he would get thirty or forty votes,' Aitken recalled.[31] Indeed, Fraser himself had hoped for fifty votes, according to his wife, the biographer Antonia Fraser.[32] Speaking days after the first ballot, Fraser showed his displeasure. The race had become a battle of 'personalities not of principles,' he declared, and Conservatism had reached a fork in the road. 'We have thought too little about what the nature of our Party is.' As it looked ahead to another few years of Labour rule, the party faced 'either extinction or rebirth.'[33] Few believed Thatcher offered the latter.

For Thatcher, although it was a triumph, it did not mean she had automatically secured the leadership. The party establishment thought the MPs had lost their minds. Reginald Maudling, the former chancellor, told Kenneth Baker it was the 'darkest day in the history of the Tory party.'[34] As such, many now expected the party to turn on Heath's assassin in the second round of voting, in which others could join the race. Willie Whitelaw immediately declared his candidacy, and was followed shortly after by John Peyton, Jim Prior and Geoffrey Howe, who Thatcher had, until then, counted as a supporter. And yet, on Tuesday, 11 February, Thatcher trumped in the second ballot even more convincingly than the first. Far from being the victim of a backlash, she who wielded the knife wore the crown. Thatcher received 146 votes to Whitelaw's 79. Prior and Howe managed nineteen and Peyton eleven.

After Thatcher's victory, Powell attributed it to luck. She had been blessed with 'supremely unattractive' opponents, he said, before adding: 'Of course, if it had been six months earlier it would have been somebody else.'[35] Yet, as Jonathan Aitken observed, her greatest piece of luck was that Powell himself was unable to stand. 'Had he still been a Conservative MP, he would have won the contest hands down.'[36]

Right or wrong, it is clear that, for those on the Powellite wing of the party, Thatcher's victory did not necessarily mean some great swing to the right. Thatcher's very first challenge was to steer the party through the upcoming referendum on British membership of the Common Market, which Harold Wilson had set for June – a referendum in which she, like her predecessor, was committed to winning for 'In'.

Chapter 5

From the moment Margaret Thatcher replaced Ted Heath, the issue of Europe presented a political challenge that would never quite go away, even if it was, for the most part, entirely manageable and of secondary importance compared to the great trials which would confront her. While there were a few Powellite ultras, the vast bulk of the parliamentary party supported British membership of the Common Market, as it was then largely known. Europe was very much Tory property at this time – after all, it was Anthony Eden who had criticized Labour for missing the boat in 1950, Harold Macmillan who had tried to clamber on board in 1960, and Ted Heath who had finally ensured Britain embarked a decade or so later. Even to win the Tory leadership, Thatcher had felt the need to declare her pro-Europeanism. If she had any private doubts about British membership – and there is scant evidence to suggest she did – she had little choice but to campaign for a Yes vote.

Thatcher's problem in 1975 was less to do with party management, and more to do with not being eclipsed by her predecessor. Heath was a flawed politician no longer popular within the Tory party, but still regarded as a genuine European statesman. Thatcher, by contrast, was seen as a provincial political lightweight, out of her depth in the contest with Wilson. And, of course, she was a woman.

For Wilson, the problem was almost entirely opposite. The referendum was the culmination of years of careful positioning to keep his party together. The bulk of the Labour Party in 1975 – both in and out of Parliament – was opposed to British membership, even though most of the cabinet were in favour. Wilson had managed this divide by opposing the supposedly Tory terms of membership that Heath had negotiated, while not opposing British membership per se. According to Labour's extraordinarily cynical (though not entirely inaccurate) manifesto, Heath had taken Britain into Europe on terms which meant 'the imposition of food taxes on top of rising world prices, crippling fresh burdens on our balance of payments, and a draconian curtailment of the power of the British Parliament to settle questions affecting vital British interests.'[1] Wilson promised to renegotiate these conditions before putting the new terms to the people in a referendum that would settle the matter once and for all. And, to keep his party onside, he promised that, if he could not negotiate better terms, he would campaign for 'our withdrawal from the Communities.'

In reality, Wilson had no intention of ever taking Britain out of Europe. 'The objective was to create conditions in which we could stay in,' one former official closely involved in Wilson's renegotiation told his biographer, Ben Pimlott, in a confidential interview.[2] Yet Wilson was limited in what he could achieve. The fundamentals of the European project had been set years in advance, in the Treaty of Rome. Wilson's renegotiation barely even tinkered, involving easier access for New Zealand dairy products and a complicated new mechanism relating to the EEC budget, which did nothing to change the basic settlement agreed by Ted Heath. In the Commons, Wilson insisted, however, that the government's objectives had been 'substantially though not completely achieved.'

When the renegotiation was put to the cabinet, he secured a majority in favour, though a sizeable minority dissented – Tony Benn, Barbara Castle, Michael Foot, Willie Ross, Peter Shore, John Silkin and Eric Varley. These were some of the biggest beasts in the party and each went on to play an extraordinary role in the political upheavals of the late 1970s and early 1980s. They were not alone in their opposition to Wilson. In the days that followed the cabinet rebellion, 145 Labour MPs voted against the government, 33 did not vote or abstained and 137 voted with the cabinet recommendation. Even junior ministers were split down the middle, thirty-one to thirty-one.

For many of the great Labour figures of this era, whether pro or anti, Europe had become central to their political identity. For the anti-Europeans, remaining inside the club meant sacrificing the very basis of their socialism. For those like Roy Jenkins and his supporters, including a young Labour MP called John Smith, Common Market membership had become the only passage to modernity left open, Britain's salvation. This was never the case for Wilson, who declared that he had 'never been emotionally a Europe man.'

Overall, the party remained sceptical. At the special Labour Party Conference called that spring to set the party's official policy on the matter, a motion was adopted by a margin of two to one, declaring Labour's opposition to membership, while recognizing the 'right to dissent'. The fact that the party's chief dissenter would also be its leader was a quirk everyone would have to live with.

With Labour's unity assured, Wilson turned to the referendum itself and his new cross-party allies, assembling 'the most powerful all-party coalition since the war' to campaign for a Yes vote. Not only did the coalition include the leaders of both the main political parties, but it would also prove to be the most professional, well-funded political campaign in British history – and the most successful, until the Leave campaign of 2016.

The campaign's president was Roy Jenkins, the Labour home secretary and former chancellor. Its vice-presidents included Ted Heath, the former prime minister, Jo Grimond, the former Liberal leader, and the popular Labour minister Shirley Williams. On top of this star-studded line-up, the campaign could count on the support of every national publication, apart from the *Morning Star* and *The Spectator*. *The Sun* told its readers the referendum was not so much about Europe but whether you wanted to side with the 'sane, sensible, moderate majority' who supported a Yes vote.[3] The campaign itself made similar claims: 'You can tell a cause by the company it keeps,' ran one of its posters.

Such an argument was not risk free. The No side had their own prominent and effective campaigners who were neither lunatic nor fringe. Enoch Powell, meanwhile, was still among the most popular, if divisive, politicians in Britain. Alongside them stood the majority of Labour MPs and trade union chiefs. More awkwardly, the Soviet Union and the National Front had both backed a vote for British withdrawal, as well as both Sinn Fein and Ian Paisley's Democratic Unionist Party.

The presence of such forces in the debate allowed the Yes campaign to crank their rhetoric to a pitch of existentialism, much of it focused on Europe's role as a bulwark against the Soviet Union. Winston Churchill MP – grandson of the wartime prime minister – declared the referendum a battle 'for the survival of democracy itself.'[4] Ted Heath said a 'vote against the Market could lead to a Soviet invasion of Europe.'[5] The pro-European *Daily Express*, meanwhile, likened No supporters to Nazi sympathizers, while Labour's George Brown claimed that, unless Europe was united, a 'concerted effort at a Communist takeover could swamp the democratic heritage of Western Europe.'[6] The threat from Soviet Russia seemed to have weighed on Thatcher too, and she warned voters that a victory for the No campaign would be 'a victory for the tribunes of the left.'[7] In 1975, the Cold War acted as a glue, binding together the Tory tribes who either saw the European Community as a force for modernization or a natural extension of their desire to oppose the Communist bloc stalking the West.

Such warnings were given short shrift by the No side. 'Surely if Communism is the main enemy,' complained one Conservative anti-Marketeer, Neil Marten, drolly, 'the Conservatives should be saying "keep away from the Common Market – it's loaded with Communists".'[8] The fact that the former Fascist leader, Oswald

Mosley, had come out in support of British membership was also a source of minor embarrassment for the Yes campaign.

Given the stakes, it is perhaps not surprising that the Yes campaign managed to assemble a vast war chest to keep Britain in the Common Market. While the No campaign had just one person to deal with the media, Britain in Europe employed seven full-time staff for this task alone – with six more working part-time. The most egregious example of Britain in Europe's largesse came with the hiring of the famous American film-maker Charles Guggenheim, who had worked with the Kennedys and was considered one of the most effective propagandists in the US. The bill for Guggenheim's broadcasts eventually totalled £105,000. In contrast, the No campaign spent £2,500 on its broadcasts, while its entire wage bill amounted to just £2,928 – barely 2 per cent of its rival's.[9]

There was a danger in this kind of disparity. As Roy Jenkins put it, rather laconically, too many on his side looked like 'well-fed men who had done well out of the Common Agricultural Policy.'[10] In 1975, being part of the establishment and loaded with money was not the best look. Indeed, for many voters, these well-fed men urging a Yes vote were the very people who had run the country into the ground over the past decade. For eleven years, Britain had been run by either Harold Wilson or Ted Heath, and few could claim that it had prospered as a result. Now, they both warned that Britain needed to join the European Communities to avoid disaster.

The No campaign's big themes, meanwhile, were self-government, cheap food and patriotism – a potentially formidable mix. As the pro-European tabloid *The Sun* lamented: '[They] have all the best tunes, if not the singers.'[11] At one point, even Thatcher seemed impressed. Those close to her at the time remember her watching one of the No broadcasts and saying, 'Gosh, that was good.' When polling day came, she even told a member of her staff she wished she didn't have to vote at all.[12]

This admission does not mean Thatcher was a closet

Eurosceptic hemmed in by her party, though she was always an intensely practical politician. It does, however, reveal a very different instinct compared to those nominally on her side, like Roy Jenkins and Ted Heath. Even in 1975, at the height of Tory Europhilia, Thatcher never displayed any visionary belief in the project. In an interview three days before the poll, she said that she favoured closer cooperation with the continent, but not a federal Europe. Her support for the Common Market was practical. 'She had a patriotic impulse and a sense of shame about what had happened to our country,' recalled the businessman John Hoskyns, who later went on to be head of her policy unit in Number Ten.[13] Thatcher's primary motivation was economic. She was not fixated on Powellite notions of national retrenchment and was wholly opposed to any of the socialist visions of modernization put forward by Tony Benn or Michael Foot. She dismissed the loss of sovereignty involved in membership as a largely 'technical' matter. Her obsession was growth and the return of British power, not some theological notion about parliamentary sovereignty, or 'a thousand years of history'.

Nevertheless, Thatcher's lack of conviction was picked up by the press at the time. *The Sun* printed a 'missing persons' notice a week before the vote. 'MISSING: One Tory leader', ran the headline: 'Answers to the name of Margaret Thatcher. MYSTERIOUSLY disappeared from the Market referendum campaign 11 days ago. Has not been seen since. WILL finder kindly wake her up and remind her she is failing the nation in her duty as Leader of the Opposition?'[14]

Thatcher found it impossible to compete with Ted Heath on the issue of Europe. She gave a number of speeches in favour of membership and even wore a woolly jumper emblazoned with the flags of the EEC's member states (standing beside one woman who wore a T-shirt bearing the words 'Europe or Bust'). Thatcher had done her bit, but she was no expert and did not pretend to be. At the Conservative Party's campaign launch on 16 April, she sat next to Heath and said, 'Naturally, it's with some temerity that the pupil speaks before the master.'[15] Europe was not an issue which exercised her. It was a practical question and at the time the sensible answer seemed to be Yes. It was this very attitude to Europe which went on to have even more profound implications than Heath's radicalism. If Europe was not a question of belief but of judgement, then it was subject to change, depending on the circumstances – and the circumstances would change.

Thatcher's attitude, far from being a break from the past, was more in line with the attitude of most of her predecessors than Heath's or that of the leaders of the Yes campaign. Indeed, it was far closer to Harold Wilson's attitude, and that of almost every other prime minister before or since. Heath stands alone among Britain's post-war prime ministers in the amount he was willing to sacrifice to join France and Germany at the heart of Europe.

Harold Wilson epitomized Britain's post-war attitude to Europe. 'I don't stand on the South Coast, look towards the Continent, and say "There's a new Jerusalem",' he declared during the campaign.[16] Wilson's Europeanism, like Thatcher's, was practical. Not for Wilson hyperbolic claims about the end of democracy or British prosperity. Being inside had been 'marginally helpful' for British jobs, he said. When it came to food prices, 'there isn't 2 ½d in it either way.' As *The Guardian* noted at the time, it was 'Mr Wilson's very scepticism about what he calls Common Market theology which makes him such a Pole Star for the wandering voter.'[17]

The other reason Wilson's dry, sceptical analysis of the economic benefits of membership seemed to resonate with voters was because Britain in 1975 was in a dire state. Though Britain had been in decline throughout the 1950s and '60s, this was only true in relative terms, and due in large part to the fact that Britain had begun this period so much richer than any other country in Europe. In these apparent years of decline before Britain joined the Common Market, the economy actually grew more quickly than at any time during the perceived recovery once it was inside.

But relative growth matters. The relentless decline of the British economy in comparison to others might not have made people's daily lives any worse, but it chipped away at the country's global status and influence, panicking the governing elite for whom this really mattered. By 1975, this erosion of power and wealth was painfully obvious. Not only had Britain's European neighbours caught up, they had also overtaken. Britain's share of global exports had plummeted, once-great industries had become uncompetitive and the pressure on the pound was unrelenting. The two principal challenges were the balance of payments – the difference between the money coming in and the money going out of the country – and runaway inflation. When Labour returned to power in 1974, the new chancellor, Denis Healey, declared the economic situation 'the worst which had ever been faced in peacetime.'[18] Although the balance of payments could be improved by lowering the value of the pound to make the country's exports more competitive, this made imports more expensive, contributing to inflation. In the short term, being part of a giant European market made the challenge even more acute, because Britain's exporters were not in good enough shape to compete with their continental rivals.

For three decades since the end of the war, the British economy had been gliding in the slipstream of its former greatness. By 1975, a sense of real economic crisis hung in the air. The Yes campaign warned that pulling out of the Common Market would trigger a collapse in the value of the pound and massive job losses. Ted Heath even warned of food shortages and a return to the ration book. Those campaigning for a No vote, on the other hand, declared that Europe was not a solution to Britain's economic woes, but a core part of the problem. After all, the country had joined the club with much fanfare two years previously, but little had improved. Tony Benn claimed 500,000 jobs had been lost in the first two years of membership, as the country adapted to its new economic surrounds. If Britain stayed in any longer, Benn warned, it would be a 'total disaster' for British manufacturing.

The problem for the No campaign at this time was that it was not plausible to argue that the country's economic problems were because of Europe. They evidently were not. Britain's problems had been building long before 1973. Indeed, the search for modernization, economic regeneration and even a new national endeavour had propelled both Harold Wilson and Ted Heath into power in the first place. The No campaign tried to deal with this problem by adopting the slogan 'Out of Europe and into the World'. But, as Enoch Powell well understood, there was no great nostalgic yearning for the glories of empire or global free trade. The root of Euroscepticism was nationalism, not imperialism.

The No campaign struggled to offer voters a coherent alternative to Europe, in large part because they didn't have one. Enoch Powell and Michael Foot admired each other and believed the most important point was sovereign democratic control. Beyond that, they could not have been further apart. Powell advocated free-market national capitalism, Foot British socialism. The public, it seemed, was uncomfortable with both.

Such political differences within the No campaign became a real problem. Tony Benn refused point blank to share a platform with Enoch Powell. In fact, as the campaign went on, Benn began to dominate, making headlines and becoming 'the focus of attention even when . . . silent himself', as *The Guardian* put it.[19] This was a disaster for the No side. Even in 1975, Benn was a divisive figure, generally disliked by the public. Barbara Castle confided to her adviser, the future foreign secretary Jack Straw, that she was 'sick of Wedgie monopolising everything.'[20] Straw, whose son Will went on to run the Remain campaign forty-one years later, replied in exasperation: 'He is losing us the referendum.' Straw, like many of his generation, was a sceptic. A young Robin Cook also campaigned for No, as did Neil Kinnock. Being a No voter in the Labour Party was a normal position to take.

In some senses, those campaigning for No simply had a harder case to make than their opponents. They were not so much arguing for change as a return to what had been before. And that was not particularly popular. *The Guardian* accused the No campaign of trying 'to cling to a world that has passed.' The Common Market, in contrast, was 'an important part of contemporary reality.'[21] Europe was progress – and progress was good.

Central to the argument was how best to protect – or resurrect – Britain's declining influence in the world. The government's own Referendum Information Unit was explicit, telling members of the public who phoned up that Britain 'needs new ways of exerting influence' in the world. 'We have to find a role to replace the one we played up to and immediately after the last war.'[22] *The Sun* put it more bluntly: 'After years of drift and failure, the Common Market offers an unrepeatable opportunity for a nation that lost an empire to gain a continent.'[23] The head of the Yes campaign, Roy Jenkins, was also consumed by notions of global influence, arguing that withdrawal would condemn Britain to 'an old people's home for faded nations.'[24] Europe was a tool to resurrect Britain as a global power. It was a way to fend off communism, save democracy, fix the economy. Europe was the means to make Britain great again.

The message was made even more potent by memories of the war, which still dominated popular culture at the time. *Dad's Army* was in its heyday, and ITV's epic twenty-six-part series *The World at War* had only finished the year before. Some on the No campaign accused the pro-Marketeers of being the new appeasers. 'Voters should not be fooled by the press bosses and the establishment politicians,' they warned. 'They were wrong about Hitler and they're wrong again.' Britain in Europe, meanwhile, plastered the poppy on its literature and used the dove of peace as its logo. One of its posters simply read: 'Forty million people died in two European wars this century. Better lose a little sovereignty than a son or daughter.'[25] In 1975, this was an extraordinarily powerful message.

On 5 June 1975, voters finally had their say. It was a landslide. The great European dilemma which had confounded Britain's political class for a quarter of a century proved to be less of a dilemma than anyone thought. Asked whether Britain should stay in the European Community, 67.2 per cent voted Yes. The country had endorsed British membership by two to one. The argument was settled. The first national referendum in British history had produced the biggest mandate ever achieved. Harold Wilson declared the debate over Europe closed for good. 'Fourteen years of national argument are over,' he said, dating the start of Britain's European debate to Harold Macmillan's first application, in 1961.[26] The argument had been raging for much longer, but few quibbled with the general point.

Every part of the United Kingdom had voted to stay in, with the exception of Shetland and the Western Isles in Scotland. It was a remarkable turnaround in public sentiment. A year earlier, in March 1974, only 12 per cent of the electorate told pollsters they believed the country had obtained any benefit as a result of membership.[27] An official at the Department of Trade and Industry had likened the public to 'a crowd of holidaymakers who, after much doubt and expense, have made a dangerous journey only to find the climate chilly, the hotel not what it was cracked up to be and the food too expensive.'[28] And yet they had voted overwhelmingly to extend the holiday.

Support for membership was most overwhelming in England, particularly in the Tory strongholds which would go on to become the areas most in favour of Brexit. Lincolnshire backed membership by 74.7 per cent; Essex by 67.6 per cent.[29] Scotland, Wales and Northern Ireland, in contrast, were the most opposed, reflecting the concerns of their nationalist leaders. Plaid Cymru and the Scottish National Party had campaigned for the UK to leave. Scotland's future first minister Alex Salmond had declared that 'Scotland knows from bitter experience what treatment is in store for a powerless region of a Common Market.'[30]

It was no surprise, therefore, that Thatcher declared the result 'thrilling'.[31] The national newspapers were just as triumphant: *The Sunday Times* called it 'the most exhilarating event in British politics since the war'; the *Evening Standard* declared it 'the best thing that has happened to British democracy for decades'; and *The Sun* concluded that, after years of debate, it was time to move on and 'make sure that we are good Europeans.'[32] Enoch Powell, of course, accepted no such conclusion. Once the public realized they had been misled, he predicted, they would 'tear apart' those responsible.[33]

It wasn't only the Europe question that conventional wisdom believed had been settled by the referendum. The poll was seen as a triumph for the moderate centre ground. In one fell swoop, both the Bennites and the Powellites had been defeated. The most encouraging lesson of all, the *Express* concluded, was also the most simple: 'The centre held.'[34] Wilsonian pragmatism had won the day on the Labour side, while Heath's star was back in the ascendency among the Tories. 'Mr Heath . . . has looked more like a party leader than he ever did when he was one,' thought *The Sun*. 'And Mrs Margaret Thatcher has looked much less like a leader than she did when she was not.'[35]

For all these reasons, the referendum was seen as a defining moment in Britain's post-war history. In his seminal account of the vote, published two years later, the political commentator and academic Professor Anthony King called it 'one of the half-dozen most important events in post-war British history,' putting to bed the great constitutional issue which had unsettled British politics since 1950, while defeating the extremes of left, right and secessionist nationalism all in one go. The referendum, he declared, had 'brought to an abrupt end, at least for the time being, the brief "Benn era" in British political history.'[36] Just imagine what might have happened had the result gone the other way, King speculated. Harold Wilson and James Callaghan – the grandees of the Labour government – would have been weakened, emboldening the Eurosceptic left. Tony Benn or Michael Foot might have emerged as leader. The party might then have split between the 'the moderate centre' and 'extreme left'. Labour's Europeans, led by Roy Jenkins and Shirley Williams, might have formed a new party, taking with them some of Labour's most popular figures, leaving the party out of power for a generation. All these traumatic events might have taken place had the No campaign triumphed, King declared with evident relief.

King was not alone in such an analysis. Even those on the No side believed the issue had been settled for good. Neil Kinnock, tribune of the left, declared the fight over. 'Only an idiot would ignore or resent a majority like this,' he said. 'We're in for ever.'[37]

Events do not unfold in such rational patterns, resolved by the results of referendums and general elections. The idiots of Kinnock's imagination would continue to have their say. People matter, decisions matter, events matter. The direction of travel was not settled by which way the winds were blowing in June 1975. Britain's painful conundrum over Europe had not ended; it merely entered a new phase.

While the Eurosceptics in 1975 were not an alternative government with an agreed and coherent vision of the future, neither was the Yes campaign. They had won a great mandate for Britain's membership of Europe, but they did not agree what Europe should be. Was it Monnet's federal Europe or the *Europe des patries* that de Gaulle had imagined? Was it a core part of the US-led Western alliance, a bulwark against communism and all its evils, or a social Europe, consensual and corporate, protected from global competition? Most profoundly of all, was the referendum an expression of the country's transition to a new and more limited role in the world, to a European identity, or was it a new platform to maintain and even grow its global relevance?

These were core questions for which the pro-European Yes campaign did not have clear answers. Nor, of course, did the European Community itself, of which Britain was now an integral part. Charles de Gaulle and Jean Monnet had disagreed about the nature of Europe from the very beginning. As the years rolled on, Thatcher's idea of Europe would prove to be different from the one that its leading continental figures were building.

The plan born in the mind of Jean Monnet in the calamity of world war and made real by Robert Schuman had achieved hegemony. With Ted Heath's idealism and Harold Wilson's pragmatism, Britain had gone further than either of these grand figures of French diplomacy thought possible and had itself become European. The great allies of Algiers had won. The vision of Jean Monnet had triumphed, and with it the moderate Toryism of Harold Macmillan. In France, de Gaulle was dead, and so too was his idea of a Europe of nations. Britain had finally eased into its place in the grand continental order. The United States continued to reign supreme, the overlord of the Western world. Enoch Powell, meanwhile, was defeated and diminished, with Powellism itself seemingly set to decay with him.

The sense of destinies being fulfilled was captured with Monnet's decision that same year to wind up his Action Committee for the United States of Europe, the campaign group he had founded twenty years earlier amid the trauma of France's rejection of his European Defence Community. His life's work was complete. He was eighty-seven and the great riddle of what to do about England had finally been answered.

After years of wavering, Britain had gone all in on Europe. It had joined a supranational organization committed to the 'ever closer union' of the peoples of Europe, and then ratified that momentous decision with the greatest democratic mandate in British history. The establishment had won. The dissidents had lost. The years of British ambiguity were over. Britain was destined to be a European power, with a European future.

Part Two

'THROUGH THE UNKNOWN GATE'

Chapter 6

While Harold Macmillan, Jean Monnet and Charles de Gaulle were thrashing out the future of Europe in the heat of a North African summer in 1943, a group of patriotic young British adventurers with far less influence, fame or glory were in the same place at the same time, serving in a little-known army unit code-named Phantom. Formally known as the GHQ Liaison Regiment, Phantom was one of those romantically unorthodox regiments of officer gentlemen we have come to associate with Britain's clandestine war effort. Part of the unit's glamour lay in its secrecy: even the word 'Phantom' was avoided, according to a study of the unit written by the military historian Philip Warner, although the recruits wore a white *P* on black cloth as their regimental sign.[1] Their purpose was to operate independently in the field, sending vital 'real time' intelligence about the state of the battle from the front line of the fighting. As is often the case with such regiments, Phantom attracted an unusual but highly impressive set of recruits.

One of those serving in Algeria at the time was Margaret Thatcher's future Conservative leadership rival, Hugh Fraser. Back in Britain, his Phantom colleagues included the Hollywood star David Niven, whose fame has somewhat eclipsed his time in the army, where he was a dedicated and professional, if still charismatically raffish, soldier. While he was undoubtedly the most famous Phantom, he was far from alone in achieving a degree of post-war notoriety. For a small unit, the list of its former members is quite extraordinary: two privy counsellors, three life peers, six hereditary peers, one master of a Cambridge college, four professors, one ambassador and one commissioner of the Metropolitan Police.[2] But what is perhaps most striking about this intelligence unit is the number of its leading members who went on to take roles in the great drama of British political life to come, including those who played key parts in the conservative counter-revolution of the 1970s and '80s.

This included not only Fraser, but also the great philosopher of British conservatism Michael Oakeshott and the influential future journalist Peregrine Worsthorne. Alongside this trio of High Tories were future Conservative MPs Jakie and Michael Astor, Carol Mather and Maurice Macmillan – son of Harold. Of these, it would be Oakeshott, Worsthorne and Fraser who would light the way to a different future for Britain than the one constructed in the aftermath of war.

Michael Oakeshott was the eldest and most erudite of these soldiering Tories. Born at the turn of the century, by the time the war came he had already established a career in academia. In fact, when Oakeshott signed up for service in 1940, at the fall of France, he was considered too old to see action, arriving in Phantom only because of an old friend from Cambridge who was already serving in the unit. For Oakeshott, his service with Phantom was 'charmed' but ultimately unfulfilling, confined mostly to administrative tasks on the home front.[3] It was not until much later that he rose to real prominence, returning to Cambridge as a fellow before a brief spell teaching at Oxford, and then to the London School of Economics, where he spent the rest of his career as a professor of political science. It was here, at the LSE, that he would develop a distinct understanding of politics that would influence a new generation of conservatives.

At the core of Oakeshott's philosophy lay a contempt for totalitarian planning, control and, ultimately, the very idea of rationality in politics. 'The imposition of a universal plan of life on a society is at once stupid and immoral,' he had written just before the war in *The Social and Political Doctrines of Contemporary Europe*. Instead, there must be balance. 'A society must not be so unified as to abolish vital and valuable differences, nor so extravagantly diversified as to make an intelligently coordinated and civilised social life impossible.'[4] Here, in essence, was the conservative faith.

In 1962, Oakeshott published what became his best-known book, *Rationalism in Politics and Other Essays*, building on this essential insight. For Oakeshott, the very idea of a 'rational' government was wrong, a false belief that politics is somehow scientific and perfectible. In contrast, Oakeshott set out the 'conservative disposition', which was not so much a doctrine as a state of mind. 'To the Rationalist', Oakeshott wrote, 'nothing is of value merely because it exists (and certainly not because it has existed for many generations), familiarity has no worth, and nothing is to be left standing for want of scrutiny.'[5] The conservative, in contrast, preferred 'the familiar to the unknown . . . the tried to the untried, fact to mystery, the actual to the possible.'[6]

In a sense, Oakeshott was expressing the instinctive Toryism that would have been familiar to most leading Conservatives in the early 1960s. Yet, there was a sense among those like Peregrine Worsthorne and Hugh Fraser that by the mid-1970s the Conservative Party had lost its way and needed to get back this older, more instinctive Toryism after the years of Heathite technocracy.

In the days after Hugh Fraser's defeat in the Tory leadership contest of 1975, the three men who had helped his campaign – Jonathan Aitken, Roger Scruton and John Casey – held a dinner to commiserate with him. The four friends agreed to set up a group to 'keep Fraser's ideas alive,' as Aitken put it.[7] 'Fraser . . . thought it would be fun to mix some of his young intellectual friends with the better class of journalist and Tory MP,' Casey explained, years later.[8] Casey hoped it would be like an Oxbridge essay-reading society. Scruton, meanwhile, wanted it to focus on the philosophy of conservatism, though many of his friends took the Oakeshottian view that there was no such thing. Whatever it was, the four friends were determined to carry forward their political project.

Fraser's own contribution might have been posthumous had an IRA bomb intended to assassinate him not exploded prematurely outside his home on Campden Hill Square on 23 October 1975, killing a neighbour instead. Fraser was one of the IRA's top targets in London for his hardline stance on dealing with the situation in Northern Ireland, which included calling for the execution of terrorists.

The attack does not appear to have intimidated Fraser. With Aitken, Casey and Scruton, he invited like-minded Tory MPs, academics, historians and journalists to join their new group. In this endeavour, one university – and one college – stood out: Peterhouse, Cambridge.

Even in 1975, Peterhouse had an air of notoriety. The year before, the satirist Tom Sharpe had published a novel called *Porterhouse Blue* parodying the almost farcically reactionary world of intrigue and opulence that existed at Cambridge. This was a time when women were still barred, candlelit meals were laid on every evening and bachelor dons quietly ran the show, cloistered from the austere realities of life.

From 1955 until 1968, Peterhouse had been run by Sir Herbert Butterfield, a close friend of Michael Oakeshott known for his fierce opposition to all Whiggish ideas of 'progress'. He was, in the words of one contemporary, a 'radical conservative'.[9] When Butterfield left Peterhouse in 1968, the job of protecting his brand of High Toryism was taken on by a new generation of dons, each with different specialisms and idiosyncrasies, but united by their loathing of liberalism. All were vigorously opposed to the admission of women, with one even opposing the very idea of 'letting the scrubbers in.' Another proudly displayed a poster of General Franco in his room.[10] One Jewish student even remembers a don's 'ironic' display of Nazi memorabilia.[11]

Among this group were the historians Edward Norman, who

would go on to extol the moral superiority of free markets, and John Vincent, one of the earliest 'tabloid intellectuals', with a polemical column in *The Sun*. Neither Casey nor Scruton were members of Peterhouse, but they were part of the wider 'Cambridge right' which was emerging at the time, alongside the fiery young historian Norman Stone. The leading member of this group, however, was Maurice Cowling, a charismatic acolyte of Oakeshott.

Cowling enjoyed his status as the doyen of the Cambridge right, processing around Peterhouse with an affected air of 'amused wickedness'. 'We must have him,' he would declare of a candidate for a fellowship, 'he is horrible!'[12] Yet he was also a serious thinker. His book *Mill and Liberalism*, first published in 1963, was hailed by conservative admirers for its controversial attack on what he saw as the 'intolerance' of the liberal mind. Cowling was an active Conservative Party member who had stood unsuccessfully for the party in the 1959 general election and had been a councillor from 1966 until 1970. But it was at Peterhouse that his influence was greatest, conspiring with colleagues to maintain things just as they had always been. In these machinations, Cowling was aided by his reputation as a well-connected intriguer, on friendly terms with sympathetic journalists. Among those were Hugh Fraser's fellow Phantom, Peregrine Worsthorne, by then an influential journalist at *The Sunday Telegraph*, and his fellow Tory commentator, T. E. Utley, whose early support for the 'Butskellism' of the 1950s, which he saw as a sensible correction to the socialism of Clement Attlee's Labour government, had developed into a hostility to the corporatism of Heath.

In this, he had a Fleet Street ally in Maurice Cowling. For a short time from 1970, Cowling had been literary editor of *The Spectator* under the editorship of George Gale, another Peterhouse alumnus. Gale had taken over the editorship of the magazine from Nigel Lawson in 1970 and quickly turned it into an organ with a distinctly Powellite flavour. Cowling and Gale were good friends and often spent their weekends at Gale's holiday home in Wivenhoe, in Essex. Together, they would be joined by a cadre of other conservative journalists and academics, including Worsthorne, who also owned a weekend cottage there. And so, over time, this pretty village on the outskirts of Colchester became the quaint meeting place for a group of like-minded Tory radicals. Paul Johnson, who had been editor of the *New Statesman* until 1970, was a regular attendee, alongside Utley and *The Spectator*'s political editor Patrick Cosgrave – another Powellite and former student at Peterhouse. Many of this band would go on to join Aitken, Scruton and Casey at the Hugh Fraser group.

At the time, however, none of them believed they were part of a 'movement', let alone a revolution in British politics. They did not meet to plot some great overthrow of the Tory hierarchy. No one would have believed any such thing remotely possible, even if it had been desirable. What they represented was a mood. They were united by a certain sensibility, a loose desire to 'wrench the public mind out of the groove it had been running in since 1940,' as Cowling later put it.[13] They were rebellious, reactionary and provocative. Together, they consciously rejected what they saw as the progressive zeitgeist. According to the conservative journalist Bruce Anderson, 'It was never a deep ingrained plot. They just wanted to enjoy themselves.'[14] Cowling himself said as much, years later: 'There is a tendency in much left-wing analysis to overestimate the novelty of the New Right, even of the economic New Right, and to ignore the extent to which its "new ideas" can be found in the thought, rhetoric and practice of the Conservative Party throughout the twentieth century.'[15] The Toryism that they embodied in 1975 did not suddenly emerge in Britain in the 1970s and 1980s; like Gaullism in France, it was woven into the national character – a 'disposition', as Oakeshott put it.

By 1975, however, this disposition was beginning to find fresh expression as ideas emerged to challenge a governing consensus. The Institute for Economic Affairs had led the way in the 1950s and '60s, with Enoch Powell as the leading voice for free-market conservatism in Parliament. But he was now a backbench Ulster Unionist MP with limited influence in the Conservative Party. The torch of resistance had been passed to Keith Joseph, the intellectual leader of the New Right in Parliament, who had stood aside from the leadership contest in 1975 to back Margaret Thatcher. Yet, in the early days of Thatcher's leadership, it was far from clear that she was the radical she would later become.

It was in this milieu that the Hugh Fraser group began to develop. It was not as important as the IEA or the CPS. It did not have the same pretensions to power and influence. But it was something they were not: a salon.

For the group's first meeting at Fraser's Holland Park home, Aitken, Casey and Scruton persuaded the biographer of Benjamin Disraeli, Robert Blake, to open the evening's discussion. It was a smart choice to focus on a character who had inspired and led a similar period of Tory introspection a century or so earlier.

In his biography, Blake charts Disraeli's ideological radicalism as a challenge to the Tory party to stand for something beyond merely 'conserving' things that have been reformed by someone else. In his early career, Disraeli had gravitated to a small and rebellious section of the party, later known as Young England. This group of Tory ultras was united in 'emotional revulsion against the liberal utilitarian spirit of the time,' Blake writes, preferring 'a sort of nostalgic escape from the disagreeable present to the agreeable but imaginary past.' For Blake, the Young England radicals did not achieve anything significant in the short term, 'but their memory will always beckon to those incurable romantics for whom political life is something more than a humdrum profession.'[16] Something similar would, in time, be true of Hugh Fraser's New Right.

When those around Thatcher heard about the Hugh Fraser group, there was some disquiet. 'What's this I hear about you starting up a splinter group to keep supporting Hugh Fraser?' Thatcher's ally and former campaign manager, Airey Neave, asked

Jonathan Aitken. Naturally, Aitken insisted it was nothing to worry about. A week or so later, a rather sheepish-looking Neave came back with a somewhat different question: 'The leader wondered whether she might be invited.'[17]

With Scruton's encouragement, the group had now changed its name to better reflect its purpose. It would be known as the Conservative Philosophy Group and would meet close to Parliament, in Lord North Street, where Aitken owned a property big enough to accommodate forty or so guests in his reception room.

Thatcher later told Aitken that she appreciated the group because it gave the party a chance to define its own philosophy rather than simply oppose someone else's. For Scruton, the romantic core of conservatism was the 'lost experience of home' – much as Powell, who rarely missed a meeting, had written to his parents during the war. Conservatism as a philosophy, Scruton argued, was the belief, however hopeless, 'that what has been lost can also be recaptured – not necessarily as it was when it first slipped from our grasp, but as it will be when consciously regained and remodelled.'[18] What the group really represented, then, was a wider challenge to the post-war consensus.

On the eve of the first ballot of the Conservative leadership contest, Thatcher had appeared on Granada Television's *World in Action*, where she spoke of this nostalgic feeling. 'All my ideas about [Britain] were formed before I was seventeen or eighteen,' she declared.[19] It was a revealing comment. The young Margaret Thatcher – or Margaret Roberts, as she then was – turned eighteen in October 1943, the year Monnet, Macmillan and de Gaulle dreamed of a new world in Algiers.

Born in 1925, Thatcher spent her entire childhood in Grantham, living above the grocery shop her parents owned. The family had no garden, hot water or inside toilet. Life was austere but respectable, and always busy, dominated by work and Methodism. 'It was all church, church, church, church,' Margaret's elder sister, Muriel, later put it.[20]

Although times were difficult nationally, the Roberts family was not impoverished. Grantham largely avoided the economic devastation of the 1930s, enjoying a mild prosperity that was not diminished as the war approached. New factories were built and full employment returned.

'I don't know why I was so staunchly Conservative,' Thatcher later speculated. 'I think it was the idea of my father that you can get on somehow.'[21] Thatcher's conservatism was unconscious, rooted in these early memories. 'I never thought that Christianity equipped me with a political philosophy,' she later reflected, 'but I thought it did equip me with standards to which political actions must, in the end, be referred.'[22] This is authentic Thatcherism.

Many have argued that Thatcher was Britain's last Victorian Liberal. There was certainly something of the austere Gladstonian about her Christian rectitude in domestic and foreign policy, which set her apart from those like Enoch Powell and Maurice Cowling, who saw no idealism in diplomacy other than the national interest.

According to Edward Norman, Thatcher was ultimately driven by the same suppressed desire that animated Scruton and Powell – namely, to 'resuscitate a world we had lost'.[23] This would always be Grantham and the memory of her father; a Britain of national unity, duty, self-reliance and endeavour. Yet, in 1975, Thatcher's convictions were not marginal, but mainstream within the Conservative Party. 'Thatcherism's chief plank is the advocacy of a free and competitive economy,' T. E. Utley later observed, 'but that simply represents one more less permanent ingredient in modern Conservative philosophy.'[24]

In late 1975, Thatcher's task of returning the Tory party to power was daunting. While she had successfully navigated the referendum campaign, she still faced a Labour Party which had won four out of the last five general elections and a prime minister who had become a wily veteran and proved survivor. Wilson was no longer the energetic modernizer he had been in the 1960s, but had become a Stanley Baldwin-type figure: managerial and sensible, skilled at holding party and country together, if not at solving underlying problems.

By 1976, there was even a slight sense that Britain might have turned the corner. Inflation had fallen from 30 per cent to 13 per cent, while the deficit had dropped from £3 billion in 1974 to £1 billion. This was not the great European promised land that many had hoped for in 1973, but it was an improvement. Harold Wilson and his chancellor Denis Healey were managing a difficult situation reasonably well, keeping the show on the road without the kind of strife that had ended Heath's time in power.

But even keeping things ticking over in this way had utterly exhausted Wilson. Among those close to Wilson at the time, there was some speculation that, after more than a decade at the top of British politics, either as prime minister or leader of the Opposition, he was looking for a way out. And yet, when the end came, it caught much of the country off guard.

On Tuesday, 16 March, less than a year after winning his referendum on Europe, Harold Wilson resigned. A partisan, academic northerner, who had emerged from the left only to become an establishment centrist, he was never beloved by the public. Yet his resignation was not celebrated. Rather, the predominant emotion was one of surprise. Typically, Enoch Powell took a more absolutist view. 'The prime ministership is a position in which you can only die fighting or die literally,' Enoch Powell said, once again drawn to the idea of martyrdom.[25]

Powell's judgement was customarily exacting, yet it did alight on something important. Wilson was one of the brightest minds ever to serve as prime minister – sharp, witty and astute. He had kept the Tories from power in four out of five general elections and outmanoeuvred both the Powellite right and Bennite left to secure Britain's place in Europe. During this time, he had somehow kept the Labour Party together, the economy moving and inflation just about under control, before quitting on his own terms at the time of his own choosing. It was a remarkable career.

Wilson was such a skilled politician that many thought his

resignation was just another trick. The truth, however, was more prosaic: Wilson had run out of steam. He was exhausted, drinking in the day just to cope, no longer able to muster the energy necessary for the job. A decade of political manoeuvring, crisis management, electioneering and national decline had taken its toll. He hadn't died in battle, but something had died within him.

Since the referendum in 1975, Wilson had been a shadow of his former self. On one occasion, talking to a friend, he'd dismissively referred to himself, tears in his eyes, as a part-time prime minister. There was some truth to this: red boxes went unopened, business delegated to senior ministers, the old spirit only occasionally roused. He looked pallid and puffy. During his first term in office, he'd enjoyed taking his dog for a walk around Chequers. Now, he couldn't even manage that. The job had taken its toll, but so too had the country's predicament. The grand plans that had fuelled his passion were now like a distant dream. In one interview at the turn of the year, he was asked about his plans for a hypothetical retirement. He replied that he hoped to write and to 'think about the problems facing the country.'[26]

Despite such admissions, and the insider speculation about his impending resignation, Wilson's announcement still came as a surprise. He was only sixty, still reasonably secure in the job, his rivals under control. And then he was gone. It was a turning point not just for Wilson, but for the country. For twelve years, Britain had been run by either Harold Wilson or Ted Heath, the modernizing men of a modern Britain. Now, both were gone, and the country was still in need of modernization.

In an interview shortly after his resignation, Wilson was asked what he most wanted his 'era' to be identified with. The first, he said, was that he had 'settled the position of Britain within the European Community once and for all'. The second was that Britain had 'established a totally new relationship between Government and people in the fight against inflation.'[27] In the years ahead, this second claim would prove to be premature, but almost no one at the time believed there was any danger to the first.

As if to prove the point, in April 1976, the European Council proclaimed Jean Monnet the continent's first honorary Citizen of Europe; its founding father. At a summit in Luxembourg, the continent's leaders declared that the progress made towards 'political unification', as they described it, was something they owed in large measure 'to the boldness and breadth of vision of a handful of men', of whom Jean Monnet was the most notable. Whether as the 'inspirer of the Schuman Plan, first president of the High Authority, or founder of the Action Committee for the United States of Europe', Monnet's genius, they said, was to give 'institutional form' to the hopes of European unity. 'Sometimes, this objective may have been lost to view amid the vicissitudes of the unification of Europe. Nevertheless, that objective has never been disavowed. Now, more than ever, it should serve as a guide, enabling us to rise above our task of daily administration and give it its true and substantial meaning.'[28]

Since the oil crisis of 1973, Monnet's Europe might have lost some of its early momentum, but his grand idea was still there, holding things together. The European Community had already pledged itself to what it called 'economic and monetary union.' This commitment had first been made in 1969, with an aspiration for completion by 1980. European leaders – including Edward Heath – had met in Paris in 1972 to inject some fresh energy into this project, following the 'Nixon shock' of the year before, when the US president unilaterally abolished the system of being able to exchange dollars for gold at a fixed price. By March 1973, the system of fixed exchange rates – created at Bretton Woods in 1944 – had collapsed. In its place came the era of free-floating currencies. It was a revolution with unforeseen consequences, as other currencies found themselves buffeted by the power of the dollar and its ultimate protector, the US Federal Reserve. In Brussels, the shock added fresh impetus to the project to build a European monetary shelter to protect the continent's exposed economies.

After Wilson's resignation in 1976, Labour's reforming former home secretary Roy Jenkins threw his hat into the ring to become

Labour leader, but was comfortably defeated by James Callaghan, who became prime minister. In January 1977, Jenkins quit British politics to become the first British president of the European Commission. One of Jenkins' most profound legacies from his time in Brussels would be the European Monetary System, including the mechanism to manage currency fluctuations that sat at its heart: the European Exchange Rate Mechanism. This system had been promoted by German Chancellor Helmut Schmidt and French President Valéry Giscard d'Estaing at a summit of European leaders in Copenhagen in 1978, although Britain, under Callaghan's agnostic leadership, opted to remain outside. The UK, once again, found itself trying to find a halfway house in which it could maintain its independence from the inside. Whether Britain eventually joined could be resolved in time. For Callaghan, there were far more pressing matters at hand.

When he replaced Harold Wilson as prime minister, he inherited a formidable set of challenges: British industry uncompetitive, the root causes of inflation untreated, a tiny majority and a Labour left on the march. In the battle to succeed Wilson, it had been the Eurosceptic left of the party which had surpassed all expectations. The great orator and polemicist, Michael Foot, had won the first round of voting, only to narrowly finish second to Callaghan in the second. Importantly, Foot comfortably defeated Tony Benn to establish himself as Labour's crown prince and standard bearer of the left.

Callaghan, meanwhile, was a man of the Labour right – a patriotic, small-c conservative trade unionist, who had served in the navy. His admiration for the Queen was deep, his discomfort with liberalism heartfelt, his feelings towards Europe pragmatic at best. He was, as Peter Hennessy wrote, a 'gnarled tree with huge, sturdy roots,' who sat squat in the centre of British politics.[29] And, for a short period, he bloomed. Uncle Jim, Farmer Jim, Sunny Jim – the undemonstrative, common-sense man of the people was almost the embodiment of the country he came to lead.

Callaghan did not shy away from addressing the nation's problems, either. 'I say to you quite bluntly that despite the measures of the last twelve months, we are still not earning the standard of living we are enjoying. We are only keeping up our standards by borrowing, and this cannot go on indefinitely. There is no soft option. I do not promise you any real easement for some time to come. There can be no lasting improvement in your living standards until we can achieve it without going deeper and deeper into debt as a nation.'[30] Bitter medicine indeed, and the kind of message that might have had Enoch Powell nodding along.

Labour had been in power for eight of the previous twelve years and had at least another two or three to run before the next general election. Its new leader was a figure of stature and experience, a man who seemed to speak for England and many of its deepest instincts. He was open to Europe but pragmatic about its benefits, alive to the challenges that lay ahead but no radical. For the Tories, James Callaghan looked just about the worst opponent imaginable. The Conservative Party, in contrast, had elected a woman who was widely seen as inexperienced, 'shrill', and even, potentially, extreme, though no one could be quite sure.

Though always careful in her pronouncements, Thatcher gave an early flash of the mettle that would play an important role in defining her in the national consciousness with a speech on foreign policy at Kensington Town Hall in 1976. In the speech, Thatcher criticized Labour's defence cuts, warned the country not to fall for 'an illusory détente' with the Soviet Union and, with a touch of George Orwell, said that Britain was lost in a 'long sleep' from which it needed to awake.[31]

The speech made the front pages of the newspapers the following day, before being picked up in the Soviet Union, where she was given the derogatory nickname of 'the Iron Lady' as a result. This in turn fed back into the Western media, much of which saw it as a badge of honour. The image of Thatcher was already being burnished.

What was less reported at the time were the influences behind Thatcher's speech. After becoming Conservative Party leader, Thatcher began to take briefings from a group of Cold Warriors led by the journalist and one-time spy Brian Crozier, alongside his friend Nicholas Elliott, a senior figure in Britain's Secret Intelligence Service – MI6 – who had been close friends with the Soviet double agent Kim Philby.[32] Crozier and Elliott had created an advisory group to brief Thatcher and other sympathetic politicians, which they called 'the Shield'.[33] The group drew much of its material from Crozier's think tank devoted to the study of communist subversion, the Institute for the Study of Conflict (ISC). In 1977, Crozier also set up a private intelligence organization called 'the 61', which worked alongside the security services 'to make up for what he perceived as the failure of western governments to counter communist Soviet propaganda effectively,' as *The Guardian* later put it.[34] Nicholas Elliott became one of its fundraisers.

Officially, Crozier's think tank was created to research what it called the 'social, economic, political and military causes and manifestations of unrest and conflict throughout the world.'[35] But, as Crozier himself later put it in his autobiography, his core objective as director was 'exposing the fallacies of détente and warning the West of the dangers inherent in a policy of illusion'.[36]

Thatcher's defiant rhetoric struck a chord with voters and, by May 1977, *The Guardian* was reporting with some alarm that the public seemed to be warming to her. According to Gallup, those who thought she was 'proving a good leader of the Conservative Party' had risen to 45 per cent from 35 per cent in March. Suddenly, the prospect of this political lightweight toppling an established figure like Callaghan no longer seemed so far-fetched. 'The spectre of Thatcher is hovering over Downing Street,' wrote the *Guardian* columnist Peter Jenkins.[37] People who had seen Thatcher only as a leader of the Opposition, were now seeing her as a prospective prime minister.

Callaghan's main problem was the unrelenting pressure on

sterling. Since Richard Nixon had ended fixed exchange rates, the pound had lost 35 per cent of its value against other major currencies.[38] Investors simply did not believe the British government would, or perhaps could, do what was necessary to stop living beyond its means. By June 1976, sterling had fallen to $1.70 and the Bank of England's reserves were almost exhausted. The choice no government ever wants to face was now unavoidable: severe public spending cuts or a bailout from the International Monetary Fund in Washington. At the time, the latter seemed to be less painful. The Americans, however, had had enough. The US Treasury secretary, William Simon, later wrote that he was simply not willing to play 'host to a parasite.'[39] Once again, just as at Suez, Britain was falling into a vortex of pain caused by its American ally.

Over the summer, the Callaghan government began a major squeeze on government spending, but the pressure on the pound continued. Many left-wingers, outraged by the austerity they were being forced to swallow, began agitating for a 'socialist alternative'. Labour's National Executive Committee called for the banks to be nationalized. Tony Benn demanded a siege economy, with tariffs and import controls to protect British industry, alongside withdrawal from the Common Market. British politics was back in turmoil, barely two years after the referendum was supposed to have tamed the extremes.

Callaghan, though, was determined to stand his ground. At the Labour Party Conference that autumn, he took the fight to the left. 'For too long, perhaps ever since the war, we postponed facing up to fundamental choices and fundamental changes in our society and in our economy,' Callaghan began, picking up on the theme of his earlier speech to the country. 'That is what I mean when I say we have been living on borrowed time. For too long this country – all of us, yes, this Conference too – has been ready to settle for borrowing money abroad to maintain our standards of life, instead of grappling with the fundamental problem of British industry.'[40]

US President Gerald Ford told the prime minister he made 'a helluva speech.'[41] Even the founding father of monetarism, Milton Friedman, who had once declared Enoch Powell the only beacon of hope in Britain, was impressed. 'That was, I think, one of the most remarkable talks, speeches, which any government leader has ever given,' he declared.[42] Even today, it marks one of those moments of national change when the scene must be slowed for a second to fully grasp its significance. Yet, as Callaghan said himself, the speech was just a reflection of reality. In 1972, there had been a sense of moral outrage as unemployment topped one million. But, three years later, it was approaching twice that.

Over the following months, the prime minister and his chancellor entered an intense process of negotiation with the IMF over the scale of cuts required. It was a painful period, the result of which was a package of austerity totalling some £1 billion in 1977–8 and £1.5 billion the following year.[43] Yet, in his methodical and collegiate manner, Callaghan brought his cabinet with him. Just as Wilson had navigated his party through Britain's tricky European dilemma, so Callaghan did now, through the IMF's imposed regime. Denis Healey thought Callaghan's performance was an object lesson for all prime ministers. Even Tony Benn was grudgingly impressed. 'Jim is a much better Prime Minister than Wilson,' he concluded that December.[44]

By January 1977, the pound was back to $1.70 and, by the end of the year, it reached $1.93. Official reserves were replenished from a low of $4 billion in December 1976 to more than $20 billion by the end of 1977. The Bank of England felt able to cut its lending rate to 5 per cent by October 1977. And, on top of this, the great white knight that might boost the British economy finally appeared: North Sea oil.

With the economy recovering, so too did Callaghan's fortunes. Britain's John Bull prime minister had steered the country through the storm. His approval ratings jumped, hitting 59 per cent in October 1977, the highest figure for any prime minister since the mid-sixties.[45] Labour had also pulled ahead in the polls. As 1977 gave way to 1978, Callaghan looked as though he might be on the verge of achieving an election victory that had appeared unlikely only a year earlier. And then it was not Callaghan who was in trouble, but his opposite number. Three years on from her victory in the leadership election, Margaret Thatcher appeared hesitant. She pushed the usual Tory lines about cutting taxes and red tape and getting the country moving again, but they were not having an impact. Indeed, it was little different from what Ted Heath had declared in 1970, or what Winston Churchill had said in his speech of 1942.

With Labour in the ascendant, the knives came out. In *The Sunday Times*, Thatcher was assailed for her 'small pawing gestures' that reminded voters of 'everyone's favourite celluloid bitch, Lassie.' In the Conservative research department, which was perceived by many Thatcherites to be dominated by their Heathite opponents, some dismissively referred to her as 'Hilda', her oh-so-provincial middle name.[46]

A collection of essays published that summer captures the mood of the traditionalist right at the time. Written by a selection of academics and journalists, including many who had dined with Thatcher at the Conservative Philosophy Group, it was edited by Maurice Cowling. The book, *Conservative Essays*, was an attempt to prod Thatcher in a more Powellite direction, with Cowling warning that Thatcher's party had 'come to seem much less conservative in tone and manner' than the Labour government.

Cowling's central argument was that Enoch Powell had set the agenda for Conservative politics before he left the party, but it had not been adhered to. Cowling argued that Powell had carved out for himself a 'special role' in British politics, 'determining the tone not just of the party with which he happens to be working but of the whole stance from which English political thinking is conducted.' What was unique about Powell, Cowling wrote, was that he attached 'the highest value to working-class opinion', regarding it as sympathetic to his stated opinions about Europe and immigration, but also, 'to the conception of a unity of national sentiment transcending the divisions of the classes.'[47] In this sense, Cowling believed Powell was a Tory in the Disraelian mould.

What is remarkable about this essay, and the volume to which it belongs, is both how much it reveals about the eventual character of Margaret Thatcher's Conservative government, and how little it corresponds to Thatcher herself. Cowling urged her to regard liberalism and Marxism as 'similar sorts of doctrine' and treat them both with the 'satire, ridicule and incredulity' he felt they deserved. He said it was important that she show a certain 'diffidence, irony or detachment' and to avoid 'ethical earnestness.'[48] If Thatcher was anything, she was earnest, and there was certainly little that was diffident or ironic about her character. She saw the world in clear moral terms and did not view liberalism and Marxism as similar sorts of doctrine. And yet, as Cowling saw, she was also a Powellite. She saw freedom through Tory eyes, not those of a libertarian. And she ultimately believed in Britain's involvement in the European Community not as an ideal, but as an instrument of the national interest, 'with no permanent claim on loyalty or attention', as Cowling summarized.

In his essay, Cowling had identified a number of resonant themes, notably the Tory party's ability to rally working-class support on the issues of Europe and immigration. He also pointed to another problem facing Thatcher: in some ways, Callaghan looked more conservative than her.

Ultimately, it was not the humiliation of the IMF bailout that cost Callaghan the premiership, nor the austerity Britain's international creditors demanded in return. Callaghan lost power in 1979 because he lost control of the country in a crisis of such chaos it would remain etched on the national memory for decades thereafter.

Just as the oil shock did for Ted Heath, so the Winter of Discontent did for Jim Callaghan. Like Heath, Callaghan believed in an orderly country, where common sense and moderation prevailed and the forces of labour and capital could be made to work in harmony for the common good. But Heath had been wrong about this in 1974, when the public had rejected him amid the turmoil of a miners' strike, and Callaghan was wrong about this now. Over the next few months, the prime minister's calls for wage restraint were first ignored and then overwhelmed in a stampede for ever-higher pay settlements. When Callaghan was finally forced to go to the country in May 1979, he did so after months of disorder, which brought the government and the unions into public disrepute.

The Winter of Discontent has become a defining image of Callaghan's Britain. But it was just the most convulsive of the ongoing battles between government and the unions. Throughout the 1970s, the number of workdays lost to strike action had been at levels not seen since the 1920s, regularly above 10 million a year, with highs of 23 million lost in 1972 and 29 million in 1979.[49] The miners had ended Heath's career in 1973. The economic reality was that Britain was living beyond its means. Successive governments had tried to deal with the problem through bargaining and consensus, pay restraint and, of course, Europe. But all had failed. Jim Callaghan was perhaps the last best hope of continuing with this model. Yet even he had failed. Confrontation was inevitable.

When Thatcher appeared on the Jimmy Young show, on Radio 2, at the end of January 1979, she offered a glimpse of steel. 'Some of the unions are confronting the British people. They are confronting the sick, they are confronting the old, they are confronting the children,' she said. 'I am prepared to take on anyone who is confronting those and who is confronting the law of the land . . . my God, I will confront them.' In a telling response, after being asked whether she might not prefer a quiet life, Thatcher replied, 'It's no earthly use saying "anything for a quiet life". I don't regard this as a quiet life. You can't even get a decent burial.'[50]

By January, the Tories had moved eight points ahead. By February, it was 19 per cent. Yet Labour had not given up hope

1. Admiral François Darlan, second-in-command to Marshal Philippe Pétain in the Vichy administration.

2. Fernand Bonnier de la Chapelle, the royalist Frenchman who assassinated Admiral Darlan.

3. General Charles de Gaulle (standing, right) and Henri Giraud (standing, left) shake hands at the Casablanca Conference in January 1943, at which the Allied strategy for the next stage of the Second World War was planned. Winston Churchill and Franklin D. Roosevelt are seated in the background.

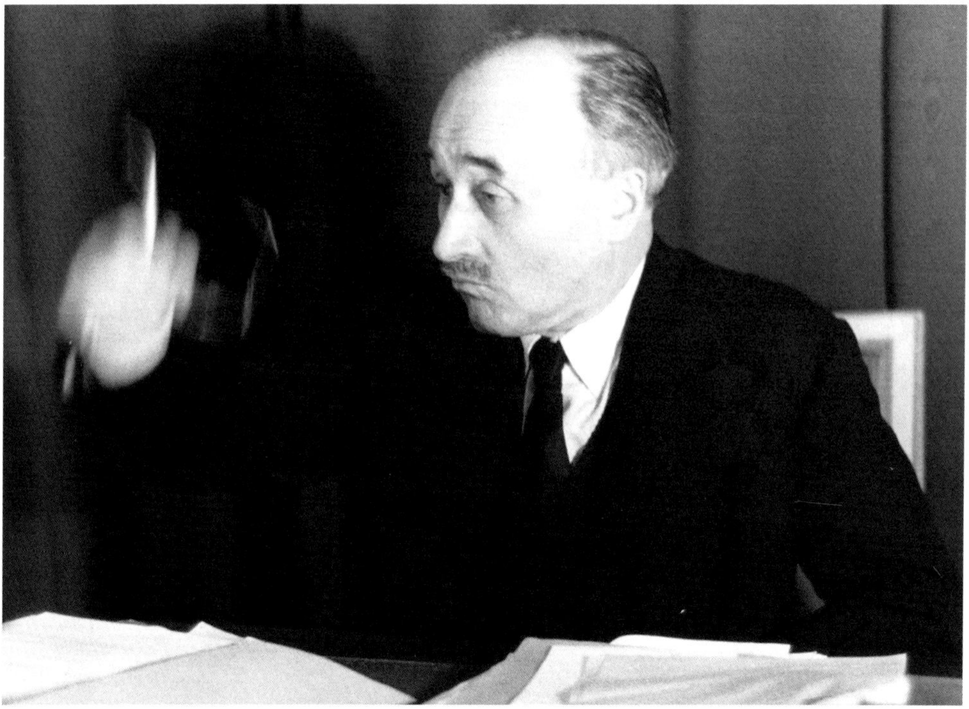

4. French bureaucrat Jean Monnet, founding father of the European Union, pictured at the Quai d'Orsay in Paris in 1947.

5. Labour's foreign secretary Ernest Bevin with French foreign minister Robert Schuman (right) and US secretary of state Dean Acheson (left) at the Quai d'Orsay, November 1949.

6. Clement Attlee meeting with Harry Truman (left), Dean Acheson (back left) and George Marshall (back right) in Washington in 1950.

7. Dwight D. Eisenhower (centre) poses for pictures with Winston Churchill (second from left) at the British Embassy in Washington in May 1959, alongside vice-president Richard Nixon (left), House speaker Sam Rayburn (second from right) and British ambassador Sir Harold Caccia (right).

8. 'The end of a thousand years of history': Hugh Gaitskell addresses the Labour Party Conference on the prospects of joining the Common Market, Brighton 1962.

9. Prime minister Harold Wilson in 1966.

10. The Big Three: former prime ministers Anthony Eden (left) and Harold Macmillan (centre) with their successor Edward Heath at the Savoy Hotel, 1973.

11. Enoch Powell and Edward Heath at the Conservative Party Conference in Brighton, 1967.

12. Meat porters in Smithfield marching to Parliament to hand in a petition backing Powell shortly after his 'Rivers of Blood' speech, April 1968.

13. Michael Foot reads *The Sun* during the general election campaign in February 1974 after Enoch Powell declared he could not stand for the Conservative Party under Edward Heath.

14. From left to right: Barbara Castle, Enoch Powell, Arne Haugestad (the Norwegian lawyer who led the victorious 'Nei' campaign in Norway's 1972 referendum), Neil Marten, Peter Shore, Jack Jones, Ronald Bell and Michael Foot at the final press conference of the referendum on British membership of the European Common Market in 1975.

15. Margaret Thatcher campaigning for a Yes vote to stay in the EEC, 1975.

16. Fathers of pro-Europeanism: Liberal leader Jeremy Thorpe, former prime minister Edward Heath and Labour home secretary Roy Jenkins during a press conference for the 'Keep Britain In Europe' campaign in May 1975.

that it could hold on for another six months, by which time its fortunes may have recovered. The end, when it came, was unexpected. A vote of no confidence, which Callaghan hoped to survive – just – had instead been lost by one. With the support of the Scottish National Party, Margaret Thatcher had her election.[51]

When polling day arrived, Thatcher was triumphant. The Tories had 339 seats to Labour's 269, a majority of 44. Labour's vote had not collapsed, but Thatcher had swept to power. Callaghan was clear: 'We lost the Election because people didn't get their dustbins emptied, because commuters were angry about train disruption and because of too much union power. That's about it.'[52] It would take fifteen years before Labour elected another leader who agreed with Callaghan's analysis.

As Peter Jenkins put it in *The Guardian*, the Winter of Discontent was a symptom of Britain's by then chronic illness. 'We are living in an expensive and increasingly poor country,' he wrote. 'It is not much use lecturing people about paying themselves more than the country can afford. A better way of putting it is that increasingly the country cannot afford to pay people enough.'[53] Even today, the theme is familiar. Narrative demands chapter breaks and sudden plot twists, moments of transformation and revolution, but the story of post-war Britain is one of gradual change.

Certainly, few in 1979 thought they were living through a great pivot in history. Labour had lost the election, but there was no reason to think it would not win again. Thatcher might be to the right of her Tory predecessors, but her manifesto was vague and her rhetoric cautious. In *The Sunday Telegraph*, Peregrine Worsthorne predicted that 'neither revolution nor counter-revolution' was likely under Thatcher and, should she manage to make any changes at all, they would be measured 'in inches not miles.'[54]

Chapter 7

On 16 March 1979, Europe's *citoyen d'honneur* took his last breath, leaving a world transformed by his presence. Jean Monnet had lived a remarkable life: international businessman, bureaucrat, politician and diplomat. He had advised some of the most powerful men of the twentieth century, proposed the union of Britain and France, worked for the British and Americans, elevated de Gaulle and founded modern Europe. At his funeral, the German chancellor Helmut Schmidt joined the French president Valéry Giscard d'Estaing in a display of shared mourning for the man who had done more than any other to ensure their two countries would never again find themselves in opposing trenches. As the leaders of the French and German republics sat in church, the American 'Battle Hymn of the Republic' rang out. Jean Monnet was the first man of Europe, but he was never just a European. Here was a man of the free world, old and new.

The Europe he left behind seemed more secure than ever before. But it was also one that felt somewhat stale, lacking the energy and optimism that had come before. The 1973 oil crisis had brought the continent's thirty-year economic miracle to an end, turning Europe's leaders in on themselves. Europe was no longer booming, but at risk of being left behind. It was not just America that was pulling ahead, but Japan too. Euro-pessimism began to creep into the discourse. The zeitgeist had shifted.

Monnet had been aware of the dangers of stagnation and had urged the continent's leaders to continue down the path of integration. By 1979, though, the aspirations of Europe's leaders were no longer so idealistic. Every country had its own problems to deal with. In Britain, the brief summer of Heathite Europeanism had long gone. For five years, Britain had been governed by a sceptical and divided Labour Party for whom even the current settlement was its limit.

Six weeks after Jean Monnet's death, the election of Margaret Thatcher appeared to offer an opportunity. The Labour Party was out; the party of Europe was back. On the surface, Britain's new prime minister offered Europe's integrationists a degree of reassurance, even hope.

For Thatcher, the one overriding objective was to rebuild the British economy, and, in 1979, she saw Europe as a potential ally in this battle, just as it was seen by most as a pillar of the Western alliance against the Soviet Union. Even future Eurosceptic hard-liners like Ralph Harris – who Thatcher made a life peer the year she arrived in Downing Street – were enthusiastic supporters of Europe as a market that could be widened and liberalized to Britain's advantage, as he saw it. Most conservative Cold Warriors were also firm supporters of British membership. Within the Conservative Party, there was no serious argument. That issue had been settled. For those in Europe who wanted to see a more engaged, positive Britain, the Conservative Party's victory was to be welcomed. If there was a threat to Britain's membership, it came from the still-powerful British left, which remained as hostile to Europe as it was to free markets themselves.

The 1979 Conservative manifesto is a testament to the Conservative Party's commitment to the European Community. Heathite in its analysis, it argued that Britain's influence in Europe had been undermined by Labour's ideological scepticism. The task ahead was to restore Britain's influence 'by convincing our partners of our commitment to the Community's success.' Here, in essence, was the pragmatic pro-European argument. While the Tory manifesto admitted that some Community policies needed to change, it argued that these were not evidence of Europe's failure. 'What has happened is that under Labour our country has been prevented from taking advantage of the opportunities which membership offers.'[1] Britain needed to return to the heart of Europe.

The sense of Thatcher returning Britain to a more open, European position was evident during the first visit of a foreign leader to Britain after the election. Helmut Schmidt, the chancellor of West Germany, arrived in London just a week after Thatcher's victory. While the new prime minister was not particularly enamoured by the prospect – 'why is he coming?' she had complained to the cabinet secretary – the event went well. Thatcher expressed none of the anti-German sentiment that would burst out in later years, and was even full of praise for the country's economic achievements. 'Ours is not a grudging acquiescence in Community membership,' she declared.[2] A new era seemed to be opening up for Britain in Europe, perhaps not as idealistic and wholehearted as had once been promised under Heath, but one that was settled at the very least.

If Thatcher had any problem with the Conservative Party at this time, it had less to do with Europe and more to do with her domestic economic agenda. Many of the leading figures on the traditionalist right had voiced their concerns about her fixation on markets and economic freedom. Indeed, Cowling had described his *Conservative Essays* as 'shots across the bows' of the free marketeers. It was also at this time that Cowling's friend Roger Scruton sequestered himself at Lake Como to work on his breakout book, *The Meaning of Conservatism*, published in 1980 to acclaim from the traditionalist right but criticism from the left, both within and beyond the Tory party. Like Cowling, the inspiration for Scruton's work was his opposition to what he saw as Thatcher's overemphasis on freedom at the expense of national identity, defence, culture and order. 'Uppermost in my mind was the freedom that had been displayed on the barricades in Paris,' Scruton later explained. 'The experience had convinced me, first that I was a conservative, and secondly that conservatism is not about freedom, but about authority.'[3]

Scruton and Cowling later came to admire Thatcher, but in the early years her focus on economic liberalization was not something of which they approved. In *The Meaning of Conservatism*, Scruton argued that the point of conservatism was to nurture the 'social organism' that was a country's culture and institutions, to protect and conserve all that was good and beautiful, not simply to balance the books or go for growth. 'Organisms can be cured by growth,' as Scruton put it, 'but they can also be killed by it.'[4]

At the same time as the Conservative Philosophy Group had got up and running, an overlapping gathering of Tory ultras had formed under the chairmanship of the Marquess of Salisbury, great-grandson of the last aristocratic Tory statesman to have run the country from the Lords. The Salisbury Group had been formed in 1976 and its founding members included Roger Scruton, Michael Oakeshott and Maurice Cowling. The purpose of this group was to give voice to Oakeshott's 'conservative instincts' in the face of what Scruton called 'their betrayal by the free marketeers'.[5]

Yet, when it came to her 'instincts', Thatcher's were certainly conservative. Though superficially pro-European, leading a pro-European government and a pro-European party, Thatcher was never a believer, being closer in temperament and feeling to her two Labour predecessors than the man she replaced as Tory leader.

The difference between the two leaders is captured in their first European summits as prime minister. In 1972, Ted Heath – invited to observe ahead of British entry – watched happily as European leaders signed up to the aspiration of a common European currency. In 1979, Thatcher went to war over Britain's budget contributions and refused to commit to taking Britain into the European Exchange Rate Mechanism. The battle over Britain's financial contributions would define Thatcher's early relationship with the European Community.

In fact, in the view of the French president Giscard d'Estaing, Thatcher was 'hostile to the European Community from the beginning.' In the new British prime minister, Giscard d'Estaing saw a vision of a provincial England for which he could hardly contain his own instinctive disdain. 'When our children were young, my family, being rather snobbish, employed an English nanny,' he recalled. 'She was very correct, very tidy, with a very neat hairdo. She was efficient, religious, always opening the windows, especially when the children were ill; rather tiresome. When I met Thatcher, I thought "She is exactly the same, *exactly* the same!"'[6]

While Thatcher was then genuinely in favour of British membership of the Common Market, it is true that she did represent a certain image of Britain that was tidy, efficient, religious and provincial. From the beginning, she found European summits frustrating and was convinced – often correctly – that her concerns were not being treated seriously. As early as September 1979, writing to her foreign affairs private secretary Bryan Cartledge, she admitted to becoming 'more and more disillusioned with the EEC'.[7]

Although she was frustrated with the reality of life inside Europe, at this stage her concerns remained practical, not constitutional. 'We are going to have a real fight over the budget,' she told Cartledge, 'we need the money.'[8] Indeed, the fight to reduce Britain's net contribution to the Community budget would dominate the first four years of her relationship with Europe.*

---

* The budgetary formula used by the Community to fund itself was particularly disadvantageous to the UK, so much so that, according to Anand Menon, Professor of European Politics and Foreign Affairs at King's College London, it appeared deliberately designed to be so. In April 1970, a few months before Ted Heath became Prime Minister, the EEC agreed a new funding formula to raise its own resources directly through a combination of agricultural and sugar levies, tariffs and VAT receipts. Britain's VAT base was proportionally higher than other Member States and its economy was more open to trade with the rest of the world, and therefore more subject to tariffs. Britain also had a smaller agricultural sector than most other Member States and most of the EEC's spending went on farming subsidies. (D'Alfonso, Alessandro: European Parliamentary Research Service: 'The UK "rebate" on the EU budget: An explanation of the abatement and other correction mechanisms', Brussels: 2016)

Beyond the prosaic question of money lay something far more important: an idea. In a speech in Luxembourg in October 1980, Thatcher set out her vision of Europe. 'The principle at the heart of our European institutions is the principle of liberty,' she declared, projecting onto the Community a narrative that bore little semblance to reality.[9] For Thatcher, Europe's great function was to bind together the free states of Europe in resistance to the Soviet Union. This idea had been a central part of the 1975 referendum campaign, particularly for the conservative right, and a core part of Jean Monnet's vision of an Atlantic Free World. Without the impetus of the Cold War and American pressure, it is unlikely the Coal and Steel Community would have emerged as it did. Yet, the notion that the 'principle of liberty' was the animating spirit of the European project was a comforting fantasy. Monnet's vision was never one of mere international cooperation to resist foreign tyranny, but something far more radical. At the heart of the European project was – and is – the idea that national interests must give way to a new shared interest called Europe. Its founders always intended to expand the nucleus of their new supranational entity, creating an ever-closer union of the peoples of Europe, as the Treaty of Rome made clear. This was not a League of Nations, dependent on international cooperation, but a new, revolutionary construct.

In Luxembourg, Thatcher insisted the idea of a United States of Europe had 'never . . . been the practical intention' of the European project, but this had been Jean Monnet's life ambition. Many of the most senior British diplomats and officials advising Thatcher at the time had become convinced European federalists. Michael Jenkins, who then worked for Roy Jenkins – president of the European Commission – later admitted that the organization '*was* trying to create a United States of Europe – with a common currency and a constitution.' And why not? This had not been some unutterable notion just a decade earlier, under Heath. 'We were Ted's children,' as Jenkins put it.[10]

Federalism was the logical conclusion to the idea that lay at the core of the Community. If it made sense to put trade and tariffs beyond mere national interest, then why not currency and defence, foreign affairs and even parliamentary democracy itself? Once the regulation of certain industries was made at a European level, surely it must be subject to democratic control at a European level? Monnet's genius was to fertilize this idea in an embryonic Coal and Steel Community, which would, in time, grow into something much more profound: first a Common Market, and then, incrementally, an ever more federal union, the animating spirit unchanged throughout.

For much of her time in office, Thatcher would avoid the constitutional and ideological implications of the project Britain had signed up to. In large part, this was because she had much more immediate problems, from the state of Britain's economy to her own political survival. But her refusal to accept the reality of the project was also partly because the political climate at the time made it difficult to attack the principle of European unity itself. In 1980, there was no appetite for anything more than a spirited defence of national interests within the Community, certainly not the rejection of the Community itself.

It was not only Giscard d'Estaing who grasped the cognitive dissonance at the heart of Thatcher's early Europe policy. At a joint press conference with German Chancellor Helmut Schmidt, in which Thatcher once again complained about the 'very unfair and inequitable' budget settlement, the German leader questioned the principle upon which she was basing her argument. Thatcher had called for a 'broad balance' between what countries put into the European budget and what they received in return. But, as the German chancellor pointed out, if he started demanding something similar 'it would mean the end of the Community in a few weeks.'[11] The budget was collective, raised collectively and spent collectively. It was a supranational budget for a supranational community. Britain was supposed to be European now, yet it was not acting like it, just as de Gaulle had foreseen.

For the first year in office, Thatcher battled for Britain's contribution to the collective budget to be brought into 'broad balance'. To do so, she threatened and harangued. At the Dublin summit in 1979, she was offered a £350 million reduction in Britain's contributions, but dismissed the offer contemptuously as 'a third of a loaf.'[12] It was then suggested that Britain could get more back if it offered the Community access to its North Sea oil reserves, to which Thatcher reacted with horror. 'To suggest that we might be allowed to keep our own money in return for giving up some of our oil is ridiculous,' she scrawled, angrily, on a memo.[13] At the Luxembourg summit in 1980, further offers were made and rejected. Finally, in May, a deal was reached. Britain's net contribution would be reduced by two thirds for three years. It was a diplomatic coup for Thatcher, but one she was never entirely satisfied with. She had accepted two thirds of a loaf.

At one level, Thatcher was struggling with a straightforward diplomatic dilemma: how to reset the financial terms of British membership, which had been set – disadvantageously – before the UK had joined. Lurking below this challenge was an altogether more fundamental conundrum: how much national sovereignty should be compromised for the sake of continuing British 'influence'? In years to come, the primary issue concerning Thatcher would move from budget contributions to the idea of a European currency and its necessary forerunner, fixed exchange rates. Should Britain risk isolation outside such a system, while all the other countries proceeded together? Or should it join despite its doubts, to maintain influence over how that currency came into being?

The extent of the Community's powers was already causing distress during Thatcher's first term in office. 'The more I read the more appalled I become,' she wrote on a memo at the time.[14] Despite the prime minister's exasperation, unabashed anti-Europeanism remained very much a minority pursuit within the Conservative Party. In November 1980, nine Conservative MPs had come together to form a new Eurosceptic caucus, the European Reform Group, or ERG. Its opening statement declared 'the urgent need for fundamental reform of the Common Market in the interest of securing genuine European co-operation based on the partnership of nation states.' ERG's driving forces were Hugh Fraser, Jonathan Aitken and Teddy Taylor.

The emergence of the group caused enough concern to be raised in the Commons. Anthony Meyer, the pro-European Conservative MP who later challenged Thatcher for the leadership in 1989, warned the government that the 'objectives of the so-called European Reform Group are irreconcilable with the settled policies of this party and this Government.' Ian Gilmour, responding for the government, agreed and went further, arguing that the prospectus put forward by the group was 'incompatible with our continued membership of the Community'.[15] Both were right. At this point, the ERG was not calling for British withdrawal, but for the restoration of national control over agricultural policy, trading practices and even the institutions of the European Community itself, as well as the complete overhaul of the budget. It was a prospectus not just for reform, but for an entirely different Europe from the one that existed. Within a month, despite being a small minority in the parliamentary party, the ERG had enough support to send thirty-six MPs to Number Ten to hold talks with the prime minister about their proposals.

A minute of the December 1980 meeting taken by Thatcher's parliamentary private secretary Ian Gow records Hugh Fraser urging the Prime Minister to put British interests first in her dealings with the European Community, telling her that while she had 'always followed this precept . . . some of your colleagues talk differently.' Fraser then implored her to go into the next election with Britain's national interests paramount. 'We must not go for a Federal Europe,' he declared. Gow's record of the proceedings records Thatcher replying: 'I agree entirely.'[16]

Once again, though, it was not Europe which principally concerned Thatcher, but the state of the British economy and the global battle with communism. For the first three years of her premiership, her economic record looked every bit as unsuccessful as that of her predecessors. Worse, in fact; the economy seemed to be deteriorating.

She had, of course, inherited a difficult situation. Inflation was in double figures, the deficit high, government spending growing and public-sector pay increases rolling over the government in waves. On top of all this, the global economy was in a bad state and even the golden goose of North Sea oil, which had once looked as though it might save the British economy, had become a double-edged sword, exposing Britain to the 'Dutch disease' whereby its oil and gas reserves would artificially increase the value of sterling, making its goods too expensive to export. The future looked as bleak as it had ever been. On her first day in office, Thatcher had been presented with documents outlining the dire state of the economy and the limited options she had to deal with it. The country's industrial performance had been so poor for so long, as one memo put it, 'that in Western industrial terms we have now become a low productivity, cheap labour, country.'[17]

In a bid to deal with the inflationary price swings that were unbalancing the British economy, Thatcher quickly deployed all the weapons in her ideological arsenal. Interest rates were hiked, foreign exchange controls lifted, spending squeezed and the 'prices and incomes' policy of the Wilson and Heath governments abandoned. Instead, the supply of money would be monitored and, at least in theory, controlled by the Treasury. This was monetarism in practice, the idea that the root cause of inflation was not wages but the amount of money circulating in the economy. Control that and inflation would disappear, even as people's wages increased.

The net result was the deepest recession since the 1930s, a collapse in manufacturing and runaway unemployment. To add to the turmoil, anti-police riots broke out in Brixton in April 1981, while Northern Ireland was in a particularly febrile state over her refusal to bend to the IRA hunger strikes. Instead of growing the economy and reducing the money supply, Thatcher achieved the opposite, as the lifting of capital controls complicated the state's ability to control how much money was flowing through the economy. Bernard Ingham, Thatcher's press secretary, complained that the government was in the worst of all worlds: 'It is criticised at once for unfeeling monetarism, while at the same time money supply, on one definition at least, is soaring.'[18]

Inevitably, sceptical grumbling about Thatcher's economic strategy began to turn into open hostility. Ian Gilmour, one of the Tory grandees left over from the Heath government, gave voice to the growing opposition to her agenda in a speech early in 1980: 'In the Conservative view, economic liberalism à la Professor Hayek, because of its starkness and its failure to create a sense of community, is not a safeguard to political freedom but a threat to it.'[19] The employment secretary, Jim Prior, warned that unemployment could hit the previously unimaginable figure of 2.6 million by 1982. In fact, by January that year, the number already stood at 3 million. Conventional wisdom at the time declared that no government could possibly be re-elected with such numbers.

As time went on, the pressure to change course became unrelenting. Harold Macmillan privately warned Thatcher that the global situation demanded 'not restriction and deflation, but powerful reflationary measures.' In a memo, he added: 'The so-called "money supply" policy may be useful as a guide to what is happening just as a speedometer is in a car; but like the speedometer it cannot make the machine go faster or slower.' For Macmillan, the answer was a return to the middle way 'consensus' politics, which he had been championing since the 1930s. Such policies might be 'sneered at by some,' he said, pointedly, 'but [they were] the essence of Tory democracy.' For Thatcher, in contrast, consensus was the worst of all aspirations, 'the process of abandoning all beliefs, principles, values and policies in search of something in which no one believes, but to which no one objects.'[20]

Thatcher rejected his advice. She was determined not to repeat

Heath's change of direction in 1972, which had become known as the U-turn. 'You turn if you want to,' she declared theatrically to the Conservative Party Conference in October 1980. 'The lady's not for turning.'[21] This *bon mot* came to define the prime minister in the public's imagination, the leader who would stay the course, unlike her predecessors. Eden had quit after Suez and Macmillan after de Gaulle's '*non*', while Wilson and Heath had both abandoned their economic strategies. For Thatcher, it was also a statement to those in her party who did not regard Heath's U-turn contemptuously, but as a sensible act of leadership.*

The Thatcher government's response to its initial failure was to double down. Her policies had failed to control the money supply, failed to reduce inflation, failed to cut the deficit and failed to stimulate growth. The situation had degenerated so far by 1981 that there were real fears of another funding crisis of the sort that had forced the Callaghan government to go to the IMF five years earlier. Despite this, Thatcher and her chancellor, Geoffrey Howe, pushed ahead with their strategy, tightening budgets and raising taxes still further. By early 1981, there was close to open revolt in the cabinet. Lord Carrington, the foreign secretary, summed up the situation: 'We've been doing this for two years, and it doesn't seem to be working.'[22] A letter to *The Times* signed by 364 economists demanding a change of direction went ignored by Thatcher.

Ironically, Britain's output reached its lowest level in the quarter that ended on the very day the letter to *The Times* was published, and then the economic recovery began. In the eight years from 1981 to 1989, real GDP growth averaged 3.2 per cent. Barely four months after declaring herself not for turning, Thatcher showed the extent of her pragmatism by stepping back from her first battle with the miners, scrapping plans to close twenty-three pits

* 'The lady's not for turning' was also a play on words, referencing the Christopher Fry play *The Lady's Not for Burning*, which had been a hit on Broadway and in the West End, with a television adaptation starring Richard Burton.

when threatened with mass walkouts. As her great admirer T. E. Utley noted in *The Spectator*, those who saw only intransigence misunderstood her skill as a politician. Like all prime ministers, Utley wrote, Thatcher put 'her ear to the ground to hear what is going on in the world and to decide how she can (however slightly) influence it.'[23]

Even as she dodged and weaved through the political challenges she faced in the early years of her premiership, Thatcher gave the impression of dogged obstinacy, particularly on foreign policy, 'handbagging' her adversaries into a British rebate, ordering the SAS to storm the Iranian embassy in London to release the hostages live on television, refusing to give way to IRA pressure over the hunger strike and, most importantly, sticking to the tenets of her 'Iron Lady' speech of 1976. In this, Thatcher was buoyed by the election of Ronald Reagan as US president in November 1980. Thatcher and Reagan were not only allies, but figureheads for the conservative movements that had grown on both sides of the Atlantic through the 1960s and 1970s, supported by institutions like the IEA in Britain and the Heritage Foundation in the United States. At the same time, nascent libertarian student movements were also taking root.

While Thatcher continued to lean on the circle of Cold Warriors around Brian Crozier, a new foreign policy think tank emerged in London in 1979 called the Institute for European Defence and Strategic Studies [IEDSS]. The IEDSS's first director was the conservative journalist Gerald Frost, who joined from the Centre for Policy Studies, while its first chairman was the Heritage Foundation's American founder, Ed Feulner. Several of Thatcher's official and unofficial advisers and speechwriters soon joined the organization's advisory council, including the Anglo-American Cold War scholar Robert Conquest, Soviet expert Leonard Schapiro and the Middle East scholar Elie Kedourie.

The organization had close ties to British intelligence. The Conservative MP Ray Whitney, who had been the final director of the Foreign Office's secret Cold War propaganda unit – the

Information Research Department – soon joined. The IRD supplied supportive journalists with information, promoted anti-communist literature at home and abroad. It was eventually closed down by the Foreign Secretary David Owen in 1977 before its clandestine operations were exposed in *The Guardian*. Peter Blaker, the Conservative MP who ran the IRD's successor, the Overseas Information Department, also joined the IEDSS board.

In March 1980, Thatcher received a report from Kedourie, Schapiro and two other historians – Michael Howard and Hugh Thomas – setting out a series of recommendations for how to respond to the Soviet Union's invasion of Afghanistan. In the report, the authors warned that 'the complete and final victory of Communism on a world scale' remained the core aim of the leaders in Moscow. They also set out their position that only 'firm resistance' offered any chance of success. Détente, Thatcher was warned, had made communism 'seem respectable again' and 'secured for the Soviet Union a legitimisation of their military control over Eastern Europe.' Together, the historians recommended Britain deepen its role in the clandestine war against the Soviet Union. 'The willingness of Britain to make a substantial contribution in this sphere might enable her to offer something to the U.S. in order to compensate for the inevitably small scale of our military effort,' the paper argued, once again drawn to the enduring flame of global influence.[24]

The report contained a warning of what might go wrong without adequate Western resolve and intelligence, by attaching a letter written by the deposed former prime minister of the Seychelles, Sir James Mancham, then living in exile in London. In the letter, Mancham complained that he had been denied support from the British government after independence, allowing a Soviet-backed coup to take over the country. Replying to Sir Michael Howard, Thatcher said she found the report 'extremely useful' because it gave her 'an independent measure against which to judge the proposals being put forward by officials.'[25]

Thatcher was certainly unusual in her determination to listen to outside sources of information, whether from historians like Howard, Kedourie, Schapiro and Thomas, or from semi-official intelligence sources like Crozier. By 1982, in fact, Thatcher had hosted Crozier at Chequers four times, receiving his briefings and passing them on to an unconvinced Foreign Office. After one report from Crozier about the situation in Angola, Thatcher responded that, 'like so much of what you send me, I found the report most interesting', while the Foreign Office simply replied: 'We doubt there is any substance in the report.'[26]

Thatcher, though, continued to seek outside advice. In February 1981, at the height of her domestic economic crisis, she attended a meeting of the Conservative Philosophy Group. Beside the group's founders Jonathan Aitken, John Casey, Hugh Fraser and Roger Scruton, and the old Phantom comrades Maurice Macmillan, Michael Oakeshott and Peregrine Worsthorne, there was the American academic Shirley Robin Letwin – mother of Oliver – T. E. Utley, Frank Johnson, Ferdinand Mount, Kenneth Minogue and Enoch Powell.

John Casey remembers this occasion for Thatcher clashing with Powell over the principles of foreign policy. Edward Norman – then dean of Peterhouse – had mounted 'a Christian argument for nuclear weapons', which prompted a wider conversation about 'Western values', which Thatcher said the bomb was necessary to defend. To this, however, Powell responded, 'No, we do not fight for values. I would fight for this country even if it had a communist government.' For Thatcher, this was an extraordinary claim. 'Nonsense, Enoch. If I send British troops abroad, it will be to defend our values.' Powell, though, was adamant: 'No, Prime Minister, values exist in a transcendental realm, beyond space and time. They can neither be fought for, nor destroyed.' As Casey wrote, Thatcher was 'utterly baffled' by Powell's response. 'She had just been presented with the difference between Toryism and American Republicanism.'[27] The exchange is a reminder that, while Powell was the intellectual godfather of the conservative counter-revolution to which Thatcher was heir, he was far outside of the

Conservative Cold War tradition to which she adhered, with the transatlantic alliance at its heart.

Five days after Thatcher declared she was not for turning, James Callaghan resigned as Labour leader. It would prove another significant moment in British politics, for the leadership would not fall to Callaghan's preferred successor and ideological soulmate, Denis Healey, but to the icon of the left, Michael Foot.

Despite his subsequent reputation for being an almost comically unelectable left-winger, Foot was a substantial figure in British politics. Before becoming Labour leader, he had been a radical journalist, polemicist, author and brilliant parliamentary orator. In 1940, he had been one of the anonymous authors of the sensational denunciation of those apparently cowardly leaders of the 1930s who had left Britain weak and exposed. *Guilty Men* was a piece of brutal, contemptuous journalism, which remains one of the most influential publications in British history. Foot was not a first-rate historian, but he was a man of intellect, nous, talent and moral clarity, a bohemian, outspoken socialist, arch anti-appeaser – and staunch opponent of the Common Market. He was also a founder, in the 1950s, of the Campaign for Nuclear Disarmament, the pressure group which, thirty years later, was leading the opposition to the placement of American cruise missiles in Britain and calling, instead, for Britain to unilaterally abandon its nuclear deterrent.

Though clearly of the left, Foot had been a collaborative minister throughout the turmoil of the Callaghan premiership, refusing to endorse the left populism of Tony Benn. He also had friendships across the aisle, including, perhaps surprisingly, with Enoch Powell, whose politics Foot generally abhorred, but whose intellect, certainty and radicalism he nevertheless admired. Foot would maintain that Powell was not a racist, despite 'Rivers of Blood'. The admiration was returned in kind. During the debates on Britain's entry into the Common Market, which Foot had opposed with persistency, Powell paid tribute to his socialist opponent as the House of Commons' first man, 'easily the first, *facile princeps*, among the parliamentarians of this day.'[28]

Above all, Foot believed in the House of Commons as the crucible of democracy and popular empowerment, a tool of progress, and the supreme representative of the British people. Any attempts to dilute that supremacy, whether through democratization of the House of Lords or the 'sharing' of sovereignty with a supranational Europe, were, to him, threats to the power of ordinary people to control the circumstances of their lives. Opposition to the Common Market was not some economic calculation, but a matter of basic principle.

In 1980, such a view was neither extreme nor nostalgic, but a mainstream sentiment within the Labour Party. To win the leadership, Foot had beaten a trio of candidates, none of whom were idealistic about Britain's membership of the Common Market: Denis Healey, a pragmatic figure who had been firmly against British membership in the 1950s; Peter Shore, a left-wing opponent; and finally John Silkin, who had not rejected membership outright in the late 1960s,[29] but had described the terms of Britain's entry as 'a betrayal of the Commonwealth'.[30]

Electing Foot was not the lunatic decision of a party that had lost its senses, but the choice of an increasingly left-wing political movement, deeply disenchanted after the trauma of austerity and the painful adjustment of the British economy then underway. Yet, by maintaining his support for unilateral nuclear disarmament, Foot opened a stark new divide in British party politics.

In the leadership contest, Foot was widely seen as the candidate best equipped to hold Labour together. But this would not prove to be the case. Ever since the defeat in 1979, there had been whispers of a new political movement that would resurrect the spirit of the triumphant 'In' campaign led by Roy Jenkins in 1975. Speculation about this new formation had grown in November 1979, when Jenkins – then president of the European Commission – gave a lecture in which he quoted Yeats's famous lines about the centre being unable to hold: 'The best lack all conviction, while the worst/Are full of passionate intensity.'[31] Jenkins, of course, was a man of passionate conviction himself. He did not support British membership of a supranational Europe because of some carefully considered calculation about the national interest, but because he believed in Europe as an idea. For Jenkins, Europe was the future; all the rest was noise.

Foot was understandably worried about a breakaway led by someone like Jenkins and worked hard to stop it from happening. Despite the sincerity of his pleas, they were destined to fail. Although not solely to blame for the split, Foot's election as leader guaranteed the emergence of the greatest third-party force in British politics since the creation of the Labour Party itself. Some in the party had already made up their minds about the necessity of a new movement in British politics. At least five Labour MPs who later joined Jenkins' new political party had voted for Foot because they believed he would help their cause.[32] His election, far from calming tensions and unifying the party, helped to lead to its break-up.

What came next changed British politics. Standing outside his east London home on 25 January 1981, the former Labour foreign secretary Dr David Owen, joined by Roy Jenkins and two other former Labour ministers, Shirley Williams and Bill Rogers, announced their intention to create a new force in British politics: the Social Democratic Party. It became known as the Limehouse Declaration. This 'gang of four' was on a mission to upend British politics, opposed to what they considered the extremes of left and right in control of the two main political parties, represented by the Labour Party's drift into open hostility to Europe and support for unilateral nuclear disarmament, and Margaret Thatcher's leadership of the Tories.*

Twenty-eight Labour MPs and one Tory would eventually join the SDP ranks. For a while, the party soared, reaching 40 per cent in the polls and winning a string of by-elections, including, most

* The term 'gang of four' was a reference to four Chinese communists who tried to launch a coup in Beijing during the Cultural Revolution, following the death of Chairman Mao.

significantly, Glasgow Hillhead in 1982, when Roy Jenkins returned to Parliament. A revolution seemed to be unfolding, endangering both Labour and the Conservative Party. Rather than providing a viable alternative to Thatcherism, however, in the end it guaranteed its success without ever wresting Labour away from its position as the principal opposition to the Conservatives. From the moment the SDP emerged, Foot's chances of winning an election were all but over. Whether that meant a Tory recovery remained unclear. And then, out of nowhere, a crisis blew over British politics from the south Atlantic with such force it would pose an existential challenge to Thatcher's government.

On 2 April 1982, Argentina invaded the Falkland Islands. Not only was this a national humiliation for Britain, but one that seemed to have been facilitated and even encouraged by the British state. In a drive to cut costs and reform the military to face the threat from the Soviet Union, the government had decided to decommission the Royal Navy's one elderly patrol vessel in the south Atlantic, the twenty-five-year-old HMS *Endurance*. Its removal, scheduled for 15 April that year, appeared to signal to the Argentine junta that Britain was no longer so committed to enforcing exclusive British control over the islands. This impression was strengthened by the fact that British diplomats had even begun discussions with Argentina at the UN for a possible 'transfer and leaseback' of the islands.

It was not obvious, therefore, that the invasion was the political gift to Thatcher that it turned out to be, but rather it was a potentially lethal threat to her premiership. The Argentinians had not attempted such an invasion under the previous Labour governments. Indeed, in 1977, Callaghan had dispatched the nuclear-powered submarine HMS *Dreadnought* to Falkland waters when it was feared that Argentina might attempt some kind of incursion.[33] This was followed by firm messages privately warning the government in Buenos Aires against any kind of military action.

What is more, the new Labour leader, Michael Foot, despite his CND affiliation, was no pacifist, but a resolute anti-fascist.

With Parliament recalled, Foot roused himself to give what his biographer Kenneth Morgan called his 'last great parliamentary performance.'[34] Today, Thatcher is so identified with the war that Foot's role galvanizing Parliament and the nation is often overlooked. But it was he, more than Thatcher, who led the House that day. Rising to his feet, Foot poured scorn on the Foreign Office and Thatcher's government. 'The Falkland Islanders have been betrayed,' he thundered. 'The responsibility for the betrayal rests with the government.'[35]

Foot described the invasion as a 'foul and brutal aggression' which could not be allowed to succeed. 'If it does,' he said, 'there will be a danger not merely to the Falkland Islands but to people all over this dangerous planet.'[36]

The rest of the story is well known. Thatcher dispatched a British task force to retake the islands in April and was able to declare victory by June. It was a do-or-die moment for her premiership. In Parliament, Enoch Powell had laid down the gauntlet, warning that her response to the invasion would reveal 'of what metal she is made.' After victory, Powell told the Commons that her character had been shown to consist of 'ferrous matter of the highest quality.' The task force's success led to the fall of the military junta in Buenos Aires and national acclaim at home. Thatcher had won and it was Michael Foot, ironically, who would pay the price.

In November of that year, first in the pages of the *New Left Review* and then as a book, Anthony Barnett published the polemic *Iron Britannia: Why Parliament Waged its Falklands War*, lamenting the culture which had taken the country to war. For Barnett, Foot's belligerent performance in the emergency debate over the Falklands revealed a country suffering from a condition 'so deeply and pervasively a part of England, so natural to its political culture, that it is difficult to see', and yet is there all the same. The condition, Barnett believed – or 'the pathology of modern British politics,' as he put it – had a name: Churchillism.[37]

'All the essential symbols were there: an island people, the cruel seas, a British defeat, Anglo-Saxon democracy challenged by a dictator, and finally the quintessentially Churchillian posture – we were down but we were not out.' Such was the power of the Churchill myth, Barnett wrote, few MPs were immune. 'They were, after all, his political children and they too would put the "Great" back into Britain.'[38]

For Barnett the response of the House of Commons in 1982 was little more than a theatrical re-enactment of May 1940. Michael Foot was not some great moral hero, but a political leader weakly playing the role the country demanded of him, a cod Clement Attlee to Thatcher's Churchill. After forty years of decline, donning these old clothes made everyone feel better, 'conjuring up the spirits of the past in the service of the present,' as Marx once described the French Revolutionary fixation on Rome.

Such an account underplays the very real parallels with May 1940, in circumstance if not in scale. Foot was not wrong to believe the Argentine junta were fascists attempting to occupy territory by force against the wishes of those who lived there. Yet Barnett does alight on something important. The crisis of May 1940 established a remarkably resilient national myth. Churchill was dependent on the support of the Labour Party and what Barnett refers to as Clement Attlee's 'Daily Express Socialism'. It is also true that all Labour leaders after Attlee had carried this strain of conservatism, from Gaitskill's 'thousand years of history' to Foot's parliamentarianism. Each were Eurosceptic, in its broader sense – sceptical of British involvement in Monnet's federal project. In moments of national crisis, the old instincts demanded support for military action and Churchillian resolution, as Barnett identified. This was one of those moments.

The Falklands War might have been an expression of latent Churchillism, but its success helped burnish a new myth that wiped away the stain of Suez and upended the perception of shrinking influence and inevitable national decline: not so much

Thatcherism, per se, as Iron Ladyism. She had shown resilience before, but victory in war took her image to a new level. This form of Thatcherism was never simply an ideology, but a memory of an instinct which would come to dominate British politics: a country standing alone, prepared to suffer in defence of its national honour, principles and sovereignty. After the humiliation of Suez a quarter of a century earlier, when Britain was forced to confront its new international weakness, here was a moment to allow Britain to believe in itself once again, a moment to prove the future did not have to be one long journey of decline and compromise, that it could draw lines in the sand, defend them and rise again. From the sick man of Europe to its military leader.

Feeding into this story of national resolution was the Thatcher government's hardening stance against Soviet expansionism following Moscow's deployment of a new generation of nuclear weapons across Eastern Europe. In response, the West determined upon what it called a 'double track' approach, threatening its own deployment of US intermediate range nuclear forces across Western Europe unless an agreement for mutual reductions could be reached. The strategy, supported by Thatcher, sparked mass demonstrations led by CND and backed by the Labour Party, the first of which came in October 1981, when tens of thousands marched through London. For the Thatcher government and its network of Cold Warriors, CND was not just an irritant but a subversive threat to the West which needed to be defeated.

The shift in the national mood after Thatcher's Falklands triumph caused a despondency among many on the left who, only a year earlier, had felt confident that the country would throw her out as soon as it got the chance. Now – or so it seemed – Thatcher was on course not only to survive, but to win with ease in a contest CND had attempted to turn into a de-facto referendum on nuclear disarmament.[39]

Writing in *The Guardian* in May 1983, the author Salman Rushdie could barely believe what was happening. 'I had always thought that the British prided themselves on their common sense, on good old fashioned down-to-earth realism,' he despaired. 'But the election of 1983 is beginning to look more and more like a dark fantasy, a fiction so outrageously improbable that any novelist would be ridiculed if he dreamed it up.'[40] Rushdie then painted the picture that he saw unfolding before him.

Thatcher had promised to get the country back to work, but had in fact driven millions more into unemployment, he wrote. Surely she should be 'hounded into the outer darkness,' rather than re-elected. Rushdie then lamented that the Britain being taken in by Thatcher was an almost completely different country from the one he had always respected from abroad. Britain in 1983 was 'nanny Britain', as he put it. He could not abide what he called 'strait-laced Victoria-reborn Britain, class-ridden know-your-place Britain, thin-lipped, jingoist Britain.'[41] To Rushdie, this was the country that lay just under the surface. When provoked, Britain had returned to its martial instincts, painting itself blue for war. Rushdie's story of provincial barbarity, the Britain of bad food, football hooligans and conservative housewives, was as simplistic a caricature as the hagiographic reverence towards Thatcher of the people he was criticizing. Just as Thatcher's Britain would always be shaped by stories of its Churchillian resolution, so too would its critics be shaped by their own myth.

To Rushdie's dismay, as the country approached the general election in 1983, Thatcher's Toryism appeared not only poised for victory, but philosophically reinvigorated. In March, a piece appeared in *The Guardian* by the journalist Martin Walker, looking with some alarm at the influence of the Conservative Philosophy Group on the prime minister's government. It was headlined, 'The unthinkable men behind Thatcher'. The piece called Maurice Cowling the group's 'godfather' and Peterhouse 'its gestation chamber', but focused most of its attention on John Casey and Roger Scruton, the two founders of the Philosophy Group and editors of two small but influential journals: Casey's *Cambridge Review* and Scruton's *Salisbury Review*, the house magazine of the Salisbury Group. By 1983, the *Salisbury Review*, in particular, had become quietly significant, despite a circulation of only about a thousand. 'One sees it in Ministers' waiting rooms, in Oxford and Cambridge colleges, in the odd Embassy,' Walker wrote.[42]

One couple who found themselves drawn to the magazine were the Douglas-Homes: Charlie, the new editor of *The Times* – cousin of Princess Diana and nephew to the former prime minister, Alec – and his wife Jessica, an artist. Charlie's politics were reactionary, Atlanticist and anti-communist. His loathing for the Soviets was not just academic, but personal. As a young journalist, he had been arrested and deported by the Soviets while covering the invasion of Czechoslovakia in 1968. As a defence correspondent, he had approached some Russian tanks parked in the Slovak countryside and, in the words of his editor at the time, William Rees-Mogg, 'simply walked over to have a look at them'.[43] The Russians assumed he was a spy and arrested him.

After his appointment as editor of *The Times* in 1982, replacing Harold Evans, Douglas-Home brought about a marked shift in the paper's political position. Its leaders took on a more outspoken tone, supportive of the Thatcher government.[44] Jessica Douglas-Home's politics were no less strident. If anything, she was even more enthralled than her husband by the new magazine he had brought home from work. 'At a time when it was generally assumed that intellectualism was the special property of the left, I was electrified by this school of political philosophers, with their compelling demolition of socialism and their shocking belief in free markets,' she later reflected.[45]

One article in particular caught her attention: an anonymous editorial on the situation in Eastern Europe, published in the magazine's very first edition. 'Buried beneath the monolith of Communism, the European spirit survives, in clandestine organizations, in the Church, in secret societies and unofficial publications, through which the memory of a European identity is kept alive,' the piece declared, before ending with a call for Western support for this underground resistance.[46]

For Jessica, the article was a window into an intoxicating struggle she had not known existed. With this vision of a 'Pimpernel world' in her mind, she arranged a meeting with Scruton, in which he revealed that he was one of a small group of academics who travelled beyond the Iron Curtain to meet dissidents, supplying them with forbidden books and other material. Formally, the group was known as the Jan Hus Foundation, named after a thirteenth-century Czech martyr, but this was a cover for what Jessica described as 'a catacomb university existing under the nose of the Communist authorities.'[47]

With Jessica's encouragement, Scruton quickly became a regular columnist for *The Times* from the beginning of 1983, where he railed against the 'progress' of modern life, lamenting the collapse of old institutions, social mores and educational standards, including the end of Peterhouse's ban on women.

From the beginning, Scruton was clear about the political objective of his conservatism and that of the *Salisbury Review*. 'It is necessary to establish a conservative dominance in intellectual life,' he wrote in the first edition. This was not because it was the quickest or most obvious way to influence the direction of the government, 'but because in the long run, it is the only way to create a climate of opinion favourable to the conservative cause.' So, here was the objective: 'Fighting a war for the Zeitgeist,' as Walker put it.[48]

While Scruton's battle for the zeitgeist brought gentle influence among a certain type of conservative intellectual, it also invited controversy – most notably in 1984, after he published an article by a teacher called Roy Honeyford, under the headline, 'Education and Race: An Alternative View'. In the piece, Honeyford attacked the values of multiculturalism for ruining education as he saw it. The piece sparked a public debate of such intensity it drew comparisons with Enoch Powell. In Honeyford's attack on multiculturalism, he criticized 'the hysterical political temperament of the Indian subcontinent' and 'the West Indian's right to create an ear-splitting cacophony for most of the night to the detriment of his neighbour's sanity'.[49]

Alongside such boorish stereotypes, Honeyford raised points which would later gain political salience, criticizing orders to 'build on and develop the strengths of cultural and linguistic diversity', which, he argued, meant turning a blind eye to a Muslim father's 'insistence on banning his daughter from drama, dance and sport'. The central point of Honeyford's lament was what he called 'the conceptual soundness of the ideas which comprise the term "multi-racial education".' He called for a curriculum which promoted what he called an 'integrated, harmonious society' instead. Honeyford was suspended from his job, and, though he was reinstated after a ruling from the High Court, his career never recovered. For Scruton, the affair left its own mark of disreputability, though one he was happy to wear.

Scruton's goal was not so much to win over the political class of the day – or, indeed, Thatcher herself – but to create the space for conservatism more generally. 'She is a practical politician who has better things to think about', he told *The Guardian*. 'Anyway, a woman's emotions are what one battles for.'[50] And yet, Scrutonism had found its epoch, just as Monnet's vision had all those years ago in Algiers.

The Conservative recovery had started before Argentina's invasion in 1982. Labour faced a formidable structural challenge to defeat the Tories, and it was in question whether it would even survive the election as the principal opposition.

On Thursday, 9 June 1983, Britain went to the polls – and 13 million people voted Tory, handing Thatcher a majority of 144, the biggest since the war. Labour, in contrast, was reduced to just 209 seats from 8.45 million votes – holding off the SDP. Although Roy Jenkins' party finished just two percentage points behind Labour, it only secured twenty-three MPs. It was a lesson in the unforgiving nature of first past the post. For Labour, the result was a disaster. But, in a red corner of north-east England, there was a shoot of future recovery for the proponents of progress: the election of a new Member of Parliament for Sedgefield, Anthony Blair.

Thatcher and Thatcherism had triumphed. The following day, *The Times* declared that her victory was a lesson in decisive government. But, to succeed in her second term, the paper warned, she needed to ensure her government was united in its mission, specifically in the Treasury and the Foreign Office. 'Economic policy and foreign affairs are too important, and too fundamental to the future of the country for their evolution under Mrs Thatcher's second administration to be subject to the uncertainties of "creative tension",' the leader warned. *The Times* was adamant that the Soviet Union remained a hostile state which must be opposed with rigour, irrespective of the dire warnings of nuclear Armageddon coming out of Moscow and its satellites.

A fortnight after Thatcher's landslide victory, an article appeared in *The Times* written by 'a citizen of Prague', warning Western readers not to be taken in by the 'World Congress for Peace', a Soviet front then holding a conference in Czechoslovakia. The author of the article was Petr Pithart, an office cleaner by day and dissident member of Scruton's underground university by night. Scruton had given Pithart's article to Jessica Douglas-Home, who had passed it on to her husband, who published it under the headline 'No Peace Without Freedom'. The last article to carry this headline in the paper had appeared in 1938 in support of an anti-appeasement speech given by Anthony Eden, in which he warned that it was 'utterly futile' to believe the European crisis then blowing in from the east would pass. Four decades later, Pithart was making the same case. After emphasizing the sham of the 'Peace' conference, Pithart finished his anonymous cri de cœur with a plea to those Western delegates making their way to Czechoslovakia: 'Visit us while you are in Prague – or try to visit us, if we have not been taken into custody or forced to leave the city.' Jessica Douglas-Home was determined to do just that.

Chapter 8

It was October 1983 when Jessica Douglas-Home finally made it to Prague for her first assignment, arriving at the city's airport carrying £600 in cash and a stash of banned philosophy books. For Jessica, the assignment was at turns nerve-racking and exciting. 'I had also a private motive for helping the Czech dissidents', she later wrote. 'I needed distraction from some shattering news at home'.[1] Her husband Charlie had been diagnosed with bone cancer. Determined to go on living as normal, the couple decided to keep his condition a secret, despite several fractures, which they explained away as mere complications from an old riding accident.

Arriving in Prague, heart racing, she made for the exit marked *Nothing to Declare*, where she was challenged by a sullen-looking border guard. 'What's your reason to be here?' he demanded. Jessica offered the answer she had practised before coming out: 'I am an artist. I've come to see the Impressionist collection in your National Gallery.'[2] It worked. She was through, into the Bohemian heart of central Europe.

From the airport, she travelled by bus into the city, where she was to meet Roger Scruton, who was coming by train from Vienna. Over the next few days, the pair moved from flat to flat, meeting 'the moving spirits' of the Czech resistance, including the anonymous *Times* author Petr Pithart, who was owed £150 from Charlie Douglas-Home for his article.[3] For Jessica, the experience was a revelation. She returned intoxicated by the city and the bravery of its dissident academics trying to keep alive the memory of their homeland. Within a month, she became a trustee of the Jan Hus Foundation, as she and Scruton began to expand their network beyond Czechoslovakia, first into Poland and then Hungary.

Through her marriage to Charlie, Jessica had occasional access to Margaret Thatcher, which she used to push the case of Eastern Europe's forgotten dissidents. After meeting the prime minister over dinner one evening, she wrote to her, setting out the extent of dissident opposition in the Eastern bloc. Thatcher had only recently returned from a visit to Hungary and Jessica was concerned she might soften her stance as a result. Thatcher replied that she had been 'a little worried that these brave people might misinterpret my visit to Hungary,' before adding: 'They need have no fear. I have no illusions about Communism and its methods.'[4]

As Jessica Douglas-Home's efforts to support her ever-expanding network of Eastern European dissidents intensified, so too did her frustration at the lack of support they were receiving from what she considered the pillars of the British establishment. Within the Foreign Office, their outfit was seen as little more than a 'potentially embarrassing nuisance', while the Church of England did not want to know.[5] Within academia, meanwhile, they were met not just by indifference, but active hostility.

One figure who shared the Jan Hus Foundation's frustration with Western academia at this time was the iconoclastic Cambridge historian Norman Stone, whose disdain for those he saw as privileged apologists for Soviet tyranny had sparked controversy following the death of the Soviet historian E. H. Carr a few months before the 1983 election.

Though Marxist in his analysis, Carr was a pillar of the British establishment: a one-time diplomat who had worked on the Treaty of Versailles before becoming assistant editor of *The Times*, and then, after swapping journalism for academia, a leading historian of the Soviet Union. Upon his death, tributes poured in from across the world. It was all too much for Stone, who despite having once been one of Carr's protégés at Cambridge, loathed his politics. On 10 January 1983, the *London Review of Books* published an obituary from Stone of such sustained polemical contempt it made international news of its own.

Not only was Carr an appeaser, Stone wrote – and his history of the Soviet Union 'clogged and pompous' – but he was so dislikable even his parents wanted little to do with him. 'It is said that they farmed him out to live with an aunt,' Stone claimed, sparking inevitable outrage.[6] Carr's daughter, Rachel Kelly, felt obliged to respond, writing to the *LRB* that much of what Stone wrote was false. 'Our father was never farmed out,' she said.[7]

The real target of Stone's animosity, though, was not Carr's personal shortcomings, as he saw them, but his political ideology. In Carr, Stone saw so much of what he believed was wrong with the left, from its flawed understanding of history to its intellectual cowardice in the face of Soviet tyranny. Stone was not the first historian of the right to criticize Carr in this way, though he was the most brutal. In 1961, Michael Oakeshott published a review of Carr's *What is History?* and drew a more philosophical conclusion. 'He believes that "history properly so-called can be written only by those who find and accept a sense of direction in history itself",' Oakeshott wrote.[8] To the conservative mind, this was preposterous: history was not a tale of linear progress, but of boundless chaos, tragedy and loss, which could only be managed, not mastered.

For Norman Stone, it was absurd to believe Soviet Russia was an agent of progress. Like Jessica and Charlie Douglas-Home, he did not simply believe this intellectually, but felt he knew it from first-hand experience. The defining moment in Stone's early adult life had come during his research for *The Eastern Front*, a study of the First World War published in 1975. It was the product of a trip Stone had taken to Austria over a decade earlier, in 1963, aged just twenty-two. He had moved to Vienna on a scholarship from Cambridge to study in the city's military archives, alongside – coincidentally – another young Scottish historian called Alan

Sked.[9] But Stone was drawn to Budapest, over the border, in February 1964, and it was here that his life changed.

Once in Hungary, Stone met a couple who pleaded with him to help them escape to the West. Over dinner, they formulated a plan. Stone would hire a car and then smuggle them over the border to Austria. The plan was as amateurish as it was foolish and quickly fell apart. Chillingly, Stone later recalled watching the man he had tried to smuggle to freedom standing in the snow, hurriedly biting his fingernails to avoid them being pulled out under torture.

The two Hungarians were given six months in prison each, while Stone escaped with just a month, after which he was expelled from the country. Stone's foolish bravery had cost him a few weeks of liberty, but the episode would never quite leave him. As he was led to his cell, he began to recite the St Matthew Passion: '*Wenn ich einmal soll scheiden, so scheid nicht von mir.*' [When I must depart one day, do not depart from me.][10]

A moral contempt for communism and those who excused it was one of the unifying threads of the New Right during the 1980s, tightening the bond not only between Thatcher and academics like Stone, Scruton and, in time, Sked, each of whom saw the Soviet Union as a barbarous threat to civilization, but also with the new generation of Conservative students inspired by the moral clarity of the Cold War. It was also on this question where the Thatcherite right rejected the views of Enoch Powell, whose amoralism in foreign policy, favouring closer ties with Moscow and opposition to Washington, isolated him from even the most hardline Tory ultras for whom he usually acted as a kind of North Star.

In 1984, Stone moved from Cambridge to Oxford to take up the position of professor of modern history. By this point, Cambridge University was only too happy for him to depart, having grown frustrated as his early academic promise was compromised by his libertine alcoholism. 'Oxford was their solution to the Norman problem,' according to Stone's friend and acolyte Niall Ferguson. 'It was only when he arrived that Oxford realized that Lord Byron had been reincarnated.'[11]

Stone quickly grew to loathe Oxford, finding it priggish and bureaucratic – even Marxist. 'I hated the place,' he said, reminiscing, years later. 'I said to my wife, two weeks after I arrived, "I made a terrible mistake" . . . the whole thing is just farce'.[12] For Stone, the spires and debating societies were not exciting bastions of intellectual enquiry, but places of plodding academic orthodoxy, snobbery and privilege: just the kind of place which still revered the likes of Carr and was happy to award Robert Mugabe an honorary doctorate, while withholding the same honour from the sitting prime minister, the first woman to hold that office and herself a graduate of the university.

Despite all of this – or perhaps *because* of all this – many students loved Norman Stone. Here was a formidable mind with an even more formidable character; a man who could be drunk and inappropriate at any time of day, holding court while in the bath or taking students on spur-of-the-moment trips to the continent to look at historical sights. The fact that at this time he also became an unofficial adviser to Margaret Thatcher and regular columnist in the national press added a certain allure of proximity to power for those ambitious students who aspired to careers in politics. For a generation of young, ideological conservatives, Stone soon became something of a mentor. Prominent among them were two young fellow Scots who would go on to play significant roles in the conservative counter-revolution already underway: an eccentric Aberdonian undergraduate called Michael Gove, who arrived in 1985, and a rebellious adventurer called Patrick Robertson, who followed three years later.

Gove in particular was quick to make his mark at Oxford, turning up for his first day in a green tweed suit bought at the Salvation Army for £1.50. In November 1985, the university newspaper, *Cherwell*, introduced readers to this strange new student: 'Michael conceals his rabidly reactionary political views under a Jane Austen cleric-like exterior.'[13]

Gove was not a typical Oxford student at that time. The adopted son of a Scottish fishing family, Gove's Toryism was openly Scrutonian – or even Powellite – when most of those around him were self-styled 'moderates' in the Tory Reform Group [TRG], actively opposed to the Conservative Party's Thatcherite direction.

As a teenager in Aberdeen, Gove had been the only *Salisbury Review* subscriber in the whole of the city. Of all the magazine's columnists, it had been T. E. Utley who had come closest to expressing his own brand of conservatism. 'He was the person whose writing I thought, Yes, that's right.'[14] In debates at the Oxford Union, Gove had taken the opposite side to Ted Heath on the merits of Europe, condemned Thatcher's Anglo-Irish agreement in 1985 and even declared his support for the 'elitism' of Oxford. 'I cannot over-emphasise what elitism is not. It is not about back-slapping cliques, reactionary chic or Old Etonian egos. It is a spirit of unashamed glamour, excitement and competition. We are all here, part of an elite. It is our duty to bear that in mind.'[15]

However, Gove was not the star draw at the Union, but the support act to the principal celebrity student of the day: Boris Johnson. Johnson had arrived at Oxford a year before Gove with his sights already on the presidency of the Union, 'the first step to being prime minister,' as Michael Heseltine had once put it.[16] The list of those who had sat on the raised dais of the president's throne certainly attested to its power: A. V. Dicey, William Gladstone, H. H. Asquith, Ted Heath, Michael Foot, Tony Benn and Hugh Fraser.

For the politically ambitious students who coveted the Union presidency as their surest stepping stone to success at Westminster, Fraser's career provided a salutary lesson that nothing is certain. He had led a remarkable life – serving in wartime, from Algeria to Arnhem; escaping IRA assassination; marrying and divorcing one of the most glamorous women in London, Antonia Fraser; and creating a philosophy group attended by the most consequential prime minister since the war. Yet, for all that, he did not rise as high as his Oxford contemporaries had expected. He remained an MP, but with little prospect of further office. Then, in April 1984, he was gone, dead at sixty-six, taken by lung cancer.

It was in 1984 that Johnson began his assault on the Union presidency, determined to be confirmed as his generation's coming man. In an essay Johnson later wrote for *The Oxford Myth*, a book edited by his sister Rachel, he describes the key to success at the Union – namely, the process of 'hacking', whereby a candidate forms a slate with other students to secure enough votes to win. And, to hack successfully, Johnson advised, was to find 'a disciplined and deluded collection of stooges' who were ready to do the grunt work for you.[17] For Johnson, his chief stooge was Michael Gove. 'I became a votary of the Boris cult,' as Gove later put it.[18]

While Johnson and Gove boosted their egos and tested their intellects amid the 'unashamed glamour' of the Union, they showed little interest in the Oxford University Conservative Association (OUCA) and even less in national student politics.[19] Much like Oxford itself, OUCA was dominated by centrists – in this case, the 'wet' TRG faction of the Conservative Party. Indeed, the main political division at Oxford was between the TRG and the Social Democrats, with neither the militant left nor the libertarian right holding much sway. The extent of 'moderate' dominance at this time is illustrated by Boris Johnson himself, who posed as a Social Democrat to win the Union presidency at the second time of asking, having lost his first attempt after being cast as a 'Tory toff' by his opponent.

Unlike the Union, however, OUCA was formally connected to national politics as an affiliate of the student wing of the Conservative Party, the Federation of Conservative Students. The FCS was composed of thousands of young Tories at universities across the country and, by the mid-1980s, had become a forum for intense ideological dispute, pitting the wets on one side – led by the TRG elite from Oxford and Cambridge – and a cadre of radical Thatcherites, mostly from less prestigious universities, on the other.

This was the period of Thatcher's rule which marked both the zenith of her power and a period of significant resistance to it. The mid-1980s were a time of mass joblessness and violent unrest, political division and renewed Conservative confidence.

For Thatcher's supporters, it was not simply her agenda that they liked, but the relish with which she pursued it. For Thatcher's enemies, meanwhile, the opposite was true. 'It was never enough to dislike her,' the novelist Ian McEwan would later say. 'We liked disliking her.'[20]

The depth of the hatred for Thatcher was made clear in October 1984 when the IRA tried to kill her by bombing the Grand Hotel in Brighton, where she was staying during the annual Conservative Party Conference. This night-time attack was intended, in part, as revenge for the deaths of the republican hunger strikers whose demands Thatcher had resisted despite enormous pressure. The attack only served to burnish Thatcher's reputation still further. The next morning, she insisted the conference should go ahead and displayed her disdain for the bombers. On television, the nation saw the prime minister once again standing defiant.

The Brighton bombing took place during a larger, more prolonged trial of strength: the miners' strike. Earlier in her premiership, Thatcher had shown her pragmatism by swerving a confrontation with the National Union of Mineworkers over pit closures at a time when coal stocks were too low to sustain the UK's power supply in the event of sustained industrial action. Yet, both sides knew the battle would soon resume. And when it did, in March 1984, Thatcher was ready. By now, any attempt to broker a compromise was futile. Thatcher had sat in Heath's cabinet as he backed down in the face of union pressure. But Thatcher's confrontation with the miners a decade later was not simply a trial of personal strength, it was an ideological battle against those, as she saw it, who continued to hold the country to ransom.

Arthur Scargill, her opponent in this battle, similarly regarded the strike as an ideological struggle: a legitimate form of extra-parliamentary action.

It was Thatcher who prevailed. After a year of bitter confrontation which convulsed the nation and divided families, communities and political parties, Thatcher won a defining victory, perhaps *the* defining victory of her premiership.

Each moment seemed to reinforce the aura of Churchillian strength which she had been cultivating since she became prime minister. But, contrary to the myth of unbending resolution, she continued to show the pragmatism that had secured her the premiership. Her government had already quietly moved away from of its monetary targets and signed the Anglo-Irish Agreement formally giving Dublin a voice in the affairs of Northern Ireland, to Enoch Powell's condemnation. Powell said Thatcher was guilty of treachery, and resigned his seat alongside his unionist colleagues to fight by-elections on the issue, marking a deterioration in relations with Thatcher. In truth, Thatcher had proved her mettle in sticking to *some* of her course, but had also shown considerable flexibility in abandoning that which she could not make work. It was always this combination of pragmatism and strength that lay at the heart of Thatcher's success as a politician.

This duality in Thatcher's character was reflected in the Conservative Party's student wing, divided between those who emphasized the pragmatism and those who preferred the resolution. Across the FCS, three broad camps had formed: the radical Thatcherite or 'sound' faction; the moderate or 'wet' opposition, which dominated the Conservative associations at Oxford and Cambridge; and, finally, the authoritarians or 'shits', as they were called by their opponents, who were, in essence, Powellite.[21]

By the mid-1980s, however, the wets were in retreat and the authoritarians confined to a small minority. Outside the last redoubts of moderate power at Oxbridge it was the Thatcherites who were in the ascendency. 'Freedom motions' would be passed at FCS conferences supporting everything from the privatization of the coal mines and the introduction of tuition fees to the liberalization of abortion and pornography, much of which would later go on to be part of the political mainstream, but at the time was considered so extreme it would often spark media controversy, to the embarrassment of Tory HQ.[22]

At the heart of the dispute was also the question of détente. To the Thatcherites, the Cold War was existential and anyone who sought an accommodation with communism was little better than an appeaser or even an enabler, the wets chief among them. Until the early 1980s, the Heathite wets had enjoyed almost full control of the FCS, although there were signs of growing Thatcherite influence as early as 1976. That year, a libertarian student called Michael Forsyth, from St Andrew's University, was elected national chairman on a platform of Cold Warrior conservatism. Forsyth's election marks the beginning of the second wave of conservative radicalism to have emerged out of Scottish politics, and St Andrew's in particular. In the early 1970s, the future founders of the Adam Smith Institute, Madsen Pirie and Eamonn Butler, had been part of a cadre of free marketeers centred around the university's Conservative Association.[23] Before them, Ralph Harris had taught at the university, too. Time and again in this story, traditional right-wing English Toryism finds itself being strengthened by sudden injections of a more robust, even combative, Scottish variant.

It was the election in 1980 of another Scot, Peter Young, a friend and protégé of Forsyth's from the University of Aberdeen, which marked the turning point in the Thatcherite student revolution, the first time the right had secured not only the chairmanship but also a majority on the national committee.

Just a few months earlier, Young had made the national news after being arrested in communist Poland smuggling banned material out of the country. He had been attending a dissident East–West 'youth seminar' in the mountains of southern Poland, which had been organized by the European Democrat Students – the organization representing conservative student groups across Western Europe – and a band of mainly Catholic anti-communist youth organizations in Poland. The meeting was held in the remote Rynias glade, accessible only by hiking from the resort town of Zakopane at the foot of the Tatra mountains.[24] Much like Jessica Douglas-Home, those that came from France, Britain, Germany and Scandinavia returned home with the conviction that the democratic opposition in the East was bigger than they had previously understood.

After Young's arrest, it emerged that he was part of a group of young Tories who had been recruited and trained by the anti-communist National Alliance of Russian Solidarists – known in Britain as 'NTS', an abbreviation from the original Russian. NTS was headed up by George Miller-Kurakin, the charismatic grandson of a Russian émigré, for whom Young had previously travelled to Moscow to pick up a microfilm of a banned novel to take out to the West for publication.[25]

Young's derring-do caused a storm of interest in the press, giving him an air of romantic intrigue and infamy that his rival for the FCS chairmanship – Anna Soubry – could not match. After Young's victory, the libertarians became the dominant faction, prompting a mass defection of wets to the newly formed Social Democratic Party the following year, including Young's defeated rival, Soubry. During his year as chairman, Young led a delegation of students to Number Ten for a meeting with Thatcher, where, according to formal government minutes, he 'questioned the role of British Embassies and Consulates, believing that they could do more [to support dissident opposition in the East]' and set out his plans to concentrate his efforts as chairman 'emphasising the philosophical side of Conservatism'.[26]

The last redoubt of wet resistance to such ideological conservatism came from OUCA, under the control of future Tory MP Richard Fuller. Allegations of libertarian dirty tricks and far-right infiltration began to drip into the press from well-connected wet students. At one point, it was even claimed that the student radicals had access to a secret 'slush fund' filled with donations from shady right-wing businessmen and, potentially, American interests – code for the CIA.[27]

By May 1982, *The Times* reported that the infighting had risen to such a pitch it had reached the prime minister's desk, and 'some powerful party voices are now being raised in support of a thorough clean-up of the FCS'.[28] An inquiry was ordered which discovered that Peter Young did have access to a secret bank account, which he had set up under the name Mycroft Holmes, the shadowy elder brother of Sherlock Holmes. The bank account had received £4,000 in donations between December 1979 and June 1981,[29] most of which came from the iconoclastic tycoon Sir James Goldsmith, though his involvement was not disclosed.[30]

Despite this controversy, the sound faction largely maintained control of the FCS, only losing one election throughout the 1980s – in 1983 – to the then wet leader Paul Goodman. In 1984, the FCS elected its most radical libertarian leader yet, Marc Glendening, who chose to up the ante in his battle against both the TRG and the left in general, attacking both at every opportunity and often in the most provocative way imaginable. One unofficial FCS pamphlet during his time as chairman captured the spirit. Styled as a 'Guide to Disrupting NUS Conference', it advised delegates to 'always be proactive': 'Remember, you are not here to persuade the closed-minded leftists. You are here to wind them up so much they lose control and disrupt the conference'.[31] In 1984, when the single 'Free Nelson Mandela' became a chart hit, some libertarians turned up at an NUS conference with stickers declaring 'Hang Nelson Mandela'.[32] On another occasion, a group of libertarian activists dropped 200 copies of the right-wing student magazine *Campus* from a balcony onto the heads of delegates below. The magazine featured a front-page cartoon of a nuclear warhead called 'Willie Warhead' shaking hands with a tampon under the headline, 'NATO guarantees peaceful periods'. The stunt caused 'pandemonium', Peter Young remembers.

Unsurprisingly, pressure began to mount on the party chairman, John Gummer, to rein in the FCS. As the 1985 FCS conference at Loughborough University approached, *The Times* reported that 'the leadership of the Conservative Party is, for the first time, contemplating drastic action to purge its student body of ultra-right-wing elements which have become an embarrassment to the Prime Minister'.[33]

At the conference, however, the Thatcherites secured another victory. Glendening's replacement was to be his friend and ally, Mark MacGregor, and another young Scottish radical called Douglas 'Dougie' Smith was elected one of two vice chairmen.[34]

Even by the standards of the Federation of Conservative Students, Dougie Smith was an unorthodox character. Born in Edinburgh in 1962, his journey into the Conservative fold started as a schoolboy when he read about Peter Young's arrest in Poland in his father's copy of *The Scotsman*. For Smith, the story was a revelation, the essence of romantic political action.

After securing a place at Strathclyde University in Glasgow, Smith joined the Conservative Association, and by 1983 had joined the FCS national executive. At the FCS, Smith fell in with other youthful recruits to the sound faction, many of whom would go on to have careers in Tory politics. The common denominator among these students was not only enthusiasm for Margaret Thatcher, but also a shared willingness to test the limits of acceptable behaviour within the Conservative Party.

Forty years later, some of them still recall with amusement the antics, some of dubious legality, that formed part of FCS's retaliation against those Thatcher called 'the enemy within'. Campaigners for unilateral nuclear disarmament who set up protest 'peace camps' outside Air Force bases were awoken in the night by screams and sirens as their tents collapsed around them. Later, they would find standpipes used to provide water blocked up by quick-drying cement.

During the miners' strike of 1984, FCS members volunteered at National Union of Mineworkers offices and Stop the Pit Closures support groups, posing as postgraduate students with Marxist sympathies. The aim was to gather intelligence, which was then collated and passed on to the flamboyant old Etonian businessman and provocateur David Hart, a close friend of Charlie and Jessica Douglas-Home, who was covertly supporting the working miners to break the strike for Thatcher.

The Thatcherite victory in the FCS elections of 1985, which brought Smith and MacGregor to prominence, was met with despair in Conservative Central Office. Commenting on the result, *The Times* reported: 'Election results published yesterday show that the 14,000-strong body has overwhelmingly voted for officers who espouse many of the controversial right-wing "libertarian" ideals, which have embarrassed the party leadership.'[35]

By this time, Tory libertarianism was certainly pushing the bounds of respectability, with some of the more hardline elements within the movement going even further than the FCS leadership, calling not just for further and faster privatization, but for the legalization of heroin, the marketization of surrogacy – or 'womb leasing' – and an end to immigration controls.[36] In 1985, an FCS deputy chairman elected alongside Dougie Smith, David Hoile, was featured in *The Guardian*, explaining how he had spent eight days on patrol with the Nicaraguan Contras.[37] During the Ethiopian famine, one libertarian journal, *Blue Touchpaper*, featured a cover image of a starving child, with the headline 'Socialism Kills – Free Markets Feed'.[38]

For much of the Conservative hierarchy, such controversies were becoming too much. In the immediate aftermath of the Loughborough conference, which elected McGregor, Smith and Hoile, there had been front-page news about rampaging Tory students trashing rooms. The allegations were particularly embarrassing for the government, coming just a day after Thatcher had publicized moves to curb football hooliganism, although it later emerged the story had been spun to the national press by a wet opponent of the leadership, a media-savvy young Oxbridge moderate called Nick Robinson. In fact, the total cost to fix the damage caused by the 'rampage' amounted to £14 for a broken door handle, a missing light bulb and some beer stains on a carpet.[39]

Still, by this point the drip-drip of stories in the media was testing even the most committed of Thatcherite ministers. A *Panorama* programme had aired on 'Maggie's Militant Tendency', exposing the radicalism of the students, but the final straw came when the renegade Russian exile, Count Nikolai Tolstoy, was interviewed for the FCS's in-house magazine, *New Agenda*. In the article, Tolstoy accused Harold Macmillan of being a war criminal for his role in the forced repatriation of Cossacks at the end of the Second World War.[40]

The Macmillan allegation was provocative, and deliberately so. For many on the Tory right at the time, the idea that Britain should sacrifice thousands of men for the sake of some vague notion of realpolitik was appalling, but, in their view, handing over thousands of anti-communists to Stalin was perfectly in keeping with what they perceived to be the amorality of the Tory left. Fighting these battles of the past, even if it meant tarnishing the reputation of one of the Tory party's post-war icons, was a central part of their struggle for the future. But the allegations sparked such a furious response from some government ministers that the Conservative Party chairman, Norman Tebbit, got a court order to stop the magazine's distribution. Tebbit then shut down the FCS altogether,[41] with *The Telegraph* later noting that he had decided it was 'too Right-wing even for him'.[42] In its place, a new student body was set up, with the Thatcherite chairman John Bercow reinstalled at its head, but with elections no longer permitted. Margaret Thatcher's government had neutered its own student wing for being too Thatcherite, turning the FCS from a democratic battleground of competing ideologies to a sterile, appointed instrument of the Conservative hierarchy. For MacGregor, there would be future electoral battles ahead; for Smith, the deputy chairmanship would be his last elected position. From that point on, he resolved to influence politics from behind the scenes.

While the FCS burned itself out, Europe played almost no part in proceedings – even though 1985 marked the beginnings of Thatcher's existential battle with the continent.

Despite the apparent lethargy that had taken hold of the European project in the 1970s, the tide of integration had continued pulling under the surface with a quiet force that would eventually drown Thatcher's premiership. This current pulled at British politics from two directions: the continent, where officials, diplomats and political leaders found ways to ensure the European project continued progressing; and at home, where Thatcher was increasingly isolated over her response to such developments.

Under Callaghan, Britain had entered the European Monetary System, though not its central plank: the Exchange Rate Mechanism. As ever with such compromises, the result was unsatisfactory for all sides. For the Europeans, monetary union was a core priority, which had been agreed in principle as early as 1969. For Britain, being inside a monetary system but not its central mechanism did not make much sense in the long run.

From the beginning of her premiership, Thatcher faced questions over when Britain would finally join the ERM. The answer eventually alighted upon was that Britain would join 'when the time is right.'[43] Such a stock answer could only last so long, inviting the inevitable question: when is that?

The episode reveals Thatcher's peculiar cognitive dissonance over Europe. She could see the direction Europe was moving and vehemently disagreed with statements produced by its leaders – but would sign them anyway, believing they did not matter very much. In 1983, she had signed a 'Solemn Declaration' committing every member state to 'continue the work begun on the basis of the Treaties of Paris and Rome and to create a united Europe.' Each of the signatories agreed that the Commission was responsible for driving this process of European integration forward – and that the integration needed to be in 'both the economic and political fields.' The declaration – two years in the making – was the culmination of the so-called Genscher–Colombo Plan of 1981, drawn up by the foreign ministers of Germany and Italy, which called for the creation of a European state, formalized with a

'European Act'. In the 1983 declaration signed by Thatcher, progress towards this goal of European union would be assessed within five years.

Thatcher, of course, hated such talk, but was persuaded not to kick up a fuss because she needed European goodwill to stand any chance of negotiating a reduction on Britain's budget contributions. 'Our overriding aim in Europe at the moment is a satisfactory outcome on the Community Budget,' wrote Lord Carrington, her foreign secretary, advising her to sign the 1983 declaration. 'We shall find it easier to persuade our partners to make the substantial moves we need from them if we can provide them with evidence of simultaneous progress on the wider, vaguer and more theological issues addressed in the Germany proposals.'[44] Her private secretary John Coles argued that it would not do 'any harm to sign this verbose document' and, besides, '[German Chancellor] Kohl will be upset if we make difficulties.' In reply, Thatcher wrote, 'I dislike it intensely' and asked whether it was possible simply to adopt this 'dreadful document'. Lord Carrington's replacement, Francis Pym, advised Thatcher to sign it because it had 'little real content.'[45] She did.

Thatcher and her officials convinced themselves that the principles they were committing to did not matter, that the aspirations were vague when they were specific, and 'theological' when they were practical. Thatcher had committed to the 'strengthening of the European Monetary System . . . as a key element in progress towards Economic and Monetary Union', even though she did not believe in economic and monetary union. In the short term, such tactics helped her achieve her objectives, just as Lord Carrington advised, but she would have to pay for them down the line.

For the first half of Thatcher's long premiership, she was able to delay damaging rows over European policy. In 1985, two things changed. In London, her most senior cabinet colleagues concluded the time was right for Britain to join the European Exchange Rate Mechanism as the best way to keep inflation under control. And, in Brussels, a new man took charge of the European Commission, determined to reinvigorate Monnet's Europe: Jacques Delors.

The push to join the ERM was the result of the Treasury's quiet abandonment of monetarism and conviction that Britain needed an external 'anchor' to protect it against the return of inflation. Thatcher, however, was opposed on principle, declaring she would not head towards an election with interest rates being put 'into someone else's hands.'[46] Undeterred, Nigel Lawson, her chancellor, introduced his own policy of 'shadowing the Deutschmark', in direct opposition to the prime minister's ideological convictions. It was an unsustainable situation.[47]

Delors emerged as the frontrunner to become the new Commission president at the very summit which seemed to confirm Thatcher's political supremacy, at Fontainebleau in 1984. It was here that she had finally secured the 'rebate' which set a standard for British diplomatic achievement – and conduct – that none of her successors were able to reach. Yet it was also here, on the margins of the summit, that she gave her blessing to Delors.

Delors had risen to prominence as the pragmatic finance minister of France's socialist president François Mitterrand, having helped rescue his administration by convincing his party that siege socialism was not viable. Nevertheless, Delors was no free marketeer. As finance minister, he had followed an incomes policy of the exact sort Thatcher had come to power rejecting. He had also committed France to the European Monetary System and its central policy, the Exchange Rate Mechanism, as a way of controlling inflation.

Delors was a man of energy and intellect who believed in Monnet's Europe. 'We all feel there is something about classical nationalism which is out of date and ill fitting,' Delors had written in an editorial for the left-wing journal *Citoyen 60*, which he founded in 1959. 'The world increasingly needs large-scale organizations, while the problems of humanity require solutions at the planetary level.'[48] *Citoyen 60*'s mission statement declared its 'guiding principle' to be 'the desire to promote the communal side of humanity.'[49] Delorsism was everything Thatcherism was not.

At first, Thatcher's support for Delors looked inspired. As Delors prepared to take over the presidency in late 1984, he began searching for the grand initiative that would define his time in charge. That autumn, he met with a group of officials and business leaders brought together by Max Kohnstamm, who had been Jean Monnet's chief assistant at his Committee for a United States of Europe. After Monnet's death, Kohnstamm had become one of the most prominent 'guardians of the sacred flame of federalism,' as Charles Grant, Delors' biographer put it. The Kohnstamm group advised Delors to concentrate his efforts on the internal market and set a timetable for its completion of no more than two terms in office – eight years. However, the group also warned Delors that, for the internal market to function, countries would have to give up their vetoes. It was not feasible for everything to be unanimous.[50]

Here was the quid pro quo: if the conservative, ostensibly free-market governments which dominated Europe at the time wanted to reduce internal trade barriers, they would need to give up some of their own national powers to keep them in place. Thatcher was as supportive of this as anyone, believing that, because of Britain's size and influence, qualified majority voting would often mean Britain getting its way.

Delors had his mission, and in Thatcher's choice for European commissioner, the Conservative peer Lord Cockfield, he also had the man to make it real. Thatcher assumed Cockfield was 'one of us', and he was, insofar as he was a believer in free markets.[51] Cockfield, though, had a very personal reason for sympathizing with Monnet's vision of a united Europe in which war had been banished. Arthur Cockfield had grown up never knowing his father, who had died fighting in the carnage of the Somme a month before his son was born.

Once in Brussels, Cockfield proved to be a formidable European administrator, unsurprisingly for a former lawyer, company director and head of the statistical section of the Inland Revenue. Within months of taking on his new role, Cockfield produced his white paper, 'Completing the Internal Market', containing 297 specific proposals on everything from the removal of physical border checks and customs formalities to the elimination of technical barriers and the creation of a 'mutual recognition' of standards across the Community. The speed and extent of Cockfield's white paper alarmed Thatcher, who began complaining that he had gone native. 'Cockfield fell out of love with Thatcher and in love with Delors,' noted Charles Powell, Thatcher's foreign-policy adviser.[52] Thatcher's complaints about Cockfield were beside the point; as Delors better understood, the very nature of 'completing' Europe's internal market did not mean less European regulation, but more – and, with it, greater sacrifices of national sovereignty.

On 14 January 1985, Delors kicked off his presidency with a speech to the European Parliament declaring his intention to bulldoze through the Community's internal barriers by the end of 1992. It wasn't purely a matter of economics; a new treaty would be needed, too. To compete, Europe needed to 'speak with a single voice and to act together.' Currency instability and hidden protectionism needed to be dealt with, and a European social space created. 'What would become of us if we didn't have a minimum harmonisation of social rules,' he demanded. 'What do we already see? Some member-states, some companies who try to steal an advantage over their competitors, at the cost of what we have to call a social retreat.'[53]

When Thatcher saw Delors for the first time after his appointment as president, she told him to be practical and avoid 'these constant references to European unity, something which could never come about.'[54] Delors does not appear to have told her she had already signed up to such references.

When Europe's leaders decided that a new treaty was needed to 'complete the internal market' – against Thatcher's wishes – German Chancellor Kohl was jubilant, declaring in a press conference after a summit in Milan that Europe would not now 'degenerate into an elevated free trade zone.' France and Germany were the motors of change, he declared. 'The mission of the founding fathers had been to slowly dismantle national sovereignty . . . At the end a European federal state could arise.'[55] Thatcher had been left no room for misinterpretation.

For Thatcher, the task was now to limit the scope of the coming treaty, keeping it focused on the single market and away from the looming question of economic and monetary union. When the summit came, Thatcher, keen not to be isolated, struck a compromise with Kohl whereby she would accept a 'symbolic' reference to monetary union, 'so long as it was accompanied by a binding provision requiring the negotiation of a new treaty . . . before any progress towards implementing it could be made.'[56] In other words, the can was kicked down the road. Thatcher had made what she saw as a symbolic concession on monetary union for the immediate benefit of the single market.

In one sense, Thatcher had achieved something significant. According to a note written by Geoffrey Howe's private office, 'Delors is reported to have told some of his associates . . . that there was only one Member State which had a clear idea of where it wanted the EC to go and was organizing its efforts to that end effectively,' and it wasn't France. 'It was the UK.' Thatcher had wanted Europe to open up its internal market, and she had succeeded in getting this. She had also avoided making any binding commitment to monetary union. Such was the victory, Delors himself complained the Single European Act agreed in Luxembourg was '*une grande deception*' (meaning 'disappointment', rather than 'deception').[57]

Yet, in the round, Thatcher could not be said to be winning the argument in Europe. Until this point in her premiership, she had proved tactically astute, willing to compromise to achieve short-term, concrete objectives. She had secured the rebate and opened Europe's internal market, while delaying the point of no return on issues which she felt were core areas of national sovereignty. Strategically, though, Thatcher had not altered Europe's direction of travel. The animating logic of European integration remained, shaping the project's development regardless of Thatcher's instinctive hostility.

While Delors felt the Single European Act's failure to lock in economic and monetary union was a disappointment, he was right to say that it was now a treaty objective. On top of this, the European Parliament had been strengthened and qualified majority voting expanded. At Luxembourg in 1985, Thatcher had accepted the greatest extension of European federalism since the Treaty of Rome in 1958.

Until 1986, Thatcher did not properly scrutinize the paradoxes in her Europe policy, believing that European integration would not develop as quickly or as radically as it did. But, from this point on, with the Commission now run by its most effective administrator since Jean Monnet, the reality of what Thatcher had agreed became increasingly impossible to ignore, with consequences that would flow through British politics for decades to come.

In February 1986, the treaty Thatcher had agreed in Luxembourg was ratified by MPs with little difficulty. Just seventeen Conservative MPs rebelled against the government.[58] These MPs included many ERG stalwarts, including Jonathan Aitken and Teddy Taylor – as well as Enoch Powell – though not, incidentally, many of the future Maastricht rebels, including the lawyer Bill Cash, the man who had replaced Hugh Fraser as MP for Stafford in 1984. Cash marked the occasion with his first attempted constitutional manoeuvre, laying an amendment that 'nothing in this Act shall derogate from the sovereignty of the United Kingdom Parliament', when it clearly had. Cash's amendment was ignored, but his journey had begun. With the exception of *The Spectator*, the press were in favour too, though T. E. Utley sent up a warning flare from his perch at *The Daily Telegraph*.

'Last week the European Communities (Amendment) Bill received the Royal Assent and is now, accordingly, part of the law of this country,' Utley wrote on 10 November 1986. 'Are you rejoicing at this leap into the future or are you sunk in gloom at the thought of having lost your national independence? I suspect neither. You have not noticed the event at all.' Utley thought his readers *should* notice, and spelled out the essential nature of the act. 'It removed the British Government's veto on a whole host of issues which come under the consideration of the European Council of Ministers,' he summarized. 'We shall be outvoted on many matters which seriously concern the domestic affairs of this country by other member states of the Common Market.'[59] In one sense, Utley was simply stating the reality of the new treaty, though the number of times Britain would be outvoted depended on the vicissitudes of diplomacy. Britain had not given away its ultimate national sovereignty – for it could always leave – but a slice had certainly been transferred for the better functioning of the single market.

Even before the single market came into existence, the stream of new regulations to create a new economically borderless Europe had started to flow. Back in Britain, the band of Conservative anti-Europeans in the ERG continued to sound a dissenting note, producing memoranda on new European regulations, attempting to convince their colleagues that the changes were bureaucratic and anti-democratic, to little effect. Every piece of European legislation sailed through Parliament with no difficulty. And then, almost out of nowhere, the anti-Europeans found a cause which grabbed Parliament's imagination: the Lawnmowers (Harmonisation of Noise Emissions) Regulations.

Jonathan Aitken had heard about the new rules – implementing a European directive – from a constituent who was worried about his business. There was then a significant domestic industry making lawnmowers, many of which would be hit by this new law, which, in Aitken's mind, was designed not just to protect continental companies, but to advantage continental companies. 'The Germans had some lawnmowers that were quieter than ours,' recalls Aitken. 'They got this through the European Commission, and so, finally, it ends up in our Parliament.'[60] Aware of the danger, Britain's lawnmower manufacturers began lobbying against the proposals. Usually, Aitken recalled, the ERG could count on a maximum of thirty or forty MPs to back their cause. But when it came to the lawnmowers, the whips suddenly got spooked, even though the government had a majority in Parliament comfortably above a hundred. Still, the ERG lost. Thatcher had been alerted and was annoyed with the rebels. It was after these shenanigans late one night that Aitken found himself with Enoch Powell. 'One day the British people will not stand for this kind of stuff,' Aitken said. Looking up from his work, Powell replied, 'You're right, Jonathan, but I fear not in my lifetime, nor in yours.'[61]

The kerfuffle over lawnmowers highlighted the political challenge in 'completing' the European internal market by 1992. On the one hand, harmonizing regulations between twelve competing European nations was just the type of deregulation Thatcher favoured. On the other, it was, by definition, intrusive and fraught with political risk. If lawnmower regulation could cause a problem, so could anything else. And each controversy would illuminate the scope and ambition of the single-market project.

In the short term, the real political challenge facing Thatcher on Europe came not from the flow of new regulations, but from the drive for further integration. The 'Solemn Declaration' she had signed in 1983 confirmed Europe's collective intent to strengthen the European Monetary System to 'consolidate an area of monetary stability in Europe and to create a more stable international economic environment, as a key element in progress towards Economic and Monetary Union.' As well as monetary union, it committed Europe's leaders to 'accord a high priority to the Community's social progress and in particular to the problem of employment by the development of a European social policy.' As an example of what such a social policy might look like, the declaration makes it clear that action to alleviate unemployment would need to be taken 'at both Community and national levels in particular by means of specific action on behalf of young people and by improved harmonization of social security systems.' If the single market appealed to conservatives across Europe, here was the offer to the left. For the Labour Party in particular, powerless at home, the Europe of Delors began to appear more attractive.

If this was not explicit enough, the 'final provision' section of the declaration made it doubly so. All the signatories of the document agreed that there was a direct 'link between membership of the European Communities and participation in the activities described'. In other words, both economic and monetary union and European-wide social policies were core parts of membership, not fringe aspirations distinct from Thatcher's own preference for open markets. The desire for European union is also explicit, which would be achieved 'by deepening and broadening the scope of European activities so that they coherently cover, albeit on a variety of legal bases, a growing proportion of Member States' mutual relations and of their external relations.' This, then, was the goal, as agreed by all members of the bloc, including the UK. What's more, all members agreed to review their progress towards these goals within five years – in other words, by 1988.

Until 1986, though there had been tensions between Thatcher and Delors, the relationship between the pair worked well enough. They had, after all, a shared goal to complete the internal market. In 1987, Delors focused on pushing through his 'Delors package', an ambitious plan to fix the Community's budgets for five years. He entitled this package *Réussir l'Acte unique* (or 'make a success of the single act'). For Delors, in other words, the new treaty could not function without a solid financial base. As ever, when it comes to money, negotiating such a package would be difficult, ultimately requiring Germany to put its hand even deeper into its pocket.[62]

'We can't make Germany move from a sense of guilt which is 40 years old,' Delors told the *Financial Times*. And yet he was also prepared to be tough. Speaking to French television, he declared, 'If you see Europe as a way of increasing your trade surplus with other countries, because you are good fellows we understand that. But if you don't understand that you also have to take part in the construction of Europe, don't be surprised if one day this Europe bursts apart and you lose your surpluses and you have more unemployed.'[63]

Here, then, is the eternal paradox – or genius – of European integration: to manage Germany's core economic strength, it must be Europeanized; but, by Europeanizing Germany, Germany continues to grow stronger, requiring ever more European integration. For the first seven years of her premiership, Thatcher had not had to properly confront this reality. Since the Treaty of Rome, European integration had only inched forward. Declarations were made and regulation harmonized, but until 1986 there had been no major change in the nature of the club. Thatcher was not burying her head in the sand by dismissing the idea that there would be a series of further leaps forward so soon after the last. For her, the Single European Act was an end in itself, opening up the European market, not being subsumed into it. It did not, in her mind, necessitate further transfers of sovereignty. But, for Delors and Europe's other true believers, the Single European Act was always just one logical step of many, the next two of which were monetary union and social union – both of which Thatcher had reluctantly accepted earlier in the decade.

Thatcher was far from being the first prime minister to have found that her vision of Europe's future was at odds with that being pursued by the continent's leaders – a thread that can be traced back to Harold Macmillan. Both Macmillan and Thatcher believed in a pragmatic accommodation with Europe and their own ability to manage its future development – and both had found out to their frustration how hard this was in practice. Still, by 1986, Macmillan appeared to be a man from another age – born in the reign of Queen Victoria, veteran of the Somme and pillar of the post-war consensus. His death, announced on 30 December 1986, marked the passing not just of a former prime minister, but of an older Britain. Macmillan was the last of the giants of Algiers who had done so much to make the world – Eisenhower had gone in 1969, de Gaulle in 1970 and Monnet in 1979. Now, only Powell remained, and he was toiling for another future entirely.

As the general election of 1987 approached, the old battles over Britain's role in Europe seemed an age away. On this subject at least, a consensus had been reached, dominated by the personality and politics of Margaret Thatcher. Yet, even at the quiet zenith of Thatcher's supremacy, the sound of the next wave approaching British politics could be detected.

The oddly vulnerable nature of Thatcher's hold on power at this time can be glimpsed in a note sent to her by her Treasury private secretary, David Norgrove, the day before voters went to the polls. 'There is a widespread assumption that we shall become full members of the EMS [European Monetary System] after the election,' he wrote. 'It will be a priority for the Chancellor.' While this would cede a major role in the British economy to Germany, he warned, she risked finding herself isolated in her own cabinet should she continue to oppose: 'You will want to consider whether that would be a sustainable position in view of the support the Chancellor would receive from the Foreign Secretary and possibly others also.'[64]

When the results of the election trickled through in the early morning 12 June, Thatcher was confirmed as the most powerful British prime minister since the war, returning with a majority of 102. No other leader had won three successive majorities. No other Tory leader that century would win a majority so large. And no other leader had followed through on their agenda quite so successfully. Yet, here she was, at the height of her powers, being warned that she would be defeated in a direct confrontation with her cabinet on a central issue of economic policy. A new era was approaching, and Thatcher was quietly powerless to stop it.

Enoch Powell, meanwhile, had lost a closely fought election in South Down by 731 votes. The constituency had a natural Irish nationalist majority and had always been marginal. It would never elect a unionist again. According to Simon Heffer, Powell's biographer, 'There had been periods of depression in Powell's career before . . . but his grief at losing his seat was unprecedented.'[65] As the ultimate parliamentarian, he treasured not only his home on the green benches, but also the almost metaphysical connection he believed existed between an MP and the people and place that elected him.

In many ways, the general election of 1987 marked the moment at which the Thatcher hegemony reached its peak and then began to unravel. A record-breaking third consecutive term started in triumph, but the uneasy compromises that had allowed the cabinet to present a united front over the previous four years were beginning to fracture under the strain of European integration. Thatcher also began to exhibit signs of dogmatism which led some supporters to think the previously unthinkable: is ten years at the top the limit before someone starts to fray?

For the time being, though, she was triumphant again, her place in history secured. For Roger Scruton and Jessica Douglas-Home, Thatcher's victory was a huge relief, not only preserving the Thatcherite domestic revolution, as they saw it, but Britain's hostility to communism. For Jessica in particular, this was doubly important because, in 1987, she had expanded her network of dissidents even further, moving beyond Czechoslovakia, Poland and Hungary into Romania, founding a new foundation with her friend, Christine Stone, the lawyer, journalist and second wife of Norman Stone. For Jessica, in fact, this work had become not only a source of meaning, but of consolation following the death of her husband, Charlie, in October 1985, aged just forty-eight.

For a little over two years following his diagnosis, Charlie had wrestled with his increasingly debilitating terminal cancer while trying to fulfil his duties at *The Times*, insisting on editing the paper and maintaining the staunch Atlanticism of its editorials,*

---

* For many Thatcherites at the time, the *Times* leaders in these final months of Douglas-Home's life were among the most important of the Cold War. On 18 March 1985, *The Times* published one particularly influential leader criticizing the

often from his hospital bed, until less than two weeks before his death.[66]

The year 1987, then, was a time of transition. The former student radicals of the FCS, having been cast out of the organization that had incubated them for so long, turned their attention to the larger prize: the Conservative Party itself. They intended to start by taking over its traditional youth wing, long a bastion of the wets: the Young Conservatives.

Back at Oxford, meanwhile, Michael Gove was gearing up for his tilt at the Union presidency, finally able to step out of the shadow of his overbearing ally, Boris Johnson; and that other young Scottish maverick destined for a walk-on part in Britain's conservative counter-revolution, Patrick Robertson, finally took up his place among the spires, ready to fall under Norman Stone's influence.

Foreign Secretary Geoffrey Howe, following a speech he had made questioning the Reagan administration's so-called 'Strategic Defence Initiative', better known as the 'Star Wars program', which envisaged building a missile defence system to protect the United States from nuclear attack. *The Times*' leader was headlined 'Howe's UDI from SDI' and accused him of unilaterally disarming Reagan's attempt to pressure Moscow into concessions. The leader argued that Howe's speech had done 'untold damage to the cohesion of the Atlantic Alliance', and that the Soviet Union could only be dealt with through strength. 'We cannot expect to achieve anything by negotiation with the Soviet Union unless we recognize that it is and always will be conducted against a background of ill will born of the incompatibility of the two systems – liberal democracy and Marxist-Leninism dedicated to the former's destruction.'

Chapter 9

Patrick Robertson arrived at Oxford in September 1987, a headstrong young Scot with dreams of a future in Parliament. The teenage Robertson had been living in the flat in Battersea, southwest London, that his ex-pat parents had bought as their retirement home, while working evenings and weekends at a supermarket in New Malden and attending sixth-form college in Kingston. He had previously been at Dulwich College, where he'd been sent to board aged thirteen, after a childhood on the continent, following his father, who worked for the British Tourist Authority.

Robertson had found Dulwich suffocating, but loved his time stacking shelves and canvassing in his spare time for the local Conservative Party. Until 1988, in fact, Robertson's experience of Britain was limited to his time at Dulwich, New Malden and the annual visits back to London that he would take with his parents as a child, feeling the country more intensely than those who knew only England.

At Oxford, Robertson got involved in various clubs: the Union, the Italian Society and, though he was not a formal member, the Edmund Burke Society, where he first met Michael Gove. The Burke Society met in the Union building every Sunday evening, where its members played an intellectual parlour game to test each other's wits, citing the most obscure references possible. To this day, Robertson vividly remembers watching the young Gove perform. 'He would recite whole sections of Burke verbatim, off the top of his head.'[1]

Gove remembers Robertson fondly as well. 'Patrick was young, sparky, ambitious, anxious to get on in the world. There was an element of the political adventurer to him.'[2] Like Gove, Robertson soon began to garner a reputation. *Cherwell* – the student newspaper – reported with evident delight that Robertson had sent a note to the visiting former prime minister Edward Heath, inviting him for a drink in the Crypt wine bar. As such, Robertson was quickly named 'Pushy Fresher' of the week.

While never close, Gove and Robertson were both eccentric Scots in awe of that other Scottish outsider in their midst, Norman Stone. 'There were always these dons who exercise a degree of influence over their undergraduates which goes beyond their teaching,' Gove recalled. 'Maurice Cowling was like that at Cambridge and, for a group of us, Norman had that influence.'[3]

When it fell on Gove to organize a Burns' Night supper in January 1988, he arranged for Robertson to sit next to Stone. Robertson soon found himself one of Stone's young apostles, invited to his home to discuss history and politics – though rarely, if ever, as Robertson recalls, Europe. The question of European integration was becoming an issue in British politics, a matter of concern to some in the upper echelons of government, but it was not yet a source of elemental Tory anguish. Certainly, in the minds of the students at the time, the issue of Europe was not particularly relevant.

Among economic historians like Niall Ferguson, there was a slight sense of unease over the government's drift towards ERM. 'Thatcherism was about monetary policy to a large extent,' he recalled. 'So, the idea you would defeat inflation and then hand over control of monetary policy was mad.'[4] Such thoughts had yet to break into the mainstream. There were other, more important issues.

For the ex-FCS radicals, the Cold War was the principal ideological battleground in their war to take over the Young Conservatives. The YC was a much bigger and less political organization than the FCS. It was open to anyone under the age of thirty, student or otherwise. By 1988, under the chairmanship of Nick Robinson, it was also the last redoubt of the Tory left.

There had long been rumours that wet domination of the YC had been maintained with the help of regular injections of cash from Tory patrician grandees and even European Christian democrats. To help with their plans for a hostile takeover, the Thatcherites turned to David Hart, persuading him to fund them through his new organization, the Committee for a Free Britain (CFB).

At first, Hart was unconvinced that control of the YC was worth the effort, given that his priority was the Cold War. What changed his mind was a photograph taken at the annual YC conference in Scarborough in 1988, where the arrival of old faces from the FCS had provoked an upsurge of factional infighting.

In this period, it was usual for the radicals to wear T-shirts and badges supporting anti-communist guerrilla movements around the world, including the Nicaraguan Contras. In response, some of the wets got hold of stickers from the left-wing Nicaragua Solidarity Campaign, which backed the Marxist regime. These proclaimed 'Nicaraguan Coffee: the Taste of Freedom' and were intended to wind up the right-wingers. One of the FCS team took a photograph of the badges and showed it to Hart, who declared it evidence of a communist effort to subvert the Conservative Party and pledged to donate as much money as was required to defeat it. In fact, it would only take a year for Dougie Smith and his allies to succeed. In 1989, the Thatcherite Andrew Tinney became the first candidate from the right to be elected national chairman of the Young Conservatives, ending a period of 'moderate' control stretching back through the 1980s and 1970s.

Beyond funding Smith's assault on the Young Conservatives, the CFB spent much of its energy on an influential Cold War newsletter it had taken over from Brian Crozier and Nicholas Elliott, which had been called 'Background Briefing'. Hart renamed it 'British Briefing' and it was edited and compiled by Charles Elwell, a former MI5 officer, and funded by donations from Rupert Murdoch, among others. Its stated purpose was 'to provide information about the threat to parliamentary democracy and the rule of law by Communists.'[5]

For Hart, whose influence with the prime minister had faded following the miners' strike, the CFB and its briefing paper was his route back to favour. He had felt his isolation acutely, writing plaintive letters to Thatcher complaining about officials who wanted to 'sow distrust between us and render me unable to assist you.'[6] Hart's efforts in the 1987 election – financing full-page anti-Labour advertisements in the national press – had bought him goodwill, but he was always greeted with distaste among those in government outside the Thatcherite inner circle. The foreign secretary Geoffrey Howe was particularly unhappy when he found himself on the front of a CFB pamphlet ahead of the Conservative Party Conference in 1988, giving what looked like a communist salute in Marxist Mozambique, though Howe insisted he was merely swatting a fly. To the young radicals, Howe's apparent salute was part of the same sordid story of communist appeasement going back to Macmillan. 'The Foreign Office is one of the last of the great British institutions that has escaped the refreshing breath of Thatcherism', the CFB pamphlet declared.[7] It is no coincidence that Howe's deputy at the time was Lynda Chalker, a decidedly wet former chairman of the Young Conservatives who was regarded with intense suspicion among Tory right-wingers. Europe, meanwhile, continued to play almost no role in the ideological struggle of the day.

Until 1986, the EEC had been an awkward and at times infuriating partner for Thatcher in her mission to overhaul the British economy and hold the line against the Soviets, but it had been a partner nonetheless. Europe was a core plank of the free world and a market that acted as a disciplining force on British industry.

One of the few voices willing to poke at this consensus over the years had been T. E. Utley. But, in the summer of 1988, aged only sixty-seven, Utley died. Thatcher was quick to lead the tributes, hailing him as 'the most distinguished Tory thinker of our time'. 'Few people have possessed such a complete understanding of the central tenets and principles of Toryism as Peter Utley,' she declared. 'Certainly no one has articulated them with more eloquence.'[8] Utley stood in the same tradition as Edmund Burke and Lord Salisbury, Thatcher wrote. Ironically, 1988 was the year Thatcher began the harder turn towards Utleyism that would, in the end, contribute to her losing the premiership.

In the same period, by contrast, Jacques Delors had grown concerned that Europe was becoming little more than a trade bloc, facilitating the kind of capitalism he had spent his life opposing. Europe had become too shallow, too economically liberal, too Thatcherite. If anything, his own programme to complete the single market by 1992, which became known as the 1992 project, was making the situation worse.

By spring 1988, Delors had begun to voice his concerns. 'I was worried that the trade unions might not continue to support the [1992] project politically,' he explained to his biographer Charles Grant a few years later.[9] At the European Trade Union Conference in Stockholm that May, Delors opened a new front in his drive for integration, promising a series of new European-wide labour laws. Thatcher, of course, hated it.

Despite her differences with Delors, she went along with his reappointment as president of the Commission at the leaders' summit in Hanover that June, calculating – correctly – that she was too isolated in her opposition to do anything about it. At this same summit, Delors was also appointed the chairman of the committee to study economic and monetary union. The decision was not to Thatcher's taste, but she succeeded in ensuring the other members of this committee would be Europe's central bankers: hard-nosed men with no interest in utopian visions of European union.

Thatcher was particularly reassured by the presence of Bundesbank president Karl Otto Pöhl, who had publicly opposed the idea of a European Central Bank, which was a prerequisite of monetary union. 'We thought the Delors Committee was a good way of sidelining the idea,' explained Charles Powell afterwards.[10]

Whatever illusions Thatcher might have had were punctured within a few weeks of the Hanover summit. Addressing the European Parliament on 6 July 1988, Delors predicted that 'ten years hence, 80 per cent of our economic legislation and perhaps even our fiscal and social legislation as well, will be of Community origin.' Here was Delors' understanding of 'completing the internal market'. To Thatcher, it was an outrage, marking a pivotal moment in the breakdown of relations between them. As she later put it, 'by the summer of 1988 he [Delors] had altogether slipped his leash as a *fonctionnaire* and become a fully-fledged political spokesman for federalism.'[11]

Before Thatcher's public bust-up with Delors, the British ambassador in Brussels, David Hannay, had arranged for the British prime minister to deliver a speech to the College of Europe in Bruges. The usual order of things would have seen the Foreign Office lead on the original drafting of the speech, but events intervened. On 20 August, an IRA bomb exploded next to a bus carrying British soldiers in Ballygawley, County Tyrone, killing eight and injuring twenty-eight more. Thatcher broke off her holiday in Cornwall to return to Number Ten, giving her the time to draft the speech with Charles Powell instead. For Thatcher, speechwriting had always formed an important part of her governing style. 'She used speeches to do what she called her "political thinking",' the former *Daily Telegraph* journalist and T. E. Utley protégé John O'Sullivan said. O'Sullivan joined Thatcher's Number Ten operation as a speechwriter at the end of 1986. 'Most of the time, the job of being prime minister was about administrative thinking, but she wanted to be able to express a basic drive of the government, which was towards a freer and more responsible society,' O'Sullivan explained. To help formulate her thinking, Thatcher relied on the support of outsiders she liked and trusted. Paul Johnson and Woodrow Wyatt would send in drafts, and Norman Stone was also regularly consulted. She also liked to include a few 'wild card' outsiders like David Hart, O'Sullivan added.[12]

In Thatcher's first draft of what would become the Bruges speech, she declared that Britain had saved Europe from being united 'under Prussian domination' and had managed its empire more successfully than other European powers. She also warned the continent's leaders to 'forget a United States of Europe'. Charles Powell sent this draft to the Foreign Office for comments, noting that it had 'been seen by the Prime Minister, who is quite attracted to it.' The Foreign Office, in contrast, was horrified. In an internal memo, Geoffrey Howe's private secretary, Stephen Wall, wrote that the speech contained 'some plain and fundamental errors.' The foreign secretary 'does not like the suggestion that we were more successful colonists' or that 'we alone fought against tyranny.' On the question of a United States of Europe, Howe agreed 'that a stronger Europe does not mean the creation of a new European super-state', but warned that it would still 'require the sacrifice of political independence and the rights of national parliaments.' This, Wall added, correctly, 'is inherent in the treaties.'[13]

From the moment the Foreign Office received Powell's draft, it went into overdrive to neuter its impact. The most senior official in the Europe department, John Kerr, arranged a meeting with other senior officials from across Whitehall to remove the 'needlessly provocative' sections of the speech. One of those involved in this effort would later tell the journalist Hugo Young that Kerr had masterfully redrafted Powell's first effort in such a way that it managed to 'retain much of the original wording, while in many cases standing Powell's meaning on its head.' Kerr sent his new draft back to Downing Street on 7 September. Number Ten then accepted '80 per cent of the suggestions set out', as Kerr put it. 'It thus looks as if our damage limitation exercise is heading for success.'[14]

Before Thatcher delivered her speech in Bruges, however, Jacques Delors arrived in Bournemouth to deliver his own era-defining address to that year's Trades Union Congress. Traditionally, the British left had been hostile to the European project, seeing the EEC as little more than a capitalist club. In September 1988, Delors set about trying to change that, with remarkable success.

Addressing the delegates, Delors returned to many of the old ideas he had been espousing for years. It was imperative that the continent 'preserve and enhance the uniquely European model of society,' he declared. This model held a 'skilful balance between society and the individual.' All this was in direct opposition to the very essence of Thatcherism, but Delors ploughed on all the same, criticizing the 'massive unemployment' levels seen across the continent – a crisis particularly acute in Britain. He then declared that 'cooperation and solidarity' were as important to a functioning market as competition, and called for new rules to protect workers. The audience loved it and began serenading the visiting Frenchman with a rendition of 'Frère Jacques', which brought him to tears.[15]

It is hard to overstate the importance of this moment. It confirmed to many on the British left that their traditional suspicion of the Common Market as a 'capitalist club' was no longer valid and that the growing supranational power of Europe, far from being a theoretical brake on British socialism, was a brake on the ambitions of Thatcherism. The 'social dimension' that Delors trumpeted in Bournemouth in 1988 had been there from the very beginning of the European project. One of the specific goals of the EEC, as spelled out in the Treaty of Rome, was to ensure not only economic integration, but 'social progress'. A European Social Fund had been set up in 1957 to 'improve job opportunities for workers and to raise their standard of living.' In 1972, the EEC declared that it was 'essential to ensure the increasing involvement of labour and management in the economic and social decisions of the Community.' In 1986, Thatcher's Single European Act gave Delors' Commission the go-ahead to 'develop the dialogue between management and labour at European level.' What Delors said in Bournemouth was not new, but its impact was profound. September 1988 was the moment the British left began its mass conversion to Europe. The stage was set for Thatcher in Bruges.

Reading Thatcher's speech today, what is most striking is just how *pro*-European it is. The British were as European as any other nation, Thatcher declared, shaped by thousands of years of war and peace, conquest and Christianity. And should there be any doubt, the prime minister went on, as bluntly as she could: 'Britain does not dream of some cosy, isolated existence on the fringes of the European Community. Our destiny is in Europe, as part of the Community.'

The Bruges speech was many things, but it was not a bugle

call to leave the EEC. The speech's principal aim was to make the case for a different Europe from the one then being built. Thatcher's vision of Europe was more liberal and free-trading than the social Europe Delors desired, more closely allied with the United States and – crucially – enlarged eastwards beyond its current borders. 'Europe', Thatcher argued, was not the same as the European Community. 'We must never forget that east of the Iron Curtain, people who once enjoyed a full share of European culture, freedom and identity have been cut off from their roots. We shall always look on Warsaw, Prague and Budapest as great European cities.' This was Thatcher the Cold Warrior, champion of liberty, national sovereignty and the idea of a wider cultural Europe as advocated by Scruton, Stone, Douglas-Home and the young Thatcherites then battling for control of the YC.

Despite the Foreign Office filtering process that had taken place, the speech retained much that was authentically Thatcher, combining prophecy, ideological clarity and willing delusion. The vision was clear and defensible, but did not correspond to the nature of the club she had campaigned to join and whose integration she had, perhaps unwittingly, helped bring about.

'The Community is not an end in itself,' Thatcher declared early in the speech. 'Nor is it an institutional device to be constantly modified according to the dictates of some abstract intellectual concept.' And yet, in a very obvious sense, that is exactly what it was. The genius of Monnet's Europe was that, rather like a nation state, its very existence created a new shared interest which bound together the previously warring states of Europe. What's more, Europe's institutions were exactly what Thatcher declared them not to be: devices to achieve the idea at the heart of the project – ever closer union. This was the bloc's animating spirit, its very life source, not something that could be wished away.

In practical terms, Thatcher was trying to slow the momentum towards further integration. In this context, she uttered perhaps the most famous line in the speech: 'We have not successfully rolled back the frontiers of the state in Britain, only to see them reimposed at a European level with a European superstate exercising a new dominance from Brussels.' On the question of monetary union, Thatcher also urged caution. Europe had many more things to be getting on with, she declared.

Delors later described Thatcher's intervention as 'a good speech, well written, beautiful phrases', and also 'very direct, very comprehensible.' Thatcher had articulated her vision of Europe, but in doing so had revealed that vision to be entirely at odds with what was actually happening. 'I think she thought she could put a stop to the European project,' remarked Delors, years later.[16]

The most remarkable thing about the Bruges speech was not its content, but rather how little it achieved initially. 'Not a single member of our own government let alone the Foreign Office was prepared to go out and argue for its ideas,' Charles Powell reflected.[17] In Europe, Delors simply doubled down on his work chairing the committee on monetary union.

Politics, though, is more than the mere art of the possible; it is a battle of ideas. While Thatcher's speech did not achieve much in the short term, it set the tone for British politics for decades to come.

At around the same time Thatcher was preparing her speech in Bruges, Patrick Robertson in Oxford had begun writing down his own thoughts on the future of Europe. The initial spark for this slightly odd endeavour for a first-year undergraduate was an article in *The Times* about Leon Brittan declaring that Britain was not opposed to a single European currency in principle. For Robertson, this was extraordinary. Was the British government really considering abolishing the pound sterling?

Robertson began working on his paper, the central thrust of which was that Delors' 1992 project was being used to impose political unity on an unsuspecting public. Robertson sent his paper to Norman Stone, seeking his advice (and contacts) on how best to set up an 'information campaign' to warn people of Delors' plans. Stone put him in touch with a number of potential supporters, including Ralph Harris.

Things then began to move quickly for Robertson. Harris liked Robertson's paper and sent it on to a series of other like-minded businessmen and Conservative donors. Robertson soon began travelling back and forth to London from his halls in Oxford, meeting with various potential supporters. Such was the interest in the group, Robertson sought special permission from Keble College to install a landline in his room to run his new campaign, going so far as to hire a secretary to take his calls, much to the amusement of *Cherwell*, which reported on the 'rather middle-aged lady' who had moved into his room.[18]

By the Christmas of 1988, Harris had agreed to become chairman of Robertson's new pressure group, and brought with him another dozen or so academics. London offices were found for the group on Jermyn Street. Eventually, on 9 February 1989, Robertson's group was launched in the grand library of the Reform Club in central London. Thirty years later, Robertson described the launch as 'a moment of total magic'.[19] Between 250 and 300 people turned up for the occasion, offering their support for the new pressure group, which Robertson had decided to call the Bruges Group.

To spell out the organization's intentions, Robertson used an updated version of the essay he'd sent to Stone. A copy is kept in the Foreign Office archives, while Robertson himself has the only remaining copy of the original fourteen-page essay. Its aspirations seem modest in comparison with what 'Euroscepticism', as it became known, would go on to achieve. 'The general public has nowhere to turn to ask its questions about what European integration will actually mean,' the pamphlet begins. 'We intend to become that point of reference for all Europeans who are supporters of 1992 but who are sceptical about the implications of European political unity.' The Bruges Group was not calling for British withdrawal.

In hindsight, the pamphlet reads like a crib sheet for the charges against Europe that would come to dominate discourse in the Conservative Party. It sets out its opposition to the withdrawal of national frontiers; the 'socialist superstructure' proposed by Delors; the single currency; the 'sheer madness' of a European army; and any permanent ceding of power by Westminster.[20]

As with Thatcher, the paper presents a particularly British understanding of the European project. 'Up until recently,' it declares, 'the question of European integration appeared limited to the issue of economic deregulation and cooperation, and therefore European unity in the economic sphere.' While this was certainly a perception that many in Britain had promoted, at no point in Europe's history had integration been limited to economics. Political integration was the objective. In the very first meeting of the European Coal and Steel Community, Jean Monnet had declared himself head of Europe's First Government.

Regardless, Robertson's essay is clear-eyed about the nature of Delors' ambitions, from removing border controls to the implementation of a European Monetary System. In light of this, Robertson set out three goals for his proposed campaign group: to raise awareness about the 'implications of the Single European Act'; to pressure all British politicians to 'state their position regarding a politically united Europe'; and to demand referendums throughout Europe 'to decide the question of national sovereignty.' For Robertson, the final demand was only an insurance policy. 'If we are forced to call for a referendum on national sovereignty,' he wrote, 'it will be because the European leaders will still be making demands for European integration.' In 1989, Robertson hoped that his support for Thatcher and the vision she set out at the College of Europe would be enough to derail this ambition. 'We are hoping that if the European Debate is properly exhausted, the issue of Federalism will recede into the background once more and we can concentrate on the business of making an economically powerful Europe.'

Over the next few months, the group's ranks would swell to include more than a hundred Conservative backbenchers, including arch Thatcher loyalists like Norman Tebbit and those long-term Eurosceptics of the ERG. Such was the success of the launch, Robertson quit his degree at Oxford to become the group's full-time secretary.

Each month, Robertson would publish reports by leading academics, usually with an introduction from Ralph Harris. A Bruges Group pamphlet published in November 1989 gives a flavour of the new group, its most prominent article a philosophical essay by the academic Alan Sked, one-time protégé of the historian A. J. P. Taylor and research companion to Norman Stone in Vienna, who was convenor of European studies at the LSE. Sked's central argument was that Europe's federalists were well-intentioned idealists guided by a mythical vision of historic unity. 'If we must worship at Europa's shrine, let us do so in the spirit of the ancient Greeks, rationally and in a balanced manner,' Sked argued.[21] In 1989, then, the Bruges Group remained a largely intellectual conservative outfit, intent on curbing what it saw as the idealistic excesses of European federalism. It was not for British withdrawal. Robertson would send the reports to the group's members, MPs and businessmen – and always to Thatcher herself. These reports would then be launched at events, often held at the Reform Club. At one of the Bruges Group's early meetings, Patrick Robertson and Dougie Smith crossed paths for the first time.

While Robertson was promoting his new campaign group, the Delors committee continued its slow, methodical work into the feasibility of European monetary union. Delors' major challenge was managing the imposing figure of Karl Otto Pöhl, who had considered boycotting the committee entirely in opposition to its aspiration of monetary union. Jacques de Larosière, the governor of the Banque de France, remembers Delors' 'extreme skill and objectivity' guiding the committee towards the conclusion he had always wanted. 'One of the great ways to make progress when your own authority is not unquestioned,' Delors later explained to Charles Grant, 'is to get others to promote your ideas.'[22]

In the end, that is what happened. The Delors committee called for economic and monetary union to be arrived at in three stages, each one leading inexorably to the next. The first stage should begin on 1 July 1990, when all member states should join the Exchange Rate Mechanism. Phase two would then begin after a new treaty had been agreed and ratified, creating a European Central Bank. Finally, each state's exchange rate would be fixed, with a single currency replacing national currencies.

All the hopes Thatcher had placed in Karl Otto Pöhl had come to nothing. The governor of the Bank of England, Robin Leigh-Pemberton, had also been swept along in the process. 'I wasn't prepared to look ridiculous and be a loner,' he later said. When he subsequently sent Thatcher a letter justifying his acceptance of Delors' report, she was so furious she refused to see him.[23]

The walls were now closing in. The next European summit was set to be held in Madrid in June, where the Delors agenda would surely be agreed. Britain either had to accept isolation or sign up to monetary union. Thatcher's two most important cabinet ministers, Geoffrey Howe and Nigel Lawson, both wanted Britain to join the ERM, though for different reasons. Howe was an instinctive European who shared the Foreign Office's preternatural allergy to 'isolation'. Lawson, meanwhile, had come to view the Exchange Rate Mechanism as a necessary tool to control inflation, but he opposed British membership of a European single currency, despite the fact that one followed the other. By the middle of 1989, in other words, the curious spectacle emerged of Thatcher raging against the reality that no one had hidden from her, while Lawson and Howe remained in denial about the implications of what was being proposed.

Thatcher had been told time and again that to maintain 'influence' she had to sign up to aspirations she did not believe in; the problem was, she was then held to what were, in reality, commitments. By 1989, she was reaching the end of her ability to maintain her own delusion. Not only did she not want to join a single European currency, but she also did not want to join a system of fixed exchange rates. Significant members of her cabinet saw things differently. A clash was all but inevitable.

On 4 May 1989 – the day Thatcher celebrated her tenth

anniversary as prime minister – Howe and Lawson met to discuss what to do about her obstinacy. The pair agreed to produce a joint paper setting out the diplomatic case for ERM membership and demanding a deadline to join. This would come to be known as the Madrid ambush.

Thatcher, however, resisted; on Friday, 23 June, two days before she was set to depart for Madrid, Howe and Lawson sent her another note demanding a further meeting, where they both threatened to resign if she did not agree to give way and set a timetable for British membership.

At the summit in Madrid that followed, Thatcher softened Britain's position on ERM, setting out, for the first time, concrete conditions for entry, but she avoided committing to a date. The move allowed the Madrid Council to agree moves towards monetary union without a date for the next 'intergovernmental council' to create a single currency having been fixed. Thatcher had lived to fight another day.

At the first cabinet after Madrid, Thatcher stood by the door to welcome Howe and Lawson. 'No resignations yet, I see,' she commented as they entered. To all intents and purposes, it looked as if she had called their bluff. The papers were full of praise, too. 'Thatcher wins hearts with charm offensive', purred *The Daily Telegraph*.[24]

From this position of strength, Thatcher decided it was time to break apart the Howe–Lawson axis. To Howe's dismay, he was summoned to Number Ten and offered the leadership of the House of Commons, while Lawson was kept in post. As Howe's replacement, Thatcher rubbed further salt into his wounded pride by promoting the inexperienced chief secretary to the Treasury, John Major. Major, Thatcher felt, was one of hers.

Though Major had all the appearances of being a modern Thatcherite, much of this came from a kind of glib assumption based on his background. In fact, Major was both more of a canny operator than many supposed and less ideological. Taken together with his inexperience, it was always unlikely that he would dissent from the institutional view presented by either the Foreign Office or, in time, the Treasury.

At the Conservative Party Conference in October, Thatcher's resistance in Europe secured her in the affections of the delegates, who chanted 'Ten more years!' An ageing Enoch Powell turned up to speak at a fringe meeting, and declared that he suddenly felt 'less on the fringe of that party than I have done for 20 years.'[25]

By October 1989, the government was running – in effect – two different policies: one through official channels, and one from Number Ten. Thatcher believed in floating exchange rates, monetarism and national sovereignty, but was pursuing a policy – officially, at least – to fix Britain's exchange rate. An explosion was coming.

The source of the ignition, in retrospect, seems odd: an article in the *Financial Times* quoting Thatcher's economic adviser, Alan Walters, criticizing the ERM as 'half baked'.[26] When Nigel Lawson saw the article, he was so outraged by what he believed to be an authorized hit job, he resigned, lamenting the incoherence of the government's policy. The exchange rate, Lawson declared, could either be treated as 'part of the maximum practicable market freedom' or 'part of the necessary financial discipline' required to control inflation. 'No case can be made for seeming confusion or for apparent vacillation between these two positions.'[27] In this, Lawson was obviously correct. To replace him, Thatcher moved John Major from the Foreign Office.

While all this was going on at home, world history shifted on its axis as the liberalizing reforms – perestroika – of Soviet leader Mikhail Gorbachev began to be felt across Eastern Europe and beyond.

In July 1989, Sir James Goldsmith delivered a speech in London warning that nationalist resentments against 'Russian ethnic domination' were growing throughout the Soviet Union and its Eastern European satellites, particularly Poland and Hungary, arguing that it would 'not be long before other colonialised [sic] people in Czechoslovakia, East Germany, and elsewhere start to stir'.

A copy of Goldsmith's speech was passed to Andrew Turnbull,

the prime minister's principal private secretary, by a member of Thatcher's Downing Street policy unit called George Guise. Guise had attached a note on top of the speech, saying 'the PM might find this interesting recess reading', before explaining that 'JG sent it to me recently and says he has had congratulatory notes from Kissinger and Nixon'.[28]

In the speech, Goldsmith had not simply predicted that seismic upheaval in the East was on its way, but warned the West not to be fooled into thinking it meant the end of the Cold War and Soviet power. Gorbachev was pursuing a carefully worked-out strategy, he argued, 'a honeytrap' to get the West to drop its guard by pretending to no longer be an enemy. Goldsmith predicted there would be a series of other manoeuvres to make the honeytrap more seductive, including, he wrote, 'the pulling down of the Berlin wall' and even withdrawal from Eastern Europe. This would all be part of Moscow's grand strategy to persuade the Americans to withdraw its forces, allowing Moscow to forge a 'pax Sovietica' with the demilitarized Western Europe.

Goldsmith's dark fantasy would prove remarkably prophetic, albeit not quite in the way he imagined. He warned that Gorbachev's grand strategy contained inherent risks for the Soviet Union in that it might unleash 'deep and widespread disturbances which even the forces of reaction would be unable to subjugate'. By the autumn, that is exactly what had happened, as Hungary opened its border with Austria, creating a breach in the wall through which millions of citizens from the old East could now pass.

Suddenly, a flood of East Germans began making their way to Hungary, demanding passage to the West – an embarrassment the East German authorities could not accept. On 3 October, the East German government banned travel to Czechoslovakia without a visa, closing off the route to Hungary. Mass demonstrations then began. By November, it was proving impossible for the East German authorities to maintain their ban on travel and the flood resumed. On 9 November, the East German government announced a new decree allowing travel across its own border into West Germany, including through West Berlin. With this, crowds began to make their way to the border. At first, guards tried to hold them back, only to then give up. The Berlin Wall had fallen and the Cold War was coming to an end.

In London, Charles Powell rushed to tell the prime minister to turn on her television. She didn't have one, so they went downstairs. According to Powell, Thatcher's first remark was, 'this is wonderful, everything we ever dreamed of, and the people are doing it, not the government.' But then, almost immediately, came the panic. 'My goodness! This is dangerous. We'd better be sure this doesn't get out of hand.' German reunification was happening, if not yet politically, then physically before her eyes. The next day, outside Downing Street, she spoke of her joy: 'A great day for freedom.' But, when asked whether she could live with a united Germany, she replied, 'I think you are going much too fast.'[29]

By this time, there was a growing realization that, to cope with a more powerful Germany, France would demand further European integration. Thatcher now faced not only the seemingly unstoppable momentum of German unification, but also a fresh impetus towards monetary union, both of which she opposed. After ten years in which she appeared to be on the 'right' side of history, able to bend events to her will, now she seemed powerless and even anachronistic. No longer was she slashing away at the obstacles to freedom, but acting as a blockage. Her moral authority, as her supporters saw it, was on the line. For those like Scruton and Stone, for example, the crumbling of the Soviet Union's European empire was a moment of great triumph for the West and for freedom – and for Thatcher.

At the Committee for a Free Britain, David Hart chartered a private plane for himself and his aides to meet the leaders of the resistance, as advised by Roger Scruton. Hart headed first to Warsaw, then to Prague, and finally to Budapest, where he met a young nationalist called Viktor Orbán.

For Dougie Smith, who accompanied Hart, the visit was an inspiration, everything he had dreamed of since reading about Peter Young's exploits a decade earlier. The old nations of Europe would soon rise again, European culture would rise again, and the barbarism of communism was coming to an end. However, Thatcher remained ambivalent, even reticent.

Thatcher was becoming isolated, not only in cabinet and Europe, but also with the United States, which under George H. W. Bush was throwing its weight behind Kohl's support for unification as part of a wider diplomatic shift towards Germany and away from Britain. For her critics at home, this was all evidence that her time was up. On 22 November, the dam burst when Conservative back-bencher Sir Anthony Meyer announced he would challenge her for the leadership. Meyer explained his challenge in *The Times*: 'Never has Thatcher's insistence on the retention of every scrap of national sovereignty seemed so dangerously unwise . . . The only safe haven for a united Germany, is a closely integrated Europe, modelled on the European Community.'[30] Here were the views of many of Thatcher's cabinet colleagues and critics. While it is obvious from her record that she had never insisted upon 'every scrap of national sovereignty', Meyer had nevertheless alighted on a deeper truth that, by this stage in her premiership, Thatcher was beginning to embrace a more fundamental critique of the EEC.

The day after Meyer announced his challenge, Thatcher flew to Washington to meet President Bush, arriving in an irritable mood after reading a Foreign Office telegram detailing Kohl's speech to the European Parliament, in which he declared the single market merely a 'staging post' on the road to 'European political union'. German and European unity, he said, were 'two sides of the same coin.' To make matters worse, President Bush then appeared to endorse Kohl's vision. 'It is my belief that the events of our time call for . . . a continued, perhaps even intensified, effort of the [EC] 12 to integrate,' he declared.[31]

Thatcher now faced a week in which both her leadership and her vision for the future of Europe were being challenged. In the leadership vote, she won the support of 314 of the 374 Conservative MPs, with thirty-three for Meyer and twenty-seven spoilt ballots. On the face of it, the result was a crushing victory. Yet, more than

15 per cent of her parliamentary party had refused to support her and, according to her whips, another forty had only supported her 'very reluctantly'.[32]

It was against this backdrop that Thatcher flew to Strasbourg for another European Council. Once again, she wanted to oppose the idea of a new 'intergovernmental conference' on the next stages of monetary union, but was advised that she was too isolated to do so. Instead, she tried to attach conditions – that she would agree to a new summit, but only if Stages II and III of Delors' plan for monetary union were delayed until the effects of Stage I could be assessed. Even here, she was unsuccessful. The Council broke up with an agreement that there would be a summit on the Delors Report, held in the Dutch town of Maastricht in December 1991. Thatcher had lost.

On New Year's Day 1990, Thatcher awoke in Chequers, where she had spent the night celebrating the new decade with family and friends. She was the most dominant and consequential prime minister since Churchill. In her first term, she had stuck to her course at home and won a war abroad. In the second, she had defeated the miners, helped create the European single market and let the City of London rip. And in her third, she had seen her vision of Cold War victory come to pass. Yet, at the dawn of the new decade, she was being swept along by events she could no longer control.

After she had returned from Strasbourg, she received a message from Enoch Powell, who told her that she had taken her place 'in the line of succession of Winston Churchill and William Pitt'. Isolation should not be a concern, he said. 'Those who lead are always out in front, alone.' Thatcher replied, 'I am deeply touched by your words. They give me the greatest possible encouragement.'[33]

Throughout the first few months of 1990, Thatcher remained fixated on the German question, but soon realized the powerlessness of her position. At a seminar on Germany, at Chequers, her opposition to unification was successfully worn down by the new foreign secretary Douglas Hurd, who counselled against becoming an 'ineffective brake'.[34] Her choice was either to maintain the illusion of British influence by going along with something she disagreed with, or to reveal the reality of Britain's diplomatic impotence by unsuccessfully opposing.

Over the next few months, Hurd and Major used all their skills to move Thatcher away from her hostility to both German unification and British membership of the ERM. On 24 March 1990, Thatcher convened another Chequers meeting on Germany, this time with voices from outside Whitehall. For those attending, the purpose was to bring her into line. Charles Powell helped draw up the guest list: Hugh Trevor-Roper, Timothy Garton Ash, George Urban and Norman Stone.

Ahead of the summit, Charles Powell wrote to Thatcher proposing some questions to consider, including whether the character and behaviour of the Germans had changed in the last forty years or whether they were 'the same old Huns'. Despite the jingoism, the summit is notable for its seriousness. 'We have to build a new framework for the future,' Thatcher wrote on the top of Powell's note, 'for defence, for cooperation beyond Europe and try to see how we can bring the Soviet Union to a real western democracy with economic as well as political freedom.' She then added: 'We must consider Central Europe and its minorities, and how our security could be upset from the Middle East.'[35]

Though Thatcher was undoubtedly trying and failing to stop unification in part because of her Germanophobia, her concerns nevertheless show more foresight than most at this time, sketching the outlines of many of the problems that would eventually come to pass.

Philosophically, she was also quick to reject the notion that the end of the Cold War had signalled an 'end of history'. Thatcher did not believe the essential nature of international affairs had changed, only the sources of power that needed to be balanced. 'We must widen the discussion to include the future of the USSR – (and of Russia),' she wrote, 'and whether we pursue spheres of influence, or alliance of democracy or geographical alliances.' Thatcher rounds off her note with a final flourish, offering one of the more revealing glimpses of her understanding of the world: 'It seems to me that while in the past, history was determined largely by the personalities and ambitions of the rulers of people, in future it will be decided much more by the character of the people.' In the democratic age, national myths and legends would not matter less; they would matter more.[36]

The experts assembled at Chequers, though of widely different character, all agreed that Britain had little to worry about from a united Germany. Even Norman Stone felt Thatcher had been too curmudgeonly about unification. 'I would really have liked her to say straightforwardly that we now had the Germany that had needed two world wars to create, that the good Germans were in charge,' Stone later wrote of the summit. Instead, he simply reassured her that Germany was not the powerhouse it looked. 'I said the unification was a good thing,' he recalled. 'In fact, the best thing that had happened in my lifetime; that there was no danger of a Fourth Reich or some such.' In the end, the conference worked. 'All right, I'll be nice to the Germans,' Thatcher declared.[37]

However nice she had resolved to be, her political problems at home did not go away, as opposition to the poll tax escalated into protests across the country and an outright riot in central London. At this time – the spring of 1990 – John Major began pushing his bid for British entry into the ERM, arguing that Thatcher needed to give way to be able to secure an 'opt in' to the single currency, which would allow the country to defer entry without rejecting the principle of a single currency. In weighing up her decision, Charles Powell cautioned about her domestic weakness. 'If the overall situation were better, you would not be hearing so much of the ERM issue', he wrote. 'The questions to be answered are whether it is politically feasible to resist this once again.'[38]

While Thatcher continued to fight against the principle of monetary union, she was being worn down on the narrower question of ERM. By June, Major wrestled out of her a commitment to enter on principle. By July, he was pushing for a date of entry. Thatcher accepted 14 September and 5 October as 'two candidates.' The Treasury took this as a green light. The momentum was now impossible to resist. A final rally of opposition came on 14 July when Nicholas Ridley, Thatcher's most important cabinet ally over ERM, resigned after giving an interview to *The Spectator* describing EMU as a 'German racket designed to take over the whole of Europe.'[39] Thatcher subsequently described Ridley's remarks as 'an excess of honesty' in her biography.[40]

As the summer lengthened, the intensity of life in Number Ten showed no sign of easing. On 30 July, her close friend and ally Ian Gow was murdered by the IRA with a bomb planted under his car. Two days later, as she travelled to Aspen, Colorado, to meet President Bush, Saddam Hussein invaded Kuwait. And, amid all of this, Major kept pushing on the ERM. The 'greatest political dividend' would come from joining before the Conservative Party Conference, he counselled. ERM was like ageing, he added: 'You don't like it, but you can't avoid it.' Once more, the argument of historic inevitability was deployed.[41]

Finally, on 3 October, Thatcher relented. Britain would go in on 5 October. It was, Charles Powell recalled, 'a necessary compromise'. But the truth was clear: 'She no longer really had the power.'[42] The date was chosen in part to overshadow the Labour Party Conference and to provide a fair wind before the Tories assembled the week after. No matter that Thatcher's Madrid conditions had not been met, or that inflation had reached 10 per cent and the value of the pound against the Deutschmark was considered by many to be too high.

At the Tory conference in October, she made the best of her decision, but insisted, to the delight of the audience, that it didn't mean accepting further integration. 'As John Major made absolutely clear yesterday,' Thatcher declared, 'this Government has no intention of agreeing to the imposition of a single currency. That would be entering a federal Europe through the back-Delors.'[43] Yet that was exactly the point of ERM: the first step on the journey to a single currency, the timetable for which would be agreed in Rome at the next summit of European leaders. Helmut Kohl was pushing for the Council to agree 1994 as the start date for Stage II.

Thatcher had to decide whether to continue fighting a losing battle to stop monetary union altogether or to sanction its creation without British involvement. As the French official Pierre de Boissieu had put it to John Kerr: 'You've lost.' Thatcher still disagreed. 'She thought she could stop it,' recalled Kerr.[44]

Before the summit, Thatcher dined with François Mitterrand at the British ambassador's residence in a philosophical mood. Their discussion that lunchtime delved into the questions of history and identity at the heart of Europe's very idea of itself. Enlargement was risky, Mitterrand told her. In his estimation, 'Eastern Europe was a different world. Nationalism was breaking out all over . . . The Teutonic Knights would ride again.' Thatcher, meanwhile, warned her counterpart that the French strategy to contain German power through European integration would fail. 'If you insisted on a Community in which we all had to give up our national sovereignty, you would soon find that Germany was dominant.' At this point in their careers, Thatcher and Mitterrand were comfortable in each other's company. It would be a different story when the summit itself began. A text was produced on monetary union, which Thatcher said was 'completely unacceptable'. Yet she was powerless to stop the others going ahead. 'I just had to say no,' she said of her refusal to support the summit's conclusions.[45]

Thatcher left the summit before it had concluded, departing after a press conference in which she denounced what had happened as 'quite absurd.' For the first time, the conclusions of the summit were released with one member dissenting. The evening after Thatcher arrived home, she bumped into Charles Moore at a reception in Downing Street. 'She asked whether I had read Enoch's speeches,' Moore recorded. She then added: 'They were so good.' Thatcher told him that she would 'never' ask Parliament to abolish the pound and was 'happy to fight the next election on Europe.'[46]

The next day, the atmosphere in Parliament had reached fever pitch. Patrick Robertson travelled to Westminster to watch the prime minister's statement. Ahead of the debate, Thatcher's office provided her with some briefing notes, including an article in *The Daily Telegraph* from its European Communities correspondent, Boris Johnson, which had appeared on 24 October under the headline, 'British right of veto faces axe in Delors plan'.[47]

In the chamber, Thatcher declared that Britain would retain its currency 'unless a decision to abolish it were freely taken by future generations of Parliament and people.' In response, Neil Kinnock – now a pro-European – argued that Britain did not have to lose the pound under the proposed single currency. 'You can perfectly well have a note or a coin which states its value in pounds,' he said, 'and its fixed equivalent in ecu [European Currency Unit].' As ever, on questions of Europe, wilful blindness affected all sides. It was in reply that Thatcher then made her famous peroration. 'The President of the Commission, Mr Delors, said in a press conference the other day that he wanted the European Parliament to be the democratic body of the Community, he wanted the Commission to be the Executive and he wanted the Council of Ministers to be the Senate. No. No. No.'[48]

It was not only Thatcher who was dismissive of Kinnock's line of argument. Rising from the Labour benches, Tony Benn told the prime minister that what was under discussion was not economic management, 'but the whole future of relations between this country and Europe.' It was not a question of the design of a currency, Benn went on, but 'whether, when the British people vote in a general election, they will be able to change the policies of the previous Government.' And he had harsh words for the prime minister:

> Given that the right hon. Lady is a member of the Government who took us into the European Community without consulting the British people, given that she was Prime

> Minister in the Government who agreed to the Single European Act without consulting the British people, and given that she has now agreed to joining the exchange rate mechanism without consulting the British people, we find it hard to believe that she is really intent on preserving democracy rather than gaining political advantage by waving some national argument around on the eve of a general election.

Thatcher replied that, while she would 'put it just a little differently from the right hon. Gentleman', she did 'recognise some of the force of some of the points that he makes.'[49]

A moment of decision was approaching. Europe was changing and with it the fundamentals of British membership. 'The Act that enabled us to go into Europe was passed on Second Reading by eight votes and it was made very clear then that we would not surrender our national identity,' Thatcher argued. 'I am afraid that it would be quite different if we went for a single European currency and a central bank and for their definition of economic and monetary union.'[50]

After watching Thatcher's performance, Geoffrey Howe declared to a friend that she was 'using her political capital to shift the centre of gravity of the Conservative Party in an anti-European direction'. Howe resigned two days later and made his position clear in a letter: 'I am deeply anxious that the mood you have struck – most notably in Rome this weekend and in the House of Commons this Tuesday – will make it more difficult for Britain to . . . retain a position of influence in this vital debate,' he wrote, explaining his decision.

Howe's resignation sparked a period of intense speculation about a fresh leadership challenge. It would fall to Howe, once again, to pull the trigger a fortnight later. On Tuesday, 13 November, Thatcher's long-serving ally stood up in the House of Commons to deliver a speech of such quiet, concentrated antagonism, it would spell the end for the most dominant prime minister of post-war Britain. Howe revealed that he and Lawson had threatened to resign before Madrid, claimed entry to the ERM should have taken place five years earlier and warned that the prime minister was leading the country into 'a ghetto of sentimentality'.

Like Kinnock, Howe argued there was a third way on monetary union: a 'common' currency rather than a single currency, as he put it, allowing Britain to keep the pound and avoid isolation. Howe accused Thatcher of fatally undermining the prospects of this compromise by ruling out the essential ingredients necessary for such a scheme to work: permanently fixed exchange rates, a central bank and common monetary policy. In her off-the-cuff remark that no one in Europe would ever actually use such a common currency, she had then further undermined her own ministers, Howe argued. 'It is rather like sending your opening batsmen to the crease only for them to find, the moment the first balls are bowled, that their bats have been broken before the game by the team captain,' Howe declared, to laughter.[51]

It is impossible to reach a definitive judgement about the veracity of Howe's argument; there are simply too many counterfactuals. Had Thatcher thrown her full support behind the 'hard ecu' common currency proposal, could Britain really have stopped the emergence of the single currency? What is clear is that Howe's optimism about a possible third way was part of a recurring fantasy in Britain's foreign policy since 1950, with little evidence to support it. Anthony Eden had insisted that the British government could join the negotiations to form a Coal and Steel Community without accepting the principle upon which it was founded. Harold Macmillan had tried to find a way to avoid the choice between integration and isolation, with grand schemes that saw the Common Market being folded into a wider European free trade area. Now, Howe was trying something similar.

Britain was approaching a choice it could not avoid: to abolish its national currency or to remain outside while the others pushed ahead. Howe argued this was a false choice being forced upon Britain by the failures of its reactionary prime minister. 'I have done what I believe to be right for my party and my country,' he declared, before plunging his rhetorical dagger at the last. 'The time has come for others to consider their own response.'[52]

The next day, Michael Heseltine launched his challenge for the leadership; with it, the endgame for Thatcher had begun. The first ballot was set for Tuesday, 20 November, when Thatcher was due in Paris for the Conference on Security and Cooperation in Europe marking the end of the Cold War. In other circumstances, it might have formed part of a harmonious final note of triumph for the prime minister and her supporters, marking their ideological victory over communism. Instead, Thatcher was in the British embassy when the results were conveyed to her over the phone. She had won, but not by enough: 204 votes to Heseltine's 152, with sixteen abstentions. Had she taken two more votes off her rival, she would have won outright, avoiding the need for a second ballot. 'For want of a nail a kingdom was lost,' wrote Alan Clark in his diary.[53] While her first instinct was to fight on, she was eventually persuaded that the game was up. On 22 November 1990, Margaret Thatcher announced she would not stand in the second round. It was all over.

Patrick Robertson remembers the moment he heard the news; he soon found himself walking the streets in a trance, the political hopes he had placed in Thatcher's vision extinguished. For the cohort of former Tory student radicals, there was a similar sense of trauma. The mystical connection they felt with Number Ten had been cut. Thatcher was their icon and protector. Some of them had even gone on Robert Kilroy-Silk's popular daytime chat show, *Kilroy*, to defend her. Now, she was gone. Those who had brought her down quickly became hate figures for the Tory grassroots, Heseltine in particular. But, more than that, the proximate cause of her downfall – Europe – became a defining issue for the right in a way that it had previously not. With the Cold War coming to an end, Thatcher had raised the banner for something new. Until then, being anti-Common Market had carried with it an air of mustiness:

an old battle that had gone. With her defenestration, everything changed.

In the press that weekend, Enoch Powell insisted that the struggle continued. 'The battle has been lost, but not the war,' he declared, much as he had always insisted.[54] The stridency of Thatcher's opposition to monetary union had played a central role in losing the premiership; the scale of Britain's isolation in Europe had been too much for her party to bear.

The job of returning Britain to the heart of Europe would fall to John Major, not Michael Heseltine, after the party's Thatcherites rallied to the man they concluded was best placed to defeat their hero's assassin. Howe had resisted Thatcher to stop the centre of gravity of the Conservative Party moving in an anti-European direction. But the battle for control of the party was only just beginning.

The sense of an era ending was compounded when the doyen of conservative philosophy and former Phantom, Michael Oakeshott, died in December. 'The death of Michael Oakeshott this week at the age of eighty-nine, so soon after the departure of the prime minister whose views owed so much to his, merits more than a passing obituary,' wrote *The Times* in its tribute. Oakeshott, the paper said, was 'nothing less than the chief reanimator of conservatism after the long dominance of socialism over political theory in 20th-century Britain.'[55]

Though Thatcher's premiership owed more to Hayek than Oakeshott at first glance, *The Times* argued, this was a misreading. 'Where Hayek, in the spirit of classic liberalism, criticised central planning and the omnicompetent state on a global scale, Mrs Thatcher and Oakeshott had more a confined and local scope,' the paper said. 'The rights and interests that concerned them are the rights enjoyed and the interests pursued by the British people, as a result of a long and unique historical process.' Thatcher's revolution, in other words, was not just conservative, but British. And it had not yet finished.

Chapter 10

From the moment Thatcher was removed from power, Patrick Robertson felt his influence drain away. MPs began to make excuses, donors' chequebooks closed and calls went unanswered. 'They could see who had the power and they gravitated towards it,' Robertson reflected.[1]

On his first day as prime minister, speaking outside Number Ten, John Major moved to define himself against his predecessor. 'I believe very firmly in the 1990s that we will have a decade of the most remarkable opportunities,' he declared, enthusiastically. 'We have in front of us the building and development of an entirely new Europe, a building and development in which this country will play a full and leading role.'[2]

In one sense, there was nothing new in Major's statement. Throughout the 1980s, Thatcher had sought to play a full and leading role in Europe. Indeed, she had declared this her policy in Bruges, two years earlier. Yet there was undoubtedly a shift in tone, masking a real shift in substance underneath. 'She disliked EMU on sovereignty and economic grounds and believed that the project was folly that should be resisted,' Stephen Wall, Major's private secretary from 1991, later reflected of Thatcher. 'Major saw that, in some form, it was inevitable and he was not going to fight an unwinnable battle to prevent Britain's partners from going ahead.'[3] The argument of inevitability was back.

For Thatcher, meanwhile, the question of Europe quickly became her chief obsession – an obsession which offered Patrick

Robertson an opportunity to recover some relevance: perhaps she could be persuaded to get involved in the Bruges Group? According to Robertson, a dinner was arranged with Ralph Harris, and a formal offer made. Thatcher was to become honorary president of the Bruges Group.

This is Robertson's version of events, though the newspapers at the time did not report it that way. 'Thatcher surprised to be made Bruges Group chief', ran the headline in *The Times*. The paper put the confusion down to the difficulties of life after power, with only a small team to run her affairs, while noting that 'some Conservatives viewed her involvement with apprehension,' worried that she would use the position to undermine her successor. Ted Heath was less concerned. 'It will allow her to show herself in her true colours,' he said. And besides, 'the Bruges Group is a very, very small minority of the Conservative Party.'[4]

The problem for the Bruges Group was that, before Thatcher's removal from power, it had managed to remain enough of a broad church to contain figures who were not Conservative. By making Thatcher honorary president, any ambivalence about its political orientation was removed, marking it out not just as an anti-federalist pressure group, but a distinctly Tory one, acting in opposition to a Tory government.

Over the course of 1991, this subtle change of identity began to eat away at its effectiveness. During that year, despite the looming Maastricht summit in December, the group only managed to release one report with unanimous support of its committee: a paper authored by Norman Stone's old friend from Vienna, Alan Sked, who had become one of the founding members of the group in 1989 and quickly established himself as one of its most effective writers.

Sked – like Patrick Robertson, Dougie Smith, Michael Gove, Niall Ferguson, Teddy Taylor and Norman Stone – was a right-wing Scot living in England; though, unlike the others, not a Tory. A Liberal in his Scottish youth, he had moved south to Oxford and then to the LSE, establishing its European studies programme.

It was in this guise during the 1980s that Sked came to see 'Europe' as anti-democratic. Soon after joining the Bruges Group, Sked became Patrick Robertson's go-to academic to author the group's papers, able to combine the rigour of academia with the polemicism of a true believer.

In this context of political division and declining influence, Robertson turned to Sked in April 1991, asking him to write a press release about the situation in Iraq, where Saddam Hussein's forces were wreaking revenge on those who had risen against his regime, most notably the Kurds.

Watching on, Thatcher had begun agitating for further Western intervention, much to her successor's frustration. 'Action was already in hand,' Major wrote dismissively in his autobiography, years later.[5] Keen to make good on his promise to place Britain 'at the very heart of Europe,' as he had declared in a speech in Germany, Major gave the Foreign Office the green light to work on a diplomatic initiative that he could launch at the upcoming European Council in Luxembourg without prior consultation with the Americans, a prospect unthinkable had Thatcher remained in power. And it worked. 'They were delighted with the novelty of endorsing a British proposal launched through the EU,' Major reflected.[6] After winning Europe's backing, he took the proposal to the Americans, who endorsed it.

For Robertson and Sked, this was all just a transparent attempt to buy influence in Europe. In response, they put together a statement condemning Major's handling of the crisis, which they sent out as a Bruges Group press release, accusing the prime minister of prematurely agreeing to a ceasefire. This decision, they said, had allowed Saddam Hussein to commit atrocities against his own people – a situation Thatcher would not have allowed to happen. 'In short, was the price paid for the overthrow of Mrs Thatcher paid for with the blood of thousands of innocent Iraqis?' the press release asked.[7] Robertson and Sked thought little of it, but then all hell broke loose. 'When I came home, I switched on *Channel 4 News*, just in time to hear Jon Snow reading out our press release in very serious tones,' Sked recalled years later, a flash of amusement still visible.[8]

The press loved it. Here was a group of Thatcherite holdouts, honorarily presided over by their heroine, attacking her successor. Robertson had overstepped the mark and was made to feel the full weight of the new Conservative Party leadership. 'It was three days of hell,' he remembers.[9] Both Ralph Harris and Thatcher distanced themselves and declared their loyalty to Major. Robertson and Sked offered their resignations – though, pointedly, Thatcher did not.

Whatever statement Thatcher was trying to make by not resigning, the Bruges Group was in trouble. *The Times* ran a feature on 'the twin angry men behind outburst', and predicted both might well be finished in British politics. 'Mr Sked will almost certainly have to leave the council,' *The Times* reported. 'Mr Robertson may rue abandoning his Oxford degree. He is no longer assured of the starry career in politics that he had assumed would be his.'[10] A leader in the same day's paper argued the Bruges Group itself was finished. 'Pressure groups are the democratic topsoil of the political landscape,' the leader ran. 'The Bruges Group may have risen too far too fast. But its more distinguished members will soon find safe havens on other mastheads.'[11]

From this point onwards, the Bruges Group was reduced to little more than firing off press releases to keep up its profile. The urbane Kenneth Minogue, a protégé of Michael Oakeshott, replaced Ralph Harris as chairman and the group tilted even further away from the type of robust political campaigning Robertson and Sked wanted.

Eventually, Robertson was offered a way out by the World Economic Forum in Switzerland. It marked the end of a remarkable journey. In a little over three years, he'd gone from a first-year student at Oxford to Thatcherite wunderkind and, finally, defeated rebel. 'We'd lost,' as Robertson recalled.[12] It would take Sked a little while longer to leave, but, as *The Times* predicted, he would quickly re-emerge.

This was a strange time for Thatcher's old guard of Cold Warriors, a moment when they felt both triumphant and powerless. Norman Stone summed up the feeling of this milieu with an article in *The Sunday Times* hailing those who had, in his view, seen the Soviet Union for what it was. As ever, Stone was scathing about the Foreign Office and its favoured think tanks, reserving his praise only for those who had dared challenge the consensus of ever-lasting détente. 'There were some, such as Brian Crozier and his Institute for the Study of Conflict, who got it right,' Stone noted, as well as the one-time CIA-backed *Encounter* magazine.[13] The irony of Stone's account, here, is that most of the individuals and institutions who stood outside the Cold War consensus in this way also took a decidedly conventional view of 'Europe', regarding European unity as a necessary bulwark against Soviet aggression. Thatcher's increasing willingness to challenge the direction of European integration made her the first great figure of the Cold War to be associated with Euroscepticism.

But, with the Cold War over, what was left for Stone, Crozier and other warriors? For many of these figures, the Cold War had been the prism through which all else was judged.

Dougie Smith, alongside another member of the Committee for a Free Britain, leading libertarian Paul Staines, had become involved in the 'Freedom to Party' campaign to protect Britain's underground rave scene from a government clampdown. Indeed, it was at a rally of thousands of people in Trafalgar Square in January 1990 that Smith would make his last public speech, while Staines turned the CFB's offices nearby into a one-day pirate radio station, broadcasting dissident acid house to his underground comrades.[14]

With the Cold War over, geopolitics had morphed into an altogether more complicated and disparate set of international challenges to bring the old communist states into the global democratic order. One such place was the tiny former British colony of Seychelles, where the one-time Soviet-aligned leader France-Albert René began making diplomatic overtures to Washington for financial help, opening the prospect of a return to multiparty democracy.

Sir James Mancham, the pro-British former prime minister, had been ousted by René in a military coup. A favourite of the Cold Warrior right, Mancham was living in exile in London at the time, but, with multiparty elections now on the cards, he contacted the Committee for a Free Britain to see if it would be interested in helping to return him to power. Several of the FCS alumni, including Smith, were only too happy to escape what they saw as the grey drudgery of John Major's Britain and signed up for a twelve-month posting.

In Parliament, meanwhile, a group of MPs had formed, calling themselves the Friends of Bruges Group, meeting under the leadership of Bill Cash, the man Thatcher considered 'the ultimate torchbearer' on European questions.[15] It was then that the term 'Eurosceptic' first began to be used in British political discourse. Cash's own journey to Thatcherite ultra is a curious one. Born on the day Winston Churchill became prime minister in 1940, he – like Norman Stone – had lost his father to the war: killed in action in Normandy, in 1944. In the early months of 1991, Cash joined Nicholas Ridley, Norman Tebbit and a backbench MP called Michael Spicer to keep the 'fire of Thatcherism burning,' as Spicer put it in his diary. By February, they had decided to set up 'a high command' to coordinate the remaining Thatcherite 'networks of journalists, MPs, academics etc'. By March, this had turned into an informal 'steering group' with two core priorities: defending the poll tax and, of course, opposing further European integration.[16]

The first meeting of the steering group took place on Monday, 15 April, at the height of the furore over the Bruges Group's attack on John Major. 'Bruges Group has recently launched personal attack on PM and view is that this was very stupid,' Spicer noted in his diary. By the following month, it was becoming difficult for any of them to even be seen associating with Robertson's outfit. 'The thought police, i.e. the whips . . . now forbid ministers to talk to the Bruges Group,' he wrote.[17]

For most of 1991, Thatcher stayed in the shadows, letting her steering group outriders do the talking. Spicer and his allies drew up anti-federalist motions, wrote letters to newspapers and gave speeches criticizing the government's policies, channelling Thatcher, but at a deniable distance.

After she left office, Thatcher suffered what John O'Sullivan described as 'something of a nervous breakdown'.[18] To keep her busy, many of those close to her began organizing conferences which she could attend and even chair, though the main source of interest was her memoirs. Over the next three years, Thatcher and her writing team, including O'Sullivan but led by the historian and former director of the Conservative Research Department, Robin Harris, would regularly retire to grand international hotels to complete this work – the Gstaad Palace in Switzerland and Lyford Cay in the Bahamas were two favourites. All the while, the looming challenge for her successor was the upcoming European summit in Maastricht.

Though a supporter of British membership of ERM, Major had concluded that the economic conditions were not yet right for British entry into the single currency itself, and so, much like Thatcher, he wanted to avoid any commitments on timing. However, unlike Thatcher, he did not oppose British membership on principle and thought it prudent to keep the option alive should he or, more likely, a future prime minister conclude it was in the national interest. While the media quickly characterized this as dithering, it was also conventional statecraft.

Major's central problem was that the rest of Europe was committed to EMU, particularly France and Germany. The British ambassador in Paris, Sir Ewen Fergusson, sent a despatch to the Foreign Office in May 1991 reporting that it had become 'axiomatic' in France that the newly united Germany would become a European superpower and therefore needed to be contained 'within reinforced European structures as quickly and thoroughly as possible'. The central thrust of this strategy was EMU, 'a means of getting a handle on German monetary policy before their economy recovers its former vigour and lest Kohl's Europeanist policies be replaced with more assertive nationalist ones'.[19] The fear of Germany was once again driving European integration.

When Kohl saw Major at Chequers in June, he told the prime minister that he understood the French concerns and was determined to assuage them. As such, he wanted Maastricht to refer to Europe's 'federal goal' – 'the process of creating the United States of Europe.'[20]

For Major, this was a nightmare in terms of party management, but what could he do about it? By early autumn, talk had turned to a mooted third way – 'the Delors compromise' – whereby Major would not veto the proposed new treaty, permitting all other countries to go ahead with the single currency, common citizenship and social charter – but with opt-outs for Britain. For Michael Spicer and those around Thatcher, such talk was unacceptable. 'This would legitimise it all,' he told the chancellor, Norman Lamont, over drinks one evening. 'The pressure for us to join this would be immense.'[21]

It was then that Alan Sked finally pushed his colleagues at the Bruges Group too far. In October 1991, he declared his intention to set up a new political party to fight Maastricht. In a letter to *The Times*, he declared 'the only way to influence government policy is to threaten it with defeat . . . I therefore propose to chair a committee to establish an anti-federalist league, open to men and women of all parties and none, with the express object of running candidates against Conservative, Labour and Liberal Democrat MPs who would vote for a Maastricht treaty.'[22]

Sked had clung on as a member of the Bruges Group since the scandal over the press release regarding the plight of the Kurds in Iraq earlier in the year. But to openly campaign against the Tories was too much. Kenneth Minogue asked Sked to stay away from the Bruges Group's executive meeting, but he decided to gatecrash the public event that followed, anyway. 'Ken, who didn't know I was there, started telling the room how much of a pity it was that I had chosen to retire,' Sked later recalled with amusement. Sked then stood up and declared he hadn't retired at all, but had been sacked for setting up the Anti-Federalist League. 'At the end of that meeting, people came up to sympathize with me'.[23] One of those was Nigel Farage. 'That was the first time I ever met him,' claims Sked, although Farage insists they first met at a meeting of the Campaign for an Independent Britain, at Westminster Central Hall, the following year. In any case, Farage soon joined Sked's new Anti-Federalist League and its executive committee.

Divorced, with two kids, strapped for cash and drinking his way through life as a metals trader in the City, Farage appeared to be just another marginal, reactionary, public-school Tory working in finance.

He was brought up in the Kentish village of Downe, which is nestled in one of the last green folds of rural Tory England before it meets the concrete sprawl of the capital. As such, Farage was able to straddle town and country, old and new, conservative and reactionary. From Downe, he was sent to Dulwich College – an unlikely starting point for one of the most significant anti-establishment insurgents ever to emerge in British politics, a man who would do more than any parliamentary leader or prime minister to upend the consensus on British membership of the European Union.

From the moment Farage arrived at Dulwich, the character that would later become famous began to reveal itself. 'He was very confident, articulate, forthright,' recalls Peter Petyt, an early classmate. 'You could tell he would be someone in life.'[24] But what really set him apart was not his character, but his politics. Many of Farage's classmates remember him as 'very Conservative', but others go further. His views were so right wing, they were seen by some as beyond the bounds of acceptability. One teacher, Bob Jope, later told Farage's biographer Michael Crick that he had thrown him out of one of his classes for yelling anti-Semitic abuse. A contemporary, Nick Gordon Brown, claimed he was 'a very vocal National Front supporter,' while another, Tim France, said

Farage openly supported the 'British Movement' – the extremist group which later called itself the British National Socialist Movement. 'He was a deeply unembarrassed racist,' another classmate, David Edmonds, told Crick.[25]

Farage has always rejected the allegation that he was a racist or extremist at school. 'Was I a difficult, bolshie teenager who pushed the boundaries of debate further than perhaps I ought to have done? Yes . . . Have I ever been a member of any extremist organisation, left or right? No.' In *Fighting Bull*, his autobiography, he claims some of the outrage was because of his 'spirited defence of Enoch Powell', who had visited the school during Farage's time there and had the young boy in raptures.[26]

What was it that Farage admired in Powell? The two figures are, in many ways, antithetical. Powell was a classicist of profound academic rigour, filled with Victorian notions of duty; a cauldron of Romantic passions just below the surface of his ascetic demeanour; a man so moved by the beauty of Wagnerian opera, for example, that he avoided listening for fear of being emotionally overwhelmed. Nigel Farage was a man nobody would describe as either a scholar or an ascetic. His teachers advised him not to go to university, but to follow his father into the City. He is a Jack-the-Lad reactionary, more comfortable fishing or going to the pub than brooding about mortality and the meaning of life. What Farage *did* share with Powell were several powerful political instincts: a deep Englishness and a corresponding hostility to immigration and Europe.

As Maurice Cowling had long understood, Powell's unique role in post-war British politics had been that of a Tory tribune, representing a certain instinct of working-class England, the leader of a rebellion against the ruling parliamentary majority.* Farage would become Powell's heir in this regard: the instinctive populist vessel of Powellism.

---

* *Tory Tribune* was the title of the first biography of Enoch Powell, written by *Guardian* journalist Andrew Roth.

Irrespective of the complaints of students and teachers, Farage has insisted he was never anything other than a mainstream Conservative during his time at school, joining the party in 1978 after listening to Thatcher's ideological mentor, Keith Joseph, who had come to Dulwich to deliver a lecture. 'I had never joined anything in my life,' Farage later said. 'But the following day I joined my local Conservative party.'[27] It seemed the natural and obvious choice for this almost cartoonishly reactionary schoolboy.

For most of the 1980s, working in the City, Farage remained a Conservative Party member, but in the elections to the European Parliament in 1989, he voted for the Eurosceptic Greens. From here, he drifted to the Bruges Group, and then into Alan Sked's Anti-Federalist League, where he began to find his voice.

For John Major, such factional intrigue was of little real concern. The Tories had a comfortable majority. The Bruges Group had been neutered, and he had a treaty to negotiate. Finally, in November, Major unveiled his plan: he would negotiate an opt-in compromise that would allow Parliament to vote to join a single currency 'when the option is a realistic one.' Major declared that 'it would be wrong now to decide to join a single currency but it would be equally wrong to decide now that in no circumstances will we ever do so.'[28]

In a debate in the House of Commons on 20 November, Major set out the nature of the choice facing Britain with a candour reminiscent of the exchanges between Attlee and Eden forty years earlier. 'For many of our Community partners,' he declared, 'the diminution of the power of national Governments and national Parliaments is not an issue.' For Britain, though, it was. '*They* accept the idea of a European federation,' he went on. '*We* have never done so.' The division between 'they' and 'we' which Heath had hoped to dissolve remained.[29]

Major then set out his position as a mildly Eurosceptic pro-European: 'When we joined, we accepted that Community law would take precedence over national law, but for that very reason we have always been concerned about the extent of Community law – precisely because it took precedence.' Britain, he said, was not opposed to reform, but was not prepared to accept 'wholesale changes in the nature of the Community which would lead it toward an unacceptable dominance over our national life.'[30] During this debate, Thatcher proposed that the way out of this conundrum was a referendum on the single currency.

The central challenge for Major, however, was that Britain's European partners were committed to exactly the 'wholesale changes in the nature of the Community' that he opposed, in large part because of the wholesale change of Europe since the fall of the Berlin Wall. The prime minister was trying to reconcile two irreconcilable policy positions: to lead in Europe, and to opt out of its central policy.

When Maastricht was finally agreed in December, the European Union was born, now formally an entity in international law, with its own citizenry, central bank and, eventually, currency.* It was Europe's Great Leap Forward, the most important step in its long evolution since the Treaty of Rome. Though Maastricht did not meet the most aspirational federalist ambitions, dividing the way the bloc was governed into three distinct 'pillars' still largely controlled by the member states rather than the Commission, it expanded the scope of its responsibilities into almost all areas of policy, from defence to asylum and immigration. As Anand Menon, Professor of European Politics and Foreign

---

* Formally, the European Union only came into being after the German constitutional court gave its assent in October 1993. Four German Green Party MEPs and a former Commission official had challenged the Treaty's constitutionality. The Court ruled that the Treaty had not created a European State with unlimited powers; this would have undermined the Bundestag's democratic authority, which was sacrosanct. The Court also stated that Germany's Basic Law allowed for further European integration, 'as long as the members of the Union remain States and do not become administrative districts of a European State,' as the *European Journal of International Law* summarized its ruling. (Wieland, Joachim: 'Germany in the European Union – The Maastricht Decision of the Bundesverfassungsgericht', *The European Journal of International Law*, Volume 5, Issue 2, Oxford University Press 1994)

Affairs at King's College London, put it: 'Maastricht marked the formal end of a period in which European integration was done by stealth. Now it was open for all to see and could no longer be said to simply impact on purely technical areas, to the extent that was ever true.'[31]

Yet, for those who wanted to see greater integration, Maastricht remains a defining moment. 'The European Union Treaty introduces a new and decisive stage in the process of European Union,' declared a triumphant Helmut Kohl, 'which within a few years will lead to the creation of what the founding fathers of modern Europe dreamed of after the last war: the United States of Europe.'[32] But, as so often had been the case, Britain did not leap with all the others, opting out of the social chapter and, most importantly, monetary union.

The result was that, for the first time since 1973, Britain was no longer in the same lane as its continental neighbours. From this moment, the nature of Britain's position within Europe changed, creating what would become a permanent separation of interests. The countries which were on the way into a monetary union with each other would be forever bound at the most existential level of national policy. The debts caused by the irresponsible spending of just one country could threaten the very stability of the new currency. Britain, meanwhile, stood aside.

As news of the deal began to leak out of Maastricht on Tuesday, 10 December, Michael Spicer was dining with Thatcher at her new home in Chester Square, along with Bill Cash, Norman Tebbit, Nicholas Ridley, Gerald Howarth and several still-serving ministers. 'Evening deteriorates into a verbal brawl between ministers and the rest about what our position should be,' Spicer recorded in his diary. 'Ridley and Tebbit try to persuade ministers to resign. They in turn argue that it would be very irresponsible for Thatcher to vote against the government. She expostulates, "But it's a matter of principle; the country is being sold down the river".'[33]

While Thatcher was fulminating against the content of the

deal, her successor was already hard at work selling his negotiation as a great triumph of statecraft. 'Game, set and match,' became the boast – a phrase which did not pass the prime minister's lips, but was instead, 'invented at three o'clock in the morning . . . by an over-enthusiastic press officer', recorded Stephen Wall.[34] With the media briefed, Major's team went to work on the Conservative Party. A paper was drawn up and distributed to every cabinet minister before Major had even set off for home. 'The deal agreed in Maastricht was a great success for Britain and a personal success for the Prime Minister,' it declared.[35]

Major's spin operation proved remarkably successful. Spicer noted in his diary that he was 'reeling' from the prime minister's 'triumphalist arrival' back in Westminster. 'I refuse to sign an adulatory EDM,' he wrote, grumpily, in his diary. The EDM – early day motion – in question congratulated the prime minister 'on having returned from Maastricht with an agreement which safeguards Britain's interest . . . and considers that this vindicates the Prime Minister's strategy of placing Britain at the heart of Europe.'[36]

The most vociferous lament about Maastricht at this time came from the *pro*-Europeans. Neil Kinnock criticized the opt-outs, which he said had isolated Britain. The Liberal Democrat leader, Paddy Ashdown, said the prime minister had 'condemned this country to be semi-detached.'[37] Both had a point, but their complaints mattered little to most Tory MPs, who felt quite comfortable with Britain's new status: a best of all worlds, it seemed.

The following day, Thatcher celebrated her fortieth wedding anniversary with a party at Claridge's, which her successor dutifully attended. 'The effect is that MT announces to the press outside that the deal at Maastricht was wonderful,' Spicer recorded in his diary with evident distress. 'God knows where that leaves us.'[38]

Though Thatcher quickly sought to row back on these remarks, the momentum was with Major. When the crucial vote came before the House the following week, the foreign secretary, Douglas Hurd, said the decision would 'match in importance the conclusions, which some of us remember, that were reached in 1971 and 1972.' By voting for the deal, in other words, a new settlement would emerge.

Finally, at 10.14 p.m. on Thursday, 19 December, a little over a week after the summit in Maastricht, MPs divided to vote on a motion which 'warmly endorses the agreement secured by the Government at Maastricht': the Ayes had 339; the Noes 253. The government had carried the day. Among those who voted in favour of the motion were Jonathan Aitken, Michael Howard, David Davis, William Hague, Edward Leigh, Peter Lilly, Francis Maude, Michael Portillo, John Redwood, Ann Widdecombe – even Teddy Taylor. Only the most die-hard opponents joined Labour in voting against, including John Biffen and Norman Tebbit. But this hardly mattered. Biffen, in particular, was a self-confessed 'euro-bore' and 'Fagin of euroscepticism', who carried quotations from Charles de Gaulle in his wallet for inspiration.[39]

Beyond those lonely Tory right-wingers willing to vote against their government, however, sat a few more who felt so uncomfortable with the new treaty that abstention was their only option. Among those were Michael Spicer, Nicholas Ridley and, most consequentially, Thatcher herself.

As Parliament broke up for Christmas in 1991, Major was triumphant. He had held the Conservative Party together through the most difficult diplomatic negotiation since Heath's push for entry in the early 1970s – and had done so despite opposition from his predecessor.

Yet, simple parliamentary arithmetic is a poor guide to analysing political trends. Maastricht was the moment that, for the first time since entry in 1971, Britain chose to stand apart from the central project of European integration. From this point, the onus would be on the pro-Europeans to make the case for unpicking the new status quo, if they wanted Britain to enter the single currency. To do so, they would need to build a British political commitment to the European project that had not existed before.

However, with a general election looming, the Conservative Party's focus turned back to domestic politics. It would be the first election since 1959 that Thatcher would not contest. For now, the show seemed to be over, although there would still be an encore from the Lords. The general election would take place on 9 April 1992; with the Maastricht Treaty not formally signed until February, Major decided to wait until after the election before introducing the legislation to bring it into law. 'The negotiations had been so well received across the House that ratification after the election appeared to present few obstacles,' Major later reflected.[40]

When the election came, to the surprise and disappointment of many Labour supporters, Major was victorious. The Conservative Party's decision to change leaders had proved electorally wise, it seemed. On the two issues which so fixated Thatcher and her ultras – Europe and the poll tax – Major's antenna had shown itself to be more in tune with the country than his predecessor. His handling of the Maastricht negotiations had won him plaudits, while his decision to replace Thatcher's Community Charge with a new Council Tax seemed to have taken the sting out of the issue.

For Alan Sked and the Anti-Federalist League, meanwhile, the election was a disappointment. The party had put up seventeen candidates and won a total of 4,383 votes, an average of just over 250 votes per candidate. Sked himself managed only 117 in Bath, where he stood against the Conservative Party chairman, Chris Patten. While Patten lost his seat, it was the pro-European Liberal Democrats who benefited – with Sked finishing sixth.

On 10 April 1992, then, Sked-style anti-Europeanism was so marginal as to seem irrelevant. Even mainstream Euroscepticism of the Thatcherite variety appeared peripheral, a hangover from an era that had passed into history. Major had just been returned with a mandate of his own, backed by more votes than any other prime minister in history, while Thatcher was no longer even an MP. Yet the margin of Major's victory was far narrower than before. Major had secured over a quarter of a million more votes than Thatcher in 1987, but Neil Kinnock had increased Labour's support by six times that amount. As a result, the Conservative majority fell from 102 seats in 1987 to just twenty-one. Major immediately sensed that this left him with a serious political problem. 'You wait,' he told Stephen Wall, 'this is where my troubles really begin.'[41]

Major was right to be concerned. The ideological currents within the Conservative Party were shifting in a Eurosceptic direction, as Geoffrey Howe had feared. Before the election, Major and his chief whip Richard Ryder had noted with some concern that 'fifty or so Members retiring from the House in 1992 were overwhelmingly loyalist or pro-European, whereas many of their younger successors in safe seats would take an opposite view.'[42] Heath's children were being replaced by Thatcher's.

As MPs prepared to return to the new Parliament, though, there was little sense of impending political drama. On Saturday, 2 May, a few days before Parliament's return and the Queen's Speech the following week, Europe's foreign ministers assembled in the pretty mediaeval town of Guimarães in northern Portugal, before the upcoming summit of the continent's leaders in Lisbon the following month. In attendance that day was Boris Johnson, representing *The Daily Telegraph*.

By 1992, Johnson had established himself as one of Fleet Street's most prominent reporters, whose dispatches from Brussels were often so colourful and popular that they prompted the editors at all the other newspapers on Fleet Street to start pressing their own correspondents to match his reports. Pascal Lamy, Jacques Delors' enforcer at the time, described Johnson's impact as that of 'a disrupter, the creator of a new style.'[43]

Johnson wrote of the European Commission's plans to build

the world's tallest building in Brussels, of new regulations on the size of condoms and a proposed ban on prawn-cocktail crisps. Many of Johnson's stories strained at the edges of veracity – and many were just false. The irony of Johnson's reputation as the inventor of 'bonkers Brussels' journalism, however, is that the very claim is something of a Johnsonian myth – a half-truth gleefully accepted by the man himself.

By the time Johnson arrived in Brussels, tabloid attacks on the city had long been a staple of Fleet Street coverage. Jonathan Aitken remembers his great-uncle, the press baron Lord Beaverbrook, receiving a report in the early post-war era of two soldiers, stationed in Germany, who had been killed in a lightning strike – 'as small a news item as you can think of,' as Aitken put it. Beaverbook thought otherwise and picked up the phone to his editor at the *Daily Express*. 'Have you read this important story about these unfortunate soldiers?' he boomed. 'I think we can make some mischief with this. Why don't you put it on page one with this headline: "British soldiers slain in *German* thunderstorm".'[44] As Aitken says, 'the story of Euroscepticism goes way, way back' – it's there in the ether of British national life, in the debates over Churchill's 'champagne' support for continentalism as much as in Johnson's journalism four decades later.

Throughout the 1960s and '70s, Beaverbrook had employed A. J. P. Taylor as a columnist for the *Sunday Express*, where he regularly railed against the European Community. At *The Telegraph*, T. E. Utley, Peregrine Worsthorne and others ploughed their Powellite furrow, albeit more philosophically than Boris Johnson, while *The Sun*, *The Times* and *The Sunday Times* deployed Eurosceptic dons to opine on the latest events, including Norman Stone and Niall Ferguson. By 1992, when Johnson arrived at Guimarães, Eurosceptic hostility had long since seeped into the marrow of Fleet Street. It was November 1990 when *The Sun* declared 'Up Yours Delors', a headline inspired not by Boris Johnson, but the paper's long experience of front-page jingo, going back at least as far as the Falklands-era 'Gotcha' in 1982.

For all his bombast, Johnson was far more nuanced and conventional in his actual opinions about the EU than is remembered. In the run-up to Major's election victory, Johnson wrote a piece for *The Telegraph* titled 'Ups and Downs of 20 Years Within Europe'. Published on 23 January 1992, Johnson wrote that, while the European Union remained undemocratic and the Common Agricultural Policy profligate, these problems were 'dwarfed by the benefits' of membership, of which the principal bonus was that it gave the country a new role in the world – to help run Europe.[45] Here, in essence, was the standard Foreign Office line, Britain's central strategic calculation from Macmillan to Major: Europe was the tool to protect British influence.

Johnson understood the inherent radicalism of Delors' efforts to 'complete' the single market. This was not some mere tidying-up exercise, but the most profound reform to Europe since its inception – until monetary union. New regulations were pouring forth, not because the Commission was madly power hungry, but because this was the inevitable consequence of creating a single market from multiple national markets. Johnson was quick to grasp the importance of this reform, the necessity for future institutional changes and the political implications in Britain. There is no doubt, too, that he also saw the opportunity to make a name for himself.

Johnson arrived in Guimarães in May 1992, then, as a high-profile journalist who understood the scale of Delors's ambition and was unafraid of stretching the bounds of credibility to get his stories noticed. On 3 May, Johnson's story was emblazoned on the front page of *The Sunday Telegraph*: 'European Community foreign ministers were stunned yesterday to learn of a plan by Jacques Delors to transform the Brussels Commission into a "European government" with himself or his successor becoming a fully fledged elected "President of the European Community"'. The piece was headlined, 'Delors plans to rule Europe'.[46]

As the *FT* later reported, the story was not so much false, but 'an exaggerated version of wishful thinking by a Delors team that was unhappy with the complex compromises of Maastricht.'[47] In other words, it reflected the federal aspirations of Delors, if not the likely reality of what he could achieve. In London, the story was picked up by a couple of MPs when Parliament returned for its first day of debate after the election. 'Mr. Delors has chosen this time of imbalance to escalate the argument for creating within Europe a separate European Government,' the Conservative MP Sir Patrick McNair-Wilson complained.[48] Overall, however, the piece had little real impact, at least in Britain.

The issue at hand was the need to ratify Maastricht. On that score, Major did not appear to have too much to worry about. Indeed, for Ted Heath, still in the House, the opportunity to gloat was too good to miss. Those resisting Maastricht had simply not got over entry and those still speaking of European 'cooperation' rather than federalism had missed the point. 'It was because Europe found that it could not rebuild itself through co-operation that the founding fathers – Jean Monnet has been mentioned – introduced the proposals for the Community.' Heath then turned to three other issues which would, over time, become of vital importance to British politics. First, he disagreed with the government's decision to opt out of the social chapter: 'I do not want this country to become the sweatshop of Europe.' Second, he did not like the government's opposition to free movement across national frontiers: 'We agreed on boundaries when we signed the treaty of Rome in 1972.' And third, once again breaking from the Thatcherite position, he came out in opposition to Europe's expansion to the east. 'The standard of living of the former Soviet-controlled territories is 32.1 per cent of the Community average,' he said. 'How can those countries be welcomed in, and how can they live on equal terms with the rest of the Community? It is just not possible.'[49]

In this intervention, we glimpse the unique character of Ted Heath, both prophetic and anachronistic, basking in the glory of the bloc's continued integration, while also placing himself outside the zeitgeist by opposing its expansion to the east. Whereas

Thatcher wanted Europe to be widened but not deepened, Heath wanted a smaller, more tightly integrated proto-state, able to act independently of the US. Thatcher correctly foresaw the prospect of populist revolts against the erosion of national borders, but supported the expansion of the Community to the east which made the mass movement of people across those frontiers more dramatic. Heath, in contrast, welcomed the end of national frontiers, but correctly foresaw that doing so in a Community with much poorer members to the east posed a first-order political challenge.

In the short term, Heath's airy confidence about Maastricht's ratification appeared well founded, with the bill comfortably sailing through its second reading, backed by 336 MPs to just ninety-two. Of the Eurosceptic holdouts, the bulk of the opposition came from the unreconciled left, led by Tony Benn, including Jeremy Corbyn, Diane Abbott and George Galloway. In fact, of the ninety-two 'noes', just twenty-two were Tories. Despite the ease of the victory, however, twenty-two was something of an ominous number. The government's majority was just twenty-one.

The next challenge for the government was the committee stage, due to begin on 4 June. Once it had got through this, the bill would get its third and final reading, and that would be that. But then everything changed.

On 2 June, Denmark voted in a referendum to reject the Maastricht Treaty by 50.72 per cent to 49.28 per cent. Suddenly, those who negotiated Maastricht had a problem. Under Danish law, there could not be a second referendum on the same question. And under European law, the treaty required unanimity to proceed. The historic integration of Europe had been blocked by a margin of 46,847 Danes.

For the Danish government, the result was a disaster, and Johnson's dispatch from Guimarães was held partly responsible, having been picked up by the Danish opposition ahead of the referendum. 'I'm sure it had an impact,' Uffe Ellemann-Jensen, the then Danish foreign minister, later reflected.[50] Johnson, of course, has delighted in the controversy ever since: 'They marched the streets of Copenhagen with my story fixed to their banners.'[51]

As ever, Johnson writes with an eyebrow raised, but, whatever the impact of his article, the Danish result was greeted with wild ecstasy among many Eurosceptics back in Britain. 'That was a moment that changed everything,' the future Conservative MEP Daniel Hannan recalled. Hannan was a student at Oxford at the time, having arrived in 1990, the year after Robertson departed to set up the Bruges Group. Like Robertson, he was an acolyte of Norman Stone and something of an outsider. Born in Lima, Peru, in 1971, the only child of Anglo-Peruvian farmers who had been in the country for two generations, he was sent to boarding school in England. Hannan had spent a gap year teaching in Dorset and travelling through Eastern Europe armed with the names of dissident academics he should visit, provided by Roger Scruton, who had come to Hannan's school to give a lecture. It was on this trip through Eastern Europe – just as the Soviet Union was beginning to unravel – that Hannan became convinced that the European Community was not moving with the grain of history, but against it: 'Those risings were primarily about sovereignty.'[52]

This is the sense of history Hannan took with him to Oxford in September 1990, just as Thatcher entered the final weeks of her premiership. For Hannan, Thatcher's subsequent removal appeared to be part of a conspiracy to protect European integration. 'It looked like an overseas army sending a signal to the resistance, saying, "Now is the time to do your rising".'[53] The following year, Hannan, the future MP Mark Reckless and their friend James Ross launched a new group on campus: the Oxford Campaign for an Independent Britain. Soon, Hannan's new group became the second biggest political society at Oxford, behind OUCA, of which he was also a member. Jacob Rees-Mogg was an early recruit. When the news broke that the Danes had rejected Maastricht, Hannan and his friends at the OCIB went wild with excitement, assuming the British government would abandon the treaty.

Major, of course, would do nothing of the sort. For the prime minister, it was not some unhappy compromise that he had agreed, but a diplomatic triumph that needed to be defended. Still, Major had a decision to make. The bill enacting the Maastricht Treaty was due to enter committee stage the very next day. Could he really go ahead with it now that the treaty might itself have to be rewritten?

A new plan was agreed: the committee stage would be delayed until the Danish government's intentions were apparent. It was a fateful decision. From this moment, events began to run away from Major. In Westminster, Michael Spicer tabled an early day motion urging the government to 'make a fresh start with the future development of the EEC,' attracting ninety-six signatures (of which five were later withdrawn under pressure from the whips), all but ten of which were from Conservative MPs. This became known as the 'Fresh Start' motion. In Paris, meanwhile, President Mitterrand announced that France would hold its own referendum on the treaty.

Thatcher began pushing ever more vocally for the treaty to be rejected. The former MP Gerald Howarth, who had, by then, set up a consultancy firm with Patrick Robertson, acted as Thatcher's go-between with MPs.* It was an extraordinary situation: 'A former prime minister openly encouraging backbenchers in her own party, many of whom revered her, to overturn the policy of her successor,' Major later complained in his memoirs.[54]

As Tory MPs lined up behind the Fresh Start motion, Labour opportunistically began changing its tune as well. At Prime Minister's Questions, Kinnock asked whether the House should debate a report on the implications of the Danish referendum 'before any further progress on the Bill is sought'. This seemingly

---

* Howarth had featured in the BBC's *Panorama* documentary about the FCS, 'Maggie's Militant Tendency', after which he sued the corporation for libelling him as a right-wing extremist. The BBC settled out of court and made an on-air apology ('BBC settles with two Tories', *The New York Times*, 22 October 1986).

innocuous question led to what became known as the 'paving debate', which almost cost Major his job. Though not at all necessary in parliamentary terms, Major believed it would offer MPs the chance to 'tug the starter cord and send the legislation chugging into life once more'. But, as Major later admitted, 'I might not have made the offer had I known of the political and economic neutron bomb that was primed to explode.'[55]

That explosion came on Wednesday, 16 September 1992 – Black Wednesday – the day Britain crashed out of the European Exchange Rate Mechanism after the government proved unable to stop the value of the pound falling below the stipulated range Major had agreed when the country joined in October 1990. It was not just a personal humiliation for the prime minister, but a defining moment in Britain's relationship with Europe. For Major, Black Wednesday was the point at which the Conservative Party turned from being merely uneasy with European integration to rejecting any further entanglement. It was, he said, when the Tory party threw logic to one side and allowed its 'emotional rivers [to] burst their banks.'[56] Contrary to Major's analysis, Black Wednesday was not simply a crisis to which people reacted overly emotionally, but one which fundamentally undermined Britain's central economic strategy, robbing Major of his legitimacy. On Black Wednesday, Major found himself desperately trying to prop up the value of sterling to keep Britain in a European policy opposed by his predecessor. His failure to do so did not just undermine the central thrust of his economic policy – controlling inflation by tying sterling to the Deutschmark – but his foreign policy too. John Major and Geoffrey Howe had consistently argued that British membership of the Exchange Rate Mechanism was a diplomatic manoeuvre to protect British influence in Europe as much as it was an economic mechanism to control inflation. Britain had joined ERM to remain 'at the heart of Europe.' But, once Britain was out of the ERM, what was left of this policy?

Black Wednesday also revealed the uncomfortable reality of German power. Major had pleaded with Helmut Kohl to help relieve the mounting pressure on sterling by cutting interest rates, without success. As Major writes in his memoirs: 'Our domestic economy required lower interest rates, but the strengthening of the deutschmark prevented this. All Europe suffered and grumbled, but the Bundesbank offered no policy change.'[57]

One obvious lesson from this was that it would be better to enter into a full-blown monetary union where currency speculation was no longer possible because there was only one currency. This was Ken Clarke's position. An alternative conclusion, though, was that Britain could avoid ever getting in such a situation by allowing the pound to float at the value the markets determined, managed by the Bank of England for the needs of the British economy.

Either way, the combination of the Danish 'no' and Black Wednesday turbocharged the Eurosceptic cause in Britain. The rebels were now being cheered on ever more loudly by the Tory press, which – in Major's eyes, at least – lost its moorings. 'Across Fleet Street, sensational and exclusive stories sold extra copies – straight reporting did not,' he complained. In this game, 'columnists of long-standing who should have known better played along,' Major wrote, saving particular ire for William Rees-Mogg, one-time editor of *The Times*, and the 'pendulum-like journalist Paul Johnson', who 'ranted in the Spectator.'[58] As ever, his critics were hysterical, emotional, devious or dishonourable. Major seems not to have questioned the assumptions upon which his economic policy had fallen apart.

The sense of mounting hostility to Maastricht was captured in a book published at this time called *Reshaping Europe in the Twenty-First Century*, containing a series of Eurosceptic essays which together acted as a shot across the bows of the government. The book was edited by Patrick Robertson, with pieces from his ideological allies Alan Sked, Kenneth Minogue, Conrad Black, Norman Tebbit, Peter Lilley and Enoch Powell. The foreword was by Thatcher herself, who left no doubt about where her loyalties lay.

Three days after Black Wednesday, Thatcher – now Lady Thatcher – piled further pressure on the prime minister with a speech in Washington in which she congratulated her successor for removing the 'economic straitjacket' of the ERM. It was hardly the endorsement Major wanted. Thatcher did little to hide her schadenfreude either. 'What we have lived through this past week has been a lesson in practical economics,' she declared, before quoting Rudyard Kipling:

> Let us admit it frankly, as a business people should,
> We have had no end of a lesson: it will do us no end of good.[59]

For Thatcher, the first and most obvious lesson of Black Wednesday was clear: fixed exchange rates do not work. 'Once that lesson is learned,' she said, 'it cannot be unlearnt.' Consequently, the second lesson was that Britain should not try to re-enter the ERM. And finally, the third lesson was to make 'as complete a reversal of policy on Maastricht as has been done on the ERM.'

If Europe's economies could not cope in a single exchange rate, she asked, how could they cope in a single currency? 'There would be chaos of the sort which would make the difficulties of recent days pale by comparison.' Huge fiscal transfers would be required. Unemployment would rise and mass migration would follow. 'The political consequences can already be glimpsed,' she warned. 'The growth of extremist parties, battening on fears about mass immigration and unemployment, offering a real – if thoroughly unwelcome – alternative to the Euro-centrist political establishment.'[60]

The speech is far more radical in tone than the one she delivered in Bruges four years earlier – and far more prophetic.

It was events that were energizing the Eurosceptic cause, not mere emotion, as Major insisted. Had the Danes overwhelmingly endorsed Maastricht, the sense of inevitability about the whole process would have remained. Had the Bundesbank acted in a spirit of European solidarity, perhaps Black Wednesday would have been avoided. But these events cannot simply be dismissed as random coincidences; they were reflections of the structural reality that existed.

On 20 September 1992, four days after Black Wednesday, Major's life got even harder when the French ratified Maastricht in a referendum by the slenderest of margins imaginable: 51.05 per cent to 48.95 per cent. Had they voted it down, the treaty would have been dead. In Britain, the Eurosceptics were on the march, now publicly encouraged by Thatcher. During the Tory conference the following month, Thatcher upped the ante even further with a newspaper article in which she claimed Maastricht would 'hand over more power to unelected bureaucrats.' As Major later wrote, 'The sub-text was clear: she would not have agreed Maastricht.'[61]

It was in October 1992 that Bill Cash created an organization that would haunt the remaining days of John Major's premiership. The College Street Group, soon known as the European Foundation, set up shop a stone's throw from Parliament, in a house owned by Alistair McAlpine, Margaret Thatcher's long-serving fundraiser, friend and ideological acolyte. Cash's new outfit was Major's 'House of Horror', as the press delightedly named it.

By the next year, the Foundation had a five-man council of management, made up of Cash, the postgraduate student John Laughland, Eurosceptic lawyers Martin Howe and Jeremy Nieboar, and a newly elected MP called Iain Duncan Smith. A separate advisory board was also established, including Ralph Harris, Kenneth Minogue, Malcolm Pearson and Norman Stone.

The aim of Cash's new group was to produce briefing papers, hold seminars, draft amendments and generally whip up opposition to the Maastricht Treaty to block its passage. Its flagship product, however, would be its monthly magazine, *The European Journal*, which set out the Foundation's stated objective: to 'resist by all lawful democratic means all and any moves tending towards the coming into being of a European federal or unitary state'.[62]

The Maastricht rebellions that would dog Major's time in office began in earnest on 4 November 1992, with the vote to resume the process of ratifying the Maastricht Treaty. The mechanism for doing this was the so-called 'paving motion', inviting the government to progress the bill to committee stage. Opening the debate, Major offered his familiar combination of candour and obfuscation, asking not whether Britain should be in or out, but 'what sort of Europe is it that we wish to help build?' The prime minister claimed there were two options: 'We can develop as a centralist institution . . . or we can develop as a free-market, free-trade, wider European Community more responsive to its citizens.'[63] Ironically, it would fall to Ted Heath to point out the contradictions in Major's account. After criticizing the prime minister for delaying ratification, he defended Jacques Delors and dismissed Major's vision of Europe. 'It is not a free market Europe and it never will be,' he declared.[64] Rather, it was a community with trade benefits for those who joined.

As the vote approached, the government appeared to be teetering on the edge, heading to a defeat that Major later insisted would have left him no choice but to resign. To avoid calamity, a last-minute promise emerged: the government would not complete the bill before the Danish position had been settled. It worked – just. When the result of the paving motion was announced, the government had won by three votes. 'Pandemonium broke out,' Major wrote.[65] He had survived, but at a cost.

The ratification process dragged on in this manner for much of 1993, with rebels determined to stop the process in any way they could, repeatedly pushing the government to the edge without quite throwing it over. This was a period of high drama and intrigue, which turned many of Major's most committed rebels into household names. The public soon got to know figures like Bill Walker, the kilt-wearing former RAF captain and MP for North Tayside, who once pretended to be too ill to vote before smuggling himself into the House of Commons to catch the Tory whips unawares.[66] Another character who became well known was the Powellite businesswoman and MP for Billericay, Teresa Gorman, who wore with pride *The Guardian*'s description of her as 'the most Right-wing member of parliament'.[67] The new MP for Chingford, Iain Duncan Smith, was another prominent rebel. For many, though, Bill Cash was the group's emblematic figurehead, dismissed by Major as an 'obsessive'. For most of the rebels, Thatcher remained their 'de facto leader,' as her former political secretary John Whittingdale later put it.[68] Yet, in the end, the rebels did not quite have the numbers.

In April 1993, with Maastricht almost certain to be ratified, Major delivered a speech to the Conservative Group for Europe, dismissing the sceptics as imperial nostalgists motivated by 'frustration that we are no longer a world power'. To Major, such fantasies were absurd. 'Fifty years from now, Britain will still be the country of long shadows on county grounds, warm beer, invincible green suburbs, dog lovers and – as George Orwell said – old maids bicycling to Holy Communion through the morning mist.'[69] Even today, it is a curious speech, mocking the politics of nostalgia with a nostalgia of its own. In *Homage to Catalonia*, Orwell had raised his fears that exactly such bucolic comfort was lulling the country into a false sense of security. Surrounded by such gentleness, Orwell thought, 'it is difficult . . . to believe that anything is really happening anywhere.' While the world convulses, the shires remain in 'the deep, deep sleep of England, from which I sometimes fear that we shall never wake.' John Major was downplaying the real changes happening around him by focusing on the superficial stability at home.

The following month, on 18 May, all the hopes the rebels had placed in Denmark were dashed when a second referendum on the treaty produced a comfortable majority for its ratification. During the British presidency of the European Council the previous year, Major had played a significant role negotiating four opt-outs from the treaty's original provisions, which helped convince the Danes to back the deal. Two days later, the Maastricht legislation made its final outing in the Commons, now backed by the Labour Party, who had run out of excuses not to support its passage. After all the noise and fury, the bill was passed with a majority of 180, though with forty-six rebel Tories – the government's worst rebellion so far. Maastricht had passed, but, just as in 1971, without a government majority of its own. From here, the bill passed through the Lords in twelve days and received royal assent on 20 July 1993.

But still there were hurdles to clear: William Rees-Mogg launched an attempted judicial review that was quickly thrown out, and Labour even tried to block the bill's passage after it had been given royal assent with an attempt to incorporate the social chapter from which Major had opted out. The proposal was supported by the Lib Dems and the SNP, which meant that, if the rebels backed it too, the effect would be to block the government from ratifying a treaty. In its leader on the morning of the vote, *The Times* backed the rebels, urging them to do what they believed was right and warning that, if Major ignored the vote, his government would be 'harried and wearied to its end'.

When the vote came, the government was defeated. 'The House was in uproar, with cheers, counter-cheers and recriminations filling the air,' noted Major.[70] But the prime minister had a final trump card to play: a motion of confidence, to be debated the following morning. It was all or nothing, and even Cash decided he had reached his limit. 'I looked at the Opposition and concluded they were worse,' he reflected, ruefully, more than thirty years later.[71]

With that, the rebellion was finally over, the prospect of bringing down the government too much even for the rebels. The Maastricht Treaty was now law. 'The longest white-knuckle ride in recent British politics was over,' wrote Major in his memoir.[72]

After a year from hell, the prime minister had won, the government had won and the pro-European majority in the Commons had won. Britain had joined the rest of Europe, at least in part. For Major, it was such a relief, he briefly lost his self-discipline. In an interview with ITN the next day, he was caught on tape criticizing the Eurosceptic 'bastards' who had caused him such difficulties.[73] 'Even a prime minister can only bite his lip for so long,' he later wrote.[74]

For the Eurosceptics, the one consoling thought was that they had caused such a stir that future British governments would be cautious about ever committing to monetary union. On 20 August 1993, Spicer received a note from a fellow Eurosceptic Tory, Peter Tapsell, to this effect. 'After such a parliamentary battle, no Conservative government in our political lifetime will attempt to venture any further down the path towards a European union of a single European currency. In that vital sense, our anti-Maastricht group are the victors.'[75] While there is a certain through-the-looking-glass quality to Tapsell's argument, there is nevertheless a perverse truth, too. Major had won, but, like Disraeli's Young England, the Maastricht rebels left an 'imaginative glow' for others to follow.[76]

For the prime minister, meanwhile, although he briefly allowed himself 'a full gloat,' as he put it, his government had been exhausted by the fight.[77] At the height of the Maastricht crisis, Major also had to deal with a shattering personal tragedy after his former political secretary, the MP Judith Chaplin, died unexpectedly. Chaplin had left Number Ten before the 1992 election to stand for Parliament in Newbury, and had not been in the House for long when she went into hospital for what was supposed to be a routine operation. Chaplin's death was a great personal blow for Major at a time of evident loneliness. The resulting by-election on 6 May then saw the Tories' 12,000 majority obliterated with the decidedly pro-European Liberal Democrats benefiting from the collapse in Tory support, sweeping up some 65 per cent of the vote to secure a 25,000 majority.

The by-election is notable for a second defeat for Alan Sked and his new Anti-Federalist League, who ended up with just 601 votes – 1 per cent of the total. It was also the first introduction to electoral politics for Nigel Farage, who found himself in the constituency for a week of leafleting. Sked had persuaded Farage's schoolboy hero Enoch Powell to come down to offer his support, and Farage was enlisted as chauffeur. He remembers Powell directing him on which route to take, enjoying a glass of wine with dinner and advising his young driver on the art of the game: 'Better to be a little late, it's all part of the act.' Sked remembers nothing of the sort. 'There was complete silence all the way, and we never exchanged a word.'[78]

Irrespective of the truth, Farage was mesmerized. Watching Powell speak 'awoke all sorts of aspirations in me which I had not even acknowledged before', Farage later wrote. By this point, Powell had been diagnosed with Parkinson's disease and, apart from one more turn at the Bruges Group, this outing in Newbury was to be his last public appearance.

Twelve weeks after Newbury, Sked stood in another by-election after the sudden death of Conservative MP Robert Adley. In this campaign, Sked had to make do with a photograph of Powell on his leaflets. He fared little better, securing just 878 votes this time.

By the autumn of 1993, Sked's Anti-Federalist League still looked lifeless, while Euroscepticism did not have an obvious political vehicle to advance its cause, having been rejected by all the mainstream parties. Labour was now led by a pro-European leader, John Smith, who had replaced Kinnock the previous year. The Liberal Democrats under Paddy Ashdown were surfing the wave of anti-establishment resentment while demanding that Britain show even more commitment to the European project. The Tory party, meanwhile, was divided, but only the most hardline sceptics were contemplating a British exit.

The fate of the Anti-Federalist League appeared to be of little or no consequence to the future of British politics. Sked was an eccentric political outsider whose appeal was more academic than populist. He admired Powell's intellect, but not his rhetoric on immigration, which had been the source of much of his public support. Sked could see his organization needed to change if it was to make any political impact. In August that year, the League decided to 'take on the name and structure of a populist party', as Farage later wrote. At a meeting in September, the decision was made to change the party's name. Farage was on holiday when several options were put forward: the British Independence Party, but that was too close to the British National Party; the Freedom Party, but this risked becoming more of a libertarian party than a Eurosceptic resistance. Farage wrote that he personally liked the Reform Party, 'which would have rung down the ages had we triumphed,' but this was rejected. In the end, the UK Independence Party was chosen, despite being a little cumbersome, 'simply because it succinctly declared our origin and our principal aim.' UKIP was born – or, as most of those at the time called it, 'The U-K-I-P.'[79]

At this meeting, one other crucial decision was made: the UKIP would try to recruit as many candidates as possible to contest the upcoming European elections set for June 1994. Wealthy individuals and organizations would also be approached for financial support. The great hope was that the billionaire businessman Sir James Goldsmith would come on board. Goldsmith had already bankrolled William Rees-Mogg's attempt to block Maastricht through the courts and was secretly backing Bill Cash's European Foundation in Westminster. He had even given a lecture on Channel 4 denouncing Maastricht. Goldsmith, however, was not interested. 'I am grateful for your suggestions,' he replied. 'I will continue to fight for the cause, but on a non-party political basis.'[80] Goldsmith's calculations would soon change.

Chapter 11

In early 1994, Patrick Robertson and Michael Gove were having lunch with Peter Lilley at his home in Normandy when Sir James Goldsmith called. Goldsmith was at his chateau in Burgundy, but wanted to see this group of Eurosceptic ultras, so he dispatched his helicopter to pick them up. Gove remembers flying into Goldsmith's estate and looking up from the book he had brought along for the journey – John Campbell's biography of Edward Heath – to see two giant initials 'J' and 'G' mown into the grass, visible only to those approaching from the air.

The whole episode is typical of Goldsmith, a man of hyper-activity, energy, ambition and bravado. Born in Paris in 1933, he was the second son of the German-born Jewish hotelier and former Conservative Party MP, Frank Goldsmith, and his French Catholic wife, Marcelle Mouiller. As his older brother Teddy would put it, the Goldsmiths grew up feeling English and French, Catholic and Jewish. 'We don't really belong,' he reflected, 'but we can look from the outside. We see what others don't see.'[1]

When the war broke out, the Goldsmiths moved to North America, and the two boys only returned to England in 1944, when it was deemed safe enough for them to begin their formal education. James was sent first to Millfield and then to Eton, neither of which suited him. Aged sixteen, he quit school after winning so much money from a £10 horse-racing accumulator that he could afford to live independently. Goldsmith won nearly £8,000 – the equivalent of around a quarter of a million pounds in 2025.[2] According to legend, Goldsmith declared to his classmates that 'a man of my means should not remain a schoolboy,' and left. Within a few years, he had squandered all his winnings and had to turn to his father to bail him out.[3]

Over the course of the next four decades, however, Goldsmith would remake his fortune and far more besides, splitting his time between London, Paris and New York. He lived with two wives, one mistress and eight children, in multiple different homes, and ran a business empire spanning the globe, including news outlets in both France and England. 'Like an Arab pasha, Goldsmith moves among all three households, supporting everyone with lavish generosity,' noted *Vanity Fair* in a profile.[4]

Throughout his career, Goldsmith had mixed politics and business, seeing the two as inextricably linked. In the 1980s, he had been among a group of businessmen and Cold Warriors who were so close to Thatcher they became known as the 'Downing Street irregulars'.[5]

Goldsmith was a particularly close friend, ally and benefactor to Brian Crozier and his private intelligence operation, the 61.* In Crozier's autobiography, *Free Agent*, he describes receiving a call from 'the great financier' at 7.45 one morning in early 1985, to tell him about a 'very important dinner at Chequers' the night before.[6] According to Crozier's account, the secret Chequers dinner had taken place on 26 February 1985 with the anonymous financier,

---

* The pair had been involved in an extraordinary legal case in which the German magazine *Der Spiegel* sued for libel and damages after Goldsmith claimed the KGB had used the publication to destroy the career of the hawkish Bavarian conservative Franz Josef Strauss in the early 1960s. Goldsmith made the allegation after being briefed about the affair by Crozier. In the end, the *Spiegel* affair dragged on for three and a half years, only brought to a close with a statement from Goldsmith that appeared in full-page adverts in British, German and American newspapers, in which he boasted that he had 'sponsored a massive international research effort' to unveil the extent of the KGB's manipulation, before describing his settlement with *Der Spiegel* as 'a famous victory for the defence of the West against its main enemy, Soviet imperialism'. (Crozier, Brian, *Free Agent: The Unseen War, 1941–1991* (London: HarperCollins, 1993), p. 252)

'another tycoon' and Keith Joseph. Thatcher's engagement diary for that day – a Tuesday – shows her in London all day. However, two days earlier, on Sunday, 24 February, Thatcher was indeed in Chequers, where her official engagement diary shows her having supper with Keith Joseph, Oliver Letwin, Rupert Murdoch and James Goldsmith.[7]

In Crozier's account of this gathering, as relayed to him by 'the financier', the theme for discussion was what he called 'an insidious domestic problem'. This was the challenge posed by what were dismissed as the 'Loony Left' councils in the tabloid press, local authorities in London, Liverpool, Sheffield and Glasgow who were using their funds to support left-wing causes like 'nuclear free zones' and what Crozier dismisses as 'minor follies, such as gay and lesbian centres'. Thatcher wanted the two businessmen's help to take these councils on.[8]

Goldsmith said what was needed was 'a full counter-subversion programme' led by Crozier and his intelligence operation, the 61.[9] Goldsmith and Murdoch then agreed to help fund the operation. Thatcher saw Crozier three days after her dinner with Goldsmith, at 9 a.m. on Wednesday, 28 February.

During the meeting, Crozier briefed Thatcher on the kind of operations his organization had already carried out, including its work to 'penetrate and defeat the Soviet "peace" fronts'. To do this, Crozier told Thatcher how he worked with 'a small group of young men', including the future Tory MPs Edward Leigh and Julian Lewis, to set up something called the 'Coalition for Peace through Security', targeting the Campaign for Nuclear Disarmament. Crozier describes the 'grand climax' of this campaign coming in 1986 at a meeting of the Soviet-backed World Peace Council in Copenhagen – just the kind of Soviet front Petr Pithart had warned against in *The Times* three years earlier.[10]

'At the opening ceremony, two of our people . . . walked towards the platform, bearing an unfurled banner,' Crozier writes. 'As the crowd read the words, which those on the platform could not see, titters and shouts of shock or approval broke out. The banner read: "Welcome to the KGB's peace conference!"' Crozier describes how the 61 had also 'packed the hall with "delegates" from imaginary peace groups, such as the "Welsh miners for Peace".'[11]

Among the young anti-communist activists there that day were some of the FCS gang, including the future BBC journalist and Downing Street director of communications Robbie Gibb, Peter Young's Russian émigré George Miller-Kurakin and Dougie Smith, who masqueraded as a steward to save any activists who might find themselves being dragged away by Soviet agents. For Goldsmith, such exploits were just what was needed in the battle against communism, embodied by his heroine in Number Ten.

By the early 1990s, Goldsmith had pulled back from business to focus more of his attention on politics. With the Cold War over, his principal obsessions were the environment, global corporatism – and Europe.

During the Maastricht debates, Goldsmith had given money to Bill Cash's European Foundation, having first bumped into him at a small conference organized by the Eurosceptic finance minister of the Czech Republic, Václav Klaus. Klaus had assembled a group of like-minded figures from across the continent for a private meeting in Prague. In a coup de théâtre, Cash had brought with him a leaked copy of the draft Maastricht Treaty. It had been delivered to his office in an envelope by a mystery figure, whose identity Cash never discovered. 'To this day, I do not know who sent it,' he recalled, smiling and shaking his head in his parliamentary office just before his retirement. 'It was someone who thought I should know.'[12]

Goldsmith's politics were as idiosyncratic as his lifestyle, departing from the usual Thatcherite script in how he saw the new European Union created by Maastricht not as a barrier to free trade, but as a great centralizing enabler of it, in hock to globalization and the corporate interests pushing it, which he believed threatened to destroy the social and environmental cohesion of Europe.

Goldsmith had not limited his political activity to Britain, either. In October 1992, he had delivered a lecture on free trade, Europe and the future for the Western world at the Grand Amphitheatre of the Sorbonne in Paris, in which he set out his case that the collapse of communism created fundamental new challenges for the industrialized world that it had not yet appreciated. In the audience that day was the editor of the economics section of *Le Figaro*, Yves Messarovitch, who became convinced that Goldsmith's ideas needed a wider audience. The pair then began work on a book that became an unlikely French bestseller in 1994: *Le Piège* – The Trap.

Reading the book decades later is a strange experience. Goldsmith's account of the world's ills manages to be both wildly at odds with the dominant economic worldview of most of his Thatcherite allies in Britain, while also prefiguring the populist conservative politics of the twenty-first century.

'The development of new technologies and economic growth are pursued as if they – and not well-being – should be the objective of human effort,' Goldsmith began. 'Social stability and sometimes entire cultures are sacrificed in the pursuit of these goals. I believe that this inversion of values is the cause of many of our ills.'[13] Goldsmith then set out three policies which he claimed had destroyed Europe's social stability: intensive agriculture, nuclear energy and, most importantly, free trade. 'Global free trade has become a sacred principle of modern economic theory,' he warned. 'If it is implemented it will impoverish and destabilise the industrialised world.'[14]

What had fundamentally shifted Goldsmith's calculus against free trade was the collapse of communism. 'During the past few years,' he declared, 'four billion people have suddenly entered the world economy. They include the populations of China, India, Vietnam, Bangladesh, and the countries that were part of the Soviet empire.'

For Goldsmith, the outcome of global free trade was obvious: giant corporations in the developed world would shift manufacturing to wherever labour was cheapest, increasing their profits while laying off workers in the West. He was also dismissive of the idea that Western consumers would benefit from cheaper goods. 'When Nike moved its manufacturing from the US to Asia, shoe prices did not drop,' he said. 'Instead profit margins rose.' Even if prices did fall, Goldsmith declared, the cost would still outweigh the benefit. 'Consumers are also citizens, many of whom live in towns,' he declared. 'As unemployment rises and poverty increases, towns and cities will grow ever more unstable.'[15]

Goldsmith's solution to all these problems was what he called 'regional free trade', whereby companies had to invest in the areas where they wanted to sell their products.[16] The oddity of Goldsmith's argument is that its central pillar resembles a defence of the very idea of Europe. Goldsmith, however, believed Maastricht had moved Europe away from this original conception – the opposite view to most British Tories.

The success of *Le Piège* prompted Goldsmith to enter the political arena himself, forming a pact with the renegade French Eurosceptic conservative Philippe de Villiers, who had broken with the governing 'Union for France' coalition in the National Assembly over Maastricht the year before. De Villiers – like Fernand Bonnier de La Chapelle – was an ardent monarchist, though from the Vendée rather than Algérie française, and he saw himself as a defender of the French way of life. At the launch of their Majorité pour L'Autre Europe party in Paris, in April 1994, Goldsmith and de Villiers were joined by Charles de Gaulle, grandson of the general – a PR coup which grabbed the media's attention.

At the press conference announcing their slate of candidates, de Gaulle insisted his grandfather would never have agreed to Maastricht and let France 'disappear into a vast supranational entity.' Reporting on this curious development across the Channel, *The Independent* wrote that Goldsmith's new party might win five or six seats in the elections if it could squeeze over the 5 per cent threshold. The headline of the piece was 'French mavericks attack free trade'.[17]

In France, however, scepticism of free trade was not as maverick as it appeared in Britain. Jacques Chirac, the leading figure of the Gaullist right at this time, had shored up his position ahead of the presidential election in 1995 by criticizing the liberal economic orthodoxy of the day, framing himself as defender of the French tradition. Goldsmith and de Villiers, then, were expressing ideas with deep resonance in French politics. Ahead of the elections, Goldsmith organized a Paris Conference for a Europe of Nation States. Alongside Goldsmith, Philippe de Villiers and Charles de Gaulle, other attendees included Bill Cash and William Rees-Mogg.

When the results of the elections were declared on Monday, 13 June 1994, their L'Autre Europe had not only comfortably surpassed the 5 per cent threshold needed to secure any seats in the European Parliament, but had reached 12.34 per cent of the vote, enough to finish third, just two percentage points behind François Mitterrand's ruling Socialist Party. It was an extraordinary result. Goldsmith, along with twelve other L'Autre Europe candidates, had been elected as members of the European Parliament, where he became leader of a Eurosceptic bloc, the 'Europe of Nations' group, comprising thirteen French MEPs, two Dutch sceptics and two Danes, but no Brits.

Though the European elections in Britain saw no such Eurosceptic breakthrough, there were two notable developments. The first was the scale of the Labour Party's victory in the first set of elections it had faced since the party's leader, John Smith, had died suddenly and unexpectedly from a heart attack the month before. Smith's replacement would not be elected until July, but Labour's victory was crushing all the same, winning 42.6 per cent of the vote and sixty-two of the eighty-seven seats up for grabs.

The second, less obvious development was the emergence of 'the UKIP' as a new force in British politics. On the same day as the European elections were held, a by-election took place in Eastleigh, Hampshire, where Nigel Farage was a candidate for the first time.

Ahead of the election, Farage followed Sked's example and wrote to Enoch Powell asking for help. 'I have everything in place to fight a good, aggressive campaign but a voice from you could transform things and put the issue to the forefront,' Farage wrote. Powell declined, though offered his assessment that the United Kingdom was finally 'consolidating against membership of the European Union.'[18]

When the results were announced, Farage fared poorly, securing a mere 952 votes, or 1.7 per cent. In the European election, though, where Farage was standing in the wider Itchen, Test and Avon constituency, he performed much better, taking home 12,423 votes – or 5.4 per cent. 'There's a new party in British politics,' Farage declared at the count.[19]

It was the first time the party had not been entirely crushed at the polls, yet Farage had still finished almost 70,000 votes behind the winning Conservative candidate, at a time when the Eurosceptic cause was becoming more salient and the government wildly unpopular. UKIP was still, in essence, a political irrelevance. Across the whole country, the party won 150,000 votes, finishing tenth, behind the Greens, Plaid Cymru and even the cumulative total for all the different independent candidates.

In 1994, then, UKIP was a small party of largely Thatcherite holdouts. Indeed, the party that seemed most in tune with the zeitgeist was not UKIP, but the refashioned and pro-European Labour Party that emerged under its new leader, Tony Blair.

John Smith had been an effective, respected and tactically astute leader of the Opposition. In contrast to his later reputation for being a lukewarm modernizer, Smith had watered down trade-union power within the party by introducing 'one member, one vote' reforms for the selection of MPs and had scrapped the union block vote. He had also set out plans for sweeping constitutional reforms to 'replace the out-of-date idea of an all-powerful nation state,'[20] committed the party to devolution in Scotland and Wales, called for the European Convention on Human Rights to be incorporated into British law and for the introduction of a

Freedom of Information Act. He was, in some ways, more reformist than his successor.

Yet Smith was a tactically cautious man and did not share the sense of urgency that some of Labour's most enthusiastic modernizers felt about internal party reform. Nor did he believe the party needed to accept quite so much of the Conservative Party's economic settlement as Blair came to advocate. Crucially, Smith also did not believe he needed to modify his life-long commitment to European integration. He had rebelled against the Labour whip in 1971 to vote for British entry and as leader had opposed John Major's opt-out from monetary union.

Smith's sudden death in May 1994 unexpectedly opened the door to the party's modernizing ultras, led by the triumvirate of Gordon Brown, Tony Blair and Peter Mandelson. Each was committed to further reforms of the party, but also to tailoring the Labour offer to Middle England.

On the face of it, then, Blair's victory in the Labour leadership race contained a curious paradox. He was young, popular and avowedly pro-European, with an overwhelming mandate from his party. Yet, on the question of Europe, Labour's commitment to 'modernization' made it both more instinctively pro-European, believing that Europe in some elemental sense represented modernity, but also more determined to win power by aligning the party with popular opinion – which contained a deep current of scepticism about further European integration.*

James Goldsmith, meanwhile, was planning his next political move, determined to build on his success in France with a

* It is possible to glimpse this latent scepticism in what economists call the 'revealed preference' of British consumers. In 1992, Disney opened a new theme park just outside Paris, which they called 'Euro Disney'. To the American mind, 'Euro' conjured up images of glamour and excitement which would draw visitors to the site. To the British mind, however, the choice of name made it sound like a greyer version of the 'real' Disney in America. After poor attendances and vast losses, the resort was forced to change its name in 1994, removing 'Euro' to become 'Disneyland Paris' instead.

campaign to transform the political dynamic in Britain. Part of the drive may well have been an acute sense of time draining away: he had turned sixty-one in February 1994 and had secretly begun treatment for cancer.

Goldsmith invited friends and family to a Lebanese restaurant in Mayfair to discuss the idea of making an intervention into British politics. Among those in attendance were the flamboyant gambling impresario John Aspinall, Dougie Smith – who had been recommended to Goldsmith as an implacable Eurosceptic and political insurgent – and Goldsmith's stepson Robin Birley.

Patrick Robertson had already got to know the Goldsmith family through Birley, a Bruges Group regular. Robertson was part of Birley's set, alongside Goldsmith's son Zac and his close friends Ben Elliot, nephew of Camilla Parker-Bowles, and Orlando Fraser, son of Hugh and Antonia Fraser.

After his stint at the World Economic Forum, Robertson had returned to London to set up a company called Taskforce Communications with the former Conservative MPs Gerald Howarth and Cecil Parkinson. Goldsmith became one of his first clients. Robertson's first job was to organize a campaign Goldsmith was running for a new national park to be established protecting the vast estate he owned in Mexico. His second project was to publish *Le Piège* in English.

After the Mayfair dinner, Goldsmith asked Robertson how much it would cost to run an election campaign. Robertson scribbled down some estimates. 'I gave him a back-of-the-envelope plan for a six-week campaign, purely in terms of advertising – £18 million to £22 million.'[21]

Robertson went away to work on a more detailed plan: VHS cassettes posted to people's homes, cinema advertising, double-page spreads in national newspapers. The central problem, though, was recruitment, given that almost all the main Eurosceptics remained within the Conservative Party. How could any new party prise them away, given they had little to no chance of winning any seats in Parliament? Goldsmith was insistent. 'The problem with you is you don't have any imagination,' he told Robertson. 'You think too traditionally.'[22]

Goldsmith finally made his move in November 1994, to coincide with the English edition of *Le Piège – The Trap*. 'Goldsmith forms a Euro referendum party,' reported *The Times* on its front page, on Monday, 28 November 1994. Goldsmith broke the news with an appearance on the BBC's flagship Sunday morning show, *Breakfast with Frost*, warning the two main political parties that, unless they pledged to hold a referendum on any further moves on European integration, he would set up his own political party that would campaign to deliver one. 'They can be 100 per cent certain that, if there is not a formal unequivocal commitment, then a new party will be formed.'

Goldsmith's intervention highlights that, even after Major's success ratifying Maastricht, the question of Europe had not gone away. By this time, the Conservative Party's Eurosceptics in the ERG had hired a full-time researcher – Daniel Hannan, fresh from Oxford. The ERG held regular breakfast meetings in the House of Lords, chaired by the Tory peer Malcolm Pearson, which were open to both Cash's Friends of Bruges and supportive journalists, including Gove. The day after Goldsmith's announcement, Major was facing rumours of a leadership challenge from Norman Lamont, his sacked former chancellor, as well as the prospect of a defeat in the Commons on a European finance bill, which he had made another matter of confidence – the only way, seemingly, he could enact any legislation concerning Europe. Such was the continuing acrimony that Major withdrew the Conservative Party whip from eight rebels after the vote. These rebels were quickly dubbed the 'whipless eight' – a moniker denoting the hardest of the hardcore, which included Teddy Taylor and Nicholas Budgen, Enoch Powell's replacement in Wolverhampton, though not Bill Cash or Michael Spicer, who abstained.*

* The whipless eight were: Teddy Taylor, Teresa Gorman, Richard Shepherd, Christopher Gill, John Wilkinson, Tony Marlow, Nicholas Budgen and Michael

Ever since Maastricht had passed into law the previous year, Major had attempted to curry favour with his Eurosceptic back-benchers with displays of chest-beating patriotism, dismissing John Smith in one notable exchange before his death, as 'monsieur oui, poodle of Brussels'. As early as September 1993, Major had tried to get back on the front foot, with a piece in *The Economist* setting his vision of Europe in terms oddly reminiscent of Thatcher's Bruges speech. In it, he poured scorn on those on the continent who were intent on further integration after Maastricht. It was time, he said, to 'put away the old slogans, dreams and prejudices' of Europe and think again. 'I hope my fellow heads of government will resist the temptation to recite the mantra of full economic and monetary union as if nothing had changed,' he declared, before adding with folksy certainty: 'If they do recite it, it will have all the quaintness of a rain dance and about the same potency.'[23]

It is impossible to know if Major believed what he was saying or whether he was merely trying to declare himself out of trouble, as if he were a caricature of the British mandarin Russell Bretherton, of '*au revoir et bonne chance*' fame. Whether he liked it or not, the central dilemma of Major's premiership was how to handle the impending reality of European monetary union. It was not Major's European partners who were performing a rain dance to avoid a meteorological certainty.

Indeed, the contrast between Major's rhetoric and the reality unfolding diplomatically became so jarring, it began to seep into the national consciousness. When Major dismissed John Smith as 'monsieur oui', he did so in a display of his own apparent patriotic virility, prepared to stand alone against the rest of the EU to stop new voting rules coming into place that watered down each country's individual ability to block new legislation. The reforms

---

Carttiss. 'Richard Body, their fellow in spirit over matters European, resigned the whip in protest and joined them,' John Major later recorded. (*The Autobiography* (London: HarperCollins, 1999), p. 603)

were due to be agreed at a summit in Greece, but Major promised all-out opposition, prompting Delors to warn of a crisis. But then, at the summit itself, Major's foreign secretary Douglas Hurd backed down, accepting a defeat he attempted to sell as a compromise. The decision prompted the normally loyal *Daily Mail* to run a front-page cartoon of Major as a poodle, held on a lead by Jacques Delors.[24]

The new voting procedures were intended to ensure the smooth running of the EU ahead of its enlargement to include Austria, Sweden and Finland the following year. For many Eurosceptics, Major's retreat was symptomatic of the Conservative Party's malaise at this time. Before Maastricht, the EEC had been something most Eurosceptics could live with. Spiritually, it was seen as an instrument of the West. Its powers were limited, its effects largely benign and economic. Britain had also been seen to have won its battles within the bloc, at least for the most part. It had got its money back and helped introduce the single market. But now the Cold War was over, the EU's power was growing and Britain was losing its arguments. To this day, many on the Eurosceptic right of the Tory party believe Major's 'surrender', as the *Daily Mail* described it, was so jarring, the idea of Westminster 'weakness' began seeping into the popular consciousness, and not only that, but also the idea that the government was actively lying about its intentions. It was not simply being weak, but deliberately so. Major's decision in 1994 to appoint Neil Kinnock to be one of Britain's European Commissioners further irritated Eurosceptic sentiment.

Bill Cash's *European Journal* was scathing about Major's interventions during this period. In the magazine's second edition, published in November 1993, it reviewed the reaction in Europe and noted that 'it would seem that John Major's rallying cry in *The Economist* and at Blackpool for a different new Europe has made little impression on continental newspapers or, indeed, continental heads of government.'[25]

Preparations for the single currency would continue regardless of what Britain thought. The question was therefore not whether it would happen, but whether Britain should join to remain at the heart of Europe, or accept life outside the mainstream. In the run-up to the European elections in 1994, Major tried to reassure Eurosceptics that the beauty of the new Europe he'd negotiated at Maastricht was that Britain did not have to integrate further because there was now a 'multi-track, multi-speed, multi-layered' community.[26] By September, however, he was telling an audience in Leiden that he saw 'real danger' in such talk: 'I recoil from ideas of a Union in which some would be more equal than others.'[27] It didn't seem to matter that this was exactly what his own policies had brought about.

By announcing the creation of a Referendum Only Party in November 1994, Goldsmith was seeking not only to maintain the political pressure on Major to avoid signing up to any further integration, but to force him to make commitments that would make it harder for *any* government to do so. If he could force a referendum commitment out of Major, Blair might follow suit.

At first, Goldsmith's pitch seemed misdirected, both too technical and too vague to gain traction. He was not calling for British withdrawal from the European Union, which would have been radical but risky, nor for a referendum on the single currency. Instead, he was calling for a referendum on the outcome of a future integration which had not yet been agreed and might not be until after the next election. What's more, he was doing so, in part, in protest against an idea supported by almost all his natural allies: free trade.

The extent of Goldsmith's political isolation on that subject was revealed in the British reaction to *The Trap*. Unlike in France, where it seemed to capture something of the Gaullist spirit, on the question of free trade, both the Eurosceptic and pro-European wings of the Conservative Party stood squarely behind the prime minister. Pro-European Tories like Chris Patten were utterly dismissive of Goldsmith's arguments, but so too were influential conservative columnists in *The Times* and *The Telegraph*. The Centre for Policy Studies, bastion of Thatcherism, produced a pamphlet called the 'Goldsmith Fallacy'.

Goldsmith wanted to rebut these attacks, so he rushed to publish a second book in Britain, *The Response*, in September 1995. He also got to work on a two-pronged strategy to force a referendum: first, by setting up a new party to fight in every seat where the sitting MP did not commit to a referendum; and second, by keeping up the pressure on the government itself to call the referendum.

The two most difficult challenges for setting up a new party were candidate selection and publicity. In this, Patrick Robertson and Dougie Smith played key roles. Robertson chaired a weekly candidate approval committee meeting, in which recommendations were made to Goldsmith about future candidates. Smith, meanwhile, brought in his friend from the Federation of Conservative Students, Marc Glendening, to join the party's political office at its headquarters on Horseferry Road. Together, Smith and Glendening took on responsibility for opposition research and attack ads. Another early recruit was a young Tory called Priti Patel, who was brought in from Conservative Central Office to head up the party's new press office.

Every day, Smith, Glendening and their researchers would trawl through the British Newspaper Library in Colindale, looking for evidence of pro-federalism. If the sitting MP was judged to be a Europhile, Smith would recommend targeting them with full-page advertisements in local papers, in which their records on Europe would be set out. If the sitting MP was considered 'sound', they would be left alone. For Smith, it was the perfect perch. With Goldsmith's money, he had the means to unseat Tory wets, thus shifting the balance of the Conservative Party in a Thatcherite direction. He took grim satisfaction from listening in as Goldsmith took calls from panicked Tory MPs pleading him not to stand against them.

The launch of the Referendum Party added to the pressure

on the prime minister to move further to appease his Eurosceptic right. Unlike UKIP, which had yet to make any real impact, Goldsmith's financial clout and connections meant he could not be so easily ignored. According to cabinet papers released at the National Archives, as early as 1 December 1994, 'attention was drawn to the need for government to take a consistent line in response to renewed speculation about a referendum on European Union issues.' The cabinet discussed the idea of a referendum on the results of the next 'intergovernmental conference,' which was set to update Maastricht and was due in 1996, or, separately, on the single currency, which was now scheduled to come into effect in 1999. 'A referendum should not be ruled out,' the cabinet agreed.[28]

In his memoirs, Major is vitriolic about the Referendum Party, dismissing its 'unthinking venom.'[29] Yet it seems Goldsmith was not so venomous that Major avoided dining with him. In October 1995, the prime minister had bumped into Goldsmith at Margaret Thatcher's birthday party at Claridge's. The Conservative Party's treasurer at the time was an old Etonian friend of Goldsmith's called Charles Hambro. The three of them agreed to meet over dinner at Charles's flat, along with Major's political secretary Howell James. At the dinner, the prime minister urged Goldsmith to recognize the divisions in the Conservative Party, and to be patient while he 'moved to a policy of promising to hold a referendum on the single currency,' as Major later recorded in his memoir. The pair 'parted amicably,' and agreed to meet after the forthcoming Madrid summit in December. 'I did not know that Goldsmith was absolutely implacable,' Major later wrote, unconvincingly.[30]

Major's behaviour during this period became increasingly erratic as he faced the consequences of his own policies, veering between thin-skinned anger at his Eurosceptic critics and expressions of patriotic populism designed to hold his party together. By 1995, with the election approaching and Blair's Labour pulling clear in the polls, pressure was mounting on Major to offer something new. Whispers of leadership challenges were everywhere: Peter Lilley was tipped to stand, as was Norman Lamont. By March, Major began hinting that he was open to a referendum, prompting fierce criticism from Blair. It wasn't enough. 'Charles Hambro began to pass on messages that Goldsmith was becoming restless,' Major writes in his memoir. Goldsmith started taking out adverts in the national media, pushing his demands. By April 1995, *The Times* was reporting that Tory Eurosceptics didn't just want a promise of a referendum, but a manifesto pledge to boycott the single currency.[31]

For the rest of 1995, Major tried to avoid going any further than saying it was 'unlikely' Britain would join the first wave of countries to enter monetary union. But, try as he might, he could not pull his party together. In June, he addressed Michael Spicer's Fresh Start group, which only made matters worse.[32] By the summer, Major had had enough. For three years since his electoral triumph, his premiership had been a calamity of crisis and division, sleaze and rebellion. His authority was shot – and, with it, his electoral appeal. In desperation, he decided to take control of the situation by resigning from the Tory leadership, daring his critics to 'put up or shut up.' And, for a moment, it worked. The leading candidates to replace him – Michael Heseltine on the pro-European left of the party and Michael Portillo on the Eurosceptic right – chose not to stand, leaving only John Redwood, the Thatcherite secretary of state for Wales, to put his name forward. In the end, it was a comfortable – if pyrrhic – victory for Major. He had seen off his opponents and bought some time, but the divisions remained – and so did the Referendum Party.

Over Christmas, Major tried once again to placate Goldsmith, calling him at his estate in Mexico and outlining why he thought his expectations of a referendum were unrealistic. 'I also reminded him once more of the damage his activities would do to his own cause if, by widening Conservative divisions, he increased the likelihood of a Labour victory,' Major wrote.[33] It was no good. On 11 March 1996, Goldsmith took full-page advertisements in every national newspaper, confirming his new Referendum Party would field 600 candidates, backed by £20 million of his own money. He also sent letters to every MP informing them of his intention to field candidates in every seat apart from those where the sitting MP had committed to supporting a national referendum on Britain's relationship with the EU.

For Conservative Eurosceptics fearful of losing their seats, there was now a direct incentive to harden their position in the hope they could avoid facing a Referendum Party challenge. According to Robertson, 'many dozens' replied to the letter trying to convince Goldsmith not to stand against them. 'We also received replies from MPs pretending they supported a referendum, which we evaluated, and from others telling us to get stuffed.'[34]

Things were already looking grim for Major when another crisis struck. On 20 March 1996, the health secretary Stephen Dorrell formally acknowledged a link between BSE in cows and the terminally degenerative disease CJD in humans. Within a week, the European Union banned the export of British beef, not just to Europe, but to the world, effectively placing Britain in quarantine. The first case of BSE had been detected in 1984, and the United States had banned British beef as early as 1989. Yet the politics of Europe banning British beef were much more explosive. Having already spent the best part of the previous three years trying to hold his party together with ineffective but theatrical displays of national chauvinism, Major decided to try again with a policy of 'non-cooperation' in Europe, whereby any decision requiring unanimity would be vetoed by Britain to grind European business to a halt.

Here was Major cosplaying de Gaulle, who had 'empty-chaired' European business in protest at his failure to reform the Community into something far more Gaullist. Yet, even for de Gaulle, the result had only been a partial success: the so-called 'Luxembourg compromise', giving member states a de facto (if not de jure) veto over issues of vital national interest. The beef ban had been imposed on Britain by a qualified majority, so there was some logic to Major's stand, even if it was ultimately doomed to failure. 'John Major himself quickly realised that the policy of non-cooperation was unsustainable,' Stephen Wall – by now Britain's permanent representative to the EU – later admitted.[35] The beef wars dragged on well into the Blair government, another wound in the relationship making it all but impossible for Major to rebuild a sense of unity in his party.

Two days after Dorrell's painful admission, Major tried one final time to get through to Goldsmith, with a letter stressing the common ground between them. 'We both agree that Europe should be built around the nation state, not a federal agenda,' he wrote, before offering a concession: he was now 'considering' a referendum on the single currency. With this point established, Major finished with a plea: 'The Labour Party's determination not to be isolated in Europe can mean only one thing for the United Kingdom. All of us who believe in a Europe of nation states should be working together at this crucial time . . . resisting the drive towards federalism and carrying forward our vision of a partnership of nations.'[36]

Major's letter to Goldsmith is striking for its criticism of Labour's 'determination not to be isolated in Europe', given that this was the policy Major had been pursuing from the moment he became Margaret Thatcher's foreign secretary in 1990, then as chancellor and then finally as prime minister.

Major finally gave way on the referendum in April 1996, pledging to hold a national poll on British entry into the single currency should the government decide to pursue this option after the election. While it should have been a great victory for the Referendum Party, this was not how it felt. 'At the time, we felt cheated,' Robertson recalled.[37] The Referendum Party wanted a vote on Britain's entire relationship with the EU. Though Major painted the future referendum as little more than a confirmatory vote should a future government recommend joining the euro, in practice he had erected a new barrier to the central objective of his premiership: to remain at the heart of Europe.

While Major insists that the emergence of the Referendum Party played no part in his decision – and, indeed, that he had been privately in favour of making this offer even before the European elections of 1994 – this seems barely credible. Major had not only dined with Goldsmith, but had phoned him in Mexico and written to him insisting upon their shared world view. Even if Major had given no heed to Goldsmith's new movement when it came to the decision to offer a referendum, the Referendum Party was a real concern among the very Tory Eurosceptics who were causing Major such trouble at this time. As *The Times* wrote in its leader column on 24 April, the government seemed stuck in Goldsmith's 'Referendum Trap'.[38] In the same edition, the paper's new leader writer and columnist, Michael Gove, wrote that Goldsmith was 'shaping events more successfully than those burdened with office.'[39] The following day's paper recorded John Major dismissing those calling for Britain's withdrawal from the European Union as 'living in cloud-cuckoo-land'.[40]

A week later, the paper showed that, while just 1 per cent of the public planned to vote for Goldsmith's party, a majority wanted a referendum on Britain's future in Europe and up to sixty Eurosceptic MPs were planning to 'rebel against their party's official line during general election campaigning – by opposing a single currency and backing a referendum on wider relations with Europe.'[41]

During this period, despite his failing health, Goldsmith cut an extraordinarily energetic figure. He would spend the week campaigning in Britain, before flying back to Paris for the weekend to rest and receive chemotherapy. Robertson only found out about Goldsmith's cancer a few weeks before the election in 1997. On the plane back to Paris–Le Bourget Airport, he remembers Goldsmith lying on his bed, exhausted, but bursting into laughter. 'They want to offer me a peerage. Those cocksuckers don't know who I am.'[42] Robertson is convinced that such an offer was made, though Major has been equally adamant that it never was. Either way, it seems implausible, given the rancour between them, that it was ever seriously considered by either side. Goldsmith had no use for a peerage, while Major had gone as far as the politics of his cabinet would allow.

Despite having no MPs or any real presence in the polls, the Referendum Party had succeeded in shaping the national conversation.

The turmoil in British politics at this time was the direct result of the most radical reform of the European project since its inception in 1958: the creation of a single European currency. Regardless of whether Britain decided to join, the very fact of its existence fundamentally altered the nature of the European Union. British politics was reacting to the continuing momentum of Jean Monnet's *grand projet*, just as it had ever since Robert Schuman's leap into the dark in May 1950. In the late autumn of 1996, Enoch Powell gave the last interview of his life to Matthew d'Ancona of *The Sunday Telegraph*, reflecting on the latest developments, arguing that he had finally lived to the age in which his ideas had become 'part of a common fashion.' Asked why, Powell replied: 'The nation has returned to haunt us.'[43]

The question of what to do about the fast-approaching prospect of the single currency was not just a problem for Conservative Eurosceptics, but for all parties. Alastair Campbell's diaries from this time are full of anguish about what the Labour Party's position should be. As early as 1994, 'the big guns' on Labour's shadow cabinet – Tony Blair, Gordon Brown, John Prescott and Robin Cook – had debated the merits of a referendum on the euro. Prescott and Cook – more old Labour than new – were in favour, but Brown was against. While pro-European, Blair's instinct was that the party could not avoid offering a vote.

By 1996, Brown was still holding out against the idea of a referendum, but the party's position was shifting nevertheless. In media interviews, shadow ministers began to speak of the need for 'popular consent' before any change of currency – language remarkably reminiscent of Heath's in the run-up to the 1970 election.[44]

In November of that year, Blair visited Paris to hold talks with the French president Jacques Chirac. It was a chance to show himself as a prospective prime minister, rather than mere leader of the Opposition. But there was a problem. 'We didn't really have a story,' as Campbell wrote. The election was coming and pressure was starting to mount. A poll in *The Times* had shown the party's lead shrinking, from twenty-seven points to eighteen. Blair felt the Tories were 'starting to get their act together'. Suddenly, the time was right to make the move on the euro, it was felt. By Saturday, 16 November, 'the referendum plan', as Campbell called it, was on. 'GB [Gordon Brown] had done an interview for the Indy on Sunday, in which he said we were coming out for it.'[45]

With that, Tony Blair made one of the most consequential decisions of his career before he had even become prime minister, joining Major in erecting a barrier he would never be able to surmount. Blair felt it was an important part of his 'modernizing agenda' – not, as many would later see it, anathema to it. 'Between 1995 and 1997 . . . I was in a perpetual motion of reassurance,' Blair later wrote in his memoir, *A Journey*. 'The more the poll lead went up, the more I did it.'[46] Reassuring Middle England *was* modernization.

Blair's less modernizing predecessor, John Smith, might have been more resistant to the idea of referendum – and therefore freer to pursue the apparent modernity of the euro – though his pro-European credentials may have forced him to move on the issue even more forcefully than Blair in order to shut down his potential weakness. At root, Britain's political leaders do not merely have to deal with the shifting political dynamics within Westminster, but the reality of public sentiment. As Blair later put it, 'Though my general posture was pro-European, I took care not to go beyond what was reasonable for British opinion.'[47]

Throughout this time, Goldsmith was keeping up the pressure as much as he could. In October, Margaret Thatcher's former Conservative Party treasurer Lord McAlpine announced he had joined the Referendum Party, infuriating Major. In November, Goldsmith unveiled his preferred referendum question: 'Do you want the United Kingdom to be part of a Federal Europe? Or do you want the UK to return to an association of sovereign nations that are part of a common trading market?' As Major later wrote, such a question was 'so ambiguous as to be meaningless', yet it was politically astute. As Major put it, the question allowed Goldsmith 'to catch each and every anti-Europe breeze that might attract votes.'[48]

Before the starting gun for the election was fired in March, the Referendum Party received another fillip in February when the Eurosceptic Conservative backbencher George Gardiner defected to join Goldsmith's new party. In truth, Gardiner only jumped once he'd been pushed by his local association, who deselected him as their candidate in January. After unsuccessfully challenging this decision in the courts, he resigned the whip and went to see Goldsmith.

By this point, the Referendum Party had announced its slate of candidates for the election, including John Aspinall, the celebrity botanist David Bellamy and Rowan Atkinson's brother Rodney. It was an eclectic, eccentric mix, with only a smattering of the kind of celebrity that would have panicked the major parties, though it did have more than enough glamour. Referendum's first and last party conference, held in Brighton, became a source of media fascination. A party hosted by Lady Carla Powell, the wife of Charles Powell – Thatcher's former private secretary – was attended by the Goldsmith clan, Lord McAlpine, Alan Walters and Charles de Gaulle, Goldsmith's colleague in the European Parliament.

Without an army of grassroots activists to rival Labour or the Conservatives, it was heavily reliant on media attention. Indeed, Goldsmith had spent £20 million on political advertising and a further £2 million on a tabloid newspaper, *The News*, that was sent to every household in the country. The Referendum Party had no actual members – just registered supporters – because

Goldsmith did not think it was right to ask people to pay him subscriptions. Equally, there was no internal democracy. Goldsmith's party would provide a template for the populist parties of the future.

Major finally called the general election on 17 March 1997, setting the date for 1 May. The following day, *The Sun* ended two decades of support for the Conservative Party by backing Labour. 'The Sun Backs Blair', ran the front page. For Murdoch's other stable, *The Times*, the decision was more agonizing. Michael Gove, who had joined as a leader writer in 1996, remembers the editor Peter Stothard arranging an awayday at the Reform Club to weigh up the merits of supporting each of the two parties. Stothard was a committed Eurosceptic who loathed Major, but could not bring himself to throw *The Times*' institutional weight behind either party. In the end, he alighted on a formula whereby the newspaper would support whichever candidate was the more Eurosceptic in each constituency, which resulted in the eccentric position of *The Times* backing Jeremy Corbyn in Islington.

For the Conservatives, the one remaining hope was the economy, which was, in Michael Heseltine's estimation, 'the best in Europe.' Blair, in contrast, said the choice was 'between a Conservative Party which most people feel has run out of ideas and is out of date, and a new and revitalized Labour Party.'[49] Neither of the two major parties wanted the election to be fought on the question of Europe.

To his annoyance, Goldsmith quickly found himself being squeezed for publicity as the structural reality of Britain's electoral system began to bite. Aware that they were likely to be outgunned as soon as the campaign got under way, Robertson had already placed an order for 6 million VHS tapes, made in the United States and shipped to Britain for the election. Goldsmith's tapes were wrapped in a dark-red sleeve with the words 'The most important video you'll ever watch' plastered over it. The video opens with sinister music, as the presenter of the BBC's *That's Life* programme, Gavin Campbell, comes into view, warning that 'what you are about to hear will both surprise and outrage you.' The British public had been lied to, Campbell tells the audience. Edward Heath had promised that entering the Common Market involved no loss of 'essential sovereignty', but it had. In fact, Britain was becoming a 'mere province' in a 'European superstate' led by Germany.[50]

As the election approached, Blair began to panic about Europe all over again – indeed, Campbell records he was 'fretting over virtually nothing else.'[51] On 21 April, Blair gave a speech in Manchester entitled, 'A New Role for Britain in the World'. Yet, in effect, Blair was offering little new. On Europe, he declared there were 'three choices open to Britain'. 'The first is leaving; the second is in but impotent; and the third is remaining in but leading.' This formulation was almost verbatim the language Major had been using for the previous five years. Blair then set out his five priorities, none of which Major would have dissented from, whether 'creating flexible labour markets' or 'CAP reform'. On the euro, Blair said there must be 'genuine sustainable convergence between the economies that take part', and he would have 'no truck with a fudged single currency.' At the same time, he said, to rule out membership would 'destroy any influence we have over the process.' Apart from support for the social chapter, there was nothing to separate the policies of the two main parties and Blair himself admitted this: 'Our position and the formal position of the Conservatives are the same. The real issue is one of leadership and clarity.'[52]

A few days before the general election, Blair tried to reassure voters even further with an article for *The Sun* entitled 'My love for the £', in which he said he would have 'no truck with a European superstate', before adding, 'If there are moves to create that dragon I will slay it.' On the issue of the single currency, he declared that he felt the same emotional attachment to the pound as others did. 'I know exactly what the British people feel when they see the Queen's head on a £10 note. I feel it too.' In the same piece, however, he also attempted to showcase his strength.

'Even if it [taking Britain into the euro] is unpopular,' he said, 'I will recommend it if it is the right thing to do.'[53] The final decision, of course, would be for the country.

In the end, Blair carried all before him with the biggest landslide victory since the war – although, with half a million fewer votes than Major had achieved in 1992. Labour secured 43.2 per cent of the vote and 418 MPs, leaving the new prime minister with a majority of some 179. The Conservative Party limped home with just 165 MPs, while the Referendum Party barely made an impression at all, winning 811,894 votes, which amounted to just 2.6 per cent of the total. The party's best result came in Harwich, where the candidate Jeffrey Titford secured 9 per cent, but still finished fourth. In Putney, Goldsmith scraped together just 1,518 votes – or 3.5 per cent of the total.

For all the passions and plots over the past three years, it was a disappointing night for Goldsmith and his supporters. The sorry nature of the result seemed to be encapsulated when Goldsmith found himself in an unseemly slanging match with his rival candidate in Putney, the defeated sitting MP David Mellor, who made an ill-tempered concession speech in which he dismissed the Referendum Party's result as 'derisory'.[54] Goldsmith shot back, jeering 'out, out, out!' while delivering a sardonic slow handclap.

The Referendum Party had underperformed – at least compared to some of the more excitable pre-election forecasts. Alan Sked's UKIP had barely registered at all, finishing eleventh overall with just 0.3 per cent or 105,722 votes. But there was one UKIP candidate who kept hold of his deposit, winning 5.7 per cent of the vote: Nigel Farage. 'I was the only one who tried,' Farage explained afterwards.[55] A more convincing explanation is that the Referendum Party did not stand in that seat.

The result left Tony Blair supreme, the most powerful incoming prime minister in post-war British history, as well as the most pro-European since Edward Heath, though guarded behind layers of populist caution. The Labour Party Blair led was no longer the fractured party of the 1970s, when it had last been in power, riven between its pro- and anti-European factions. For the first time in its history, it was largely united and overwhelmingly pro-European. Robin Cook, the new foreign secretary, neatly embodied this new reality. Having campaigned for 'No' in 1975, he was now a pragmatic, mainstream European social democrat. One of his first acts was to dispatch his deputy, the new Europe minister Doug Henderson, to the negotiations over the next set of reforms, due to be finalized in Amsterdam within weeks. 'I come to this meeting as the representative of a new government with an overwhelming mandate,' Henderson declared. 'One of the most important priorities we have identified is to make a fresh start to Britain's relations with the rest of the EU and draw a line under the recent past.'[56] Britain would end its opt-out from the social chapter, support a new employment chapter in the treaty and support enshrining a commitment to human rights. After years of turmoil, Britain suddenly seemed comfortable in Europe.

'England arose yesterday,' declared *The Guardian* in triumph. 'Perhaps there is a God, after all.'[57] Across Europe, there was also barely concealed relief. Alain Juppé, the French prime minister, said there was 'new hope for social Europe', while German Chancellor Helmut Kohl was even more blunt: 'This should be a lesson for all those who want to win votes with anti-European polemics.'[58]

For Britain's Eurosceptics, of course, the result offered the dismal prospect of a decade in Opposition, leaving the Labour Party of Tony Blair to navigate the political challenge of the impending single currency. Watching the election results at home, a frail and mournful Enoch Powell turned to his wife and declared, 'They have voted to break up the United Kingdom.'[59] Powell was not only concerned with the question of Europe but of the future of Britain itself, wary of Blair's proposed constitutional reforms on the House of Lords, elected regional mayors and devolution.

As Powell entered the dusk of his life, his dream of Britain was fading from memory, just as his dreams of empire had faded long before. Those who had taken inspiration from Powell appeared similarly lost amid the triumphant euphoria of their opponents. Nicholas Budgen, Powell's Eurosceptic successor as MP for Wolverhampton South West – and the last candidate Powell publicly supported – had lost his seat alongside many of his colleagues. UKIP, the last party for whom Powell campaigned, was defeated, dejected and mutinous, split between two rival factions of old Skeddite loyalists and a new band of populists battling for control under the leadership of the coming man in the party: Nigel Farage. For the Referendum Party, though, the defeat was more final.

A fortnight after the election, Goldsmith hosted a lunch for his main lieutenants at which he confided that he was withdrawing from politics, closing down the party and turning it into a 'movement', which would be run by his wife, Lady Annabel Goldsmith.

Two weeks later, the news finally broke that Goldsmith was terminally ill. On Friday, 18 July 1997, he flew to Malaga, where a helicopter was waiting to take him to the Spanish estate and to the bed in which he had been born sixty-four years earlier. Within hours of his arrival, he was dead.

At Goldsmith's packed memorial service in London on 13 November 1997, Thatcher led the tributes, praising her friend as 'a giant among men' who had 'brought to bear on politics the same intellectual clarity that had stood him so well in business'. She called Goldsmith 'one of the bravest men I ever met', adding that the measure of his success could be judged by 'the fear he inspired in the political-bureaucratic class that opposed him'. Thatcher was also clear that Goldsmith was responsible for having 'dragged both main parties to concede the referendum they'd earlier refused.' She went as far as to declare that, 'Above all he was right about "Europe" – the word upon which hang so many questions fundamental to our national identity and future.' Goldsmith was 'a Great European on a continent which the Little Europeans claimed as their own'.[60]

The following day's *Times* carried a report of the service on its front page, under the headline 'Goldsmith – and all that jazz'. 'The 700 guests who gathered to celebrate his multifaceted life found themselves in a carnival atmosphere, punctuated by jazz, a band and impromptu dancing,' the paper reported. In attendance were his two surviving wives, Annabel Goldsmith and Ginette Lery, and 'a clutch of his children' led by his daughter Jemima, accompanied by her husband Imran Khan, though not his long-standing mistress Laure Boulay de la Meurthe, who had been asked to stay away. Rupert Murdoch, Conrad Black, Lord McAlpine, Bill Cash, Neil Hamilton and Jonathan Aitken were all in attendance, alongside Goldsmith's brother Teddy, Henry Kissinger and John Aspinall. But it was the music most of all that branded the event with an air of celebration. From a conventional start with 'Jerusalem', the programme proceeded through Verdi's 'Chorus of the Hebrew Slaves' and Gershwin's 'Summertime' to a Mexican mariachi band and thence to Duke Ellington's 'Mood Indigo'. The service closed to the spectacle of Chief Mangosuthu Buthelezi, political leader of South Africa's Zulus, leading dancing in the aisles.

For Patrick Robertson, Goldsmith's death was not just a personal tragedy, but a political bereavement bringing to an end a wild decade in which he had risen from young Eurosceptic student to Thatcherite protégé and, finally, political revolutionary. Robertson had been planning to stand for the Referendum Party at the next European elections, due in 1999. Now, Goldsmith was gone, his party had been disbanded and the Conservative Party disempowered. Robertson returned to his PR firm. Meanwhile, Britain's Eurosceptics could do little but prepare for a long, painful resistance, protected only by the final barrier of a referendum which they had erected at the last.

For Enoch Powell, too, the resistance had come to an end. Now eighty-five, his mobility was limited and even simple acts of reading and writing proved an immense effort. During the night of Friday, 6 February 1998, he suffered an aneurysm and was taken to hospital, where he died two days later, taking with him the memories of his dreams which had not yet come to pass.

Like those other titanic figures who had been with him in

Algiers in 1942, Enoch Powell had blazed a trail through twentieth-century Britain. He had longed for the glory of martyrdom in the war and had seemed almost determined to seek it out in the peace that followed – if not for empire, then at least for England and the union.

His death in 1998 seemed not only to bring an end to his long life, but also to that of the kind of country he had longed to die for. The Labour Party was ascendant and Toryism powerless. The future was Europe and devolution, not the old nation state. Further integration seemed an inevitability. Powell remains a singular figure in Britain's post-war politics, burning with the determination of a man intent on keeping alive his dream of Britain. In doing so, he created new dreams for others to seize.

Powell's funeral in London was attended by almost all the leading figures of British Euroscepticism at the time: Lord Salisbury, Michael Portillo, Michael Howard, Peter Lilley, Jonathan Aitken, Iain Duncan Smith, Charles Moore, Simon Heffer and Bill Cash. The widow of T. E. Utley was there, as well as John Major. At the funeral, Powell's daughter read out 'Loveliest of Trees', a passage from Housman's *A Shropshire Lad*, reflecting on the fleeting nature of life. Powell was then laid to rest in the uniform of a brigadier of the Royal Warwickshire Regiment, in which he fought during the war.[61]

Housman's epic closes with a more melancholy reflection on mortality than 'Loveliest of Trees', brooding over the legacies we leave behind when we're gone:

> I Hoed and trenched and weeded,
> And took the flowers to fair:
> I brought them home unheeded;
> The hue was not the wear.

For decades, Powell had honed his ideas into the soil of British politics, but for the most part they had not been taken up to wear. Housman continues:

So up and down I sow them
For lads like me to find,
When I shall lie below them,
A dead man out of mind.

Some seed the birds devour,
And some the season mars,
But here and there will flower
The solitary stars,

And fields will yearly bear them
As light-leaved spring comes on,
And luckless lads will wear them
When I am dead and gone.[62]

When John Enoch Powell passed what he had once called the separating flame on 8 February 1998, many of the seeds he had laid in his long life in Parliament had flowered into the mainstream of public life, from the scepticism about the Commonwealth he had displayed in his early years as an MP, to the monetarism he championed in the 1960s. Yet, some of his other causes had badly marred, from the imperial delusions of his youth to his prophecies of civil war and national suicide in 1968. Regardless, by the time of his death, the fields of British politics had been forever altered by his presence, most consequentially of all on that greatest question of post-war British politics: Europe.

Part Three

'HISTORY IS NOW'

Chapter 12

In the years running up to her husband's death in 1985, Jessica Douglas-Home had found solace in her underground partnership with Roger Scruton.[1] In the years that followed, their partnership developed into something more. In one sense, the match was obvious; they were bound together in a mission to protect the fading memories of Europe's forgotten East. But they were also very different characters: he, distant, impractical and prone to solipsistic flights of fancy; she, a widowed mother of two, who could not afford to be too removed from the realities of life. And, by the late 1980s, Scruton was not the only man vying for her affections.

Born in Dublin in 1934, the wealthy businessman Rodney Leach was educated at Harrow and Balliol before entering the world of high finance, where he rose to become an executive at the global conglomerate Jardine Matheson. While Scruton preferred the world of Nietzsche and Wagner, Leach liked to spend his evenings at the Portland Club, playing bridge. One was solitary and somewhat stiff in company; the other was gregarious and urbane.

For Jessica Douglas-Home, they offered different visions of the future. The nature of the choice she faced was brought home to her in a moment of familial anguish. In 1989, her eldest son, Tara, was almost killed in a car crash near the family's country home in Gloucestershire. As Jessica and her family gathered in desperate anxiety, scrambling to do all they could to help, Scruton called from London. He had been due to stay at Jessica's home that weekend to go hunting. His message, though, was not to cancel the plan, but to reassure everyone that he would be sure not to disturb them. The call infuriated Jessica's closest family, who told him he could not possibly think it was acceptable to come to stay in such circumstances. When Jessica was told about the conversation, she began to cry. 'Oh, he's just so damaged,' she said.[2] Leach, in contrast, offered practical help.

When later asked why she and Scruton had never married, Jessica would say, 'Because he never asked.'[3] Yet, those closest to her pinpoint this crisis as the real turning point in their relationship. Scruton's eccentricities and tendency to live in his own mind had become too much for Jessica. Three years after the accident, with Tara recovered, Jessica married Rodney Leach.

Rodney Leach was not without political convictions of his own. As a young classics tutor at Oxford in the 1950s, he had been so moved by the accounts of communist terror in Budapest that he had set up the Oxford Hungarian Relief Fund to help refugees fleeing the Soviet advance.[4] Once he entered the business world, he retained an interest in politics and was part of the set which backed Margaret Thatcher throughout the 1980s.

Yet, it was not until his marriage to Jessica that Leach became a political figure in his own right, drawn into the higher echelons of Tory activism just as the focus of the right began to shift from the Cold War to Europe. With Jessica's encouragement, he began to apply his forensic corporate mind to the small print of the Maastricht Treaty. By 1993, he had joined the advisory board of Bill Cash's European Foundation, along with Ralph Harris, Kenneth Minogue and Norman Stone. And, by 1994, he was publicly intervening in European affairs, first publishing *After Maastricht*,[5] a pamphlet for Cash's Foundation, and then delivering a lecture entitled 'City Concern over Federal Europe'.[6] In it, Leach went as far as to raise the prospect of withdrawal from the EU, insisting that 'the $64,000 question' – should we continue? – could not be avoided much longer.

The central argument of Leach's intervention in 1994, however, was not to advocate leaving the EU, but to call for a new organization to look at the pros and cons of British membership. 'We need an accurate cost–benefit analysis of withdrawal.' The seed had been planted, though it would not flower until after the Labour landslide of 1997.

By then, the debate over Europe was not over Maastricht or withdrawal, but the specific issue of the single currency. For Eurosceptics like Rodney Leach, the great danger was that Blair would try to drive Britain into the single currency in time for its launch in 1999. Not only did Blair have an even greater majority than Thatcher, but he was also just as radical.

The extent of the Labour government's ambition was revealed within days of victory. First came independence for the Bank of England, and then, in the first meeting of the new cabinet, the creation of a new 'joint consultative committee' with the Liberal Democrats.[7] This was the beginning of what Blair hoped and believed would be a progressive realignment of British politics. After these opening salvos came devolution in Scotland and Wales and an intensification of the push for peace in Northern Ireland. In Europe, too, there was a clear sense that Britain was entering a fresh era. During his first EU summit, in Amsterdam, in June, Blair signed up to the social chapter and agreed new powers for the European Parliament. A new dawn really had broken.

And yet, in most other respects, Blair was not as radical as he seemed. In Amsterdam, he held fast to most of the traditional British positions: opposing any loss of sovereign control over welfare policy and any dilution of NATO's role in European security. Ahead of the Labour Party Conference that autumn, the co-chairman of the Bruges Group, Martin Holmes, even wrote in Bill Cash's *European Journal* that Blair's policies were little more than a continuation of Majorism. 'I am not saying Tony Blair is one of us,' Holmes wrote, 'but at least he is not a John Smith.'[8]

At the conference, Blair gave credence to Holmes's theory, telling the audience that, while Britain was destined to lead the continent into its future – 'to be nothing less than the model twenty-first century nation, a beacon to the world', as he put it – the economic conditions had to be right before Britain would join the single currency.[9] Britain, then, was both the dashing new face of modern Europe and the same old cautious partner it had always been.

Still, for Britain's Eurosceptics, Blair's energetic early months in office exposed their own sudden powerlessness. Most of the groups which had played such pivotal roles in the dramas of the Major years had either been neutered or appeared irrelevant. The Eurosceptic 'bastards' of John Major's ire no longer held the balance of power.[10] The Bruges Group had long since been tamed. Goldsmith's Referendum Party had been reduced to a 'movement' without an obvious leader, ultimately controlled by Robin Birley, but largely run by the old FCS comrades Dougie Smith and Marc Glendening.

Yet, the scale of Blair's power coupled with his radical constitutional reforms and the extent of his modernizing ambition injected a fresh sense of purpose into the Eurosceptic movement. If Blair had a mission, so did they: to stop Britain's entry into the euro.

Some of those who had worked for Goldsmith remained employed by the new entity and had close connections to the cadre of Eurosceptic journalists then emerging into positions of influence on Fleet Street. By 1997, Dougie Smith and Michael Gove had become close, having been introduced by one-time FCS wet turned more right-leaning comment editor of *The Daily Telegraph*, Paul Goodman, and his fellow *Telegraph* leader writer Dean Godson who had moved into journalism after working for Sir James Goldsmith as his personal librarian in the early 1990s. The journalists Matthew d'Ancona, Daniel Johnson and Martin Ivens were also part of this young, right-leaning friendship group united by a shared opposition to further European integration.

'We were all, in different ways, to a greater or lesser extent Eurosceptic,' Gove later reflected.*

Gove was also part of a dining society organized by Jessica Douglas-Home and Roger Scruton, which often met at Rodney Leach's Holland Park home. Gove remembers Scruton as the 'guru' of their evenings, as they discussed the state of the Conservative Party and how to save it.[11] To begin with, Leach was a marginal figure, only joining late in the evening after returning home from the Portland. Yet, over time, he became something of an éminence grise: a quiet, pragmatic voice of influence from a world largely alien to the journalists and philosophers around the table.

With the question of British membership of the euro hanging over everything, the overwhelming priority for the group in 1997 was to stop Ken Clarke securing the Tory leadership.[12] Opposing Clarke were a series of Eurosceptic candidates, ranging from Michael Howard to Peter Lilley, John Redwood and, finally, William Hague, then only thirty-six. Though Hague had not been expected to stand at first, he quickly spotted an opportunity for generational change. His pitch was attractive to a party that had just suffered a near-mortal defeat, promising a fresh start and party unity by establishing a clear position on the single currency. 'I think it's important to lead the party away from squabbles about that issue,' he said. 'My choice would be very clear: we should not be part of a single European currency.'[13] Hague made it through to the final round against Clarke, and this was enough to win the backing of Margaret Thatcher. 'I am supporting William Hague,' she declared to the media. 'Have you got the name? Vote

---

* In the historian Andrew Roberts' 1995 novel, *The Aachen Memorandum*, which imagines a dystopian future in which Britain has been subsumed into a United States of Europe, a dissident group of nationalists called the 'Bonchurch Group' are jailed for what Roberts calls 'Anglo-patriotism'. The name is a reference to the flat on Bonchurch Road near Ladbroke Grove where Michael Gove was living at the time. Roberts, Andrew, *The Aachen Memorandum* (pp. 117–18). (London: Biteback Publishing)

for William Hague to follow the same kind of government I led. Vote for William Hague on Thursday. Have you got the message?'[14] It seemed they had.

Ahead of the vote, *The Times* had warned that, even though Hague's leadership was likely to be 'a poor, weak thing', Clarke could not be leader. The winner needed a 'decisive view on Europe' and the ability to motivate the party's activists. 'The Tory party cannot unite with vigour around any European policy Mr Clarke is likely to adopt.'[15] The author of this intervention was Michael Gove.

In the final vote, William Hague defeated Ken Clarke. It was a pivotal moment. Hague's victory ensured that any move to take Britain into the euro via a referendum would not be a repeat of 1975, in which most of the political establishment had lined up behind the Labour prime minister. Had Clarke won the leadership in 1997, his plan was to give Conservative MPs a free vote on the euro – and to campaign to join himself. By electing Hague, the Conservative Party guaranteed that any future referendum would be contested at the elite level as well as among the public.

For Blair, the challenge of leading Britain into the euro had been complicated by Hague's election, but the internal politics of the Labour Party were not straightforward either. Contrary to later perceptions, the general impression in the media at the time – as reflected in *The European Journal* – was that Blair was more sceptical about the economic case for joining the euro than his chancellor, Gordon Brown. Blair had pushed for the party to match the Conservative Party's referendum pledge in the run-up to 1997, while Brown had resisted. Brown had also supported British membership of the ERM in the run-up to Black Wednesday.

Brown's decision to hire a young journalist called Ed Balls from the *Financial Times* as his special adviser in 1994 stiffened his scepticism, at least on monetary matters. Balls had published a Fabian pamphlet in 1992 criticizing the single currency,[16] and had continued in this vein in his position as an *FT* leader writer.* After joining Brown, Balls was instrumental in devising the 'five economic tests' that would need be passed before Labour could recommend joining the euro. Blair and Brown were as one in believing that, to stand any chance of convincing the public to join the euro, the economic case had to be watertight. This, in turn, required the economic tests to be met in a way that would be seen as credible, which was unlikely in the short term. As Stephen Wall, Britain's permanent representative to the EU, later concluded, 'EMU was probably always going to be an issue of the second term.'[17] Weighing on Blair's mind at this time was also the simple reality of public hostility to the idea of giving up sterling, set out in the polling reports he received from his influential adviser Philip Gould.

By the autumn of 1997, Brown was becoming ever more irritated by media reports caricaturing him as a gung-ho pro-European, which, he felt, placed him on the wrong side of a political dividing line with Blair. Blair, in turn, did not want the issue permanently hanging over the government.[18] After much agonizing, a decision was taken to publicly rule out joining the euro in the first wave of countries in 1999, while keeping open the prospect that Britain could join later in the parliament if the conditions were right. The story was given to *The Times* in an 'interview' with Brown, which, for the most part, was a series of quotes agreed with Number Ten and faxed to the paper's political editor. Without Blair's knowledge, however, Ed Balls had gone further, briefing the paper that Britain would not be joining the

---

* 'If countries are affected differently by an economic event – such as an oil shock or German unification – then the desired policy response will not be the same,' Balls had written in the Fabian pamphlet. 'Tying countries together under these circumstances means large and persistent regional problems – slow growth and huge unemployment in different European countries, precisely what has occurred in Europe since German unification . . . In short, monetary union, in the manner and timetable envisaged in the 1991 Maastricht Treaty is an economically and politically misconceived project.'

single currency before the next election. The story landed the following day, the paper splashing with the headline: 'Brown rules out single currency for lifetime of this parliament'.[19] The Treasury had spun the government into a position Number Ten had not agreed.

When Blair saw *The Times*' headline that evening, he erupted in anger, but Brown refused to take his calls. The following morning, Blair met with Alastair Campbell, Peter Mandelson and Jonathan Powell to discuss how to respond. If they said nothing, it would confirm the story, but if they denied it, they would be at war with the chancellor. They were stuck. On 17 October, Jonathan Powell wrote in his diary: 'We may regret that we took the biggest decision of this government in this most haphazard of ways.'[20]

In an attempt to wrestle back control of events, Blair demanded that Brown make a formal statement clarifying that the government remained committed to joining the euro in principle, even if that was unlikely to be within the parliament. 'If a single currency would be good for British jobs, business and future prosperity, it is right, in principle, to join,' Brown told the Commons. As *The Times* noted the next day, this was 'the first endorsement by any British Government of the principle of European monetary union coupled with a promise to prepare for entry.'[21] Yet it was also a decidedly conventional way of understanding the dilemma of European integration: a question of pragmatic economic judgement and not political commitment. Blair was declaring Britain's 'destiny' to lead Europe – but only when the economic conditions were right.

Despite this setback, Blair remained dominant. To many observers of British politics, it seemed only a matter of time before the country accepted the euro. From the moment Robert Schuman had proposed a European Coal and Steel Union in May 1950, Britain had been slow to accept its fate, but always did so eventually. This sense of inevitability was promulgated in an influential history of Britain's relationship with Europe, *This Blessed Plot*, written by the respected *Guardian* columnist Hugo Young, first published in 1998. In it, Young set out the Blairite case that Britain's destiny was European: 'This is not an opinion,' he wrote, 'but surely incontestable fact . . . proved by the outcome, Britain's presence inside the European apparatus.'[22]

Young's account remains the urtext of Britain's relationship with Europe, capturing a moment in time when narratives of historical teleology fired the Western imagination. In his concluding thoughts, he set out his hope that Blair's failure to take Britain into the euro the year before would prove little more than another blip in Britain's relentless journey of integration, a mere tactic that would allow a sense of inevitability to build.[23] The book, however, was not only influential among those who shared Young's pro-Europeanism, but also among many of the most committed Eurosceptics, who admired its account of Britain's entry – 'a subterfuge most foul', guided by a political elite which had never been entirely honest about the project's true nature. In *The Daily Telegraph*, Boris Johnson praised Young for 'rootling out the federasts at the heart of the British establishment'.

This, then, was the situation in 1998 as Blair entered his second year as prime minister. To realize his political vision for Britain's future, he needed to build an economic case for the single currency. To stop him, the Eurosceptic alliance needed to make the opposite case: for the retention of sterling. And, to do that, they required a think tank of the sort Rodney Leach had suggested four years earlier.

The Eurosceptic resistance at this time remained broad but inchoate, made up of Hague's Conservative Party and a broader constellation of journalists and Thatcherite activists. Beyond this were the near dormant groups like the Campaign for an Independent Britain, a few remaining Labour Eurosceptics and the marginal UKIP. Yet, within this wider milieu, two new political forces emerged. The first was the brainchild of Dougie Smith; the second, of Rodney Leach.

In 1998, the Referendum Movement merged with another

insurgent anti-euro organization, the Euro Information Campaign, funded by the millionaire businessman Paul Sykes, and became the Democracy Movement. The principal figures in this new organization were, once again, Dougie Smith and Marc Glendening.

At the Referendum Party, the pair had tried to engineer a change in the balance of power in the Conservative Party by standing Goldsmith-backed candidates selectively against their factional opponents, pumping resources into seats where the Conservative was pro-European, while providing only token or even no opposition to Eurosceptic Tories. But, with the Referendum Party gone, Smith and Glendening needed to devise a new instrument to shape the Conservative Party. Smith's key insight was that the Conservative grassroots were now so solidly Eurosceptic that they would do the job themselves by selecting future MPs who shared their beliefs, if they had access to information that enabled them to identify the genuine views on Europe of every candidate.

In 1997, Smith and Glendening had used the abundant funds of the Referendum Party to build a large database containing details of hundreds of Tory candidates and their stated positions on Europe. Now, the Democracy Movement intended to turn this into a publicly available resource which could be used by members of local Conservative associations to research any Tories who applied to be parliamentary candidates.

To its critics, this endeavour was an almost McCarthyite inversion of the democratic process, surreptitiously tipping the scales against the old Europhile 'moderates' in favour of Smith's fellow travellers. Yet, the power of Smith's idea lay in the simple fact that the Conservative grassroots were no longer the Heathite Europhiles of yesteryear, but the children of Thatcher for whom Britain's integration into Europe had reached the limits of tolerability. Even the more pro-European candidates appeared to understand this shift in the party, loudly declaring their own hostility to European federalism before the selectors.

Over the course of 1998, Smith began work on his project, which he called 'Candidlist'. At the same time, Rodney Leach's idea for a new European think tank finally found its moment. Back in 1994, in his original pamphlet for the European Foundation, Leach had argued that business in particular would be crucial in shaping the public debate. 'Business leaders, who have seen their sycophantic pro-Government generalizations quoted back as objective testimony to the rightness of the Government's position, have a particular responsibility to start saying in public what so many of them say in private,' Leach had declared.[24] Now, four years later, the government had set out its stall and business had a duty to respond.

Through his contacts in the City, Leach already knew many of the most influential Eurosceptic tycoons of the day, including fellow Portland Club regulars Stanley Kalms and Stuart Wheeler. Through his marriage to Jessica Douglas-Home, Leach also knew the circle of Tory academics around Roger Scruton and Norman Stone, including, most importantly, Stone's close friend, the former MP and Tory grandee Viscount Cranborne, scion of the last great aristocratic family still involved in British politics, the Cecils, and son and heir of the Marquis of Salisbury.

Though no longer an MP, Robert Cranborne remained influential in Tory circles as leader of the House of Lords and an inveterate organizer and fixer. Together, the pair had the connections, financial backing and respectability to set up the kind of venture Leach demanded. And so, in June 1998, a decade after Margaret Thatcher had electrified the Eurosceptic cause in Bruges, a new organization was born: Business for Sterling.

After an uneasy start, it found its feet by poaching the campaigning young Tory, Nick Herbert, from the Countryside Alliance as its chief executive. Leach made the move at the urging of his confidant, Alex Hickman, a close friend of Jessica Douglas-Home's youngest son Luke, who had been one of the first to join Leach's new venture, charged with looking after the high-value donors who were providing the financial firepower of the organization. Yet, it was the appointment of a third figure early the next year which turbocharged Leach's new venture: Dominic Cummings.

Cummings had been back in England for just a few months when Tony Blair swept to power with his promise to remake Britain. Since December 1994, he had been in Moscow, trying and failing to make his fortune. The inspiration for Cummings' Russian adventure was his tutor and friend at Oxford, Norman Stone, who had travelled to and from the Russian capital after the fall of the Soviet Union, trying to access the KGB's Second World War archives, returning in wonder at the chaotic energy he had witnessed. 'He realized there was all this unbelievable stuff which the Russians had nabbed in 1945,' Cummings recalled. 'He'd say to me, "This place is totally fucking crazy, it's like a gold rush."'[25]

Cummings had entered Stone's orbit after turning up at one of his lectures and asking whether Stone would be his tutor. Slightly taken aback, Stone told Cummings that this wasn't usually how things worked, but if his college was fine with it, he'd be happy to, having received glowing reports from his colleague Robin Lane Fox. Thus began a lifelong friendship. Cummings paid Stone with a bottle of whisky at the end of each term. 'He taught me a lot of twentieth-century history out of the kindness of his heart, really,' Cummings later reflected.[26] Cummings and Stone shared a love of history, an admiration for Thatcher and a loathing of Labour.

Encouraged by Stone, Cummings travelled to Moscow, initially staying with a young academic called Liam Halligan who was already there. Halligan remembers Cummings as 'bright and analytical, asking tons of questions'. Cummings was particularly interested in what Halligan called 'the emerging state of nations'. 'We were all told to believe this thesis about the end of history, but what was happening in the post-communist world was history on speed.' Cummings was also struck by the disconnect between Western perceptions of the situation in Russia and what was really happening. 'Yes, for a lot of people what was happening was terrible, but for others it was a boom,' as Halligan put it. 'So, while there was a collapse going on, there was also a release. I think that was quite a formative moment for him.'[27]

In Moscow, Cummings alighted on his plan to make his fortune: a new airline allowing rich Western businessmen to bypass Moscow. Cummings chose the formerly closed city of Samara, 1,000 kilometres south-east of the capital, as the host city for his new airline. Samara had been a centre for Soviet airspace technology; Cummings believed that, if Russia was going to open up, it would be just the kind of place that would be attractive to foreign investors. The plan soon fell apart as those with deeper pockets and better connections took control. 'We got fucked by the EPRD [European Bank for Reconstruction and Development], Lufthansa and the KGB,' Cummings later reflected.[28]

While in Russia, Norman Stone got in touch with Cummings to ask a favour. Robert Cranborne's daughter, Eyzie, was coming to Moscow: would he make sure she was OK? Cummings was happy to help and thought little of it; yet, through this seemingly unexceptional connection, his life would change – and with it, perhaps, the fate of British politics.

Chastened by his failed attempt at setting up an airline, Cummings arrived home in late 1996 and began to study for the bar. By 1998, however, he had grown bored of his chosen new profession and, visiting Eyzie one evening at her father's house, fell into conversation with Cranborne, who suggested that he come to work for him instead. 'He and some friends had just started up this campaign to stop Blair taking us into the euro, and he said, "If you're looking for something to do, why don't you go do this?"'[29]

The businessmen involved in the new group appealed to Cummings' sense of adventurism. 'They were entrepreneurs, not CBI, hired-manager types,' he said.[30] Alongside Stanley Kalms and Stuart Wheeler, there was the Thatcherite tycoon James Hanson and one-time British Leyland chairman Michael Edwardes, as well as the hotelier Rocco Forte and Labour peer Dick Marsh. Rodney Leach, though, was the lynchpin who brought not only 'worldly success', as Michael Gove put it, but respectability. 'For some, Euroscepticism was always a gambler's cause,' Gove reflected. 'But Rodney was not a gambler. He was a bridge player and shrewd reader of the cards.' Leach was 'successful, polished and credible'.[31] The energy of the organization, however, came from its staff, each of whom brought different attributes to the table. Alex Hickman ensured the flow of donations from Leach's friends in the City. Nick Herbert brought professional campaigning experience. And Dominic Cummings injected an ideological fervour and strategic discipline not seen in British politics since the early days of the Bruges Group.

One of Cummings' strengths was getting to know the national media, and soon he had struck up a close working relationship with the Anglo-Australian political editor of *The Sun*, Trevor Kavanagh. For Cummings, this relationship was crucial. Not only was Kavanagh one of the most influential figures on Fleet Street, but he was known to have the ear of Rupert Murdoch himself. 'People knew that he was the journalist upon whom Rupert Murdoch most relied for an understanding of UK politics,' Gove explained.[32] But the relationship was not all one way. Despite his youth, Cummings soon became a trusted source and confidant for Kavanagh.

Just as Cummings' influence grew in Fleet Street, so too did his power within Business for Sterling. Soon, strategy notes began pouring forth, filled with insights from his heroes Otto von Bismarck and Sun Tzu. 'Avoid keen energy'; 'Disrupt their alliances'; 'Strike the slumping and receding'; 'Win without fighting'. Cummings' strategy was to split the left, destroy the CBI and starve Business for Sterling's Eurosceptic rivals of cash and airtime – anything which could be used to undermine the group's core policy: not ideological hostility to the EU, which was marginal, but pragmatic opposition to the single currency, which was mainstream.

Such was Business for Sterling's impact, Dougie Smith's circle at the Democracy Movement soon became engaged with Leach's new outfit. In Cummings, Smith saw a kindred spirit. Alongside Cummings were two young men from Huddersfield and Derby, Neil O'Brien and James Frayne. But, as well as these new faces in Conservative politics, some older ones were reappearing.

In 1998, Hague had reshuffled his shadow cabinet to promote Francis Maude into the shadow chancellorship. Maude, in turn, brought with him Smith's former FCS ally Robbie Gibb as his chief of staff. Smith had also quietly rejoined the Conservative Party. After the years of angst and division, the Conservative constellation appeared to be quietly reforming, this time with a distinctly Eurosceptic hue.

For Rodney Leach, the whole process was electrifying. Though he had grown rich in the City, he was a largely anonymous fixer, a consigliere for the Keswick family, which controlled Jardine Matheson. Now, to his surprise, he was the lynchpin of the Eurosceptic resistance, connecting the worlds of finance and philosophy, media and politics. Though Leach had called for a dispassionate 'cost–benefit analysis' of Britain's place in Europe, he was far from dispassionate himself. 'If 750 years of almost unbroken constitutional continuity are to come to an end,' he had declared in a speech in 1994, 'let it be done with all the implications candidly before us, not under the cover of black smoke put up by politicians who lack the courage to face Oliver Cromwell's unnerving plea: *I beseech you, in the bowels of Christ, think it possible you may be mistaken.*'[33]

Business for Sterling's first skirmish in the battle to 'save the pound' came in the June 1999 European elections, the first to be held under a new electoral system after Blair forced onto the statute book the innocuous-sounding European Parliamentary Elections Bill, just in time for voting.

The bill made good on Labour's manifesto commitment to introduce what it called a 'proportional voting system' for the European elections. Contrary to later claims, Blair was not compelled to introduce this. The Treaty of Rome had always included an aspiration for European elections to take place 'in accordance with a uniform procedure in all Member States', but this had never become a fully fledged requirement. Still, changing the electoral system was the kind of thing a good European would do, especially after the bungled handling of the euro announcement. It was also good politics. At the core of Blair's vision of becoming a great reforming leader lay two foundational aims: securing Britain's place at the heart of Europe; and 'reuniting these two wings of progressive social democracy' with the Liberal Democrats, as he later wrote, to usher in a century of hegemony for the centre left.[34] The European Parliamentary Elections Bill was a first step towards both. It also had the immediate political benefit of giving the Labour leadership more control over candidate selections. High and low political considerations had merged.

Labour's 1997 manifesto had committed to a referendum on changing the voting system for the House of Commons, and an independent commission chaired by Roy Jenkins was set up in December 1997 and tasked with recommending a preferred electoral model. But changing the voting system for European elections required no such referendum and was deemed important for Blair's wider strategy to keep Paddy Ashdown's Liberal Democrats onside.[35]

Watching these changes to the voting system with particular interest, however, was someone far removed from Blair's progressive alliance: Nigel Farage. After UKIP's meagre showing in the 1997 election, a poisonous battle for control of the party had erupted, which finally came to an end with the resignation of its founder and leader, Alan Sked. 'I have no wish to lead a lunatic fringe in which temporary divisions are fought to the bitter end,' he wrote in his farewell address.[36] In his place, Sked appointed thirty-year-old Craig Mackinlay as interim leader until new elections the following year. What was left to lead, however, was open to question; in a by-election in July, UKIP had finished in tenth place, with just thirty-nine votes.

Six weeks before that by-election, a television exposé on ITV's *Cook Report* revealed that the party had been infiltrated by the far right. The programme showed one of Sked's closest allies, the seemingly affable student Mark Deavin, boasting about his secret double life as a BNP activist. For Sked, the revelation was particularly devastating; not only had he brought Deavin into the party, he had also been his academic supervisor at the LSE, as well as a mentor and friend.

After the party's drubbing in 1997, Farage had been part of the 'lunatic fringe' agitating for Sked's removal, and he agreed to meet Deavin for lunch in the hope of picking up some valuable information. Farage's naivety led him into a trap. Deavin had brought a friend along. Not only was this associate a BNP member, he was a figure so notorious that even other activists on the far right were wary of him. Tony 'The Bomber' Lecomber had been sentenced to three years in jail in 1986 for possession of bombs and grenades, and another three years in 1991 for assaulting a Jewish teacher. As the three men spoke, a photograph was taken covertly. Farage did not realize that, while he was trying to use Deavin, Deavin was using him. Once the meeting was set, Deavin and his mentor in the BNP, Nick Griffin, had arranged for Lecomber to turn up. 'The photo was partly and primarily to give Farage problems,' Griffin later admitted to Farage's biographer Michael Crick.[37]

The whole sordid affair discredited all those involved, but it also revealed how toxic and divided UKIP had become. Its founder had departed under a cloud. It had been infiltrated and exposed on national television and repeatedly rejected at the ballot box. The party's prospects were bleak. But then came salvation, thanks to Blair's reform of the electoral system. 'The key to our revival was PR [proportional representation],' Farage reflected. 'After 1997 we were all thinking this might be a complete waste of time. But suddenly, with PR, it all became rather interesting again.'[38]

Given the size of Labour's majority, the European Parliamentary Elections Bill was sure to sail through the Commons. The House of Lords, however, was a different matter, and peers repeatedly rejected the government's proposals. Initially, the home secretary Jack Straw – a lifelong sceptic of proportional representation – announced the government wouldn't force through the legislation before the European elections in 1999, meaning they would go ahead under the old first-past-the-post system.

For Paddy Ashdown, however, being denied even this small victory would have been a humiliation too far. By early 1999, he had little to show for the closeness of his partnership with Blair. Not only had he not secured a single Liberal Democrat seat in the cabinet, but it was also far from clear whether the government was going to make any serious move on electoral reform. When Roy Jenkins concluded his commission into voting reform in December 1998 with a recommendation for 'AV+' – a system which topped up the number of MPs to make it more proportional – Blair said he was 'unpersuaded'.[39] With the European elections fast approaching, it seemed as though Ashdown might not even get voting reform for European elections. 'Paddy was back onto TB, saying the Lib–Lab game was dead if he could not get PR for the European elections,' Alastair Campbell noted in his diary. 'He was in a real panic.'[40] To keep the Lib Dems onside, Blair ordered the use of the Parliament Act to force the bill onto the statute book. On only four other occasions in British history had the Parliament Act been used.[41] To Ashdown's relief, PR was introduced into British politics in February 1999, just four months before the European elections.

For William Hague, the elections were a test he could not afford to fail. For much of the two years since he had won the leadership, his poll ratings had been very poor. To prop up his support, Hague and his advisers decided to focus on the one major policy question in British politics where they appeared to be more in tune with the electorate than the prime minister: the euro. To secure the Tory crown, Hague had promised not to take Britain into the single currency for the duration of the parliament. He had since hardened this position to insist that Britain should not enter 'for the foreseeable future.'[42] Privately, Hague believed Britain should never enter, but for the sake of party unity he could not say as much. For the European elections, he ran a simple campaign to 'save the pound'.

The campaign was no less make-or-break for UKIP. Failure and dissolution beckoned.[43] And then, just five days before polling day, disaster struck for Farage as the story of his meeting with Lecomber was passed to *The Times*.[44] Three days later, Alan Sked plunged the knife still further, urging people to vote Tory and shun the party he founded, writing in *The Times*, 'I believe that it is now impossible to support UKIP in Thursday's elections.'[45]

When the election results were announced, not only had the Tories comfortably surpassed expectations with 33.5 per cent of the vote, they had pushed Labour into second place. Among the new Conservative MEPs were Daniel Hannan, Chris Heaton-Harris, Roger Helmer, Timothy Kirkhope and Nirj Deva, all of whom would go on to play roles in the Brexit battle to come. William Hague's leadership was secured alongside his Eurosceptic strategy. In the same election, a pro-euro Conservative splinter party had finished tenth, with just 1.3 per cent of the vote. As the *Times* columnist Tim Hames wrote, 'in many ways it is Kenneth Clarke and Michael Heseltine not Tony Blair or Paddy Ashdown who are the biggest losers.'[46] After the election, Hague even felt confident enough to promote Michael Portillo to shadow chancellor following his return to Parliament earlier in the year in a by-election.

UKIP, however, were the other surprise winners of the night. Three of its candidates would now enter the European Parliament: Michael Holmes, the party leader, in the south-west; former Referendum Party candidate Jeremy Titford in the east; and Nigel Farage in the south-east. 'If you asked me, what was the most significant moment in my career,' Farage said, 'there's absolutely no question about it – getting elected to the European Parliament.'[47] UKIP had been saved, thanks to Tony Blair's determination to modernize Britain.

For Blair, much as the European elections of 1999 were a disappointment, they were hardly a disaster. By October 1999, according to an ICM poll, his approval ratings had fallen, but only from an unprecedented 80 per cent to a still historically high 52 per cent.[48] Blair remained the future and Euroscepticism remained the past. Roger Scruton's reputation may have been enhanced by the revelations of his exploits during the Cold War, but many of those associated with him were still figures of respectable disdain. Among Scruton's Conservative Philosophy Group founders, Hugh Fraser was dead and John Casey remained marginalized in his reactionary redoubt.[49] And then, just a few days before the 1999 European elections, Jonathan Aitken was sentenced to eighteen months in prison for perjury, after he was found to have lied in court in a failed attempt to sue *The Guardian*.[50] For Hague, even electoral victory could not dispel the lingering aura of Tory sleaze.

On the surface, then, the European elections of 1999 changed little. Support for the euro remained weak among the public, despite the launch of Blair's cross-party 'Britain in Europe' campaign with Ken Clarke and Michael Heseltine. The semi-detached status feared by many in Westminster appeared to suit the electorate just fine. If anything, the essentials of British politics seemed set: Blair was cruising to re-election, but the obstacles standing in the way of his ambition to take Britain into the single currency remained formidable.

For Blair, 1999 was not primarily the year of the European elections, but the moment he became a war leader. Indeed, the elections were little more than a sideshow, given the situation in Kosovo, where NATO had intervened to push back an advancing Serbian army, stirring recollections of the 1995 massacre at Srebrenica which had lain uneasily on the Western conscience ever since. In Europe, Blair had been the leading voice calling for Western intervention – and had won out. After seventy-eight days of NATO bombing, Slobodan Milošević agreed to an unconditional withdrawal of his forces, allowing 30,000 NATO troops into Kosovo. In July, Blair visited the country and was greeted as a hero. Babies were soon being named 'Tonibler'.[51] What were the European elections compared to this?

Blair was not acting in a vacuum of his own ego, either, but in a world transformed by the end of the Cold War. NATO had acted in Kosovo in large part because it could. During the war, Blair delivered a speech in Chicago, setting out what he called a new 'doctrine of the international community'.[52] Number Ten had approached Lawrence Freedman – then head of the war studies department at King's College London – to help prepare the text, which would later be seen as the height of Blairite hubris. But, as Freedman subsequently explained, the question in his mind – if not in Blair's – was not how to empower the growing 'interventionist impulse', but how to keep it under control and stop it spreading into what he feared might be its next stage: toppling dictators.[53]

Blair's Chicago speech and his approach to the crisis in Kosovo reveal the scale of his ambition to shape the new world order. The turn of the millennium marked a moment of extraordinary Western supremacy and confidence. The collapse of the Soviet Union had already reshaped Europe, unifying Germany and adding impetus to the push for a new single currency. But the end of the Cold War had two other important consequences.

First, it erased the unique circumstances that had brought Monnet's Europe into being. As early as April 1998, the pro-European historian Timothy Garton Ash had sent up a warning flare about the wisdom of further integration, pointing out that the nations of Western Europe had been driven together because of circumstances that no longer existed: the threat from Moscow and the encouragement of Washington. Together, this had created 'a historical constellation that was particularly favourable to a particular model of West European integration,' wrote Garton Ash. With the fall of the Soviet Union, that constellation had gone.[54]

Second, irrespective of how they felt about this thesis, Europe's leaders had to deal with the reality of the EU's imminent expansion east. This was the central focus of the preparations for the Nice summit in December 2000, especially the question of how to adapt the EU's structures for the ten new states that would enter the bloc in 2004. The challenge for Blair was that, by widening the bloc, the EU would either have to move towards a looser federation, as Britain had long championed, or deepen its integration further to ensure it could still function. For a project founded on the ambition of 'ever closer union', there could only be one answer. And so, for Britain's newly elected Eurosceptic MEPs, an opportunity arose to make trouble.

For much of their first year in Brussels, life for UKIP's new MEPs was hard going, their influence marginal at best. Farage and his colleagues had joined a small group of continental sceptics who called themselves the Europe of Democracies and Diversities (EDD). It was led by the veteran Danish anti-federalist Jens-Peter Bonde. Bonde represented Denmark's June Movement, which had grown out of the referendum against Maastricht in June 1992. Ultimately, however, Farage and Bonde were a tiny minority in a European Parliament dominated by the two main blocs representing the continent's overwhelmingly pro-European conservatives and socialists. The EDD made little impact.

Though UKIP's presence in the European Parliament provided important financial support, status and media profile at home – most notably on *Question Time* – life in Brussels remained a dispiriting slog of small battles and marginal gains. Yet, on the margins, new relationships were beginning to be forged across party lines.

One example of this was an initiative called 'SOS Democracy', which brought together Eurosceptics from a broader cross-section of MEPs than the Europe of Democracies and Diversities grouping. It included Conservative MEPs like Daniel Hannan. Another was the so-called 'Fishing Group', made up of a handful of 'sound' Eurosceptic staffers from different parties and groupings, whose purpose was to share information and gossip about Brussels away from official channels – much of which was then leaked to the British media, as hungry as ever for new tales of

European overreach.[55] For the Tories, two aides in particular regularly attended: Gawain Towler, who had moved to Brussels with the new Tory MEP Nirj Deva, and Lee Rotherham, who split his time between the Conservative shadow Foreign Office team in London and working for Daniel Hannan in Brussels. Whenever Rotherham returned to London, he would first brief Michael Howard, the shadow foreign secretary, and then the Eurosceptic press. Alongside Towler and Rotherham, a Frenchman called Emmanuel Bordez was a regular attendee. Bordez worked for the royalist Philippe de Villiers, who had joined forces with James Goldsmith and the young Charles de Gaulle, the general's grandson, in 1994. He went on to become Nigel Farage's chief of staff in Brussels.

For much of 2000, the focus for Hannan, Towler, Rotherham and everybody else in Brussels was the impending summit in Nice. Whatever dreams of European leadership Blair might have harboured, when the summit came, he soon found himself playing the role expected of all British prime ministers: defending British sovereignty from Europe's federalist assault. 'Britain finally saw off an attempt by European Union leaders to remove the national veto on taxation measures last night,' *The Times* reported as the summit began.[56] Blair's aides briefed that his success in seeing off this pressure had come because of his willingness to accept reforms in other areas. William Hague, meanwhile, gave an indication of the election campaign he intended to run the following year by denouncing the agreement as a major step towards a European superstate.[57]

The Nice summit was a dispiriting affair for all those involved and, before he left for home, Blair publicly demanded an overhaul of European summitry itself. All-night negotiations which lasted until someone finally cracked were no way to run an organization, he declared.[58] His remarks served to prepare the ground for the next round of negotiations, which had quietly been signposted in the small print of the Nice conclusions. Attached to the treaty was a declaration on the future of the Union. While the Nice summit had opened the way to enlargement, Europe's leaders said 'a deeper and wider debate about the future of the European Union' was now needed.[59] This process would try to find 'a more precise delimitation of powers between the European Union and the Member States', simplify the treaties 'with a view to making them clearer and better understood', consider the role of national parliaments in the bloc and improve the 'democratic legitimacy and transparency of the Union and its institutions'.[60]

Welcoming this declaration, the European Parliament issued a response two months later arguing that the failures in Nice demonstrated that 'the purely intergovernmental method has outlived its usefulness for the purpose of revising the Treaties.' This had even been 'implicitly recognised' by Europe's leaders in the declaration, the MEPs said. In its place, a new 'constitutional development process' should be initiated.[61] The stage was being set for a European constitution, though not until the beginning of 2002, following the British general election widely expected to be called for May 2001.

This, then, was the European context for Blair's first re-election. Facing overwhelming odds, William Hague resorted to a rerun of his 1999 strategy, campaigning to 'save the pound'. As election day approached, Hague went so far as to warn that, should Labour be re-elected, the country would soon resemble a 'foreign land' in which Britain had been swallowed up into a European superstate. 'Let me take you on a journey,' Hague began in his speech to the Conservative Party's spring conference in Harrogate. 'The Royal Mint melting down pound coins as the euro notes start to circulate. Our currency gone forever. The chancellor returning from Brussels carrying instructions to raise taxes still further. Control over our own economy given away.'[62]

For Dominic Cummings, Hague's 'save the pound' tactics were a disaster, contaminating opposition to the euro by aligning it with support for the unpopular Conservative Party. By this point, Cummings was the campaign director for a wider 'No' campaign – an umbrella group merging Business for Sterling with another cross-party outfit, called New Europe, which opposed the euro and was supported by a formidable cast of serious men from Britain's recent past, including the former foreign secretaries David Owen and Malcolm Rifkind and former chancellors Denis Healey and Nigel Lawson. The No campaign's strapline was simple: 'Europe Yes. Euro No'. This, in 2001, was the limit of mainstream Eurosceptic ambition – in public, at least.

At the No campaign, Cummings grew frustrated with the Conservative Party's election strategy. On 31 May 2001, *The Times* reported him complaining about the Tory tactics: 'I have lost count of the number of times I have said that if the No Campaign were to be right wing and based on sovereignty and the Union Jack – while the other side focus on jobs and living standards – we will lose.'[63] For Cummings, this essential lesson would never change.

For Hague, such concerns were of secondary importance as he tried to up the ante during the campaign itself, warning of 'two weeks to save the pound' before polling day and declaring the election a de facto referendum on the currency.[64] For Cummings, such talk was so potentially disastrous he released a statement on the day of the election rejecting Hague's central argument. 'Late desertion,' ran the front-page headline in *The Times*. 'The No campaign . . . issued a statement contradicting Mr Hague's claim that the election had been a referendum on the Euro,' the paper reported. 'Dominic Cummings, campaign director . . . said: "This campaign is not a referendum on the euro – Tony Blair says so, we say so, and the public know it's true."'[65]

Hague's campaign message simply would not land. It was too vulnerable to the obvious Labour rejoinder that the real referendum on the euro was still to come. When the result was announced, the Tories had been crushed once again. For all his efforts, Hague had managed to increase the number of Conservative MPs by one. Among those who did not make it was the one-time student radical, Mark MacGregor, who lost again, this time in Thanet South, which was held by Labour. Yet, among those who were elected were George Osborne, Boris Johnson and

David Cameron, the latter of whom had been helped by support from an unlikely source: Dougie Smith's Candidlist.

By the time of the general election, Candidlist was headed up by the eccentric and unbiddable editor of *Free Life*, the journal of the Libertarian Alliance, Dr Sean Gabb. As Gabb later wrote, he was first approached about the project in late September 1999, by someone he described as 'a friend who had spent his adult life despairing over the Conservative Party'.[66]

Smith and Glendening understood that their links to Goldsmith meant they were ill-suited to trying to influence Conservative Party candidate selections themselves. Gabb, in contrast, carried no such baggage. He lost no time building a website, where he uploaded Smith's old Referendum Party database and compiled every additional scrap of information he could find.

By doing so, Gabb later wrote, 'it would make knowledge gathered over many years, but so far confined within a small circle of the informed, available to selection committees.'[67] Gabb divided his list of prospective parliamentary candidates into 'sceptics', 'Europhiles' and 'don't knows' – those who would follow the party line whatever it might be. For David Cameron – hoping to be selected in the leafy Oxfordshire seat of Witney – it was important not to be marked as a Europhile.

The seat had become available in late 1999, when the sitting Conservative MP Shaun Woodward – who had only been selected as the Tory candidate in 1997 – took his demotion from the shadow cabinet so badly that he defected to the Labour Party. Two figures quickly emerged as the frontrunners to replace him: Cameron and the former junior whip Andrew Mitchell, who had lost his seat in 1997. For Smith, in particular, Mitchell represented everything that was wrong with the Conservative Party: he was entitled, careerist and, in Smith's view, lacking any desire to fight EU integration. In the run-up to the selection, Mitchell had attempted to display his apparent Euroscepticism by claiming that he had been approached to serve on Business for Sterling's national council. He would later argue that this claim had been 'over-interpreted'.[68] During the contest, however, in a move orchestrated by Smith, a letter from Business for Sterling emerged, denying Mitchell's claim.

Cameron, though, did not have it all his own way from Candidlist either. At first, Gabb did not classify Cameron as a Eurosceptic. Cameron was so concerned about the damage this might cause, he emailed Gabb to protest, 'on the basis that I oppose the single currency and any further transfer of sovereignty from the UK to the EU', even if, as he conceded, he did not support withdrawal. Cameron also accepted that EU law was supreme. 'I don't like it, but it's a fact.'[69]

For Gabb, this admission was tantamount to acquiescence. 'Your complacent tone does you no credit whatever', he replied. 'It is only because I believe you are sincere in what you say that I do not reclassify you as a Europhile.' Cameron attempted to reassure Gabb: 'I am not a lawyer and perhaps my original email put it the wrong way. But these are my views – no to the single currency, no to further transfer of powers from Westminster to Brussels and yes to renegotiation of areas like fish where the EU has been a disaster for the UK. If that is being a Europhile, then I'm a banana.'[70]

Cameron's victory over Mitchell was part of a pattern of Eurosceptic success in Tory selections at this time. As individual selection meetings played out, the Candidlist team would often receive updates from Conservative associations by telephone. They tuned in as if listening to the Saturday football results, delighted by their progress. By October 2000, *The European Journal* found that, of the 170 most winnable seats at the next election, 46 per cent of the candidates selected were Eurosceptics and a further 47.5 per cent were party-line loyalists prepared to stick to Hague's script. Only 6.5 per cent were Europhiles. The author of the piece, Allister Heath, concluded that, after the next general election, 'a new generation of radical Euro-realists will take seats in Parliament.'[71]

In 2001, then, even though on the surface the Conservative

Party appeared to be stuck, unable to increase its parliamentary presence, the party was in fact changing from the ground up.

This evolution did not go unnoticed. In the aftermath of the general election, Chris Patten and Michael Heseltine quickly came out to criticize the party's 'kamikaze' Eurosceptics, blaming them for the result.[72] As if to prove their point that there were no votes in Euroscepticism, UKIP had also performed poorly. The party finished fifth, with just 1.5 per cent of the national vote, a sharp drop on its performance in the European elections two years earlier. Without PR, the party had no chance of securing representation. In Bexhill and Battle, Nigel Farage limped home in fourth place, with 3,474 votes, or 7.8 per cent, despite being a sitting MEP for the region. The party had secured fewer than half the number of votes won by the Referendum Party four years earlier.

In the summer of 2001, although Euroscepticism was gaining traction in the Conservative Party overall, it looked to be as far from power as the Tories themselves. The day after the election, *The Independent* published what Ed Balls later described as an 'extensive and very well-briefed story', setting out what Blair hoped to be his legacy: the campaign to take Britain into the single currency.[73] Now that the election was out of the way, *The Independent* reported, Blair would throw himself into the campaign to lead Britain back into the heart of Europe, beginning with a speech to the TUC on 11 September. By this time, Blair believed joining the euro was 'almost existential', his European adviser Roger Liddle recalled.[74]

The same day, Hague quit as leader of the Conservative Party, accepting the blame for his party's defeat, setting in train another Tory leadership election – an event, once rare, that would become a familiar ritual in the years ahead. This one would conclude in time for the party's conference in September 2001. British politics was gearing up for its moment of reckoning on the euro and the choice of Conservative Party leader would, once again, be crucial. Ken Clarke was expected to stand, opposed by the Maastricht hardliner Iain Duncan Smith from the right of the party. The favourite, however, was Michael Portillo, the choice of the new 'modernizing' cadre of one-time Thatcherites who had concluded that the Tory party needed to change far more dramatically than either Clarke or Duncan Smith understood.

The essence of the modernizers' case was captured in a rare public intervention by Dougie Smith, who wrote an article in *The Daily Telegraph* attacking the 'soulless, selfish and smug' candidates who had represented the party in that year's election. Smith was particularly scathing about Jacob Rees-Mogg, who, 'thought it would be clever to announce to the Scottish mining seat he aspired to represent that he was being assisted in his campaign by his nanny'.

'The Conservative Party is in a deeper hole than even the sneerers and jeerers of the Guardian claim,' Smith argued. 'The world's oldest and most successful political party has become estranged from the country it aspires to govern.' To win again, the party needed to look and sound like modern Britain, he wrote. 'Unless the Conservative Party is able radically to diversify its appearance it will not attract the support of those who feel that they don't belong.' An A-list of candidates needed to be recruited, 'biased towards the sections of the population where the party is weakest – women, ethnic minorities, young people and, yes, gays.' Smith's argument was that, by presenting a narrow and monochrome slate of candidates to the public, the Tories were not only alienating ethnic minorities, but much of the rest of the country besides, who simply thought the party looked odd. To conclude, Smith suggested that the next generation of Conservatives could simply try being 'nice'.[75]

Here was 'modernization', as it came to be known, and its earliest advocates were not left-leaning wets, but young Thatcherite right-wingers – Dougie Smith, Mark MacGregor, Robbie Gibb, Dominic Cummings and Michael Gove. And, for many of these figures, although not all, Michael Portillo was their great hope.

This was the first Tory leadership election under the new rules introduced by William Hague, which gave party members the final say in a run-off between the top two candidates chosen by MPs. In the opening two rounds of voting, Portillo topped the polls, finishing comfortably ahead of Iain Duncan Smith in second and Kenneth Clarke in third. He seemed set for victory.

Then, on 15 July 2001, two days before the final ballot of MPs, the *Sunday Telegraph* ran a story which looked like it could be decisive. 'Thatcher says Portillo is the right leader,' ran the front-page headline. The editor of the *Daily Telegraph*, Charles Moore, was not convinced. Moore got hold of Thatcher directly to check the story, which she forcefully denied. 'Portillo's hopes hit by angry Thatcher denial,' the *Daily Telegraph* ran the following day, while revealing that, in fact, it was Duncan Smith who was her preferred choice. The next day, Duncan Smith beat Portillo by a single vote in the final ballot of MPs to go into a final run-off against Clarke. 'Because it was so close, it would probably not be an exaggeration to say we swung it for him,' Moore later reflected.[76] Indeed, under Moore's editorship the *Daily Telegraph* had established itself as the most influential Conservative newspaper in the country.

Moore had become editor of the paper in 1995, replacing the patrician pro-European Max Hastings. Under his editorship, the paper became far more hostile to European integration, mirroring the scepticism of the title's Canadian media mogul Conrad Black. As early as November 1996 Moore had written a piece titled, 'Tell Us Why We Should Stay'. Two years later, Black went further in a speech to the Centre for Policy Studies calling for withdrawal.[77]

Whether Moore's intervention was decisive or otherwise, Duncan Smith's victory left the party's modernizers in dismay. With a final between Clarke and Duncan Smith, they now faced a choice between abandoning their modernizing electoral project and abandoning their Eurosceptic principles. 'It was a hopeless situation,' David Cameron later noted in his memoirs. 'One couldn't unite the party; the other couldn't win over the country.'[78] Cameron joined many of the modernizers in support of Duncan

Smith, while Boris Johnson sided with Ken Clarke. The result of the election would be announced on 11 September – the same day Blair was due at the TUC to unveil his Europe strategy for his second term.

And then everything changed: domestic politics was rendered irrelevant as a spectacle of terror was beamed across the world from New York. September 11, 2001, would not be remembered for Blairite dreams of Europe, nor the election of a Conservative leader, but as the day a new world came into being.

In Britain, Blair cancelled his speech to the TUC and the Conservative Party delayed its leadership announcement. 'The events of September 11 . . . marked a turning point in history,' Blair later told the Labour Party Conference.[79] The future would be determined by the battle between freedom and terror, he said. Blair's response to 9/11 was a new defining mission that would utterly transform his relationship with Europe.

Two days after 9/11, the Conservative Party announced that its next leader would be Iain Duncan Smith – although, understandably, the result barely touched the front pages. Duncan Smith's victory was the third election in a row in which the Conservative Party had chosen a leader from the centre right of the party, not on the basis of their particular talents or electoral appeal, but to prevent the pro-European left of the party regaining the control it had lost when Heath was defeated.

To the young, modernizing Eurosceptics, this remained the ultimate priority. As they saw it, the 'Blessed Plot' to integrate Britain into Europe required a political consensus in Westminster. But, as long as the Conservative Party resisted further integration – or even sought to reverse it – there would always be an open national debate in which, they believed, the country's deepest instincts might emerge.

It was for this reason that Dougie Smith and those in his circle had thrown in their lot with Duncan Smith to stop Clarke. Once he was elected, they set about trying to salvage their modernizing agenda. Business for Sterling's Stanley Kalms was appointed Tory party treasurer, and he immediately brought in his allies. Mark MacGregor was made chief executive of the party and Dominic Cummings received a call to join the team. 'Stanley said 9/11 has happened, the euro is on the back foot, bin Laden has killed that issue for a bit, you should go over to CCHQ to try to sort out the Tory party,' Cummings recalled.[80] It was a dramatic turnaround. The day of the election, he had gone on the record undermining the central message of the Conservative Party leader. Now, he was in the new leader's office trying to save the party from oblivion.

Iain Duncan Smith had prevented the party from falling into the hands of the pro-Europeans, but he was never comfortable as the standard bearer for the modernizing project being enacted by the team around him.

It would not prove a happy time for any of those involved.

Chapter 13

Three months before 9/11, on 26 June 2001, the Belgian prime minister Guy Verhofstadt had beamed for the cameras at the first meeting of his 'Laeken group' of wise men, assembled to advise on how the EU should make good on the declaration agreed in Nice the year before.[1] Alongside Verhofstadt stood the dominant figure of Jacques Delors, the *bon papa* of modern Europe, while in the background the newly elected MP for South Shields, David Miliband, smiled awkwardly for the photographers. He was present as Tony Blair's representative.

Instead of making specific recommendations for reform, Verhofstadt's group called for Europe's leaders to establish a 'constitutional convention' with a mandate to simplify the existing treaties into a constitution for Europe.[2] When Europe's leaders met in December 2001, the idea was signed off and the former French president Valéry Giscard d'Estaing was made chairman of the new convention, with Britain's Sir John Kerr – the mandarin who had been permanent representative to the EU under John Major – as his most senior official.

Alongside Giscard d'Estaing and Kerr, the EU's leaders agreed there should be a representative from each of the fifteen national governments, plus two from each parliament, sixteen from the European Parliament and two from the Commission. From this extensive group of European politicians, a thirteen-strong executive committee, or presidium, would be formed to drive the convention forward. The first meeting would take place in Brussels in February 2002.

The choice of who to send to this grand European affair demanded careful political balancing. Britain's sole MEP slot on the convention went to a pro-European Tory, Timothy Kirkhope. To ensure a more sceptical presence, however, the Tories sent David Heathcoat-Amery as their parliamentary representative, nephew of the former chancellor and wartime Phantom, Derick Heathcoat-Amery. The Labour Party, meanwhile, sent the Europe minister Peter Hain as the government representative, with the final spot going to a Labour MP who seemingly could not have been more suited to the job: the German-born modernizer Gisela Stuart, who represented Birmingham Edgbaston.

On the surface, Stuart was the embodiment of Blairite metropolitan liberalism, a European representative of contemporary Britain. As one of the few socialist women at the convention, Stuart found herself being invited to sit on the governing presidium responsible for drawing up the final proposal for a constitution.

Though few spotted the significance of Stuart's appointment at the time, *The Times'* William Rees-Mogg noted that the British government's influence on the convention would largely depend on whether it was Stuart's voice that was listened to or Peter Hain's. Of the two figures, Rees-Mogg noted, 'Stuart is more interesting': 'Her father was a Bavarian farmer; her mother was a Czech; she speaks good French. We shall see how her thinking develops as the Convention proceeds.'[3]

On the conservative side, meanwhile, ideas were developing too. To support his work on the convention, Timothy Kirkhope, who represented Yorkshire in the European Parliament, hired a young researcher from Leeds, who had helped in his office before the 1997 election: Matthew Elliott. Then just twenty-three, Elliott had been working for Bill Cash's European Foundation in Westminster for the previous two years.

The convention opened in Brussels in February 2002, with Chairman Giscard d'Estaing setting out the historic opportunity that lay before them. 'If we succeed, in twenty-five years or fifty years – the distance separating us from the Treaty of Rome – Europe's role in the world will have changed,' he told the delegates. 'It will be respected and listened to, not only as the economic power it already is, but as a political power which will talk on equal terms to the greatest powers on our planet.'[4] It was a grand vision, one that was, at its core, similar to that of Ted Heath and, indeed, Tony Blair. The future was too big for countries like Britain or France to compete, the argument ran. Europe was the only answer.

By October 2002, Giscard d'Estaing had published a first draft of the proposed constitution. It did not lack ambition. Article one described the bloc as 'a union of European states' which would 'closely coordinate their policies at the European level and administer certain common competences on a federal basis.'[5] Britain's Eurosceptics were aghast. David Heathcoat-Amory said the draft contained 'all the attributes of a state' and refused to endorse it.[6]

What power the Conservative Party had to stop the constitution was less obvious. At the convention, Heathcoat-Amory had few allies, while, at home, Iain Duncan Smith's leadership was already running into trouble. In September, the month before the draft constitution's unveiling, Dominic Cummings quit in disgust as Duncan Smith's director of strategy. 'I was completely wasting my time,' he later reflected. 'Iain himself obviously couldn't do the job and the whole entity just seemed dead, brain dead and organizationally dead.'[7] A few months later, in February 2003, Mark MacGregor followed suit. For Duncan Smith's defenders, the twin resignations were all part of a plot by the disgruntled 'modernizers' who had supported Michael Portillo's leadership campaign. In the press, Norman Tebbit resurfaced to rage against MacGregor, the 'spotty teenager' whose FCS faction had caused him such trouble in the 1980s. The loony right were now, apparently, the modernizing left.

By this point, the modernizers had begun to organize

themselves into a more formal grouping, centred around a new think tank, Policy Exchange, founded in 2002 by the leading Portillistas of the day: Francis Maude, who had run Portillo's leadership campaign, Nick Boles, a modernizing Westminster councillor, and Michael Gove. Dougie Smith, meanwhile, took charge of a sister unit called 'C Change', focused specifically on reforming the Conservative Party.

To begin with, Policy Exchange was little more than a few desks in a room in the basement of Methodist Central Hall in Westminster, staffed by Boles, Smith and the former *Economist* journalist and Russia specialist, Anna Reid. Its first major promotional push came in 2002, when the team put together a roadshow on the need for modernization, with data from former Conservative HQ staffer Andrew Cooper, then running the polling company Populus alongside the ex-FCS activist Michael Simmonds. Simmonds' boyfriend at the time – and later husband – was Nick Gibb, the future education minister and brother of Robbie.

Policy Exchange quickly became the organizational core of Tory modernization, the place where friendships and political ambition overlapped. By early 2002, Gove and Smith, for example, were not only friends, but flatmates, Smith having moved into the flat which Gove shared with his wife Sarah Vine, following their marriage the previous year. Gove and Smith were also regulars at a Wednesday-night poker game in Aspinall's, the Mayfair gambling club founded by John Aspinall. Other regulars included Smith's Democracy Movement friends, Ben Elliot and Zac Goldsmith, as well as – rather incongruously – Kate Moss and the Australian cricketer Shane Warne.

An indication of the modernizers' growing influence in the party came at the 2002 Conservative Party Conference that autumn, when the party chairman, Theresa May, gave what became known as the 'nasty party' speech, warning members of its reputation in the country. 'The truth is that as our country has become more diverse, our party has remained the same,' May warned.[8] The author of the speech was Dougie Smith. While

Portillo may have lost his leadership bid, the battle for control of the party had not been settled.

While the Conservatives continued their long-running fight for the soul of Toryism, the world beyond was being dragged ever further into Osama bin Laden's millenarian mire. By late 2002, Blair had been prime minister for five years and had led Britain into four major military campaigns: Iraq in 1998, Kosovo in 1999, Sierra Leone in 2000 and Afghanistan in 2001. None of these interventions had caused him any real political harm, and in fact had furthered his political ambition to become the martial leader of Europe. Britain had become a beacon of action, just as he promised, and the world seemed to applaud Blair's muscular approach.

But Iraq in 2003 was different. As the US began its preparations for war, French and German opposition intensified. Now, the British prime minister faced a choice: to fight alongside the US and risk diplomatic isolation in Europe, or join with France and Germany and risk diplomatic isolation in America? Blair chose to stick with his ally, George W. Bush. After the initial success of the invasion and ousting of Saddam Hussein, Iraq began its descent into anarchy, dragging Blair's reputation in Europe down with it. Abroad, Britain was no longer a beacon of leadership, but a facilitator of chaos. And, at home, Blair was no longer the mastermind of modernity.

The decision to go to war without a second UN resolution in the face of French and German opposition remains the defining moment in Blair's premiership. As Iraq slid into a quagmire of sectarian chaos and the death toll – including that of British troops – mounted, Blair's authority drained away and, according to Peter Mandelson, he became 'terribly down'. The suicide of Dr David Kelly in July, after reports that the government had 'sexed up' its justification for war by misusing his work, was particularly devastating. From this moment, Blair was simply too weak to lead Britain into the euro. He had spent his political capital on another project to remake the world.

It was during these most difficult months of 2003 that Gordon Brown made his move to finally kill off the prospect of British entry altogether, dispatching a courier to deliver the Treasury's latest 300-page assessment of the 'five tests' to Number Ten without even the courtesy of a formal meeting. It was an extraordinarily crass move, revealing the depth of the bitterness which had consumed the Blair–Brown relationship. 'In retrospect, it was one of the more heavy-handed and un-collegiate things that I was ever involved in,' Balls later admitted. The team around Blair exploded in anger, culminating in a face-to-face showdown two days later which became so heated that Brown was left unsure whether he'd resigned or been sacked. 'Then Tony blinked,' as Balls later put it. Number Ten got in touch to ask for the language to be softened. 'Not only was Gordon still the Chancellor, but the issue was settled,' wrote Balls. 'The debate on the euro was comprehensively won.'[9] After a decade of political agony and upheaval about the UK's place in the new Europe, Britain had chosen to stick with its Majorite status quo: yes to Europe, no to the euro. It had settled for being semi-detached.

When the Treasury analysis was finally published that summer, it did not show a decision weighed delicately in the balance, but one tilted decisively against British membership – at least for the foreseeable future. Of the five tests, only one had been met – the impact on the City of London. On the most important question of all – whether the UK had achieved durable and sustainable convergence with the eurozone – the answer was a definitive 'No'.

Two weeks after Brown set out his negative assessment of the merits of joining the single currency, the final draft of Valéry Giscard d'Estaing's proposed constitution was unveiled, to wild acclaim in Brussels. 'We have a draft constitution that is worthy of the word historic,' declared Joschka Fischer, the German foreign minister, while Johannes Voggenhuber, an Austrian member of the convention, went even further, likening Giscard d'Estaing to Socrates.[10]

Throughout the process, Gisela Stuart, Peter Hain and the

British government had worked to blunt Giscard d'Estaing's more radical ambitions. The usual British 'red lines' had been drawn and reassurances sought. As ever, this foot-dragging had caused frustration on the continent. The French MEP Alain Lamassoure quipped that, unlike the Europeans, the Americans had had the sense to deal with the British problem *before* drafting their own constitution.[11]

After the final text was published, the UK government maintained its tradition of claiming victory while downplaying the significance of what had been agreed. Peter Hain admitted it was a 'modernising and reforming' document, but played it down as a 'a tidying up exercise'.[12] But, for Gisela Stuart, the experience had been more profound: dispiriting to the point of disillusion.

She had gone into the convention 'agnostic' about the outcome, and even, as a Bavarian, open-minded to the prospect of a federal future, if it did not encroach on what was best left to national parliaments. Democratically, though, she believed that, if the European Union was going to develop the constitutional character of a state, there had to be a proper mechanism for countries to leave. Downing Street had not been keen on the idea. 'Number Ten kept saying the exit clause thing was not a priority, so I was freelancing a bit,' Stuart recalled.[13] And after some last-minute negotiations, a concession was made and Article I-60 was born, establishing a two-year period for member states to negotiate withdrawal, should they so wish, which later became Article 50.[14] So marginal was the idea at this time, however, that few paid any attention.

Despite this moment of success, Stuart left the negotiations disconcerted by the process she had witnessed: the charade of consultation as she saw it; the sense of impotent inevitability; the same men in charge, pursuing the same agenda. For months, she stewed in silence on her complaints, before deciding to go public in a pamphlet for the Fabian Society: 'From my experience at the convention it is clear that the real reason for the constitution – and its main impact – is the political deepening of the union,' she wrote. 'The convention brought together a self-selected group of the European political elite, many of whom have their eyes on a career at a European level, which is dependent on more and more integration and who see national governments and national parliaments as an obstacle.'[15]

Stuart's opposition was an unexpected problem Blair could do without. Yet, the constitution was, in essence, the EU's chosen answer to the impending arrival in 2004 of ten new member states from the former Eastern bloc, which had been one of Britain's foreign-policy objectives since Margaret Thatcher's Bruges speech of 1988. Indeed, by 2003, with these poorer countries due to join the Union, one of the main questions for European governments – irrespective of any constitution – was how to manage the inevitable flow of people from east to west that would come the following year. Each member state had the option to introduce 'transitional controls', lasting up to seven years, restricting the rights of those new citizens from the East to work.

To try to gauge the number of people who might migrate to Britain, the Home Office commissioned a study to forecast the likely increase in numbers once the ten new countries joined the bloc. Ministers were advised that Britain could expect between 5,000 and 13,000 new arrivals, net, per year. David Blunkett, the home secretary at the time, was told about these figures and thought nothing of it. 'When they start talking about 13,000 you just start blanking out,' he recalled.[16] The headline figure may have been reassuringly low, but there were also caveats that should, perhaps, have rung alarm bells. The report did not forecast a maximum of 13,000 in all circumstances – only if all member states opened their labour markets at the same time. The authors added that, if the German government imposed transitional controls and Britain did not, a third of the 100,000 migrants expected to travel to Germany might instead come to the UK. In this case, Britain might see 46,000 migrants arriving each year from the ten new EU member states, amounting to almost half a million new people over a decade.[17]

When the decision came before the cabinet in late 2003, it caused barely a ripple of concern. The government had plenty on its mind at this point: Iraq; the Hutton report that Blair had commissioned on the death of Dr David Kelly; a growing rebellion over university 'top-up fees'; even the problem of illegal immigration from outside Europe, which had been an ongoing issue since Blair became prime minister. Did the government really need to worry about the prospect of a few thousand Polish plumbers?

For Number Ten and the Foreign Office, the diplomatic case for not imposing transitional controls was powerful: many of the ten new member states had backed Britain over Iraq and were potential allies around the EU table. Britain had been keen to widen Europe to dilute the power of France and Germany. Now it had achieved that goal, could Britain really turn its back on its new allies? For the Treasury, meanwhile, keeping the British labour market open was good economics. The economy was booming, new workers were needed and, besides, they would help in the fight against inflation, a perennial concern. Even the Home Office was supportive; the last thing it needed was to try to enforce a ban on tens of thousands of new EU citizens working in Britain.[18]

The decision not to impose transitional controls would prove one of the most consequential ever taken by a post-war British government. Over the course of the next seven years, the number of people living in Britain who had been born in the EU would grow by more than a million, from 1.49 million in 2004 to 2.68 million in 2011 – an average increase of 170,000 a year, much of it caused by large-scale immigration from Eastern Europe.[19] For many, this remains the key moment on the road to Brexit. It is a plausible story, and one that Nigel Farage certainly believes. As a narrative, it contains an important truth, even if it fails to account for significant nuance in the historical record.

First, while Blair made the decision not to impose transitional controls, he did not create the conditions for a mass movement of people from east to west in the decade after 2004. As Heath had foreseen, this was the inevitable result of the EU's expansion following the fall of the Soviet Union and its eastern empire, accompanied by the euphoric sense that the end of history had arrived. Second, Britain was always going to be one of the more attractive destinations for Eastern Europeans, with or without transitional controls. The British economy, operating outside the euro, open to international flows of capital and with a liberalized, flexible labour market, was a magnet for foreign workers. The result of this model's success – one largely constructed under successive Conservative governments – was an increase of immigration.

Finally, by 2004, net migration had already been rising steadily for a decade and would have remained at unprecedentedly high levels throughout this period no matter where the new citizens of Europe chose to move. Up until the mid-1990s, the number of new arrivals into Britain had roughly been in balance with the numbers leaving. After the explosions of anti-immigration sentiment in the 1960s, there had been an undeclared policy of 'zero immigration', in the phrase of the immigration barrister and author Colin Yeo.[20] The 1968 and 1971 Acts of Parliament had effectively restricted legal entry into Britain to the almost exclusively white offspring of people who had emigrated from the UK. Although 'zero immigration' is a misnomer, given that there was a steady flow of immigration into the UK throughout this period, it nevertheless indicates that, for most of this time, the numbers of people arriving in Britain tended to be matched by an equivalent, or usually larger, number of people leaving. This began to change at the margins in the 1980s, as the economy improved, before taking off in 1994 – the moment net immigration into Britain began its long upward trajectory as the economy thrived in the new, globalized, post-Cold War world.

By 1997, migration had risen to around 50,000 a year, net, largely composed of people moving to Britain from outside the EU. Between 1997 and 2003, after Blair liberalized immigration rules, the numbers rose, reaching 185,000 a year before the EU's expansion in 2004, with most, again, coming from outside the EU. From 2004, immigration from Eastern Europe increased the overall figure still further, to more than 200,000 a year, net, according to the government's official figures.[21] Modern Britain had never experienced immigration on anything like this scale. In the census of 1991, there had been 3.6 million people living in England and Wales who had been born outside the UK, amounting to 7.3 per cent of the population.[22] By 2001, this had risen to 4.6 million people, or 8.9 per cent of the population. In 2011, this had jumped again to 7.5 million, or 13.4 per cent of the total.[23]

The decision not to impose transitional controls in 2004 therefore contributed to a steadily building wave, making it larger than it would otherwise have been. But, even if Blair had imposed controls, between 2004 and 2011 net immigration into Britain would still have been historically unprecedented. If Britain's post-war history is anything to go by, it is implausible to believe that such a change could have happened without any political consequences. It is surely not a coincidence that the years of 'zero immigration' came after Enoch Powell built his own political funeral pyre in Birmingham with his visions of inevitable race war.

At the level of political narrative, however, the decision not to impose controls turned an issue that had always been incendiary into one that became bound up with the question of Europe for the first time. 'After 2004, it became obvious to people that large numbers of people were moving [to Britain] from the EU and there was a specific reason that they could pin it on,' James Frayne, a colleague of Dominic Cummings from Business for Sterling, recalled. Frayne was spending much of this time doing polls and conducting focus groups, and specifically remembers the sudden change in mood. 'This was a date stamp for them,' he said. 'From that point on, you would get people saying they were worried about the effect of Eastern European immigration.'[24]

It would not be Iain Duncan Smith, however, who would get the chance to challenge Blair on the issue. After he declared himself 'the quiet man . . . turning up the volume' at the Conservative Party Conference of 2003, his opponents in the party decided to turn him off instead.[25] After a vote of no confidence, Duncan Smith resigned, ending the brief shadow ministerial career of Bill Cash, who returned to the backbenches. In Duncan Smith's place came the one-time hard man of the Home Office, Michael Howard, chosen, without a vote, on a pitch of party unity.

Howard was a man of the moderate right, promising to 'lead the party from its centre'. Yet, as the commentator Andrew Rawnsley noted in *The Observer* shortly after Howard's triumph, the fact that Howard now represented the party's centre was revealing in itself: 'The inability of One-Nation, pro-European Tories to find an alternative standard bearer, underlines how weakened they are in today's Conservative Party.'[26]

The party was not simply divided between one-nation pro-Europeans and Thatcherite Eurosceptics, however, but between the 'modernizing' Portillistas, many of whom were deeply Eurosceptic, and the traditionalists like Duncan Smith, who were often similarly inclined. In 2003, Michael Howard was an acceptable unity candidate, but one whose destiny would be to prepare the path for the next generation. 'Perhaps, just as Labour produced Blair and Brown in 1994, in an ideal world the Conservative Party would now produce two bright young things, unsullied by having held office in a previous administration,' Portillo reflected in an *Observer* article praising the party's removal of Duncan Smith. 'We have George Osborne and David Cameron, but they aren't ready.'[27]

The most important figure in Howard's leadership team, however, was neither Cameron nor Osborne, but Rachel Whetstone, his formidable political secretary, who had worked with him in the Home Office. Whetstone was the granddaughter of Antony Fisher, founder of the Institute of Economic Affairs, and daughter of the feted libertarian campaigner Linda Whetstone. She had joined Conservative Central Office after university, where she met her future husband Steve Hilton as well as David

Cameron. As Howard's most influential official, Whetstone encouraged the promotion of those she knew and rated: Cameron, Osborne, and her friends Ed Vaizey and Kate Fall, who were brought into Howard's private office. Alongside Steve Hilton, Michael Gove, Nick Boles and Oliver Letwin, these figures would go on to form the core of the modernizing set who saw themselves as the future of the party, much to their colleagues' annoyance.

Dougie Smith, although a modernizer, was not one of them. At this time, he was kept busy by a more exotic sideline he had developed: organizing 'elite orgies'. Smith had made no secret of his extracurricular activities, but they threatened to impact his role as a behind-the-scenes political fixer when, in 2003, he found himself on the front page of *The Sunday Times* as the 'king of the urban swingers'.[28] 'By day Dougie Smith, 41, is the respectable co-ordinator of Conservatives for Change (Cchange), the influential Tory think tank whose board members include Theresa May, the Conservative party chairman,' ran the paper's exclusive exposé in the summer of 2003. 'However, by night Smith runs Fever Parties, a London-based organization that hosts "five-star" orgies for swingers.'

Smith's boss, Francis Maude, was approached for a quote. Maude was not only a modernizer, but a social liberal by conviction, and was quoted saying that he had no idea what Smith got up to in his private life, but 'as long as it's legal I don't care'. Ann Widdecombe, the most outspoken of the party's traditionalists, was less forgiving. 'For those who wonder if the modernising agenda of C-Change is going too far, this is precisely the sort of thing that gives cause for that wonder,' she said.[29]

In the meantime, Howard began to assert his authority over the party, with Portillo's backing. Indeed, the most important advantage Howard brought to the role, Portillo argued, was that he had not relied on the votes of party members to establish his authority. 'The fact that the leader will not this time be elected by the party's masses provides a useful precedent,' Portillo declared. 'We should now be able to dismantle the daft electoral system which pits MPs against party activists.' Portillo would not get his wish on this count, but, in any case, there appeared to be little unhappiness – and even some relief – from the Tory base at Howard's elevation. 'For a majority of party members the most important thing is that the leader should be against the euro,' Portillo noted.[30] The centre of the party was now Eurosceptic.

Howard was certainly against the single currency. In his first major foreign-policy speech as leader, in Berlin, in February 2004, he set out his pitch for a radically different Europe from the one that existed, confirming his opposition to the proposed constitution and repeating his call for a referendum on its introduction. Like Thatcher and Major and Blair, Howard's vision in one sense was decidedly conventional: Europe needed to be less bureaucratic and more liberal. Yet, in another way, Howard's speech marks an important change in British thinking. Thatcher had sought not simply to stop British membership of the euro, but to stop the euro itself, because she did not want Britain to find itself in the outside lane in Brussels. John Major had negotiated an opt-out, but saw it as a pragmatic piece of diplomacy to keep the option open should Britain want to join at a later date, and warned of the dangers of a multi-speed Europe. Blair, too, feared being locked out of the leadership of the continent and wanted to make joining the euro the defining achievement of his premiership. But, in Berlin, Howard set out a fresh approach. 'Faced with a new EU initiative, our traditional response has often been to oppose it, to vote against it, to lose the vote, then sulkily to adopt it while blaming everyone else,' Howard said, warning that this was not sustainable. Instead, those members who wanted to integrate further should go ahead, while those that did not – like Britain – should be left alone. 'The nations of Europe should come together as a series of overlapping circles: different combinations of member states should be able to pool their responsibilities in different areas of their own choosing.'[31]

Britain's decision not to join the euro was not an aberration,

Howard argued. It was a model for a new relationship. Just as Europe had nothing to lose from this arrangement, nor did Britain. 'Britain is the second largest economy in Europe. It is also the strongest military power in Europe. So we should not have any fears about our influence.'[32]

Here was the new model for Britain's European future: forget trying to be at the 'heart' of every European decision and happily adopt a compromise position outside the integrated core. Howard's vision was not revolutionary – John Major had flirted with something similar following Maastricht. But Major had never been comfortable following through with the logic of his argument.

Howard's speech, however, did not answer the obvious question of what he would do about the European constitution if it were to be enacted before the election. In March, Howard finally gave his answer: he would seek to renegotiate the constitution. In trying to break out of the trap that had caught all British party leaders when it came to Europe, Howard found himself back with the same old solution: renegotiation. He would not be the last.

With Blair at his weakest and most dejected, the Conservative Party buoyed by its new leader, and the negotiations over the European constitution dragging on ahead of the summit in June, pressure began to mount on Number Ten to allow a referendum. One such source of pressure was a new group called Vote 2004, founded by Dominic Cummings' former ally at Business for Sterling, Neil O'Brien. Even the Liberal Democrats came out in support of a national vote. The constitution amounted to 'a significant transfer of powers' to the EU, Charles Kennedy wrote in a letter to *The Guardian*, and therefore must be approved by a referendum.[33] Internally, Jack Straw began arguing that Blair needed to give way. Roger Liddle remembers Blair exploding in anger at Straw at one gathering in Chequers, dismissing the idea of a referendum as 'idiotic'.[34] Straw, though, persisted. Jonathan Powell remembers a note appearing on his desk one day, making the case for a referendum; thinking little of it, he left it there while he went away to do something else, only to find that it had gone by the time he was back. Blair had picked it up.[35]

Blair finally gave way in farcical circumstances reminiscent of the euro announcement of 1997. According to Mandelson and Liddle, Blair was weakened and exhausted, suffering from a heart condition and under relentless pressure from Rupert Murdoch, who was threatening to pull *The Sun*'s support ahead of the next election.[36] Finally, in April, there was an apparent miscommunication between Blair and his press secretary David Hill – who had replaced Alastair Campbell following Dr David Kelly's death – which led to *The Sun*'s Trevor Kavanagh being briefed that Blair had changed his mind on the question of a referendum. Peter Mandelson had been flying to Majorca for an Easter holiday and missed a call from Blair at the airport. When the story appeared the next day, he rang Blair demanding to know what had happened. Blair insisted the briefing had been a mistake, but there was no retraction. To this day, Mandelson does not know whether it was really a mistake on Hill's part or whether Blair had simply given in to pressure and did not want to admit it.[37]

'With deep misgivings, I accepted we had to promise a referendum on it,' Blair later explained in his memoir. 'We wouldn't get the Constitution through the House of Lords without it, and even the Commons vote would have been in doubt.'[38] As justifications go, this is only part of the story. The truth, Blair admits, is that he wasn't strong enough to resist at this point. 'I couldn't avoid it,' Blair wrote, 'and as Jack Straw insistently advocated, better to do it apparently willingly than be forced to do it by a vote.'[39]

The decision placed French President Jacques Chirac in an invidious position, forcing him to match Blair's offer. It also erected another barrier to Blair's dreams of European leadership. Neil O'Brien's short-lived Vote 2004 was wound up – and replaced by a new organization, Vote No, to campaign against the constitution whenever the referendum came.

The fact that Blair had to grant a referendum on the European constitution, he later wrote, 'reminded me how far I had to go to persuade British opinion of the merits of being in the mainstream of Europe'.[40] Blair began dreaming of a political counterpunch to seal his legacy: an all-or-nothing referendum on EU membership, including the euro. 'Tony held a flame for the euro far longer than people realize,' Jonathan Powell recalled. 'In hindsight, we'd lost it back in 1997, but that's not how Tony saw it. He had this idea that he could tie everything up together: in or out. This was his great idea.'[41]

Another consideration was the upcoming elections to the European Parliament, scheduled for June 2004. These were taking place on the same day as a series of local elections in England and the election for London mayoralty. They were the first major set of elections since the invasion of Iraq, the first since Michael Howard had replaced Iain Duncan Smith as Tory leader and the first since Europe's expansion east on 1 May. They were also the first real test for UKIP since 1999.

In the run-up to the vote, the headlines could hardly have been worse for Blair. Images of Iraqi prisoners being tortured in Abu Ghraib had leaked and calls were being made for yet more British troops to be sent in to restore order. Blair was 'worn down', weaker than at any point in his premiership and looking for a way out. He and Cherie had even had an offer on a house accepted. 'My feeling at that point was to announce around conference time that I would go, and be out by Christmas,' Blair later wrote.[42] First, he had to get through the European elections.

In early May, the former Labour MP and daytime television presenter Robert Kilroy-Silk announced he would stand as a UKIP candidate. For almost seventeen years, the one-time Labour MP had presented one of the most watched daytime shows on British television, attracting audiences of up to a million people. In the 1970s, he had been a fiery left-winger. After leaving Parliament in 1986 to present his new show, his political career seemed behind him, until an article he'd written for the *Sunday Express* in April 2003, defending the Iraq War, was reprinted early in 2004. In the piece, Kilroy-Silk claimed Arabs should be thankful for 'the munificence of the United States' liberating their country. 'What do they think we feel about them?' he asked. 'That we adore them for the way they murdered more than 3,000 civilians on September 11 and then danced in the hot, dusty streets to celebrate the murders?'[43]

Despite the original article receiving no complaints, when it was reprinted eight months later it caused outrage, and the BBC sacked him on the spot. Unemployed and relaxing at his holiday home in southern Spain, Kilroy-Silk was invited to lunch by a fellow British holidaymaker who owned a place nearby. Richard Bridgeman, the Earl of Bradford, was a businessman, hereditary peer and UKIP activist who had stood for the party in 2001 and was standing again in the upcoming European elections.

Having heard Kilroy-Silk's wife, Jan, was a UKIP voter, Bradford chanced his arm and suggested Kilroy-Silk could stand for the party. Kilroy-Silk liked the idea, so Bradford rang Nigel Farage to arrange a meeting. Despite some misgivings, Farage saw it as too big an opportunity to turn down. Above all, UKIP needed attention, and Kilroy-Silk guaranteed it. 'I might have a few fans, but he would command the worship of thousands,' as Farage later put it.

Kilroy-Silk proved a natural campaigner, drawing crowds and media attention, while being utterly at ease with the public. He was brought in to present one of the party's election broadcasts and took Farage's place on a pre-election *Question Time*. In their account of the 2004 elections, the political historians David Butler and Martin Westlake wrote that, within days of his announcement, 'the UKIP/Kilroy-Silk combination had become the phenomenon of the elections'.[44] James Frayne remembers the sudden shift in focus groups. 'You had people voting for UKIP who did not know they were Eurosceptic, but knew they were anti-immigration. This was the key.'[45]

The European elections in 2004 were the first time UKIP made immigration a central part of its campaign. 'IMMIGRATION SET

TO SOAR', the party's first election leaflet declared, above a cartoon of Eastern Europeans flooding through the 'Channel funnel'.[46] And it worked.

The Conservative Party finished first, but with eight fewer seats than last time, while Labour slumped to an even worse showing than in 1999. Robert Kilroy-Silk's UKIP, meanwhile, surged into third place, with 2.6 million votes – 16.1 per cent of those cast – pushing the Liberal Democrats into fourth. UKIP now had twelve seats in the European Parliament, up from the three it had won in 1999. In Kilroy-Silk's East Midlands base, the party had won 26.1 per cent of the vote. 'Not since former Conservative Enoch Powell urged people to vote Labour in the February 1974 election had someone who wasn't a party leader had such an impact on a British nationwide contest,' wrote Michael Crick.[47]

Unlike Powell, though, Kilroy-Silk's influence would not last, burning brightly for a brief moment, before fizzling out in the deep waters of his own ego. Within days of being elected, Kilroy-Silk began trying to oust the sitting UKIP leader, Roger Knapman, setting off an internal battle for control which ended in a humiliating defeat months later. In early 2005, Kilroy-Silk finally stormed out and set up his own party, Veritas.

When Europe's leaders assembled in Brussels a few days after the elections, however, there were bigger concerns than UKIP. Across the bloc, just 45 per cent of voters had cast their ballot, the lowest on record, dragged down by a lack of enthusiasm among the new voters of the east. In the Czech Republic, Estonia and Slovenia, less than a third of voters turned out, while in Poland it was just 20 per cent and in Slovakia 17 per cent.[48]

For Roger Scruton, who had devoted much of his life to Eastern Europe, and particularly the Czech Republic, such scenes were no real surprise. 'The Poles, Czechs and Hungarians have elected to join the European Union: not in order to throw away national sovereignty, but under the impression that this is the best way to regain it,' he wrote in *The Need for Nations*, published in 2004. 'They are wrong, I believe. But they will be able to see this only later, when it is too late to change.' The book was a development of the theme Scruton had been setting out for some time: that the nation state was essential for democracy and that those who spoke of 'progress' inevitably moving towards new and transnational forms of government were endangering something precious. 'Everywhere the idea of the nation is under attack,' he wrote, 'either despised as an atavistic form of social unity, or even condemned as a cause of war and conflict, to be broken down and replaced by more enlightened and more universal forms of jurisdiction.'[49]

Among EU leaders, the low turnout in the east was seen as a spur for further integration. The need to 'strengthen a sense among the citizens of Europe of the importance of the work of the Union and its relevance to their daily lives' had been one of the central tasks of Giscard d'Estaing's new European constitution, finally agreed by Europe's leaders in June.[50] 'The Treaty establishing a Constitution for Europe is an historic step forward in the process of integration and cooperation in Europe,' EU leaders had declared. 'It completes the process which began when the Treaty of Rome established the basic framework for European integration.'[51]

Despite this sentiment, the summit in Brussels in the summer of 2004 was marked more by continuing division than hopeful expectation. First, there was a curiously bitter disagreement between Blair and his German counterpart, Gerhard Schröder, over the appointment of the next Commission president. The German chancellor and the French president Jacques Chirac had agreed on the appointment of Guy Verhofstadt, but Blair successfully resisted by corralling a blocking coalition of states – including many from the new east. 'New Europe sides with Blair over old Europe', ran the headline on the front page of *The Times*.[52] Britain's great push to expand the EU was bearing fruit. But when a compromise candidate emerged in the form of Chris Patten, Chirac refused his appointment on the grounds that Europe could not have a president from a country 'which doesn't take part in all European policies'.[53] The diplomatic fallout spilled over into the discussions on the constitution itself, with Britain refusing to give up national vetoes on tax and social-security measures, much to the frustration of France and Germany.

For Blair, the summit ended as a qualified success – politically, at least. He had resisted French and German pressure, even at the cost of a breakdown in relations with Berlin. 'This was the first time that the twin-engine motor of Europe had been stalled in respect of such a big issue,' Blair later claimed in his memoir. 'My relationship with Gerhard Schröder never recovered.' For Blair, the summit was a lesson in the importance of being at the centre of Europe. 'As a result of being in the middle, we could achieve. On the periphery, counting for nothing, we achieve nothing.'[54] It was a curious conclusion. After the summit, a Downing Street spokesman had been sent out to rebuke the French and Germans for their behaviour. 'We all have to accept that we operate in a Europe of 25 – not a Europe of six, or two, or one,' the unnamed spokesman told the assembled press, dismissing the suggestion that Britain's decision not to join the euro meant it could no longer expect to see its citizens take on leadership roles in the Commission. 'There are no first- or second-class members of the EU.'[55] Yet this was exactly the logic driving Blair towards the euro – the belief that, without being as integrated as the rest of the EU, as central to its decision-making, Britain's influence would diminish.

The problem for Blair was, the more he championed Britain's economic and diplomatic successes, the weaker he made the argument for changing the status quo. Blair faced a challenge simply to maintain Britain's current place by ratifying the European constitution. Around the time of the European elections, a new think tank called the New Frontiers Foundation had begun to appear in newspaper articles criticizing Giscard d'Estaing's proposed constitution. 'Most businesses say "no"', ran the headline in *The Times* in April, citing a poll conducted on behalf of this new foundation, which it described as 'a Eurosceptic think-tank likely to generate the official "no" campaign against the constitution.'[56]

Dominic Cummings had re-entered public life in late 2003, establishing the New Frontiers Foundation with the support of his old friend Robert Cranborne and with generous funding from the betting magnate and close friend of Rodney Leach, Stuart Wheeler, who had made headlines in 2001 by donating £5 million to the Conservative Party – the biggest donation in British political history at that time.[57] Cummings' new foundation stirred some media attention about the 'mercurial figure' in charge, who had already proved his worth at Business for Sterling.[58]

Cummings had chosen the name of his new think tank in honour of John F. Kennedy's 1960 Democratic Convention speech, in which he declared the beginning of 'a new frontier, a frontier of unknown opportunities and perils.' This was the sentiment behind much of Cummings' analysis: the idea that the European Union represented an old world which risked being swept away in the age of globalization after the fall of the Berlin Wall. Cummings believed that, to thrive in the new world, the British state needed to be overhauled and the country turned into the 'school of the world', focusing on high-end science and technology.[59] This was the vision he would outline at the NFF in a regular email sent to supporters, as they prepared the ground for the expected campaign against the European constitution.

Cummings quickly moved to rehire his old friend from Business for Sterling, James Frayne, who joined in March 2004. According to Frayne, Cummings' central analysis was that, while Business for Sterling and the 'No' campaign had been good at stopping things, Euroscepticism needed to do more than this if it was to triumph in the long term. It needed its own vision of the future and what it looked like. 'It was a think tank to get Eurosceptics on the front foot,' Frayne said. 'To be forward thinking and to counter the idea that Eurosceptics were obsessed with heritage and Britain's past.' Cummings set about this task with his usual energy and quickly became fixated on the process of leaving the EU, which he believed was far more complicated than most Eurosceptics understood. Cummings became particularly obsessed by a 1988 report on deepening the European internal market, called the Cecchini report. 'He would say things like, "We'll need a Cecchini report in reverse" to leave,' Frayne recalled. 'Dom's view was that you can't just sign a document with a quill pen and suddenly you've left the EU.'[60]

The NFF's first home was in a set of shared offices on Wilton Road, near Victoria, in central London. In February 2004, Cummings and Frayne were joined by another new organization which moved into offices on the same corridor: the TaxPayers' Alliance. The TPA, as it quickly became known, was the brainchild of Matthew Elliott, who had stopped working for Timothy Kirkhope when the European convention concluded the previous year. Elliott's idea was to have a non-partisan pressure group in favour of a smaller state and lower taxes, shining a spotlight on government waste, as he saw it, whether in London or in Brussels.

Elliott and Cummings were the new faces of Euroscepticism, less animated by questions of parliamentary sovereignty, of the sort that burned in figures like Michael Foot, Enoch Powell or Roger Scruton, than what they saw as the bureaucratic nature of the EU, which was either too big, in Elliott's view, or too anachronistic, in Cummings' analysis. Neither was driven by visions of the past, and both looked to the US for inspiration. This was twenty-first century Euroscepticism, though it would rely on a revival of that deeper romantic tradition for its eventual triumph.

Although Cummings' NFF and Elliott's TPA were separate organizations, with separate ambitions, they were operating in the same ecosystem and naturally influenced each other's thinking. One of the first moves Elliott made to secure the TPA was to create a mailing list from all those who had publicly backed Business for Sterling. From this alone, he received enough money in donations to keep him going for the first three months of the new organization's existence. Many of those figures giving money to the TPA would be needed to fund the expected 'No' campaign against the European constitution.

The TPA published a *Bumper Book of Government Waste and Useless Spending* in February 2004, which claimed that 'at least £50bn' of taxpayers' money had been wasted by the government the previous year.[61] The crucial point, the TPA would claim repeatedly over the years, was that this waste could be avoided 'without closing a single hospital, firing a single teacher or cutting pensions.'[62] There had been Hayekian free-market think tanks before – the IEA, CPS and Adam Smith Institute – but none so ruthlessly focused on the consumer, and none with such an evident understanding of small-state conservatism's core political weakness: people's reliance on public services. The TPA was the conservative answer to the Blairite ascendancy.

Before the referendum on the European constitution could take place, the government was committed to another referendum, this one on whether to establish a regional assembly in the north-east of England – the first step in what it saw as the eventual answer to the West Lothian question created by devolution in Scotland and Wales. For those opposed to English devolution, the north-east was a tricky problem: a virtual one-party state, where organized opposition was difficult. Apart from two rural Northumberland MPs, every other seat in the region was Labour, including Blair's in Sedgefield, Peter Mandelson's in Hartlepool and David Miliband's in South Shields.

The lack of space for a conventional campaign run by MPs, however, opened up an opportunity – and Dominic Cummings, himself a native of the region, grabbed hold of it, seeing in the north-east referendum a 'test run' for the real thing to come. Cummings assembled a shoestring operation to begin campaigning. 'I got my uncle as finance director,' he recalled with a laugh, 'and my girlfriend answering the phone.'[63] James Frayne was made campaign director. Together, they set to work on one of the most extraordinary campaigns in modern British history, crushing the opposition with a message of clean populist anger.

'The north-east has been let down by politicians for years,' the campaign's ultra-low-budget election video declares. 'Remember 1997? We were told that things can only get better. But politicians have failed us. Now, politicians want even more power for themselves by creating a regional assembly made up of more full-time professional politicians. It's time to say no.'[64]

The video then set out the No campaign's central argument: cost. The assembly would cost '£1 million a week', paid for with higher council tax. The £1 million a week calculation seems to have been arrived at through government estimates that the new assembly would cost £30 million to set up and £20 million a year to run, while ignoring the savings that would come from closing other layers of local government. 'The equating of money spent on more politicians instead of doctors resonated,' said Graham Robb, the campaign's chief spokesperson, who voiced the election video. 'It isn't about, to the penny, what slogan you use about the NHS. It's about the principle of it.'[65] Cummings learned a valuable lesson.

Robb later described the referendum as 'Britain's first populist campaign', though there had already been warning flares of growing anti-politics sentiment – specifically in the north-east, where Hartlepool had responded to the imposition of a new directly elected mayor by voting for the football-club mascot, H'Angus the Monkey, in 2002. During the referendum campaign, Cummings and Frayne deployed a giant inflatable white elephant and burned a million pounds in fake £50 notes to display the cost of the proposed venture. 'Politicians talk, we pay,' ran one slogan. Another declared, 'More doctors, not politicians.' Whatever the merits of the campaign, it is impossible not to marvel at its brute success. Early in the campaign, polls showed Yes leading two to one. By October, Newcastle's local newspaper, *The Journal*, carried a poll showing the No campaign in the lead. When the result came in, No had won with 78 per cent of the vote. 'It was a training exercise that turned out surprisingly well,' Cummings later reflected. But what lessons were learned by the losing side?

'SW1 100% ignored it,' Cummings wrote, gleefully, though Matthew Elliott at the TPA had not.[66]

For much of 2004, Blair had been in a desperate state: worn out, despondent and uncertain about the future, having promised Brown in a moment of weakness that he would leave before the next election. Yet, by the summer, he had begun to have second thoughts about giving way, and in July finally plucked up the courage to tell Brown that he would be staying on. The decision set up a highly charged conference in October, where Blair confirmed not only that he would be fighting his third election, but also that he would not contest a fourth. At the same conference, he also revealed that he had bought a new home for his post-premiership life and that he needed minor heart surgery. It was a whirlwind, but provided an indication of his re-energized frame of mind.

For Blair, the challenge now was to win the coming general election to secure a defiantly New Labour package of reforms at home, before launching into the referendum on the European constitution. In his memoirs, he sets out why he placed such emphasis on Europe: 'In a world of new emerging powers, Britain needed Europe in order to exert influence and advance its interests. It wasn't complicated.' Blair regarded those who questioned this logic as 'hopelessly, absurdly out of date and unrealistic', but also parochial. Euroscepticism, he wrote, was 'the product of a dangerous insularity, a myopia about the world . . . a kind of post-empire delusion.'[67]

Ironically, Blair did not question whether his vision of European leadership might itself be the product of a post-imperial delusion about British power. Nor did he question whether twenty-first-century modernity might demand entirely different structures from those assembled in the twentieth.

For Tony Blair, the 2005 general election was not just a last hurrah, but the necessary precursor to the coming battle over the constitution – and perhaps even the euro. For Michael Howard, the election was the opportunity to put the Conservative Party on the road back to power. To help during the election, he brought in Dougie Smith as his speechwriter. Smith was the indirect beneficiary of battlefield promotions. Michael Gove had originally taken the job, only to be selected as the Conservative Party candidate in Surrey Heath. The role had then gone to Ed Vaizey, only for him to be selected as a candidate too. And so it went to Smith, a safe choice insofar as he had never had any interest in seeking elected office.

Howard decided that his best chance of securing a surprise victory was to target Blair's weakest point: immigration. 'Are you thinking what we're thinking?' asked the party's infamous campaign poster. 'It's not racist to impose limits on immigration.' The attack, masterminded by the Australian election guru Lynton Crosby, who had been hired to lead the campaign – his first major role in British politics – posed a difficult challenge for the Labour Party: should they condemn the poster, thereby suggesting that they did believe it was racist to impose limits on immigration? Or should they ignore it and run the risk of looking out of touch?

Blair decided to deal with the Tory attack head-on, with a speech in Dover. 'Concern over asylum and immigration is not about racism,' he declared. 'It's about fairness.' Blair insisted that he understood people's concerns. He promised to introduce 'strict' new points-based immigration controls after the election. He then turned his fire on Howard. 'Their campaign is based on the statement that it isn't racist to talk about immigration,' he declared. 'I know of no senior politician who has ever said it was. So why do they put it like that?' Blair said it was an attempt 'to suggest that, for reasons of political correctness, those in power don't dare deal with the issue . . . when actually the opposite is true.'[68]

The speech risked talking up the subject to the Tories' advantage; instead, it snatched back some of the momentum. 'Because our position was sophisticated enough – a sort of "confess and avoid", as the lawyers say – we won out,' Blair later explained. Still, the poster, and Blair's response, mark an important turning point, with immigration centre stage in an election campaign in a way not seen since the years of 'zero immigration' consensus. Blair might have dealt with the immediate political challenge, but it would not go away if immigration remained as high as it was. Confessing and avoiding would not be enough.

When the results started to come through on 6 May 2005, it was clear Blair had won a third consecutive term, but with a significantly reduced majority – down more than a hundred seats – with the lowest vote share of any majority-winning party in modern history.

Despite disappointment for the Tories, for the first time since 1997 they could see a possible route back to power. In terms of vote share, Michael Howard had won just 2.8 per cent less than Blair, and in England had finished first – a portent of things to come.

For UKIP, it was another poor showing, scoring just 2.2 per cent of the vote – up from the 1.5 per cent it had achieved in 2001, but a disappointment nonetheless. Standing in Thanet South, Farage managed 5 per cent, just enough to cost the Tory candidate, Mark MacGregor, the seat. One consolation for UKIP was the death of Kilroy-Silk's Veritas, which was returned with 0.1 per cent of the vote nationally, comfortably behind the new force emerging on the far right of British politics: Nick Griffin's BNP, which increased its votes from 47,000 to 197,000. It was an early warning sign. For those paying attention, a similar story had already played out in the European elections the year before, when the BNP narrowly missed out on winning a seat after securing 4.8 per cent of the vote to finish sixth.

Despite the historic nature of Blair's victory – no previous Labour leader had won three consecutive elections – the 2005 election left a peculiar sense of deflation, and the mood in the Labour Party turned sour as Brown's outriders hit the airwaves claiming a different leader would have obtained a better result. 'The media treated me as if I had lost,' Blair later wrote. 'I allowed myself to be caught up in this mood.' But then Michael Howard announced he would resign. 'Suddenly people remembered the Tories had lost.'[69] There would be yet another Conservative Party leadership election.

A few weeks later, on 29 May 2005, Blair was relieved to receive the helpful news that France had unexpectedly rejected the European constitution by a margin of 55 per cent to 45 per cent. Three days later, the Dutch followed suit by a far greater margin, 61.5 per cent to 38.5 per cent. 'I knew at once I was off the hook,' he later wrote.[70] For Dominic Cummings and the wider Eurosceptic movement, meanwhile, it meant the loss of their main campaign focus. They had been confident they could win a referendum and, in doing so, not merely end further European integration but, perhaps, even turn the political tide in favour of eventual withdrawal. But, now, the European constitution had been defeated and the euro had been kicked even further into the long grass. Neil O'Brien's Vote 2004 had morphed into Vote No, and now even that seemed redundant. So, what next? While they could all agree on what they did not want, there was little consensus about where they should go from here. The Eurosceptics had lost their chance to draw their enemy into open battle. Now, they feared no government would ever put themselves in a position where they would have to fight a referendum. The long march of integration that Edward Heath had begun in 1971 seemed stuck.

Chapter 14

On 17 July 2005, Edward Heath died, aged eighty-nine, the last prime minister to have served in Britain's battle for survival against Hitler the century before. While the soldiers of the First World War generation had long since passed – Winston Churchill in 1965, Clement Attlee in 1967, Anthony Eden in 1977 and Harold MacMillan in 1986 – the veterans of the Second World War had also now gone: Harold Wilson* in 1995 and James Callaghan in March 2005. Heath, fittingly, was the last of Britain's soldier statesmen to pass.

Though Heath had only served four years in Number Ten, British membership of the new Europe marked him out as one of the most transformative prime ministers of post-war Britain. Through ambition, skill, determination and luck, he had led Britain into the Community. He was also the only British prime minister who believed in the idea of Europe not simply as a source of power, but as a shared identity and destiny. Throughout his life, Heath raged at the philistines who could not see Europe in this way. 'She is so ignorant that she does not realise we have a European culture,' Heath had said of his nemesis, Margaret Thatcher, at the height of the drama over Maastricht in 1992, when she was leading the opposition to the bill from the Lords.[1]

Here was the real Heath: not the dour technocrat of parody,

---

* Wilson did not see active service. After volunteering for the war effort, he was placed in the civil service rather than the military.

but a passionate believer in Europe. It is fitting, perhaps, that Heath's final illness was first diagnosed in Salzburg, Austria, when he became unwell attending the city's annual Mozart festival. In 1994, when Heath was admitted to the Order of the Garter, his coat of arms included a cloud with beams of sunlight bursting forth, representing Britain's entry into the European Community. At his funeral in Salisbury Cathedral, Bishop David Stancliffe observed that no one could doubt his commitment to Europe: 'In this he exerted his fullest force.'[2]

It was not until a few months after his funeral, at a service of thanksgiving in Parliament, that Europe was able to return his esteem, as the European Union's Youth Orchestra played to a cast list of long-retired characters from British politics: Edward du Cann, who might have been something more but wasn't; Jonathan Aitken, who briefly played a part only to fall in disgrace; Robin Chichester-Clark, the last MP from Northern Ireland to serve in the cabinet, who departed government with Heath in 1974. Here were members of an older cast, long since replaced by the newer men of England who were also in attendance that day, from Tony Blair to the outgoing Conservative Party leader Michael Howard.[3]

A month after Heath's death, another figure from this lost world departed the stage. Maurice Cowling, the one-time leader of the Peterhouse right, died in August, aged seventy-eight. In life, Cowling had taught or inspired many of the leading figures in the Thatcherite counter-revolution opposed to Heath, from Norman Stone to the darling of the new modernizers, Michael Portillo, himself a Peterhouse alumnus, who led the tributes at Cowling's memorial service alongside Peregrine Worsthorne, Cowling's great friend and fellow Cambridge radical.

In a tribute in *The Times*, William Rees-Mogg claimed the new generation of Tory MPs vying for control of the party were, in many respects, 'Cowling's intellectual grandchildren'.[4] Whether these grandchildren would take control was another matter.

The backdrop to the leadership election was not one of cuddly liberal modernity, however, but murderous violence, in the single most deadly act of terrorism on British soil since the Lockerbie aeroplane bombing in 1988. Britain had suffered its first suicide attack: 7/7, as it came to be known, immediately understood in relation to its American forebear. The spectre of jihad had hung over the country since 9/11. In Madrid, the year before, 200 people had been killed in a series of coordinated train bombings. Now, Britain had fallen victim to this dark inflection of modernity, as four Islamist bombers – three of whom were British born – struck during the rush-hour commute, killing fifty-two people and injuring 700 more. The image of a destroyed double-decker bus, its roof blown apart by the ferocity of the explosion, became the symbol of the attack: a picture of England, prostrate.

The news of the attack came as world leaders gathered in Gleneagles, Scotland, for a meeting of the G8. As Tony Blair delivered a solemn joint statement in response, he was flanked by US President George W. Bush, German Chancellor Gerhard Schröder, European Commission President José Manuel Barroso and China's Hu Jintao to his right, and French President Jacques Chirac, Italian Prime Minister Silvio Berlusconi, Russian leader Vladimir Putin and India's Manmohan Singh to his left. The world's leaders, once divided by Iraq, had come together to offer symbolic unity against terrorism, which threatened them all.

It is a strange quirk of history that news of the 7/7 bombings came a matter of hours after the International Olympic Committee, meeting in Singapore, announced that London would host the 2012 Games. 'It's not often in this job that you punch the air and do a little jig and embrace the person next to you,' Blair had declared earlier that morning.[5] For Blair, the Games represented the very future he envisaged: Britain back at the centre of the world, not as the hegemon of old, but as the beacon of enlightened liberalism. To secure victory, he had flown to Singapore to present London in this light: the world's city. 'As a leader in government or sport, we have a duty to reach beyond our own time and borders, to have a vision which serves those who come after us,' Blair had declared in his final pitch, drawn once again to the future of his dreams. This vision of modern Britain would survive the Tube and bus bombings – indeed, it would survive Blair's own departure from power – to reach its apotheosis with the staging of the Games in 2012. Yet, the carnage that shook Britain from its reverie that day would also implant itself in the national consciousness as a gnawing challenge to the Blairite dream.

This was the context of the Conservative Party leadership campaign of 2005. David Davis was the early favourite, and his principal rivals were Ken Clarke – again – and Liam Fox, representing the Thatcherite right. David Cameron, meanwhile, was the anointed leader of the modernizers, though he was not expected to win.

Cameron and the Tory modernizers were not particularly popular in the parliamentary party. 'This is what we call the Notting Hill Tory set,' said the Conservative MP and Davis ally, Derek Conway, before the election. 'They sit around in these curious little bistros in parts of London, drink themselves silly and wish they were doing what the rest of us are getting on with.'[6] The name stuck: the Notting Hill Set.

In *The Guardian*, Cameron and George Osborne were named as the set's 'leading lights', along with Rachel Whetstone, Ed Vaizey and George Bridges, a close friend of Robert Salisbury.[7] Bridges was also a regular attendee at the dinner parties organized by Jessica Douglas-Home and Roger Scruton. The aspiring MP Danny Finkelstein and pollster Andrew Cooper were also named, alongside the journalists Alice Thomson, of *The Telegraph*, and her husband, Edward Heathcoat-Amory, of the *Mail*. Michael Gove, who had won his seat of Surrey Heath, was also a core member.

Gove was, in many ways, the most incongruous figure in the group. Bright and ambitious, his politics were far from 'modern' in the Blairite sense. Even after university, he had remained defiantly 'sound'. Before being elected to Parliament in 2005, he had written a Powellite condemnation of the Good Friday Agreement and had begun a polemical critique of Islamism, which he called *Celsius 7/7*. Yet, it was less the conservatism of his politics which set him apart from most of the Notting Hill Set than the circumstances of his birth.

Gove had been born Graeme Andrew Logan, in Edinburgh, in the summer of 1967, but was almost immediately placed in care and was then adopted by Ernest and Christine Gove of Aberdeen when he was just four months old. Gove himself has speculated about the circumstances of his adoption lying at the root of his radicalism. Though he seems to have felt no sense of trauma or rejection because of this start in life, he is far from the only figure in this story to have experienced a form of parental loss. Norman Stone, Bill Cash and Robert Kilroy-Silk all lost their fathers in the war. Nigel Farage's dad was an alcoholic who left the family when he was four.

'It's the fiery chariot!' Gove declared, emphatically, when asked about this link.[8] *The Fiery Chariot* is the title of a book by the Conservative writer Lucille Iremonger, which argued that children who had suffered a childhood trauma developed a 'Phaeton complex': a fateful desire to prove their worth in the eyes of the world.[9] 'Like so many things, it is broadly true,' Gove said.[10] Phaeton or otherwise, Michael Gove was unique among the Notting Hill Set for the stridency of his politics.

Unlike most of the Cameroons, he was also something of a political flaneur, moving from one social circle to the next. There were those he knew from university: Nick Boles, Matthew D'Ancona, Ed Vaizey and Boris Johnson. Many of these figures, including Cameron but not Johnson, were also part of an ironically named Eurosceptic dinner club: the Roy Jenkins Appreciation Society. Then there was the circle around Dougie Smith and the Democracy Movement – Ben Elliot, Robin Birley and Zac Goldsmith – and the Scrutonians. Finally, there was the group around Business for Sterling, including Nick Herbert, Robert Salisbury and Dominic Cummings. 'I suppose it was like a Venn diagram of overlapping groups, with only some of us who fitted into all, of whom I was one,' Gove recalled.[11]

In the leadership election, the main obstacle in the way of the modernizers was the figure of David Davis, who had gained the admiration of many of his colleagues by standing aside in favour of Michael Howard for the sake of party unity in 2003. Davis was a party loyalist who had risen to become Europe minister under John Major in the years before the Labour flood. He also had the kind of life story that appealed beyond Westminster: abandoned by his father and brought up in poverty in York, before working his way near to the top of British politics.

Such was Davis's popularity within the party in 2005 that, if Cameron was going to win, he needed time to raise his profile, which only the leader Michael Howard could provide. Having fallen out with Davis during the general election campaign, Howard felt free to do all he could to help Cameron. Immediately after the election defeat, Howard reshuffled the shadow cabinet, promoting all of Davis's main rivals, including George Osborne, who became shadow chancellor at just thirty-three, David Cameron, who became shadow education secretary aged thirty-eight, and Liam Fox, who was made shadow foreign secretary aged forty-four. Howard then announced that the leadership election would take place after the next Conservative Party Conference, which was not until October.

Still, the chances of Davis being beaten remained low. Following the reshuffle, *The Times* stated that 'Mr Osborne and Mr Cameron have a tough task to convince older members of the Tory parliamentary party that they should get their chance of a run at the leadership this time.' Their problem, *The Times* wrote, was that they had been 'derided as members of the so-called Notting Hill Set, a group obsessed with talking and writing about the party's problems rather than doing anything about them'.[12]

A poll of Tory MPs in *The Sunday Times* on the first weekend in September found that Cameron had the support of only nine MPs.[13] He was being squeezed not only by Davis, but by Ken

Clarke and Liam Fox, too. In the last week of September, Fox had set out his Eurosceptic credentials by promising to lead the Tories out of the centre-right bloc in the European Parliament, the European People's Party (EPP). This proposal had been kicking around for some time, the brainchild of Daniel Hannan, who had persuaded Iain Duncan Smith to embrace the idea in 2001, only for him to be removed as leader before the policy could be enacted.

Cameron was so worried that Fox's embrace of this policy might push him out of the contest, he broke his unofficial 'no promises' rule to match it.[14] David Davis, however, refused to follow suit. Suddenly, the main modernizer in the contest was trying to stay in the race by outflanking the favourite from the right.

In one sense, such a move seemed incongruous. In later years, modernization would come to be associated with the left of the party – a 'centrist' project against the traditionalist right, supported by those like Finkelstein and Cooper, who had once been in the SDP. Yet, as with Tony Blair's drive to reform the Labour Party a decade earlier, the question of Europe never had a simple 'modernizing' answer. At Policy Exchange, the intellectual heart of the Tory modernization project, Francis Maude, Michael Gove and Dougie Smith were all long-standing Eurosceptics. For them, modernization was not about abandoning core tenets of their faith, but reconciling the Tory party to the country it aspired to lead. Cameron had never been shy in his scepticism, opposed to both the euro and the European constitution. According to George Eustice, Cameron's then press secretary – who had started his career at the Referendum Party and stood for UKIP in the 1999 European elections, before working under Cummings at Business for Sterling – Cameron had already privately indicated his support for leaving the EPP when he made his pledge, but did not want to announce it out of loyalty to Michael Howard, who had put a lot of effort into renegotiating the Conservative Party's membership of the EPP.[15] After Fox's endorsement, though, he had no choice.

Cameron had displayed his instinctive Euroscepticism in a series of light-hearted diary pieces he wrote for *The Guardian* between 2001 and 2004, in which he had described himself as a 'passionate believer' in the pound,[16] argued for a referendum lock against further European integration and described Tony Blair as a 'Euro-fanatic'.[17] Apart from his self-deprecating insistence that these views were not the result of 'too much time spent alone with Bill Cash,' Cameron's arguments were uncomplicatedly Eurosceptic in a way that would have been considered distinctly right wing only a decade earlier.[18] Indeed, Cameron's pragmatic Euroscepticism had been crucial in him becoming an MP. His decision to match Liam Fox's pledge was not intellectually inconsistent.

The decisive moment in the leadership contest, however, came at the party conference in Blackpool, in October. In later lore, this is the moment Cameron pulled the sword from the stone with a display of Etonian bravado, wowing the Tory delegates with a speech delivered without notes. Almost as important was a *Newsnight* focus group conducted by the American pollster Frank Luntz, which found the public preferred Cameron to Davis, much to the surprise of many observers. Both of these developments helped see Cameron through to a final run-off against Davis, though it was far from certain he would win. In November, *The Times* reported that Cameron had fallen behind among party members once again, after Davis made a series of eye-catching pledges on tax cuts and referendums on European integration.[19]

When the result was announced in December, however, it was Cameron who had triumphed – and convincingly, by a margin of more than two to one. The modernizers were now in control of the Conservative Party. What this meant for Europe, however, remained unclear.

The Eurosceptic movement was going through its own period of change. Dominic Cummings and James Frayne had come back from the north-east in 2004 convinced that the time was ripe for a more aggressively 'anti-politics' message to wrest back more powers from the EU. On this point, however, they had been unable to convince the old Thatcherite tycoons who had funded Business for Sterling. On the one side, Cummings and Frayne wanted a more assertive Eurosceptic campaign to start immediately. But, on the other, those involved in Vote 2004 and Vote No, led by Alex Hickman and Neil O'Brien, argued that Euroscepticism needed to remain consciously cross-party and moderate.

Unable to persuade Leach and the other donors, Cummings departed the New Frontiers Foundation and closed it down. Frayne, meanwhile, joined Matthew Elliott at the TaxPayers' Alliance, leaving Leach and others to plough their money into a new think tank called 'Open Europe', which was keen to maintain close ties to Cameron's Conservative Party. Open Europe's first director was Neil O'Brien. O'Brien remembers the early sense of energy as they began shaping opinion with simple but effective tactics. 'We did a European press summary every day,' he recalls. 'Blair and Brown liked to say European integration was dead, but this was such an insular, British view, because all you had to do to show the continued commitment to ever closer union was to translate what was being said in *Le Figaro* and *FAZ* and *La Repubblica*.'[20] As Hugo Young had noted, Britain's myopic attitude to Europe was far from simply a Eurosceptic trait, but was just as prevalent among EU supporters in the UK, many of whom could not shake themselves from their very British assumptions about what the project entailed.

In Cameron's first reshuffle, William Hague was brought back as shadow foreign secretary, while modernizers Francis Maude, Oliver Letwin and Andrew Lansley were all given key jobs. Two other promotions caught the media's eye: Michael Gove became shadow housing minister, just seven months after entering the Commons, and Boris Johnson returned to the front bench as higher education spokesman. For Johnson, in particular, this appointment was not just a promotion, but something of a resurrection.

Only the year before, Johnson's political career seemed to be over, after he was sacked from Michael Howard's front bench for lying about an affair with the journalist Petronella Wyatt. At first, Johnson dismissed the allegation as an 'inverted pyramid of piffle' and assured Howard it was untrue, only for Wyatt's mother to publicly confirm the opposite. When Howard discovered the lie, he demanded Johnson's resignation. Johnson refused and was sacked.

'The episode brings an end to an unlikely but uniquely engaging political career,' reported *The Guardian* the next day, under the headline, 'Have we got news for you'.[21] Johnson was a joke, famous mostly for his appearances alongside Paul Merton and Ian Hislop on the BBC's *Have I Got News for You*. And yet the fame mattered; the jokes were a source of strength, not weakness.

In his first appearance on the show in 1998, Johnson was tormented by Hislop over a recording of him agreeing to hand over a journalist's address to a friend who wanted to have him beaten up. 'Ha, ha, ha, yes, yes, richly comic,' Johnson squirmed. Far from damaging Johnson, such moments cemented his image as 'a lovable, self-mocking buffoon', as the novelist Jonathan Coe observed in an essay looking back at this period, published almost a decade later. In Coe's estimation, Johnson was the first politician in Britain able to turn the culture of satire on its head. 'Boris Johnson has become his own satirist: safe, above all, in the knowledge that the best way to make sure the satire aimed at you is gentle and unchallenging is to create it yourself.'[22]

Johnson was not some throwback clown, but an emblem of modernity. No matter how many scandals came his way, he seemed able to shrug them off with a wink and a joke. After his public skewering by Hislop, Johnson was appointed editor of *The Spectator* on the condition that he didn't stand for Parliament, only then to do so. He became shadow arts minister while remaining editor, during which time he was forced to travel to Liverpool to apologize for an editorial accusing Liverpudlians of wallowing in their 'victim status' after the murder of the aid worker Ken Bigley in

Iraq.[23] Johnson dubbed this trip 'operation Scouse grovel'.[24] Cameron's decision to bring him back in 2005 seemed to fit the pattern of his life.

But why did Cameron do it? While they knew each other, they were hardly close. Johnson had always been the senior, more famous figure. At Oxford, he'd been the star, much as he had been at Eton. It was at school, in fact, that *Boris* had emerged from the chrysalis of *Alexander*, the name in which he had sheltered happily until then.

As Alexander, before Eton, Johnson had been a much quieter, bookish boy, moving around the world with his family, following the ego and ambition of his erratic, philandering father. In all, the family moved thirty-two times in fourteen years during Johnson's childhood. The one constant in his life was his mother, Charlotte. But then, in 1974, Charlotte suffered a breakdown, forcing her to leave her children and their home in Brussels for psychiatric treatment in London. While there, Charlotte produced a series of disturbing paintings. In one, *Hanged by Circumstances*, Stanley, Charlotte and the four children are strung up by their arms, with pained expressions on their faces. Another depicts 'Dark Stanley'.[25]

Charlotte later rejoined the family, but suffered health problems for the rest of her life: depression, obsessive–compulsive disorder and finally Parkinson's disease, diagnosed when she was only forty. Three years later, Stanley and Charlotte's marriage collapsed, just as their son was settling into life at Eton. 'I was so, so close to the children,' Charlotte told her son's biographer Andrew Gimson, 'and then I disappeared.'[26] Years later, Charlotte gave an interview to the BBC for a 2013 documentary, in which she spoke of her son's oft-stated ambition to be 'world king'. 'I often thought that the idea of being a world king was a wish to make himself unhurtable,' she said, 'invincible, somehow, safe from the pains of life, the pains of your mother disappearing for eight months, the pains of your parents splitting up.'[27] Alexander had become Boris and the mask had moulded to his face, as the philosopher John Gray noted.[28] The brooding and vulnerable loner had protected himself through self-satire.

From Eton onwards, Boris rose to national fame through force of personality, wit, hyperbole and falsehood. Until 2005, he had never been Cameron's junior. Cameron bringing Johnson into his team could be seen as an act of confidence, but also of beneficence, of clemency, of power.

Cameron's principal goal as leader was to show the country that he led a changed Conservative Party. During the leadership election, he had promised to 'share the proceeds of growth' between public spending and tax cuts, so that voters didn't have to choose between them.[29] Here was Tory Blairism. In his first party conference speech as Tory leader, in 2006, Cameron urged the party to stop 'banging on about Europe' and focus on the priorities of the public: 'safer streets, schools that teach, a better quality of life, better treatment for carers.'[30] These were the issues people were talking about, he said.

The entire offer, however, was predicated on the idea that the economy would continue to expand, as it had for the past decade. At the time, this seemed reasonable: the British economy was among the strongest in Europe and seemed structurally well placed to thrive in the new, globalized world. London was the richest city in Europe, the engine of an open, liberal economy producing enough wealth to support the country. By remaining outside the euro, the UK even seemed to have accidentally alighted on a 'best of all worlds' model. Yet, in October of that year, the governor of the Bank of England, Mervyn King, felt concerned enough to warn that the 'NICE' years of 'Non-Inflationary Consistently Expansionary economic growth' were coming to an end.[31] 'The business cycle has not been abolished,' King warned, pointedly.[32]

Although Britain's economic growth figures still looked healthy on paper, median real wages – the after-inflation earnings of the average worker – had already started to stagnate and private debt was exploding. For a country in the middle of a period of unprecedented stability and growth, these were signs that all was not well.

Politically, too, there was a striking disconnect between the consensus in Westminster and the mood in the country. While on the face of it both main parties were now firmly in the 'centre ground', a new force was growing on the extreme right: the British National Party. In the 2002 local elections, the BNP had gained its first councillors in almost a decade: four in total. A year later, it added thirteen more. At the 2004 European elections, the party had won 800,000 votes. And, while it did not achieve the breakthrough it wanted in the general election of 2005, the 2006 local elections offered another opportunity. Across the country, Griffin's party gained 220,000 votes, winning another thirty-three councillors. Long before the financial crash, a malaise was beginning to spread over the country.

This was the backdrop, in the summer of 2006, when Hezbollah launched a cross-border attack into Israel, setting off a chain of events that would eventually force Tony Blair from office. In response to Hezbollah's incursion, Israel launched a ground invasion of Lebanon, which turned into a month-long war, sparking condemnation from much of the global left, though not, significantly, from Blair. Blair later reflected that his response to the crisis did him more damage than anything had since Iraq. Ultimately, he believed the civilized world was still locked in an existential battle with Islamist extremism. 'To me, Lebanon was embroiled in something far bigger and more portentous than a temporary fight with Israel,' he wrote.[33]

The horror of Iraq, in other words, had not weakened his belief in the righteousness of his mission, but rather had convinced him still further. By not calling for an immediate ceasefire, Blair realized 'how far I had swung from the mainstream of conventional Western media wisdom and from my own people.' Reading his account of this episode in his memoirs, it is clear that Blair no longer had the will to do what was necessary to remain in power. 'I had my determination to comfort me,' he later wrote, 'which is, I suppose, what always happens to leaders when the final hubris overwhelms them.'[34]

A month later, after Blair had refused to set a date for his departure, Gordon Brown's allies launched the 'coup', with waves of resignation letters and calls for Blair to go. 'He had me trapped,' Blair reflected.[35] A few days later, on 7 September, Blair announced that that year's Labour Party Conference would be his last as prime minister.

The sense of one epoch giving way to another was captured in October of that year when another of the great characters of British politics was lost to the passage of time. Ralph Harris was eighty-one when he died, a founding member of not one political revolution, but two: the Thatcherite insurgency of the 1980s, and the Eurosceptic revolt that followed. At his memorial service at St John's, Smith Square, the tribes who had taken part in both turned out in force. Margaret Thatcher herself attended, as well as the man who had done more than anyone to remove her from power, Geoffrey Howe. Neil Hamilton, Simon Heffer and Edwin J. Feulner of the Heritage Foundation gave speeches, while the founders of Business for Sterling all paid their respects: Stanley Kalms, Malcolm Pearson, Rocco Forte and Rodney Leach. Enoch Powell's widow, Pamela Powell, also attended.

The month before Harris's death, Nigel Farage was finally elected UKIP leader. His victory came after a difficult few years for the party, squeezed from its left by the resurgent Conservatives under David Cameron and from its right by the BNP. In his first interview after taking over as leader, Farage set out his new strategy: to divide the Tories and win over the disaffected voters who had abandoned both main parties.

In April 2006, in the run-up to the local elections, a new group of Tory MPs had formed: Better Off Out.[36] The group had grown out of a conference fringe meeting in Blackpool the year before, when Philip Davies had defied the Tory whips and publicly backed British withdrawal from the EU. The MPs included Philip Hollobone, Bob Spink, Ann Winterton, Nicholas Winterton and the new MP for Harwich – where Enoch Powell had launched his campaign against Britain's European membership in 1968 – Douglas Carswell.

Farage went out of his way to praise these MPs and pledged not to stand against anyone else who followed their lead. 'These are not enemies of ours,' he declared, while alighting on the group of voters he believed could propel the party in the years ahead: 'The nine million people that voted in 1992 and didn't vote in 2005.' For the first time, Farage also claimed he had been offered a safe Tory seat to join the Conservative Party.[37]

In Europe, things were also about to change. First, in January 2007, Romania and Bulgaria joined the EU, though this time Britain placed transitional controls on their citizens, limiting their right to work in Britain for another seven years. Then, marking the start of the German presidency, Angela Merkel arrived in Strasbourg and declared that 'the period of reflection' since the French rejection of the European constitution in 2005 was finally over.[38] New reforms were coming.

Since September 2006, an action group of the usual wise men had been meeting to find a way out of the mess caused by the French and Dutch vetoes. Under the stewardship of Giuliano Amato, the former Italian prime minister who had worked on the European constitution under Giscard d'Estaing, the group set out to streamline the original 63,000-word document into something less controversial. The committee published its proposal in early June 2007, just in time for the summit of European leaders later that month – the last significant act of Tony Blair's premiership – where it was intended to form a new draft EU treaty, which would be finalized before the next summit, in Lisbon, later that year.

Almost immediately, the opposition began back in Britain. Neil O'Brien's Open Europe dusted off their old Vote 2004 plan to create their new campaign: 'I want a Referendum'. The campaign stuck to its tried and tested cross-party approach, securing the support of MPs from each of the main parties, including Tony

Blair's former economic adviser Derek Scott and his partner Gisela Stuart, as well as David Heathcoat-Amory, Greg Hands and Michael Gove.

Having entered Number Ten with the grandest of European ambitions, there is a touch of pathos to Blair's final few weeks in office. After being forced from power and then kept on a tight leash by his chancellor at the final European summit of his premiership, Blair resigned, admitting that his European idealism had never quite been accepted by the country. 'With Europe, where I believe Britain should keep its position strong, you know you are fighting opinion,' he said in his resignation address. Overall, Blair defended his record and said he had achieved something facts and figures could not capture: modernization. 'Look at our economy,' he declared. 'At ease with globalization. London the world's financial centre.' Britain understood the modern world, he added, 'able not just to be proud of its past but confident of its future'.[39] Blair's Britain had, in other words, finally reconciled the past it could not forget with the future it could not avoid.

This Blairite vision of a liberal, open and global new century was shared in almost all its essentials by both Gordon Brown and David Cameron. After finally becoming prime minister, Brown stood outside Number Ten and declared Britain would be 'the great global success story of this century'.[40] Yet, amid such visions of the future, Roger Scruton published his latest shot across the bows of British politics: *Culture Counts*. 'Challenged from the outside by radical Islam and from within by "multiculturalism", Western societies are experiencing an acute crisis of identity,' he argued. For Scruton, the main purpose of modern conservatism was to protect the sense of a national identity and national culture from these threats. 'Culture has become not just precious to us, but a genuine political cause, the primary way of conserving our moral heritage and of standing firm in the face of a clouded future,' he wrote, mapping the contours of future politics more closely than Blair or Brown.[41] As Gordon Brown settled into the job, however, Scruton's warnings were little more than background noise.

Brown was baptized into power with a series of crises over issues far more immediate than those of modern deracination. On his second full day in the job, there was an attempted bomb attack in London; the day after, an attack on Glasgow Airport. These were followed by floods, and a case of foot-and-mouth disease. To each of these crises, Brown reacted 'swiftly and effectively', as Cameron himself later admitted.[42] The mood of the country seemed to shift. The Conservative MP Quentin Davies defected to Labour. Cameron, meanwhile, flew to Rwanda to promote his 'modern, compassionate conservatism', even as his own constituency lay under water from the floods.[43]

Suddenly, Labour was back ahead in the polls and speculation began to mount about an early election. 'The wheels are falling off the Tory bicycle,' Brown joked at Prime Minister's Questions.[44] Even the first run on a British bank in almost 140 years, which began in mid-September outside branches of Northern Rock, did not seem to derail Brown's momentum. Brown's successor at the Treasury, Alistair Darling, announced the government would guarantee all Northern Rock deposits. Once again, it seemed, the government had acted swiftly and decisively.

To try to knock Labour off course, Cameron and Osborne pulled out all the stops at that year's Tory conference. Osborne announced an eye-catching inheritance-tax cut. Cameron delivered his entire speech without notes, again. Some polls suggested Brown would likely win a small majority if he called the election early, but others pointed to a hung parliament. A decisive poll, published in the *News of the World*, showed Labour losing ground in the all-important marginal seats.[45] Brown had told Ed Balls the election was on, but then he blinked. Having led his troops to the top of the hill, he ordered them back down.[46] The 'election that never was' cost Brown both his momentum and his public image as a man of selfless strength.

Cameron had meanwhile taken the opportunity to reshuffle

his top team in preparation for the next election. Former Business for Sterling chief Nick Herbert and one-time OUCA president Jeremy Hunt were both brought into the shadow cabinet, despite having only been elected in 2005. The most significant promotion, however, was saved for Michael Gove, who moved from housing to Cameron's former brief, education, and brought with him the man he had first met at a Business for Sterling briefing eight years earlier: Dominic Cummings.

The new Tory generation was on the march, but one figure was not: Boris Johnson, who was left with the same job he had been given in 2005. Having had his cake and eaten it for so long – journalist and politician, editor and minister, husband and philanderer – he found he had given up the editorship of *The Spectator* only to be stuck in a boring, mid-ranking position, going nowhere. Two days later, he announced he wanted to run for London mayor.

Before Johnson's announcement, the clear front runner for the mayoral nomination had been Cameron's ally and Policy Exchange modernizer, Nick Boles. But, just two weeks before the close of nominations, Boles had to withdraw after being diagnosed with cancer. Only then did Johnson put his name forward.

Johnson insisted the idea to run 'did not come from David Cameron or anyone in his office,' but Cameron disputes this.[47] 'George and I were keen to persuade him, and we worked hard to do so.' According to Cameron, he also promised Johnson 'the best-financed and organised campaign that money could buy'.[48] And he needed it.

Before Lynton Crosby's introduction in January 2008, Johnson's campaign seemed unfocused and beset by attacks on his character and suitability. Doreen Lawrence, the mother of the murdered black teenager, Stephen Lawrence, said he was 'not an appropriate person to run a multicultural city like London'.[49] But, over the next few months, under Crosby's instruction, Johnson tidied himself up, had a haircut and even underwent media training. Crime became a key focus, with pledges that he would cut it by 20 per cent in his first term or not stand again. Then began a series of extraordinary exposés about Ken Livingstone's mayoralty, in the *Evening Standard*, by the journalist Andrew Gilligan, who had resigned from the BBC after being criticized by the Hutton Report for his claim that the government had 'sexed up' a dossier on Iraqi weapons of mass destruction. When the election finally came, in May 2008, Johnson had won 53.2 per cent of the vote after second preferences. 'I was elected as New Boris and I will govern as New Boris,' Johnson declared, with a characteristically satirical flourish.[50]

Johnson's mayoral victory, though significant, was quickly overshadowed by the enormity of the crisis that erupted on 15 September 2008 when the US investment bank, Lehman Brothers, collapsed, causing an implosion of the global financial system 'akin to a massive electrical power failure', as Professor Adam Tooze put it in his chronicle of the first great crisis of globalization, *Crashed*.[51] Despite an emergency bank bailout package worth £500 billion in Britain, it emerged that London's banks had grown so reliant on US dollars that the British government alone could not save them: the US Federal Reserve would need to step in. Facing a global crisis, Ben Bernanke, the chairman of the Fed, intervened, and trillions of dollars began to flow across the Atlantic. In the moment of maximum crisis, the true structure of the global economy had been revealed: London was not the world's financial centre, but an offshore hub in an American order. For years, Britain had been wrestling with the question of monetary sovereignty in relation to the euro, but all while it had grown ever more exposed to another currency altogether.

For Britain, the implosion of the City of London not only upended an entire economic order, but the political and social consensus that had been built upon it. Blair, Brown and Cameron had all believed Britain's strength was its interconnected, open, flexible economy. Now, the house of cards had collapsed.

In November 2008, as the economy spiralled into the worst recession since the 1930s, David Cameron abandoned his entire political pitch. The Tories would no longer match Labour's spending plans, he declared. 'Sharing the proceeds of growth' was out and spending cuts were in. The central argument behind this strategy was that Labour was racking up debts on the country's credit card that would have to be paid back later. A Tory poster unveiled in January 2009 featured a giant picture of a baby, with the line: 'Dad's nose. Mum's eyes. Gordon Brown's debt.'[52]

While Brown had hosted a successful G20 summit in April 2009, committing the world's leaders to a $1 trillion stimulus package, his budget a few weeks later revealed the scale of the challenge to protect public finances at home. Under Labour's plan, the deficit would rise to 12.4 per cent in 2009/10. Austerity was coming – the question was simply how severe it would be. In the meantime, the banks saved by the state were continuing to pay salaries and bonuses unimaginable to most ordinary voters.

These ripe conditions for electoral rebellion were further inflamed by the next crisis to grip Westminster: the parliamentary expenses scandal of 2009. *The Daily Telegraph* revealed, in a series of well-documented exposés, that MPs had been paid to have their moats cleaned, rabbit fences repaired, swimming pools maintained and much more besides. The revelations unleashed a barrage of public antipathy like few MPs had ever experienced.

In response, Cameron showed his skill as a political operator, bolstering his image as a man of action with the help of two figures from the Conservative research department: Oliver Dowden, its chief, and his deputy, Dougie Smith, who had moved to Conservative Central Office in 2008 after a stint working as Cameron's speechwriter. Cameron trusted the pair to act with speed to limit the damage of the scandal to the Tory brand. They were to set up a 'Star Chamber' to adjudicate on the party's MPs, dispensing summary justice to protect the Tory party's chances of winning power. Every MP's expenses were examined, explanations demanded and ultimatums delivered: apologize and repay in full, or lose the whip and be deselected.

The scandal came close to costing Michael Gove his career, after it emerged that he had claimed £7,000 for redecorating his second home in North Kensington. Embarrassingly, for Gove, around a third of the sum was spent at Oka, the high-end interior-design company set up by Lady Annabel Astor, David Cameron's mother-in-law. When the details were published in *The Telegraph*, they showed Gove had claimed £331 for a Chinon armchair, £134.50 for a pair of elephant lamps and £238.50 for a birdcage coffee table.[53] Gove later credited Cummings with rescuing him from this crisis, having 'put together a strategy for him not having to resign': repaying the money, apologizing and surviving.[54]

Gordon Brown, meanwhile, moved more slowly, offering Whitehall's favourite solution: an independent inquiry. This approach was quickly overwhelmed by the ferocity of public outrage.

It was in this context that the TaxPayers' Alliance published its latest attack on government largesse. The sequel to the 2004 *Bumper Book of Government Waste*, which had been followed with second and third editions, was a European special in 2009: *The Great European Rip-off: How the Corrupt, Wasteful EU is Taking Control of Our Lives*, published to coincide with the European elections. The book attempted to present itself as neither pro- nor anti-EU, merely interested in the facts. Underneath this apparent fact-finding exercise lay a distinct radicalism:

> Many ordinary citizens instinctively sense that something is not right in the way we are now being governed and feel a growing unease at the way the EU seems to be trying to transform itself from being an innovative, reasonably effective way for free, independent countries to cooperate for the benefit of their citizens and instead appears intent on becoming a monolithic, authoritarian and censorious superstate that mainly serves the interests of those fortunate enough to be members of the ruling euro-elite.[55]

'It was all part of a drum beat to raise people's awareness,' Matthew Elliott, one of its authors, recalled. He even put a figure on the cost of the EU: '£1,000 billion a year . . . £2,000 for every man, woman and child in Europe.'

The yet-to-be ratified Lisbon Treaty was another target for populist ire, on top of the expenses scandal, the financial crisis and Elliott's 'Stop the EU Rip-Off' campaign. David Cameron argued that the new treaty was '90 per cent the same' as the previous constitution and therefore should only be ratified after a referendum. Even the Labour-chaired parliamentary European Scrutiny Committee agreed, ruling that the Lisbon Treaty was 'substantially equivalent' to the EU constitution. But, by the time of the European elections in June 2009, Cameron's hopes of putting the new treaty to a referendum were hanging by a thread. Unlike Blair, Gordon Brown had seen off public pressure for a referendum, ratifying the treaty in Parliament in mid-2008. This left Ireland and the Czech Republic as the last remaining holdouts: Ireland because voters had rejected the proposed treaty at the first time of asking; the Czechs because the country's president and old friend of Bill Cash, Václav Klaus, was refusing to sign it off.

Ahead of that year's European elections, the conditions could hardly have been better for an anti-establishment, Eurosceptic insurgency of the sort offered by Nigel Farage. Yet UKIP seemed to be on its last legs, destined to be sunk by a combination of its own inadequacy, the menace of the BNP, and the Conservative Party's Eurosceptic turn under David Cameron. The Tories were offering a 'cast iron' promise of a referendum on Lisbon, and each Conservative MEP had been forced to agree to leave the pro-European centre-right grouping in the European Parliament, the EPP.[56]

Under Farage's leadership, meanwhile, UKIP had been slipping further and further from relevance. In the Sedgefield by-election following Tony Blair's resignation from Parliament in 2007, the party finished in sixth place, with 1.9 per cent of the vote, significantly behind the BNP, which came fourth, with 8.9 per cent. In the summer of 2008, UKIP had won 2.2 per cent in the Crewe and Nantwich by-election, and 2.4 per cent in Henley-on-Thames, after Boris Johnson left to become mayor of London. Even in the comfortable heart of the Tory Home Counties, the BNP finished ahead of UKIP. Over the course of 2006, 2007 and 2008, UKIP picked up six council seats to the BNP's fifty-eight. In Brussels, meanwhile, UKIP had been beset by a series of arrests and investigations, accused of expenses fraud and corruption. Farage began to talk about resigning if he could not turn things around, and there was internal concern that the party could lose all its MEPs in a surge of support for the BNP.

But, with Westminster in turmoil over the expenses scandal, those voters who seemed to have been drifting away from UKIP over the previous few years suddenly flooded back for the 2009 European elections. UKIP leapfrogged Labour into second place behind the Tories, winning 16 per cent of the vote and thirteen seats. At the same time, Nick Griffin entered the European Parliament in the most important electoral victory for the extreme right in British democratic history. 'Have we hit a political tipping point?' asked Labour's Jon Cruddas, MP for Dagenham. 'The election of two BNP members to the European parliament has given fascism a foothold.'[57]

Four months after the European elections, the Irish finally ratified the Lisbon Treaty in a second referendum, which left only the Czech president holding out against his own parliament's ratification. Cameron wrote to Václav Klaus, 'pleading with him to wait until after a UK general election before he ratified the treaty,' but Klaus had run out of road.[58] He could not wait that long without causing a constitutional crisis. When the Czech Constitutional Court ruled against the final legal challenge to the treaty, Klaus signed and the die was cast. On 1 December 2009, the Lisbon treaty became law. 'Our promise to hold a referendum on it was redundant,' Cameron reflected.[59]

For some Eurosceptics, the failure of the Czechs to hold out long enough for Cameron to become prime minister remains a tantalizing 'what if' moment in the wider Brexit story. According to George Eustice, Cameron believed that a referendum in Britain would almost certainly block the ratification of the Lisbon Treaty, forcing the EU into a negotiation with Britain that would result in a looser relationship that Britain could have lived with, without having to resort to threats of withdrawal.[60] Such counterfactuals are impossible to disprove, but at no point in the EU's history – from Schuman to Lisbon – had Brussels let Britain either carve itself out of its legal system or block the continent's integration by threat of veto.

Once Lisbon had been ratified, it was William Hague who argued that Cameron could not continue with his plan to hold a referendum, because to do so would effectively mean rejecting the terms of Britain's membership of the EU, thereby raising the prospect of an accidental withdrawal. 'At least I wouldn't have to worry about my legacy,' Cameron quipped.[61]

The ratification of the Lisbon Treaty hardened David Cameron's attitude. In a speech, he criticized what he called 'the steady and unaccountable intrusion of the European Union into almost every aspect of our lives' and pointedly raised the prospect of a referendum on 'a wider package of guarantees to protect our democratic decision-making'.[62] The ghost of renegotiation had returned. A few months later, Cameron went further and became the first Conservative Party leader to declare Britain would 'never' join the euro on his watch.[63] Britain's room for manoeuvre within the EU was narrowing.

The Eurosceptic right was certainly not going to allow Cameron off the hook just because of the Lisbon Treaty's ratification. In the run-up to the European elections, Matthew Elliott had commissioned a poll on public attitudes to the EU which found opposition to the euro reaching its highest level on record, with 75 per cent now opposed to Britain joining and just 23 per cent in favour.[64]

Overall, the poll found many of the arguments which would come to dominate the Brexit campaign had strong, instinctive support among the public. By two to one, the public preferred 'control' over the British economy to making trade easier. They also preferred 'taking back power' to 'influencing the EU' by a similar margin. Interestingly, however – and much to the surprise of Elliott – the poll found that people supported the free movement of people in the EU by 51 per cent to 47 per cent, and were in favour of British membership of the European Convention of Human Rights by 51 per cent to 44 per cent.[65]

What struck Elliott the most was the Eurosceptic tilt among the public compared to a decade earlier, during Blair's first term in office. 'People are much more hostile to the EU than they were a decade ago,' he wrote at the time. 'Public hostility to the EU will be a major factor for any future government and there is no force to change this unless the EU undertakes some sort of fundamental reform, comparable in scale to the great leap forward it took under Delors with the Single Market.'[66]

The Lisbon Treaty, meanwhile, had created new jobs which now needed filling: a new president of the European Council had to be chosen to be the political face of the EU, as well as a 'High Representative of the Union for Foreign Affairs and Security Policy', which would, in effect, be the bloc's first foreign secretary.

For Tony Blair, the presidency of the European Council – the first man of Europe – offered the tantalizing prospect of political resurrection. In 1999, he had become only the third British prime minister to win the Charlemagne Prize for services to European integration, after Winston Churchill and Edward Heath. Since leaving office, he had spent an underwhelming two years as Middle East Quartet's special envoy, but the job had limited responsibilities. With Peter Mandelson back from Brussels as Gordon Brown's first secretary of state, having served four years as European commissioner for trade, he had the support of the British government and natural allies across the continent. Blair also believed the new role offered a way to finally realize his dream of European leadership. 'Blair had a clear view of the role – the Council providing a clear strategic direction for the EU, which the Commission would implement,' Peter Mandelson recalled. 'He saw Britain finally forming a triumvirate with Germany and France in providing the leadership Europe needed. And he thought it was in the bag. And then it wasn't. It was a real shock.'[67] Blair could not bring Angela Merkel and Nicolas Sarkozy along with him. They wanted their own man, from their own conservative bloc.

In the end, the job went to Herman Van Rompuy, the little-known former Belgian prime minister. Where there had been concerns that Blair would dominate the European Council, there were no such fears about Van Rompuy. 'Harmless Herman is now leader of the pack', reported *The Times*.[68] Nigel Farage took up the theme when Van Rompuy visited the European Parliament for his maiden appearance. 'I don't want to be rude, but really you have the charisma of a damp rag and the appearance of a low-grade bank clerk,' Farage spat.[69]

Videos of the exchange quickly began to spread on social media. 'We'd spent years plugging away in the European Parliament with little impact,' Gawain Towler reflected. 'Suddenly, Nigel is rude and everyone's watching. It was extraordinary.'[70]

Buried within Farage's ad hominem attack on Van Rompuy was a passing reference to the unfolding situation in Greece. 'Since you took over, we've seen Greece reduced to nothing more than a protectorate,' Farage claimed. By February 2010, Greece was certainly in the grip of an economic crisis of such major proportions it would eventually plunge millions of its citizens into unemployment and poverty as the price of a bailout package from the EU and IMF.

What had started as a financial crisis in the United States had morphed into a sovereign debt crisis for Europe, which soon began to threaten the eurozone. If Greece defaulted on its debts, the fear was that Europe's banks would be hit all over again. 'The risk of contagion was serious,' as Adam Tooze put it in *Crashed*.[71]

What intensified the crisis was that the eurozone was a monetary union operating without a state. The Maastricht Treaty had specifically included a 'no bailout' clause (article 125) and the Lisbon Treaty had reinforced this principle. The Greek crisis also exposed the limits of Europe's will to share the pain of perceived 'Greek irresponsibility'. When the German finance minister Wolfgang Schäuble proposed the creation of a European Monetary Fund to ensure the continent did not have to rely on the US, he was shot down by Angela Merkel, who had no appetite for reopening the terms of the Lisbon Treaty. Finally, at a European summit in March, Merkel forced through the involvement of the IMF, over the objections of the French, who complained that it was a 'humiliation'.[72] The new arrangement saw a joint EU–IMF bailout of Greece, enforced by a 'troika', which included the European Central Bank, in which Athens would continue paying off the debts it could not afford with vast new loans, at the cost of previously unimaginable austerity, sending the Greek economy into a depression that sparked riots.

In 1992, after Britain's withdrawal from the ERM, Margaret Thatcher had warned that the single currency would not be able to contain the divergent economies of Europe, for in a single currency there is no 'escape hatch'. 'Europe will be forged in crises, and will be the sum of the solutions adopted for those crises,' Jean Monnet had written in his memoirs.[73] Now, that was being put to the test.

When the crisis of global capitalism crossed the Atlantic and threatened to burn down the EU's monetary union in early 2010, the bloc revealed the extent to which national interests still dominated, particularly those of Germany. Faced with the choice of taking control of the continental crisis at the cost of Europeanizing the debts of the eurozone periphery, or internationalizing the crisis with American help, Berlin chose the latter.

This was the backdrop for the British general election of 2010, finally called by Gordon Brown in April. Cameron warned that Britain was in danger of following Greece over the cliff unless urgent action was taken to bring down government spending. Britain, of course, did not face the same dangers as Greece, for the very reason that Cameron had long opposed British membership of the euro: Britain retained sovereign control of its currency.

17. Peregrine Worsthorne, influential journalist at *The Sunday Telegraph* and member of the secret 'Phantom' army unit.

18. Prominent Conservative journalist T. E. Utley.

19. Professor Michael Oakeshott, philosopher of British conservatism and fellow 'Phantom', pictured in 1961.

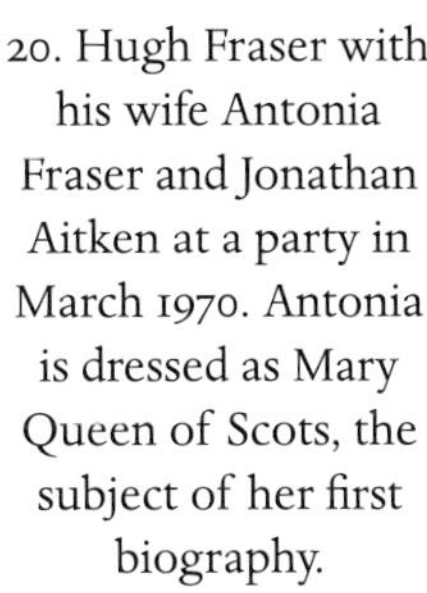

20. Hugh Fraser with his wife Antonia Fraser and Jonathan Aitken at a party in March 1970. Antonia is dressed as Mary Queen of Scots, the subject of her first biography.

21. Peter Young (far left) with a group of conservative student leaders from across Europe at a secret anti-Soviet conference in Poland over New Year 1979/80.

22. George Miller-Kurakin (far left) and other conservative activists disrupt the 1986 Copenhagen Peace Congress organized by the Soviet-controlled World Peace Council.

23. Scottish journalist Charles Douglas-Home, the future editor of *The Times*, with his fiancée Jessica, December 1965.

24. Conservative philosopher Roger Scruton in 1989.

25. Norman Stone, iconoclastic historian and Eurosceptic mentor, in 1997.

26. Rodney Leach, businessman, Tory activist and second husband of Jessica Douglas-Home, pictured in 1969.

27. Margaret Thatcher giving the 'Bruges speech' in September 1988.

28. President of the European Commission Jacques Delors addressing the TUC conference in Bournemouth, September 1988.

29. Patrick Robertson of the Bruges Group in 1991.

30. Foreign secretary Douglas Hurd and prime minister John Major at the Maastricht summit in 1991.

31. Eurosceptic ultra Bill Cash in 1996.

32. Conservative candidate Jacob Rees-Mogg canvasses support on a housing estate in Central Fife during the 1997 UK General Election campaign.

33. Scottish historian Dr Alan Sked at an early UK Independence Party conference in April 1997.

34. Scottish radical Dougie Smith, a key modernizer of the Conservative Party.

35. James Goldsmith campaigning for the Referendum Party in Newlyn, south-west Cornwall, in 1997.

36. Gordon Brown and Tony Blair rule out entering the single currency during a press conference in 2003.

37. Dominic Cummings poses for a photograph as campaign director at Business for Sterling in 2001.

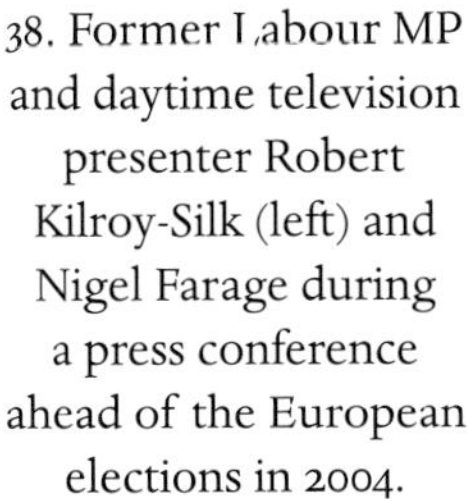

38. Former Labour MP and daytime television presenter Robert Kilroy-Silk (left) and Nigel Farage during a press conference ahead of the European elections in 2004.

39. David Cameron announces his resignation as prime minister the day after the EU referendum, 24 June 2016.

40. Gisela Stuart and Michael Gove listen to Boris Johnson at Vote Leave's headquarters in central London on 24 June 2016.

Unlike Greece, it could not run out of its own money. Monetary sovereignty did not insulate Britain from debt crises; the British economy had almost collapsed in 2008 because it had run out of American dollars. However, Britain not being in the euro meant its challenge was structurally different from the one tearing Greece apart.

By the time of the election in 2010, the choice being offered to British voters was not between austerity and Keynesian spending, but between the degrees of pain necessary to reassure global bond markets that British debt was safe. The Tories were promising to eliminate the bulk of what they called the structural deficit, taking into account the immediate impact of the recession. Under Labour's plan, this was already due to fall from 8.4 per cent of GDP to 3.1 per cent, so, depending on the definition of 'bulk', the Tory plans amounted to another couple of per cent of GDP in cuts or tax rises. Here was the choice facing the British public in 2010: more or less austerity.

There were, of course, other differences, particularly over Europe. Labour spoke of the need for a strong Europe, while the Tories promised to 'never join the euro' and described the Lisbon Treaty as a 'shameful episode' which they would neuter by introducing a new referendum lock against further erosion of sovereignty. A future Tory government would even seek to return powers to Westminster on criminal justice and employment rights.

Another difference was on immigration, the Conservatives pledging to 'take net migration back to the levels of the 1990s', which they defined as being in the 'tens of thousands a year, not hundreds of thousands.' David Cameron had made the pledge during an appearance on the BBC's *Andrew Marr Show* in January.[74] The idea of the 'right amount' of immigration had been gaining traction in Parliament since 2008: MPs Frank Field and Nicholas Soames had created a cross-party parliamentary group calling for 'balanced migration', which meant, in effect, a return to the 'zero net immigration' of yesteryear. This new technocratic formula to determine the right amount of migration had the political benefit of sounding distinct from the race issue raised by Enoch Powell.

To achieve their aim, the Tories promised to set a new cap on the number of migrants coming from outside the EU, while applying transitional controls 'as a matter of course' in any future EU expansion. Labour, in contrast, boasted of its 'Australian-style points-based system' for those coming from outside the EU. It was not this manifesto commitment which stuck in the minds of voters, however, but a dramatic incident on the campaign trail: Gordon Brown dismissed an elderly Labour supporter in Rochdale, Gillian Duffy, as 'some bigoted woman', after she challenged him about benefits and the number of Eastern Europeans arriving in the town.[75] With that remark, caught on tape by a microphone left on his jacket, Brown had inadvertently revealed the disconnect between Labour and its voters.

The distance between the rulers and the ruled had grown into something almost spiritual in nature, it seemed. The governing elite was not resented so much for its power or prestige, but for the sense that it held the ordinary man or woman in disdain.

The idea had established itself in British political life and, like a drumbeat, it grew louder and more intense with each passing year. Its sound can be heard as far back as the 1980s, in the saga of Ray Honeyford, the teacher whose attack on multiculturalism in education was published in the *Salisbury Review*, and the attempts by Scruton to cast him as a kind of English martyr. By the time of Gordon Brown's premiership, high-profile cases such as that of Abu Hamza, the jihadist preacher whom the British government was unable to extradite to the United States on terrorism charges, had become a source of acute public anger. Hamza caught the public's attention in part because he wore hooks in place of the hands that had been blown off by a bomb.

From 2007, meanwhile, the bodies of British servicemen and women killed in Iraq and Afghanistan had begun to be repatriated to RAF Lyneham, in Wiltshire, from where they would be transported to John Radcliffe Hospital, in Oxford, in coffins covered with a Union flag, passing through the town of Wootton Bassett on their way. In response, the Royal British Legion began to show their respects to the soldiers as their bodies were driven through the town. Soon, others began to join, hundreds gathering in mournful respect for the fallen. To many on the Eurosceptic right, the atmosphere captured in these moments was more important to the future trajectory of British politics than any given piece of parliamentary legislation or political manoeuvre in London or Brussels. Brown's accidental moment of candour merely opened a valve to a set of feelings already searching for expression.

For those then working at the very top of the Conservative Party machine, 'bigotgate' is less important in the longer narrative of British politics than the furore that came the previous year, when Brown was sent into a headlong retreat after declaring that his government would promote 'British jobs for British workers'. This seemingly anodyne declaration sparked howls of disgust within Westminster. Brown's Blairite opponents said they were 'appalled' by his language, the MP Keith Vaz said it amounted to 'employment apartheid' and David Cameron accused Brown of borrowing language from the National Front.[76] When Brown uttered the word 'bigot', the power lay not in the fact that it exposed his own prejudices, but that it gave expression to the prejudices of the wider political class. Roger Scruton would later write that ordinary voters felt their government was failing to defend what they considered their inherited rights. Disparate feelings of anger and betrayal over a range of issues, from immigration to Islam and Europe, had morphed into a wider sense that their government was no longer on their side, creating a bubbling resentment that had yet to find its expression. And, in 2010, it was Gordon Brown who paid the price.

In the election, Labour's support plummeted from its 1997 peak of 13.5 million to a nadir of 8.6 million, or just 29 per cent of the vote. However, David Cameron's Conservative Party had not secured a majority. The only way to guarantee its return to government was to strike a deal with the Liberal Democrats, now led by Nick Clegg, who had entered the European Parliament alongside Nigel Farage back in 1999 and had become an MP in 2005.

It took four days for the coalition agreement to be reached – a remarkably short period, but enough time for the crisis in Europe to develop even further. On Sunday, 9 May, the day before Gordon Brown finally resigned, Alastair Darling travelled to Brussels for an emergency meeting of Europe's finance ministers, to find a way to stabilize the crisis threatening to overwhelm the eurozone. The idea was to agree to a bailout fund of such magnitude it would finally reassure the bond markets. Was this the kind of Great Leap Forward Monnet had foreseen, a stride towards shared eurozone debt? No. Berlin was not prepared to go that far. Instead, most of the money would pile into a private 'special purpose vehicle' registered in the tax haven of Luxembourg, supported by EU states, without any overarching federal 'European' commitment. A separate, much smaller fund would be created, backed by the European Union itself, though strictly limited in size to a maximum of €60 billion, of which Britain's liability was 12.5 per cent, or €7.5 billion. Only in the case of a default would Britain lose any money. Politically, however, the emergence of this small fund backed by the EU was dynamite. Britain had found itself on the hook – theoretically, at least – for the failures of the eurozone.

Incoming chancellor George Osborne quickly condemned the agreement, insisting Britain should not have to pay for the folly of the eurozone. As had been clear from 1992, the very existence of the euro without British participation had created an irresistible internal logic which would in due course place a strain on Britain's membership of the EU.

When the new coalition government was formed, with David Cameron as prime minister and Nick Clegg as his deputy, they agreed Britain would play a 'leading role' in Europe, but would not transfer any further powers without a referendum. The Liberal

Democrats accepted the Conservative Party's austerity plans, while the Conservatives were prepared to enact some of the Liberal Democrats' long-held ambitions for political reform. A Fixed-term Parliaments Act would be introduced and the House of Lords democratized. Finally, there would be a referendum to introduce the 'alternative vote' for elections to the House of Commons. With the advent of the coalition, a new world had been born – young, liberal and modern. David Cameron was forty-three, the youngest prime minister in almost 200 years; Nick Clegg was the same age. 'We are both committed to turning old thinking on its head and developing new approaches to government,' they declared in the foreword of their agreement.[77]

One person who would not be joining the new government was Dominic Cummings. 'David said, "Oh, you're going to be education secretary, but – by the way, bad news – you can't take Dom into government with you",' Michael Gove recalled. Cameron and his communications director, Andy Coulson, felt Cummings could not be trusted. 'Dom took it remarkably philosophically, but I was hurt,' Gove later commented.[78] But it would not be long before Cummings was back.

Chapter 15

By the summer of 2010, Dominic Cummings had returned to his bunker and British membership of the euro was a fading Blairite dream. As part of the coalition deal, the Conservatives and Liberal Democrats had not only agreed that Britain would not join the single currency, but that the civil service would not be permitted even to prepare for the future possibility.[1]

For the countries using the euro, meanwhile, the question of British membership was little more than a marginal concern. 'The euro is in danger', ran the front-page headline in *The Times* on 20 May, a fortnight after the general election, picking up on the warning from Angela Merkel of an 'existential' danger now threatening the single currency.[2] The big fear was that the fire which had started in Greece would spread through the periphery of the eurozone, before engulfing the core. Even outside the single currency, Britain was not entirely safe. Not only would an economic slowdown in the eurozone harm British growth, but, to deal with the crisis, further treaty changes might be necessary, which could then trigger the 'referendum lock' that Cameron had insisted on including in the coalition agreement.

Even without this, Cameron had enough problems of his own to deal with. The coalition had inherited a deficit which had reached 11 per cent of GDP in 2009/10. To eliminate the bulk of it, George Osborne announced an emergency budget just weeks after the election: VAT would rise, benefits would be cut and every area of government spending – apart from the NHS and overseas aid – would be reduced by a quarter.

Within weeks, the consequences of such austerity began to bite. In education, Michael Gove found himself drowning in the details of a nationwide school-building programme he had chosen to scrap as a cost-saving measure. In defence, Liam Fox began the first comprehensive review in twelve years, resulting in cuts that reduced the army to its smallest size in a century. Funding for police fell by 20 per cent over four years, while the justice department cut the number of prison places by 3,000. Then came the most explosive issue of all: university funding.

The Liberal Democrats had gone into the election promising to abolish tuition fees, but in government agreed a policy which would allow universities to triple them, from £3,000 to £9,000 a year. While they understood there were risks involved in such a choice, it remains a decision of extraordinary political naivety and self-harm. A party that had surged in popularity on the back of student support because of its opposition to the Iraq War had not only broken one of its central pledges within a year of taking office, but had done so in such an egregious way. Nick Clegg would never fully recover.

The party had long been aware of the electoral dangers of joining a coalition. As early as 1997, the astute campaign director for the Liberal Democrats, Chris Rennard, had warned that the only way a formal coalition could be justified was if the party could secure electoral reform to insure itself against oblivion.[3] Having studied the fate of junior coalition partners in governments across Europe, Rennard had observed in an internal party memo that 'in every case the junior coalition partner loses support.' He then concluded, 'the loss of support may be acceptable in return for PR and with it permanent influence. But it is suicidal without.'

After the calamity over tuition fees, this necessity became even more acute. The lesson for Clegg was clear: if the electoral system was not changed, the Liberal Democrats would almost certainly suffer major losses at the next election. By November 2010, when

45,000 students took to the streets around Westminster to vent their anger at the government over tuition fees, the party was acutely aware of the existential importance of winning the alternative vote referendum due the following year, as set out in the coalition agreement.

Of all the available reforms, the alternative vote was the least radical. The proportional 'plus' element included in the original Roy Jenkins plan from 1998 had been removed to assuage Conservative concerns. All that was left was a preferential voting system. To begin with, Cameron kept his distance from the referendum campaign to protect relations with the Liberal Democrats. The scale of the hostility towards Clegg and his party over the student fees increase could become a threat to the coalition itself if panicking Liberal Democrat activists forced Clegg to withdraw from the government. Michael Gove even offered to come out in support of AV to help shore up Clegg's position.[4] Yet, with the polls putting the two sides of the referendum neck and neck, Cameron began to feel the heat from his own party, so his calculus changed.

To help run the 'No' campaign, Cameron had secretly turned to the one man he knew could organize such an operation at arm's length from the Conservative Party: Rodney Leach. After his success at Business for Sterling and the original No campaign against the euro, Leach had become something of an éminence grise in Tory politics. When Dominic Cummings returned from the north-east in 2004 convinced the time was right to pursue a more aggressive, populist campaign against the political establishment, Leach had instead spent his time and money on the self-consciously moderate Open Europe think tank, which built ties with Cameron's leadership. Despite his independent reputation, Leach was even ennobled by the Tories in 2006 for his efforts. He was the perfect man to help assemble the 'No to AV' campaign.

Leach's first thought was to ask James Frayne, Cummings' right-hand man at 'North East Says No', to run the campaign. But, after attending a few chaotic early meetings dominated by

Tory MPs of the sort he and Cummings loathed, Frayne turned down the opportunity.[5] At this point, Leach approached another figure who had made his name as an insurgent Westminster campaigner: Matthew Elliott. Unlike Frayne, Elliott had no qualms about taking on the job. 'I jumped at the opportunity,' he recalled.[6]

At first, with the referendum still months away, there were only murmurings of discontent from the Tory backbenches. But when the bill for the referendum cleared the Commons in November, there was an ominous rebellion from the Conservative right, led by Bill Cash, who demanded a minimum threshold be inserted into the bill to ensure AV could only win if there was a 40 per cent turnout in the country – a device successfully used in the original Scottish devolution referendum in 1979. 'If we do not tell the British people the entire truth,' Cash declared, 'I fear they will be misled in the referendum campaign.'[7]

Few paid much attention. Cash was in a small minority, and by far the bigger story at the time was the ongoing controversy over votes for prisoners, following a ruling from the European Court of Human Rights which found Britain's blanket ban unlawful. For Matthew Elliott and the No campaign, the principal concern was to ensure the issue of voting reform did not become what James Frayne had feared: an irrelevance to all but the most hardline of Tories. Elliott's initial focus was to bring as many Labour politicians into the campaign as possible. John Prescott, David Blunkett, John Reid and Margaret Beckett were all quickly recruited. The Yes campaign, meanwhile, denied a role to its most prominent backer outside the political mainstream: Nigel Farage. One side was self-consciously widening its appeal, the other was not.

Elliott then launched the central thrust of his campaign, claiming the switchover to AV would cost £250 million, which would be better spent on the NHS. This figure was made up of £130 million for new electronic voting machines and £26 million for a publicity campaign that would be necessary to explain the new system to voters. Add in the £91 million cost of running the referendum (a sunk cost, either way), and Elliott's campaign argued that money could provide 2,503 doctors, 6,297 teachers or 8,107 nurses.[8] One poster featured a newborn baby in intensive care, next to the words: 'She needs a new cardiac facility NOT an alternative voting system.'[9] The tactic was a carbon copy of Cummings' own in the north-east. Leach and many others in the campaign viewed with distaste what they saw as the irrelevant populism of the message, but were prepared to accept it as long as it was effective.

While the strategy caught the media's attention, the polls remained tight until well into 2011, prompting further stirrings of rebellion on the Tory backbenches. A delegation from the Conservative Party's 1922 Committee paid a visit to Downing Street and 'expressed their fears about a loss'.[10] Cameron took it as a warning. A Tory leader is only ever as strong as his support in Parliament. He could not afford to float above the campaign any longer.

It was then – and in a 'moment of weakness', as Cameron later described it – that he sanctioned Dominic Cummings' return to government.[11] Crucially, the man who had originally vetoed Cummings' appointment – Cameron's director of communication, Andy Coulson – had resigned from the government over growing allegations about his role in phone hacking during his time as editor of the *News of the World*. Cummings joined Gove at the Department for Education in January 2011. Two months later, James Frayne followed suit.

Meanwhile, to sharpen Elliott's No campaign, Tory election expert Stephen Gilbert advised Cameron that, while Elliott's focus on the costs of the new electoral system had been effective, to secure victory, the No campaign needed to go after the Yes campaign's biggest weakness: Nick Clegg. 'Do it,' Cameron replied, though admitted to 'wincing' when he saw the result: a photograph of Clegg holding a sign saying he wouldn't vote for tuition fees, with the words, 'AV will lead to more broken promises.'[12]

The referendum result was a crushing defeat for the Yes campaign: 68 per cent against and just 32 per cent in favour. On the same day, the Liberal Democrats suffered a bloodbath in the local elections, losing 750 of the 1,850 seats the party was defending: the worst results since the founding of the Liberal Democrats. The party's worst fears were coming to pass.

The AV referendum marks an important moment in Cameron's premiership. He had secured his political goals through a referendum for the first time, but 2011 also offered valuable insights for those who wished to learn from the experience. While Cameron had other problems to deal with, on Monday, 20 June, around six weeks after the vote, Matthew Elliott sat down to compose a confidential five-page note on the lessons of the referendum for prospective future donors. Though it was 'embarrassing to admit', Elliott wrote, there were many similarities between the Eurosceptic cause and that of the electoral reformers. 'Both are highly passionate about a subject which, to the rest of the population, is a third-tier issue', he noted. While this meant voters could be more easily 'frightened' into changing their minds during a campaign, it also meant that, unless they could be persuaded to care more about the EU, the government would not feel the need to offer a referendum on British membership in the first place.[13]

The first goal for Eurosceptics who wanted to withdraw from the EU, therefore, was to increase the salience of 'Europe' by showing voters how it affected their everyday lives. The second goal was to convince the Conservative Party leadership that it was in its best interests to offer a referendum on British membership. This could be achieved by a pincer movement of internal and external pressure. 'UKIP remains an extremely useful and important force for reminding Conservatives what their EU policy should be and for pressuring them into taking a more Eurosceptic stance,' Elliott wrote. Euroscepticism within the Conservative Party was also crucial. 'You may recall that the No to AV campaign was left high and dry by the Conservative Party

Leadership until backbench MPs and Conservative associations started to express concern about the lack of campaigning,' Elliott wrote. 'A similar dynamic should be encouraged for an EU referendum.' Elliott then finished with a proposal to immediately carry out a research project into both public and Conservative parliamentary opinion.

Events, meanwhile, were piling pressure on Cameron. First, in March, he agreed what he called a 'small amendment' to the European Treaties, creating a permanent bailout fund to protect the euro.[14] Though Britain would not have to contribute, the possibility of treaty change to meet British demands was now real. Then, in July, the European Central Bank released a policy paper calling for clearing houses trading in euros to be based only in the eurozone – and therefore not in Britain. The fear of eurozone power being used to undermine Britain's place within the single market seemed to be coming true. And then, finally, a public petition calling for a referendum on Britain's membership of the EU passed 100,000 signatures, triggering a debate in Parliament under a new reform passed by the coalition. The outcome of the resulting vote was the biggest rebellion on Europe since 1945, with eighty-one Conservative MPs ignoring the whip to signal their support for a referendum – more than half of all Tory backbenches. Cameron could have ignored the vote, which was not binding on the government, but he had tried to make it a test of strength by ordering his MPs to vote down the motion in favour of a referendum. The status quo was becoming increasingly untenable.

This was the context for a defining moment in Cameron's premiership, when the eurozone – led by Germany – began pushing for further treaty change to protect the single currency. What Cameron had called the 'remorseless logic' of greater fiscal integration was coming to pass.[15] Yet, if there was remorseless logic to eurozone integration, there was also remorseless logic to its consequence: British isolation. Much like John Major and Tony Blair, Cameron became fixated on the prospect that eurozone integration would create a permanent caucus within the EU, weakening Britain's influence over the rules governing the single market, specifically those concerning its principal source of prosperity: the City of London. To insure against such economic isolation, Major had negotiated his 'opt-in' at Maastricht, giving future prime ministers the power to join the single currency if necessary. Now, Cameron concluded that, because Britain would never join, it needed to extract specific legal protections to ensure it would not end up trapped in a single market governed by rules made purely for the eurozone. As the next EU summit approached, Cameron settled on his strategy: in return for agreeing new rules to protect the eurozone, he would demand corresponding rules to ensure the eurozone could not abuse its power.

From Cameron's perspective, this was entirely reasonable. And yet, just three years after the global financial crisis, the British prime minister was effectively demanding special protections for its financial sector in return for agreeing to reforms to save the euro. From the eurozone's perspective, they were drowning and Cameron was trying to negotiate a price for the life raft. 'It was a parting of the ways,' noted Adam Tooze.[16]

Watching this scene unfold back in London was the former Whitehall mandarin Ivan Rogers, who had agreed to return to government to be Cameron's Europe adviser after a six-year spell in the City. Rogers seemed to be everything Cameron needed: a pragmatic Treasury veteran, with experience of both the UK's financial sector and the EU machine. In the late 1990s, Rogers had worked in Brussels under Leon Brittan, alongside Nick Clegg, after which he had been the Europe director in Gordon Brown's Eurosceptic Treasury.

Rogers replaced outgoing adviser Jon Cunliffe, who was leaving to become Britain's permanent representative in Brussels after the December summit. In fact, Rogers' first day in the job would be the day after the European Council had ended.

As the summit had approached, Cunliffe drew up a draft protocol with six British demands which Cameron wanted in return for the changes the EU was working up to protect the eurozone. The demands involved opt-outs from new EU financial services regulations and changes to ensure future rules could only be agreed by unanimity – in effect giving London a veto over the regulation of its most important industry. In the run-up to the summit, the six-page protocol was sent to Berlin in the hope that Angela Merkel would be able to persuade French President Nicolas Sarkozy to accept it.[17]

Merkel, however, rejected Cameron's draft outright. From Berlin's perspective, the British prime minister was trying to blackmail the EU by exploiting the turmoil in the eurozone to advance long-standing British objectives. Faced with backing down or persisting, Cameron chose to double down and make his case to EU leaders directly at the summit. It was a decision that led to a serious miscalculation.

Once in Brussels, he stated to the leaders that he would not agree to a new treaty for the eurozone if they did not give him the guarantees he wanted. The eurozone leaders replied that they would simply do what they wanted anyway, outside the European Union's formal infrastructure. The illusory nature of Britain's veto had been revealed. Just as Margaret Thatcher had been warned she could not stop the euro coming into existence, even if she vetoed its introduction, now Cameron discovered that he could not stop the eurozone integrating, if that is what participating countries wanted. The European project never had been and never would be dependent on British approval. From the moment Robert Schuman made his declaration in 1950, this had been the lesson Britain seemed incapable of learning. Worse, like Anthony Eden in 1956, Cameron had inadvertently exposed Britain's fundamental weakness. His reaction would set in motion the revolution that would define his legacy: Brexit.

The irony of Cameron's diplomatic failure is that the 'fiscal compact' which emerged from the December summit of 2011 upset the federalist heirs of Jean Monnet more than it did the Conservative Party's allies on the continent. If Europe was to be forged in crisis, as Monnet had predicted, then the one that was emerging was not the one he had dreamed of. Gone was the old Delorist focus on solidarity, growth and the European ideal. In its place, so it seemed, was little more than grinding Teutonic austerity. Indeed, in March 2012, Delors himself felt moved enough to intervene with a speech making clear his displeasure in Brussels. Dismissing the compact as an *'usine à gaz'* – a gas factory – he accused those behind it of 'killing Europe' by abandoning the federal idea at the heart of the project. Delors ended by saying the EU that now existed was 'the reverse' of what he'd tried to achieve, and even criticized the dominance of Germany itself. 'Europe is built on diversity,' he concluded with exasperation. 'Should it live on this diversity, or should it accept an implicit rule of Germany, that is the question.'[18]

Back in Britain, meanwhile, Cameron was being hailed a hero for his apparent display of resolute statecraft. Here was Churchillism reincarnate: *Very well, alone.* Boris Johnson declared that Cameron had 'played a blinder',[19] while Nick Clegg said Britain's demands had been 'modest and reasonable'.[20] And while Ed Miliband, the Labour leader who had replaced Gordon Brown after narrowly defeating his brother, David, in 2010, criticized Cameron's failure to build alliances, it was left to Nigel Farage to highlight the true extent of the diplomatic calamity. 'It's quite untenable for us to remain in a union alone, on the outside, having laws made for us, in a permanent voting minority', he said.[21] Untenable or not, this was indeed the fear which had driven Cameron to make his futile stand.

Nevertheless, Cameron played up to the role of Eurosceptic hero into which circumstance had cast him. He had said *No* to the EU's new treaty, he told MPs. And not only that, but he would fight to stop the EU's institutions being used to police the new 'compact' that emerged in its place. The Tory benches were delighted; the Eurosceptic press, too. Cameron's poll ratings went up. And yet, it was all a sham. As Cameron later admitted, in Brussels he had been told by the EU's lawyers that Britain could not stop the institutions being used to support the new compact.* 'Though he rather superbly turned what could have been a moment of public humiliation into a moment of triumph, Cameron knew he'd screwed up,' Ivan Rogers later reflected.[22] Jeremy Heywood, the cabinet secretary, launched an internal post-mortem. Sessions were held to determine who had been responsible for the errors of fact and judgement. No resolution emerged. Better to let the episode be quietly forgotten, it was thought.

Britain was now in the worst of all worlds, as Farage had indicated: it had deployed its most powerful weapon, the veto, and discovered it did not work. The eurozone had the reforms it wanted, and Britain had lost its leverage to get the changes it needed. 'The EU's decision to bypass Cameron in 2011 is the moment the final Brexit crisis began, even if questions about the long-term sustainability of the UK's hybrid semi membership were present long before 2011,' Ivan Rogers reflected.[23] From the moment Rogers started in the Cabinet Office after the summit, he began warning his European counterparts that they had to start taking seriously not just what had become known as 'Grexit' – Greek exit from the euro, which was their principal concern at the time – but also what he termed 'Brexit'.

After December 2011, Cameron concluded that Britain's relationship with the EU was becoming 'increasingly unsustainable'. He decided that, when the next push for treaty change came, he needed to renegotiate the terms of Britain's membership – and to put the results to the people in a referendum. The month

* In Cameron's memoirs, he complains that the head of the European Council's legal service, Hubert Legal – 'his actual name,' as Cameron writes – had been called to give his judgement on whether Britain could block the EU's institutions from being used. 'At a pre-meeting the day before, Mr Legal had been categorical about the constraints on forming a pact outside the EU treaties that used the EU institutions. He had said that it was full of difficulties and potentially illegal. However, he now proclaimed from on high – holding some sacred-looking EU text – that their use probably was in order.' Cameron then complains that 'anyone who says that the EU is an organisation based on law and not politics has never seen it act under pressure.' (Cameron, *For the Record*, p. 337)

after the summit, Cameron put his feelings on the issue on record.* 'My long-term view is that Europe is changing and Britain is changing in its relation to Europe because of the creation of the euro and a multi-speed Europe', he dictated. 'At some stage, altering Britain's relationship with the European Union in some regards and then putting it to a referendum I think would be good Conservative policy for the next Parliament'.[24]

Cameron's idea was not new, of course. Blair had also weighed up an in–out referendum, as part of a wider strategy to settle the same fundamental tensions in Britain's membership – albeit, in Blair's case, by leading the country into the eurozone itself. Yet, even after December 2011, was Britain's position any more 'unsustainable' than it had been for the previous twenty years? There were certainly systemic risks based on Britain's position outside the single currency that were becoming more obvious, but it was Cameron who chose to make these challenges existential.

Still, by 2012, Europe was merely one in a series of crises destabilizing Cameron's government. In March, George Osborne delivered what became known as his 'omnishambles' budget, imposing a series of small but unpopular tax rises on everything from pasties to caravans. Talk of a 'double dip' recession had entered the national conversation, as the problems in the eurozone continued to undermine growth. Even Barack Obama was privately concerned that the economic fallout from the crisis could cost him re-election. Confidence only began to return in July 2012, with a simple sentence uttered by the president of the European Central Bank, Mario Draghi: 'The ECB is ready to do whatever it takes to preserve the euro,' he declared.[25]

Another cause for political optimism for Cameron was the re-election of Boris Johnson as London mayor in May 2012, when he squeezed home by a margin of just 60,000 votes over Ken Livingstone.

* Throughout his premiership, Cameron met with the journalist and Conservative peer Daniel Finkelstein to record his thoughts in private. These sessions were recorded on a series of mini-discs.

After congratulating his old rival, Cameron claims Johnson declared, with sweeping certainty, 'And that's me done with public life'. Unsurprisingly, Cameron 'took it with a huge pinch of salt'.[26]

A further boost for the government came in July, when London played host for the 2012 Olympic Games. The opening ceremony, the brainchild of Scottish film director Danny Boyle, displayed to the world a vision of Britain that was everything Blair had showcased to secure the Games in Singapore seven years earlier: modern, multicultural and finally comfortable in its own skin. After the horrors of Iraq and 7/7, Britain had become the beacon Blair had foreseen in 1997. The Games were hugely popular and became such a success that some even wondered whether they might be a turning point in Britain's post-war history. 'Perhaps historians might record this strange, heady fortnight as the moment when we finally laid to rest a national myth that had dogged us so long,' wrote Jonathan Freedland in *The Guardian*, 'concluding a narrative that began with one London Olympiad and ended in another: the age of decline, 1948–2012.'[27]

Forty-four years after Enoch Powell's prophecies of national suicide, the British state had given its formal response. Enoch had *not* been right. Britain was not dead; it was thriving. And yet, the vision of British modernity on display in 2012 was also, by necessity, fantastical – an echo of a promise that had already melted away by the time it reached its theatrical realization in Stratford.

Only two weeks before Boyle's 'Isles of Wonder' opening ceremony, the giant government contractor G4S had sparked panic at the top of government when it admitted it could not supply the number of staff required to provide security, prompting Cameron to order in the army. For those of a more cynical persuasion, this was the real morality tale of the Games, exposing the threadbare nature of the British state, patched up after a last-minute act of crisis management, while actors playing nurses danced around a giant 'NHS' symbol and were beamed to the world.

In 2011, the year before the Games, London had been gripped by riots, revealing a face of Britain far more menacing than the harmonious vision of easy contentment displayed by Boyle. It was also the year the 'grooming gangs' scandal first came to light, offering a disturbing glimpse of the divisions that existed in the forgotten corners of provincial England.

Even as the Games opened, there was an uneasy sense of fragility that hung over the 2012 Olympics. One Conservative MP, Aidan Burley, found himself under attack – including from Number Ten itself – after condemning the opening ceremony as 'multicultural crap'.

For those who would come to play prominent roles in the Brexit revolution to come, 2012 remains a symbolic moment on the road to the coming revolt. The Games, in their view, were not merely a colourful display of sporting prowess, but a metropolitan power play; a declaration of liberal ownership of modern Britain – *We are the masters, now* – which they resolved to challenge.

Underneath it all, the structural reality remained bleak: the British economy was still performing far below its pre-crisis levels; the deficit was proving much harder to reduce than Cameron and Osborne had hoped; Scotland was gearing up for a referendum which could result in the break-up of the United Kingdom; and the question of Europe remained. Cameron was facing something of an omnicrisis. The sense of disconnect between the Olympic fantasy and the governing reality was captured during the Paralympic Games, which opened on 29 August, when George Osborne was booed by the crowd as the face of the austerity. The Games were a golden moment for the fading liberal consensus, but not a turning point, for the reasons popularly understood at the time.

In June, just before the Olympics, another European Council summit had thrown up a plan for a new European banking union, something that Britain would be politically unable to join. In the end, Cameron ensured that it would only apply to the eurozone. Still, his anxieties were rising. The more he kept Britain outside the arrangements to protect the eurozone, the more detached the country was becoming from the core of the EU and the more vulnerable it was to single-market regulations that could damage Britain's interests. Back in Britain, support for an in–out referendum was growing, with opinion polls now regularly showing leaving the EU running fifteen to twenty points ahead of remaining.[28]

In the press conference after the summit, Cameron tried to get back on the front foot, arguing that, while he understood calls for a referendum on British membership, 'the trouble with the argument about the in/out [is] it is only those two options, whereas I think what we want is a government that stands up and fights for Britain in Europe, gets what we want.'[29] Here was the first solid indication that Cameron was ready to pursue the strategy he had raised after the ratification of Lisbon, three years earlier: renegotiation. The press, though, largely missed the point, and so, the following day, Cameron published a piece in *The Telegraph* to 'set the record straight'. He was not opposed to a referendum in principle, he wrote, 'but let us give the people a real choice first.'[30] That summer, Foreign Secretary William Hague also announced there would be a government 'balance of competences review', which would act as 'an audit of what the EU does and how it affects the UK'. The gears of state were beginning to grind.

It was at this time – in August 2012 – that Jessica Douglas-Home and Rodney Leach hosted a weekend gathering for their friends at Jessica's seaside retreat on the north Norfolk coast. Roger Scruton joined, with his wife, Sophie, whom he had married in 1996. Alongside these old friends, the Conservative MPs Jesse Norman and Andrea Leadsom were invited, the latter of whom was leading the backbench Fresh Start project alongside David Cameron's old communications director, George Eustice, who had become an MP in 2010. The project's aim was to assess the structural changes Britain needed from its membership of the EU.

Its first big report, 'Options for Change', with a foreword by William Hague, had been published in July.[31] It called for a series of 'emergency brakes' to be negotiated to guard against future EU regulations which might affect financial services, social and employment law. It also demanded an opt-out from all existing EU policing and criminal justice measures, as well as a new legal safeguard to ensure it could not be discriminated against because it was not in the euro.

Joining Norman and Leadsom that weekend were two other leading Eurosceptic friends: the MEP Daniel Hannan and Matthew Elliott. On a walk one afternoon, Hannan implored Elliott to turn his attention to the referendum that Cameron had hinted was coming.[32] Elliott and Hannan asked Rodney Leach to help set up a new organization which would form the basis of an eventual Referendum campaign, as he had done with Business for Sterling in 1998. Leach, though, did not want to jump the gun. He was committed to Open Europe, which had brought him close to the heart of the Tory leadership, and he still believed Cameron might be able to win reforms that would allow Britain to remain in the EU.[33]

Elliott, though, had been weighing up the creation of a new organization for months and decided to push ahead regardless, establishing Business for Britain. The inspiration was clear. Fifteen years after the formation of Business for Sterling, its successor had arrived. Though the organization was not formally established until April 2013, Elliott began work finding donors to back his new venture, which had the same strategic goal as Leach's original outfit: to challenge what they saw as the establishment monopoly that purported to represent business opinion.

Ahead of its launch, 500 business leaders were brought on board, including long-time Eurosceptics like Peter Cruddas and Rocco Forte, but also those like Stuart Rose, the former Marks & Spencer chairman, who did not support withdrawal. Indeed, Rose would go on to chair the Remain campaign in 2016. Elliott was able to bring such figures together by ensuring that Business for Britain was not an explicitly 'Out' organization, but one principally focused on reform, much like the original 'No' campaign.

Before Cameron could make any commitment to renegotiation or a referendum, he needed to square off his most senior cabinet allies. Though George Osborne cautioned against the plan, fearing Cameron would not be able to negotiate a good enough deal to convince voters to vote to remain, he was also concerned the Tories could find themselves isolated at the next election in not offering a referendum. 'Like me, he believed that ultimately a referendum was probably inevitable anyway,' Cameron later wrote.[34] He received the support of William Hague and Oliver Letwin, the man Cameron relied upon more than any other to develop his policy agenda. With the fateful decision made, his next challenge was timing. Before going public with his plan, Cameron needed to get through the autumn European Councils. Realistically, this meant he would not be able to announce anything until early the following year. And so it was that Cameron locked in January 2013 as the month to bind himself to fate.

In a speech at Bloomberg's offices in central London on 23 January, Cameron made his pitch. The EU was 'a family of democratic nations . . . whose essential foundation is the single market rather than the single currency', he declared, more in hope than reality.[35] Apart from Britain and Denmark, every other member state was under a legal obligation to eventually join the euro. The treaties left no doubt about the centrality of the euro to the European project. 'The Union shall establish an economic and monetary union whose currency is the euro,' article two of the Lisbon Treaty declared.

In essence, Cameron's aspiration to recast the EU as a multi-currency bloc rather than a group of states converging around the euro worked as a diplomatic and political manoeuvre – as did his plan to formally remove Britain from the EU's commitment to 'ever closer union' – but, like Thatcher's Bruges speech twenty-five years earlier, it aimed in an almost completely different direction from the one most EU leaders wanted to go in at the time. Cameron wanted a new treaty 'freeing those who want to go further, faster, to do so, without being held back by the others'. At heart, Cameron's vision of a new treaty would have been entirely recognizable to every prime minister bar Heath: 'A flexible union of free member states who share treaties and institutions and pursue together the ideal of cooperation.'

While Cameron's agenda was undoubtedly ambitious, the detailed asks were also carefully calibrated to remain diplomatically deliverable. In this, he was advised by Ivan Rogers, Jon Cunliffe and Tom Scholar, who had replaced Rogers as Europe adviser after Rogers became Britain's permanent representative to the EU. All three were determined Britain would avoid the mistakes of 2011. As such, Cameron purposefully avoided challenging any of the EU's sacred 'four freedoms' protecting the free movement of goods, labour, capital and people – and he did not even mention immigration as a source of concern. Jean Claude Juncker, the influential European power broker and prime minister of Luxembourg at the time, subsequently declared that much of what Cameron was asking for was possible within the existing treaties. Experts in EU law back in Britain agreed, pointing out that EU leaders had adopted special provisions for Denmark and Ireland after the referendums rejecting Maastricht and Nice, and could do something similar for Britain. Angela Merkel responded cautiously, talking up the prospect of a 'fair compromise', though the French were much more hostile. 'Europe has to be accepted as it is,' François Hollande declared. 'We cannot dismiss it or diminish it under the pretext of proposing to stay in it.'[36]

The part of the speech that was genuinely radical, and not just a rerun of Bruges, was the implicit threat: give us what we want or we might leave. While the details of Cameron's strategy were designed to avoid the mistakes of 2011, Cameron was dramatically upping the ante in a way that even Margaret Thatcher as prime minister never did. In 2011, Cameron's threat had been the veto that never was; now, it was British withdrawal. Ivan Rogers says he advised Cameron not to box himself in to any specific timetable for the referendum, arguing that to do so would almost inevitably mean he would not have enough time to negotiate anything substantive and this would, in turn, undermine his chances of winning a referendum. Cameron countered that, politically, his party – and voters more generally – would only believe he was serious if he set out a specific timetable.

In the Bloomberg speech, Cameron promised there would be a referendum before the end of 2017 and made clear that his commitment was a red line in any future coalition agreement should he not secure a majority at the next election. 'I would not continue as prime minister unless I can be absolutely guaranteed that this referendum would go ahead on an in–out basis,' he later said.[37] The Lib Dems had already promised such a referendum if there was 'fundamental change' in Britain's relationship with the EU. In fact, in 2008, the party's then foreign affairs spokesman Ed Davey had even staged a protest in the Commons chamber of such theatricality that he was ejected, after the Speaker refused to allow a vote on a referendum on EU membership.[38]

Cameron later reflected that he had made two big mistakes in the speech. The first was that he had not set out why the 'caucusing of euro countries' was such a threat to British interests. Though this was the central reason for his entire renegotiation, his failure is at least partly explicable because the problem remained essentially notional. Cameron was trying to fix a crisis that had not yet happened. The second omission, however, was almost inexplicable. Cameron had entirely ignored the question that would come to dominate the EU debate by the time of the referendum: immigration. 'At that moment it was immigration from outside the EU that was driving the numbers,' Cameron later tried to explain, by way of mitigation.[39] Even on the official figures available at the time, though, net migration from the EU was running at 108,000 in 2012 – slightly below the number from the rest of the world, but still higher than Cameron's total immigration target. It later became clear that even these numbers were a dramatic underestimate. Revised figures showed that net migration from the EU in 2012 was, in fact, 206,000.

By 2013, Cameron was contending with demographic currents far more powerful than he realized. Immigration had been a perennial source of anxiety in post-war British politics, felt particularly acutely in the 1960s and 1970s when an uneasy political consensus emerged, treating black and Asian Commonwealth citizens differently from white 'patrials'.* From the 1990s, this consensus began to fracture as globalization and EU expansion brought a fresh rise in the numbers arriving and settling in Britain before the country became a 'labour market of last resort' during the eurozone crisis.[40] Cameron came to power as the tide was rising quickly and had little power to do anything about it.

The most likely explanation for the apparent myopia of Cameron's Bloomberg speech in the face of these deeper trends is that he hoped the numbers arriving from the EU would taper back down to more politically acceptable levels. He also knew that freedom of movement was an integral aspect of membership of the EU, therefore any reforms in this direction would be much harder, if not impossible, to negotiate. While these portents were troubling, Cameron was satisfied with how his speech had gone on the day.

In Cameron's own telling, the next few months showed he could still get his way in Europe, despite Britain's apparent isolation. In February, he led a successful charge to reduce the EU's next seven-year budget, going some way to meeting the demands of Conservative rebels. Much like Blair, Cameron feared British diplomatic weakness in private, but trumpeted British diplomatic strength in public.

After Cameron's budget success, he began his diplomatic offensive with a tour of the continent's capitals to try to sell his vision of a new Europe. One of his first stops was Madrid, and it was here, on 8 April 2013, that news reached him of Margaret Thatcher's death after she suffered a stroke at the Ritz, where she had been staying for the previous few months because she was no longer able to use the stairs at home. The Conservative Party's first great European martyr had gone, just as her successor was

* The name dreamed up by the Heath government to define Commonwealth citizens with a familial tie to Britain through a parent or grandparent.

battling with the forces she had helped create. Cameron immediately cancelled the rest of his trip, recalled Parliament and led the tributes. Before Thatcher, 'there was a sense that the role of Government was simply to manage decline', Cameron declared. 'Margaret Thatcher rejected this.'[41] Here is a key tenet of contemporary Conservatism's cosmology: not simply the arresting of decline, but Thatcherite resurrection. As Norman Stone put it in his account of post-war Europe, *The Atlantic and its Enemies*, published in 2010, Thatcher had been 'a force of tissue-regeneration' that even he had not thought possible.[42]

Decades on, the simple narrative that Britain was declining in the years before 1979 and regenerating thereafter looks, at best, overly two-dimensional.[43] Had there really been an alternative to Britain's relative decline in the years after 1945? Was it British capitalism that recovered in the 1980s or had Britain merely become a receptacle for the rest of the world's money? Whether Thatcher arrested British decline or not, the one act of restoration that is hard to dispute is that of the authority of the British state itself. After the humiliations of Suez, the IMF and the Winter of Discontent, Thatcher reimposed dominion at home and abroad. This, alone, was transformative.

And, although Thatcher also fought for a vision of Europe that she could not deliver – and against a single currency she could not stop – even in defeat she succeeded in 'shift[ing] the centre of gravity of the Conservative Party in an anti-European direction', just as Geoffrey Howe had feared.[44] Now, she was gone. After Cameron had spoken, Thatcher's Eurosceptic disciples rose in the Commons, one after another, to hail their prophet. Bill Cash said that 'she lived out her retirement in the certain knowledge that on the issue that primarily brought about her fall – that of Europe – she had been right.'[45] The newly elected MP for Rochester, Mark Reckless, Daniel Hannan's ally from Oxford, went further still and said her only real fault was that she had been too pro-European until her about-turn at the last.

Thatcher's funeral was the grandest non-royal laying-to-rest since Churchill's in 1965, her coffin draped in the Union flag and carried by gun carriage to St Paul's for a service attended by the Queen. In its dignified symbolism, the state had conferred on Thatcher a status beyond that of any other peacetime prime minister. Conservative lore was passing into the national story. From Churchillism to Thatcherism, each recognizable to the other – obstinate, defiant, independent – and hard for their successors to live up to.

A month later, Cameron returned to the grim reality of government. In May 2013, a twenty-five-year-old soldier called Lee Rigby was walking near his barracks in Woolwich when he was deliberately run over and stabbed to death by two British-Nigerian Islamists. The depravity of the murder repulsed the nation. Every year since Cameron had become prime minister, a terrorist attack comparable to the 7/7 Tube and bus bombings of 2005 had been averted by the security services. This was the first to slip through their net.

In response, Cameron became 'obsessed with the barriers that prevented us from dealing with Islamist extremism', as he put it.[46] Chief among those was the European Court of Human Rights. The government had still not found a way to extradite Abu Hamza, who, by now, had become embedded in popular consciousness, his case regularly brought up by voters in focus groups as an emblem of government failure. Rage against the seemingly ineffectual nature of the system was building.

Then, in August 2013, events once again intruded from abroad when the Syrian president Bashar al-Assad launched a chemical-weapons attack on his own people in Ghouta. Cameron forced himself to watch the horrifying footage – 'infants fitting and foaming at the mouth, parents hysterical with fear and grief'.[47] When Barack Obama asked Cameron to join the US in a surgical 'punish and deter' attack shortly afterwards, Cameron readily agreed. At first, the mission was supposed to take place within thirty-six hours. But then the timings began to slip – and then slip again. Pressure mounted to recall Parliament before any British action with authorized. After initially resisting, Cameron relented. But Ed Miliband was opposed and, without Labour's support, Cameron did not have the numbers. 'It is clear to me that the British Parliament, reflecting the views of the British people, does not want to see British military action,' Cameron responded when MPs voted against British involvement.[48] A few days later, deprived of British support, Obama postponed the military action altogether.

In the aftermath, there was much agonized reflection about the consequences of the vote, particularly for Britain's international standing – a perennial concern. George Osborne said the vote should prompt a period of 'national soul searching about our role in the world'. If Britain was not the hegemon's reliable, martial partner – standing sentry in Europe for Washington – what was it? After empire, there was influence: this was the goal, the axiomatic first principle of British foreign policy. Now, it seemed, Britain's political class was losing its stomach to fulfil the role it had created for itself. In an echo of Enoch Powell, the Conservative rebel Crispin Blunt said he hoped the vote would 'relieve [us] of some of this imperial pretension that a country of our size can seek to be involved in every conceivable conflict.' The vote would not prove as consequential as either side believed at the time. Domestically, focus quickly returned to more prosaic matters: the economy, energy prices – and the future of Dominic Cummings.

In October 2013, Gove's controversial aide announced his departure from government – and, it seemed, public life – with a 135,000-word, 237-page valedictory essay-cum-manifesto, railing against the quality of Britain's political class and media establishment and calling for the UK to find a new role for itself in the world. 'The romantic pursuit of "the special relationship" and the deluded pursuit of a leading EU role have failed,' he wrote in *The Times* shortly after.*

---

* The essay was published on his blog: https://dominiccummings.com/2014/12/. Throughout the essay, Cummings cites those who did know how to grip complex bureaucratic machines to achieve their aims: Sun Tzu, Bismarck, Steve Jobs – and

The same year also saw the revival of Roger Scruton's Conservative Philosophy Group, driven by the same instinct expressed by Cummings: that there was a lack of seriousness about the Cameron government and the country at large. Scruton was assisted by Rodney Leach, Jessica Douglas-Home and Robert Salisbury, who offered his home as an early venue. The party had spent thirteen years in Opposition, Scruton lamented, but did not seem to have learned anything. 'There was a need to re-examine the core beliefs and assumptions of Tory politics, and to reconnect with the instincts and values on which the Tories had in the past depended for their support,' he wrote.[49]

For Cameron, in late 2013, there was a sense that events were running against him. After losing the vote on Syria, the prime minister had been backed into a corner by Ed Miliband's pledge to cap energy prices. To get back on top, Cameron turned to the man he had first met in 2005, running Michael Howard's general election campaign: Lynton Crosby. Crosby told Cameron that the government was not explaining to people what it was doing. It was all too haphazard. There had been painful cuts and rows over Europe, but what was the vision? What was it all for? The country needed to know there was a plan.

And so, on 1 January 2014, Cameron welcomed in the New Year with a speech setting out this vision. He had a 'long term economic plan', he declared.[50] The message was simple: the economic recovery had begun so stay the course. He had sixteen months to persuade the country.

But what was the plan? Cameron had inherited an economy in crisis after the global financial system's implosion in 2008. He did not yearn for a more national economy, but rather a new and even more international model, which conserved and strengthened the position Britain had ended up in after Black Wednesday in 1992: as an off-shore financial capital for both the US and the eurozone. By

---

Jean Monnet. Cummings is still full of awe for Monnet to this day: 'He was a genius,' he said, in an interview with the author.

2014, however, Cameron had concluded that, for this strategy to survive, a reset with the EU was required to protect Britain's place within the single market but outside the eurozone, while also dealing with the public's unhappiness with the settlement.

To reassure backbench critics that the European dimension of his plan was working, Cameron needed to show at least some diplomatic progress. Once again, though, events began to work against him.

In February 2014, a crisis broke out in Ukraine when men in Russian army fatigues stripped of their official insignia began appearing across Crimea and pro-Russian separatists seized Ukrainian government buildings in Donetsk and Luhansk, declaring independence and signalling the start of Europe's biggest land war since 1945. It was amid such scenes that Angela Merkel arrived in London to deliver an address to both Houses of Parliament, as Cameron tried to charm his way to a breakthrough. Merkel's message was not what Cameron wanted to hear, however. While much of the press picked up Merkel's optimistic insistence that 'where there's a will, there's a way,' the central thrust of her speech was far more cautious. Merkel told MPs she could accept only 'limited, targeted and swift' reform of the European Union.[51] This was not enough for Cameron.

In March 2014, Cameron set out a series of apparently 'specific changes' he wanted from his renegotiation, including fresh controls to stop 'vast migrations' of people after new countries joined the EU and tighter rules to protect 'free movement, not free benefits'. In this task, Cameron leaned on the advice and judgement of Ivan Rogers. In November 2013, Rogers had replaced Jon Cunliffe as Britain's permanent representative to the EU and therefore shouldered much of the burden of the renegotiation. Throughout this time, Rogers was on guard against what he regarded as Number Ten's institutional ignorance over how the EU operated and what was diplomatically possible. All the while, politics at home were becoming ever more challenging, as Nigel Farage's UKIP continued to climb in the polls.

With the May 2014 European elections approaching, Nick Clegg decided he had so little left to lose that he challenged Farage to a series of live TV debates on the merits of the EU. 'I've spent years being told I'm a nutcase,' Farage declared delightedly. 'Yesterday the deputy prime minister challenged the fruitcakes to take part in a national debate.'[52]

When the debate came, on 26 March 2014, the public preferred the fruitcake. 'Farage is the winner', declared *The Times* the next day.[53] The moment of the night came when Clegg challenged Farage over UKIP's claims, published on one of its leaflets in a recent by-election, that 29 million Romanians and Bulgarians could come to Britain. 'There aren't even 29 million Romanians and Bulgarians living in Romania and Bulgaria,' Clegg declared. Farage hit back. 'I'm not claiming that 29 million people have the right to come to Britain,' he said. 'I am claiming that 485 million people have the total, unconditional right to come to this country if they want to.' For Cameron, it was a moment of clarity. 'This election wasn't about gay marriage or HS2. It wasn't about the credibility of Nigel Farage or UKIP,' he later wrote. 'It wasn't even really about Europe, at least not all the European issues. It was about immigration and its link to Europe.'[54] The result of the second debate, a week later, was even worse for Clegg, with a poll for *The Guardian* finding 'a clear-cut 69% to 31%' split in favour of the UKIP leader.[55] Clegg's plan to cut Farage down to size had spectacularly backfired.

When the 2014 European elections came, UKIP topped the poll for the first time in its history, securing 26.6 per cent of the vote and twenty-four seats – narrowly ahead of Labour, which won 24.4 per cent and twenty seats, and the Tories, who gained 23.1 per cent and nineteen seats. Clegg's Lib Dems collapsed, finishing fifth, with just 6.6 per cent and one seat. Farage hailed the result as an 'earthquake' and announced that, ahead of the following year's general election, he would launch the party's manifesto in Doncaster, Ed Miliband's constituency, where UKIP had finished first.[56] In the space of twenty years, Nigel Farage had gone from the political neophyte whose job was driving Enoch Powell around by-elections, to leading UKIP to victory in national elections.

A similar earthquake shook the political establishment in France that year, as Marine Le Pen's National Front secured a result that almost exactly matched UKIP's, with the same tally of twenty-four seats on a slightly lower vote share. At a summit in Brussels after the election, both Cameron and Hollande cautioned Europe not to ignore the warning. Even Tony Blair felt the need to intervene, stating that the results needed to serve as a 'wake-up call' for Europe to reform.[57]

In the aftermath of the elections, Cameron went on the offensive, attacking the leading candidate to become the new Commission president, Jean-Claude Juncker, and warning that, should his appointment be confirmed in the face of British opposition, it would only further inflame Eurosceptic opinion. Once again, however, Cameron had launched into a crusade he could not win. 'Britain nears EU exit', splashed *The Times* the day after Juncker was confirmed in his post with Merkel's backing.[58]

Such stories may have antagonized voters in Britain, but they were already irritated. Before the European elections, Matthew Elliott at Business for Britain approached Dominic Cummings asking him to conduct a research project to gauge the public's attitude to the arguments they would hear over the course of the campaign. Cummings reflected on his findings in a blizzard of blogs, interviews and op-eds over the summer, setting out his thoughts about British politics and the potential referendum after the next election.[59] His first intervention came in an interview with *The Times* in which he accused Cameron of bumbling 'from one shambles to another without the slightest sense of purpose' and said everything you needed to know about him was revealed by the fact he had a picture of Harold Macmillan on his wall.[60] Shortly afterwards, he published a blog railing against the 'hollow men' of Westminster leading the country to disaster, quoting T. S. Eliot's poem of the same name.

Cummings' overall sense was that Britain was driving headlong towards another of its great post-war political calamities, the first of which, in his view, had been the Foreign Office's 'historic misjudgement' about the formation of the European Coal and Steel Community, when it had 'arrogantly dismissed Monnet who understood better than them how to change the world'. Cameron's strategy, Cummings complained, was the worst of all worlds: 'Whining, rude, dishonest, unpleasant, childishly belligerent in public while pathetically craven in private.' The result, he predicted, would be a failed 'renegotiation'. 'Hollow, hollow, hollow . . .'[61]

Cummings followed this post with another shortly after, setting out in more detail what voters felt about the EU. While Cameron was fixated on the issue of British influence, voters' overwhelming concern was immigration. Indeed, throughout the European election campaign, Nigel Farage and UKIP had talked about 'taking back control' of immigration, and Cummings and Elliott had been keen to test this message with voters. 'We saw how much it resonated,' Elliott later explained.[62] In fact, immigration had become 'such a powerful dynamic in public opinion', Cummings wrote, there was no need for any future Out campaign to focus on the issue, because voters had already made up their minds. The problem was not that voters needed persuading on the question of immigration, it was that they remained worried about the economic consequences of withdrawal. The 'one essential task' of any Leave campaign, Cummings wrote, was therefore 'to neutralise the fear that leaving may be bad for jobs and living standards.'[63]

This was where Business for Britain came in: neutralizing the issue as best they could. Voters needed to conclude that business was, at the very least, divided on the issue of EU membership, Cummings wrote. If this happened, 'then OUT should win'. It was, in essence, the same conclusion he had reached in 1998 at Business for Sterling, when his goal was to lodge in people's minds that the CBI did not reflect business opinion on the euro. Indeed, a decade and a half on from those original debates, the dire warnings from the CBI about the consequences of not joining were now actively helpful. 'Whenever you read "the CBI said . . .", remember they also said 1997–1999 that we HAD to join the euro or else inward investment would flood out', Cummings noted.

Finally, in an op-ed in *The Times*, Cummings set out his view of what a successful referendum campaign would look like for Out and why Cameron's renegotiation strategy was doomed to fail. Not only had voters concluded that immigration was 'out of control', but they believed it was putting public services under 'intolerable strain', Cummings wrote. A new argument had arrived in British politics: 'We can save a fortune [by leaving the EU] and spend that money on the NHS or whatever we want.'[64]

Cummings was sanguine about the potential for Cameron's renegotiation to change the terms of the debate. In fact, because Cameron could achieve nothing on either freedom of movement or financial contributions, voters were likely to become more hostile after his renegotiation. 'Cameron hoped that the referendum promise would push the EU issue beyond the election and he would not have to infuriate people by revealing how little he wants to change,' Cummings wrote. 'Wrong. People have already concluded he doesn't want to change much.' Worse, in fact: as the renegotiation went on, Cameron was almost certain to come under pressure from his own side to achieve things he could not deliver. Cameron's fate, Cummings concluded, was unavoidable. 'The country wants more back from Europe than he wants to ask for, or Europe wants to give.'[65] A crisis was coming.

In Brussels, Ivan Rogers had already arrived at a similar conclusion. At the heart of Rogers' concern was a sense that Cameron might have learned the lessons of 2011 diplomatically – not asking for more than he could deliver – but he was abjectly failing to manage domestic political expectations of what was possible.

Rogers says that, increasingly exasperated, he sought out Nick Clegg, who he had worked with at the European Commission in the 1990s, to urge him to begin preparing for the prospect of a British withdrawal, but Clegg rejected the proposal. Rogers then went to Jeremy Heywood, the head of the civil service, urging him to at least commission the work necessary to understand the most pressing areas of concern for the British state in the event of a vote to leave. Heywood, though, was adamant that he could not authorize such work without Cameron's approval – and equally adamant that Cameron would not give it.[66]

Despite Cameron's troubles in Europe, his position at home remained relatively secure, aided by the improvement in the British economy, which had finally returned to the level it had been in March 2008 – fully six years earlier, marking the slowest economic recovery since the Great Depression of the 1930s. By summer, the economy was growing 3.2 per cent over the year – the biggest annual expansion since 2000. As the economy picked up, so did Conservative support. Even as the party fell behind UKIP in the European elections, it had retaken a narrow lead over Labour in voting intention for the coming general election.

From this position of relative strength, Cameron carried out his first major reshuffle since 2012, most notable for the rise of the next generation of Tory women, including Esther McVey, Nicky Morgan, Priti Patel, Penny Mordaunt and Liz Truss, as well as the painful demotions of figures like Owen Paterson, Dominic Grieve, Ken Clarke, Andrew Lansley – and Michael Gove.

In Cameron's telling, Gove had become something of a nuisance, ranging well beyond his brief, annoying colleagues and dragging the government into controversies it did not need, including a public row with Theresa May over radicalization in schools. Dominic Cummings' attacks were not helping Gove's cause. By July, Cameron had had enough and moved him to the role of chief whip. Gove was devastated and, in the minds of many close to him, never entirely forgave Cameron.

Meanwhile, the decade of destruction that had gripped the Middle East since the Iraq invasion reached its apotheosis in June 2014. ISIS had emerged. Soon after, the first images of Westerners in orange jumpsuits, waiting to be executed, became public. The nightmare that had stalked the West since 9/11 had morphed into something frighteningly familiar: 'Jihadi John' from St John's Wood. It was in this context that Cameron authorized British airstrikes on ISIS, just a year after failing to win MPs' approval to punish Assad. Britain was fighting again in the Middle East.

At the same time, Cameron found himself back in the trenches over Europe, while simultaneously fighting simply to ensure the very survival of the British state. First, in August, and seemingly out of nowhere, the Conservative MP Douglas Carswell strode onto the stage to join Nigel Farage at a hastily arranged press conference in Westminster to announce he was leaving the Conservative Party to join UKIP. Four weeks later, Daniel Hannan's school friend and fellow plotter, Mark Reckless, became the second Conservative MP to defect, prompting a caustic reaction from David Cameron, who accused him of betraying the Tory activists who had 'knocked on doors, stuffed envelopes, licked stamps to get his fat arse on the Commons benches'.[67] The pressure on Cameron was unrelenting. The Bloomberg speech had been the grand strategy to stem the bleeding over Europe and allow Cameron to set up the election as a straight fight on the economy. But it did not seem to be working.

At the same time, the union with Scotland was in jeopardy. After the SNP's victory in the Scottish parliamentary elections of 2011, Cameron had played obliging genie to Scotland's first minister, Alex Salmond, granting not only his wish for an independence referendum, but also his preferred timing, wording and his demand that sixteen-year-olds be allowed to vote for the first time in British history. As the referendum approached, Cameron's confidence began to wane as the polls first narrowed and then, with weeks to go, flipped to give the Yes campaign the lead.

In a panic, Cameron joined with Ed Miliband, Nick Clegg and Gordon Brown to sign a last-ditch pledge to save the union – 'the vow' – promising to give Scots more powers over their own affairs should voters reject independence. Far from killing Scottish nationalism 'stone dead',[68] as had been the original boast of Blair's Labour Party, devolution had brought Scotland to the brink of secession, prompting a last-minute offer to devolve even more power in the hope of avoiding separation.[69] The extent of the constitutional upheaval that resulted from this promise only became clear in the aftermath of the referendum.

Scotland voted to reject independence by 55 per cent to 45 per cent. The morning after, on 19 September 2014, Cameron strode out to the podium in Downing Street determined to take back the initiative. 'Just as Scotland will vote separately in a Scottish parliament on their issues of tax, spending and welfare, so too England as well as Wales and Northern Ireland should be able to vote on these issues.'[70] This was not part of the deal presented to Scotland just days earlier. But Cameron was clear: 'The question of English votes for English laws, the so-called West Lothian question, deserves a decisive answer.' The question, first raised by Tam Dalyell and coined by Enoch Powell in 1977, had apparently received an answer, though not one that would last.

For the Scottish Thatcherites who had given the Eurosceptic vanguard a distinctly Caledonian flavour, the fact that Scotland had almost been lost to the Union confirmed their intuitive sense that the nation was a fragile organism that required constant vigilance to protect.

Before the Scottish referendum was even over, Matthew Elliott wrote a briefing note on the lessons of the campaign, building on Cummings' work earlier in the summer. Elliott had observed how the Better Together organization had built a narrative of uncertainty about the consequences of independence, which had proved decisive. To win, any future 'Out' campaign needed to turn the tables on the 'In' side on this question. 'We need to make sure that we seize the initiative – and the early months of the campaign must establish the dangers of *staying in*.'[71]

Elliott was particularly concerned about a future 'In' campaign copying Better Together's tactics by making claims about threats to specific areas of economic or national life, whether defence or the NHS or people's savings and pensions. In his conclusion, echoing Cummings' research, Elliott returned to his central observation: 'The question has to be what happens if we DON'T leave. The other side will launch a fear campaign. We will need to beat them at their own game.'

At Business for Britain, Elliott was still ostensibly supporting Cameron's renegotiation strategy, yet he was also continually upping the pressure for reforms which went far beyond those Cameron was pursuing, much as Cummings had argued was inevitable earlier in the summer. A 1,000-page policy document, published by Business for Britain in September, set out the reforms the UK would need in order to make remaining in the EU more attractive than leaving. This was then followed up with a letter, signed by 500 business leaders, demanding that all the main party leaders commit to an EU referendum.[72]

The original policy document was called 'Change, or Go' and was designed to present the group as the reasonable centre ground of British politics, between what they described as the 'in at all costs' federalists and the 'out at all costs' anti-Europeans. Much of the 'Change, or Go' prospectus was the work of the Fresh Start group, whose proposals had been welcomed by William Hague earlier in the parliament.

Elliott's 'Change, or Go' pamphlet included many ideas that were deliverable within the existing EU treaties, such as securing fresh protections for the City of London and reducing the EU's budget.[73] But many more were not. Indeed, the paper argued that 'unless Treaty change is secured, any reform agenda would amount to little more than the status quo', which it said was unacceptable. In one area in particular, little of significance could be achieved without treaty change: immigration.

Elliott's agenda demanded that the treaties be rewritten so that free movement no longer applied to citizens, but only to 'workers', reducing the flow of people across borders to those who already had job offers. 'Alternatively, the UK could seek to reach a new settlement where it could democratically control the number of people coming in,' the paper wrote.

By October, Cameron felt he had no choice but to make

immigration an additional part of his renegotiation. In his speech to the Conservative Party Conference, he had announced it would 'be at the very heart of my renegotiation strategy for Europe,' adding: 'When it comes to free movement – I will get what Britain needs.'[74]

All Ivan Rogers' fears about Cameron's political mismanagement were coming to pass. He had drawn up hundreds of pages of policy options he felt Cameron could deliver, but on one thing he was clear: freedom of movement was sacrosanct. Throughout 2013 and 2014, Rogers had warned Cameron that there was 'zero chance' of EU leaders agreeing to any cap on numbers of the sort Business for Britain was suggesting. Cameron, though, seemed determined to test the water. At a meeting with Angela Merkel in the UK delegation room in Brussels in October 2014, he raised the idea, prompting a defiant response. 'There's no way, David,' she told him.[75] It was at this point that Cameron turned his attention to a different plan: restricting benefits for new arrivals from the EU.

Cameron, though, had promised his backbench MPs a 'game-changing' announcement on immigration, which both *The Times* and *The Sun* had been briefed could be an 'emergency brake' on freedom of movement.[76] Instead, in a speech in November, Cameron proposed the more limited aim of removing benefits from new arrivals from the EU until they had been in the country for four years. This proposal was the final move in Cameron's grand strategy to clear the immigration 'boulder' out of the way with a 'reasonable' demand that could hold his party together through the general election campaign. He wanted this to be, as he later described it, a 'classic election campaign offer: Britain is on the right track, don't turn back'.[77]

A surge in support for the SNP after the independence referendum offered another opportunity to sharpen the Conservative message: not voting Tory risked a Labour government propped up by the Scottish nationalists. To ram home this claim, the Tory advertising agency M&C Saatchi produced the defining image of the campaign: a giant Alex Salmond with a tiny Ed Miliband poking out of his breast pocket. Yet, despite Cameron's growing confidence in his message, the polls did not shift. By the middle of April, Labour had retaken the lead. After five years of austerity and seemingly endless turmoil over Europe, the election appeared to be on a knife-edge – and so, therefore, was the prospect of an EU referendum.

At 10 p.m. on 7 May 2015, election day, the BBC announced the result of the exit poll. When the final results came in, the Conservatives had won 330 seats to Labour's 232, not just finishing as the largest party, but winning an overall majority. The Conservative campaign had defeated Labour and crushed the Liberal Democrats, who were reduced to a rump of eight MPs, while the SNP won fifty-six of Scotland's fifty-nine MPs. UKIP won 12.4 per cent of the vote, but finished with just one MP – Douglas Carswell. Nigel Farage had lost again, falling almost 3,000 votes short of his old UKIP colleague Craig McKinley in Thanet South. Cameron was victorious. His gambles had paid off. He had done a deal with the Liberal Democrats when required, dashed their hopes of electoral reform, defeated Scottish independence, hacked away at public spending and returned the economy to growth. He had the first Conservative majority in twenty-three years. All he had to do now was win the EU referendum and his legacy would be secured. David Cameron would be the prime minister who taught Britain to live with its contradictions: a devolved but somehow unitary state, floating comfortably in a supranational bloc in which it alone did not have to accept the premise of ever closer union. Powellite certainty had never been possible or desirable. Lofty ambiguity was Britain's destiny. Britain would be with Europe, but not of it. The future seemed set. And it would not be Nigel Farage's version.

After the result was announced, Farage said he was quitting as leader of UKIP. 'I feel an enormous weight lifted from my shoulders,' he declared. A delighted heckler shouted out from the crowd: 'Bye, bye, Nigel!'[78]

Chapter 16

In the early afternoon of Friday, 8 May 2015, David Cameron strode out from Number Ten to deliver the victory speech he never expected to give.[1] This was the outcome he and his friends had been working towards for fifteen years: a Conservative majority. 'Our manifesto is a manifesto for working people and as a majority government we will be able to deliver all of it,' he began. 'All of it. Yes, we will deliver that in/out referendum on our future in Europe.'[2]

Until that point, all but the most optimistic Brexiteers had convinced themselves that a referendum remained unlikely, at least in the short term. Dominic Cummings thought a Conservative election victory was so unlikely that securing the Conservative leadership for a committed Brexiteer following a Tory defeat remained the priority. At Business for Britain, Matthew Elliott was working on the assumption that either Ed Miliband would become prime minister or Cameron would return at the head of a patched-up government too weak to deliver the referendum promise. Like Cummings, Elliott thought the real battle would be the next Tory leadership contest.

Nigel Farage, meanwhile, had resigned as leader of UKIP, Nick Clegg had stood down as leader of the Liberal Democrats and Ed Miliband had quit as leader of the Labour Party. In one sweeping move, Cameron had scythed down each of his opponents. Merkel was 'full of praise', though she avoided any substantive talk about the referendum in her first call after the election. Obama was more direct: 'I hope you've got a plan to keep Britain in Europe,' he told Cameron.[3]

In truth, few were betting against Cameron's ability to do so. Those like Norman Stone, who had dismissed Cameron as a 'transitional nobody', appeared to have underestimated him.[4] Cameron had returned the Tories to power, seen off Scottish independence and was on track – it seemed – to secure Britain's place in the EU for another generation. If anything, it was Cameron's critics who seemed to have lost their relevance.

After its revival in 2013, Scruton's Conservative Philosophy Group had struggled to recover its old energy. Scruton had once reflected that the romantic core of conservatism was the hopeless attempt to recapture that which had been lost. The Conservative Philosophy Group seemed to be living proof.

In truth, Scruton himself seemed a little passé. This was the year he published *Fools, Frauds and Firebrands*, an update of his 1985 book, *Thinkers of the New Left*. Thirty years earlier, such invective was considered wildly provocative, but, by 2015, it seemed rather old hat, even a little antiquated. Of the other Conservative Philosophy Club founders, Jonathan Aitken had become a repentant priest and John Casey a retired academic, 'getting steadily less conservative with age', as one reviewer put it.[5] Norman Stone was in Istanbul, drinking three bottles of wine a day – still the sardonic wit of old, but no longer the influential tabloid don and mentor to the next generation of conservative rebels. Even those intellectual bandits who had once sat at his feet were now either marginal or subordinate to Cameron. Patrick Robertson was a largely anonymous businessman living in Switzerland, Michael Gove an apparently committed Cameroon, Dougie Smith an employee of the Conservative Party and Dominic Cummings little more than a rebel campaigner.

Nigel Farage had led a peasants' revolt, but, like Wat Tyler, had fallen short, winning nearly 4 million votes but only one MP. Now, he was being urged by his own party to stay out of the coming referendum because he was 'toxic' for the Brexit cause.

Only one figure in British politics could credibly claim to challenge Cameron in terms of national appeal – Boris Johnson. But even he had been cast into the shade by Cameron's triumph.

Cameron, meanwhile, had momentum on his side and the power of the state at his back. In Ivan Rogers and Jeremy Heywood, he had two formidable operators. Rogers, though, was increasingly alarmed by what he saw as the institutional complacency over the risk Cameron was running. Even Heywood seemed unaware of the scale of the challenge Britan's withdrawal posed, Rogers believed. When Rogers warned him that it would take two parliaments just to disentangle Britain's regulatory system from the EU, Heywood was dismissive. After the election, Rogers asked him to begin drawing up a series of potential post-exit models that Britain's political leaders could consider in the event of a vote for Out, but Heywood refused. To this day, Rogers believes the failure to prepare was a dereliction of duty from everyone concerned.[6]

There was at least one leading proponent who shared Rogers' understanding of the bureaucratic challenge of withdrawal: Dominic Cummings. Since his time at the New Frontiers Foundation, Cummings had been obsessed with the technical aspects of withdrawal, and as late as July 2015 was blogging about the complexities of the process. 'Escaping the supremacy of EU law enshrined in the 1972 European Communities Act will be a complicated process stretching over years,' he wrote.[7]

In 2015, few seemed willing to face up to this reality. Many Eurosceptics argued that Britain had integrated far more deeply than any government liked to admit, but paradoxically claimed that cutting loose from this arrangement would be easy. Pro-Europeans, in contrast, argued that the scale of Britain's European entanglement was exaggerated but that leaving would be impossibly complex.

Cameron's first post-election European problem did not take long to surface. A report was published by the bloc's 'five presidents' in June 2015, setting out the next stages of the EU's plan to 'complete' its economic and monetary union.[8] The first stage would see the eurozone integrate under the existing treaties before June 2017. After this point, new rules of 'a legal nature' would be introduced. The treaty changes Cameron had long believed inevitable were back on the table – only they would not come in until *after* his own renegotiation deadline had passed.

Despite the importance of Juncker's report, it received little coverage in the British press, which was focused on the continuing crisis in Greece and the growing wave of refugees arriving in Europe from the Middle East. Yet, as Cummings spotted, the report was a crucial development. 'These plans will leave Britain as a permanent second-class member state, subject to EU law but condemned to be constantly outvoted in the EU's institutions,' Cummings wrote on his blog.[9] True or not, this was the essence of Cameron's concern which had led him to call the referendum in the first place.

At his first summit of EU leaders after his election victory, Cameron was given ten minutes to set out his pitch for reform, after which Europe's leaders 'agreed to revert to the matter in December.'[10] But there was a catch: there would be no *treaty* change. 'I underestimated the desire of the EU's leaders to avoid changes they would have to consult their own voters about,' Cameron later admitted.[11] This was not some small oversight either, but a structural flaw in Cameron's entire strategy.

To deal with the fact that reform via immediate treaty change was now off the table, Ivan Rogers had come up with the only alternative he could think of: the Danish solution. This was the fix Europe's leaders had found in 1992 after Denmark's rejection of Maastricht, whereby specific changes would be agreed for Denmark and then inserted into the *next* treaty whenever it was eventually negotiated. It was a neat diplomatic solution, though Dominic Cummings quickly spotted the problem: 'A promise before the end of 2017 to change the treaties at some point in the future is the political equivalent of "the cheque's in the post, and it will be paid in a few years' time if 28 people still agree to pay it",' Cummings wrote. 'The NO campaign will be able to say simply, "If you trust all these politicians' promises vote YES, if you suspect they may be lying as usual, vote NO to get a better deal."'[12]

For Matthew Elliott, Cameron's failure to secure treaty change was the excuse he needed to order his troops over the top. Within Business for Britain, a significant number of people supported Cameron's renegotiation, but after it was confirmed that there would be no treaty change, Elliott could argue that the 'Change, or Go' prospectus for reform could not be delivered and the only logical option was to campaign for Out. The logistical challenge was also weighing heavily by this point; to wait any longer before committing to supporting withdrawal, Cummings argued, was tantamount to accepting defeat. As early as May, Cummings had already pledged himself to help set up and run the campaign.

On the final day of the summit, the backdrop of Cameron's entire renegotiation strategy darkened as news of simultaneous terrorist attacks in France and Tunisia filtered through to the delegates. 'Oh God, not again,' Cameron thought.[13] Only six months earlier, gunmen loyal to ISIS had murdered twelve people at the Paris offices of the satirical French magazine *Charlie Hebdo*. This time, a lorry driver in Lyon had beheaded his boss. In Tunisia, meanwhile, Islamist gunmen had charged along a popular tourist beach, shooting holidaymakers indiscriminately, killing thirty-eight, including thirty British citizens.

The European Council of June 2015 is a moment which captures many of the structural problems that would undermine Cameron's strategy until his defeat and departure, a little over a year later. With Cameron relegated to the end of the discussion, the rest of the summit was devoted to Europe's primary challenges at that time: the migrant and monetary crises it continued to face. The inherent vulnerabilities in the EU's single currency and borderless travel area were being exposed by the wave of human suffering breaking over the continent from Syria. This was the unpropitious background reality against which David Cameron was attempting to deliver both a successful renegotiation and a referendum victory.

Cameron could always delay the referendum until 2017 in the hope of more benign conditions, but it had become clear that Europe's leaders would not be wasting any more time dealing with Britain's concerns when they had such challenges of their own to deal with, as well as French and German elections in 2017. In the end, after consultation with Lynton Crosby, Cameron decided that 2016 was 'as good a time as any' to take the plunge.

For many of Europe's leaders, the disconnect between the long-term ambition of Cameron's renegotiation and the immediacy of their own crisis was a source of acute frustration. Through his own diplomatic miscalculation, Cameron had found himself isolated and ignored in 2011, but, from the perspective of Europe's leaders, this was not their fault. Besides, Britain already had a set of special arrangements to protect its sovereignty on the twin issues that were now causing the leaders such political pain: migration and monetary control. As far as the EU was concerned, there was simply no immediate threat to British interests which required an emergency renegotiation in 2015.

The fact that Cameron was also making additional demands about restrictions to free movement grated, too. Across much of the continent, EU citizens crossing borders for work were not considered 'immigrants' in the same way that those arriving from Africa, the Middle East and beyond were. In Britain, however, the sense of huge numbers was exacerbated by the fact that all incomers were viewed by the public as migrants, whether from Europe or anywhere else. Ted Heath's idealistic ambition that Britain's entry into Europe would finally rub away the distinction between 'we' in Britain and 'they' in Europe was as far away as ever.

The immigration question might have been voters' number one concern, but on its own, as both Cummings and Elliott had noted, a promise from the 'Out' side to stem the numbers arriving would not be enough to win the referendum. The economy remained central.

One way to reassure voters, Cumming speculated, was to offer them a second referendum on the terms of any future divorce settlement. Cummings worried this would give the government an unfair advantage because it could afford to lose the first referendum and still stop Britain leaving the EU. Yet, it brought advantages for Out, too. If voters knew there would be a second referendum, they would be more likely to take a risk in the first. 'Further,' Cummings wrote, 'as a matter of democratic accountability, given the enormous importance of so many issues that would be decided in an Article 50 renegotiation – a far, far bigger deal than a normal election – it seems right to give people a vote on it.'[14] Boris Johnson soon began to talk about the idea too. For Cameron, though, such a formula increased the chances of an initial defeat. 'Leave means leave,' a spokesman for the prime minister declared, shutting down Cummings' twin-referendum speculation.[15]

Back in July, a rival Eurosceptic group, utterly dismissive of Cummings' thoughts, had burst out of the blocs. Initially calling itself 'In the Know', the new organization – run by multimillionaire businessman and UKIP donor Arron Banks – rejected Cummings' logic about the need to neutralize the Out side's economic vulnerability before turning to immigration. Despite multiple attempts to bring the two camps together, each effort foundered. The clashes of personality and strategy were too great. And so, as the referendum approached, there would be two rival campaigns: a 'respectable' Tory outfit and a UKIP-aligned alter ego, the latter with a more fundamentalist approach which Cummings believed was preaching to the converted. The two campaigns were separate, but never entirely so.

The rival campaign caused Elliott considerable consternation: Banks tried to poach Cummings; he secured the support of the left-wing railway workers' union, the RMT; and he hired the big-data firm Cambridge Analytica and the American pollster Gerry

Gunster. So concerned was Elliott that he and his team drew up a giant organogram of Banks's operation, which they stuck to the wall of their offices as if they were running a police investigation. On it, brightly coloured red and blue lines connected Banks to a series of obscure companies based in places like Gibraltar, Belize, Lesotho and the Isle of Man, peppered with question marks and suggestive pound signs.[16]

For Cameron, all of this was a dream. His opponents were at each other's throats before he had even started his renegotiation; if he could deliver a substantive set of reforms, he would surely have the upper hand. By this stage, Cameron had begun his tour of Europe's capitals and, with each visit, he returned encouraged by what he was told. Ivan Rogers, ever the Eeyore to Cameron's Pooh, repeatedly warned the prime minister to treat all such personal promises sceptically. In Rogers' view, the real negotiation would not take place between leaders, but between officials who did not have to worry so much about the diplomatic niceties. In a negotiation like this, personal relationships meant little, he argued. To understand the underlying reality, look to the behaviour of the institutions.[17] As such, Rogers set up a 'shadow' negotiation in Brussels. After each of Cameron's diplomatic trips, Rogers made sure to host the same country's officials at the British residence in Brussels, where he would wine, dine and mine them for information. Rogers then typed up his intelligence in a long note for Cameron, intended to temper his expectations. Cameron quickly grew frustrated by this process. 'Often I would report back to Ivan or Tom [Scholar] after a tête-à-tête with a fellow prime minister, only to be told that their officials refused to accept what had been agreed,' Cameron later wrote. 'Merkel and Hollande, surrounded by officials deeply imbued with Brussels orthodoxies, were the worst for this.'[18]

At the same time, Cameron was dealing with the relentless demands of the premiership. In August, he authorized the RAF to conduct a drone strike on Syrian soil to kill a twenty-one-year-old British jihadi called Reyaad Khan. The strike was, as Cameron later wrote, 'the first time a British citizen had been killed by the British state in a country with which the UK was not at war'.[19] More significantly, by August 2015 the early waves of refugees arriving in Europe had turned into a tidal surge, with hundreds of thousands piling onto small boats and dinghies along the Turkish coast, heading for Europe. In 2014, the EU had received around 625,000 asylum applications from Syrian and other refugees, the highest number since the Yugoslav Wars in 1992; over the course of 2015, this number topped a million, prompting two emergency interventions from Angela Merkel that upended German and European politics. First, Merkel unilaterally suspended the requirement for refugees from Syria to claim asylum in the first safe country they arrived in. Then, as refugees began heading in ever greater numbers towards Germany, she uttered the phrase that came to define her handling of the crisis: '*Wir schaffen das*.' We can do this.[20]

It was then that a Turkish photographer captured a moment of horror that shook European politics: the limp, lifeless body of a two-year-old boy called Alan Kurdi, lying face down in the Turkish surf, dead, discarded and alone. Alan had drowned with his five-year-old brother, Ghalib, and their mother, Rehanna, as they attempted to cross the Aegean Sea to Kos. Their deaths were not unique; over the course of 2015, 3,700 people would die trying to make it to Europe. Yet the photograph weighed on the conscience of a complacent continent. Three days after Alan's death, Angela Merkel dropped Germany's border controls entirely, and the crisis reached its apogee.

Though Merkel's decision was notionally for Germany alone, it had implications far beyond that country's own borders. Faced with tens of thousands of refugees arriving in Germany every week, Merkel forced through a new EU quota plan for the resettlement of 120,000 migrants across the bloc, bypassing opposition from Eastern Europe, which then simply refused to implement the order. Viktor Orbán's Hungary was particularly incensed by the decision and began to construct a giant fence along its border.

Though Britain was largely exempt from the crisis, because it was not in Schengen and, therefore, not required to take part in the relocation scheme, Cameron quickly understood he was not immune to the political challenge it posed. The re-emergence of 'the Jungle' – a refugee camp near Calais – soon began to fixate the media. Cameron came under intense pressure to do more to help the refugees fleeing the Middle East and eventually offered to take in 20,000 of them over the course of the parliament – 4,000 a year.[21] At the height of the crisis in 2015, Germany was taking 13,000 refugees every day. After leaving office, Cameron wrote that one of his biggest regrets as prime minister was not making more of the fact that he had entirely rejected Merkel's approach to the crisis.[22] Yet to have highlighted this would have been to define the benefits of Britain's EU membership negatively: showing it to be acceptable only because it was *not* part of other European-wide schemes, from refugee resettlement programmes to Schengen, bailout funds and, of course, the euro.

By the autumn of 2015, Cameron still appeared largely unscathed by the refugee crisis, even going as far as to later dub this period the 'halcyon days' of his premiership. At Balmoral for the annual weekend with the Royal family in September, Cameron went shooting, walking over the moors with a borrowed shotgun in one hand and his BlackBerry in the other. It was here that he received another apparent political fillip: Jeremy Corbyn had been elected Labour Party leader. Cameron even began to think the previously unthinkable: 'What would be so wrong about a third term?'[23]

Though Cameron claims he quickly swatted away such thoughts, that they had intruded into his imagination at all reveals his high spirits. These were then buoyed further by the state visit of China's president, Xi Jinping. For Cameron and George Osborne, Xi's arrival encapsulated their wider political project. Economically, they were Thatcher's children, committed to her vision of Britain as the most open, flexible and globally integrated economy in Europe. The financial crisis hadn't undermined their faith in this model; if anything, they only became more committed to its success. Since 2010, Osborne had set about making Britain even more attractive to global capital, cutting corporation tax from 26 per cent to 20 per cent and reducing the top rate of tax from 50 per cent to 45 per cent.

In the 1980s, Margaret Thatcher had targeted Japan as the great source of untapped investment. Now, Cameron and Osborne were doing the same with China. In 2014, London had become host to the first clearing bank for the Chinese currency outside Asia – an initial step, it seemed, for the City to become the global centre for offshore renminbi trading. Then, in early 2015, Britain had become a founder member of China's Asian Infrastructure Investment Bank, despite American protests. These moves, however, seemed to be little more than early flirtations: Xi's state visit was the consummation of the affair. Britain would become China's preferred gateway into Europe and the global financial system, and would go into partnership with Beijing in areas of high sensitivity, including nuclear energy. 'The UK has stated that it will be the western country that is most open to China,' Xi declared. 'This is a visionary and strategic choice that fully meets Britain's own long-term interest.'[24]

All the elements of Cameron's wider strategy were now in place. He had survived the most difficult moments of his first term: the veto that wasn't; the double-dip that wasn't; and the lost Syria vote that certainly was. Now, he was at the height of his power, the Opposition weaker than at any time since the 1980s, and his economic strategy was coming together, just as it had for Thatcher.

Elliott and Cummings, meanwhile, were scrambling to keep up. They had been caught on the hop when Nigel Farage had taken to the stage at UKIP's annual conference in September to announce the party would back Arron Banks's rival group, which had become Leave.EU. 'Leave' had emerged into British politics after the Electoral Commission rejected Cameron's proposed referendum question – borrowing a trick from Alex Salmond – which would have asked voters whether they wanted to remain in the EU, Yes or No. Instead, voters would be asked whether they wanted to Leave or Remain in the EU, a more neutral question.

At this point, the Elliott–Cummings group had not yet even been launched. That would come in October, when Matthew Elliott unveiled Vote Leave, backed by an underwhelming group of MPs and businessmen, including the Business for Britain stalwarts Stuart Wheeler and John Mills, and, as interim chairman, Nigel Lawson, the one-time chancellor who battled Thatcher over her opposition to British membership of the Exchange Rate Mechanism. At the launch, Vote Leave unveiled its slogan for the campaign: 'Take Control'.[25] This was soon updated by Cummings to read 'Take Back Control', intended to trigger a strong 'evolved instinct' against the loss of what was previously considered safe.[26] It was not a new slogan. Cummings had been playing with similar catchlines for almost twenty years, while Nigel Farage had deployed it during the 2014 European elections. The central purpose of taking back control was also revealed: to spend more money on the NHS. Many Tory MPs disliked it, but Cummings was insistent. It was the combination of control, money and public services that voters were most interested in. This was not guesswork, but the result of the research projects he had undertaken for Elliott's Business for Britain since quitting government in 2014. To reinforce the message, Cummings and Elliott put a number on the money that could be saved and spent on the NHS: £350 million a week. This was the gross sum that Britain contributed to the EU budget – not counting the roughly £100 million a week it received back in the rebate or the other £100 million a week that was spent in Britain by the European Commission.

To begin with, Vote Leave's eye-catching message was not the focus of media attention. The following day's newspapers were more interested in Vote Leave's decision to endorse votes for sixteen- and seventeen-year-olds than its slogan or £350 million claim. For Cameron, meanwhile, his focus was directed towards his renegotiation. Having been warned by Ivan Rogers not to repeat the mistakes of 2011, when he had made a set of demands the EU was never going to accept, Cameron carefully split his negotiating demands into four 'baskets', which he set out in a letter to the president of the European Council, Donald Tusk, in November.

The first of these baskets was the core of the negotiation: 'fairness', to ensure the eurozone could not tip the rules of the single market in its favour and against Britain. Cameron asked for 'legally binding principles that safeguard the operation of the Union for all 28 Member States'. The second basket was 'competitiveness' – an eternal British concern – that was already all but empty by November, with Cameron asking for little more than targets to cut red tape and boost productivity. The third basket – 'sovereignty' – contained more substance, including a demand for a 'formal, legally binding and irreversible' guarantee that Britain was no longer obliged to work towards ever closer union. But the final basket was the trickiest of all and the only one absent from his original Bloomberg speech in 2013: 'immigration'.[27] Having accepted defeat on an emergency brake, Cameron instead demanded a four-year benefit ban for new EU citizens arriving in Britain and an end to 'the practice of sending child benefit overseas'. The proposal was carefully calibrated to be both diplomatically deliverable and politically sellable, answering voters' concerns about the perceived unfairness of immigration. Cummings had also spotted that voters felt particularly strongly on the issue of child benefit.

Just three days after Cameron had sent his letter, ISIS launched the deadliest attack on French soil since the Second World War. During a night of terror, 130 people were killed across Paris, as suicide bombers and gunmen carried out a coordinated assault, attacking cafes, restaurants, the national stadium and the Bataclan theatre. Many of the killers had smuggled themselves into Europe posing as refugees, using false Syrian passports.

For Cameron, these scenes contributed to a nagging doubt about the referendum. 'Could I really persuade the people of

Britain that we were protected from illegal immigration when the issue had become so prominent?'[28] Cameron needed something to show for his negotiation, but was unhappy with the progress achieved. The December European Council was the summit he and Ivan Rogers had earmarked to secure his deal, but there remained too much opposition to Britain's welfare proposals. And so Cameron delayed the moment of truth until February – his last chance to secure an agreement, if he was to hold the referendum on his preferred date of 23 June.

Back home, Cameron had other concerns. Over New Year's Eve, he and Samantha hosted some of their closest friends at Chequers. Margaret Thatcher had celebrated New Year in the same way to welcome in 1990; by then, she was the most dominant figure in post-war British politics, yet was powerless to halt the forces of history about to wash her away. Among Cameron's guests that night were Michael Gove and his wife Sarah Vine. Cameron had become concerned about Gove's intentions and asked Vine directly whether her husband would stick with him and back the 'Remain' side when the time came. 'Sarah said that he would,' Cameron later wrote.[29]

Cameron, though, remained concerned enough about Gove to ask Osborne to 'work on him' over the next few weeks. Cameron eventually invited him to his flat in Downing Street. 'My head is in a strange place,' Gove admitted to Cameron. 'For once, I find it hard to articulate.'[30] Cameron could not believe what was happening. Gove was part of his inner circle. Sarah Vine was godparent to one of his children. If Gove could not be counted on, who else would he lose? Gove, though, had never been narrow in his friendships. While he was being 'worked on' by Osborne and Cameron, his other friendship circles were doing the same – not least Dougie Smith and Dominic Cummings. Cummings and Smith calculated that securing Gove's support for Leave doubled the chances of getting Boris Johnson. And, with Johnson, Vote Leave stood a chance of victory. Gove, then, was the key.

Throughout this period, there were many meetings at Gove's family home in North Kensington, with Dominic Cummings, Dougie Smith, Nick Boles and others debating his next move. For Gove, the calculation was personal as well as professional. He knew that, if he went against the Notting Hill Set, Vote Leave would still probably lose, but it would cost him his political career. Cameron would never trust him again. Yet, he had been a Eurosceptic since childhood. He blamed the collapse of his father's trawler business on the Common Fisheries Policy. As a boy, he had subscribed to Scruton's *Salisbury Review*. At Oxford, he had challenged Edward Heath over British membership. At *The Times*, he had pushed for anyone but Ken Clarke. Cameron and Osborne were his professional circle, the men who had implemented the modernizing project close to his heart. But his political model had been Michael Portillo, not David Cameron, and his ideological soulmates were Dominic Cummings and Dougie Smith. Gove was an outsider with a sense of mission. Cameron demanded fealty, much as Boris Johnson had once demanded of his stooge at Oxford. But Cummings and Smith wanted him to lead, to be something more. They sent him a regular stream of exhortatory messages. 'Here I stand, I can do no other', read one, quoting Martin Luther, a figure calculated to appeal to Gove's Presbyterian antecedents.* History was now.

Gove, though, needed to wait to declare his hand. As a member of the government, he remained bound by collective responsibility. In February, though, Cameron removed this initial hurdle when, under pressure from his most Eurosceptic ministers, he announced a temporary suspension of the normal rules of government for the duration of the EU referendum campaign, following the precedent set by Harold Wilson in 1975. Much now

* The quote is attributed to Martin Luther, refusing the demand by the Holy Roman Emperor Charles V to recant his rejection of Catholic authority: 'My conscience is captive to the word of God. To go against conscience is neither right nor safe. I therefore cannot, and I will not recant! Here I stand. I can do no other.'

depended on the success or failure of the renegotiation, and Ivan Rogers was growing concerned. In January, he fired off a long memorandum, warning the prime minister that, unless expectations were brought into line with the reality of what was possible, the renegotiation would be dismissed irrespective of its wider merits, much as Cummings had written. While the British negotiating team was spending much of its time winning assurances about Britain's place in the single market, Rogers warned that the Leave campaign would ignore this to focus on 'money, migration and the lack of treaty change', as he later put it.[31]

But the Leave campaign was facing its own crisis, after a group of Eurosceptic MPs launched an attempt to force Cummings out of his position as campaign director. They were infuriated by his abrasive manner and opposed his strategy to focus on the NHS. Cummings was summoned to a meeting and asked to sign an agreement which would have sidelined him in the campaign. He refused, warning that there would be a mass walkout if he was removed and Vote Leave would lose its chance to get Michael Gove – and therefore Boris Johnson. Dougie Smith and his allies went into overdrive to rally support for their comrade. When the MPs discovered the scale of backing for Cummings within the organization, the 'coup' fell apart. From then on, Cummings was in full and unchallenged control.

For Cameron, meanwhile, the point of maximum danger was approaching. Ivan Rogers had warned him that the key moment would be when Donald Tusk produced the draft text of the agreement in February. 'That's where the shit hits the fan,' as he put it.[32] When the draft was published, the reaction from the Tory press was scathing. 'Who do EU think you are kidding Mr Cameron?' ran the front-page headline in *The Sun*, next to a mocked-up image of Cameron in a *Dad's Army* costume.[33] Cameron had 'caved on all his immigration demands', the paper reported. There was little support elsewhere either. *The Times* splashed with 'Brussels will have right to reject benefit curbs' and focused entirely on the welfare element of the deal, without a single mention of the original purpose of the negotiation: the eurozone.[34] Cameron's strategy was unravelling.

For the remainder of the month, however, Cameron was locked in negotiations not to improve the deal, but to stop it being watered down further. And yet, even in that, he failed. At the summit in Brussels to finalize the agreement, Cameron accepted that, rather than ending the practice of EU migrants claiming child benefit and then sending it to their children abroad, the amount they could claim would merely be reduced to reflect the economic conditions of their country of residence. Cameron also accepted a compromise where, instead of his original proposal in which new arrivals would get no benefits for the first four years in the country, their benefits would instead be gradually tapered from nothing to full eligibility over this time period. Lynton Crosby urged Cameron to reject these compromises and try again, but Cameron decided to do the deal – a decision he later regretted. 'I should have held firm,' he wrote.[35]

The problem was not so much the scale of the concessions made during the negotiations, but that the entire package was now too weak to sell to voters, exposing the reality of Britain's limited influence. By accepting the compromise at the first time of asking, Cameron had also failed to play the role expected of him by the public. 'To accept a third of a loaf when you are asking for a whole loaf, is no settlement of a problem,' Thatcher had declared dismissively in 1979, before eventually settling for two thirds a year later. Cameron, though, had bargained down, not up.

Whether he could ever have got a full loaf, or even two thirds, is doubtful. Even less clear is the impact a better deal would have made to the eventual result. Cummings would later write that, had Cameron held firm, the cracks in Vote Leave would have opened up once again, clearing the way for a Remain victory. By this time, however, even the draft agreement had been dismissed by the press, MPs and the public. A ComRes poll published before Cameron had finished the negotiation found that 58 per cent of the public expected him to get a 'bad deal'.[36] By his own admission, Cameron failed at the politics of the negotiation; he did not meet the expectations he had set, nor adequately explain his central purpose. Addressing the inherent weakness of Britain's position in the EU outside the eurozone was legitimate, but by turning the negotiation into a wider renegotiation of Britain's entire membership, Cameron repeated – indeed, compounded – his mistakes from 2011, raising expectations beyond what he could deliver and the stakes beyond the price he could pay.

Ironically, Cameron's negotiation did secure a number of substantive protections. According to the text published at the end of summit, Britain would be under no obligation to ever take part in further integration to stabilize the eurozone. Furthermore, any form of discrimination 'based on the official currency of the Member State' was formally prohibited, while future 'intergovernmental agreements' of the sort agreed in 2011 would have to show they did not 'constitute a barrier to or discrimination in trade between Member States.' Some of Cameron's concerns – and those of the British system more generally – had been addressed. The European Central Bank's role imposing a banking union would be applicable 'only to credit institutions located in Member States whose currency is the euro'. There was also a bail-out clause which guaranteed that future measures to safeguard the euro area 'will not entail budgetary responsibility for Member States whose currency is not the euro'.[37]

Cameron also won concessions in his sovereignty basket. Britain's 'specific situation' in the EU meant that it was not committed to 'further political integration into the European Union'. The agreement even stated that 'references to ever closer union do not apply to the United Kingdom' and, in a clause to stop judicial overreach, it stated that references to 'ever closer union among the peoples of Europe' could not be used in future to offer 'a legal basis for extending the scope of any provision of the Treaties or of EU secondary legislation'.[38]

For some federalists, in fact, these concessions went too far.

Former Liberal Democrat MEP Andrew Duff, the former chair of the Union of European Federalists, believes the agreement would have eventually caused a crisis within the EU itself. 'It could not have been implemented,' Duff later reflected. 'In itself, it was a kind of soft Brexit, which was going to lead to a much bigger political crisis than Tusk realized . . . It was a time bomb, which would have exploded in the EU, had the United Kingdom voted to remain.'[39]

For Duff, the central problem was that Cameron had secured an opt-out from the very purpose of the European Union – political integration – and so, in his estimation, it guaranteed a future crisis. 'Without any doubt, it would have gone to the Court of Justice,' he said. 'The EU was going off in some other direction, but we were staying put, so it just wasn't sustainable.'[40] This, though, was the central problem of British membership from the beginning: the EU was always heading in a direction Britain did not want to commit to. As ever, the only exception to this rule was that brief period of supranational enthusiasm under Ted Heath.

For Cameron, of course, none of this mattered. He just had to sell his deal as best he could. Standing at the press conference in Brussels, 'two Union Jacks on either side of me, a European flag pushed into the corner,' as Cameron wrote, he turned to the arguments he wanted to make for the next four months before referendum day. Britain had guaranteed its 'special status' within the EU. It had 'the best of both worlds' and, as such, was 'stronger, safer and better off' inside than out. At the podium in Brussels, on 2 February 2016, Cameron confirmed that he would be campaigning for Remain.[41] The starting gun had been fired.

Michael Gove, however, was already up and out of the blocks for Leave, the decision having leaked into the press, much to Cameron's surprise. In Brussels, Cameron sought to make light of Gove's decision. 'Michael is one of my oldest and closest friends but he has wanted to get Britain to pull out of the EU for about 30 years,' he said. 'I am disappointed but I am not surprised.'[42] In private, though, he was surprised. 'I didn't anticipate who would be quickest out of the stalls,' Cameron later wrote. 'As soon as I had sealed the deal in Brussels – indeed, while I was still in the building – it was Michael Gove who was the first on the media condemning it.'[43]

The following day, Cameron held an emergency cabinet meeting to formally agree the deal, lift cabinet responsibility to campaign for it and confirm the date of the referendum: 23 June. Shortly afterwards, he watched on television as his old friend joined Iain Duncan Smith, Chris Grayling, Priti Patel, Theresa Villiers and John Whittingdale at the headquarters of Vote Leave, looking for all the world like a parallel cabinet, with a parallel prime minister: Michael Gove.

Attention then turned to Boris Johnson. 'The last thing I wanted was to go against David Cameron or the government,' Johnson declared to the waiting press outside his home at 5 p.m. on Sunday. 'But after a great deal of heartache, I don't think there's anything else I can do. I will be advocating Vote Leave. Because I want a better deal for the people of this country.'[44] Cameron immediately understood the seriousness of this moment. 'He was the only leading politician whose favourability rating was higher than mine.'[45] Any remaining hope of a poll bounce from his renegotiation was gone. 'It meant all we really had was the economy,' Cameron's pollster Andrew Cooper reflected.[46]

Cameron had called a referendum to deal with Britain's structural weakness in the EU, end the Tory civil war over Europe and put the question to bed for a generation. Instead, over the next few weeks, almost 140 Conservative MPs joined Johnson and Gove in supporting Leave, including the man both Cameron and William Hague had picked out as the future of the party: Rishi Sunak. 'At that point the project had already failed,' one of Cameron's advisers admitted.[47] Cameron yearned to be the one to settle matters, but the waves of history were washing over him instead.

In the opening skirmishes of the campaign, 'Stronger In' – as the Remain campaign was titled – revealed its formidable power, with letter after letter from business leaders warning about the dangers of Brexit, as it had come to be known. Vote Leave began to label all such interventions 'Project Fear' – borrowing another slogan deployed by Alex Salmond in the Scottish referendum – but, by March, the warnings seemed to be having an effect, as Remain gained around a 5 per cent lead in the polls.

The other problem for Vote Leave was one of respectability. Ever since Enoch Powell, a whiff of sulphur had attached itself to anyone in British politics who appeared too hung up about immigration. UKIP had broadened its appeal as immigration rose from the mid 1990s, but even in 2015 it had only managed a little over 12 per cent of the vote. There was, it seemed, a ceiling on support for any party – or project – associated too heavily with stopping immigration. One of the main objectives of Vote Leave was therefore to avoid any such hint of disreputability. For Cummings, this was part of the importance of Gove and Johnson: they were Tories, not demagogues, and liberal Tories at that. Gove was a modernizer and Johnson an amiable jester who mocked the self-importance of anyone who took anything too seriously, including immigration. Farage, meanwhile, was not part of the campaign, but off doing his own thing. In early March, Vote Leave was further inoculated against the charge of xenophobia with the emergence of a third figurehead to helm the campaign: Gisela Stuart.

On 9 March, it was announced that Stuart would become chair of Vote Leave. After her experience on the European convention, Stuart had taken a back seat on Europe, serving on select committees and defending her marginal seat in Birmingham. By 2016, she had little to do with the wider Eurosceptic movement, and her initial aim had been to steer clear of the referendum debate entirely. But then her friend David Owen told her he was joining the Vote Leave board – 'the man who had left Labour because it was not pro-European enough,' as Stuart put it – and he began to exert pressure on her to meet the moment.[48] It was

OK for Mrs Stuart from Birmingham to stay silent, he told her, but not the honourable member for Edgbaston. She had a duty.

Shortly after, Stuart got a call from Nigel Lawson, asking whether she would join the board; Stuart replied that, if she was to do so, she had to chair it. 'That wasn't like me,' Stuart reflected later. 'But this organization had to show that it was cross-party to get the official designation. Having a Labour woman who is German has got to help.' Stuart brought the former Liberal Democrat MP, Paul Keetch, on board, too. 'The charge that this was a group of little Englanders fell away,' Stuart said. 'I was genetically incapable of that.'[49]

With a cross-party board assembled, Vote Leave was in a strong position to secure the designation from the Electoral Commission as the official Leave campaign, ahead of Banks's more hardline outfit. And, in mid-April, it did so. Nigel Farage – 'Mr Brexit' – had been denied his chance to lead the revolution. For Vote Leave, it was not just a relief, but a moment of high significance. 'You can tell a cause by the company it keeps,' ran one of the Yes campaign's posters in the first EU referendum of 1975, reminding voters of the divisiveness of Tony Benn and Enoch Powell, who led the No campaign. Farage's exclusion from the main campaign organization did not make it harder to persuade those who liked Farage to vote for Brexit, but it made it easier to persuade those who disliked him to do so. Yet, it also liberated Farage to campaign as he saw fit: 'The campaign not being united left me completely free to go off and do my stuff around the country.'[50]

Vote Leave's victory also cast immigration into the background of the campaign, at least to begin with. For Cummings, the central task was to neutralize the Remain campaign's warning about the economic risks of leaving. Stronger In still had the full force of the state at its back; the Treasury had published a 200-page document on the 'long term economic impact' of leaving the EU, which argued that the UK would be 'permanently poorer' if it left the EU and that each household would be £4,300 worse off by 2030 if it left the single market.

Then, on 8 May, Michael Gove appeared to make the Remain campaign's case even easier by explicitly making clear, for the first time, that Britain would leave the single market if the country voted for Brexit. This was the moment Stronger In had been waiting for. 'Leave will never hear the end of it,' Cameron's director of communications, Craig Oliver, texted journalists.[51] George Osborne called the decision 'catastrophic'. Yet, as Cummings had told Vote Leave insiders, it was far from clear anyone in the country even understood why it mattered. 'No one knows what the single market is,' he said. 'The MPs don't know what the single market is! No one knows! No one will know what it is by the end of this campaign. Period.'[52]

By the end of the month, Stronger In was starting to panic that he was right. A second report from the Treasury spelling out the 'immediate implications' of Brexit argued there would be an 'immediate and profound economic shock' in response to a vote to leave.[53] The UK would be pushed into an instant recession, the pound would fall in value by 12 per cent and unemployment would rise by 500,000. But the message didn't seem to be getting through. On 25 May, Ryan Coetzee, the Remain campaign's director of strategy and former adviser to Nick Clegg, presented evidence from focus groups showing that voters were 'very sceptical about our warnings on the economy . . . They don't trust these reports. They don't trust the numbers. They don't trust the Treasury. And many don't like the messengers.'[54] Even Barack Obama's warning during a visit to London that Britain would be at 'the back of the queue' in future trade negotiations seemed to backfire, prompting an angry reaction from the public. Voters could not be convinced that leaving the EU posed a fundamental risk to their livelihoods.

For the remainder of the campaign, immigration would dominate the agenda. Only by leaving the single market could Britain end free movement. On 22 May, Vote Leave unveiled a startling new poster claiming that 'Turkey (Population 76 Million) is Joining the EU.'[55] The poster featured a giant open door, shaped like a passport. This came a few days before the publication of the official immigration statistics for 2015, showing the net total had reached a record 333,000 the year before – three times higher than Cameron had promised in both 2010 and 2015. It was a major blow for the Remain campaign. Johnson and Gove seized on the figures by writing a letter, with Gisela Stuart, accusing the government of deceiving voters that it was possible to meet its immigration target while being in the EU. 'Voters were promised repeatedly at elections that net immigration could be cut to the tens of thousands,' they wrote. 'This promise is plainly not achievable as long as the UK is a member of the EU, and the failure to keep it is corrosive of public trust in politics.'[56] On 30 May, YouGov found Leave had drawn level in the polls.

Seizing on the momentum, Vote Leave issued a series of policy pledges, starting with an 'Australian points-based system' to manage immigration, followed by a promise to scrap VAT on household energy bills and to plough an extra £100 million a week into the NHS from the savings made from not contributing to the EU budget. By the end of the second week of June, YouGov, ICM and Ipsos MORI all had Leave ahead by anything from five to seven percentage points. In a desperate attempt to save the campaign, Osborne unveiled the content of an 'emergency budget' on 15 June, which he insisted would be necessary in the event of a vote to Leave. There would be spending cuts of £15 billion, with reductions in the health, defence and education budgets, as well as a 2p rise in the basic rate of income tax and increases in alcohol and petrol duties. It was wild, unbelievable stuff.

Rodney Leach had grown impatient with such apocalyptic warnings. Having been supportive of Cameron's renegotiation and concerned about the British state's ability to cope with the demands of withdrawal, some had assumed he might even back Remain, albeit reluctantly. Privately, however, he had finally resolved to vote Leave. 'Brexit will not be an economic disaster and it will not be a utopia,' he wrote to a friend. 'Withdrawal from the EU is likely to result in an initial economic cost but

Britain can prosper if it takes a liberal approach to trade, immigration and regulation.'

Leach hadn't shared this view widely as he continued in his role as chairman of Open Europe, which had maintained a neutral stance on the referendum. But then fate intervened. 'Poor, poor Rodney,' recalled his wife, Jessica. 'He was speaking about the forthcoming referendum and then fell down and died.' Leach passed away on 12 June. For almost twenty years, he had funded, chaired and campaigned for the Eurosceptic cause, only to die eleven days before the referendum. In his final messages to friends, Leach had argued that the question was far deeper than simple economics. 'We aren't ever going to sacrifice our democracy, and the EU cannot ever develop a democracy,' he wrote, shortly before his fatal stroke. 'So it has to be exit, painful though that may temporarily be.' Just a few days before his death, Leach's friend, dining partner and one-time love rival, Roger Scruton, was knighted for his services to 'philosophy, teaching and public education'.

Facing the prospect of defeat, Cameron and Osborne contemplated further emergency measures, including asking Angela Merkel for a last-minute 'vow' of the sort Cameron had arranged with Ed Miliband, Nick Clegg and Gordon Brown to save Scotland in 2014. In the end, Cameron and Osborne decided it was not worth it. Merkel would not agree, and the risk of a failed request leaking was too great. The immigration debate had reached such a fever pitch that even Labour figures were starting to demand a tougher line. In the *Daily Mirror*, Ed Balls said that Britain would 'have to find a way in which to have managed migration, not free migration'. Theresa May, meanwhile, who had been keeping a low profile and hedging her bets – in part, thought some observers, to avoid alienating voters in any future leadership contest – used her one and only intervention of the campaign to call for 'further reform' of Europe's migration rules. Even before the referendum was over, the idea of further renegotiation was back on the table. Cameron had hoped to finally settle Britain's relationship with Europe, but no such thing was possible.

On 16 June, the campaign's turn to immigration reached its culmination when Nigel Farage unveiled a Leave.EU poster featuring a stream of migrants moving into Europe under the slogan 'Breaking Point'. But then, just a few hours later, came an event which stopped the whole referendum campaign in its tracks: an MP had been attacked and was in a critical condition. The MP was Labour's Jo Cox, and the attacker was a fifty-two-year-old neo-Nazi. Four hours later, Cox was dead. It was the first political assassination in Great Britain since Ian Gow had been murdered by the IRA in 1990.

Though all campaigning was suspended, the recriminations soon began. Had the tone of the campaign contributed to her murder? Had Nigel Farage crossed a line with his final campaign poster? Cox had been a passionate pro-European and supporter of Syrian refugees. The attacker, Thomas Mair, had screamed out 'Britain First' during his assault. The incident had occurred in Cox's Batley and Spen constituency. The private reaction of many Leavers that afternoon was not simply one of sadness, but helpless dejection. That night, a dinner had been organized at Mosimann's private dining club in Belgravia to thank those who had helped Vote Leave, but the atmosphere was funereal – not only for the death of an MP, but the possible death of their campaign.

In the days afterwards, polls showed the two sides back in a virtual dead heat. Campaigning resumed on Sunday, 19 June, with the focus on each side's final pitch to the country. The Remain campaign chose to double down on the economy, publishing a letter on the final day, signed by 1,280 executives and company directors, warning against Brexit, while Vote Leave claimed there would be an additional 261,000 children from EU countries in UK schools by 2030 if the UK remained in the EU – swelling to 571,000 if Albania, Macedonia, Montenegro, Serbia and Turkey were to join in the near future. Cummings was swinging what he called his 'baseball bat marked Turkey / NHS / £350 million' as vigorously as he could.

The campaign was brought to a close at Wembley Arena on 22 June in the BBC's *Great Debate*, pitching Boris Johnson, Gisela Stuart and Andrea Leadsom against the London mayor Sadiq Khan, Scottish Tory leader Ruth Davidson and head of the Trades Union Congress Frances O'Grady. Not a single current or former prime minister, chancellor, Conservative leader or Labour leader formed part of the cast for Remain in the final pitch to voters, each considered too toxic or too divisive to take part. Wise or not, it left Boris Johnson as the biggest beast on the stage, tasked with making the closing argument and reaching into the soul of the Leave campaign. 'They say we can't do it; we say we can. They say we have no choice but to bow down to Brussels; we say they are woefully underestimating this country.' Then came the closing line of the entire campaign: 'If we vote Leave and take back control, then I believe this Thursday can be our country's Independence Day.'

On referendum day, the conventional wisdom was still that Leave would lose – just. An on-the-day poll from YouGov, released at 10 p.m., suggested there would be a 52–48 vote to Remain, following a small but significant shift against Brexit at the last. 'It looks like Remain will edge it,' Nigel Farage predicted.

The first indication that this was wrong came from the north-east of England at around midnight. In Downing Street, Cameron was poring over a list that had been drawn up for him by the US pollster Jim Messina, showing how well Remain needed to do in each area if it was to win nationally. In Newcastle, Messina's list suggested Cameron needed a 52–48 win to be on track to win nationally. Yet, when the result was announced, it was much tighter: 50.7 per cent to 49.3 per cent. Then came Sunderland, which was worse. For Remain to avoid defeat, Leave should not get above 60 per cent; yet they had won with 61 per cent of the vote. Result by result, the pattern repeated itself across the country. Cameron's supreme gamble had failed. A year earlier, he had been king of all he surveyed. The economy had been resurrected and a fresh wave of prosperity from globalization was about to reach the country from China. Britain was finally back on the road to where it felt comfortable, a beacon of liberalism, just as Blair had hoped, only one that was happy being a part of Europe without ever quite being *of* it. But now a very different future beckoned. Cameron had lost. Leave had won.

Anchoring the BBC's referendum coverage, as he had done for every general election since 1979, David Dimbleby uttered the words few had thought possible. 'At twenty minutes to five, we can say the decision taken in 1975 by this country to join the Common Market has been reversed by this referendum to leave the EU.' There was no way back for Remain. 'It looks like the gap is going to be something like fifty-two to forty-eight, so a four-point lead for leaving the EU, and that's the result of this referendum which has been preceded by weeks and months of argument and the rest of it. And the British people have spoken, and the answer is: we're out.'

Shortly afterwards, Farage emerged from the Leave.EU offices to declare a revolution. 'We have done it without having to fight . . . without a bullet being fired,' he said – jarringly, given recent events – rocking back on his heels, face thrust forward. Across the river, in the Vote Leave offices in Westminster tower, Johnson was 'punching the air like Maradona'. Cummings chose that moment to tell Johnson that, on the first day of his premiership, he must announce the extra £100 million per week for the NHS that Vote Leave had pledged. 'Absolutely,' Johnson replied, in Cummings' recollection. 'Absolutely. We must do this, no question, we'll park our tanks everywhere.'

Just a few hours later, that prospect was in sight as Cameron walked out of Number Ten and announced his resignation. 'I do not think it would be right for me to try to be the captain that steers our country to its next destination,' he declared, voice wobbling. A new prime minister would be in place by the Conservative Party Conference in October, and he would leave it to them to decide how and when to leave.

Over at Vote Leave, Johnson paid tribute to his old school

friend, saying he agreed that the formal process of withdrawal – the triggering of Gisela Stuart's exit clause – should not begin just yet. The Labour leader Jeremy Corbyn – who, like Theresa May, had played a distinctly low-profile role in the campaign – had other ideas, however, and called for the process to begin immediately. This declaration sparked such indignation that it almost swept him from office, as Labour shadow ministers began resigning from the front bench and declaring no confidence. Over the course of that day, billions of pounds were wiped off the stock market, the pound plunged to a thirty-one-year low and Scotland's first minister Nicola Sturgeon announced that a second independence referendum was now 'highly likely'.

Boris Johnson, meanwhile, went to play cricket, his own dreams of glory seemingly coming together without the need for panic. On Saturday, Gove called to offer his full support, striking a deal to become Johnson's campaign manager, chancellor *and* future lead Brexit negotiator. With Theresa May emerging as the only real alternative candidate, Johnson and Gove were keen to bring Andrea Leadsom on board to show a united Vote Leave front. By Wednesday afternoon, Leadsom had been promised a 'top three' job in government to join the ticket – either deputy prime minister, chancellor or lead Brexit negotiator, only one of which was available. She asked that Johnson make the offer public, but, when that did not happen, Leadsom declared her own leadership bid. When Gove discovered what had happened, he told friends he was dismayed by Johnson's mismanagement and then called a meeting of his advisers to consider whether he too should stand. Tellingly, neither Dougie Smith nor Dominic Cummings was invited.

The basic atoms of life, as Dominic Cummings called them, were colliding. In the turmoil of revolution, 'fear, self-interest and vanity' had been let loose. And the rest is history: Gove's 'stab in the back'; the sugar rush of political adrenalin; and then the crash that followed, as Boris Johnson took to the stage that had been prepared for his campaign launch to declare instead that his leadership ambitions were over. In a flash, British politics had turned on its axis. After Johnson announced his withdrawal, he went to ground. Gove's extraordinary gambit, meanwhile, backfired. He did not have the numbers, as Dominic Cummings and Dougie Smith had always warned, which is why they had not been consulted. But there Gove stood, he could do no other. He had not accepted his destiny, but he scorched the earth all the same, finishing third behind Theresa May and Andrea Leadsom in the second ballot of MPs.

The revolution finally appeared to come to a conclusion when Andrea Leadsom pulled out of the race after giving a disastrous interview in which she seemed to suggest that being a mother gave her more of a stake in the future of the country than her opponent, who had no children. The leadership was May's. The dashing generals of Vote Leave had won their revolution, only to turn on each other instead of securing the crown.

With Leadsom's departure, the Brexiteers had lost their last representative in the leadership race. She had been there with Roger Scruton and Matthew Elliott at Jessica Douglas-Home's country home when Business for Britain was born. She had led the 'Fresh Start' group of Conservative MPs drawing up plans for the future. Now, she was just another minister, much like Boris Johnson, who had been offered yet another political lifeline as foreign secretary. Watching with sardonic amusement, Dominic Cummings hunkered down at home to think and read. The job of enacting Brexit would fall to others. Leaving was not in doubt, it seemed. Theresa May had committed herself to enacting the result of the referendum – 'Brexit means Brexit' – and so had Jeremy Corbyn, even if he was now fighting to remain as Labour leader. Each side agreed there would be no second referendum.

His part in the Brexit revolution now complete, Cummings typed out a note to the man who had made it possible: Norman Stone. 'Dear Norman,' he began. 'Just wanted to say that you were the intellectual godfather of our victory and thanks again and again for the fantastic tutorials you gave me – I was clearly one of your thickest students but I learned a thing or two from the old monster Bismarck along the way that proved v useful!' Stone, who had recently moved to Hungary for what he hoped to be his retirement, replied shortly after. 'Oh you. SOOO much to say, I've followed it all of course from Turkey and now Budapest. Superb performance, a line-up of all the right enemies.'[57]

Neither Cummings nor Stone were in attendance when the Brexit tribes came back together in September for Rodney Leach's memorial service in Knightsbridge, as Jessica Douglas-Home endured the loss of a second husband. The list of attendees reads like a shadow cast from a lost world: the Earl of Home, cousin of Jessica's first husband Charlie, and nephew of the former prime minister and foreign secretary who helped take Britain into the EU under Heath; Baroness Rawlings, a regular at Jessica and Rodney's Norfolk gatherings; Lord Powell and Lord Lawson, the two Thatcherite greats providing the connection to the Lady whose shadow continued to fall on British public life. Then there were the MPs: Michael Gove, the teenage Powellite who entered Leach's world through Jessica and her band of High Tory philosophers; Andrea Leadsom, the accidental history maker; Jacob Rees-Mogg, future carrier of the Brexit flame; and even David Cameron, the man who toiled for Remain, but was levelled by the wind.

It was left to Rodney's daughter, Alice, to capture the moment by reading T. S. Eliot's 'Little Gidding':

> We are born with the dead:
> See, they return, and bring us with them.
> The moment of the rose and the moment of the yew-tree
> Are of equal duration. A people without history
> Is not redeemed from time, for history is a pattern
> Of timeless moments. So, while the light fails
> On a winter's afternoon, in a secluded chapel
> History is now and England.[58]

Five years earlier, Roger Scruton had written of his awe for this poem, claiming that its atmosphere 'stays in the mind of every cultivated Englishman'. For Scruton, the importance of 'Little Gidding' was not just that it captured an atmosphere he cherished about England, but also 'the core belief of modern conservatism' as he understood it. This was the belief in inheritance and history, what Edmund Burke described as the contract between the living and the dead and those yet to be born. 'We are born with the dead.'

For Scruton, Eliot's poem captured this insight. A people cannot escape their history, for they *are* their history. 'Therefore, we must listen to the voices of the dead, and capture their meaning in those brief, elusive moments when "History is now and England",' Scruton wrote.[59] Little comes closer to capturing Britain's long, painful relationship with Europe than this image, 'a pattern of timeless moments' stretching back through those men and women from another time – Ted Heath and Margaret Thatcher, Jean Monnet and Enoch Powell – and beyond them, to the England that came before. The pattern will continue, for we too are born with those that came before.

Conclusion

'What we call the beginning is often the end.' So it proved in 2016. The elevation of Theresa May to the premiership was not the beginning of a new story for Britain, for the old one had not yet finished.

The month after mourners had assembled to pay their respects to Rodney Leach, May delivered her first speech to the Conservative Party Conference as prime minister. She had been in the job for a little over two months, but, like James Callaghan forty years earlier, seemed comfortable in the role history had handed her.

In her first act as prime minister, she had promised a country that worked 'not for a privileged few, but for every one of us.' And with that, the Cameron era was brought to a close. By August, the Conservative Party had surged into a fourteen-point lead in the polls and May was at the height of her powers, redefining conservatism, 'in terms appropriate to the times', as Tom Nairn had once put it.[1] 'Brexit means Brexit – and we're going to make a success of it,' May declared at the Conservative Party Conference. Iron Britannia was back: *Very well, alone*.

At this point, May staked out four Brexit principles that she hoped would define her premiership. The United Kingdom would leave as one country, she said. Free movement would end. EU law would no longer apply after Brexit. And the formal process of withdrawal would begin no later than March 2017. The audience loved it.

Watching on in Brussels, however, Britain's ambassador Ivan Rogers was in despair. Setting a timetable to enact Article 50 of the Lisbon Treaty – the formal mechanism for departure – 'forfeited at a stroke any leverage over how that process would run,' he declared.[2] Dominic Cummings thought similarly, insisting the British government should only begin the process of withdrawal once it had agreed its future relationship with the EU. 'We will negotiate the terms of a new deal before we start any legal process to leave,' the Vote Leave prospectus read. By October, May had concluded this was not feasible.

The decision would be the first of many that May would take over the course of her first year as prime minister that would lead not only to her own downfall, but to one of the most ignominious periods in British public life since 1945. From the moment Britain gave notice of its intention to leave on 29 March 2017, the government entered a process it could not control.

Was there ever a realistic alternative? As early as 11.57 a.m. on 24 June 2016, EU leaders had released a statement ruling out any talks on the future relationship until formal notification of Article 50 had been received. Perhaps, with more determination, a prime minister of greater substance could have changed their minds. Or perhaps not.

Either way, the extent to which the EU had taken control of the process emerged in April 2017 when the continent's leaders met in Brussels to respond to Britain's formal notice of withdrawal. A set of 'negotiating guidelines' were unveiled, setting out how the process would work. There would be a 'phased approach' to the talks, the EU declared. The UK would have to settle all its outstanding debts and guarantee the rights of EU citizens living in Britain before the EU would discuss Britain's priorities. It would also have to agree a solution to the Irish border dilemma.[3]

The problem was that May had made two seemingly contradictory pledges: one, that there would be no return 'to the borders of the past' in Ireland; but also, two, that the UK as a whole would leave the EU's customs union and single market, creating the need for border controls in Ireland.

Before negotiations began, Theresa May made the next fateful – and ultimately fatal – decision of her premiership: a snap election. The casus belli was, apparently, a speech from the shadow Brexit secretary Keir Starmer, threatening to vote against a future withdrawal agreement unless it met the new Brexit secretary David Davis's promise that Britain would retain the 'exact same benefits' outside the EU as it had inside. The seven-week campaign that followed was among the most extraordinary in British electoral history, as Jeremy Corbyn clawed back a twenty-point deficit in the polls to deny Theresa May a majority. For the next two years, May would stagger on, trying to lead Britain out of the EU, without the strength to do so.

As the scale of Britain's weakness in the negotiations became apparent, Westminster was slowly consumed by a paralysis it seemed powerless to reverse. By December 2017, desperate to move to the next phase of the negotiations, May agreed to what became known as the Irish 'backstop', promising to maintain 'full alignment' in all areas necessary to keep the border open.[4] At a stroke, she had broken at least one of the red lines she had set out in her speech to the Conservative Party Conference the year before. Either EU law would continue to apply to the whole of the UK after Brexit, or, at the very least, to Northern Ireland alone.

The consequences of May's concession became clear in February 2018, when the EU released its first draft withdrawal agreement. 'The territory of Northern Ireland . . . shall be considered to be part of the customs territory of the [European] Union,' the proposed text declared.[5] Later that day, May told MPs that 'no UK prime minister could ever agree' to such a clause.[6]

The scale of Britain's proposed integration with the EU after Brexit became even clearer over the summer of 2018 with the publication of May's 'Chequers proposal' for the future relationship, calling for a 'common rule book' between the UK and EU.

The first cabinet resignations began soon after. First, David Davis quit in protest; twenty-four hours later, Boris Johnson followed suit. May was no longer conjuring up the spirit of Margaret Thatcher, but that of John Major.

After the terms of withdrawal were finally reached in November 2018, the inevitable leadership challenge came. Though May survived, her position was now fatally weakened. When she put the withdrawal agreement to MPs in January 2019, it was rejected in the biggest parliamentary defeat for a British government in history. Still May stumbled on, putting a revised withdrawal agreement to MPs in March, only for it to be rejected again. A third attempt was made a few weeks later, with the same result. Soon, MPs began agitating for different forms of Brexit, but no majority could be found for any. Over the course of March 2019, MPs voted against not only a 'no deal' exit, but eight alternative forms of withdrawal. The paralysis was complete.

In 1969, as Britain weighed up entry into the Common Market, Enoch Powell condemned the country for becoming 'a nation of ditherers who refuse to make up our minds.' Almost half a century on, his judgement – in this regard, at least – seemed to have come to pass. The cause of Britain's paralysis, however, was not so much indecision as division. Unlike 1975, the decision of 2016 had never been fully accepted by its opponents. Rival camps had formed, Remainers and Leavers, each committed to their cause – but neither could assemble a majority in the House of Commons.

Watching this spectacle unfold was Nigel Farage, who had quit UKIP that year because, as he put it, it had become 'obsessed with the issue of Islam' and the figure of Tommy Robinson. Instead, Farage had formed a new party, the Brexit Party, which would stand in the European parliamentary elections in May 2019, demanding that Brexit be enacted. Farage's new party stormed to victory. The Conservatives were pushed into fifth place and were now facing potential annihilation. A day after the European election, May announced her resignation. Britain would soon have its third prime minister in four years.

A few weeks later, one of the great characters of Britain's Brexit drama departed the stage. Norman Stone was seventy-eight when he died in Budapest, in June 2019, after a short illness. He had moved to Hungary from Turkey a few years earlier, but he was growing tired of life abroad. At the end of his wanderings, Stone's mind was turning to home.

For many who knew and loved him, his passing was a moment of deep sadness. For others, it was an opportunity for revenge. In *The Guardian*, the former Regius professor of history at Cambridge, Richard Evans, dismissed Stone as a second-rate historian concerned with little more than his own personal prejudices. Four decades after Stone's evisceration of E. H. Carr, the left had paid him back in kind. Evans' obituary concluded that, while Ted Heath may have been wrong about many things in his life, he was surely right to have been 'both horrified and disgusted that the higher education of our children should rest in the hands of such a man.'[7] Even in death, the enmities of Stone's life lived on.

Whatever Heath's views about Stone, many of his former students, friends and colleagues appeared to feel otherwise. At a memorial service at St Martin-in-the-Fields that October, his fellow travellers turned out to show their respects, from John Casey to Roger Scruton, Nikolai Tolstoy, Jessica Douglas-Home, Bill Cash, Peter Lilley, Alan Sked and Robert Salisbury. Alongside them were figures who had been with Stone at significant moments of recent history: Niall Ferguson and Andrew Roberts at Oxford and Cambridge in the 1970s and '80s; Timothy Garton Ash and Charles Powell from the Chequers summit of 1990; and then, the men of the moment, Michael Gove and Dominic Cummings.

By the time of Stone's memorial service, Cummings was chief of staff to the new prime minister, Boris Johnson, and Gove, the errant stooge, was back as his votary running the Cabinet Office. Dougie Smith, meanwhile, was regularly moving between Number Ten and his base at Conservative Campaign Headquarters. To try to break the constitutional logjam, the new prime minister and Cummings pushed and probed, threatened and cajoled, before eventually ordering Parliament to be prorogued for five weeks from the beginning of September. In a moment of high drama, the Supreme Court ruled Johnson's prorogation unlawful and therefore null and void.

In the space of a few months, Johnson's premiership appeared to have collapsed. In a panic, he unleashed on Cummings in a telephone call from New York. 'You fucked me! You told me it would be fine.' Cummings urged calm. 'This is a win–win.'[8] He understood that the sight of the highest court in the land apparently handcuffing the prime minister would be the proof that Leave voters needed that Boris Johnson was the real deal. One person on the call that day said, from this moment until the election, Johnson backed Cummings without question.

Still, Johnson needed a deal with Brussels to break the impasse: 'Extracting a policy from a need,' as the French had remarked of the Schuman Plan seventy years earlier. To do so, Johnson delved deep into his stores of cynicism, agreeing a deal that was, at first glance, remarkable, removing the backstop entirely. On closer inspection, however, the price was that Northern Ireland would remain anchored to the EU. The sea border was back. It was, as Peregrine Worsthorne had written of Harold Wilson in 1976, 'another characteristic confidence trick.'[9]

Though Northern Ireland would remain, explicitly, part of the UK's customs territory under the terms of the new agreement – and Stormont given the right to reject its new, special status – the fact remained that EU law would continue to apply in Northern Ireland after Brexit, but not in mainland Britain. Faced with a choice between purity and pragmatism, Johnson had chosen the latter.

'Does the Right Honourable Lady understand – if she does not yet understand she soon will – that the penalty for treachery is to fall into public contempt?' Powell had demanded of Thatcher in 1985, as she prepared to sign the Anglo-Irish Agreement. There is little doubt that Powell, the intellectual godfather of Brexit, would have thought similarly of Johnson's deal with the EU.

Once Boris Johnson had secured his Brexit agreement in October 2019, he recalled Parliament for its first Saturday sitting since the Falklands War. Outside Parliament, meanwhile, a million people had gathered to protest in a final howl of resistance. The long-term sense of loss and dislocation that led so many to support Brexit had suddenly been reversed. Now, it was great swathes of liberal Britain that had lost their country and their sense of control.

Brexit was an expression of another England. Maurice Cowling had once written that Enoch Powell's unique role in the Tory party had been to attach 'the highest value to working-class opinion' because of its sympathy for his own opinions about Europe and immigration, but that he also understood 'the conception of a unity of national sentiment transcending the divisions of the classes.' Something similar is true of Brexit. Yet, much as the resistance to Powell had been intense, so too was the resistance to Brexit.

Inside Parliament, MPs postponed the moment of decision once more, passing a new law forcing Johnson to apply for yet another delay to Britain's withdrawal. A new exit date emerged: 31 January 2020. Yet, the resistance had passed its high-water mark. Sensing his opportunity, Johnson pushed for a general election.

The Liberal Democrats were first to break, then the Scottish National Party, forty years after it had cleared the way for Thatcher. Then, finally, Jeremy Corbyn's Labour. Johnson had the election he wanted – and on the terms he wanted, too. He promised to 'Get Brexit Done'. Labour, meanwhile, fell back on the tried and tested: another renegotiation and another referendum – 1975 in reverse.

As the general election of 12 December 2019 approached, Nigel Farage faced a defining moment in his career: to continue his own resistance to the terms of the withdrawal package by standing in every seat, risking Jeremy Corbyn as prime minister and thus losing Brexit; or to compromise by entering a pact with the Conservative Party. Farage chose to make a deal. His party would not stand in the 317 seats the Tories had won at the last general election. Farage later complained about the pressure he came under to go further: 'It was a guy called Dougie Smith.'

The result was decisive: the biggest Tory victory since 1987. The resistance was over. Tony Blair, who had led the push for a second referendum, raised the white flag and declared Britain now had to make the best of Brexit, his dreams of Britain's future at the heart of Europe little more than a fading memory from another age. When Parliament returned, MPs quickly backed Johnson's withdrawal agreement. Britain would leave the EU at 11 p.m. on 31 January 2020, forty-three years after it had joined the Common Market. Before it did so, however, another giant of the Brexit march passed from the scene.

Roger Scruton was seventy-five when he died from cancer. His funeral was held at Malmesbury Abbey, Wiltshire, near his family farm. In the year before his death, Scruton had been honoured by the nations whose memories he had fought to save. The Polish government presented him with the Grand Cross of the Order of Merit; the Czech parliament followed suit with its own award; and finally, in a ceremony in London just weeks before his death, Viktor Orbán presented him with his country's Order of Merit.

The Hungarian leader returned to Britain a few weeks later to attend the funeral, joining those other counter-revolutionaries who had been drawn to Scruton's struggle to recapture what had been lost, as he once described the romantic core of conservatism. Without this 'consciousness of death', as he put it, 'the world *cannot be loved for what it is.*'[10] Now, Scruton himself was gone. At the funeral, one of his young apostles, Samuel Hughes, read from 'Little Gidding'.

Before he died, Scruton had written 'a personal response to the "Brexit" decision'. Published in 2017, *Where We Are* argued that the referendum was never about economics or geopolitics, but identity: 'Who are we, where are we, and what holds us together?'

The answers to these questions, Scruton wrote, did not lie in ideology or sociology, but history. 'It is a noteworthy fact about our country, that those with designs on its present have generally been inspired to adopt a vision of its past,' he observed. This was certainly true of Enoch Powell.

For Powell, what held the country together was the Crown-in-Parliament: the connecting thread which stretched back into the mists of old England. In Powell's mind, Britain's imperial adventure had left no real lasting mark, a mere passing phase in time, 'strange and brief.'

Yet, as Philip Larkin had once observed, the very experience of elsewhere serves to sharpen the experience of home. 'Lonely in Ireland, since it was not home,' Larkin had written of his time in Belfast, two decades before Powell's arrival in Northern Ireland: 'Their draughty streets . . . prove me separate'.

> Living in England has no such excuse:
> These are my customs and establishments
> It would be much more serious to refuse.
> Here no elsewhere underwrites my existence.[11]

Like Larkin, Britain was proved separate by its experience in Europe: lonely in Brussels, because it was not home. Yet, the question remains: *why* did Britain feel so lonely in Europe, when other countries did not?

One way to answer this question is to ask why 52 per cent of the country voted to leave the European Union on 23 June 2016. In Dominic Cummings' account, published six months after the vote, he dismissed any argument that alighted on 'one big factor'. It was, he said, largely a story of 'men going at it blind' as the great waves of history crashed over them.[12]

The decision by Michael Gove to join Vote Leave had been crucial. Gove cleared the way for Johnson. Together, the pair ensured that Nigel Farage did not have a more prominent role, which, Cummings argued, might have been enough for Remain to win. David Cameron's ineptitude was also a necessary condition: the decision to call the referendum in the first place, the choice of timing, the failed renegotiation, the weakness. Yet, in Cummings' estimation, 'the closest approximation to the truth' is that Leave won because 'three big powerful forces' collided to create the conditions in which Brexit was possible: the immigration crisis, the financial crisis and the euro crisis.

Much of Cummings' analysis is hard to dispute. Each crisis which washed over Europe in the years after 2007 served to reinforce the others. In 1992, Margaret Thatcher had warned that a Europe without internal borders, bound together by a single currency, risked the emergence of a 'thoroughly unwelcome alternative to the Euro-centrist political establishment' – which all came to pass.

Hanging over the long story of Britain's struggle with Europe, then, is a curious sense of dramatic tragedy: the doomed struggle against a future foretold. In 1990, Geoffrey Howe saw in Thatcher a rebel leader who could become an icon of Eurosceptic resistance if she was not stopped. And yet, by removing her from power, he only served to turn her into the very icon he feared. It was not Thatcher who created the conditions for Britain's eventual withdrawal, but those who ignored her warnings about the risks they were taking. Britain did not radicalize itself in a vacuum. Had the City of London and immigration policy been better regulated, and the European Union more limited in its ambition, the conditions for Britain's rebellion would not have existed.

Still, the waves which crashed over Britain from 2007 to 2016 crashed over much of the continent, too. So, the nagging question remains: why did Britain choose to leave the EU, when no other country did?

There are practical answers. Britain had not joined the euro, which made the prospect of withdrawal more plausible. As Ed Balls has argued, had Britain joined the euro before the financial crisis, the pain required to remain inside might well have been too great for the public to accept and Britain might have crashed out of the EU even earlier than 2016 – though, such counterfactuals are of course impossible to prove.[13]

At the heart of it all, an elemental truth remains. Membership of the EU and its institutions demands a *political* commitment to the European Union. 'Europe' is a project animated by a principle, Clement Attlee told MPs in 1950: 'A principle of the supranational authority.' As Attlee declared, the question was always: should Britain accept the principle? Britain never quite could.

For Scruton, the reason lay in the unique circumstances of Britain's history. Its island home, its language and common law, its Crown and its Parliament, each a layer of sediment creating a nation that could not feel at home in the Europe of Jean Monnet.

In 1950, when Monnet's Europe was born, no country on the continent was as powerful as Britain. Nor did any other country have a global nation beyond its borders, as Britain did. No other country had an Australia or a New Zealand, let alone a Commonwealth the size of Britain's. And no other country had a colony which had become an imperium. Each of these worlds pulled at Britain's imagination, begging that most elemental of questions: who are we?

On the continent, there was always a sense of British exceptionalism. 'What to do about England,' Monnet had wondered as he looked over his maps in Algiers, contemplating the future. When Helmut Kohl, the second honorary Citizen of Europe, died in 2017, eight current and former political leaders were asked to speak, including Emmanuel Macron, Angela Merkel, Bill Clinton and even Dmitry Medvedev. Theresa May was not asked, nor was John Major. When Jacques Delors, the third of Europe's *citoyen d'honneurs*, passed away in 2023, not a single UK government representative turned up to pay their respects. The lonely figure of Charles Grant, Delors' biographer, was the one Englishman who did.

For many in Britain, such stories are emblematic of the country's isolationism after 2016, its withdrawal from the world in pursuit of a fantasy of former glory. 'This is the story of fifty years in which Britain struggled to reconcile the past she could not forget with the future she could not avoid,' Hugo Young wrote in *This Blessed Plot* in 1998. In Young's account, the struggle against membership was a story of 'high political misjudgement'; this was not an opinion, he wrote, but surely an incontestable fact, 'proved by the outcome, Britain's presence inside the European apparatus.' With Britain now back outside the European apparatus, Young's thesis falls away on its own merits: if not disproven, then certainly unproven.

As Young himself wrote, Britain's relationship with 'Europe' is, in the end, a story about 'an attitude to history itself.' On the one hand, there is the Young view of history, the progressive account: a country struggling *against* its past to reach its future. This is the story that was displayed in technicolour in Danny Boyle's opening ceremony of 2012, and subsequently set out in hostile accounts of Brexit written in the aftermath of the referendum: Britain, nostalgic for empire, lost in the memories of its faded past.

The alternative story is the conservative one: 'The proud people, who defended their "sceptred isle" for a millennium,' as Scruton put it. Here we find the country born in the vicissitudes of war, mythologized by Churchill, its warrior bard. As Scruton acknowledged, *both* stories contain essential truths and, just as importantly, 'Both look backwards, in order to offer a story of how we have become what we are.'[14] Britain's attitude to its own history is neither static, nor inevitable, but contested. 'We live with two rival conceptions of our past,' Scruton wrote, 'standing to either side of the central icon, like warring heraldic beasts.'

Each story was on display as the day of Britain's withdrawal from the European Union arrived: 'Brexit Day', 31 January 2020. 'A New Dawn For Britain', ran the *Daily Mail*, above an image of the White Cliffs of Dover. *The Sun* declared '30 years of resistance to the creeping danger of a European superstate' finally over. For *The Daily Telegraph*, meanwhile, a more poetic epitaph was chosen: 'This is not an end, but a beginning'.

For *The Guardian*, another mood was captured: 'Small Island'. *The Herald* declared Britain 'isolated, worse off, weaker and divided'. *The Independent*, meanwhile, asked whether it was 'inevitable that we will rejoin?'

For all the passion of the previous three years, the climax was remarkable more for the bathos of the moment than the drama. 'Britain bows out with a mixture of optimism and regret', ran the *Financial Times*. VE Day had not arrived. Britain had entered a transition period in which yet more negotiations were required, this time over the trade deal that would replace EU membership. Britain had entered the Common Market in 1973 with a weary shrug of acceptance, and, after a tumultuous few years, it was leaving in much the same way.

It is tempting, therefore, to reach for the Powellite conclusion to this tale: wandering Britain, returning home to the Shire, unaffected by its journey. Yet, just as this account of Britain's imperial legacy appears fantastical today, so too does the idea that Britain's European adventure has left no mark at all, or is, somehow, finally settled. The most ironic quirk of Brexit, perhaps, is that it sparked Britain's first populist movement for Europe, not simply as a sensible economic arrangement, but a source of belonging and identity. The continent itself, meanwhile, cannot be wished away, nor can the project at its heart: the Europe of Jean Monnet.

In the end, Britain's years of wandering *did* matter. A new layer of sediment was added to the nation's history, which in turn will shape the future. The story of Britain and Europe is not one of destiny, in or out. It is one of timeless moments washing over the country, 'for history is a pattern.' The tide will roll on, the same dilemmas repeating themselves, each new and yet familiar; Britain standing between the waves of a past it half remembers and a future it cannot know.

Acknowledgements

This book is the product of many years of work, during which I have leaned on the advice, patience and support of so many people – from family and friends to colleagues, mentors and those I consider inspirations. I am thankful to them all.

I realize now that the idea for the book was born in a period when I was reading obsessively about American politics. Like so many others, I had become infatuated with the work of Robert Caro: the scale of his ambition; the sweeping scenes of the Texas Hill Country; the Shakespearean characters. From Caro I moved to Rick Perlstein and his account of the great conservative counter-revolution of the 1960s, *Before the Storm*. I remember marvelling once more at the size of the canvas on which these American writers were working.

It was at about this time, not long after Britain had voted for Brexit, that I came across Hugo Young's *This Blessed Plot*. It was a revelation. What a piece of work. What ambition. What writing. I was stunned by the clarity of Young's account and the honesty of his analysis. And yet there was also a gaping hole that had opened up in his history of Britain's relationship with Europe. 'High political misjudgement is the thread running through this history,' Young wrote from his vantage point in 1998. 'This is not an opinion, but a surely incontestable fact. It is proved by the outcome, Britain's presence inside the European apparatus.' This sentence stopped me in my tracks. *Proved by the outcome*. So what would Young write today?

These were the influences for *Between the Waves*. Could I tell the story of how Britain's Eurosceptics went from the defeated and divided outsiders to unlikely victors, much as the American conservatives had done in Rick Perlstein's account? And could I do so while capturing the deeper historical currents at play? These were my goals when I began thinking about this book.

I was helped by a number of fortuitous events in my life which – together – made this book possible. The first was being made redundant. At the time, of course, I didn't see it quite like this. In 2015 I had landed my dream job: political editor of the first newspaper I had ever worked for, the *Independent on Sunday*. Under the guidance of James Hanning – my first mentor – and Lisa Markwell, my editor, I first began to stretch my legs, journalistically. And then, four months into the job, the newspaper folded.

The next great influence on my career was Matt Kaminski, the editor in chief of *Politico Europe*. Matt introduced me to the world of American magazine writing, allowing me to bury into the world of Brexit and its personalities with an eye on the historic nature of what was happening, without which this book would not have been possible. Matt also gave me the space to write my first book with Tim Ross, *Betting the House: The Inside Story of the 2017 General Election*. This was my first taste of book writing – and the source of my craving for more.

From *Politico*, I made perhaps the most important move of my career after the *Independent on Sunday*, joining the *Atlantic* in 2019, where I fell under the influence of Jeff Goldberg. It was at the *Atlantic* where I finally found the confidence to write in my own voice and at scale. For that alone I will be for ever indebted to those who made that possible: Jeff, of course, but also my editor Prashant Rao, Yoni Applebaum, Denise Willis, Matt Seaton, John Hendrickson, Helen Lewis and many others.

During my time at the *Atlantic*, three further fortuitous events occurred. First, I got to know Tom Holland. Then Helen Thompson. And finally my agent, Toby Mundy. Tom, Helen and Toby have each been crucial influences on this book. First, over a number of beers at the best pub in London – the Blythe Hill Tavern – Tom encouraged me not only to take the plunge, but to write the most ambitious book I had in me. It was this advice which turned this book from a work which I first envisaged beginning in London in 1990 to the one that opens in Algiers in 1942. It was Tom who brought me together with Helen over dinner, for which I will for ever be grateful. Helen is a genius and a lovely person who has offered advice and inspiration from beginning to end. I want to dedicate a special thank you to Helen.

And then a word for Toby, without whom this book would never have got off the ground. Toby has encouraged and guided me through the entire process and is both a pleasure to work with and excellent at his job. It was also Toby who guided me into the hands of Picador and my editor, George Morley, who has been a delight, improving the book and steering it to publication with skill and wisdom, alongside Alpana Sajip.

While I began this book at the *Atlantic*, much of it was written during my time at *UnHerd*, where I was supported with patience and understanding by Freddie Sayers, Sally Chatterton, Jacob Furedi and the rest of the team. Thank you to them all for bearing with me. A special mention here must go to Nick Harris, who read and re-read (and re-read again) the early drafts of this book until I felt as though he knew it better than I did. Nick has provided excellent suggestions throughout, improving the book in immeasurable ways, for which I am both grateful and impressed. Thank you.

Beyond all of these people, I would like to thank the following people for their guidance, advice, expertise and willingness to hear me out: Dominic Sandbrook, John Gray, Anand Menon, Dean Godson, John Bew, Paul Bew, James Vitali, Anthony Barnett, Luke Douglas-Home, Simon Heffer, Charles Moore, Jonathan Rutherford, Colin Yeo and many others who know who they are.

I would also like to thank the many people I have interviewed – including those who showed considerable patience as they agreed to re-interviews: Patrick Robertson, Jonathan Powell, Andrew Duff, Dominic Cummings, Nigel Farage, Michael Gove, Peter Mandelson, Roger Liddle, Gisela Stuart, Matthew Elliott, James Frayne, Ed Balls. There are others who, again, know who they are.

Throughout the writing process I've also relied on the work

of journalists and historians, without which this book would be far poorer. There are too many to name in full, but special mention must go to the work of Charles Moore, Simon Heffer, Ben Pimlott, Charles Grant, François Duchêne, Tom Nairn, D. R. Thorpe, Michael Crick, Tim Shipman, Mark Dooley, Sonia Purnell, John Campbell, Stephen Wall, Simon Kuper, Robert Saunders, Philip Warner, Andrew Gimson, Peter Hennessy, David Edgerton and Duncan Weldon.

Finally, I would like to thank my friends and family who have looked on as I have disappeared into this book many times over the course of the past few years. To my parents, who gave me everything and continue to do so; my brother and sisters whom I love; my Nan, who is an inspiration beyond words; Leo, Phoebe and Annabel, the shining lights of my life. And, most importantly of all, to Louise. We are not good at being soppy, but she is the best thing to have ever happened to me: the heart and brain of our partnership in life. Without her taking the strain in a way that has often been beyond reasonable, I simply could not have written this book and stayed sane. I fear it will not be the last time I write something like this.

Between the Waves has one name on the cover, but many authors. To all of those who made it possible, I can only finish with a simple thank you – you let me dive deeply into a world I did not know existed. Hopefully it was worth it.

Tom McTague
London
May 2025

Bibliography

Ackroyd, Peter, *T. S. Eliot* (London: Penguin Books, 1993)

Aitken, Jonathan, *Margaret Thatcher, Power and Personality* (London: Bloomsbury, 2013)

Aitken, Jonathan, *Pride and Perjury* (London: HarperCollins, 2000)

Ashdown, Paddy, *A Fortunate Life: The Autobiography of Paddy Ashdown* (London: Aurum Press, 2009)

Ashdown, Paddy, *The Ashdown Diaries: Volume Two 1997–1999* (London: Allen Lane, 2001)

Balls, Ed, *Speaking Out: Lessons in Life and Politics* (London: Arrow Books, 2016)

Barrington, Nicholas, *Envoy: A Diplomatic Journey* (London: Bloomsbury Publishing, 2014)

Bew, John, *Realpolitik: A History* (Oxford: Oxford University Press, 2016)

Blair, Tony, *A Journey* (London: Arrow Books, 2011)

Blake, Robert, *Disraeli* (London: Faber & Faber, 1969)

Bogdanor, Vernon, *The Monarchy and the Constitution* (Oxford: Oxford University Press, 1995)

Cameron, David, *For the Record* (London: William Collins, 2019)

Campbell, Alastair, *The Alastair Campbell Diaries, Volume One: Prelude to Power 1994–1997* (London: Random House, 2010)

Campbell, Alastair, *The Alastair Campbell Diaries, Volume Two: Power and the People, 1997–1999* (London: Hutchinson, 2011)

Campbell, John, *Edward Heath, A Biography* (London: Jonathan Cape, 1993)

Churchill, Winston S., *Secret Session Speeches* (New York: Rosetta Books, Kindle Edition, 2013)

Churchill, Winston S., *The Hinge of Fate* (New York: Rosetta Books, Kindle Edition, 2013)

Churchill, Winston S., *Winston Churchill's Speeches: Never Give In!* (London: Pimlico, 2007)

Collin, Matthew, *Altered State: The Story of Ecstasy Culture and Acid House* (London: Serpent's Tail, 1998)

Connelly, Toby, *Brexit and Ireland* (London: Penguin, 2018)

Corthorn, Paul, *Enoch Powell: Politics and Ideas in Modern Britain* (Oxford: Oxford University Press, 2019)

Cowling, Maurice, ed., *Conservative Essays* (London: Cassell, 1978)

Cowling, Maurice, *Mill and Liberalism* (Cambridge: Cambridge University Press, 2nd edn., 1990)

Craig, David and Elliott, Matthew, *The Great European Rip-Off: How the Corrupt, Wasteful EU is Taking Control of Our Lives* (London: Random House, 2009)

Crick, Michael, *One Party After Another: The Disruptive Life of Nigel Farage* (London: Simon & Schuster UK, 2022)

Crowley, Alex, *Victory in London: The Inside Story of the Boris Campaign* (Epsom: Bretwalda Books, 2012)

Crozier, Brian, *Free Agent: The Unseen War 1941–1991* (London: HarperCollins, 1993)

Daniel, Mark, *Cranks and Gadflies: The Story of UKIP* (London: Timewell Press, 2005)

Dooley, Mark, *The Roger Scruton Reader* (London: Continuum, 2009)

Douglas-Home, Jessica, *Once Upon Another Time: Ventures Behind The Iron Curtain* (Norwich: Michael Russel Publishing, 2000)

Duchêne, François, *Jean Monnet, The First Statesman of Interdependence* (New York: W.W. Norton, 1994)

Duff, Andrew, *Britain and the Puzzle of European Union* (London: Routledge, 2022)

Eade, Charles, *The War Speeches of Winston Churchill. Volume 2* (London: Cassell, 1965)

Eden, Anthony, *Full Circle: The Memoirs of Sir Anthony Eden* (London: Cassell, 1960)

El-Enany, Nadine, *(B)ordering Britain: Law, Race and Empire* (Manchester: Manchester University Press, 2020)

Eliot, T. S., 'Little Gidding', *Four Quartets* series (London: Faber & Faber, 1942)

Elliott, Francis and Hanning, James, *Cameron: Practically a Conservative* (London: Fourth Estate, 2012)

Elliott, Matthew & Rotherham, Lee, *The Bumper Book of Government Waste: The Scandal of the Squandered Billions from Lord Irvine's Wallpaper to EU Saunas* (Petersfield: Harriman House, 2006)

Etheridge, Bill, *The Rise of UKIP* (Epsom: Bretwalda Books, 2014)

Evans, Timothy, *Conservative Radicalism: A Sociology of Conservative Party Youth Structures and Libertarians 1970–1992* (Oxford: Berghahn Books, 1996)

Farage, Nigel, *Flying Free* (London: Biteback, 2011)

Fernández-Armesto, Felipe, *A History of England 1945–2000* (London: The Folio Society, 2001)

Fraser, Hugh, *A Rebel For The Right Reasons, A Selection of Speeches and Writings of Hugh Fraser* (Stafford and Stone Conservative Association, 1975)

Gardiner, George, *A Bastard's Tale: The Political Memoirs of George Gardiner* (London: Aurum Press, 1999)

Goldsmith, James, *The Response* (London: Macmillan, 1995)
Goldsmith, James, *The Trap* (London: Macmillan, 1994)
Gordon, Lyndall, *The Imperfect Life of T. S. Eliot* (London: Virago, 1998)
Gove, Michael, *Michael Portillo: The Future of the Right* (London: Fourth Estate, 1995)
Grant, Charles, *Delors: Inside the House That Jacques Built* (London: Nicholas Brealey, 1994)
Guicciardini, Francesco, *Maxims and Reflections (Ricordi)* (Philadelphia: University of Pennsylvania Press, 1992)
Halcrow, Morrison, *Keith Joseph: A Single Mind* (London: Macmillan, 1989)
Harris, Ralph, *Ralph Harris In His Own Words, The Selected Writings of Lord Harris* (Cheltenham: Edward Elgar Publishing, 2008)
Heath, Edward, *Travels: Peoples and Places in My Life* (London: Sidgwick & Jackson, 1977)
Heffer, Simon, *Like the Roman: The Life of Enoch Powell* (London: Faber & Faber, 2014)
Hutchins, Chris & Midgley, Dominic, *Goldsmith: Money, Women and Power* (London: Neville Ness House, 2015)
Iremonger, Lucille, *The Fiery Chariot* (London: Secker & Warburg, 1970)
Jackson, Julian, *A Certain Idea of France, The Life of Charles de Gaulle* (London: Penguin Books, 2019)
Jackson, Julian, *France: The Dark Years 1940–1944* (Oxford: Oxford University Press, 2001)
Johnson, Boris, *Have I Got Views for You* (London: Harper Perennial, 2008)
Kuper, Simon, *Chums: How a Tiny Caste of Oxford Tories took over the UK* (London: Profile Books, 2022)
Larkin, Philip, *Collected Poems* (London: Faber & Faber, 2003)
Laws, David, *Coalition: The Inside Story of the Conservative–Liberal Democrat Coalition Government* (Hull: Bitebac,k 2016)
Leach, Rodney, *Europe: A Concise Encyclopaedia of the European Union from Aachen to Zollverein* (London: Profile Books, 1998)
Ledwidge, Frank, *Losing Small Wars: British Military Failure in Iraq and Afghanistan* (London: Yale University Press, 2012)
Levitas, Ruth, *The Ideology of the New Right* (Cambridge: Polity Press, 1986)
Liddle, Roger, *The Europe Dilemma: Britain and the Drama of EU Integration* (London: I.B. Tauris, 2014)
Macmillan, Harold, *Tides of Fortune 1945–1955* (London: Macmillan, 1969)
Macmillan, Harold, *War Diaries: The Mediterranean 1943–1945* (London: Macmillan, 1984)
Major, John, *John Major: The Autobiography* (London: HarperCollins, 1999)

Mayne, Richard & Pinder, John, *Federal Union: The Pioneers* (London: Macmillan, 1990)

Miller, David W., *Queen's Rebels* (Dublin: University College Dublin Press, 2007)

Monnet, Jean, *Memoirs* (New York: Doubleday, 1978)

Moore, Charles, *Margaret Thatcher, The Authorized Biography, Volume One: Not For Turning* (London: Allen Lane, 2013)

Moore, Charles, *Margaret Thatcher, The Authorized Biography, Volume Two: Everything She Wants* (London: Allen Lane, 2015)

Moore, Charles, *Margaret Thatcher, The Authorized Biography, Volume Three: Herself Alone* (London: Allen Lane, 2019)

Morgan, Kenneth O., *A Life: Michael Foot* (London: Harper Collins, 2007)

Nairn, Tom, *The Break-up of Britain: Crisis and Neo-nationalism* (Champaign, Illinois: Common Ground Publishing, [1997], 25th Anniversary Edition, 2015)

Oakeshott, Michael, *Rationalism in Politics and Other Essays* (London: Methuen, 1962)

Oakeshott, Michael, *Social and Political Doctrines of Contemporary Europe* (Cambridge: Cambridge University Press, 1939)

Parkinson, Roger, *A Day's March Nearer Home: The War History from Alamein to VE Day Based on the War Cabinet Papers of 1942–1945* (London: Granada Publishing Limited, 1974)

Perlstein, Rick, *Before the Storm* (New York: Nation Books, 2009)

Pimlott, Ben, *Harold Wilson* (London: William Collins, 2016)

Powell, John Enoch, *Collected Poems* (London: Bellew Publishing, 1990)

Powell, John Enoch, *Dancer's End and The Wedding Gift* (London: The Falcon Press, 1951)

Priestly, J. B., *The Edwardians* (London: William Heinemann, 1970)

Purnell, Sonia, *Just Boris: A Tale of Blond Ambition* (London: Aurum, 2011)

Rentoul, John, *Tony Blair: Prime Minister* (London: Warner Books, 2001)

Robertson, Patrick, *Reshaping Europe in the Twenty-First Century* (London: Macmillan, 1992)

Robinson, Colin, *Arthur Seldon: A Life for Liberty* (London: Profile Books, 2009)

Rogers, Ivan, *9 Lessons in Brexit* (London: Short Books, 2019)

Rotherham, Lee, *Ten Years On: Britain Without the European Union* (London: The TaxPayers' Alliance, 2009)

Rutherford, Jonathan, *Forever England. Reflections on Masculinity and Empire* (London: Lawrence and Wishart, 1997)

Sandbrook, Dominic, *Seasons in the Sun: The Battle for Britain, 1974–1979* (London: Allen Lane, 2012)

Sandbrook, Dominic, *State of Emergency: The Way We Were: Britain, 1970–1974* (London: Penguin, 2011)

Sandbrook, Dominic, *White Heat: A History of Britain in the Swinging Sixties* (London: Abacus, 2006)

Saunders, Robert, *Yes to Europe! The 1975 Referendum and Seventies Britain* (Cambridge: Cambridge University Press, 2018)

Scruton, Roger, *Against the Tide: The Best of Roger Scruton's Columns, Commentaries and Criticism* (Bloomsbury: Continuum, 2022)

Scruton, Roger, *Culture Counts* (New York, NY: Encounter Books, 2018)

Scruton, Roger, *Gentle Regrets: Thoughts from a Life* (London: Continuum, 2005)

Scruton, Roger, *The Meaning of Conservatism Third Edition* (South Bend, Indiana: St. Augustine's Press, 2002)

Scruton, Roger, *The Need for Nations* (London: Civitas, 2004)

Scruton, Roger, *Where We Are* (London: Bloomsbury, 2017)

Shipman, Tim, *All Out War: The Full Story of How Brexit Sank Britain's Political Class* (London: William Collins, 2016)

Shipman, Tim, *Fall Out: A Year of Political Mayhem* (London: William Collins, 2017)

Shipman, Tim, *No Way Out. Brexit: From The Backstop to Boris* (London: William Collins, 2024)

Shipman, Tim, *Out: How Brexit Got Done and the Tories Were Undone* (London: William Collins, 2024)

Sisman, Adam, *Hugh Trevor-Roper: The Biography* (London: Orion, 2010)

Spicer, Michael, *A Treaty Too Far: A New Policy for Europe* (London: Fourth Estate, 1992)

Spicer, Michael, *The Spicer Diaries* (London: Biteback, 2012)

Stone, Norman, *The Atlantic and Its Enemies* (London: Allen Lane, 2010)

Thompson, Helen, *Disorder: Hard Times in the 21st Century* (Oxford: Oxford University Press, 2022)

Thorpe, D. R., *Eden, The Life and Times of Anthony Eden First Earl of Avon, 1897-1977* (London: Pimlico, 2004)

Thorpe, D. R., *Supermac: The Life of Harold Macmillan* (London: Pimlico, 2011)

Tombs, Robert, *This Sovereign Isle: Britain In and Out of Europe* (London: Allen Lane, 2021)

Tompkins, Peter, *The Murder of Admiral Darlan, A Study in Conspiracy* (New York: Simon and Schuster, 1965)

Tooze, Adam, *Crashed: How a Decade of Financial Crises Changed the World* (London: Penguin, 2019)

Utley, T.E., *A Tory Seer, The Selected Journalism of T.E. Utley, Edited by Charles Moore and Simon Heffer* (London: Hamish Hamilton, 1989)

Verrier, Anthony, *Assassination in Algiers, Churchill, Roosevelt, de Gaulle, and the Murder of Admiral Darlan* (London: Macmillan, 1990)

Wall, Stephen, *A Stranger in Europe: Britain and the EU from Thatcher to Blair* (Oxford: Oxford University Press, 2008)

Walters, Simon, *Tory Wars: Conservatives in Crisis* (London: Politico's, 2001)

Warner, Phillip, *Phantom* (Class War, 2014)

Webb, W. L., *The Beside Guardian 22* (London: Collins, 1973)

Webb, W. L., *The Bedside Guardian 24* (London: Collins, 1975)

Webb, W. L., *The Bedside Guardian 32* (London: Collins, 1983)

Webster, Philip, *Inside Story* (London: William Collins, 2016)

Young, Hugo, *This Blessed Plot: Britain and Europe from Churchill to Blair* (London: Macmillan, 1998)

Notes

Introduction

1 Churchill, Winston, *Secret Session Speeches* (London: Cassell & Co., 1946), p. 3
2 Verrier, Anthony, *Assassination in Algiers* (New York, NY: W. W. Norton & Co. 1990), p. 195
3 Ibid., p. 182
4 Ibid., p. 190
5 Ibid., p. 191
6 Ibid., p. 192
7 Ibid., p. 226
8 Tompkins, Peter, *The Murder of Admiral Darlan* (London: Weidenfeld & Nicolson, 1965), p. 185
9 Ibid., p. 186
10 Eliot, T. S., 'Little Gidding', *Four Quartets* series (London: Faber & Faber, 1942)
11 Heffer, Simon, *Like the Roman* (London: Weidenfeld & Nicolson, 1998), Chapter 3
12 Tompkins, *The Murder of Admiral Darlan*, p. 195
13 Churchill, Winston, *The Hinge of Fate* (London: Penguin, 2005), p. 680

Chapter 1

1 Heffer, Simon, *Like the Roman* (London: Weidenfeld & Nicolson, 1998), Chapter 3
2 Ibid.
3 Ibid.
4 Ibid.
5 Powell, Enoch, *Dancer's End* (first published 1951)
6 Rutherford, Jonathan, *Forever England* (London: Lawrence & Wishart, 1997), p. 104
7 Heffer, *Like the Roman*, Chapter 2

8 Ibid.
9 Ibid.
10 Ibid.
11 Ibid.
12 Ibid.
13 Ibid.
14 Ibid.
15 Ibid.
16 Ibid.
17 Powell, Enoch, *Collected Poems* (Ashford: Bellew Publishing, 1990), p. vii
18 Ibid., p. 5
19 Heffer, *Like the Roman*, Chapter 2
20 Ibid., Chapter 3
21 Eade, Charles, *The War Speeches of Winston Churchill*, Volume 2 (London: Cassell, 1952), pp. 425–37
22 Ibid.
23 Macmillan, Harold, *Tides of Fortune* (London: Macmillan, 1969), p. 154
24 Duchêne, François, *Jean Monnet* (New York, NY: W. W. Norton, 1994), p. 108
25 Ibid., p. 71
26 Ibid., p. 83
27 Ibid., p. 120
28 Ibid.
29 Ibid., p. 127
30 Ibid.
31 Ibid.
32 Ibid., p. 183
33 Heffer, *Like the Roman*, Chapter 3
34 Ibid., Chapter 4
35 Ibid.
36 Ibid.
37 Ibid.
38 Powell, Enoch, 'St. George's Day Banquet', 22 April 1961, published by the literary executors of J. Enoch Powell, file 6, 1957–61
39 Eden, Anthony, Schuman Plan debate, Hansard, vol. 476, 26–27 June 1950
40 Cripps, Stafford, ibid.
41 Churchill, Winston, ibid.
42 Ibid.
43 Heffer, *Like the Roman*, Chapter 5

Chapter 2

1 Jackson, Julian, *A Certain Idea of France* (London: Penguin, 2019), p. 421
2 Ibid., p. 63
3 Duchêne, François, *Jean Monnet* (New York, NY: W. W. Norton, 1994), p. 228
4 Bogdanor, Vernon, 'From the European Coal and Steel Community to the Common Market', Gresham College lecture, November 2013
5 Duchêne, *Jean Monnet*, p. 235
6 Ibid.
7 Ibid., p. 236
8 Monnet, Jean, *Memoirs* (London: Collins, 1978), p. 377
9 Jackson, *A Certain Idea of France*, p. 63
10 Duchêne, *Jean Monnet*, p. 259
11 Thorpe, D. R., *Eden* (London: Pimlico, 2004), p. 368
12 Young, Hugo, *This Blessed Plot* (London: Macmillan, 1998), p. 73
13 Bogdanor, Vernon, *The Monarchy and the Constitution* (Oxford: Oxford University Press, 1995), p. 291
14 Ibid.
15 Heffer, Simon, *Like the Roman* (London: Weidenfeld & Nicolson, 1998), Chapter 5
16 Ibid.
17 Young, Hugo, *This Blessed Plot* (London: Papermac, 1999), p. 80
18 Ibid., p. 81
19 Butler, R. A., Cabinet Paper: European Integration, 29 June 1955 (National Archives: CAB/129/76 https://webarchive.nationalarchives.gov.uk/ukgwa/20221101212600/http://filestore.nationalarchives.gov.uk/pdfs/small/cab-129-76-cp-55-55-5.pdf)
20 Young, *This Blessed Plot*, p. 89
21 Ibid., p. 92
22 Duff, Andrew, *Britain and the Puzzle of European Union* (Abingdon: Routledge, 2022), p. 16
23 Young, *This Blessed Plot*, p. 93
24 Ibid., p. 91
25 Ibid., p. 93
26 Thorpe, *Eden*, p. 452
27 HM Queen Elizabeth II, Prorogation: Her Majesty's Speech, Hansard, vol. 183, 29 October 1953
28 Heffer, *Like the Roman*, Chapter 5
29 Thorpe, *Eden*, p. 490

30 Ibid., p. 481
31 Ibid., p. 503
32 Ibid., p. 513
33 Ibid., p. 488
34 Bogdanor, Vernon, 'The Suez Crisis, 1956', Gresham College lecture, November 2015
35 Jackson, *A Certain Idea of France*, p. 449
36 Ibid., p. 464
37 Ibid., p. 465

Chapter 3

1 Thorpe, D. R., *Supermac* (London: Pimlico, 2011), p. xv
2 Heffer, Simon, *Like the Roman* (London: Weidenfeld & Nicolson, 1998), Chapter 6
3 Harris, Ralph, *Ralph Harris in His Own Words* (Cheltenham: Edward Elgar Publishing, 2008), p. 4
4 Ibid., p. viii
5 Heffer, *Like the Roman*, Chapter 7
6 Utley, T. E., *A Tory Seer* (London: Hamish Hamilton, 1989), p. 2
7 Ibid.
8 Economic Steering (Europe) Committee, 121 Memorandum, 25 May 1960 (Published by the Australian Government's Department of Foreign Affairs and Trade: https://www.dfat.gov.au/about-us/publications/historical-documents/volume-27/Pages/121-memorandum-by-economic-steering-europe-committee)
9 Thorpe, *Supermac*, p. 514
10 Bevan, Aneurin, *Back to Free Markets and the Jungle* (Tribune: 30 August 1957)
11 Wilson, Harold, European Economic Community debate, Hansard, vol. 645, 3 August 1961
12 Ibid.
13 Ibid.
14 Bogdanor, Vernon, *Learning from History? The 1975 Referendum on Europe* (Gresham College lecture, 23 May 2016)
15 Jackson, Julian, *A Certain Idea of France* (London: Penguin, 2019), p. 572
16 Ibid., p. 592
17 Thorpe, *Supermac*, p. 537
18 Utley, *A Tory Seer*, p. 5

19 Ibid., p. 16
20 Pimlott, Ben, *Harold Wilson* (London: HarperCollins, 1992), p. 356
21 Ibid., p. 438
22 Scruton, Roger, *Gentle Regrets* (London: Continuum International Publishing, 2005), p. 34
23 Ibid.
24 El-Enany, Nadine, *Bordering Britain* (Manchester: Manchester University Press, 2020), p. 107
25 Ibid.
26 Heffer, *Like the Roman*, Chapter 11
27 Ibid.
28 Ibid.
29 Utley, *A Tory Seer*, p. 40
30 Powell, Enoch, *The Speeches of John Enoch Powell, January–April 1969* (POLL 4/1/5 File 4), available at the Enoch Powell Speech Archive (http://www.enochpowell.info/), p. 51
31 Ibid.
32 Heffer, *Like the Roman*, Chapter 12
33 Ibid.
34 Ibid., Chapter 13
35 'France Mourns De Gaulle', *New York Times*, 11 Nov 1970 (New York Times Archive https://www.nytimes.com/1970/11/11/archives/france-mourns-de-gaulle-world-leaders-to-attend-a-service-at-notre.html)

Chapter 4

1 Sandbrook, Dominic, *State of Emergency* (London: Allen Lane, 2010), p. 61
2 Campbell, John, *Edward Heath* (London: Pimlico, 2013), p. 31
3 Ibid., p. 42
4 Ibid., p. 48
5 Heath, Edward, *Travels: People and Places in My Life* (London: Sidgwick & Jackson, 1977), p. 115
6 Campbell, *Edward Heath*, p. 398
7 Ibid., p. 400
8 Ibid., p. 403
9 'The World: Common Market: A Great Day for Europe', *Time* magazine, 8 November 1971
10 Sandbrook, *State of Emergency*, p. 166

11 Barrington, Nicholas, *Envoy: A Diplomatic Journey* (London: Radcliffe Press, 2013), p. 174
12 'UK unemployment tops one million', BBC Archives, 20 January 1972 (http://news.bbc.co.uk/onthisday/default.stm)
13 Sandbrook, *State of Emergency*, p. 7
14 Heffer, Simon, *Like the Roman* (London: Weidenfeld & Nicolson, 1998), Chapter 15
15 Ibid.
16 Ibid., Chapter 16
17 Corthorn, Paul, *Enoch Powell: Politics and Ideas in Modern Britain* (Oxford: Oxford University Press, 2019), p. 136
18 Ibid., p. 145
19 Wilson, Harold, Broadcast on the Ulster Worker's Council Strike, 25 May 1974 (published on the Ulster University International Conflict Research Institute's CAIN archive https://cain.ulster.ac.uk/index.html)
20 Heffer, *Like the Roman*, Chapter 16
21 Ibid.
22 Moore, Charles, *Margaret Thatcher: The Authorized Biography, Volume One* (London: Allen Lane, 2013), p. 270
23 Ibid., p. 275
24 Ibid., p. 276
25 Patrick Cosgrave, 'Margaret Thatcher: clear choice for the Tories', *The Spectator*, 23 January 1975
26 Heffer, *Like the Roman*, Chapter 16
27 Moore, *Margaret Thatcher: The Authorized Biography, Volume One*, p. 302
28 Fraser, Hugh, *A Rebel for the Right Reasons* (Stafford: Stafford and Stone Conservative Association, 1975), p. 72
29 Ibid.
30 Walker, Martin, 'The Unthinkable Men Behind Mrs Thatcher', *The Guardian*, 1 March 1983, as reproduced in Webb, W. L. (ed.), *The Bedside Guardian 32* (London: HarperCollins, 1983), p. 85
31 Aitken, Jonathan, interview with author
32 Moore, *Margaret Thatcher: The Authorized Biography, Volume One*, p. 282
33 Fraser, Hugh, *A Rebel for The Right Reasons* (Stafford: Stafford and Stone Conservative Association, 1975), p. 73
34 Ibid., p. 283
35 Heffer, *Like the Roman*, Chapter 16
36 Aitken, Jonathan, *Margaret Thatcher* (London: Bloomsbury, 2014), p. 174

Chapter 5

1 Bogdanor, Vernon, 'The Referendum on Europe, 1975', Gresham College lecture, April 2014
2 Pimlott, Ben, *Harold Wilson* (London: HarperCollins, 1992), p. 654
3 Saunders, Robert, *Yes to Europe!* (Cambridge: Cambridge University Press, 2018), p. 124
4 Ibid., p. 123
5 Ibid., p. 15
6 Ibid., p. 16
7 Thatcher, Margaret, Speech to Conservative Group for Europe, 16 April 1975 (available at the Margaret Thatcher Foundation website, www.margaretthatcher.org)
8 Saunders, *Yes to Europe!*, p. 16
9 Ibid., p. 105
10 Ibid., p. 106
11 Ibid., p. 143
12 Moore, Charles, *Margaret Thatcher: The Authorized Biography, Volume One* (London: Allen Lane, 2013), p. 306
13 Ibid., p. 302
14 Saunders, *Yes to Europe!*, p. 112
15 Moore, *Margaret Thatcher: The Authorized Biography, Volume One*, p. 306
16 Saunders, *Yes to Europe!*, p. 29
17 Ibid., p. 115
18 Ibid., p. 18
19 Ibid., p. 13
20 Ibid., p. 150
21 Ibid., p. 122
22 Ibid., p. 18
23 Ibid., p. 254
24 Ibid., p. 18
25 Ibid., p. 13
26 Pimlott, *Harold Wilson*, p. 660
27 Saunders, *Yes to Europe!*, p. 7
28 Ibid.
29 Ibid., p. 9
30 Ibid., p. 10
31 Pimlott, *Harold Wilson*, p. 660
32 Saunders, *Yes to Europe!*, p. 366
33 Ibid., p. 373

34 Ibid., p. 3
35 Ibid., p. 2
36 Ibid.
37 Ibid., p. 367

Chapter 6

1 Warner, Philip, *Phantom* (Kindle Edition: Class Warfare 2014), location: 124.
2 Phantom Living History Group (website), www.phantomghq.co.uk
3 Warner, *Phantom*, Chapter 13
4 Oakeshott, *The Social and Political Doctrines of Contemporary Europe* (Cambridge: Cambridge University Press, 1939), pp. xviii–xix
5 Oakeshott, *Rationalism in Politics and Other Essays* (London: Methuen, 1962), p. 4
6 Ibid., p. 169
7 Aitken, Jonathan, interview with author
8 Casey, John, 'The revival of Tory philosophy', *The Spectator*, 17 March 2007
9 Sisman, Adam, *Hugh Trevor-Roper* (London: Phoenix, 2012), p. 456
10 Ibid.
11 Confidential interview with author
12 Ibid.
13 Cowling, Maurice, *Mill and Liberalism, Second Edition* (Cambridge: Cambridge University Press, 1990), p. xviii
14 Anderson, Bruce, interview with author
15 Cowling, *Mill and Liberalism, Second Edition*, p. xvii
16 Blake, Robert, *Disraeli* (London: Eyre & Spottiswoode, 1966), p. 171
17 Aitken, Jonathan, *Margaret Thatcher* (London: Bloomsbury, 2013), p. 205
18 Scruton, Roger, 'Why I became a conservative', *The New Criterion*, February 2003
19 Moore, Charles, *Margaret Thatcher: The Authorized Biography, Volume One* (London: Allen Lane, 2013), p. 289
20 Ibid., p. 7
21 Ibid., p. 17
22 Thatcher, Margaret, 'I BELIEVE – A Speech on Christianity and Politics', St Lawrence Jewry, London, 30 March 1978 (available at the Margaret Thatcher Foundation website, www.margaretthatcher.org)
23 Moore, *Margaret Thatcher: The Authorized Biography, Volume One*, p. 349

24 Utley, T. E., *A Tory Seer* (London: Hamish Hamilton, 1989), p. 76
25 Pimlott, Ben, *Harold Wilson* (London: HarperCollins, 1992), p. 681
26 Ibid., p. 677
27 Ibid., p. 684
28 European Council Conclusions, 2 April 1976 (Published by the University of Pittsburgh's Archive of European Integration available at https://aei.pitt.edu/)
29 Sandbrook, Dominic, *Seasons in the Sun: The Battle for Britain, 1974–1979* (London: Allen Lane, 2012), p. 463
30 Ibid., p. 435
31 Moore, *Margaret Thatcher: The Authorized Biography, Volume One*, p. 332
32 Bellamy, Chris, 'Brian Crozier: Intelligence and security expert who fought communism and founded his own spy network', *The Independent*, 12 August 2012
33 Crozier, Brian, *Free Agent: The Unseen War, 1941–1991* (London: HarperCollins, 1993), p. 128
34 Norton-Taylor, Richard, 'Obituary: Brian Crozier', *The Guardian*, 9 August 2012
35 Michaels, Jeffrey, 'The Heyday of Britain's Cold War Think Tank: Brian Crozier and the Institute for the Study of Conflict, 1970–79', in van Dongen, L., Roulin, S., Scott-Smith, G. (eds.), *Transnational Anti-Communism and the Cold War*, Palgrave Macmillan Transnational History Series (London: Palgrave Macmillan, 2014), pp. 146–60
36 Crozier, *Free Agent*, p. 96
37 Jenkins, Peter, 'Up She Goes', *The Guardian*, 25 May 1977
38 Sandbrook, *Seasons in the Sun*, p. 467
39 Ibid., p. 470
40 Ibid., p. 477
41 Ibid., p. 479
42 Ibid.
43 Ibid., p. 489
44 Ibid., p. 499
45 Ibid., p. 652
46 Ibid., p. 667
47 Cowling, Maurice, *Conservative Essays* (London: Cassell, 1978)
48 Ibid.
49 'Labour disputes; working days lost due to strike action; UK (thousands)', published by the Office for National Statistics (Source dataset: Labour market statistics time series)
50 Sandbrook, *Seasons in the Sun*, p. 763

51 Hattersley, Roy, 'The party's over', *The Guardian*, 22 March 2009
52 Sandbrook, *Seasons in the Sun*, p. 803
53 Ibid.
54 Ibid., p. 808

Chapter 7

1 Conservative Party General Election Manifesto 1979 (available at the Margaret Thatcher Foundation website, www.margaretthatcher.org)
2 Moore, Charles, *Margaret Thatcher: The Authorized Biography, Volume One* (London: Allen Lane, 2013), p. 443
3 Scruton, Roger, 'Why I became a conservative', *The New Criterion*, February 2003
4 Scruton, Roger, *The Meaning of Conservatism* (South Bend Indiana, St. Augustine's Press, 2002), p. vii
5 Scruton, Roger, *Gentle Regrets* (London: Continuum International Publishing, 2005), p. 51
6 Moore, *Margaret Thatcher: The Authorized Biography, Volume One*, p. 444
7 Ibid., p. 485
8 Ibid.
9 Ibid., p. 487
10 Ibid.
11 Ibid., p. 489
12 Ibid., p. 491
13 Ibid., p. 492
14 Ibid., p. 494
15 Gilmour, Ian, European Community debate, Hansard, vol. 995, 3 December 1980
16 'Ian Gow record of conversation between Margaret Thatcher and members of Conservative European Reform Group', 15 December 1980 (available at the Margaret Thatcher Foundation website, www.margaretthatcher.org)
17 Moore, *Margaret Thatcher: The Authorized Biography, Volume One*, p. 455
18 Ibid., p. 536
19 Ibid., p. 522
20 Ibid., p. 529
21 Ibid., p. 533
22 Ibid., p. 629
23 Utley, T. E., *A Tory Seer* (London: Hamish Hamilton, 1989), p. 77

24 Howard et al., *Western Strategy in the Wake of Afghanistan*, 14 March 1980 (available at the Margaret Thatcher Foundation website www.margaretthatcher.org)
25 Ibid.
26 Angola: Margaret Thatcher letter to Brian Crozier, 3 May 1980 (available at the Margaret Thatcher Foundation website, www.margaretthatcher.org)
27 Casey, John, 'The revival of Tory philosophy', *The Spectator*, 17 March 2007
28 Powell, Enoch, European Communities Bill debate, Hansard, vol. 840, 13 July 1972
29 Silkin, John, European Communities (Membership) debate, Hansard, vol. 746, 10 May 1967
30 'Anti-Market Laborites Force Special Party Meeting on Entry', *The New York Times*, 24 June 1971
31 Yeats, W. B., 'The Second Coming' (1919), *The Poems* (London: Everyman, 1994)
32 Crewe, Ivor and King, Anthony, *SDP: The Birth, Life and Death of the Social Democratic Party* (Oxford: Oxford University Press, 1995), as recorded by Kenneth O. Morgan in *Michael Foot: A Life* (London: HarperPress, 2007), p. 379
33 'How Britain averted a Falklands invasion in 1977', *The Guardian*, 1 June 2005
34 Morgan, *Michael Foot: A Life*, p. 411
35 Ibid.
36 Ibid.
37 Barnett, Anthony, 'Iron Britannia', *New Left Review* (special issue I/134), July/August 1982
38 Ibid.
39 Bloomfield, Jon, CND briefing note, April 1983, published by the LSE: https://www.lse.ac.uk/ideas/Assets/Documents/project-docs/cnd-archives/009-0003.pdf
40 Rushdie, Salman, 'Woadicea rides again', *The Guardian*, 23 May 1983
41 Ibid.
42 Walker, Martin, 'The Unthinkable Men Behind Mrs Thatcher', *The Guardian*, 1 March 1983, as reproduced in Webb, W. L. (ed.), *The Bedside Guardian 32* (London: HarperCollins, 1983), p. 85
43 Douglas-Home, Jessica, *Once Upon Another Time* (Wilby: Michael Russell Publishing Ltd., 2000), p. 10
44 Apple, R. W., 'Obituary: Charles Douglas-Home, 48, Editor of Times of London', *The New York Times*, 30 October 1985
45 Douglas-Home, *Once Upon Another Time*, p. 10

46 Ibid., p. 13
47 Ibid., p. 15
48 Walker, 'The Unthinkable Men Behind Mrs Thatcher', *The Guardian*, 1 March 1983
49 Honeyford, Roy, 'Education and Race – an Alternative View', *Salisbury Review*, 1984
50 Walker, 'The Unthinkable Men Behind Mrs Thatcher', *The Guardian*, 1 March 1983

Chapter 8

1 Douglas-Home, Jessica, *Once Upon Another Time* (Wilby: Michael Russell Publishing Ltd., 2000), p. 38
2 Ibid., p. 18
3 Ibid.
4 Ibid., p. 57
5 Ibid., p. 41
6 Stone, Norman, 'Grim Eminence', *London Review of Books*, 10 January 1983
7 Kelly, Rachel, 'Letters', *London Review of Books*, 3 February 1983
8 Oakeshott, *What Is History? And Other Essays: Selected Writings* (Exeter: Imprint Academic, 2004), pp. 321–2
9 Sked, Alan, interview with author
10 Stone, Norman, *The Atlantic and Its Enemies* (London: Allen Lane, 2010), p. 378
11 Ferguson, Niall, interview with author
12 Professor Norman Stone, *In the Psychiatrist's Chair*, BBC Radio 4, 3 August 1997
13 Kuper, Simon, *Chums* (London: Profile Books, 2022), p. 82
14 Gove, Michael, interview with author
15 Kuper, *Chums*, p. 85
16 Ibid., p. 64
17 Ibid., p. 79
18 Kuper, Simon, 'The final act in the Gove–Johnson psychodrama', *New Statesman*, 13 July 2022
19 Kuper, *Chums*, p. 85
20 McEwan, Ian, *Margaret Thatcher: we disliked her and we loved it*, 9 April 2013
21 *A Burst of Freedom*, BBC Radio 4, 2 August 2006
22 Evans, Timothy, *Conservative Radicalism* (Oxford: Berghahn Books, 1996)

23 Ibid.
24 Confidential interviews with Federation of Conservative Students activists, conducted by author
25 Buchanan, Kirsty, 'The senior Tories with the secret Soviet past', *The Telegraph*, 19 March 2021
26 Minutes of the meeting between Margaret Thatcher and Peter Young and Federation of Conservative Students, 8 July 1980, available at https://www.margaretthatcher.org/
27 'Tory inquiry into alleged offences by students', *The Times*, 5 May 1982
28 Ibid.
29 Evans, *Conservative Radicalism*, p. 27
30 Confidential interviews with Federation of Conservative Students activists, conducted by author
31 Evans, *Conservative Radicalism*, p. 33
32 Ibid., p. 70
33 'Tory student body could face purge of extremist wing', *The Times*, 30 March 1985
34 Evans, *Conservative Radicalism*, p. 36
35 'Tory students vote in more right-wingers', *The Times*, 4 April 1985
36 Evans, *Conservative Radicalism*, p. 43
37 Ibid., p. 40–1
38 Ibid., p. 73
39 *A Burst of Freedom*, BBC Radio 4, 2 August 2006
40 Evans, *Conservative Radicalism*, p. 44
41 'Tebbit severs links with student group', *The Times*, 13 November 1986
42 'Meet the most influential couple in Downing Street you've never heard of', *The Daily Telegraph*, 4 February 2022
43 Moore, Charles, *Margaret Thatcher: The Authorized Biography, Volume Two* (London: Allen Lane, 2015), p. 420
44 Ibid., p. 389
45 Ibid.
46 Ibid., p. 420
47 Ibid., pp. 409–21
48 Grant, Charles, *Delors: Inside the House that Jacques Built* (London: Nicholas Brealey Publishing, 1994), p. 23
49 Ibid.
50 Ibid., p. 66
51 Moore, *Margaret Thatcher: The Authorized Biography, Volume Two*, p. 392
52 Grant, *Delors*, p. 70
53 Ibid., p. 67

54 Moore, *Margaret Thatcher: The Authorized Biography, Volume Two*, pp. 393–406
55 Ibid.
56 Ibid.
57 Ibid.
58 Ibid.
59 Utley, T. E., 'Duped by a European Smokescreen', *The Daily Telegraph*, 10 November 1986
60 Aitken, Jonathan, interview with author
61 Ibid.
62 Grant, *Delors*, pp. 77–8
63 Ibid.
64 Moore, Charles, *Margaret Thatcher: The Authorized Biography, Volume Three* (London: Allen Lane, 2019), p. 95
65 Heffer, Simon, *Like the Roman* (London: Weidenfeld & Nicolson, 1998), Chapter 20
66 'Royalty and commoners remember editor of *Times*', *The Times*, 26 November 1985

Chapter 9

1 Robertson, Patrick, interview with author
2 Gove, Michael, interview with author
3 Ibid.
4 Ferguson, Niall, interview with author
5 Hollingsworth, Mark, 'Thatcher's unsung hero who broke the miners' strike – but always stayed in the shadows', *The Daily Telegraph*, 25 January 2024
6 Obituary: David Hart, *The Daily Telegraph*, 5 January 2011
7 Ibid.
8 Utley, T. E., *A Tory Seer* (London: Hamish Hamilton, 1989), p. ix
9 Grant, Charles, *Delors: Inside the House that Jacques Built* (London: Nicholas Brealey Publishing, 1994), p. 84
10 Ibid., p. 120
11 Moore, Charles, *Margaret Thatcher: The Authorized Biography, Volume Three* (London: Allen Lane, 2019), p. 130
12 O'Sullivan, John, interview with author
13 Young, Hugo, *This Blessed Plot* (London: Macmillan, 1998), p. 346–51
14 Ibid.
15 Ibid.

16 Moore, *Margaret Thatcher: The Authorized Biography, Volume Three*, pp. 150–1
17 Ibid.
18 Kuper, Simon, *Chums* (London: Profile Books, 2022), p. 103
19 Robertson, interview with author
20 Robertson, Patrick, *Campaign for a Europe of Sovereign States*, 1988 (personal essay shared with the author)
21 Sked, Alan, 'Good Europeans?', Bruges Group, Occasional Paper 4, November 1989
22 Grant, *Delors*, pp. 121–4
23 Moore, *Margaret Thatcher: The Authorized Biography, Volume Three*, p. 300
24 Ibid., pp. 311–22
25 Heffer, Simon, *Like the Roman* (London: Weidenfeld & Nicolson, 1998), Chapter 20
26 Moore, *Margaret Thatcher: The Authorized Biography, Volume Three*, pp. 341–50
27 Ibid.
28 No.10 Policy Unit minute to Andrew Turnbull (Speech by Sir James Goldsmith: the situation on Europe, as seen from Moscow), 27 Aug 1989 (available at the Margaret Thatcher Foundation website, www.margaretthatcher.org)
29 Moore, *Margaret Thatcher: The Authorized Biography, Volume Three*, p. 484
30 Ibid., p. 353
31 Ibid., p. 490–7
32 Ibid., p. 356
33 Heffer, *Like the Roman*, Chapter 20
34 Moore, *Margaret Thatcher: The Authorized Biography, Volume Three*, p. 510
35 Ibid., p. 526
36 Ibid.
37 Stone, Norman, 'Germany? Maggie was absolutely right', *The Sunday Times*, 23 September 1996
38 Moore, *Margaret Thatcher: The Authorized Biography, Volume Three*, p. 582
39 Ibid., p. 551
40 Ibid., p. 592
41 Ibid., p. 626
42 Ibid., p. 631
43 Thatcher, Margaret, Speech to Conservative Party Conference, Bournemouth, 12 October 1990 (available at the Margaret Thatcher Foundation website, www.margaretthatcher.org)
44 Moore, *Margaret Thatcher: The Authorized Biography, Volume Three*, pp. 640–5
45 Ibid.
46 Ibid.

47 'Article by young Boris Johnson helped inspire Thatcher's "No, no, no"', *The Guardian*, 29 February 2020
48 Thatcher, Margaret, European Council (Rome) debate, Hansard, vol. 178, 30 October 1990
49 Ibid.
50 Ibid.
51 Moore, *Margaret Thatcher: The Authorized Biography, Volume Three*, pp. 648–62
52 Ibid.
53 Ibid., p. 683
54 Heffer, *Like the Roman*, Chapter 20
55 Leader on Michael Oakeshott, 'Pragmatic Thatcherite', *The Times*, 22 December 1990

Chapter 10

1 Robertson, Patrick, interview with author
2 Major, John, Doorstep Interview, 28 November 1990 (available at the John Major Archive website, www.johnmajorarchive.org.uk)
3 Wall, Stephen, *A Stranger in Europe* (Oxford: Oxford University Press, 2008), p. 114
4 'Thatcher surprised to be made Bruges Group chief', *The Times*, 7 January 1991
5 Major, John, *The Autobiography* (London: HarperCollins, 1999), pp. 242–3
6 Ibid., p. 269
7 'Bruges Group blames Major', *The Times*, 11 April 1991
8 Sked, Alan, interview with author
9 Robertson, Patrick, interview with author
10 'The twin angry men behind outburst against Major', *The Times*, 12 April 1991
11 'Beyond the Fringe', *The Times*, 12 April 1991
12 Robertson, interview with author
13 'The evil empire', *The Sunday Times*, 1 September 1991
14 Collin, Matthew, *Altered State* (London: Serpent's Tail, 2009), pp. 99–121
15 Moore, Charles, *Margaret Thatcher: The Authorized Biography, Volume Three* (London: Allen Lane, 2019), p. 802
16 Spicer, Michael, *The Spicer Diaries* (Hull: Biteback, 2012), pp. 178–81
17 Ibid.
18 O'Sullivan, John, interview with author
19 Wall, *A Stranger in Europe*, pp. 117–22
20 Ibid.
21 Spicer, *The Spicer Diaries*, p. 186

22 Sked, Alan, 'Debate for Maastricht', letter to *The Times*, 12 October 1991
23 Sked, interview with author
24 Crick, Michael, *One Party After Another* (London: Simon & Schuster, 2022), pp. 19–33
25 Ibid.
26 Ibid.
27 Ibid.
28 Wall, *A Stranger in Europe*, pp. 130–1
29 Ibid.
30 Ibid.
31 Menon, Anand, interview with author
32 Young, Hugo, *This Blessed Plot* (London: Macmillan, 1998), p. 389
33 Spicer, *The Spicer Diaries*, p. 193
34 Wall, *A Stranger in Europe*, p. 135
35 Ibid.
36 Spicer, *The Spicer Diaries*, p. 193
37 Ashdown, Paddy, Maastricht: European Council debate, Hansard, vol. 533, 11 December 1991
38 Spicer, *The Spicer Diaries*, p. 193
39 Young, *This Blessed Plot*, pp. 376–7
40 Major, *The Autobiography*, p. 346
41 Wall, *A Stranger in Europe*, p. 138
42 Major, *The Autobiography*, p. 346
43 Brunsden, Jim, 'How Boris Johnson's Brussels years helped pave the way to Brexit', *Financial Times*, 1 July 2019
44 Aitken, Jonathan, interview with author
45 McTague, Tom, 'The Minister of Chaos', *The Atlantic*, July/August 2021
46 Brunsden, 'How Boris Johnson's Brussels years helped pave the way to Brexit', *Financial Times*, 1 July 2019
47 Ibid.
48 McNair-Wilson, Patrick, First Day debate, Hansard, vol. 207, 6 May 1992
49 Heath, Ted, European Communities (Amendment) Bill debate, Hansard, vol. 208, 21 May 1992
50 Brunsden, 'How Boris Johnson's Brussels years helped pave the way to Brexit', *Financial Times*, 1 July 2019
51 Johnson, Boris, 'Europe: my part in its downfall', *The Daily Telegraph*, 15 September 2003
52 Hannan, Daniel, interview with author
53 Ibid.
54 Major, *The Autobiography*, pp. 350–2
55 Ibid.

56 Ibid.
57 Ibid., p. 314
58 Ibid., p. 359
59 Kipling, Rudyard, 'The Lesson' (1901). In her speech, Thatcher actually misquoted the poem, the first line of which should be 'Let us admit it fairly'.
60 Thatcher, Speech to CNN World Economic Development Conference, 19 September 1992 (available at the Margaret Thatcher Foundation website, www.margaretthatcher.org)
61 Major, *The Autobiography*, p. 361
62 *The European Journal*, First Issue, October 1993
63 Major, John, European Communities (Amendment) Bill debate, Hansard, vol. 213, 4 November 1992
64 Heath, Ted, ibid.
65 Major, *The Autobiography*, p. 383
66 Obituary: Group Captain Bill Walker, *The Times*, 23 June 2017
67 Obituary: Teresa Gorman, Tory MP, *The Daily Telegraph*, 28 August 2015
68 Moore, *Margaret Thatcher: The Authorized Biography, Volume Three*, p. 782
69 Major, John, Speech to Conservative Group for Europe, 22 April 1993 (available at the John Major Archive website, www.johnmajorarchive.org.uk)
70 Major, *The Autobiography*, p. 383
71 Cash, Bill, interview with author
72 Major, *The Autobiography*, p. 384
73 Routledge, Paul and Hoggart, Simon, 'Major hits out at Cabinet', *The Guardian*, 25 July 1993
74 Major, *The Autobiography*, p. 343
75 Spicer, *The Spicer Diaries*, p. 236
76 Blake, Robert, *Disraeli* (London: Eyre & Spottiswoode, 1966), p. 168
77 Bowcott, Owen, 'John Major had a "full gloat" after defeating rebels on Maastricht', *The Guardian*, 24 July 2018
78 Crick, *One Party After Another*, p. 57
79 Farage, Nigel, *Flying Free* (Hull: Biteback, 2011), pp. 78–9
80 Crick, *One Party After Another*, p. 68

Chapter 11

1 Bedell Smith, Sally, 'Billionaire with a Cause', *Vanity Fair*, May 1997
2 Bank of England inflation calculator (www.bankofengland.co.uk/monetary-policy/inflation/inflation-calculator)

3 Hutchins, Chris and Midgley, Dominic, *Goldsmith: Money, Women and Power* (London: Neville Ness House Kindle Edition 2015), p. 20
4 Bedell Smith, 'Billionaire with a Cause', *Vanity Fair*, May 1997
5 Crozier, Brian, *Free Agent: The Unseen War, 1941–1991* (London: HarperCollins, 1993), p. 252
6 Ibid., p. 250
7 Margaret Thatcher's engagement diary for 24 February 1985 (available at the Margaret Thatcher Foundation website, www.margaretthatcher.org)
8 Crozier, *Free Agent*, pp. 239–58
9 Ibid.
10 Ibid.
11 Ibid.
12 Cash, Bill, interview with author
13 Goldsmith, James, *The Trap* (London: Macmillan, 1994), p. 3
14 Ibid., p. 15
15 Ibid., pp. 16–25
16 Ibid., p. 35
17 'French mavericks attack free trade', *The Independent*, 11 April 1994
18 Crick, Michael, *One Party After Another* (London: Simon & Schuster, 2022), pp. 61–2
19 Ibid.
20 Barnett, Anthony, 'John Smith and the path Britain did not take', Open Democracy, 12 May 2019
21 Robertson, Patrick, interview with author
22 Ibid.
23 Major, John, Article on the European Union, published by *The Economist*, 25 September 1993 (available at the John Major Archive website, www.johnmajorarchive.org.uk)
24 James, Barry, 'Major's Hold on Tories Shaken by EU Reversal', *The New York Times*, 31 March 1994
25 'What the Continental Papers Say', *The European Journal*, November 1993
26 'Portrait of the Week', *The Spectator*, 4 June 1994
27 Major, John, Speech in Leiden, 7 September 1994 (available at the John Major Archive website, www.johnmajorarchive.org.uk)
28 Bowcott, Owen, 'John Major's cabinet considered holding EU vote, papers reveal', *The Guardian*, 28 December 2018
29 Major, John, *The Autobiography* (London: HarperCollins, 1999), p. 587
30 Ibid., p. 704
31 'Portillo rocks the boat on Europe', *The Times*, 3 April 1995

32 Major, *The Autobiography*, p. 614
33 Ibid., p. 704
34 Robertson, interview with author
35 Wall, Stephen, *A Stranger in Europe* (Oxford: Oxford University Press, 2008), p. 156
36 Major, *The Autobiography*, pp. 704–5
37 Robertson, interview with author
38 'The Referendum Trap', leader for *The Times*, 24 April 1996
39 Gove, Michael, 'Goldsmith, Redwood and a Blue Funk', *The Times*, 24 April 1996
40 'Major derides call for EU withdrawal', *The Times*, 25 April 1996
41 'Right-wing Tory MPs plan to campaign with rebel election agenda', *The Times*, 29 April 1996
42 Robertson, interview with author
43 Heffer, Simon, *Like the Roman* (London: Weidenfeld & Nicolson, 1998), Chapter 20
44 Campbell, Alastair, *The Alastair Campbell Diaries, Volume One: Prelude to Power, 1994–1997* (London: Hutchinson, 2010), p. 434
45 Ibid., pp. 717–20
46 Blair, Tony, *A Journey: My Political Life* (London: Penguin, 2010), p. 96
47 Ibid., p. 536
48 Major, *The Autobiography*, p. 705
49 Blair, Tony, *BBC News*, BBC 1, 17 March 1997
50 Taylor, Ros, '"The most important video you'll ever watch": the 1997 roots of British Euroscepticism', LSE Blog, 14 October 2019
51 Campbell, *The Alastair Campbell Diaries, Volume One*, p. 804
52 Wall, *A Stranger in Europe*, pp. 162–3
53 Blair, Tony, 'My Love for the £', *The Sun*, 17 April 1997
54 Garner, Clare, 'No fun for Mellor as he is ousted from his Putney seat', *The Independent*, 1 May 1997
55 Crick, *One Party After Another*, p. 73
56 Wall, *A Stranger in Europe*, pp. 163–4
57 'A political earthquake', *The Guardian*, 2 May 1997
58 'Europe hopes for a chance to kiss and make up', *The Times*, 3 May 1997
59 Heffer, *Like the Roman*, Chapter 20
60 Thatcher, Margaret, Speech celebrating the memory of Sir James Goldsmith, 13 November 1997 (available at the Margaret Thatcher Foundation website, www.margaretthatcher.org)
61 Heffer, *Like the Roman*, Chapter 20
62 Housman, A. E., *A Shropshire Lad* (1919)

Chapter 12

1 Douglas-Home, Jessica, *Once Upon Another Time* (Wilby: Michael Russell Publishing Ltd., 2000), p. 64
2 Confidential interview
3 Ibid.
4 Obituary: Lord Leach of Fairford, *The Daily Telegraph*, 13 June 2016
5 Leach, Rodney, *After Maastricht*, the European Foundation, February 1994
6 Leach, Rodney, '"Europe as 1996 Approaches": A Speech Made by Rodney Leach on 13th May 1994', the European Foundation, June 1994
7 Rentoul, John, *Tony Blair: Prime Minister* (London: Warner Books, 2001), p. 332
8 Holmes, Martin, 'Whither the Eurosceptics', *The European Journal*, July/August 1997
9 Blair, Tony, 'Leader's speech, Brighton 1997' (available at the British Political Speech website, www.britishpoliticalspeech.org)
10 Routledge, Paul and Hoggart, Simon, 'Major hits out at Cabinet', *The Guardian*, 25 July 1993
11 Gove, Michael, interview with author
12 Heffer, Simon, interview with author
13 'Hague Brings Youth to Leadership Challenge', Politics 1997, BBC News
14 'Thatcher endorses Hague "to stop Clarke"', *The Independent*, 18 June 1997
15 Gove, Michael, 'Principle and Pique', *The Times*, 18 June 1997
16 Balls, Ed, *Euro-monetarism: Why Britain was Ensnared and how it Should Escape* (London: Fabian Society, 1992)
17 Wall, Stephen, *A Stranger in Europe* (Oxford: Oxford University Press, 2008), p. 170
18 Webster, Philip, *Inside Story* (London: William Collins, 2016), pp. 171–86
19 Ibid.
20 Powell, Jonathan, interview with author
21 Webster, *Inside Story*, pp. 171–86
22 Young, Hugo, *This Blessed Plot* (London: Macmillan, 1998), p. 3
23 Ibid., p. 493
24 Leach, '"Europe as 1996 Approaches": A Speech Made by Rodney Leach on 13th May 1994', the European Foundation, June 1994, p. 8
25 Cummings, Dominic, interview with author
26 Ibid.
27 Halligan, Liam, interview with author
28 Cummings, interview with author
29 Ibid.
30 Ibid.

31 Gove, interview with author
32 Ibid.
33 Leach, '"Europe as 1996 Approaches": A Speech Made by Rodney Leach on 13th May 1994', the European Foundation, June 1994, p. 9
34 Blair, Tony, *A Journey: My Political Life* (London: Penguin, 2010), p. 119
35 Campbell, Alastair, *The Alastair Campbell Diaries, Volume Two: Power and the People, 1997–1999* (London: Hutchinson, 2011), p. 567
36 Crick, Michael, *One Party After Another* (London: Simon & Schuster, 2022), p. 79
37 Ibid., p. 96
38 Farage, Nigel, interview with author
39 House of Commons Library, 'Voting Systems: The Jenkins Report', Research Paper 98/112, 10 December 1998
40 Campbell, *The Alastair Campbell Diaries, Volume Two*, p. 567
41 The Government of Ireland Act 1914, Welsh Church Act 1914, Parliament Act 1949, War Crimes Act 1991 (Source: The House of Commons Library)
42 'We care too, claims Hague', *The Guardian*, 11 October 1997
43 Crick, *One Party After Another*, p. 84
44 'BNP link allegation hits Euro party', *The Times*, 5 June 1999
45 Sked, Alan, 'I would advise people voting on Thursday to help the Tory revival. It may be the one useful thing to emerge from this useless election', *The Times*, 8 June 1999
46 Hames, Tim, 'Hague's euro gamble pays off', *The Times*, 14 June 1999
47 Farage, interview with author
48 'Blair "losing the common touch"', *The Guardian*, 27 October 1999
49 The first edition of the *Salisbury Review* published a talk by Casey in which he called for the 'repatriation of a proportion of the immigrant and immigrant-descended population' to avert 'the possible destruction of civilised life in the centres of the big cities'. Malik, Kenan, 'The uncomfortable truths about Roger Scruton's conservatism', *The Observer*, 18 January 2020
50 Harding, Luke and Pallister, David, 'He lied and lied and lied', *The Guardian*, 21 June 1997
51 Borger, Julian, 'Meet the Kosovan Albanians who named their sons after Tony Blair', *The Guardian*, 20 June 2014
52 Blair, Tony, 'Doctrine of the International Community', speech delivered to the Economic Club, Chicago (available at the British Political Speech website, www.britishpoliticalspeech.org)
53 Freedman, Lawrence, 'From Kosovo to the May doctrine, when is it just to go war?', *New Statesman*, 8 April 2017

54 Young, *This Blessed Plot*, p. 496
55 Rotherham, Lee, interview with author
56 'Marathon summit in chaos', *The Times*, 11 December 2000
57 'Blair to EU: We can't go on like this', *The Times*, 12 December 2000
58 Ibid.
59 Treaty of Nice, Declaration on the future of the Union, *Official Journal of the European Union*, 10 April 2001
60 Ibid.
61 'Resolution on the Treaty of Nice and the future of the European Union', European Parliament, 31 May 2001
62 'Hague's "foreign land" speech', *The Guardian*, 4 March 2001
63 'Anti-euro group keeps distance from Tory leader', *The Times*, 31 May 2001
64 Jones, George, 'Two weeks to save the pound, says Hague', *The Daily Telegraph*, 26 May 2001
65 'Defeat may leave Hague facing his own exit poll – Late desertion', *The Times*, 7 June 2001
66 Gabb, Sean, 'Political Notes No. 172', 3 November 2000 (available on the Libertarian Alliance website https://libertarianism.uk/)
67 Ibid.
68 Elliott, Francis and Hanning, James, *Cameron: Practically a Conservative* (London: Fourth Estate, 2012), location 2912, Kindle edition
69 Ashcroft, Michael (Lord), 'Did I really say that about Europe?', https://www.lordashcroft.com/, 4 October 2015
70 Ibid.
71 Gabb, 'Political Notes No. 172', 3 November 2000
72 'Old guard blames defeat on "kamikaze" Eurosceptics', *The Times*, 9 June 2001
73 Balls, Ed, *Speaking Out: Lessons in Life and Politics* (London: Arrow Books, 2016), p. 166
74 Liddle, Roger, interview with author
75 Smith, Dougie, 'Soulless, selfish and smug – today's Tory candidates', *The Daily Telegraph*, 18 June 2001
76 Harry de Quetteville, 'The Inside Story of The Telegraph and Brexit,' *The Daily Telegraph*, 31 January 2020
77 Conrad Black, 'Britain's Final Choice: Europe or America?', Centre for Policy Studies, July 1998 (London: The Chameleon Press)
78 Cameron, David, *For the Record* (London: William Collins, 2019), p. 57
79 'Full text: Tony Blair's speech', *The Guardian*, 2 October 2001
80 Cummings, interview with author

Chapter 13

1 'Verhofstadt holds inaugural meeting of "Laeken Group"', Euractiv (website), 28 June 2001
2 Fuller, Thomas, 'Paving Way for a "Constitutional Convention"', *The New York Times*, 14 December 2001
3 Rees-Mogg, William, 'Bismarck, Bonaparte or British freedom?', *The Times*, 4 March 2002
4 'From Laeken to Copenhagen', Institute for Security Studies, February 2003
5 'Giscard unveils draft for "United Europe"', *The Guardian*, 29 October 2002
6 'Giscard's first volley starts battle for Europe', *The Times*, 29 October 2002
7 Cummings, Dominic, interview with author
8 'Full text: Theresa May's conference speech', *The Guardian*, 7 October 2002
9 Balls, Ed, *Speaking Out: Lessons in Life and Politics* (London: Hutchinson, 2016), pp. 170–1
10 Black, Ian, 'Giscard hailed as the Socrates of new Europe', *The Guardian*, 14 June 2003
11 Graff, James, 'Toward A More Perfect Union', *Time* magazine, 15 June 2003
12 'Voters can decide in Euro poll, Hain says', *The Times*, 28 May 2003
13 Stuart, Gisela, interview with author
14 'Treaty establishing a Constitution for Europe', *Official Journal of the European Union*, 16 December 2004
15 Stuart, Gisela, 'I am not convinced', introduction to Gisela Stuart's Fabian pamphlet, *The Guardian*, 8 December 2003
16 Watt, Nicholas and Wintour, Patrick, 'How immigration came to haunt Labour: the inside story', *The Guardian*, 24 March 2015
17 Ibid.
18 Portes, Jonathan, interview with author
19 'EU Migration to and from the UK (Analysis of Annual Population Survey 2004–2022)', the Migration Observatory at the University of Oxford, 20 November 2023
20 Yeo, Colin, interview with author
21 'EU Migration to and from the UK', the Migration Observatory at the University of Oxford, 20 November 2023
22 'Ethnic Group & Country of Birth, 1991 Census of Great Britain', Office for National Statistics, figures provided to the author by the ONS on request, 16 January 2025
23 'The changing picture of long-term international migration, England and Wales: Census 2021', Office for National Statistics, 27 January 2023
24 Frayne, James, interview with author

25 'Quiet man "turning up volume"', *The Guardian*, 9 October 2003
26 Rawnsley, Andrew, 'A caretaker, not a saviour', *The Observer*, 2 November 2003
27 Portillo, Michael, 'Ruthless and right', *The Observer*, 2 November 2003
28 'Top Tory aide is king of the urban swingers', *The Sunday Times*, 22 June 2003
29 Ibid.
30 Portillo, 'Ruthless and right', *The Observer*, 2 November 2003
31 'Full text: Michael Howard's speech on Europe', *The Guardian*, 12 February 2004
32 Ibid.
33 Kennedy, Charles, 'Letters: Choice for Eurosceptics', *The Guardian*, 21 April 2004
34 Liddle, Roger, interview with author
35 Powell, Jonathan, interview with author
36 Liddle, Roger and Mandelson, Peter, joint interview with author
37 Mandelson, Peter, interview with author
38 Blair, Tony, *A Journey: My Political Life* (London: Penguin, 2010), p. 501
39 Ibid.
40 Ibid.
41 Powell, interview with author
42 Blair, *A Journey*, p. 504–5
43 Whitaker, Brian, 'Kilroy-Silk investigated for anti-Arab comments', *The Guardian*, 8 January 2004
44 Crick, Michael, *One Party After Another* (London: Simon & Schuster, 2022), p. 149
45 Frayne, interview with author
46 Crick, *One Party After Another*, p. 151
47 Ibid., p. 155
48 'Turnout by country', information provided by Verian for the European Parliament, updated on the European Parliament website (https://results.elections.europa.eu/en/turnout/), 6 September 2024
49 Scruton, Roger, *The Need for Nations* (London: Civitas, 2004)
50 'The Presidency Conclusions of the Brussels European Council', published by the European Commission (https://ec.europa.eu/commission), 18 June 2004
51 Addendum to 'The Presidency Conclusions of the Brussels European Council', published by the European Council (https://ec.europa.eu/councils/bx20040617/addendum_en.pdf), 17 and 18 June 2004
52 'New Europe sides with Blair against old Europe', *The Times*, 18 June 2004
53 'Leaders hammer out EU's new look', BBC News, 17 June 2004
54 Blair, *A Journey*, p. 537

55 'A first constitution for Europe', *The Times*, 19 June 2024
56 'Most businesses say "no" to Europe constitution', *The Times*, 28 April 2004
57 'Tories' spotty teenager takes on Europe: the final frontier', *The Times*, 16 December 2003
58 Ibid.
59 Lambert, Harry, 'What Dominic Cummings was thinking in 2004', *New Statesman*, 23 January 2020
60 Frayne, James, interview with author
61 *The Spending Plan* (London: TaxPayers' Alliance, 2015)
62 TaxPayers' Alliance press release, 2004
63 Cummings, interview with author
64 McDevitt, Johnny, 'Dominic Cummings honed strategy in 2004 vote, video reveals', *The Guardian*, 12 November 2019
65 Ibid.
66 Ibid.
67 Blair, *A Journey*, p. 533
68 'Full text: Tony Blair's speech on asylum and immigration', *The Guardian*, 22 April 2005
69 Blair, *A Journey*, p. 529
70 Ibid., p. 531

Chapter 14

1 Campbell, John, *Edward Heath* (London: Pimlico, 2013), p. 797
2 'An ancient feud is buried at Sir Edward Heath's funeral', *The Times*, 26 July 2005
3 'Service of Thanksgiving for Sir Edward Heath', *The Times*, 9 November 2005
4 Rees-Mogg, William, 'Ideas are the decisive force', *The Times*, 29 August 2005
5 'Blair hails UK's Olympic victory', BBC News, 7 July 2005
6 'Veteran Tories hit out at Howard's "Notting Hill set"', *The Guardian*, 27 July 2004
7 Watt, Nicholas, 'Tory central', *The Guardian*, 28 July 2004
8 Gove, Michael, interview with author
9 Iremonger, Lucille, *The Fiery Chariot* (London: Martin Secker & Warburg, 1970), p. 13
10 Gove, interview with author
11 Ibid.
12 'Tory talent contest gives youth a shot at leadership', *The Times*, 11 May 2005

13 Elliott, Francis and Hanning, James, *Cameron: Practically a Conservative* (London: Fourth Estate, 2012), Chapter: 'Blackpool leadership election 2005'
14 Ibid.
15 Eustice, George, interview with author
16 'Boredom with a purpose', David Cameron Diaries, *The Guardian*, 10 June 2003
17 'A safe bet', David Cameron Diaries, *The Guardian*, 28 May 2003
18 Ibid.
19 'Davis races ahead in Tory poll', *The Times*, 9 November 2005
20 O'Brien, Neil, interview with author
21 Hinsliff, Gaby, 'Boris Johnson sacked by Tories over private life', *The Guardian*, 14 November 2004
22 Coe, Jonathan, 'Sinking Giggling into the Sea', *London Review of Books*, vol. 35, no. 14, 18 July 2013
23 'Bigley's fate', *The Spectator*, 16 October 2004
24 Taylor, Ros, 'Operation Scouse-grovel', *The Guardian*, 21 October 2004
25 McTague, Tom, 'Boris Johnson Meets His Destiny', *The Atlantic*, 22 July 2019
26 Gimson, Andrew, *Boris: The Adventures of Boris Johnson* (London: Simon & Schuster, 2016), p. 27
27 *Boris Johnson: The Irresistible Rise*, BBC Two, 9 November 2013
28 Gray, John, interview with author
29 Elliott and Hanning, *Cameron: Practically a Conservative*, location 5293, Kindle edition
30 Cameron, David, 'Leader's speech', Conservative Party Conference, Bournemouth, 2006 (available at the British Political Speech website, www.britishpoliticalspeech.org)
31 Thompson, Helen, *Disorder: Hard Times in the 21st Century* (Oxford: Oxford University Press, 2022), p. 139
32 'Bank cannot avert downturn, warns King', *The Times,* 12 October 2005
33 Blair, Tony, *A Journey: My Political Life* (London: Penguin, 2010), p. 599
34 Ibid., p. 600
35 Ibid., p. 618
36 'Let's recall how the idea of brexit went from taboo to reality', Brexit Central (website), 26 January 2020
37 'UKIP leader "offered Tory seat"', BBC News, 5 December 2006
38 'Merkel wants EU Constitution deal by 2009', Euractiv (website), 18 January 2017
39 Blair, Tony, 'Resignation speech', Sedgefield, 2007 (available at the British Political Speech website, www.britishpoliticalspeech.org)
40 'In full: Brown speech', BBC News, 27 June 2007

41 Scruton, Roger, *Culture Counts* (New York, NY: Encounter Books, 2018)
42 Cameron, David, *For the Record* (London: William Collins, 2019), p. 104
43 Ibid. p. 105
44 Ibid.
45 Ibid.
46 Balls, Ed, *Speaking Out: Lessons in Life and Politics* (London: Hutchinson, 2016), p. 260
47 Woodward, Will, 'Indecisive Johnson adds to Tory confusion over London mayor', *The Guardian*, 5 July 2007
48 Cameron, *For the Record*, p. 109
49 Wintour, Patrick, 'Johnson "would destroy London's unity" as mayor', *The Guardian*, 4 August 2007
50 Wintour, Patrick, 'London chooses Mayor Boris', *The Guardian*, 3 May 2008
51 Tooze, Adam, *Crashed: How a Decade of Financial Crises Changed the World* (London: Penguin, 2019), p. 165
52 Sparrow, Andrew, 'Gordon Brown hits back at Tory debt accusations', *The Guardian*, 12 January 2009
53 'Michael Gove "flipped" homes: MPs' expenses', *The Daily Telegraph*, 11 May 2009
54 Lambert, Harry, 'Dominic Cummings: The Machiavel in Downing Street', *New Statesman*, 25 September 2019
55 Craig, David and Elliot, Matthew, *The Great European Rip-Off* (London: Random House, 2009), pp. 7–8
56 Cameron, *For the Record*, p. 119
57 Cruddas, Jon and Lowles, Nick, 'The myth of the BNP "protest" vote', *The Guardian*, 8 June 2009
58 Cameron, *For the Record*, p. 119
59 Ibid., p. 20
60 Eustice, interview with author
61 Ibid.
62 Cameron, *For the Record*, p. 120
63 'Cameron says would never join euro', Reuters, 12 February 2010
64 'Public attitudes on the EU: Implications for Political Campaigns Between the 1st and 4th May 2009', poll conducted for the TaxPayers' Alliance by ICM, 22 May 2009
65 Ibid.
66 Ibid.
67 Mandelson, Peter, interview with author
68 'Harmless Herman is now leader of the pack', *The Times*, 6 November 2009
69 'Ukip's Nigel Farage tells Van Rompuy: You have the charisma of a damp rag', *The Guardian*, 25 February 2010

70 Towler, Gawain, interview with author
71 Tooze, *Crashed*, p. 322
72 Ibid., p. 333
73 José Manuel Barroso, president of the European Commission, referenced Monnet's remark in a speech to the EU heads of delegation, in Brussels, on 30 November 2011 – the speech was titled 'A Europe for all weathers'
74 'Tories would limit immigration to "tens of thousands" a year, says Cameron', *The Guardian*, 11 January 2010
75 Curtis, Polly, 'Gordon Brown calls Labour supporter a "bigoted woman"', *The Guardian*, 28 April 2010
76 Summers, Deborah, 'Gordon Brown's "British jobs" pledge has caused controversy before', *The Guardian*, 30 January 2009
77 'The Coalition: our programme for government', HM Government, 20 May 2010
78 Gove, interview with author

Chapter 15

1 'We rule out joining or preparing to join the European Single Currency for the duration of this agreement.' 'The Coalition: our programme for government', HM Government, 20 May 2010
2 'The euro is in danger', *The Times*, 20 May 2010
3 Laws, David, *Coalition: The Inside Story of the Conservative–Liberal Democrat Coalition Government* (Hull: Biteback, 2016), Chapter: 'Political Reform: Progress and Potholes'
4 Cameron, David, *For the Record* (London: William Collins, 2019), p. 292
5 Frayne, James, interview with author
6 Elliott, Matthew, interview with author
7 Cash, Bill, Parliamentary Voting System and Constituencies Bill debate, vol. 517, Hansard, 2 November 2010
8 'No to AV' leaflet, titled 'Keep One Person, One Vote: Vote NO in the referendum on 5 May'
9 The poster sparked indignation and some mockery in the press. 'No to AV's new campaign is beyond parody', *New Statesman*, 22 February 2011
10 Cameron, *For the Record*, p. 292
11 Ibid., p. 222
12 Ibid., p. 293
13 Elliott, Matthew, 'Thoughts on an EU referendum', confidential memo shared with author, dated 20 June 2011
14 Cameron, *For the Record*, p. 325

15 Ibid., p. 329
16 Tooze, Adam, *Crashed: How a Decade of Financial Crises Changed the World* (London: Penguin, 2019), p. 417
17 Rogers, Ivan, interview with author
18 'Delors points the finger at Europe's "killers"', Euactiv (website), 29 March 2012
19 'EU treaty: David Cameron has played a blinder says Boris Johnson', *The Daily Telegraph*, 9 December 2011
20 Traynor, Ian, Watt, Nicholas et al., 'David Cameron blocks EU treaty with veto, casting Britain adrift in Europe', *The Guardian*, 9 December 2011
21 'David Cameron blocks EU-wide deal to tackle euro crisis', BBC News, 9 December 2011
22 Rogers, interview with author
23 Ibid.
24 Cameron, *For the Record*, pp. 339–40
25 Tooze, *Crashed*, p. 438
26 Cameron, *For the Record*, p. 357
27 Freedland, Jonathan, 'London 2012: we've glimpsed another kind of Britain, so let's fight for it', *The Guardian*, 10 August 2012
28 Wells, Anthony (head of European political and social research at YouGov), 'How people would vote in an EU referendum', an analysis on the trends in EU referendum voting intention, 11 March 2014 (the analysis shows a consistent lead for 'Leave' from December 2011: https://yougov.co.uk/politics/articles/8820-how-people-would-vote-eu-referendum)
29 Kirkup, James, 'The night that David Cameron sealed Britain's Brexit fate', *The Spectator*, 29 June 2022
30 Cameron, *For the Record*, p. 410
31 Fresh Start Project, 'Options for Change: Renegotiating the UK's relationship with the EU'. A copy of the original has been archived by the Wayback Machine: https://web.archive.org/web/20140921193622/http://www.eufreshstart.org/downloads/fullgreenpaper.pdf
32 Shipman, Tim, *All Out War: The Full Story of How Brexit Sank Britain's Political Class* (London: William Collins, 2016), p. 27
33 Elliott, interview with author
34 Cameron, *For the Record*, p. 408
35 Cameron, David, 'EU speech at Bloomberg', published by the Prime Minister's Office, 23 January 2013
36 Watt, Nicholas, Traynor, Ian and Wintour, Patrick, 'EU speech: let's talk, says Merkel after Cameron's referendum gamble', *The Guardian*, 24 January 2013

37 Mason, Rowena, 'David Cameron to refuse coalition without EU referendum backing', *The Guardian*, 28 April 2014. In his memoir, Cameron explains that he made this commitment 'very clear from the outset, in public and in private, that if I didn't get a majority, this was a red line: this policy was so important, so unlike any other, that I would not become prime minister after the next election in a government that was not committed to do it.' (Cameron, *For the Record*, p. 399)
38 Sparrow, Andrew, 'Lib Dem frontbencher thrown out of Commons', *The Guardian*, 26 February 2008
39 Cameron, *For the Record*, pp. 412–13
40 Menon, Anand, interview with author
41 Cameron, David, 'Tribute to Lady Margaret Thatcher by Prime Minister', published by the Prime Minister's Office, 10 April 2013
42 Stone, Norman, *The Atlantic and Its Enemies* (London: Allen Lane, 2010), p. xix
43 For further discussion about this, see Bernstein, George L., *The Myth of Decline: The Rise of Britain Since 1945* (London: Pimlico, 2004)
44 Moore, Charles, *Margaret Thatcher, The Authorized Biography: Volume Three* (London: Penguin 2020)
45 Cash, Bill, Tributes to Baroness Thatcher debate, vol. 560, Hansard, 10 April 2013
46 Cameron, *For the Record*, p. 420
47 Ibid., p. 459
48 Ibid., p. 465
49 Scruton, Roger, 'Conservatives must think. So come and do so at the second Conservative Renewal conference', published by Conservative Home (website), 7 April 2013
50 Cameron, *For the Record*, p. 496
51 'Merkel offers Cameron hope over EU reform', *The Times*, 27 February 2014
52 Mason, Rowena, 'Nigel Farage accepts Clegg's challenge to debate Britain's EU membership', *The Guardian*, 21 February 2014
53 'Farage is the winner of round one in TV tussle with Clegg', *The Times*, 27 March 2014
54 Cameron, *For the Record*, p. 513
55 Wintour, Patrick, Watt, Nicholas et al., 'Clegg and Farage are both "quite extreme" over Europe, says Cameron', *The Guardian*, 3 April 2014
56 Wintour, Patrick and Watt, Nicholas, 'Ukip wins European elections with ease to set off political earthquake', *The Guardian*, 26 May 2014
57 'Tony Blair to call for EU reform after election "wake-up"', *Financial Times*, 1 June 2014
58 'Britain nears EU exit', *The Times*, 28 June 2014

59 Cummings' blogs can be read on his website, including 'My report for Business for Britain on the dynamics of the debate over the EU', 30 June 2014: https://dominiccummings.com/2014/06/

60 'Cameron bumbles from one shambles to another with no sense of purpose', *The Times*, 16 June 2014. In the full quote, Cummings says: 'As Bismarck said about Napoleon III, Cameron is a sphinx without a riddle – he bumbles from one shambles to another without the slightest sense of purpose. Everyone is trying to find the secret of David Cameron, but he is what he appears to be. He had a picture of Macmillan on his wall – that's all you need to know.'

61 Cummings, Dominic, 'Gesture without motion from the hollow men in the bubble, and a free simple idea to improve things a lot which could be implemented in one day (Part I)', 16 June 2014: https://dominiccummings.com/2014/06/16/

62 Elliott, interview with author

63 Cummings, Dominic, 'My report for Business for Britain on the dynamics of the debate over the EU, and a small but telling process point on the EU', 30 June 2014: https://dominiccummings.com/2014/06/30/

64 Cummings, Dominic, 'Cameron's empty Euroscepticism fools no one. Voters don't believe the prime minister when he says he'll get a better deal for Britain in Europe', *The Times*, 26 June 2014

65 Ibid.

66 Rogers, interview with author

67 Sparrow, Andrew, 'Mark Reckless wins Rochester and Strood byelection for Ukip', *The Guardian*, 21 November 2014

68 The claim was made by Labour's then shadow home secretary for Scotland, George Robertson, who said that devolution would 'kill the SNP stone dead', discussed by Brian Taylor, the BBC's Scotland editor, in a piece published by BBC News on 4 February 2015, titled, 'How is the "killing the SNP stone dead" project going?' (https://www.bbc.co.uk/news/uk-scotland-31129382)

69 The offer was splashed across the *Daily Record* as 'The Vow', as Cameron records in his memoir *For the Record*, p. 553

70 Cameron, David, 'Scottish Independence Referendum: statement by the Prime Minister', published by the Prime Minister's Office, 19 September 2014

71 Elliott, Matthew, confidential memo shared with the author

72 'Business leaders demand cross-party pledge on EU vote', *The Daily Telegraph*, 8 November 2014

73 Published by Business for Britain in June 2014, the 1,030-page report was described by Douglas Carswell as the document which contained much

of the Eurosceptic cause's 'intellectual capital' (Carswell, Douglas, 'The Mandate for Brexit', UK in a Changing Europe (website), 18 June 2016, https://ukandeu.ac.uk/the-mandate-for-brexit/)

74 'David Cameron promises "one last go" at EU migration curbs', BBC News, 16 October 2014

75 Rogers, interview with author

76 'No 10 seeks emergency brake on immigration', *The Times*, 16 October 2014. The BBC report (op. cit.) states: 'The Sun newspaper goes further, saying Mr Cameron will "demand the right to limit European immigration" as the "price of staying in the EU".'

77 Cameron, *For the Record*, p. 564

78 'Nigel Farage quits – to consider becoming leader again', *The Independent*, 8 May 2015

Chapter 16

1 Cameron and this team had considered three scenarios: one, that the Conservative Party would finish with enough MPs to form a coalition; two, 'the zone of uncertainty', in which an alliance with the Lib Dems and the DUP was not enough to secure a majority; and three, coming behind Labour. On the day of the election, Cameron then asked George Osborne and Ed Llewellyn whether they should consider what would happen if the Conservatives won enough seats 'not to need the Lib Dems'. 'This was the scenario no one had even mentioned,' Cameron wrote in his memoir. 'Ed told me not to be ridiculous.' Cameron, David, *For the Record* (London: William Collins, 2019), pp. 574–5

2 Cameron, David, 'Prime Minister's speech following the results of the 2015 general election', published by the Prime Minister's Office, 8 May 2015

3 Cameron, *For the Record*, p. 581

4 Evans, Richard J., 'Obituary: Norman Stone', *The Guardian*, 25 June 2019

5 Wood, James, 'What's next?', *London Review of Books*, vol. 33, no. 8, 14 April 2011

6 Rogers, Ivan, interview with author

7 Cummings, Dominic, 'On the referendum #11: new ICM poll on a second referendum idea, Boris etc', 20 July 2015: https://dominiccummings.com/2015/07/

8 European Commission press release, 'Five Presidents' Report sets out plan for strengthening Europe's Economic and Monetary Union', published on the European Commission website, 1 July 2015

9 Cummings, Dominic, 'On the referendum #17: The state of the campaign', 26 September 2015: https://dominiccummings.com/2015/09/
10 European Council meeting conclusions, published by the General Secretariat of the European Council, 26 June 2015 (https://www.consilium.europa.eu/media/21717/euco-conclusions-25-26-june-2015.pdf)
11 Cameron, *For the Record*, p. 627
12 Cummings, Dominic, 'On the referendum #9: Cameron begins his renegotiation, the Commission sets out its timetable for new Treaty pre-2025, BJ & SJ make moves, a Greek "no"', 6 July 2015: https://dominiccummings.com/2015/07/06/
13 Cameron, *For the Record*, p. 595
14 Cummings, Dominic, 'On the Referendum #6: Exit plans and a second referendum', 23 June 2015: https://dominiccummings.com/2015/06/23/
15 Helm, Toby, 'Cameron insists: no means no in EU vote', *The Observer*, 25 October 2015
16 Organogram provided to the author
17 Rogers, interview with author
18 Cameron, *For the Record*, p. 640
19 Ibid., p. 598
20 Ibid., p. 614
21 Ibid., p. 616
22 Ibid., p. 618–19
23 Ibid., p. 592
24 Phillips, Tom, 'Britain has made "visionary" choice to become China's best friend, says Xi', *The Guardian*, 18 October 2015
25 Shipman, Tim, *All Out War: The Full Story of How Brexit Sank Britain's Political Class* (London: William Collins, 2016), p. 54
26 Cummings, Dominic, 'How the Brexit referendum was won', *The Spectator*, 9 January 2017
27 Cameron, David, 'PM's letter to President of the European Council Donald Tusk', published by the Prime Minister's Office, 10 November 2015
28 Cameron, *For the Record*, p. 621
29 Ibid., p. 650
30 Ibid.
31 Rogers, interview with author
32 Ibid.
33 Newton Dunn, Tom, 'Who do EU think you are kidding Mr Cameron? Our deal turns to farce as PM caves on immigration demands', *The Sun*, 3 February 2016
34 'Brussels will have right to reject benefit curbs', *The Times*, 3 February 2016

35 Cameron, *For the Record*, p. 647
36 Kroet, Cynthia, 'Britons expect a bad deal for EU membership: poll', Politico, 14 February 2016
37 European Council conclusions, published by the General Secretariat of the Council, 18 and 19 February 2016 (https://www.consilium.europa.eu/media/21787/0216-euco-conclusions.pdf)
38 Ibid.
39 Duff, Andrew, interview with author
40 Ibid.
41 Cameron, *For the Record*, p. 644
42 Watt, Nicholas, Traynor, Ian and Rankin, Jennifer, 'Cameron "disappointed, but not surprised" as Gove heads towards Brexit', *The Guardian*, 19 February 2016
43 Cameron, *For the Record*, p. 656
44 Shipman, *All Out War*, p. 175
45 Cameron, *For the Record*, p. 656
46 Shipman, *All Out War*, p. 175
47 Ibid., p. 185
48 Stuart, Gisela, interview with author
49 Ibid.
50 Shipman, *All Out War*, p. 226
51 Ibid., p. 242
52 Ibid., p. 240
53 'EU referendum: Brexit "would spark year-long recession"', BBC News, 23 May 2016
54 Shipman, *All Out War*, p. 251
55 Ibid., p. 295
56 Ibid., p. 284
57 Private email exchange, shared with the author
58 Eliot, T. S., 'Little Gidding', *Four Quartets* series (first published 1942)
59 Scruton, Roger, 'T.S. Eliot as Conservative Mentor', The Imaginative Conservative, 3 January 2023

Conclusion

1 'Tory lead grows as May extends her honeymoon', *The Times*, 4 August 2016
2 Rogers, Ivan, lecture to the University of Liverpool, 13 December 2018 (https://news.liverpool.ac.uk/2018/12/13/full-speech-sir-ivan-rogers-on-brexit/)
3 European Council (Art. 50) guidelines for Brexit negotiations, press

release, European Council, 29 April 2017 (https://www.consilium.europa.eu/en/press/press-releases/2017/04/29/euco-brexit-guidelines/pdf)

4 'Joint report on progress during phase 1 of negotiations under Article 50 TEU on the UK's orderly withdrawal from the EU', presented jointly by the negotiators of the European Union and the United Kingdom, published by the Prime Minister's Office, 8 December 2017

5 European Commission Draft Withdrawal Agreement, European Commission, 18 February 2018 (https://commission.europa.eu/publications/european-commission-draft-withdrawal-agreement-withdrawal-united-kingdom-great-britain-and-northern_en)

6 'Theresa May: No UK PM could ever agree with EU draft', BBC News, 28 February 2018

7 Evans, Richard J., 'Obituary: Norman Stone', *The Guardian*, 25 June 2019

8 Shipman, Tim, *Out: How Brexit Got Done and the Tories Were Undone* (London: William Collins, 2024), p. 91

9 Sandbrook, Dominic, *Seasons in the Sun: The Battle for Britain, 1974–1979* (London: Penguin Books Ltd., p. 426)

10 Scruton, Roger, *Gentle Regrets* (London: Continuum International Publishing, 2005), p. 56

11 Larkin, 'The Importance of Elsewhere', *The Whitsun Weddings* (London: Faber, 1964)

12 Cummings, 'How the Brexit referendum was won', *The Spectator*, 9 January 2017

13 Balls, Ed, interview with author

14 Scruton, Roger, *Where We Are* (London: Bloomsbury, 2017), p. 14

Index

Acheson, Dean 29
Action Committee of the United States of Europe 43–4, 123, 138
Adam Smith Institute 184, 354
Adams, Harold 32–3
Adenauer, Konrad 57
Adley, Robert 264
Afghanistan 161, 335, 388
Aitken, Jonathan 108, 109, 129, 130, 132–4, 156, 162, 196–8, 247, 250, 294, 295, 318, 361, 428
Algiers, Algeria 3–10, 11–13, 20–21, 23, 28, 36–8, 40, 41, 56, 58–60, 61, 70, 92, 95, 96, 123, 127, 134, 173, 180, 201, 271, 294–5, 469
Allies, Second World War ix, 3–4, 5, 6, 7, 18, 21, 22, 23, 26, 38
alternative vote (AV) 316, 391, 392–8
Amato, Giuliano 374
Amsterdam, European Council summit in (1997) 292, 301–2
Anderson, Bruce 132
Anglo-Irish Agreement (1985) 180, 183, 465
Anti-Federalist League 240–41, 243, 248, 263, 264
Ashdown, Paddy 246, 264, 314, 316, 317
Asian Infrastructure Investment Bank 437
Aspinall, John 275, 288, 294, 334
Aspinall's, Mayfair 334
Assad, Bashar al- 413–14, 422
Astor, Lady Annabel 380
Atkinson, Rodney 288
Atlantic Charter (1941) 4
Atlantic Free World 24, 36, 39, 153
Attlee, Clement 25, 27, 30, 34, 35, 44, 46, 47, 51, 52, 67, 93, 131, 168, 243, 360, 469
austerity programmes 76, 142, 143, 145, 164, 378–9, 386–7, 391–3, 401, 405, 426, 450

Background Briefing (newsletter) 206
bailouts, bank 142, 145, 378, 385–6, 390, 398, 436
Baker, Kenneth 108–9
balance of payments 111, 117
Balls, Ed 304–6, 305*n*, 326, 336, 376, 451, 468–9
Bank of England 142, 143, 217, 257, 301, 371
Banks, Arron 433, 437
Barnett, Anthony: *Iron Britannia: Why Parliament Waged its Falklands War* 167–8
BBC 4, 255*n*, 269, 348, 370, 378, 426
Beaverbrook, Lord 70, 250
Bech, Joseph 50
Bellamy, David 288
Benn, Tony 111, 115, 117–18, 121, 136, 139, 142, 143, 163, 180, 228, 253, 448
Bernanke, Ben 378
Better Off Out 373–4
Better Together 423–4
Bevan, Aneurin 67, 77
Beveridge Report (1942) 18–19
Bevin, Ernest 30, 67
Bigley, Ken 369–70
bin Laden, Osama 330, 335
Birley, Robin 275, 302, 364
Black, Conrad 257, 294, 328
Black Wednesday (16 September 1992) 256–9, 304, 415
Blair, Tony 354, 418, 422, 454
Brexit and 403, 466
Brussels summit (2004) and 350–51

Blair, Tony (*cont.*)
Cameron and 366, 367, 368, 371, 403, 411
Chicago speech (1999) 319
elected as Member of Parliament for Sedgefield (1983) 174
European constitution referenda and 345–7
European Parliament elections (1999) and 313–18
European Parliament elections (2014) and 418
European single currency (euro) and 286, 287, 290–91, 292, 301–2, 304–7, 311, 322, 323, 326, 336, 344, 346, 351, 392
general election (1997) and 289, 290–92, 310
general election (2001) and 322, 326
general election (2005) and 356–9
immigration and 339–41, 357–8
Iraq War and 335, 339, 347, 372
Kosovo, NATO intervention in (1998–9) and 318–19, 335
Labour Party leader, becomes 273, 274–5, 281, 282
Nice summit (2000) and 321–2
9/11 and 329
Olympics (2012) and 362–3, 404
presidency of the European Council, bid for 384–5
resignation as prime minister 372–5
resignation from Parliament 381
7/7 and 362–3
voting system reform and 313–14, 315, 316
Blake, Robert 133
Blaker, Peter 161
Blue Touchpaper 188
Blunkett, David 338, 395
Blunt, Crispin 414
Body, Richard 96, 277*n*
Boissieu, Pierre de 227
Boles, Nick 334, 343, 364, 377, 441
Bonde, Jens-Peter 320
Bonnier de la Chapelle, Fernand 5–6, 271
Bordez, Emmanuel 321
Boyle, Danny 404
Bradford, Richard Bridgeman, Earl of 348
Brandon mission (1942–3) 6
Bretherton, Russell 52–4, 277
Bretton Woods Conference (1944) 138
Brexit 85, 120, 317, 362, 363–4, 400
Better Together and 423–4
'Breaking Point' poster 452
Brexit Day (31 January 2020) 470–71
campaign 427–58
Great Debate 453
immigration and *see* immigration
Jo Cox murder and 452
Leave.EU 437–8, 452, 454
origins 339, 402, 403, 405, 410, 427
Project Fear 447
referendum question 437–8
second referendum on terms of divorce settlement, possibility of 433
Stronger In 446–9
Take Back Control slogan 438, 453
term 402
£350 million a week claim 438
Treasury document on 'long term economic impact' of leaving EU 448
Vote Leave 438–9, 440, 441, 442, 443, 446–56, 460, 467–8
withdrawal agreement 461–6
withdrawal process 459–66
See also individual names of participants
Brexit Party 462–3
Bridges, George 363
British Briefing (newsletter) 206
British Movement 241–2
British National Socialist Movement 242
British National Party (BNP) 83*n*, 265, 315, 358, 372, 373, 381, 382
British Supply Council 22
Brittan, Leon 213, 399

Brixton riots (1981) 157
Brown, George 113
Brown, Gordon 342, 368, 401
  euro and 286, 287, 304–6, 336
  general election (2010) and 386, 388, 389, 399
  prime minister 356, 358, 373, 375–6, 378, 379, 380, 381, 384
  resigns as prime minister 390
  Scottish independence referendum and 422, 451
  Smith's death and 274
Brown, Nick Gordon 241
Bruges, Thatcher speech at (1988) 208–13, 233, 258, 277, 309, 338, 408, 409
Bruges Group 213–14, 216, 234–6, 238, 240, 243, 254, 264, 275, 301, 302, 312
Brussels, Belgium 54, 59, 96, 97, 99, 138, 139, 152*n*, 192–4, 209, 213, 249, 250, 251, 277, 320–22, 325, 344, 353, 370, 382, 383, 384, 389, 390, 399, 400, 401–2, 420, 425, 434, 442, 443, 445, 446, 453, 460, 464, 467
  EU constitutional convention in (2002) 332–3, 336
  European Council summit in (2004) 349, 350–51
  summit in (2014) 418
  Treaty of Brussels (1948) 99
BSE 285
Buchan-Hepburn, Patrick 35
Budgen, Nicholas 276, 276*n*, 293
Bulgaria 374, 417
Bumper Book of Government Waste and Useless Spending 354
Bundesbank 208, 257, 258–9
Burley, Aidan 405
Bush, George H. W. 222, 226
Bush, George W. 335, 362
Business for Britain 407, 418, 419, 424, 425, 427, 431, 438, 456
Business for Sterling 309–10, 312, 313, 322–5, 329, 341, 345, 352, 353, 364–6, 368, 373, 377, 394, 407, 419
Butler, David 348
Butler, Eamonn 184
Butler, R. A. 'Rab' 50–52, 61, 62, 63
Butskellism 62, 131
Butterfield, Sir Herbert 130

Callaghan, James 80, 121, 139–47, 159, 163, 166, 190, 360, 459
Cambridge Analytica 433
Cambridge Review 108, 170
'Cambridge right' 131
Cameron, David 323–4
  alternative vote and 394, 396–7
  austerity and 378–9, 391–3
  Bloomberg speech (2013) 408–9
  Brexit referendum and 390–91, 392, 397–8, 403, 406–10, 420, 426, 427–54, 457, 468
  China and 436–7
  coalition agreement with Liberal Democrats 390–91, 392
  Cummings and 391, 396, 415, 419, 420, 421, 423–4, 427, 430–31, 442, 443
  Duncan Smith and 328–9, 342
  Euroscepticism, instinctive 367
  European elections (2014) and 417–18
  fiscal compact and 399–402
  general election (2001), elected to Parliament 323–5
  general election (2010) and 386–7, 389–91
  general election (2015) and 425–6, 427
  Islamist extremism and 413–14, 421–2, 431, 434–5
  Johnson and 370, 371, 377, 403–4, 454–5
  leadership election (2005) 363–8, 371
  Lisbon Treaty and 381–3
  omnishambles budget and 403
  parliamentary expenses scandal and 379
  party conference speeches 371, 376
  public petition calling for referendum on Britain's membership of the EU and 398
  renegotiation of terms of EU membership 402–3, 402*n*, 406–13, 416, 418, 419, 420, 421, 424–6, 427–34, 438–40, 442–6, 450, 451

Cameron, David (*cont.*)
resignation as prime minister 454, 457, 459
Reyaad Khan killing and 434–5
Scottish independence referendum and 405, 422–3, 451
'stop banging on about Europe' comment 371
Syrian Civil War and 413–14, 415, 431, 434–5, 437
West Lothian question and 423
Whetstone and 342–3
Campaign for an Independent Britain 241, 254, 307
Campaign for Nuclear Disarmament (CND) 163, 166–7, 169, 268
Campbell, Alastair 286, 287, 306, 316, 346
Campbell, Gavin 289–90
Campbell, John 92, 266
Campus 186
Candidlist 309, 324, 325
Cann, Edward du 105, 361
Carr, E. H. 176–7, 179, 463; *What is History?* 177
Carr, Robert 104
Carrington, Lord 159, 191
Carswell, Douglas 374, 422, 426
Cartledge, Bryan 152
Casey, John 108, 129–30, 131, 132, 133, 162, 170–71, 318, 428, 463
Cash, Bill 196, 238, 245, 259, 261, 262, 269, 272, 276, 294, 295, 342, 364, 367, 381, 395, 412, 463
Castle, Barbara 111, 118
Catroux, Georges 58–9
Cecchini report (1988) 353
Centre for Policy Studies (CPS) 106, 133, 160, 280, 328, 354
Chalker, Lynda 207
Chamberlain, Joseph 14, 84
Chamberlain, Neville 16
'Change, or Go' policy document 424, 431
Chaplin, Judith 263
Charlemagne Prize 384
Charlie Hebdo, terror attacks on (2015) 431
Chequers, Buckinghamshire 56, 137, 162, 240, 267, 268, 345, 440
Chequers proposal, May (2018) 462
Chequers summit (1990) 223–4, 225, 433
Cherwell 179, 205, 214
Chichester-Clark, Robin 361
China 31, 165*n*, 270, 362, 436–7, 454
Chirac, Jacques 272, 287, 346, 350, 362
Churchill, Winston 44, 47, 49, 107, 113, 144, 238, 250, 470
Atlantic Charter, signs 4
Beveridge Report and 18–20
Boris Johnson and 401
Charlemagne Prize 384
Churchillism 167, 168, 401, 413
Council of Europe, on 19
death 73, 360, 413
Eden and 44
general election (1945) and 25, 27
general election (1951) and 36, 50
Monnet and 22
Queen's Speech (1953) and 55
Schuman Plan and 32–5
Second World War and 4, 5–6, 7, 10, 18–20, 21, 22, 30, 31, 58, 66, 168
Thatcher and 167–8, 170, 183, 223
wartime broadcast (21 March 1943) 18–21, 40, 66, 96, 144
Churchill, Winston (grandson of wartime prime minister) 113
CIA 186, 237
Citoyen 60 192
City of London 223, 336, 378, 399, 412, 424, 468
Clark, Alan 231
Clark, General Mark 3–4
Clarke, Kenneth 257, 303, 304, 317, 318, 325–7, 328–9, 363, 365–6, 421, 441
Clegg, Nick 390–91, 393, 394, 396, 399, 401, 417, 420–21, 422, 427, 449, 451
Coalition for Peace through Security 268–9
coalition government (2005–10) 390–426
Cockfield, Lord 193–4
Coe, Jonathan 369
Coetzee, Ryan 449

Cold War (1946–91) 29, 38, 113, 153, 220–21, 223–4, 231, 269, 278, 300, 319, 340
  Cold Warrior conservatism 141, 149, 160–63, 169, 178, 184, 202–203*n*, 205, 206, 212, 237, 238, 267, 318
Coles, John 191
College of Europe, Bruges 208, 215
College Street Group 259
Comité Français de Libération Nationale (CFLN) 21
Committee for a Free Britain (CFB) 206, 207, 221, 237, 238
Committee for a United States of Europe 193
Common Agricultural Policy (CAP) 57, 114, 156, 251, 290
Common Fisheries Policy (CFP) 441
Commonwealth 19, 27, 32, 34, 38, 40, 46, 47, 48, 53, 54, 57, 66, 68, 70, 73–4, 75, 76, 80, 82*n*, 86, 87, 94, 164, 296, 411, 411*n*, 469
  Commonwealth Immigrants Act (1962) 79
'Completing the Internal Market' white paper (1985) 194, 209
Conference on Security and Cooperation in Europe (1990) 231
Conquest, Robert 160
Conservative Party 20, 26–7, 34, 35
  Brexit referendum and 427–58
  Central Office 26, 188, 280, 342, 379
  Cold War tradition within 141, 149, 160–63, 169, 178, 184, 202–203*n*, 205, 206, 212, 237, 238, 267, 318
  Conservative Group for Europe 261
  Conference (1968) 84
  Conference (1971) 94
  Conference (1980) 159
  Conference (1984) 182
  Conference (1988) 207
  Conference (1989) 219
  Conference (1990) 226–7
  Conference (1992) 259
  Conference (2001) 326
  Conference (2002) 334–5
  Conference (2003) 342
  Conference (2005) 365, 367
  Conference (2006) 371
  Conference (2014) 376
  Conference (2015) 425
  Conference (2016) 454, 459, 461
  defections to UKIP 422
  elections *see individual election name*
  EU constitution and 333–5
  EU withdrawal agreement and 459–72
  euro and *see* euro
  European Exchange Rate Mechanism (ERM) *see* European Exchange Rate Mechanism
  European Reform Group (ERG) 155–6, 196, 197, 198, 215–16, 276
  Euroscepticism and *see* Euroscepticism
  Federation of Conservative Students and *see* Federation of Conservative Students, The (FCS)
  leaders *see individual leader name*
  leadership election (1965) 74
  leadership election (1975) 104–9, 110, 129, 134, 144
  leadership election (1989) 156, 222–3
  leadership election (1990) 229–32
  leadership election (1997) 303–4
  leadership election (2001) 326–9
  leadership election (2005) 359, 361–2, 363–8, 371
  leadership election (2016) 455–6
  leadership election (2017) 462
  MPs *see individual MP name*
  New Right and 132–4
  1922 Committee 105, 396
  Research Department 27, 144, 239, 379
  summits, European *see individual summit name*
  think tanks *see individual think tank name*
  treaties, European *see individual treaty name*
  Young Conservatives, The (YC) 203, 205–6, 207
  Young England 133, 263

Conservative Philosophy Group 134, 144, 151, 162, 170, 318, 415, 428
Conservatives for Change (Cchange) 343
Conway, Derek 363
Cook, Robin 118, 286, 292
Cook Report 315
Cooper, Andrew 334, 363, 366, 446
Corbyn, Jeremy 253, 289, 436, 455, 456, 461, 465, 466
corporatism 131, 269
Cosgrave, Patrick 105, 132
Coulson, Andy 391, 396
Council of Europe 19, 40
Countryside Alliance 309
Cowling, Maurice 131–2, 135, 151, 170, 205, 242, 361, 465
  Conservative Essays 144–5, 150
  Mill and Liberalism 131
Cox, Jo 452
Cranborne, Eyzie 311
Cranborne, Robert, Viscount 309, 311, 352
Crewe and Nantwich by-election (2008) 381–2
Crick, Michael 241–2, 315, 349
Crimea 416
Cripps, Stafford 31–2
Crosby, Lynton 357, 377, 415, 432, 443
Crossman, Richard 77, 84
Crozier, Brian 141, 160, 162, 206, 237
  Free Agent 267–9, 267*n*
Cruddas, Jon 382, 407
Cummings, Dominic
  Boris Johnson and 440, 441, 447, 454, 455, 456, 463–4, 467–8
  Brexit and 429–33, 437–43, 447–9, 452, 454, 456–7, 460, 463–4, 467, 468
  Business for Sterling and 312–13, 341, 345, 352, 364, 366, 377
  Cameron and 391, 396, 415, 419, 420, 421, 423–4, 427, 430–31, 442, 443
  coalition government (2010–15) and 391, 392, 394, 396, 414, 414*n*, 415, 418–20, 421, 423–4
  Conservative Party, joins 330
  Gove and 312, 380, 391, 396, 421, 440, 441, 447, 455, 456, 463, 467–8
  immigration question and 432–3
  Juncker report and 430–31
  Monnet, on 415*n*
  Moscow, time in 310–12
  New Frontiers Foundation 352–3, 354, 355–6, 359, 368, 429
  No campaign (euro) and 322–3, 352
  North East Says No and 354–6, 394, 396
  quits as Duncan Smith's director of strategy 333
  Stone and 310–11, 456–7, 463
  technical aspects of withdrawal from EU, obsession with 429
Cunliffe, Jon 399–400, 409, 416
currencies
  European Exchange Rate Mechanism *see* European Exchange Rate Mechanism
  exchange rates *see* exchange rates
  free-floating 79, 85, 87, 138
  single currency *see* euro
  See also individual currency name
customs duties 25, 53, 57, 194, 461, 464
customs union, EU 461, 464
Czech Republic 269, 332, 349, 381, 382, 466
Czechoslovakia 17, 171, 172, 174, 175, 176, 202, 219, 220

d'Ancona, Matthew 286, 302, 364
d'Estaing, Valéry Giscard 139, 148, 151–2, 154, 331, 332–3, 336–7, 350, 351–2, 374
Daily Express 113, 121, 168, 250
Daily Telegraph, The 64, 189, 196, 209, 218, 228, 249, 250, 251, 280, 302, 307, 327, 328, 363, 379, 380, 406, 471
Daladier, Édouard 22
Dalyell, Tam 423
Darlan, Admiral François 3–7, 23
Darling, Alistair 376, 390
Davey, Ed 410
Davies, Philip 373
Davies, Quentin 376

Davis, David 247, 363, 365–6, 367, 462
de Gaulle, Anne 36–7, 89
de Gaulle, Charles
  death 89, 96, 123, 201
  death of daughter and 36–7
  European Defence Community and 38, 42
  Maastricht Treaty and 271
  Major and 283
  Monnet and 9, 21, 22, 23, 24, 25, 25, 28, 122, 148
  Powell and 86
  prime minister, return as (1958) 59–60, 61
  resigns 78, 93
  Rome, Treaty of and 58–60
  Schuman and 29
  Scruton and 77–8, 86
  Second World War and 4, 7–9, 20–25, 28, 37, 127, 134
  vetoes British application to EEC (1963) 62, 70–73, 159
  vetoes British application to EEC (1968) 77, 78, 86, 154
  wilderness years 37–8, 39
de Gaulle, Charles (grandson of General Charles de Gaulle) 271, 272, 288, 321
Deavin, Mark 315
Delors, Jacques 192–6, 208–13, 215–17, 226–8, 249–52, 260, 278, 331, 384, 401, 469
  Delors Commission 208, 211, 216
  'Delors compromise' 240
  Delors package ('*Réussir l'Acte unique*') 199–200
  Delors Report (1989) 217, 223
  Thatcher and 192–4, 199, 200, 208–9
  'Up Yours Delors' headline 250
Democracy Movement 308, 313, 334, 364
democratic socialism 20, 67
Democratic Unionist Party (DUP) 102, 113, 213
Deniau, Jean-François 53
Denmark 253–4, 255, 257, 258, 260, 261, 320, 408, 409, 430
Department of Trade and Industry 120
détente 140, 141, 161, 184, 237
deutschmark 192, 226, 256, 257
Deva, Nirj 317, 321
devolution
  English/regional 292, 354–6, 394, 396
  Scotland and Wales 273–4, 295, 301, 354, 395, 422–3, 426
Dien Bien Phu, battle of, Vietnam (1954) 43, 59
Dimbleby, David 454
Disraeli, Benjamin 107, 108, 133, 145, 263
Dorrell, Stephen 283, 284, 285
Douglas-Home, Alec 73, 74, 107, 171
Douglas-Home, Charlie 171, 175, 176, 177, 188, 202–3, 457
Douglas-Home, Jessica 171–2, 174–7, 185, 187, 188, 202, 202*n*, 212, 299–300, 303, 309, 363, 406, 415, 451, 456, 457, 463
Douglas-Home, Luke 309
Dowden, Oliver 379
Draghi, Mario 403
Dreadnought, HMS 166
Dublin, EEC summit in (1979) 155
Duff, Andrew 445
Duffy, Gillian 388, 389
Duncan Smith, Iain 259, 261, 295, 327, 328–30, 333, 341–2, 347, 366, 446

East Germany 219, 220–21
Economist, The 104, 277, 278, 334
Eden, Anthony 62, 107, 110, 174
  becomes prime minister 48
  death 360
  Europe and 5, 30, 31, 33, 35, 40, 42, 44–5, 46, 47, 50–51, 230, 243
  resigns 44, 56–7
  Suez Crisis and 44, 55–7, 58, 159, 400
Edmonds, David 242
Edmund Burke Society 204
Edwardes, Michael 311
Egypt 12, 54–6, 58
Eisenhower, General Dwight 3, 6, 20, 36, 38, 201

Electoral Commission 437–8, 448
Eliot, T. S.
  'Hollow Men' 418–19
  'Little Gidding' 8–9, 10, 457, 458
Elizabeth II, Queen 45–7, 55, 75, 88, 139, 413
Ellemann-Jensen, Uffe 253
Elliot, Ben 275, 334, 364
Elliott, Matthew 332, 353, 356, 368, 380–81, 383, 384, 395–8, 407, 418, 419, 423–4, 427, 431–4, 437–8, 456
Elliott, Nicholas 141, 206
Elwell, Charles 206
'emergency brakes' 406–7, 425, 439
Encounter magazine 237
Endurance, HMS 166
energy prices 414, 415
Euratom Treaty (establishing the European Atomic Energy Community) (1957) 58
euro
  Brexit and 468–9
  Bruges Group and 215
  Business for Britain and 419–20
  Business for Sterling and 312
  Cameron and 325, 366, 383, 386, 392, 398, 403, 408, 410, 431, 436, 444, 468
  coalition government deal (2010) and 392
  Delors compromise and 240
  euro crisis 392, 398, 399, 402, 468
  Exchange Rate Mechanism and 217, 225–7, 258, 386–7
  'five economic tests' for British membership of 305, 336
  Hague and 303, 304–8, 316–17, 322, 323
  Howard and 344
  Howe on 230
  Kinnock on 228
  Labour/Blair and 286–7, 290–91, 292, 301, 302, 304–8, 311, 314, 318, 319, 323, 326, 335, 336, 344–5, 347, 351, 356, 392, 403
  lack of British participation places strain on membership of EU 390
  Madrid Council and 218
  Major and 239, 240, 243, 279, 281, 282, 284, 399
  'opt in' 225, 243, 399
  referendum on proposed 244, 282, 284, 286, 322, 323, 347, 394
  Thatcher and 218, 225, 226–7, 228, 230, 239, 240, 244, 386–7, 400, 412, 468
Euro Information Campaign 308
Europe of Democracies and Diversities (EDD) 320
European Assembly 41, 57
European Atomic Energy Community (EAEC) 57, 58
European Bank for Reconstruction and Development (EBRD) 311
European Central Bank (ECB) 208, 217, 386, 398, 403, 444
European Coal and Steel Community (ECSC) 24–5, 28–35, 38–42, 43, 46, 49, 51, 93–4, 153, 154, 215, 230, 306, 419
  European High Authority (EHA) 28, 29, 30, 31, 32, 35, 38, 41–2, 50, 67, 97, 138
  Monnet and birth of 28–9, 30, 31, 32, 34–5, 38–9, 40–43, 44, 48–9, 215
  Schuman Plan 28–35, 39, 50, 51, 68, 122–3, 138, 286, 306, 383, 400, 464
  Six, The (founding members) 39, 40, 48, 50, 51, 57, 65–6, 71
European Commission 57, 139, 153, 164, 190, 192, 193, 196, 197–8, 208, 211, 228, 244, 244*n*, 249–50, 251, 331, 350, 351, 362, 384–5, 418, 420–21, 438
  Kinnock as European Commissioner 278
European Communities Act (1972) 429
European Convention on Human Rights (ECHR) 273–4
European Council 138, 197, 223, 235, 261, 399, 402*n*, 405, 408, 431–2, 439, 440
  Blair bid for presidency of 384–5
European Court of Human Rights (ECHR) 395, 413
European Court of Justice (ECJ) 41

European Defence Community (EDC) 38–44, 48, 49, 50, 57, 123
Messina meeting (1955) and 48, 50, 52
Pleven Plan 38–9, 42
European Democrat Students 184–5
European Economic Community (EEC) (Common Market)
Britain joins (1973) 98–9, 106, 109
Britain/Macmillan seeks to join (1959–63) 65–71
Britain reapplies for membership of (1966–8) 76–7
British prime ministers and *see individual prime minister name*
budget contributions/British rebate 151, 151*n*, 152*n*, 154–5, 160, 192, 195
Common Agricultural Policy (CAP) 57, 114, 156
currency, single European/euro and *see* euro
de Gaulle vetoes British application (1963) 62, 70–73, 159
de Gaulle vetoes British application (1968) 77–8, 86, 154
Delors Commission 208, 211, 216
'Delors compromise' 240
Delors package (*'Réussir l'Acte unique'*) 199–200
Delors Report (1989) 217, 223
economic and monetary union, pledges itself to 138
European Exchange Rate Mechanism (ERM) *see* European Exchange Rate Mechanism
European Monetary System *see* European Monetary System
Euratom Treaty (establishing the European Atomic Energy Community) (1957) 58
'ever-closer union', pledges itself to 57–8, 97, 123
Genscher–Colombo Plan (1981) 190–91
Maastricht Treaty *see* Maastricht Treaty
1992 project and 208, 213
origins of 48–53, 57–8, 59, 60
Paris, Treaty of (1954) and 43, 190
Powell and *see* Powell, Enoch
referendum on British membership (1975) 99, 109, 110–23, 135, 136, 137, 142, 153, 441, 465
Rome, Treaty of (EEC Treaty) (1957) *see* Rome, Treaty of (EEC Treaty)
Single European Act (1986) 195–6, 200, 211, 215, 229
social progress aim of 198, 211
Solemn Declaration (1983) 190, 198–9
Spaak/Spaak Report (1956) and 49, 50–54, 57, 59, 60
summits/meetings *see individual location name*
Treaty of Accession 96
European Exchange Rate Mechanism (ERM)
Black Wednesday (16 September 1992) 256–9, 304, 415
Blair and Brown and 304
Major and 224–6, 239, 256–9
origins 139
European Exchange Rate Mechanism
Thatcher and 151, 190–92, 205, 217, 218, 219, 224–7, 229, 230, 239, 258, 386, 438
European Foundation 259, 265, 269, 300, 309, 332
European Free Trade Area (EFTA) 62, 65, 230
European High Authority (EHA) 28, 29, 30, 31, 32, 35, 38, 41–2, 50, 67, 97, 138
European Journal, The 259, 278, 301, 304, 325
European Monetary Fund (EMF) 386
European Monetary System (EMS) 139, 190, 191, 192, 198, 201, 215
European Parliament 152*n*, 194, 196, 208–9, 222, 228, 243, 272, 288, 301, 313–16, 317, 320, 322, 331–2, 347, 349, 366, 381, 382, 385, 390
elections (1989) 243
elections (1994) 265, 271–3, 279, 285

European Parliament (*cont.*)
elections (1999) 294, 313–19, 326, 347, 349, 366, 390
elections (2004) 347–51, 358, 372
elections (2009) 380, 381, 382, 383
elections (2014) 417–18, 419, 421, 438
elections (2019) 462–3
European Parliamentary Elections Bill, UK (1999) 313–16
European People's Party (EPP) 366, 381
European Reform Group (ERG) 155–6, 196, 197, 198, 215–16, 276
European Social Fund (ESF) 211
European Scrutiny Committee (ESC) 381
European Trade Union Conference (1988) 208
European Union (EU)
banking union 405, 444
Brexit and *see* Brexit
British beef exports banned by 283–4
Cameron renegotiation with 402–3, 402*n*, 406–13, 416, 418, 419, 420, 421, 424–6, 427–34, 438–40, 442–6, 450, 451
constitution 322, 331–2, 333, 336, 337–8, 344–7, 350–52, 354, 356–7, 359, 366, 374, 381
customs union 461, 464
elections *see* European Parliament
euro and *see* euro
euro crisis and 385–7, 392, 398, 399, 402, 430, 468
expansion to east of Europe 319–20, 338–42, 349–50, 374, 388
fiscal compact 400–402
free movement of people 57, 252, 384, 409, 416, 424, 425, 432, 449, 459–60
Grexit, possibility of 402
origins 244–7, 244*n*, 269
single market 195, 197, 198, 199, 208–13, 216–23, 251, 278, 384, 398, 399, 406, 408, 416, 439, 442, 448, 449, 461
social chapter 245, 252, 262, 290, 292, 301
summits *see individual place name*
treaties *see individual treaty name*
troika 386
veto, British 283, 321, 351, 383, 400, 402, 409, 437
See also individual institution name
Euroscepticism 34, 70, 77, 85, 94, 96, 115, 118, 121, 122, 139, 149, 155, 168, 243
AV campaign and 397–8
Blair and 292, 294, 302–3, 318, 356
Brexit and 429, 433, 441, 442, 447
Brexit Party *see* Brexit Party
Bruges Group and 214–16, 238
Business for Britain and *see* Business for Britain
Cameron and 324, 325, 366, 367, 412, 418
EU constitution and 333, 359
Fishing Group and 320
Gove on 312
Hague and 313, 317
Howard and 342–4
Lisbon Treaty and 381–4
Maastricht Treaty and 253, 254, 257, 258, 259, 263, 269, 277, 278, 279
Major and 243–4, 249, 276, 277, 278, 279, 281, 282, 285, 289
New Frontiers Foundation and *see* New Frontiers Foundation
origins of 127–47, 250
press and 250–51, 321, 401
Referendum Party *see* Referendum Party
SOS Democracy and 320
term, origins of 238
Thatcher and 237, 248–9, 309, 412, 468
UKIP *see* UK Independence Party (UKIP)
Eustice, George 366, 383, 406
Evans, Harold 171
Evans, Richard 463
Evening Standard 120–21, 378
'ever-closer union among the peoples of Europe' (Article one, Treaty of Rome) 57–8, 97, 123, 212, 320, 368, 408, 426, 439, 444

exchange rates 138, 139, 142, 151, 155, 157, 158, 190, 191–2, 217, 219, 229, 230, 256, 258, 438
ERM and *see* European Exchange Rate Mechanism (ERM)
fixed 138, 142, 155, 217, 230, 258
exports 117, 157, 283

Fabian Society 304, 305*n*, 337
Farage, Nigel 241, 321
alternative vote referendum and 395
Anti-Federalist League and 241, 243, 263–5
Brexit Party and 462–3
Brexit referendum and 428, 429, 437, 438, 447, 448, 452, 453, 454, 468
Cameron renegotiation and 401, 402
childhood 241, 364
Clegg challenges to series of live TV debates on merits of EU 417
Conservative Party, joins 243
Dulwich College 241–3
Eastleigh by-election (1994) and 272–3
elected UKIP leader 373
Enoch Powell and 242, 264, 273, 293
Europe of Democracies and Diversities (EDD) and 320
European Parliament elections (1999) and 317
European Parliament elections (2014) and 417–18, 438
European Parliament elections (2019) and 462–3
Fighting Bull 242
general election (1997) and 291, 293, 314, 315
general election (2001) and 326
general election (2005) and 358
general election (2015) and 426
general election (2019) and 465–6
Kilroy-Silk and 348
Lecomber and 315
Newbury by-election (1992) 263–4
offered safe Tory seat to join the Conservative Party, claims 374
racism, accused of 241–2
resigns as leader of UKIP 426, 427, 462
Sedgefield by-election (2007) and 361
Sked and 241, 263–4, 315
'taking back control' of immigration, on 419
Tory defections to UKIP and 422
transitional controls, on decision not to impose 339–40
UK Independence Party origins and 265
Van Rompuy, attacks 385
Falklands War (1982) 166–70, 250, 465
Fall, Kate 343
Federal Reserve, US 138, 378
Federation of Conservative Students. The (FCS) 181–9, 203, 205, 206, 238, 255*n*, 269, 280, 302, 313, 333, 334
Ferguson, Niall 179, 205, 234, 250, 463
Fergusson, Sir Ewen 239
Feulner, Ed 160, 373
Field, Frank 387–8
Financial Times (*FT*) 199–200, 219, 251–2, 304, 305, 471
Finkelstein, Daniel 403n
First World War (1914–18) 15, 21, 22, 61, 177, 360
Fischer, Joschka 336
Fisher, Antony 63, 342
Fishing Group 320
'five economic tests', single currency membership and Brown's 305, 336
Fixed-term Parliaments Act (2011) 391
Foot, Michael 70, 111, 115, 118, 121, 139, 163–8, 180, 353
Ford, Gerald 143
Foreign Office 5, 92, 160–62, 167, 174, 176, 207, 209–10, 212–14, 217, 219, 222, 235, 237, 239, 251, 321, 339, 419
Forsyth, Michael 184
Forte, Rocco 311, 373, 407
Foucault, Michel 77–8
Fox, Liam 363, 365, 366, 393

France
  Algeria and 58–60
  Brussels summit (2004) and 350–51
  Cameron renegotiation and 409
  Churchill offers 'indissoluble union' to 22, 57
  de Gaulle and *see* de Gaulle, Charles
  Dien Bien Phu, battle of and 43, 59
  European constitution and 351, 359, 374
  European Defence Community and 38–43
  European Economic Community and *see* European Economic Community
  European Monetary System and 192
  Fifth Republic 60
  Fourth Republic 36, 58–60, 61
  German reunification and 221, 227, 239, 240
  Goldsmith and 271–2
  Iraq War and 335
  Maastricht Treaty and 196, 240, 255, 259, 271–2
  Majorité pour L'Autre Europe party 271–2
  Mollet offers union with Britain 57
  Monnet Plan and 28
  National Assembly 29, 37, 42, 43, 44, 50, 58, 95, 271
  National Front 418
  pied noirs 58, 59
  post-war origins of European project and 28–33, 36, 37, 38, 41, 42, 43, 44, 48, 49, 50, 58
  Rome Treaty and 59, 60
  Second World War and 3–25, 128
  student protests (1968) 77–8, 150
  Suez Crisis and 56, 57, 58
  terrorist attacks in 431, 439
  Third Republic 4, 37
  Treaty of Paris and 43
  Vichy 3–7
France, Tim 241–2
Fraser, Antonia 108, 180–81, 275
Fraser, Hugh 91, 92, 106–8, 127–34, 156, 162, 180–81, 196, 275, 318
Fraser, Orlando 275
Fraser, Sir Michael 71–2, 91
Frayne, James 313, 341, 348, 352, 353, 354, 355, 367–8, 394–5, 396
Free Life 324
free markets 63, 67, 85, 87, 90, 94, 104, 106, 118, 131, 133, 149, 150, 151, 171, 184, 188, 192, 193, 260, 354
free movement of people, EU 57, 252, 384, 409, 416, 424, 425, 432, 449, 459–60
Freedland, Jonathan 404
Freedman, Lawrence 319
Freedom of Information Act (2000) 274
'Freedom to Party' campaign 237
Fresh Start Project/Fresh Start Group 255–6, 282, 406, 424, 456
Friedman, Milton 143
Friends of Bruges Group 238, 276
Frost, Gerald 160
Fuller, Richard 185–6

Gabb, Dr Sean 324–5
Gaitskell, Hugh 62, 67, 69–70
Gale, George 105, 131–2
Galloway, George 253
Gardiner, George 288
Garton Ash, Timothy 224, 319, 463
general elections, UK
  (1945) 25, 27, 107
  (1950) 93
  (1951) 63
  (1955) 63
  (1959) 61, 62, 131, 248
  (1964) 73, 74–5
  (1966) 76
  (1970) 85, 87, 88–9, 93, 286
  (1974, February) 98–9, 100, 102, 106
  (1974, October) 100, 103–4, 106
  (1979) 140, 144, 146–7, 148–50, 164
  (1983) 170, 173–4, 176
  (1987) 201–2, 207
  (1992) 248–9, 251, 252, 263, 282

(1997) 281, 284, 285–6, 287, 288, 289–91, 292, 301, 310, 314, 332, 389
(2001) 321, 322–6, 327
(2005) 346, 356–9, 363–4, 365, 372, 415
(2010) 386–90, 392, 393
(2015) 421, 425–6, 427–8, 430
(2017) 461
(2019) 465–6
Genscher–Colombo Plan (1981) 190–91
George VI, King 45–6
Germany
Black Wednesday and 256–7
Brussels summit (2004) and 350–51
Cameron renegotiation and 400, 409
eternal paradox of European integration and 200
European army and 38
European Exchange Rate Mechanism and 139
European Monetary Fund and 386
France turns increasingly to as partner 57
Heath visits 91, 92
Iraq War and 335
post-war rehabilitation of 29
Schuman Plan and 28–30
Second World War and 3–9, 15, 16, 22, 23, 24–5, 26, 27, 28–31, 33, 37, 42
Syrian refugee crisis and 435–6
Treaty of Rome and 58
unification (1990) 220–27, 239–40, 305*n*, 319
G4S 404
Ghouta chemical-weapons attack (2013) 413–14
GHQ Liaison Regiment. *See* Phantom
Gibb, Nick 334
Gibb, Robbie 269, 313, 327, 334
Gilbert, Stephen 396
Gilligan, Andrew 378
Gilmour, Ian 156, 158
Giraud, General Henri 3, 6, 7, 20–21, 23, 24, 37
Gladstone, William 135, 180
Glasgow Hillhead by-election (1982) 166
Glendening, Marc 186, 187, 280, 302, 308, 324
global financial crisis (2008) 378–9, 381, 385, 399, 436–7, 468
Godson, Dean 302
gold 138
Goldsmith, Lady Annabel 293
Goldsmith, Frank 266
Goldsmith, Sir James 186, 219–20, 265, 266–76, 267*n*, 279–91
birth and background 266
death 293–4
Le Piège (*The Trap*) 270, 271, 275, 276, 279
Referendum Party and 279–90, 293–4, 302, 308
The Response 280
the 61 and 267–9
Goldsmith, Zac 275, 334, 364
Good Friday Agreement (1998) 364
Goodman, Paul 186, 302
Gorbachev, Mikhail 219, 220
Gorman, Teresa 261, 276*n*
Gould, Philip 305
Gove, Michael 234, 312, 327, 343, 375, 394, 421, 428, 463
birth and background 234, 363–5
Brexit and 440–42, 445–7, 449, 450, 455, 456, 457, 467–8
Cabinet Office, runs 463–4
Cummings and 312, 391, 396
Dougie Smith and 302–3, 303*n*
education secretary 377, 378–9, 393, 396, 421
expenses scandal and 379–80
Goldsmith and 266, 276, 285
Oxford University 179–81, 203, 204–5
Policy Exchange and 334, 366
selected as Conservative Party candidate 357, 363
shadow housing minister 368
The Times journalist 289, 304
Gow, Ian 156, 226, 452
Grant, Charles 193, 208, 216, 469
Gray, John 370–71

Great Debate 453
Great European Rip-off, The 380–81
Greece 28, 30, 55, 278
economic crisis 385–7, 392, 402, 430
Grexit (Greek exit from the euro) 402
Griffin, Nick 315, 358, 372, 382
Grimond, Jo 112
'grooming gangs' 405
G20 summit (2009) 379
Guardian, The 108, 116, 118, 119, 141, 147, 161, 169–70, 173, 188, 242*n*, 261, 292, 306–7, 318, 327, 345, 363, 367, 369, 404, 417, 463, 471
Guggenheim, Charles 114
Guicciardini, Francesco: *Maxims and Reflections* ix
Guimarães, Portugal, EU foreign ministers conference in (1992) 249–54
Guise, George 220
Gummer, John 186–7
Gunster, Gerry 433–4

Hague, William 247, 303–4, 307, 313, 316–18, 321–3, 325, 326, 328, 368, 383, 406, 408, 424, 446
Hailsham, Quintin Hogg, Lord 63
Hain, Peter 332, 336–7
Halligan, Liam 310–11
Hambro, Charles 281, 282
Hames, Tim 317
Hamza, Abu 388, 413
Hannan, Daniel 254, 276, 317, 320, 321, 366, 407, 412, 422
Hannay, David 209
Hanover, European leaders' summit in (1988) 208
Hanson, James 311
Harris, Ralph 63–4, 81*n*, 149, 184, 213–14, 216, 234, 236, 239, 259, 300, 373
Hart, David 188, 206–7, 209, 221–2
Have I Got News for You (television programme) 369
Hayek, Friedrich 63, 158, 232, 354; *The Road to Serfdom* 63
Healey, Denis 75, 117, 136, 143, 163, 164, 323
Heath, Allister 325
Heath, Edward 9, 121, 123, 129, 136, 137, 138, 144, 150, 151, 152*n*, 153, 157, 158, 184, 205, 243, 247, 249, 266, 286, 290, 291, 308, 329, 333, 339–40, 359, 384, 408, 411*n*, 432, 441, 445, 457
birth and background 91
Bruges Group and 234
budget (1972) and 97–8
Conservative Party candidate, Bexley 93
Conservative Party leadership election (1965) and 74
Conservative Party leadership election (1975) and 104–9, 110
Conservative Party manifesto (1979) and 149
corporatism 131
death 360, 361
EEC, UK bid to join (1963) and 66, 70
EEC, UK bid to join (1968) and 93–9, 110, 111
European vision of Britain's future 90–91
general election (1950) and 93
general election (1966) and 76
general election (1970) and 85, 87, 88–9, 93
general election (February, 1974) and 98–9, 102
general election (October, 1974) and 103–4
Germany trip (1937) 91
Gove and 180
House of Commons vote on motion supporting entry into Common Market (28 October 1971) and 94–8
Maastricht Treaty and 252–3, 260
maiden speech in Commons, Schuman Plan and 33–5, 93
miners' strike and 98, 146, 182
music and 91
Northern Ireland and 98, 100–103
oil crisis and 98, 145
Order of the Garter 361

Oxford University 91
Powell, 'Rivers of Blood' speech and 83–4, 94, 100
pro-Europeanism, uniquely open 33–4
referendum on British membership of Common Market (1975) and 111, 112, 114, 115–18
Second World War military service 91–3
'Selsdon man' 90
special relationship and 90
Stone and 463
Travels: People and Places in My Life 93
U-turn (1972) 159

Heathcoat-Amery, David 332, 333
Heaton-Harris, Chris 317
Helmer, Roger 317
Henderson, Doug 292
Henley-on-Thames by-election (2008) 382
Hennessy, Peter 139
Herbert, Nick 309, 312, 364, 377
Heritage Foundation 160, 373
Heseltine, Michael 180, 231, 232, 282, 289, 317, 318, 326
Heywood, Jeremy 402, 421, 429
Hezbollah cross-border attack into Israel (2006) 372
Hickman, Alex 309, 312, 368
Hill, David 346
Hillary, Edmund 45
Hilton, Steve 342–3
Himmler, Heinrich 91
Hiroshima, atomic bombing (1945) 26
Hirsch, Étienne 24
Hislop, Ian 369
Hitler, Adolf 3, 15, 16, 17, 21–2, 56, 91, 119, 360
Hoile, David 188
Hollande, François 409, 418, 434
Hollobone, Philip 373
Holmes, Martin 301–2
Holmes, Michael 317
Home Office 338, 339, 342
Honeyford, Roy: 'Education and Race: An Alternative View' 172–3, 388
Hoskyns, John 115
House of Commons 30, 31, 46, 54, 70, 79, 94–5, 100, 107, 111, 156, 163–4, 167, 168, 218, 229, 243, 260–62, 276, 306, 314–16, 346, 368, 391, 395, 410, 412, 422, 462
House of Lords 151, 164, 248, 262, 276, 292, 309, 315–16, 346, 360, 391
Housman, A. E.: *A Shropshire Lad* 15, 17, 295–6
Howard, Michael 161, 162, 247, 295, 303, 321, 342, 343, 344–5, 347, 356–7, 358–9, 361, 365, 366, 369, 415
Howarth, Gerald 245, 255, 255*n*, 275
Howe, Geoffrey 63, 109, 159, 203*n*, 207, 210, 217, 218, 229–32, 249, 256, 373, 412, 468
Howe, Martin 259
Hungary 176, 178, 202, 219, 220, 300, 349, 435, 457, 463, 466
Hunt, Jeremy 377
Hurd, Douglas 88–9, 224, 247, 278
Hussein, Saddam 226, 235, 335
Hutton Report (2003) 339, 378

immigration
'balanced migration' 387–8
Brexit and 419, 420, 424–5, 431, 432, 433, 435, 439, 440, 442, 443, 447–52, 465, 468
Cameron and 387–9, 409, 410–11, 417, 419, 420, 424–5, 431, 432, 439–40, 442, 443
Commonwealth, origins of 73–4, 79–81
Commonwealth Immigrants Act (1962) 79
East African Asians 80
EU expansion east and 338–42, 374
European parliament elections (2014) and 417
general election (2005) and 357–8
general election (2010) and 387–9
Immigration Act (1968) 80, 340
Immigration Act (1971) 80, 340
Maastricht Treaty and 244
net migration 339–40, 387, 410

immigration (*cont.*)
Powell, 'Rivers of Blood' speech and 78–9, 81–5, 81*n*, 82*n*, 86, 87, 88, 94, 100, 145,
242, 264
racism and 80
transitional controls, decision not to impose 339–42, 374
UKIP and 348–9
'zero immigration' 340, 341, 358
In the Know 433
India 11, 12, 13, 26–7, 45, 47, 86, 101, 270; independence (1947) 27, 102
inflation 64, 97–9, 106, 117, 136–7, 139, 157, 159, 191–2, 205, 217, 219, 226, 256, 339, 371
Information Research Department (IRD) 160–61
Ingham, Bernard 158
Institute for Economic Affairs (IEA) 63, 64, 81, 106, 132–3, 160, 354
Institute for European Defence and Strategic Studies (IEDSS) 160, 161
Institute for the Study of Conflict (ISC) 141, 237
interest rates 157, 192, 257
International Monetary Fund (IMF) 142, 143, 145, 159, 385, 386, 412
International Olympic Committee (IOC) 362
IRA 130, 157, 160, 180, 182, 209, 226, 452
Iraq 235–6, 240, 339
Iraq War (2003–11) 335, 339, 347–8, 362, 369–70, 372, 378, 388, 393, 404, 421
Ireland, Republic of 45, 381, 409, 461
Irish 'backstop' 461, 464
Iremonger, Lucille: *The Fiery Chariot* 364
ISIS 421–2, 431, 439
Israel 56, 98, 372
Ivens, Martin 302

Jan Hus Foundation 172, 176
Jardine Matheson 299, 313
Jenkins, Michael 153
Jenkins, Peter 141, 147
Jenkins, Roy 69, 76, 96, 112, 114, 115, 119, 121, 138–9, 153, 164–6, 173, 314, 316, 364, 394
Job, Charles 93
Johnson, Boris
Brexit referendum and 433, 440, 441, 442, 446–7, 453, 455–6
Brexit withdrawal agreement and 462, 464–6
Cameron and 370, 371, 377, 401, 403–4, 429, 441, 446, 454–5
childhood 370–71
Conservative Party leadership election (2001) and 329
Conservative Party leadership election (2016) and 455–6
Daily Telegraph journalist/'bonkers Brussels' journalism and 228, 249–54, 307
elected to Parliament (2001) 323–4
Eton 370
general election (2019) and 465–6
Have I Got News for You and 369
higher education spokesman 368–71
Liverpool, apologizes to 369–70
London Mayor 377, 378, 382, 404
Oxford University 180–81, 203, 364, 441
prime minister 463, 464–5
sacked from Howard's front bench 369
self-satire, protects himself through 369, 370–71
shadow arts minister 369
The Spectator, appointed editor of 369
'Ups and Downs of 20 Years Within Europe' 251, 253–4
Johnson, Charlotte 370
Johnson, Daniel 302
Johnson, Frank 162
Johnson, Paul 132, 209, 257
Johnson, Rachel 181
Johnson, Stanley 370
Jones, Clement 81
Jope, Bob 241
Joseph, Keith 104, 106, 133, 243, 268
Juncker, Jean Claude 409, 418, 430

June Movement 320
Jungle, the (refugee camp near Calais) 436
Juppé, Alain 292

Kalms, Stanley 309, 311, 329–30, 373
Kavanagh, Trevor 312, 346
Kedourie, Elie 160, 161, 162
Keetch, Paul 448
Kelly, Dr David 335, 339
Kelly, Rachel 177
Kennedy, Charles 345
Kennedy, John F. 107, 114, 352
Kennedy, Joseph 91
Kenya 80
Kerr, John 210, 227, 331
Khan, Reyaad 434–5
Kilroy-Silk, Robert 231, 347–9, 358, 364
Kim Il Sung 31
King, Professor Anthony 121, 122
King, Mervyn 371
Kinnock, Neil 118, 122, 228, 230, 246, 249, 255, 264, 278
Kipling, Rudyard 258
Kirkhope, Timothy 317, 332, 353
Klaus, Václav 269, 381, 382
Knapman, Roger 349
Kohl, Helmut 191, 194–5, 222, 227, 240, 245, 256–7, 292, 469
Kohnstamm, Max 193
Korean War (1950–53) 31
Kosovo, NATO intervention in (1998–9) 318–19, 335
Kurdi, Alan 435
Kuwait, Saddam Hussein invades (1990) 226

Labour Party 20
  Brexit and 451, 452, 453, 455, 456, 461, 465, 466
  Conference (1961) 67
  Conference (1962) 69–70
  Conference (1975) 112
  Conference (1977) 142
  Conference (1990) 226
  Conference (1997) 301–302
  Conference (2001) 329
  Conference (2004) 356
  Conference (2006) 373
  democratic socialism as central ideology of 67
  elections *see individual election name*
  euro and 286–7, 290–91, 292, 301, 302, 304–8, 311, 314, 318, 319, 323, 326, 335, 336, 344–5, 347, 351, 356, 392, 403
  European Coal and Steel Community and 28–35
  EEC membership and 67–70, 93, 96, 99, 110–13, 117–18, 121–2
  EEC referendum (1975) and 99, 110–13, 117–18, 121–2
  leaders *see individual leader name*
  leadership election (1977) 138–9
  leadership election (1980) 164
  Maastricht Treaty and 240, 247, 248, 255–6, 262
  MPs *see individual* MP name
  National Executive Committee 142
  SDP and 165–6
  summits, European and *see individual summit name*
Lacoste, Robert 59
Laeken group 331
Lamassoure, Alain 337
Lamy, Pascal 249
Lane Fox, Robin 310
Larkin, Philip 467
Larosière, Jacques de 216
Laughland, John 259
Lawnmowers (Harmonisation of Noise Emissions) Regulations (1992) 197–8
Lawrence, Doreen 377
Lawrence, Stephen 377
Lawson, Nigel 131, 192, 217, 218, 219, 230, 323, 438, 448, 457
Le Pen, Marine 418
Leach, Rodney 299–301, 303, 307–13, 352, 368, 383, 394–6, 406, 407, 415, 450–51, 457, 459
Leadsom, Andrea 406, 407, 453, 455, 456, 457

League of Nations 21, 41, 153
Leave.EU 437–8, 452, 454
Lebanon, Israel launches ground invasion of (2006) 372
Lecomber, Tony 315, 317
Lee, Sir Frank 65
Lehman Brothers 378
Leigh, Edward 247, 268
Leigh-Pemberton, Robin 217
Letwin, Oliver 162, 268, 343, 368, 408
Letwin, Shirley Robin 162
Lewis, Julian 268
Liberal Democratic Party 240, 246, 248, 262, 263, 264, 301, 314, 316, 345, 349, 390, 391, 392, 393–4, 397, 410, 417, 426, 427, 445, 448, 465
Libertarian Alliance 324
Liddle, Roger 326, 345, 346
Lilley, Peter 257, 266, 282, 295, 303, 463
Limehouse Declaration (1981) 165
Lisbon European Council Summit (1992) 249, 374
Lisbon Treaty (2007) 374, 381–7, 406, 408, 460
  Article 50 337, 433, 460
'little Englanders', Euroscepticism and 14, 31, 34, 50
Livingstone, Ken 378, 403
local elections, UK
  (2002) 372
  (2004) 347
  (2006) 373–4
  (2010) 397
London conference (1950) 29
London Review of Books (*LRB*) 177
London riots (2011) 404–5
Lovat, Simon Fraser, 14th Lord 92
Luntz, Frank 367
Luxembourg 38, 49–50, 195, 235, 390, 409
  European Coal and Steel Community inaugural ceremony (1952) 41
  European Council summit (1976) 138
  European Council summit (1980) 153, 155
  European Council summit (1985) 196
  High Authority of the European Coal and Steel Community in 38, 41–2, 67
  'Luxembourg Compromise' (1966) 283

M&C Saatchi 425–6
Maastricht Treaty (1992) 301, 305*n*, 326–7, 385
  birth of EU and 244–8, 244*n*
  Britain signs 248
  Bruges Group and 234, 240
  Goldsmith/Referendum Party and 265, 269, 271, 276–9
  Maastricht summit (1992) 223, 234, 239
  Major and 239–40, 243–8, 252, 255–6, 257, 258, 259–63, 274, 276–9, 344, 345, 399
  MPs vote on 247–8, 255–6, 261–3, 269
  ratification of 252–65, 276, 320, 409, 430
  Thatcher and 245–7, 254, 255, 261, 360
  Tory rebels 196, 245, 259–63, 265, 269, 277–9, 300
McAlpine, Alistair, Lord 259, 287–8, 294
McEwan, Ian 182
MacGregor, Mark 187, 188, 189, 323, 327, 330, 333, 358
Mackinlay, Craig 314
Macmillan, Harold 35, 207, 230, 251, 418
  Algiers, plots out future of Europe in (1943)/Second World War and 7, 9, 18, 20, 21, 23, 25, 40, 127, 134
  Churchill's cabinet, joins 36
  Commonwealth Immigrants Act (1962) and 79
  death 200–201, 360
  EEC, attempts to join 66, 67–8, 69, 70, 71–3
  EEC, Heath's attempts to join and 93, 95, 96, 110, 120, 123
  family background 61–2
  First World War and 61
  general election (1959) and 61–2
  Macmillisma 74, 90
  middle way 64
  Pleven Plan and 39
  Profumo sex scandal and 73

resigns as prime minister 73, 159
Suez Crisis and 55
Thatcher and 158–9, 162, 189, 200
'The Grand Design' 66
Macmillan, Maurice 128, 162
McNair-Wilson, Sir Patrick 252
Madrid, Spain
European Council meeting (1994) 281
European Council meeting (2019) 217, 218, 226, 230
Madrid ambush (1989) 218
train bombings (2004) 362
Mair, Thomas 452
Major, John 295, 301, 302, 331, 336, 365, 398, 462, 469
'bastards', criticizes Eurosceptic 263, 302
Black Wednesday and 256, 257, 258
Bruges Group attacks 235, 236, 238
Chancellor of the Exchequer 219, 224, 225, 226
ERM and 225, 226, 239–40, 256, 257, 258
general election (1992) 248–51, 291
general election (1997) 289, 291
Goldsmith and 281, 282–3, 284–6, 288
Iraq and 235–6
Maastricht Treaty and 239–40, 243–7, 248, 252, 255–6, 257, 258, 259, 260–63, 274, 276, 277–9, 344, 345, 399
prime minister, becomes 232, 233
Referendum Party and 281–6, 288
resigns from Tory leadership 282
Thatcher and 218–19, 224, 225, 232, 233, 235, 236
Majorité pour L'Autre Europe 271–2
Makins, Roger 41–2
Mancham, Sir James 161, 238
Mandelson, Peter 274, 306, 335, 346, 354, 384–5
Marsh, Dick 311
Marshall Plan (1948) 28–9
Marten, Neil 96, 113
Marxism 145, 176, 179, 187, 203*n*, 206, 207
Massingham operation (1942–3) 6
Mather, Carol 128
Maude, Francis 247, 313, 334, 343, 366, 368
Maudling, Reginald 74, 108
May, Theresa 334–5, 343, 421, 451, 455, 456, 459–63, 469
Mellor, David 291
Mendès-France, Pierre 43
Menon, Anand 152*n*, 244–5
Menzies, R. G. 45
Merkel, Angela 374, 385, 386, 392, 400, 409, 416, 418, 425, 427–8, 434–6, 451, 469
Messarovitch, Yves 270
Messina, Italy, foreign ministers of Coal and Steel Community meet in (1955) 48–50, 52
Messina, Jim 453
Meurthe, Laure Boulay de la 294
Meyer, Sir Anthony 156, 222
MI5 206
Miliband, David 331, 354, 401
Miliband, Ed 401, 414, 415, 417, 422, 426, 427, 451
Miller-Kurakin, George 185, 269
Milošević, Slobodan 318
miners' strike
(1974) 98, 146
(1984–5) 159–60, 182–3, 187–8, 207, 223
Minogue, Kenneth 162, 236, 240, 257, 259, 300
MI6 (Secret Intelligence Service) 141
Mitchell, Andrew 324, 325
Mitterrand, François 58, 192, 227, 255, 272
Mollet, Guy 57, 58–9
monetarism 79, 85, 87, 143, 157, 158, 192, 219, 296
Monnet, Jean 50, 62, 66–7, 70, 94–5, 153–4, 168, 192–3, 196, 212, 252, 286, 319, 386, 390, 471
Action Committee of the United States of Europe, creates 43–4, 123, 138
Algiers, plots future of Europe in (1943)/Second World War and 7–8, 9, 18, 21–5, 28, 127, 134, 173, 469
citoyen d'honneur, first honorary Citizen of Europe 138, 148

Monnet, Jean (*cont.*)
Cummings on 415*n*, 419
death 148–9, 201
Europe forged in crisis, foresees 400–401
European Coal and Steel Community origins and 28–9, 30, 31, 32, 34–5
European Defence Community origins and 38–43, 44, 48–9
First World War and 21
Fortune magazine profile 'Mr Jean Monnet of Cognac' 25
Fourth Republic, influential figure of 36
High Authority of the European Coal and Steel Community, first president of 38–9, 40–43, 44, 48–9, 215
League of Nations and 21
Monnet Plan 28
Schuman Plan and 30, 31, 32, 34–5
Treaty of Paris (1954) and 43, 44
UK entry into Common Market and 95, 96, 122–3
Moore, Charles 227–8, 295, 328
Morgan, Kenneth 167
Morning Star 112
Mosley, Oswald 62, 64, 113–14
multiculturalism 172–3, 375, 388
Murdoch, Rupert 206, 268, 289, 294, 312, 346
Murphy, Robert 7, 21, 56

Nairn, Tom 87–8, 459
Nasser, Gamal Abdel 55, 56
National Alliance of Russian Solidarists (NTS) 185
National Front 113, 241–2, 389, 418
National Union of Mineworkers (NUM) 182, 187
nationalism 14, 21, 24, 25, 44, 47, 50, 54, 58, 87, 101, 107, 118, 120, 121, 192, 201–2, 219, 221, 227, 240, 303*n*, 422–3, 425
Neave, Airey 104–5, 133–4
New Agenda 189
Newbury by-election (1992) 263–4
New Europe 323
New Frontiers Foundation 351–2, 368, 429
New Left Review 87, 167
New Party 62
New Right 132–4, 178
New Statesman 132
News, The 288
Newsnight 367
Nicaragua Solidarity Campaign 206
Nicaraguan Contras 188, 206
Nice European Council summit (2000) 320–22, 331, 409
Nieboar, Jeremy 259
Nietzsche, Friedrich 15, 299
9/11 329, 330, 331, 362, 421–2
1992 project 208, 213
Niven, David 127
Nixon, Richard 138, 142, 220
Norgay, Sherpa Tenzing 45
Norgrove, David 201
Norman, Edward 130–31, 135, 162
Norman, Jesse 406
North Africa 3–12, 23, 58, 127
North Atlantic Treaty Organization (NATO) 38, 66, 186, 318–19, 335
North Sea oil reserves 143, 155, 157
Northern Ireland 98, 100–103, 130, 157–8, 183, 301, 361, 423, 461, 464, 467
Anglo-Irish Agreement (1985) 180, 183, 465
EU withdrawal agreement and 461–2, 464
general strike (1974) 102–3
Good Friday Agreement (1998) 364
IRA campaigns 130, 157, 160, 180, 182, 209, 226, 452
Northern Ireland Executive 102
Stormont parliament abolished (1972) 100–101
Sunningdale Agreement (1973) 102
Northern Rock 376
Notting Hill Set 363, 364, 365, 441
nuclear energy 270, 437
nuclear weapons 162, 163, 164, 165, 166, 169, 174, 186, 187, 203*n*, 268

O'Brien, Neil 313, 345, 346, 359, 368, 374
O'Sullivan, John 209, 239
Oakeshott, Michael 128–30, 131, 132, 151, 162, 177, 232, 236
  Rationalism in Politics and Other Essays ix, 129–30
Obama, Barack 403, 413, 414, 428, 449
oil-price crisis (1973) 98–9, 138, 145, 148
Oliver, Craig 449
Olympic Games (2012) 362–3, 404–5
Open Europe 368, 374–5, 394, 407, 451
Options for Change report (2012) 406–7
Orbán, Viktor 221, 435, 466
Organisation for European Economic Co-operation (OECD) 54
Orwell, George 140
  Homage to Catalonia 261
Osborne, George 323, 342, 343, 363, 365, 376, 390, 392–3, 403, 405, 408, 414, 436, 437, 440, 441, 449, 450, 451
Overseas Information Department 161
Oxford Myth, The 181
Owen, David 161, 165, 323, 447
Oxford University 73, 91, 92, 107, 128, 171, 178–83, 203, 213, 214, 216, 236, 276, 300, 310, 370, 412, 441, 463
  Edmund Burke Society 204
  Oxford Campaign for an Independent Britain (OCIB) 254
  Oxford Union 180–81
  Oxford University Conservative Association (OUCA) 91, 181, 185, 254, 377

Paisley, Ian 102, 113
Panorama 189, 255*n*
Paris, France
  Paris Conference for a Europe of Nation States 272
  terror attacks (2015) 439–40
  Treaty of Paris (1954) 43, 190
Parkinson, Cecil 275
parliamentary expenses scandal (2009) 379–81, 382
Patel, Priti 280, 421, 446
Patten, Chris 248, 279–80, 326, 350
paving motion 260
Pearson, Malcolm 259, 276, 373
Pétain, Marshal Philippe 3, 4, 22, 58
Peterhouse, Cambridge 130, 131–2, 162, 170, 172, 361
Petyt, Peter 241
Peyrefitte, Alain 71
Peyton, John 109
Pflimlin, Pierre 59
Phantom intelligence unit (GHQ Liaison Regiment) 5, 92, 127–8, 131, 162, 232, 332
Philby, Kim 141
Pimlott, Ben 111
Pirie, Madsen 184
Pithart, Petr 174, 175, 268
Plaid Cymru 120, 273
Pleven, René 38–9
Pleven Plan 38–9, 42
Pöhl, Karl Otto 208, 216, 217
Poland 22, 91, 176, 184–5, 187, 202, 219, 339, 349, 466
Policy Exchange 334, 366, 377
Political Warfare Executive (PWE) 5
poll tax 225–6, 238, 246
Portillo, Michael 247, 282, 295, 317, 327–8, 333, 334–5, 342–4, 361, 441
Portland Club 299, 303, 309
pound and sterling 51, 72, 117, 141–3, 157, 213, 226, 228, 230, 232, 256–7, 290, 305, 307, 313, 317, 322, 323, 367, 449, 455
  devaluation of 75–7, 83
Powell, Carla, Lady 288
Powell, Charles 194, 208, 209–10, 213, 221, 224, 225, 226, 288, 463
Powell, John Enoch
  absolutism 17, 27, 47, 88
  Anglo-Irish Agreement and 183
  birth 14
  Cambridge University 15
  childhood 14–15
  Collected Poems 17
  conservatism 18, 133
  Conservative Party, joins 26–7

Powell, John Enoch (*cont.*)
- Conservative Party leadership election (1965) and 74
- Conservative Party leadership election (1975) and 105, 109
- Cowling on 144–5
- death 294–6
- EEC, UK attempts to join and 67, 85–8, 95–6
- enters Parliament (1950) 27–8
- Falklands War and 166–7
- Farage and 242, 264, 273, 293
- Foot and 163
- general election (1970) and 88–9
- general election (February, 1974) and 99
- general election (October, 1974) and 103
- general election (1987) and 201–2
- general election (1997) and 292–3
- Harwich Conservative Association's women's rally, addresses 85–6
- health minister 67
- Heath and 83–4, 94, 100
- IEA and 64
- imperialism 11–18, 26–7, 47–8, 55, 84, 86–8, 102, 118, 292–3, 295, 296, 467, 471
- India and 11, 12, 13, 26–7, 47, 86, 102
- last interview 286
- loss, sense of 17, 27, 135
- loses Parliamentary seat 202
- martyrdom, fascination with 17–18, 136, 295
- nationalism to replace imperialism, calls for 47, 102
- Newbury by-election (1992) and 264
- Nietzsche and 15
- Northern Ireland and 100–102
- poetry 17
- Powellism 63, 64, 79, 84, 88, 89, 106, 123, 242
- referendum on British membership of EEC (1974) and 110, 118, 123
- *Reshaping Europe in the Twenty-First Century* and 257
- resigns as chief secretary to Treasury 62–3, 64, 67
- 'Rivers of Blood' speech (1968) 78–9, 81–4, 83*n*, 94, 163
- 'Saving in a Free Society' 64
- schooldays 15
- Schuman Plan and 35
- Second World War and 9–14, 16–18, 26, 92, 292–3
- speech, House of Commons (3 March 1953) 46–7
- Suez Crisis and 55
- Thatcher and 72, 162–3, 167, 183, 223, 227, 232
- Ulster Unionist, stands as 100, 133
- University of Sydney 15–16
- West Lothian question and 423
- Wilson resignation and 136

Powell, Jonathan 306, 345–6, 347
Powell, Pam 89
price controls 79, 87, 106
Prior, Jim 109, 158
prisoners, votes for 395
Profumo sex scandal 73
proportional representation (PR) 315–16, 326, 391–8
Pym, Francis 191

Question Time 83*n*, 320, 348

racism 80, 83, 84, 163, 242, 357
Rawnsley, Andrew 342
Reagan, Ronald 160, 203*n*
recession 157–8, 378, 387, 403, 449
Reckless, Mark 254, 412, 422
Redwood, John 247, 282, 303
Rees-Mogg, Jacob 254, 327, 457
Rees-Mogg, William 171, 257, 262, 265, 272, 332, 361
referenda
- alternative vote (2011) 394–8
- Brexit (2016) 427–58, 465–70
- British membership of EU, push for in lead-up to Brexit 397–8, 403, 406, 407–10, 418, 420, 424–6

euro, single currency and 244, 279, 281, 282, 284, 286, 287, 304, 323, 344
EEC, British membership of (1975) and 99, 109, 110–22, 135–7, 142, 153, 441, 465
European constitution and 345–7, 354
Gaitskell and concept of use in European debate 70
Lisbon Treaty 381, 382–3, 387
Maastricht Treaty 253, 255–6, 259, 261–2, 320, 409
referendum lock against further European integration, Cameron and 367, 387, 390–92
regional assembly, north-east of England (2004) 354–6, 359
Scottish independence (2014) 405, 422–3, 425
second Brexit referendum, push for 456, 466
Referendum Movement 307–8
Referendum Party 274–91, 293, 294, 302, 307–8, 317, 324, 326, 366
Reform Club 214, 216, 289
Reid, Anna 334
René, Albert 237–8
Rennard, Chris 393
Reshaping Europe in the Twenty-First Century 257
Réussir l'Acte unique (Delors package) 199–200
Ridley, Nicholas 226, 238, 245, 247
Rifkind, Malcolm 323
Rigby, Lee 413
RMT 433
Robertson, Patrick 179, 428
Bruges Group and 213–16, 223, 233–6, 238, 254, 255, 257
Oxford, arrival at 203, 204–5
Referendum Party and 266, 275–6, 280, 283, 284, 285, 289, 294
Thatcher resignation and 231, 233
Robinson, Nick 188, 205
Robinson, Tommy 462
Rogers, Bill 165
Rogers, Ivan 399–400, 402, 409, 416, 420–21, 425, 429, 430, 434, 438–9, 440, 442, 460
Romania 202, 374, 417
Rome, Treaty of (EEC Treaty) (1957) 53*n*, 57–60, 66–68, 70, 93–7, 111, 153, 190, 196, 200, 211, 244, 313–14, 333, 350
Rommel, Erwin 92
Roosevelt, Franklin D. 4, 6, 7, 22, 23, 26
Rose, Stuart 407
Rotherham, Lee 321
Roy Jenkins Appreciation Society 364
Royal British Legion 389
Royal Society of St George 87
Rushdie, Salman 169–70
Ryder, Richard 249

Salan, General Raoul 59
Salisbury Group 151, 170–71
Salisbury Review 170–71, 172, 180, 388, 441
Salisbury, Robert, Lord 208, 295, 309, 363, 364–5, 415, 463
Salmond, Alex 120, 422
Sarkozy, Nicolas 385, 400
SAS, storm Iranian embassy in London (1980) 160
Scargill, Arthur 183
Schapiro, Leonard 160–62
Schäuble, Wolfgang 386
Schengen area 436
Schmidt, Helmut 139, 148, 150, 154
Scholar, Tom 409, 434
Schröder, Gerhard 350, 351
Schuman, Robert, and Schuman Plan 28–35, 39, 50, 51, 68, 122–3, 138, 286, 306, 383, 400, 464
Scotland 62, 92, 96, 101, 120, 147, 184, 205, 425, 426, 453, 455, 465
devolution 273, 301, 354, 395, 422–3
independence referendum (2014) 405, 422–3, 428, 447, 451
Scott, Derek 375
Scottish National Party (SNP) 120, 147, 262, 425–6, 465

Scruton, Roger 8, 77–8, 86, 150, 389, 469, 470
 Conservative Party leadership contest (1975) and 108, 129
 Conservative Philosophy Group and 134, 162, 170, 318, 415, 428
 Culture Counts 375–6
 de Gaulle and 77–8, 86
 death 466–7
 'Education and Race: An Alternative View' and 172–3, 388
 Fools, Frauds and Firebrands 428
 Gove and 180, 303, 363, 441
 Hannan and 254
 Hugh Fraser group and 129–31, 132, 133, 134
 Jessica Douglas-Home and 172, 174, 175–6, 202, 212, 299–300, 303, 406
 knighted 451
 Leadsom and 456
 'Little Gidding' and 8–9, 458, 466
 Memoires de Guerre and 77–8
 'No Peace Without Freedom' 174
 Salisbury Review and 170–71, 172, 180, 388, 441
 Thatcher and 134, 135, 150–51, 178, 202, 212, 221
 The Meaning of Conservatism 150–51
 The Need for Nations 349–50
 The Times, writes for 172
 Thinkers of the New Left 428
 Where We Are 466–7
SDP (Social Democratic Party) 164–6, 173, 185, 366
Second World War (1939–45) 3–25, 26, 28, 30, 31, 37, 44, 50, 56, 58, 91–4, 107, 119, 122, 127–8, 134, 173, 189, 310, 360, 439, 469
Sedgefield by-election (2007) 381–2
Seldon, Arthur 64
7/7 362–3, 364, 404, 413
Seychelles 161, 237–8
Sharpe, Tom: *Porterhouse Blue* 130
Sherman, Alfred 106
Shield, the 141
Shore, Peter 111, 164
Shuckburgh, Evelyn 45
Silkin, John 111, 164
Simmonds, Michael 334
Simon, William 142
Single European Act (1986) 195–6, 200, 211, 215, 229
single market, EU 195, 197, 198, 199, 208–13, 216–23, 251, 278, 384, 398, 399, 406, 408, 416, 439, 442, 448, 449, 461
Sinn Fein 113
Six, The (founding members of Coal and Steel Community) 39, 40, 48, 50, 51, 57, 65–6, 71
61, the (private intelligence operation) 141, 267–9
Sked, Alan 177–8, 216, 234–6, 240–41, 243, 248, 257, 263–4, 273, 291, 314, 315, 317, 463
Smith, Douglas 'Dougie' 234
 Brexit and 440–42, 455, 456, 463–4, 466
 Bruges Group and 216
 Business for Sterling and 313, 329–30
 Candidlist and 324–5
 Committee for a Free Britain and 221–2, 238
 Conservative research department and 379, 428
 Democracy Movement and 308, 334, 364
 'elite orgies', organizes 343
 FCS and 187–9, 206, 238, 269
 Freedom to Party campaign and 237
 general election (2005) and 357
 Goldsmith and 275
 'nasty party' speech, authors 334–5
 Policy Exchange and 334, 366
 Referendum Party and 280, 302, 307–9
Smith, John 112, 264, 272, 273–4, 277, 287, 301
Soames, Nicholas 387–8
Social and Political Doctrines of Contemporary, The 129
socialism 20, 33, 34, 57, 67, 72, 74, 76, 112, 115, 118, 131, 142, 163, 168, 171, 188, 192, 211, 215, 232, 320, 332
Solemn Declaration (1983) 190, 198–9

SOS Democracy 320
Soubry, Anna 185
Soviet Union 19, 20, 23, 24, 29, 56, 113, 140, 141, 149, 153, 160, 161, 166, 171, 177, 185, 189, 203*n*, 207, 219–21, 224, 237–8, 252, 254, 267*n*, 268, 269, 270, 300, 310–11, 319, 340
Spaak, Paul-Henri 49, 50–54, 57, 59, 60
Spaak Report (1956) 57
Special Operations Executive (SOE) 5–6
Spectator, The 64, 72, 105, 112–13, 131, 132, 160, 196, 226, 257, 369, 377
Spicer, Michael 238–40, 245, 246, 247, 255, 263, 276, 282
Spink, Bob 373
Staines, Paul 237
Stancliffe, Bishop David 361
Starmer, Keir 461
Stone, Christine 202
Stone, Norman 202, 216, 234, 238, 250, 309, 361, 364
  Brexit and 456–7, 463–4
  'Cambridge right' and 131
  Cameron and 428
  Carr and 176–7, 463
  communism, moral contempt for 177–8, 221, 237, 310
  Cummings and 310–11, 456–7, 463
  death 463–4
  Delors 1992 project and 213, 214
  European Foundation and 259, 300
  German unification and 225
  Gove and 179, 205
  Hannan and 254
  Heath and 463
  Oxford University and 178–9, 205, 310
  Thatcher and 179, 209, 212, 224, 225, 237, 310, 412
  The Atlantic and its Enemies 412
  The Eastern Front 177–8
Stop the EU Rip-Off campaign 381
Stop the Pit Closures support groups 187
Stothard, Peter 289
Strachan, Michael 12–13, 26
Strasbourg European Council (1989) 223
Straw, Jack 118, 316, 345–6
Straw, Will 118
Stuart, Gisela 332, 336–7, 375, 447, 450, 453, 455
Sturgeon, Nicola 455
Suez Crisis (1956) 54–6, 57, 58, 69, 86, 102, 142, 159, 168, 169, 412
Sun, The 112–13, 114, 115, 119, 121, 131, 250, 289, 290, 312, 346, 425, 442, 470–71
Sunak, Rashvir 80
Sunak, Rishi 80, 446
Sunak, Usha 80
Sunday Express 70, 250, 347–8
Sunday Telegraph, The 72, 84, 131, 147, 251, 286, 328
Sunday Times, The 120–21, 144, 237, 250, 343, 365–6
Sunningdale Agreement (1973) 102
Sykes, Paul 308
Syria 413–14, 415, 431, 434, 435, 437, 439, 452

Tapsell, Peter 263
tariff, common European 57
Taskforce Communications 275
TaxPayers Alliance, The (TPA) 353–4, 356, 368, 380
Taylor, A. J. P. 70, 216, 250
Taylor, Edward 'Teddy' 96, 156, 196, 234, 247, 276, 276*n*
Tebbit, Norman 189, 215, 238, 245, 247, 257, 333
Thatcher, Denis 104
Thatcher, Margaret 62
  Anglo-Irish Agreement and 180, 183, 465
  birth 134
  Black Wednesday and 257, 258
  Bruges Group honorary president 234, 235, 236
  Bruges speech (1988) 208–13, 258, 277, 309, 338, 408
  budget contributions to Europe and 151–2, 151*n*, 154–5, 191, 195–6
  career in Parliament 105–6
  childhood 134–5

Thatcher, Margaret (*cont.*)
CND and 169
cognitive dissonance over Europe 190
Conservative Cold War tradition/ communism/Soviet Union and 160–63, 169
Conservative Party leadership election (1975) and 104–9, 110, 133, 134, 144
Conservative Party leadership election (1989) and 156, 222–3
Conservative Party leadership election (1990) and 231–2
Conservative Philosophy Group and 134
Cowling on 144–5, 150
death 411–12
Delors and 192–4, 199, 200, 208–9
dogmatism 202
Dublin summit (1979) and 155
eastern expansion of European Community, supports 253
economy and 156–60, 170
EEC, backs Britain's accession to 106
enters Parliament (1959) 62
European Exchange Rate Mechanism (ERM) and 151, 190–92, 205, 217, 218, 219, 224–7, 229, 230, 239, 258, 386, 438
European Reform Group and 156–7
Falklands War and 166–9
fortieth wedding anniversary 246
funeral 412–13
general election (1979) and 146–7, 148–50
general election (1983) and 170, 173–4
general election (1987) and 200–202
German unification and 221–2, 223–5
Goldsmith and 267, 268, 269, 270, 293
Grand Hotel, IRA attempt to kill at (1984) 182
Hague, backs for leadership of Conservative Party 303–4
Harris memorial service and 373
Howe's resignation and 229–30
Iraq and 235–6
'the Iron Lady' 140, 160
Kensington Town Hall speech on foreign policy (1976) 140–41
Luxembourg speech (1980) 153, 155
Maastricht Treaty and 245–7, 254, 255, 261, 360
Madrid ambush (1989) and 216
memoirs 239
miners' strike and 146, 159–60, 182–3
nervous breakdown 239
political convictions 134–5, 150–51
poll tax and 225–6
Powell and 64, 72, 83, 106, 135, 162–3
pragmatic accommodation with Europe, belief in 200
practical conservative 106
pragmatism 183
referendum on British membership of EEC (1975) and 109, 114–16, 135, 151–2, 151*n*, 154–5, 191
removed from power 231–2, 233, 239, 254
Reshaping Europe in the Twenty-First Century and 257
Shield, the and 161
Single European Act and 195–6, 200
Solemn Declaration (1983), signs 190, 198–9
'The lady's not for turning' 159
Washington speech (1992) 258
wets and 183–4
World in Action, appearance on 134
Thatcher, Muriel 134
Thesiger, Wilfred: *Arabian Sands* 13–14
Thomas, Hugh 161, 162
Thorpe, D. R. 61
Times, The 89, 159, 171, 172, 174, 176–7, 186–8, 202–3, 202*n*, 203*n*, 213, 222, 234, 236, 240, 250, 257, 262, 268, 276, 280, 282, 285, 287, 289, 304, 305, 306, 317, 321, 323, 332, 350–52, 361, 365, 367, 385, 392, 414, 417, 418, 420, 425, 441, 442, 459
Tinney, Andrew 206
Titford, Jeffrey 291, 317
Tolkien, J. R. R. 15

Tolstoy, Count Nikolai 189, 463
Tooze, Professor Adam: *Crashed* 378, 385, 399
Towler, Gawain 321, 385
Trades Union Congress (TUC) 210–11, 328, 329, 453
Treasury 51, 62–3, 65, 75, 97, 98, 142, 157, 174, 192, 201, 218, 219, 226, 306, 336, 339, 376, 399, 448, 449
Trimble, David 101
'troika' 386
Truman, Harry 26
tuition fees 184, 393–4, 396
Tunisia 6, 9, 18, 431
Turnbull, Andrew 219–20
Tusk, Donald 439, 442, 445

UK Independence Party (UKIP) 307
  Brexit and 433, 437–8, 447, 462
  Brexit Party and 462–3
  Carswell defects to 422
  Cook Report exposé 315–16, 317
  Crewe and Nantwich by-election (2008) and 381–2
  Europe of Democracies and Diversities (EDD) and 319
  European Parliament elections (1994) and 273
  European Parliament elections (1999) and 315, 317, 366
  European Parliament elections (2004) and 347–9
  European Parliament elections (2009) and 382
  European Parliament elections (2014) and 417–18, 421
  Farage elected leader 373–4
  Farage resigns as leader 426, 427, 462
  general election (1997) and 291, 293, 314, 315
  general election (2001) and 326
  general election (2005) and 358
  general election (2015) and 426
  Henley-on-Thames by-election (2008) and 382
  Kilroy-Silk and 347–9, 358, 364
  origins 265, 272, 273, 281
  proportional representation and 315, 317
  Reckless defects to 422
  Sedgefield by-election (2007) and 381–2
  Sked resignation 314
Ukraine, war in (2014–) 416
Ulster Unionism 100, 101, 102, 133
Ulster Volunteer Force (UVF) 103
Ulster Workers' Council 102
unemployment 97, 143, 157, 158, 170, 198–9, 200, 211, 258, 271, 305*n*, 348, 385, 449
Union of European Federalists 445
United Nations (UN) 19, 20, 56, 166, 335
United States of America (USA) 91, 92, 107, 123, 142, 148, 153, 162, 163, 186, 203*n*, 212, 220, 222, 235, 283, 289, 335, 337, 348, 385, 388, 437
  Marshall Plan 28–9
  NATO and 38
  9/11 329, 330, 331, 362, 421–2
  origins of post-war Europe and 19–26, 28–30, 34, 42, 65, 66, 71, 72, 79
  presidential election (1952) 36, 38
  presidential election (1956) 56
  presidential election (1980) 160
  Second World War and 3, 4–5, 7, 11, 12, 19
  'special relationship' with UK 75, 90, 94
  Suez Crisis and 56–7, 86
University of Sydney in New South Wales 15–16
Utley, T. E. (Peter) 64–5, 72–3, 84, 131, 132, 135, 160, 162, 180, 196–7, 207–208, 209, 250, 295

Vaizey, Ed 343, 357, 363, 364
Van Rompuy, Herman 385
Vanguard Party 101
Vaz, Keith 389

Verhofstadt, Guy 331, 350
Veritas 349, 358
Villiers, Philippe de 271, 272, 321
Vincent, John 131
Vine, Sarah 334, 440
Voggenhuber, Johannes 336
Vote Leave 438–9, 440, 441, 442, 443, 446–56, 460, 467–8
Vote No 346, 359, 368
Vote 2004 345, 346, 359, 368, 374

wages 157, 371
Walker, Bill 260
Walker, Martin 170, 171, 172
Wall, Stephen 210, 233, 246, 249, 284, 305
Walters, Alan 219, 288
Warner, Philip 127
West Germany 51, 150, 221
West Lothian question 354, 423
Western Union 38
Westlake, Martin 348
Wheeler, Stuart 309, 311, 352, 438
Whetstone, Linda 342
Whetstone, Rachel 342–3, 363
Whitelaw, Willie 109
Whitney, Ray 160–61
Whittingdale, John 261, 446
Williams, Shirley 112, 121, 165
Wilson, Harold
  death 360
  devaluation crisis/economic policies 75–6, 88, 157, 159
  Britain's attempt to join EEC (1963) and 67–9, 86
  Britain's attempt to join EEC (1968) and 76–7, 85–6, 87
  general election (1964) and 74–5
  general election (1966) and 76
  general election (1970) and 85, 87, 88–9
  general election (February, 1974) and 99
  general election (October, 1974) and 100, 103–4
  National Plan 75–6
  Northern Ireland and 100, 102, 103
  Powell and 87, 100
  prime minister, becomes 73, 74–5
  Profumo sex scandal and 73
  referendum on British membership of EEC (1975) and 99, 109, 110–12, 114, 116, 118, 120, 121, 123, 137, 143, 441, 464
  replaces Gaitskell 70
  resigns as prime minister 136–7, 138
  'white heat of technology', promise to unleash 73, 85
  Wilsonism 76
Winter of Discontent (1978–9) 145–6, 147, 412
Winterton, Ann 373–4
Winterton, Nicholas 373–4
Woodward, Shaun 324
World Congress for Peace 174
World Economic Forum 236, 275
World in Action 38, 134
Worsthorne, Peregrine 128, 129, 131, 132, 147, 162, 250, 361, 464
Wyatt, Petronella 369
Wyatt, Woodrow 209

Xi Jinping 436–7

Yom Kippur War (1973) 98
Young, Hugo: *This Blessed Plot* 210, 306–7, 368, 470
Young, Peter 184, 185, 186, 187, 221, 269
Young Conservatives. The (YC) 203, 205–6, 207
Young England 133, 263